A SIGNIFICANT CASUALTY

A SIGNIFICANT CASUALTY

PETER J. PILKINGTON

To order additional copies of this book, contact:
Xlibris Corporation
1-888-795-4274
www.Xlibris.com
Orders@Xlibris.com
80821

CONTENTS

Introduction..11

Dedicated to 13

Chapter 1   United Arab Emirates..15

Chapter 2   Onions 24

Chapter 3   Abu Musa Island 34

Chapter 4   West Cameron Block 83..46

Chapter 5   Bellevue, Washington..74

Chapter 6   Houston 77

Chapter 7   Home 87

Chapter 8   Mile Posts...90

Chapter 9   Searching for the truth..106

Chapter 10   Fort Eustis, Virginia..115

Chapter 11   What is a man worth?..116

Chapter 12   The Depositions 117

Chapter 13   Settlement Hearing..153

Chapter 14   Provost Umphrey..158

Chapter 15   Port Arthur, Texas...164

Chapter 16   Getting Ready...174

Chapter 17   U.S. Coast Guard-Marine Safety Office 177

Chapter 18   U.S. Coast Guard Investigation 216

Chapter 19   Day 2 295

Chapter 20   Proceedings Day Three...379

Chapter 21   Findings in fact...408

Epilogue 413

Appendix...415

Index 521

For
Colonel Frederick A. Pilkington
Army of the United States

A failure first and foremost of management, a failure of oversight and a failure of laws so riddled with loopholes that companies repeatedly can violate safety regulations without penalty.

—*Barack Obama*
(regarding the mine disaster in West Virginia, April 2010)

Introduction

In a perfect world a story such as I am about to relate could never have happened and would never have needed to be told, but this is not a perfect world, and life does not always treat us in the manner to which we feel we deserve. We have become accustomed to accepting mediocrity and bureaucratic incompetence. Indifference and ambivalence are becoming the accepted norm. We live in a democratic society where less than half the eligible members actually participate, and as a result, the officials we elect owe more allegiance to the special interests that fund and support them than to the constituents they purport to represent.

As a result we have enabled a system to exist where the interests of business overshadow the rights of the individual; a system where we permit industry to write the regulations intended to control their activities. We live in a society where human life is measured and analyzed, compared and evaluated against the cost of doing business—where litigators feed on the misery of others while doing little to prevent the carnage on which they feed and depend while a "kinder and gentler"[1] government stands idly by protecting the special interests that feed the political system while hiding behind "cost to benefit" studies to justify their inaction.

Under current United States Coast Guard policy, a significant casualty is one that may involve multiple deaths, the loss of a ship of five hundred gross tons or larger or one that if properly investigated could lead to the implementation of changes in current standards of safety. And it is only these significant casualties that by regulation merit proper investigation.

The following is a story of a young man who went off to work one morning and never to return. But mostly it is the story of a man who, like all men, should never be allowed to be remembered as only another statistic. This is the story of one such significant casualty.

---

[1]   George Herbert Walker Bush

Dedicated to

Allen Anderson

Martin Anderson

Al Arnold

David Baney

Marc Begnaud,

Bob Bowes

Walter Canfield

Dennis Carnwright

Ron Clark

Phil Clegg

Michael Climer

Harold Cook

Dave Copeland

Martine Cote

Kyle Cronlund

Ron Cummings

Edward Cwick

David Dahl

Ted Davis

John Devine

Brian Diebol

Steven Duque

Troy Elwood

Victor L. Fountane

B. J. Gogne

Skip Guille

John Lipscomb,

James Little

Brent R. Louis

Michael Mahoney

Nicole Marie

David May

Darlene McAuliffe

John McCarty

John J. McHazeltt

Scott Mercer

Tim Nordeen

Dave Norton

Steve "Pearly" Perlewitz

Brian S. Pilkington

Hans Ploeg

Tommy Poore

Eric J. Primavera

G. R. Rogers

Richard Roost

Kevin Sass

Bert Scofield

Jay Shapcotte

Josh Sieber

Lee Snowman

Woody Stangle, Sr.

Adolph Stolz

Albert Harjula

Jude Herpin

Lt. Jessica Hill

Bill "Muffy" Honts

Tom T. Hostetter

Neil Huffman

Bill Juse

Edward King

Roger Kustka

John Lentz

Ron Liest

William L. Stoner

Charles Sturgis

Jim Sugrue

Danny Sullivan

Elwin Swint, Jr.

George C. Tomlinson

Matthew Warzack

Todd Washburn

Lyle Wheeler

Kevin G. Whitney

Frank Zimmerman

And all the men and women that make their living at the end of a hose.

Chapter 1

UNITED ARAB EMIRATES

SEPTEMBER 1976

Desert sand raised in a vortex of gray, gritty fury clinging to every inch of our sweat-covered bodies, clothes flapping in the torrent, heads bowed, hands clasped about our ears, eyes closed as we awaited the rotors to slow and the hatch to be opened. The day was hot and humid as it always was here on the Island of Abu Musa. Even in the early fall of the year, temperatures rarely dropped below eighty-five degrees, and now as the sun was high in sky, it was closer to ninety-five with the humidity approaching 100 percent. Clinging to my right hand was the older of my two sons, Brian, who was about to experience his first flight in such a curious craft with its whirling blades, whining jet turbine engine, gauges, and assorted gizmos. A craft that might have been envied from afar but never so close as this by the four-year-old whose only thoughts at that moment lay in the anticipated flight on which we were about to embark.

As Jack Brooks forced open the forward starboard hatch, pushing against the upwelling wind-driven sand and desert *subca*.[2] Brian lunged forward with me in tow, eyes focused on the pilot and the empty seat to his right. With little or no assistance from anyone he scampered aboard and claimed his throne of honor, scanned the array of gauges, switches and dials as though he knew for what purpose each was intended. To his left sat Jack, peering through mirrored aviator sunglasses, a man in his early thirties who had honed his aviation skills while flying Huey gunships for the United States Government over South East Asia followed by four years of

---

[2]   Sweet sand capable of supporting life

employment with Bell helicopter at their Teheran sales and maintenance facility in Iran.

He was a likable sort of fellow hired by our employer, Rashid Construction of Dubai, to transport construction personnel between our numerous building sites dotted along the northern Arabian Peninsula. Although we had worked together for some four months and would continue to do so for an additional two years, I don't think I ever observed him without the glasses. I'm sure behind them lay the compassionate eyes of a man who now was assisting his youthful copilot with the headset and seat belt as I slipped through the rear door to the passenger compartment.

The craft was a Bell Jet Ranger II, complete with air-conditioning that we never used because of the power required to operate. The brutally hot, thin air through which we flew required that all resources be conserved to maintain the lift required to propel this mechanical marvel. What little power remained precluded the operation of the AC unit meant only to make our flight more bearable. All this was of little consequence to Brian who was more concerned with his preflight preparations. Hands were gyrating in all directions as he reached for switches beyond his grasp, tapped the numerous gages and dials to verify their individual accurateness. On occasion he stopped to admire his own reflection in those mirrored glasses resting on Jack's nose just above the pilot's wide, smiling jaw.

The bright blue ear cups nearly covered the copilot's diminutive head, and the attached microphone would have been more effective at detecting his heartbeat than voice; but to him, it was a perfect fit, to me an image never to be forgotten. Together they reached forward, Brian's hand firmly about the stick, Jack's firmly over Brian's. With a twist of the wrist and a push forward, our craft lunged ahead and upward, quickly rising above the desert, leaving behind the swirling sand. At an elevation of five hundred feet, we turned 180 degrees to the south passing back over the island. Abu Musa is a small and otherwise insignificant dot of land except for its location amid one of the world's largest offshore oil fields—a point of land less than two miles wide with but a single tree. On the southern shore, surrounding one of the island's two shallow bays was the village of Abu Musa inhabited by some fifty Arab fishermen, their families, and an array of emaciated chickens, goats, and one lonely cow. To the northwest around the island's other natural harbor lay the navy base currently under Iranian control. A strange place at best, this little outpost of humanity, half under the authority of the Iranians to the north, the United Arab Emirates to the south, Abu Musa, surrounded by oil wells with eternally burning natural gas flares that bathe the island in twenty-four-hour artificial daylight is a stone's throw from the mouth of the Persian Gulf.

As we gained altitude, Brian looked back down through the gray afternoon mist to this curious place he had only arrived at that morning, a place with houses built of coral and driftwood encompassing the bay with no particular order or pattern. Sandy roads were lined with privacy walls meant to protect the inhabitants from the glances of the occasional passerby. These same walls would cast the slimmest of shadows in the heat of the day protecting the livestock huddled tightly against the base from that merciless yellow orb circling above. To the immediate north of the old village, just south of Abu Musa's only tree, Brian could see the newly surveyed grid of roads that would soon serve the homes we had contracted to build, a brightly painted yellow crane and a half-loaded tractor trailer. Just below we could see a smiling young man waving farewell and a pickup speeding toward some unknown location followed by a cloud of desert dust. As we continued our ascent, the island was quickly obscured by the ever-present mist and shimmering heat and quickly disappeared from view.

Our copilot had lived with us in the United Arab Emirates for less than half a year, but already he had lost his Long Island accent, replacing it with that of something more like a school boy's from east London rather than that of one from eastern New York. The change could be contributed to his exposure to the large contingent of expatriates, primarily British, with whom we lived and worked as well as the faculty and students of the international school he was currently attending in Dubai. Attended, that is, when not obligated to fly such an important mission and protect his father on days such as this. The workforce in the Gulf area was made up primarily of European supervisory personnel along with Pakistani and Indian labor. Although we lived in an Arab country, we rarely associated with the local indigenous population finding ourselves more likely consorting with the European community or expatriate Indians educated under the British system. This British accent would remain with Brian for years after we left the gulf. Remain, perhaps from habit, but I think more likely from choice.

The preceding summer's relentless hours of sunshine through cloudless skies had altered the young man's once brown hair to a golden blond; it hung neatly trimmed straight and long, flowing midway across his ears just below the rim of the bowl his mother would use to keep it just so. Just the way he liked it and contrary to the unruly mess his young brother, Jamie, would permit atop his head. Jamie had been left on the mainland with his mother as he was not yet old enough or responsible enough to accompany his father on such important missions as this. These chores would be left for Brian, and Brian alone, until little Jamie would grow to be the mature young man Brian perceived himself to be. Brian's once-pale complexion was now bronzed from hours of play with little brother and their neighborhood friends along the Ajamanie beach, which was now their front yard. It was a front yard bordered along its northern edge by the Arabian Gulf with an armada of merchant vessels along the northern horizon waiting their turns to be unloaded at the Port of Dubai.

The neighborhood friends consisted of two brothers hailing from Ohio now living next door and an only child, originally from Florida, two doors away. The five boys were all close in age—with Jamie the youngest, Brian the oldest. But it was to Brian that Jamie would turn for guidance and assistance in all things that only a brother older by two years could know. How to escape the crib without being heard, how to get to the cookies, how the bike worked and best of all how to take it apart? The latter was a task left totally to the older brother with the mechanical aptitude. There would be no need for Jamie to learn the functions of pliers, screwdrivers, wrenches, chains, or wheels, as the all-too-willing older sibling was invariably ripe to take advantage of any opportunity to display his mechanical wizardry.

As we flew above the waters of the Arabian Gulf (better known as the Persian Gulf to those not living in Arabia), Brian's hands remained fixed, beneath Jack's. Firmly in control of our craft with his deep blue eyes scanning the array of dials, switches, gizmos, and gadgets, Brian occasionally peered beyond the cockpit to check our location as if he could ascertain exactly where we might be even though we were now well out of sight of land and the seemingly endless sea stretched below us in a monotone of green gray shrouded in that veil of heavy mist created by the evaporating ninety-six-degree waters of the gulf below. Although cruising at two thousand feet above this steamy caldron at 180 knots, there was no relief from the afternoon heat. Our bodies remained mired in gritty desert sand and perspiration collected during our stay on Abu Musa.

Twenty-four hours earlier, his great adventure had begun when, together, we had boarded the *Umm Khanur*, a rusty excuse for a ship capable of carrying four, forty-foot trailers, a crew of eight, and enough fuel for twenty hours of fully laden cruising. A flat-bottomed landing craft, the *Umm Khanur* could enter the shallow bays of remote islands and dispatch its cargo of much-needed building supplies shipped by Rashid Construction from their manufacturing plant in Sharja.

The *Umm Khanur*'s sides more closely resembled a half-completed building than a ship, with exposed beams and columns supporting an overhead bridge crane capable of traversing the length of the cargo deck. If she had ever been painted no evidence now remained for the only portions not covered with the insidious reddish brown cloak of rust were the parts recently scraped clean by an improper docking or covered with some undefined lubricant or fuel. My job was to oversee the manufacture of the building elements required for the new village at Abu Musa, organize their delivery and coordinate the construction. Brian's job was to fly the helicopter, operate the cranes, sail the ship, or do whatever else would normally be expected to be done by a man just seven months short of his fifth birthday.

After boarding the vessel empty of cargo, we left the port of Sharja and proceeded up the man-made Sharja Creek, a river of sorts created so that the people of Sharja might have something to build a bridge across. Dubai had recently constructed its bridge connecting it to Diera and unifying the two-city state. The people of Sharja demanded equal status and, thus, the creation of this man-made tributary to nowhere. Dubai, Sharja, Abu Dhabi, Ajman, Rus Al Khaymah, Al Fujayrah, and Umm Al Qaywayn made up this loose federation of states now known as the United Arab Emirates. Although now somewhat united, the centuries of conflict among the seven tribes now manifested itself in the form of mindless spending to achieve status rather than the senseless killing of one another. Oil and the revenue it produces had made all this possible: rivers to nowhere, bridges to cross the rivers to nowhere, roads to connect the city-states, and then there was the housing. First to house the myriad of workers required to build the housing for the local population and then the high-rise apartments to house the employees necessary to manage the new bureaucracies. It was to this end that we were there, prefabricating houses of concrete panels, constructing low—and high-rise structures of concrete beams and columns all to house the ever-increasing population of expatriates and indigenous nomads. But Abu Musa was different.

The small fishing village nestled around the shallow bay on the southern shore of this remote desert island had been there for centuries. Protected from the warring mainlanders by its shielding expanse of water and local poverty, there was no need to exploit these simple fishermen. There were no herds of livestock, no possessions of value, but then came the oil. Abu Musa found itself strategically located halfway between the Arabian Peninsula to the south and Iran to the north just east of the Strait of Hormuz. The Persian Gulf cannot be entered or left without passing this insignificant atoll, a fact that did not go unnoticed by the Shah's government in Teheran. The Iranians struck a deal with Sheik Abdullah in Sharja who claimed sovereignty over the island and set out to construct a naval base to protect the straits and the offshore oil fields in the region.

Seeing the construction of twentieth-century housing for the Iranian naval personnel the simple fishermen of the island mustered all their collective courage and set sail for Sharja. Once there they demanded and received an audience with their sovereign and cousin at the daily *majlis*. While seated to the right of the sheik, hours of time were spent and innumerable cups of thick black Arabian coffee sipped through tiny cubes of sugar clenched tightly between rotting teeth. Honored guests and members of the family would be granted the privilege of these places of distinction while all others sat to the left.

Whether seated left or right, all were treated to the never-ending cups of coffee, each containing more grounds than liquid while waiting quietly for their individual opportunity to address the monarch. I had often thought it was not the importance of what you were there to say but the size of your bladder that determined when your audience would be granted. The fishermen sat patiently on the hand-built chairs of unfinished teak. Accepting all the coffee served from the long spouted brass pots dutifully carried by black-faced servants dressed in long-flowing white cotton robes, they engaged in the small talk of the day until finally able to present their case.

It was within the monarch's magnificent power to grant them new homes—homes equal to those he was providing to others within his rule. Were they less equal because they lived on an island? Because they were but mere fishermen? Their village was old, and was it not the ruler's responsibility to provide equally for all his subjects? And then there was the matter of the newly constructed Iranian naval base on the northern bay. If perhaps they, the original inhabitants of the island—the longtime, obedient subjects of this ruler and his father before him—were not treated at least as well as these new arrivals by their government in far off Iran, perhaps it might be necessary to move the one mile north, cross the border, beyond the island's only tree, and ask for housing from the Shah. It made little difference to these simple fishermen what authority or what nation claimed control of their village. They lived from day to day, catch to catch with little or no contact with any government agency or control—save the single police officer assigned to the village. If the Shah were willing to provide for them, surely they would be willing to swear allegiance to a new master.

The following day George Putti walked into the Sharja plant office. George was a barrel-shaped man in his late forties, well-groomed except for the knot in his tie that remains forever pulled to one side and never quite sufficiently tightened. The twisted remains of a once-broken nose now well tanned from too many hours in the relentless Arabian sun angled in much the same direction as the tie. Hungarian by birth, Canadian by choice, George was the man for whom we all worked, the man who had convinced me to leave the States some six months before and join him here. Armed with the two briefcases always in his possession and a look of determination, he hurried past the receptionist, and through to the space, I called my office. Both cases were thrust on my cluttered desk. Without so much as a greeting, he grabbed a scrap of paper from the disorder, placed it atop one of the two unopened cases, and drew a small circle.

"This is Abu Musa, a military helicopter will be here in twenty minutes to take you and Mohammed to lay out the new village. Make it four houses to the block, each block should be fifty meters square, each lot twenty-five. Make the roads ten meters wide. They don't have cars, so that should work. We need to fit in a total of 110 houses. Don't go north of the tree, the Iranians control everything up there."

George didn't breathe much; it would take too much time. But after this battery of instructions, he took a deep breath, snatched up the cases, leaving the hastily drawn plan to fall to the desk, and headed for the door. Still in amazement, I called after him, "Where the hell is Abu Musa?"

Without slowing or turning, he lifted the left briefcase pointing it northward and said, "The pilot knows."

"Does it matter where I lay out this new village? I asked.

There was no retort either by choice, or perhaps he was already beyond the range of my voice or his hearing. Quickly following him through the door, I caught up as he hurried away the Pakistani laborer who had decided to wash the dusty brown Jaguar recently parked alongside the temporary-steel Quonset hut used to house the office.

"Just make it fit, make them happy. When you get back, see engineering about the building plans. First units must be started within thirty days." The half-washed car rearranged the gravel of the lot as George and his two unopened bags of importance headed to their next meeting.

Now one month later, the *Umm Khanur* was motoring up Sharja Creek preparing to accept the second of 121 shipments bound for Abu Musa. Brian immediately found his way to the wheelhouse perched well above the empty cargo deck. From here, all the excitement of the loading of the trailers could be observed. The control of the ship and its overhead crane could be monitored. More switches and dials, levers and handles, all the wonders that once were only to be imagined were now in reach. Under Brian's watchful gaze the four-hundred-ton hulk was skillfully run aground at a point where a newly constructed road terminated just below the high tide line. One after another the four loaded trailers were to be backed down the tarmac ramp, then up the steel gate that, when raised, formed the bow of the craft. The loading was not as uneventful as might be expected since this was the first time such a loading had been attempted by both the newly appointed crew of the ship and the inexperienced Pakistani drivers.

The loading gate had been recently extended to accommodate the longer trailers and unusual loading conditions. The drivers were uncomfortable, backing down the steep beach and then up the slick new steel ramp into the undulating cargo deck. On first attempt wheels spun, the trailer slid diagonally across the steel ramp, and the door to the tractor flew open, revealing a turban-headed driver dressed in long loose-fitting garb with sweat pouring from his dust-covered forehead. Leaping to the firm ground below, he headed up the beach in search for dry land and safety from the wrath of Mr. Bill.

Mr. Bill was a young man in his early twenties who had come from Canada to look after the trucks, cranes, heavy construction equipment, and the people that would be hired locally to operate them. His real name was Bill Portingale, but the Pakistanis would refer to each of us by our given names preceded by *mister* as a sign of respect. This was to be the first loading of trailers on the *Umm Khanur*, but Mr. Bill was a veteran as he personally had loaded the craft with an all-terrain crane, a tractor, a four-wheel drive pickup, and a portable office-housing unit twenty-four hours earlier, initiating the maiden voyage to Abu Musa. Never showing any trepidation, Mr. Bill climbed into the now-empty seat, pulled the tractor and trailer forward straightening the rig, and backed directly down to the appointed location on the deck of the ship, blowing both outboard tires on the trailer. Unnoticed, a series of steel gusset plates projected from the superstructure to just above the cargo deck creating a particularly unfriendly environment for the sidewalls of truck tires.

Cutting torches were summoned, and Mr. Bill and I set to modifying the craft still further so that such an occurrence would not be repeated. The tractor was detached from the now-safely-loaded trailer and driven by the now-remorseful original driver to retrieve the second trailer load of cargo. Although not done as skillfully, the remaining trailers were successfully loaded without incident—all under the watchful direction of the newly self-appointed master of the ship, Brian, who had left the wheelhouse during the commotion and assumed a new vantage point atop the ship's unused overhead crane. From his new perch, he supervised the loading and cutting, tire changing and load binding. The craft was now secure and the oversized boarding ramp hoisted to its upright position obscuring all vision directly forward. Both ship engines had been utilized during the loading to maintain contact with the beach as the tide slowly filled the man-made estuary. With the first Abu Musa home now safely aboard the *Umm Khanur*'s, transmissions set to reverse, engines roared to life under the strain and slowly the hulk of a craft creaked and groaned as it freed itself from the sandy bottom. Once liberated the craft—along with Mr. Bill, Brian, I, and the original crew of four—proceeded down Sharja Creek and into the Arabian Sea to begin the eight-hour crossing to the obscure little island amid the sea of steel dinosaurs.

Chapter 2

ONIONS

Once under way and clear of the hazards of the harbor, Brian, the self-appointed young master of the ship, was introduced to Masude, captain of the *Umm Khanur*. Masude was of Indian extraction, slight of build with long dark flowing hair, jet-black skin accented his smiling grin filled with huge glistening white teeth. Looking more like he should be attending high school than commanding a commercial vessel on the high seas, this was the man to whom we would be entrusting our cargo and, at least for this trip, our safety. Brian was most intent on following his newfound friend as they toured the ship together on the first of many inspections. They descended down to the bowels of the freighter containing the twin Detroit diesel engines that were housed in a cavernous space with oil-stained walls. The air was filled with and the smells of grease, salt water, and spilled fuel oil. Not an inch of space was wasted. Tools hung from the walls, chains and pulleys from the ceiling. Seawater leaked through unkempt stuffing blocks only to be returned to the sea via the constantly running bilge pump along with the absorbed fuels and lubricants encountered along the way. The roar of the engines' deafening drone as first one piston fired followed by the next, drowned out any conversation that may have been attempted.

Up the ship's ladder to the galley went Brian back to the chart room that doubled as wardroom, down to the crew quarters with its assortment of hammocks, blankets, and bedding—and finally, once again, ascending and through to the bridge. If the engine room was the heart of the craft, this surely was the brain. Here were found not only all the mechanisms that controlled the craft but also the navigational equipment, communication

gear, and radar—some working and others long abandoned. Dust-covered charts lay on the ledge beneath the expansive window that ran the length of the space. A brass-encased clock with a glass face adorned the wall reading 6:23 and would continue to read the same for the entirety of the voyage. A black ball with the white markings of the compass rose floated in a liquid-filled glass orb prominently mounted to the left of the helm. Just beyond the broad windows overlooking the deck were metallic arms that once directed the rubber blades meant to keep the glass free of rain drops and salt spray but now permanently frozen in place by years of corrosion and salt. Both port and starboard doors were tied in the "open" position with well-used oil-stained cotton lines. Any sign of order was purely accidental on the *Umm Khanur*. But this was to be our home for the night and into the next morning. It was a wondrous place where a young imagination would be free to explore, evolve, and expand. Masude instructed his young pupil in the correct manner of steering and, once learned, turned the responsibility over to him. Although no matter how much Brian turned this great chrome wheel with its radiating, rope-covered spokes the ship would only continue on the preset course north-northeast. No mention of this electronic autopilot was ever made, but Masude was clearly amused by the antics of his new helmsman as Brian would spin the wheel sharply in one direction and then the other.

The helm stood amid ships, behind and high enough above the cargo deck to see over the collection of building components sufficient to assemble the first of the Abu Musa homes. However, it was not high enough to see over the immense loading ramp that served as the craft's bow while under way. As a result the helmsmen required the eyes of the lookouts perched on both the port and starboard flying bridges for visual-hazard recognition. Brian soon became weary of piloting while seeing nothing but the backside of the huge boarding ramp and his attention became redirected to the unmanned radarscope to his left. Seeing Brian's interest, Masude explained the intricacies of this electronic marvel although I question if he himself really understood how it worked, relying more on the visual signals to which he was more accustomed. As no one seemed to have the responsibility of manning this green marvel with its revolving white stripe and knowing the importance of protecting us from some unseen hazard, our young helmsman gave up his position of importance to become the *Umm Khanur*'s full-time radar operator. After several minutes with calves strained from standing straight-legged atop pointed toes, Brian briefly abandoned his position of importance. Scurrying aft through the open hatch to the galley, he quickly reemerged with a half-filled crate of overly ripe onions. Once positioned at the base of the console containing his newly discovered assignment, this wooden crate would provide the additional altitude required to more comfortably complete his self-appointed mission.

Perched low off the starboard rail, the late-afternoon sun dropped into the sea like a free-falling stone. At these latitudes sunrises and sunsets are anything but spectacular. One second there, the next gone, but not so our radar operator. He would leave his post only to scamper to either the port or starboard flying bridge to confirm the existence of one of the blips he might have observed. The late-afternoon waters were filled with returning fishing boats and commercial sailing dhows hurrying to port for protection from the darkness. Few craft in this part of the world contained any sort of navigational equipment much less someone that might be capable of understanding what to do with the apparatus if they did. Rumor had it that even the United Emirates' newly formed navy was under operational orders to conduct activities only in daylight hours and within sight of land. Brian would watch each blip as it would appear, then follow its progress as it moved across the screen and eventually disappeared.

Bill and I joined Masude in the wardroom for the evening meal of fish and rice. The concoction was covered with clarified butter, onions, tomatoes, and an assortment of spices. A single aluminum tray containing the meal was placed on a low table in the confines of the diminutive dining room with the three of us gathered round. A shelf on the inboard wall contained an unused chart case and various electronic components of questionable origin and the remains of a previous meal. Next to the shelf a free-swinging door gave sporadic glimpses of the even smaller galley with its once-gas-fired cooktop now converted to burn the more readily available wood. The walls were covered with multiple layers of white paint completed with drips running down to a metal floor polished by years of use by shoeless feet. Forward, an open hatch led to the bridge where Brian continued his relentless vigil.

On the outboard wall a single porthole with three steel dogs clogged with the same white paint that adorned the walls permitted an occasional view of the stars suspended in the darkness beyond. The aft end of the room contained an open hatch leading to a companionway and then down to the engine room below permitting an occasional burst of unburned diesel fuel to penetrate the space further adding to the ambiance of the meal.

As is customary, only three fingers of the right hand could be used to scoop up the mixture and form it into golf ball-sized bits for consumption. Bill had a habit. While engaged in thought, he would, on occasion, pinch the base of his nose between the thumb and forefinger of his right hand. It was a habit he had learned to regret some weeks before while consuming another equally spicy subcontinent meal while we dined together as the guests of a collection of our Pakistani site agents. Now, aware of how sensitive his nose membrane was, I took great delight in watching him resist the urge to repeat the old habit. Brian had elected to remain at his post and did so for the remainder of the evening. Perhaps he had made the wisest choice. The meal was at best filling, the tea almost warm, but the wardroom with its proximity to the galley much too hot, so Bill and I retired to the port flying bridge to enjoy the freshening evening air.

The evening was calm and clear. The moonless sky was illuminated only by distant gas flares from some oil field over the horizon; the constant sound of the great engines below and the vibrating deck the only reminders that we were in motion. Brian was glued to his post, Masude half-asleep sitting behind the automatically controlled helm. Mr. Bill and I still recovering from the evening meal relaxed while swapping stories and vowing not to return to the confines of the wardroom and the certain sea sickness that awaited us there. At about 2:00 AM, Brian hopped down from the crate that had afforded him access to the green cathode-ray tube and scampered to the starboard watch, then back to his screen and again to the starboard bridge. Finally, he shook Masude with alarm to warn him of the certain danger approaching. Masude, trusting the eyes of his own posted watch, explained to his newest crewmen how false images can be created by waves, birds, or other objects and there was no reason for alarm. Brian returned to his post. But still the blip remained and was getting ever closer. There was no wind, no waves; surely, he had to be correct. He would not take another excuse. Masude must accompany him to the starboard bridge or change course to avoid this unseen object.

Finally, the captain pulled himself from the comfort of the only padded piece of furniture on the vessel and proceeded with the help of his radar operator to the starboard watch. When they did not return for some time, Bill and I followed. The seas remained glassy calm with but a single ribbon of light created by that faraway gas flare. But just to the north, if you strained to see, there was a shadow. No lights, no sound, just a shadow, and it was getting closer. As the shadow passed across the stream of light reflecting over the sea from that distant oil field, the intensity of the light was absorbed by the shadow and then reappeared on the opposite side as this unseen object continued directly into the path of the *Umm Khanur*. Masude raced to the helm, switched off the autopilot, and spun the wheel hard right in an attempt to turn behind the object. Bill looking into the darkness calmly said, "Wonder if that guy knows just how much trouble he's in, eh?" in his best Western Canadian accent.

At that same moment, the captain of the unlit dhow turned hard left. The resulting impact sounded like a thousand wooden kitchen matches being crushed. Mr. Bill and I remained on the starboard bridge—Masude, ramrod straight with teeth firmly clenched, white-knuckled at the helm. Brian, who had already returned to his post looked across to the captain on his right, leaned closely and said with his best British accent:

"Told you so."

All engines had been stopped. Not by Masude, who remained stiff and motionless behind the helm, but by a mate whose presence had gone unnoticed until now. Springing to the deck of the wheelhouse from a compartment high above, originally intended to contain life jackets, this boy had sprung into action throwing both engines hard astern momentarily and then to stop perhaps preventing additional carnage to the as-yet-unseen obstruction in our path. Deck lights were turned on revealing a plume of oily black smoke pouring over the starboard rail just forward of our number two trailer.

Mr. Bill and I, without speaking, dropped down the starboard ship's ladder to the cold steel cargo deck heading for the source of smoke. Squeezing between and then under our consignment of trailers, we finally reached our destination. Preceding us to the point, two of the *Umm Khanur*'s crew had already begun securing the remaining section of the crippled dhow preventing what appeared to be its inevitable sinking.

Persian Gulf dhows have remained unchanged for centuries. They are primarily hand-hewn mahogany planks stretched across teak superstructures with long protruding and distinctive bow sprints. Each plank is individually cut, shaped, drilled, caulked with cotton fibers and oily putty to keep out the ever-invasive sea. The open cargo holds are capable of transporting all nature of things from produce to people, dry goods to machinery, complete with the smells of oil and fish, sweat and exotic spices permeating each board and fastener. In recent years the once-romantic sails had been replaced with the clanging reliable propulsion contraptions common to all modern vessels of commerce. It was just such a craft that had had the misfortune to cross our path that early moonless morning. Probably this dhow had been traveling from some unknown port to some equally unknown destination with a cargo that might only be moved under the veil of darkness.

Together we ventured uninvited to provide aid and assistance and to see to the cause of the persistent oily smog that now invaded every pore and orifice. Damage was confined to the bow sprint that clearly made up one third of the entirety of the craft. Sheared off just above the water line the splintered remains of the bow floated, undulating closely below its once-proud position. But still the black pestilence persisted. Peering below the deck beyond the canvas draped, rope bound bundles of uninvestigated commerce could be seen the hulking antique diesel engine meant to provide propulsion to the craft. Valve covers had been removed to expose the metal shafts and lifters of twelve small springs each compressed and released in turn as the relic continued to operate. The once-necessary oil pump needed to provide the required lubrication had been replaced by a mate with a Maxwell House coffee can. Dressed in little more than sweat-covered rags pulled tightly around his waist and loosely draped over greasy shoulders, he would first scoop up oil deposited in the bilge and then methodically spread it over each exposed moving part. The heat of the engine caused the water bearing oil to vaporize mixing with the unruffled exhaust, thus creating the greasy mist.

Not speaking the language of the unidentified crew but understanding their displeasure with our presence, we quickly retreated to the safety of our own vessel. Lines were cast off, and as quickly as this ship of midnight commerce had appeared, she slipped back into the protective cover of night never to be seen again.

Upon our return to the bridge, we found Masude as we had left him, stiff and motionless, eyes fixed forward, teeth knit tightly together. To his left, with newfound confidence and an air of respectability, standing atop a half-filled crate of overly ripe onions, the radar administrator carefully monitored the departure of the once-ominous blip to the edge of the screen.

Time was of the essence. High tide would be 6:45 AM and access to the harbor was only possible for ninety minutes either side of that appointed hour. Any later and we would have to secure offshore, await the next tide, or risk running aground. Unknown to Mr. Bill and me, Masude had arranged a short diversion along the way. Although the sun was still some two hours away from being thrust once again to the heavens, the cloudless skies became unnaturally bright as we approached the first of the oil fields with their sentinels of gas flares burning off the unwanted methane. Platforms could be seen in all directions—some producing, some drilling, but all active. Alive with life and lights, each appeared to be a great floating Christmas tree. It was an eerie seascape filled with shimmering shadows, clanking steel, voices calling out in unknown tongues, streams of water pumped over the sides with plumes of smoke and steam being projected skyward. Merchant ships would normally avoid fields such as this, but our captain was on a mission.

Masude was now once again in control of not only himself but also our vessel, one hand on the wheel, the other tightly wrapped about the handset suspended from the radio overhead. He spoke in one of the two hundred Indian dialects shouting orders to the assembled crew of eight (make that nine counting the radar technician still manning his position of importance). Instructions crackled over the antique speakers, our course was changed, lookouts posted, engines slowed—all to the bewilderment of our electronics expert. Why was he not informed of this change in course? Why this deviation from plan? What were these mechanical dinosaurs that changed his once-green monitor to now almost white? Confusion was the order of the day. No one paid mind to the youngest member of the crew as attentions were focused on a single platform directly ahead: the one with the recently illuminated spotlight aimed directly toward us.

Seeing no point in monitoring his position any longer, Brian hopped down from the half-filled wooden box that had been his home throughout the night.

He rushed to the starboard flying bridge to peer skyward with wide-eyed awe at the ever-approaching marvel. From his new vantage point, the solitary monster could be observed and monitored as, slowing to a crawl, the unwieldy *Umm Khanur* was maneuvered closely to the side of this giant shape. Our proximity only magnified the size of this machine meant to drill miles below the surface of the earth in search for the oil known to be there. Three great legs projecting up from the unseen shallow seafloor below, then thrusting skyward from the surface of the inky black sea to the underside of the open steel deck some twenty meters above Brian's head. Open steel framing extended in all directions connecting legs to legs and legs to deck. Diminutive work platforms with temporary pipe railings suspended from above suggested a giant erector set out of control. The open steel trusses, bolts, nuts and cables too large for any young man to have assembled also challenged immediate comprehension. Sparks from welder's torches, drilling mud, and discarded liquids of all description poured from above as the crew that provided life for this monster continued on with their assigned tasks. Surely, if the *Umm Khanur*'s engines, dials, hoists, and other assorted equipment had been a source of awe and inspiration to spark a young imagination, now they were but simple toys and gadgets compared to this dinosaur lurking off the starboard bow.

Lights blazed on not only the *Umm Khanur* but also streamed down from the halogen lamps strung like holiday lights between and around the base of the monster's deck high above. Hovering at some predetermined location midway between two of the giant legs the *Umm Khanur* held position. Overhead, the monster swung a great steel arm complete with pulleys, cables, and a rope-woven basket for a hand. Voices called out in some  unknown tongue as a worker released the arm in a controlled fall to our vessel's deck. Boxes and burlap sacks filled with produce appeared from one of the forward stowage lockers and were quickly loaded in the waiting basket. Masude hurried from the bridge followed closely by his young prodigy. Once on deck, our captain joined the cargo of supplies now safely loaded for the trip up and aboard the menacing monster. Brian, as he had the previous night, followed his newly found friend in eager anticipation of what was to be experienced in the continuation of his tour.

The gentle rolling of the ship gave slack to the line supporting the basket and again tightened as the vessel dropped following a passing swell and then slacked again. Engines growled as the helmsmen switched from forward to reverse in an attempt to hold a steady position. Voices called out from above intermingled with the clanging of steel pipes and the banging sounds of chains. Masude cautioned his fellow voyager as the cable from above was once again tightened and the pair along with the cargo was propelled skyward into the bowels of the awaiting monster.

Deposited unceremoniously between a pile of drill rod and casing, the mates emerged on the first solid surface encountered since leaving the dock in Sharja. A young Indian boy with flowing jet-black hair protruding from beneath a bright yellow hard hat immediately embraced Masude. With similar facial features and of equal stature to our captain, he was neatly dressed in coveralls bearing a logo matching the ones emblazoned on most all the objects in sight as well as on the crew that hurriedly emptied the basket. The two apparent brothers continued in animated conversation, ignoring the boy who had come to explore. From the protective shadow of the captain's thigh, the curious young sojourner could see this alien city on the water stretched before him. There were buildings and equipment of all description. Tools, forklifts, great drums of oil, and assorted lubricants were everywhere: all the things needed to find the black gold of the twentieth century.

The precious cargo of fresh produce was quickly spirited away to one of the white aluminum-clad structures. Curious, other similar buildings containing housing, dining facilities, offices, and community services lay in orderly rows. Some were bolted to the open mesh steel deck, others stacked above and still more above them. Railed ramps, ship ladders, and companionways connected all, creating a complex maze that would have been the envy of any domesticated rat. Other men in similar coveralls, except for the covering of mud and grease, continued on wrapping chains around the vertical casing extending from the seafloor up to the main deck, hoisting pipes, cutting, welding, and moving equipment. The sun was still hours from beginning its daily trek across the sky, but this was a city that never sleeps. The pursuit of oil kept this metropolis alive with activity twenty-four hours a day. The delivery of the produce had provided a momentary break in the prepackaged, preserved, and mediocre cuisine available on this man-made island of exploration. But as quickly as Masude and Brian had arrived, the boarding party was hurried back to the elevator cab constructed of rope and wood for the short trip down to the rolling deck of the *Umm Khanur*. Farewells exchanged and a parting hug interrupted by the roaring diesel engine of the drilling platforms crane followed by the whine of cable racing through well-oiled pulleys separated the brothers once more. Once swung clear of the platforms deck the basket and its precious cargo were allowed to free-fall to the awaiting ship below.

Quickly regaining their individual positions of responsibility, both captain and mate prepared to depart the realm of the lurking giants and continue the journey as contracted. Engines were brought back to life, and a course set for north-northwest leaving the strange half-light of the oil flares and electric lights behind. Masude had made a few extra dollars or perhaps just kept a family promise. Brian had experienced his first oil well, his first exposure to the larger-than-life world of the business of oil.

Brian's monitor once again regained its green hue as the steel giants faded to the edge of the screen. The second mate returned to his post nestled between the life jackets in the overhead locker. Masude resumed his vigilant watch from the comfort of the only padded seat on this relic of a craft. Watches assumed their previous posts and all returned to the way it had been prior to our encounter with the midnight ship of commerce. Mr. Bill and I pondered the prospect of the 120 subsequent trips that would be required to complete our mission—required, that is—if this one was ever to be completed.

Almost simultaneous with the first light of day on the eastern horizon an ever-enlarging blip appeared on the top of Brian's radar screen. The events of the evening had not tired the young traveler but only caused him to be more attuned to his surroundings. Again, fearing a second collision or better yet another encounter with a monster of the sea, he jumped down. Scampering past the napping captain, he slipped out the starboard hatch where he climbed the rail currently supporting the sleeping mate assigned to the watch. There, unfolding before him in the first light of day, lay the island of Abu Musa. Hanging tightly to the top rail, Brian leaned forward pointing and shouting so that all might be aware of his discovery. It would be hard to believe that even the top watch on the Santa Maria could have been more excited than our mate at that moment. With wide-eyed amazement, feet planted atop the bottom rail, hands wrapped about the top rail, windblown golden hair glowing with the light of a new day, he stood erect watching his new discovery as it developed along the northern horizon.

With the knowledge that he had safely protected us from the dangers of the night and delivered us to our destination, Brian climbed down from the rail reentered the bridge and filled the space left by the departing first mate, along with the few remaining life jackets safely stored in the overhead compartment. The young self-appointed master of the ship now with his task complete, rearranged the pile of orange-covered cork-filled vests to form a makeshift throne high above the awakening nerve center of his vessel. For now his work was done, and with fingers laced behind his head, he peered passed his crossed legs through the compartment's open hatch to the awakening throng below. Time for a well-deserved nap while the mundane task of docking and unloading could be left to the remaining members of the crew.

Chapter 3

ABU MUSA ISLAND

The morning incoming tide continued to fill the small harbor along the northern shore of Abu Musa as the *Umm Khanur* slowly churned closer to the entrance. Rashid construction, through the government at Sharja, had negotiated an agreement with the Iranian military permitting us to use their facilities for unloading cargo. This had become necessary as the soft coral sand beaches that ringed the atoll had been considered too soft and unstable to support the weight of our loaded trucks and trailers. The now-completed naval base contained not only a row of neatly constructed barracks, so coveted by the original inhabitants, but also warehouses, piers, bulkheads, and a concrete slipway leading from the island's only paved road to the low watermark. This slipway had been constructed to permit the expeditious launching of small shore-based speedboats that could and would be used to protect or harass passing ships. It would also provide for the *Umm Khanur* the safest, most secure place at which to unload her bulky, top-heavy baggage.

With full knowledge of the agreement and with the understanding that twenty-four hours earlier our vessel had safely discharged her cargo of rolling stock, we still proceeded with caution not knowing if the word had been spread to this day's military field personnel manning the recoilless rifles that were currently tracking our every movement. The government in Teheran was still firmly in the control of Mohammad Reza Pahlavi, but each day rumors spread that Muslim extremists were threatening that control. However, our task was not to understand the politics of the day but rather to unload our four trailers and proceed to the safety of the south side of the island's only tree. Then we were to begin the construction of Abu Musa's first new home built in this century on the Arab-controlled side of the island.

Past the harbor markers, slowly approaching the ribbon of concrete extending beneath the surface of the gulf, Masude, our vessel's captain, directed his craft to the second of many landings in this strangest of ports. Awakened by the scraping of the steel hull against the gritty sand bottom and the revving of our two great engines, Brian sprung once again to the ready. Running his fingers through his disheveled hair, straightening his shirt and trousers, he left his bed of life jackets and dropped to the cold steel deck below. The *Umm Khanur* had once again found a steady berth to call home, if for only as long as it would take to unload her cargo and then escape before the tidal flow would leave her stranded. The deck was now once again firm and motionless, the undulating cadence of the sea now only remembered by our legs as we attempted to adjust to the stationary surface. Scampering forward along the starboard catwalk, Brian sought out his perch atop the motionless unused bridge crane from which he had directed the loading the previous day.

From this vantage point, he could see the lowering of the battering ram used earlier that morning to drive off that strange ship of midnight commerce. Beyond the concrete key lay a sort of village unlike any he had seen before, monotonous buildings standing stark and sterile, monotone in color with writing consisting of strange curves and slashes painted in a dark color above each door. Barred windows and metal portals provided the only relief through the thick, heavy walls meant to provide protection from the sun and possible intruders. There were rows of small identical boats each carefully placed atop its individual trailer. Multi sand colored four-wheeled vehicles with canvas tops and empty gun mounts stood at the ready. This was no village but rather the home of the garrison sent to protect the Shah's interests here in the northern Gulf. The people in evidence were not dressed in the long-flowing robes of the Arabs to the south or the loose-fitting, baggy trousers and shirts of the Pakistanis to the east. Each man standing along the key was dressed the same, neatly shined black boots, desert brown trousers tightly bloused just above the ankle, heavy-starched tunics of the same color with razor-sharp creases. The shirtsleeves were rolled into four-inch cuffs midway up the biceps. And squarely mounted on the head of each soldier of the Shah's navy was a round lid with a flat top and a blunt bill. Each cap was emblazoned with the two-thousand-year-old seal of the Persian empire. Beneath each cap, in stern defiance, stared a pair of brown eyes framed by what appeared to be several days' growth of beard. No matter how often these men of Central Asia would shave, their cheeks would all too often look as those belonging to this line of spectators. This inherited five o'clock shadow coupled with the stern appearance and military bearing only further intimidated our crew of misfits from India.

No assistance was asked and none offered from these men of the Shah as our rag tag crew scurried about in preparation for the discharge of cargo. Not only were the tides now of concern but also there was this assembled group of militaristic observers each bearing either a side arm or an assault rifle. In addition, there was no sign of the necessary island-based crew needed to pull the trailers to shore.

They were supposed to have been in place with a tractor at the ready to reverse the operation conducted twelve hours earlier on the beach up the Sharja River. In the distance and far up the road could be seen an approaching cloud of dust preceded by the yellow Daihatsu four-wheel-drive pickup delivered to the island the previous day. At the wheel sat Mr. Martin in semi control of his vehicle as he hurried to meet our already arrived craft. At some distance behind followed the lumbering tractor needed to extract the trailers now being unlashed from the deck of the *Umm Khanur*. Mr. Martin, Martin Neal, was actually the company electrician. A boy of twenty-one, whose father worked for Tarmac Limited, a multinational British firm, currently building the Dubai International Airport, had been sent along with Mr. Bill to assist in the construction and assume responsibility in Bill's absence. It was a responsibility he apparently had failed to acknowledge, at least on this early morning.

Upon Masude's order, the great loading ramp was lowered once again giving us access to dry land. Mr. Bill hurried ashore to greet if not admonish his tardy cohort who, at that moment, was attempting to bring to a halt the out-of-control pick up. Once at a standstill amid the cloud of dust, words were exchanged as the two reached a temporary understanding, and they assessed the situation. Every second was now critical, missing a tide could and would cost another day's delivery. If on the first day, a day was lost, how would they ever regain the schedule? Although only minutes away the tractor should already have been unloading the first trailer. The tractor should have been standing by, awaiting the ship's arrival not still lumbering down the dusty road.

Brian stood above still perched on the overhead crane as he watched the chaos unfolding below him. This was a time for action as both Mr. Bill and the newly arrived Martin were being surrounded slowly by the ominous men previously only watching from their positions on the key. Back across the cat walk into the bridge, down the ship's ladder, across the deck, and finally down the ramp while Brian found his way to his old friend's side as Bill and Martin continued their animated conversation. Already on the deck I slowly followed behind as Brian got ever closer to these foreign soldiers. He stopped at a respectful distance, looked them up and down as he straightened his trousers and tucked in his shirt. He checked to see that his shirt buttons were properly aligned with his fly, his collar standing tall. He wiped his dusty shoes on the backs of his pant legs and then carefully and methodically rolled his shirtsleeves into four-inch cuffs or as close as he could get to that necessary arrangement. Then too he stared and waited, watching to see what these strange men would do. They were perhaps more perplexed than he to see such a young person in this outpost of desolation—not only one so young but one with blue eyes and blond hair shaped like an overturned pot. Brian brought his hands slowly to their respective sides; positioning them just above his hips. And then without warning, he quickly reached and drew his imaginary guns just like he had watched John Wayne do a thousand times.

"Bang bang, I got you."

The silence that followed seemed to last an eternity but, in reality, was probably less than a second as the assembled solders burst into a chorus of uncontrolled laughter. Each in turn approached the little man touching the top of his head, messing the golden locks Brian was so proud of. Never again would these men of the Shah's navy seem so ominous. Never again would we ever encounter a hostile stare or an unfriendly gesture. Brian would never again pass through this port, but on my own subsequent visits, I would always be asked, "And how is Mr. Brian? We miss him."

The frivolity of the day subsided as the tractor finally arrived and the reason we were there returned to the forefront. Unloading was quick and proceeded far more easily than had the loading twelve hours earlier. Now, the only backing up required was with the trailerless tractor. In turn, each of the four units was extracted amid the shouts of direction in various tongues from members of the crew and the assembled military observers. The Island-based driver spoke Urdu, a Pakistani dialect, and maybe a little English when he chose to. The crew of the *Umm Khanur*, save the captain, spoke only a collection of Indian languages and the soldiers on the key only Farsi, the official Persian language. Despite this questionable assistance, the first three trailers loaded with building components were parked along the sandy shoulders of the paved road just beyond the slipway. Surrounded by a cloud of dust and fine sand propelled skyward by escaping exhaust and compressed air, the rag-draped driver would in turn uncouple the newly arrived load and then remount his ride to retrieve the next. The fourth load would be taken directly to the new town site short two kilometers away. Mr. Martin, Brian, and I did not stay to watch the completion of the unloading but rather opted to leave that task to Mr. Bill. Without our companion of the perilous sea journey, we climbed aboard Martin's orange-painted pickup to find our way to the construction site.

Martin was in the driver's seat, I to his right, and Brian hanging tightly to one of the two-side mounted crew seats fastened to the bed of this company-owned vehicle. Trapped on this desert island, the only function of our truck was to expedite the numerous anticipated trips from job site to the Iranian port and back. There was nowhere else to go that could not be more easily reached by the more-conventional method of transportation used by the island's original inhabitants. Their feet had served them well, and no other mode of land transit was ever really necessary. Before we arrived, there was no need to follow a schedule, no sense of urgency, or even time to clutter up the day. The entire island was less than four square miles, and now truly half of that was under the watchful control of these new neighbors to the north. The only other mechanical means of land transportation found on the island were our tractor, an old Bedford utility truck used to deliver water, and the Toyota Land Cruiser operated by the local police. As might have been expected, months later on one of Martin's hurried excursions to meet an already-arrived shipment, he would be involved in the only recorded traffic accident on the island. The account of his head-on collision with the Land Cruiser while both were attempting to negotiate the narrow wall lined lanes of the old village in opposite directions was one of unbelievable amazement, improved with each retelling. But today, with both my young son and me aboard, he drove with great care as we left the port heading for the border crossing.

Following the asphalt-paved surface through the naval base between the rows of military structures, each painted with the same monotone hue displayed on the buildings along the key, we found our way to the edge of this outpost of the Shah. Entering the interior of the island, the road continued straight and flat, terminating at a point marked with twin concrete monoliths. Projecting between them was a single four-inch-diameter steel pipe painted alternating red-and-white stripes. The left end of the pike projected beyond a pilaster, supporting a great concrete counterweight and to the left of that a small guardhouse. Hurrying from the protective shade of his post, a single soldier appeared, with one arm adjusting the weapon slung about his shoulder, the other projected skyward signaling us to stop. Without a word and under the curious eyes of our young passenger, the guard circumnavigated our vehicle, slowly peering into each space of this open truck that had passed by his post just minutes before going the other way. He continued to walk, once clockwise, then once around in the opposite direction, but on the return trip more interested in our passenger than on some unseen contraband that might be hidden somewhere within the vehicle. Brian followed each step as he straightened once again his freshly cuffed shirtsleeves, adjusted his collar, all while sitting ramrod straight trying to look taller than his four feet, one inch would permit. Martin, impatient to continue and knowing the guard could not speak a word of English, began a diatribe in the King's worst English relative to the similarities between this man with the gun and a camel. He emphasized in particular the relationship of appearance and odor, all done with a smile and spoken in a most sincere tone. Brian, hearing every word, broke into laughter as I bit my lip and held tight to my seat not knowing of what to expect. Mr. Martin continued to smile as the armed man, not understanding a word, joined in the laughter and patted the top of the young voyager's golden locks as he turned to open the gate permitting us to pass.

Pressed back against our seats by the force of the accelerating truck, we passed beneath the uplifted pole leaving the paved road behind as we entered the Arab side of the island. Although still early in the day, the sun had already assumed its place of prominence overhead in the cloudless sky as the cool morning air quickly retreated, replaced by that heat of the day—a heat to which we would never be able to become fully accustomed. Dry desert dust and sand became mixed with the scattering gravel of the road and petrol exhaust created by our speeding truck as we hurried to our destination. Why we were in such a hurry, I will never completely understand, but then Martin was always in need of doing things with great dispatch. And the speed, rushing wind, raising dust, and the roar of the engine only caused his young passenger, firmly strapped to the rear seat, to shout out in delighted encouragement. Faster and faster, Martin sped down this poor excuse for a road until we reached the site of what was to be the new village at Abu Musa. As quickly as we had left the control point to the north, Mr. Martin brought his truck to a screaming halt. The backend swerved to the right as the front brakes dug deeply into the soft sand creating two furrows in what would someday be the main street. Brian released himself, jumped to his feet and congratulated his new friend on this wonderful ride of exhilaration as the cloud of dust that had been following a safe distance behind now engulfed all three of us and, at least momentarily, blocked out all reminders of that relentless sun above.

Directly to our front, standing at the ready was the never-before-used all-terrain crane delivered to the island twenty-four hours earlier. Two turban-headed operators interrupted their morning maintenance to admonish the driver of the newly arrived vehicle as the accompanying dust settled on their newly polished source of pride. Martin responded with comments of a nature similar to those used with the guard to the north as he dusted himself off and wiped the sand from his tightly closed eyes. Brian remained firmly in place, grasping the roll cage suspended above the head of the driver, inquiring if perhaps there was somewhere else Mr. Martin would be in need of going.

I climbed to the safety of the dry sand as Brian filled my vacated seat, and with great care, my son and his newly found friend slowly pulled away.

"Martin where the hell are you going?" I called after them.

"I'm an electrician, there be nothing for me to do until you guys build something for me to pull wires in. And this boy, he needs to see the island, you know all the sights, downtown that sort of thing. We'll be back for tea. Maybe."

As Brian pulled hard to secure the seat belt around his waist, Martin once again displayed the full power of his trucks 1800 cc engine as he turned to the east heading for the far side of the island and the beach he had discovered the day before. Never had Brian been allowed to be in a moving vehicle without first being securely fastened in. His mother would always be so insistent. "Young man, this car will not be moving one inch until that belt is fastened, and you are sitting straight and tall in that seat," she would say, followed by some comment about keeping his hands to himself and leaving little Jamie alone. But today was different; he was in the company of men, doing man things, driving in a vehicle with no doors across a desert landscape with no apparent road to confine them and no mother to direct or control his actions. He completed the last tug on the belt, grabbed hold of the handgrip mounted on the dash, giving out another yell of joy further encouraging his newly found partner to drive even faster.

The morning's activity proceeded somewhat as planned as first one tractor and trailer arrived and then another, each having its cargo removed and set in its final place forming the first of the new homes. Our predetermined schedule allowed one workday to complete the basic construction of each building. Then in turn, one day would be allowed for each of the subsequent operation required to turn the structure into a livable home. A total of twenty-one such operations, including the erection of the frame, would be required, resulting in a completed home every day, following the initial start up. As Mr. Bill instructed his crew, made up of Pakistani laborers and Indian equipment operators, in the method by which assembly should proceed, we would catch an occasional glimpse of a speeding open truck. Following closely behind there was an ever-present cloud of swirling dust that needed to be kept at bay and the sound of two young men yelling encouragement to each other. There was as yet nothing for an electrician to do and his young associate exhibited a greater interest in speed and exploration than in watching the laborious efforts of the yellow crane and cautious riggers as they pieced together the first of the 110 units.

Standing at a safe distance from the yellow monster, the town fathers watched. Thirty days earlier, these men of importance had presented themselves to the ruler, respectfully requesting new homes for their families. Today they stood protected from the relentless sun by their peasant rags, watching the fruition of that request. Half of the first structure was complete as the sun reached the noonday sky and the midday break began. In this part of the world, centuries of experience had taught the wisdom of an extended departure from work in order to avoid the heat of the day. This time would be spent eating, relaxing, socializing, or sleeping until the midday heat subsided. The third trailer had just been moved beneath the hook of the waiting crane when all engines stopped and crew ceased work to find a place in the shade. With no words passed, the most senior looking of the local observers approached the now-lifeless crane followed by the remaining members of his entourage. Continuing past, each in turn touched the smooth concrete walls in reverent recognition of their first new home. With proud approval, the leader turned to Mr. Bill and me motioning for us to follow. Surrounded by the entourage, we were directed from the new town site following the well-beaten trail to the original village only a hundred meters away. Past the rough coral walls protecting the old residences from view, down the narrow lanes meant to support only foot traffic, we traveled to the old town square.

Prominently placed on the site stood Abu Musa's only public building standing in defiance of years of salt spray emanating from the adjacent harbor. Rusty bits of steel reinforcing projecting from craters once filled with locally manufactured concrete, pock marked the exterior walls. Small almost-insignificant windows shielded with iron bars provided the only fenestration and a single steel door, the only means of entrance or exit on this otherwise lifeless-looking structure. Haphazardly parked to the left of the door stood the black-and-white-painted Toyota Land Cruiser that two days before had been Abu Musa's only truck—only truck, save for the old rusted-out Bedford used to haul water. Alongside the Toyota a passengerless open pickup covered in dust sat motionless.

The purpose for which we had been directed to this ominous structure still remained unclear. Not a word had passed between us two North Americans and the surrounding Arab peasants during the short hike from the construction site to the old town center. Not a word could have been passed as Bill and my combined Arab language skills were confined to the Arab words for "yes," "no," "peace be with you," and the numbers one through ten. However, I always suspected Mr. Bill had also mastered a few local expressions not generally found acceptable in polite conversation. But here was our pickup parked in front of this building, which looked more like a prison than a place for social gathering, and its last two occupants were nowhere to be seen. Passage into the structure was possible only through that single door constructed of steel plate with decorative welded appliqués. Although carefully adorned to present some aura of opulence on the face of this otherwise austere structure, the door required a considerable amount of persuasion from two of our hosts to open it. Once the task had been completed, Bill and I were beckoned to enter. The entry hall, illuminated only by the light streaming through the open door, was paved with coarsely laid marble blocks surrounded by plastered walls that appeared to have been painted at one time. A small wood desk constructed of unfinished mahogany and a single chair were the only furnishings. Two closed interior doors and a passage leading to the rear of the building completed the space. Standing at the ready, dressed in complete military attire was Abu Musa's lone policeman. Words were passed between our hosts and this outsider who had been posted here by the ruler to protect the islanders from themselves. Then a nod of the head and out through the open door the policeman scurried on what appeared to be a mission of importance as Mr. Bill and I were directed down the darkened hall past more closed doors.

The last of these doors was pushed opened by the leader of the entourage to reveal a room as stark and barren as the entry we had just left, except that this room had a window. Perched high on the rear wall of the space, a single opening permitted the midday sun to penetrate the space, revealing another room paved in cast marble aggregate blocks and crudely plastered walls. In the center of the space sat a solitary wood table with stubby legs too short to permit the use of chairs, and against the side wall stood a pair of beds constructed of rough timbers and rope-woven mattresses. Seated on the bed closest to the door with hands neatly folded in their laps were the two young men last seen traveling, unabated on their unescorted tour of the island. They appeared to be in good health, but in less than happy spirits. I began with a series of questions first directed to the fellow employee who was obviously responsible for this current situation and then to my young son who was experiencing his first incarceration in something other than a room filled with his toys. As my interrogation continued, neither Mr. Bill nor I realized that the heavy wood door through which we had just passed was now closed. The men who had accompanied us were now gone and we too, apparently, had become prisoners for some crime not yet revealed.

I was twenty-seven years old at the time and more concerned with my responsibilities as a builder than with my obligations as a father. Continuing my tirade with more concern for the schedule, which we would not be capable of maintaining while locked up in the local jail, with Mr. Bill and me cooling our heels in the can, who would complete the first structure? Who would be responsible for the delays, the costs, the crew, tomorrow's sailing? Brian sat on the rope-woven mattress and watched. He had seen me lecture before and probably listened, as before, not hearing a word but rather dreaming of the story he would have to tell little Jamie upon his release from prison. He was the oldest, and it was his responsibility to blaze all the trails, then teach his sibling the ways of the world. Without his help, Jamie could never have figured out how to get out of the crib, how to torment the cat, how to disassemble all nature of things. But this would be great! Not only had he accompanied Dad on a ship, but he, personally, had sailed through a field of hazards avoiding them all—well, most all. Then he had confronted a foreign military force and won. Then he had learned to drive fast, really fast, and off the road. Jamie would not need to know about the seat belt part. Now we were in jail, what could be better? More new experiences in one day to relate than ever before. Jamie would be so proud of his big brother—that is, if we were ever able to get out of here.

As my tirade continued, the door once again swung open as two young men dressed in local attire entered and with sandaled feet turned over the table with the all-too-short legs dumping the loose sand and dirt to the floor. Then righting the table they wiped the surface with a discolored, gritty rag. Once that task had been completed, they disappeared as quickly as they had entered, leaving the door open as they departed. Through the open door, the original entourage of village elders entered, beckoning for us to join them as they selected their individual places to squat around the freshly cleaned table. The oldest of the group selected his place at the head of the table with the window above and behind him. A place was left for us four captives on the left side and all the others sat to the right across from us. Martin had selected his place immediately to the left of the man seated at the table's head. This arrangement displeased this man of obvious importance as he motioned Martin to change places with me so that the final seating arrangement would place me at the elder's elbow.

Coffee appeared carried by the boys who had earlier cleaned the room so efficiently. Each carried a brass tray supporting traditional spouted pots, clear glass cups, some empty, some filled with white blocks of sugar. The thick warm beverage was offered and accepted by all, including the four-year-old young man seated to my left. Blocks of sugar were clinched between the blackened teeth of our guests, and pleasantries were exchanged. None of us understood what the others were saying, and I suspect none of them understood what we said unless it involved a yes, a no, or a number. After several rounds of coffee, a platter of rice appeared and was placed prominently in the center of our table. This presentation was followed quickly by small plates containing a concoction of tomatoes, overcooked goat, and a selection of spices. An individual plate containing this mixture was placed to the right of each diner. This would be Brian's first meal consumed under Arab etiquette, so I quickly instructed him regarding the finer points of eating with your hand so as not to offend our hosts. As had appeared to be the case earlier, my young companion was preoccupied with thoughts of his own as he stared past me not hearing a word.

"Dad, I know all that stuff. Look at your plate. You gonna eat that?" exclaimed my young man of the world.

Apparently, I had misread the intent for our being brought to this place. We were not prisoners, but rather guests being treated to the best this island had to offer. I looked to the item of so much interest to young Brian on the plate to my right. Peering back at me was a single eye placed carefully among the tomatoes and charred goat flesh. Slowly I lifted my vision from this most uncommon entrée only to catch the smiling grin of our host and the blackened remains of his teeth. Clutched between thumb and forefinger of his right hand was the match to the hors d'oeuvre so splendidly displayed on my plate. Holding it up high, he slowly passed this symbol of esteem from left to right and then dropped it into his own open mouth, swallowing it like a freshly shucked oyster. Once the assembled elders had assured him of a job well done, he redirected his attention to me and motioned to do the same. I complied.

Brian would remind me of that incident in his young life many times over the following years. This recognition of importance, being permitted to swallow an eye of the meat offering of the meal was a sign of respect and manhood. Years later, the family would be traveling through Turkey on our way to Greece and would have occasion to stop at a small restaurant on the banks of the Bosporus just outside Istanbul. Traveling with us was a young couple from New Zealand, and together we made a party of six. The restaurant was small and infrequently visited by English-speaking guests, and as a result, no one there was able to converse with our language-challenged party. As we had done so many times before, the six of us invited ourselves to the kitchen to preview what might be available for our consumption. There among the varieties of produce, meat, and fowl was this fish—big and ugly with clear, glowing eyes, obviously freshly caught. I pointed to the fish and directed they prepare it along with some vegetables. Even in this Muslim country a bottle of suitable wine was located from a seldom-used shelf, and we all made our way to the dining room to await the feast.

Some time later, the fish arrived. It was looking much the way it had in the kitchen, only now completely cooked swimming in a sauce of blood red tomatoes, onions, garlic, and spinach, tail and fins still attached and those two great eyes peering at those preparing to feast on this denizen of the deep. Brian looked at me and I to him. No words needed to be exchanged as I pried the eyes of this fish from the protection of their sockets and placed them on the plate to my left. Now Brian would have the chance to show not only young Jamie but also his other dinner guests the proper method of consumption and the appropriate etiquette required of the man of honor.

The Abu Musa cell was comparatively cool compared to the heat of that September afternoon in 1976. The United States had just completed celebrating its two hundredth birthday. Microwave ovens had just been introduced as the newest must-have consumer item and eight-track tape players were being replaced by cassette players in all the newest cars. But here on Abu Musa, we passed the afternoon eating boiled rice, goat and stewed vegetables, enjoying the occasional zephyr passing through the open widow of our dining room. Electricity had not yet arrived here at Abu Musa, neither had the window screen. So as we passed the afternoon attempting to communicate with these longtime residents of this island using the right hand to eat, the left to shoo away the flies and in between using both to gesture in animated conversation. Their way of life had remained essentially unchanged for centuries, but we had a schedule to keep, crew to manage, and homes to build. So after a respectful interlude, we excused ourselves from our relaxing hosts and retraced our steps down the darkened hall through the entry and back to the blazing midday sun just beyond that magnificent steel door. Martin trotted ahead to retrieve his recently impounded truck. His young associate attempted to follow only to be caught by the collar as he tried to scurry past his now somewhat more-attentive father.

"Not this time, Brian, perhaps you need to stay a little closer. You don't what to miss the helicopter, do you? Martin, perhaps you might think about staying a little closer too, you might learn something, that is, if you haven't already. I'll only be here another hour or two. Try to make me think it wasn't a mistake to send you out here." I called as we all started back the way we had come. With Brian in tow and Mr. Bill in conversation, we proceeded down the narrow lanes, past the homes built of local coral and mortar. Goats and chickens still huddled in the slivers of shadows, seeking protection from the heat of the day; the balance of the population continuing the time honored practice of midday relaxation with little concern for these men that had come to so improve the style of life on this sleepy outpost of humanity.

The silence of the afternoon was interrupted as the whine of a distant turbine engine and the telltale sounds created by air forced down against a canopy could be heard coming from the south. Flying low on the horizon could be seen the company's helicopter. Mr. Bill would have to complete the first unit on his own. Brian and I would need to rush to the prearranged landing site and return to the mainland. We bid farewell to Mr. Bill and Abu Musa with the traditional Arab salutation: "*Salumalicun* [peace be with you], Mr. Bill, and try not to go native on us."

Chapter 4

WEST CAMERON BLOCK 83

NORTH 29 DEG. 34 MIN. 7 SEC. W
MARCH 4, 1996
(EIGHTEEN YEARS LATER)

The spray of salt water mixed with the fresh smells of the new morning as the high-speed aluminum crew boat propelled through roughening seas. Approaching the jetty demarcating the end of the pass and the entrance to the Gulf of Mexico, the morning breeze was turning to a gusty zephyr, wiping up waves in its path. Not a particularly remarkable day, but then Mondays never were particularly remarkable when following such a glorious weekend. This day was unseasonably cool for the southeastern Texas Gulf Coast for this time of the year. Aboard was the pilot, doing his best to control the craft, and the three-man inspection team, the pilot was entrusted to deliver along with their equipment to an offshore drill rig. Kirk Austin, leader of the team, sat amid ships wrapped in a heavy slicker, protecting himself from the chilly mist of gulf water emanating from the ever-worsening seas. A man in his mid thirties, Austin had recently established a testing company to service the ever-increasing needs of the oil industry for inspecting and recording the structural integrity of their equipment. Government regulations had been established in an attempt to protect the nation's waterways requiring that all structures placed or working offshore be regularly inspected and certified as sound. Around this set of regulations, an emerging industry of small business began proliferating. Austin, armed with a collection of electronic gadgets seized the opportunity and entered the market.

Up forward, crouched among the assembled dive equipment, Dan Wiitala tightened the bindings of his bouncing cargo. A man also in his mid thirties, he was along to do some of the actual diving required to deliver the testing equipment to the underwater points of interest. With fourteen years of experience, this volatile ride to an offshore facility was nothing he had not encountered before. As he struggled with the task, the boat turned sharply to starboard, exposing the underside of the hull to the stiffening wind, completing a 180 turn, rising up on a passing wave and aimed directly back to the pass and the safety of the Sabine river beyond left only twenty minutes before. A feeling of elation filled Dan's thoughts. Surely, they must be heading back to pick up the two missing divers. This was supposed to be a five-men job to be conducted over three days. The other divers were not there to catch the boat earlier. But this was a Monday. Men were known to be late on Mondays. Just the evening before, Dan had engaged his employer in a heated discussion over the personnel to be used on this last-minute project. All G&G's equipment had been committed to previously scheduled jobs. All the other divers had already been dispatched. Gilbert had assured him there would be five-man dive team made up by the three divers Austin's company was to provide a tender from G&G to manage the above water operations and Dan as a backup diver if needed. But Dan had been sent out shorthanded before, without adequate equipment, and he had threatened Gilbert that night before that he would not conduct another operation without the proper staff, without the adequate equipment. Gilbert assured him that this would not be the case. This was Kirk Austin's contract. Kirk was a diver. He had two other divers working with him and the necessary equipment. All Dan and the tender were to do was provide backup assistance and the required video equipment.

The sudden violent change in course unceremoniously woke the third passenger, who, moments before, was carefully nestled among the life jackets stowed in the bow lazaret. Although only eight in the morning, Brian had already put in the better part of a day's work: arising at 2:00 AM and hurrying to the shop to collect the necessary backup dive equipment, driving the truck two hours from Houston to Port Arthur, picking up Dan Wiitala along the way, unloading the truck at the dock at the offshore dock facilities at Sabine Pass and then loading the boat. But this was the task of the tender: do what had to be done, complete the tasks no one else wanted to do, sleep when you could, be ready for whatever might be needed. Finding another comfortable position, unaware of the change in course, he returned to his half sleep and to the remembrances of the day before.

Sunday had been an uncommonly warm and sunny day, perfect for being outdoors. Friends had woken Julie with the suggestion of a picnic. Brian had slept through the call. They had been married just over eight months now. And they had been in a hectic six months. There had been the move from Seattle to Texas—finding an apartment and, for Brian, finding a new job. Sears had transferred Julie after she had requested a position somewhere close to either Houston or New Orleans. If Brian were to continue on working as a diver, he would need to be in one of those cities. Sears was everywhere and willing to accommodate Julie as she moved through the corporate structure. Brian had spent his first year after graduating from divers school working out of New Orleans. Most of the entry-level jobs could be found there or in Houston—close to where majority of the U.S. offshore oil fields were located. The jobs there were plentiful and good for an entry-level diver.

Brian had begun his career as a diver twenty years before in the temperate waters of the Persian Gulf and Arabian seas. Starting at the age of four, he would accompany his father on hours of exploration among the unspoiled fields of coral that lined the shallow eastern shores of the Emirates. By the time he was five, he had his own mask and snorkel. Once old enough, he was certified in scuba three times—once on his own, the second time to accompany a hesitant friend, Julie, who would later become his wife, and finally, a third time while attending commercial dive school in Seattle. After graduation from high school, his father advised him to find something he loved to do and then find someone willing to pay him to do it. Diving was his choice, so off to commercial dive school to enhance his abilities, develop the skills needed, and gain the knowledge to enable him to be a valuable member of a diving team.

But this Sunday was not a day to dive for recreation or profit. The apartment was complete. All the furniture purchased and arranged. Stereo set up and operational. His grandfather's artwork hung, all was in order. In order except for the not-so-shiny red car with the chrome wheels. There could be no frivolity while the car was in need of cleaning. Better to be late in a clean, polished car than early in a dirty one. Much to the dismay of his new bride, the picnic would have to wait.

Buckets and sponges, towels and polish made short work of the job that would have been left undone by anyone else. But then there was the pickup. Setting next to the newly polished car, it didn't look as good as it had. Its candy apple red finish was also in need of polish, and its chrome wheels had looked better. The labor of love continued until both his vehicles were in order.

As the task neared completion, the ever-present pager announced that the office was looking for him. The pager had been a good investment. Employers were always able to find him no matter where he was. It was Brian that would get the job when no one else could be found. And after all, that's what he was there to do. Work, get the needed experience and make some extra money to pay for his new dive helmet.

The page was from G&G Marine. There was a job going out on Monday. G&G had been contracted at the last moment to provide backup personnel for the primary divers on an underwater structural inspection to be carried out on a jack-up oil drilling rig somewhere off the coast of Texas. There were no company vehicles available, so Brian would need to be there that evening to pick up the equipment and necessary tools. The newly polished little red truck with the chrome wheels was not large enough to carry all the equipment necessary to provide for a complete dive package, but they would only be a backup to the primary team. The camera, video equipment, and cables were all they would really need. The other divers and equipment would be supplied by the inspection service, Texas Non-Destructive Testing. Texas NDT was a small company owned by Kirk Austin and would often contact G&G to supply extra divers to support their underwater inspection teams. In addition, this particular inspection was being carried out under the watchful eye of the American Bureau of Shipping in conjunction with the United States Coast Guard. The agreement called for underwater video record keeping, assuring the accurateness and thoroughness of the inspection as well as providing a permanent record. Texas NDT was a newly established venture and relied on companies like Brian's employer for not only personnel but also extra equipment. The need of video equipment, someone to man the above-water monitoring and backup dive support, had prompted the call from Kirk that Sunday afternoon to Gilbert, owner of G&G Marine. Unlike Texas NDT, G&G Marine was a well-established company with years of experience in the Gulf area and possessed much of the equipment the younger firm had yet to purchase. In turn, G&G called the young tender with the mechanical aptitude and a pickup to check on his availability. Brian assured the caller Dan Gilbert that he was up to the task and set out to pack three days worth of clean clothes to accompany him on the venture before attending to the now-twice-postponed picnic.

The canvas bag that had served so well to carry soccer uniforms, track shoes, and tennis gear during the high school years was once again retrieved from the entry closet. A well-worn flannel shirt given by Uncle Bob for a birthday years ago was packed first, then a woolen sweater, three pairs of sox, underwear, and jeans. The coveralls would go in last, leaving just enough room for the shaving kit and maybe a book or two. Not that he would read the books, but he had intentions to start reading more someday. No, forget the books, he would rather spend the spare time with his camera. So from the same closet, he pulled down the old Minolta with the dented focus ring, checked the battery indicator and looked for an extra roll or two of film. The camera was old and had been around the world a time or two, first with his father and now in his care. It may not have been state of the art any longer, but it took great pictures just the same, and there was always so much to photograph: boats at the dock, birds in flight, great oil rigs with their cables and cranes, and always a sunset. There was something special about those moments just before darkness when the sun would slowly drop below a watery horizon. Yes, the camera would be a good choice; the books can come next time.

Leaving the partially packed bag of necessity by the entry door, he made his way to the deck and the outside storage locker. The olive drab duffel bag hanging over the balcony rail was almost dry from its last use, but then it was almost never allowed to completely dry—from out of the locker and into the moist container rubber boots, neoprene gloves, a webbed work harness, and an Eddie Bauer wool hat given to him by his mother. He liked the hat but really never wore it much. Why cover up that great-looking hair? Hats were for guys losing their locks or for Jamie, that little brother who never had the time to comb, not for Brian. But he packed it any way just in case the weather should turn. The majority of the remaining space would be filled with the farmer john suite with the blue neoprene patches on the knees. The same suite that he had used back at Divers Institute and recreationally in the cold waters of Puget Sound. The legs may have been tattered, but it still kept him warm. Once packed and zipper secured, the old duffel that had years before been used by his father to carry military garb was placed alongside the bag of clothing at the front door. One more item to go and then on to the picnic. Back on the deck, he pulled out the baby blue milk crate that had years before been liberated from an Albertson's grocery store. Neatly arranged in the bottom of the old plastic crate were six five-pound lead weights each connected to the next on a blue-woven belt. He pulled the assembled weights and carefully inspected the quick-release buckle. This was no ordinary buckle, but rather a self-adjusting one he had found years before in a dive shop in faraway Renton, Washington. Unlike the standard buckle everyone else had, this one was meant to adjust as the pressures of depth compressed or expanded the neoprene suit, maintaining the proper fit regardless of depth. So proud of his find of this bit of mechanical wizardry that he had purchased two—one for his own uses, the other as a birthday gift for his Father.

One quick pull of inspection and it was obvious that the buckle was in need of service. The mechanism was slow to respond and the self-adjusting springs stiff and clogged with salt and corrosion. From the top shelf of the locker, the can of WD40, stored next to the duct tape, was retrieved. Spray a little of this wonder stuff and anything could be fixed. So the belt was returned to the blue crate, leaving the buckle hanging free and a liberal coat of good old WD40 applied, left to do its work in the hot dry air of that East Texas morning on the deck bathed in sunshine. Julie would appreciate that noxious smell remain outside where it belonged.

The necessities of the day now completed. The bags were packed, the vehicles cleaned, apartment in order. Now was the time to find Julie and head for that twice postponed picnic. But the hour was late and the best part of the day now spent. He would need to drive up to the office and pick up the gear needed for the following three-planned days of work. The others had long gone in search for a place to party, and he would need to be up by four in the morning to meet his Monday commitment. There would always be another chance to picnic.

He enjoyed these early-morning rides although had never become fully accustomed to waking quite so early. Noon, that was a good time to start a day but jobs offshore always require an early start. The first microscopic rays of sun were piercing the low gray cloudbank hovering above the eastern horizon, a foreshadowing of the blustery day to come. The flat countryside with sparse vegetation streamed, pasted the freshly tinted windows. Windows he had tinted himself with supplies purchased at the local auto parts store so that he might keep the suns damaging rays off his truck's newly customized interior. Tinting that would never have been needed in the gray days back in Western Washington State, but this was Texas, and he was quickly adjusting to this, his new home. The early-morning hour meant for few cars to hinder his passage as he raced along the interstate. Driving east along Highway 10, even the full load in the cargo bed of his little red truck did not slow the progress as he proceeded to the prearranged meeting with Dan Wiitala.

Enjoying the music emanating from the newly installed speakers connected to the equally new CD player, he was sitting on his recently acquired leather bucket seat so carefully modified to fit the interior of this his first truck. Bucket seats made necessary to fit his six-foot-five-inch frame in his diminutive first truck. There is always something special in that first truck, something that remains with every boy no matter how old he may be. The joy of ownership, the knowledge of the little things that make this ride as special as a first kiss. To his right, on the second of the newly acquired bucket seat, tightly sealed in its protective neoprene case was the newest of his possessions. A Kirby Morgan SuperLite 27 helmet, or dive hat as the old salts referred to this piece of equipment, meant to provide protection from the harsh underwater environment. He had contemplated purchasing a used older model and refurbishing it to meet his needs and save a few dollars. There was nothing he couldn't fix, make better than it was, in his estimation; but after analyzing the actual savings, it only made sense to purchase new. After all, it was through these brass fittings, springs, and diaphragms he would be drawing life-giving air while working below. The internal communication would all be state of the art, permitting him clear verbal contact with those above. That is, if he were permitted to dive. But on this trip, he was to be the tender, and there were no dives to be on his schedule. The hat would come anyway. You never know what opportunities might arise. Things always seem to change, and at the last minute, he could get the chance to get wet. The pay was better, the work more interesting than manning communication gear or pulling lines for those fortunate enough to be down. Things had already changed on this job, and the work had not as yet begun.

The plan, prearranged on Sunday night, had only included picking up the required video camera, cabling, monitor, and recording device. But stowed in addition to the video equipment was a complete dive set: compressor, dive rack, umbilical, assorted hoses, back high-pressure air cylinders, all the things required to support a single diver on a shallow dive. When picking up the gear at G&G the night before, Dan Gilbert had suggested the extra equipment to supplement what Texas NDT was scheduled to bring. G&G Marine was a member of the Association of Dive Contractors; in fact, one of the owners was the executive director of the organization. The ADC had created rules required to be followed by all members regarding safe-dive practice, business practice, and conduct. They also publish a list of all those members who had signed their safe-diving consensus and distributed this list of names to the professional dive schools throughout the country. It was from this list that Brian had found Dan Gilbert and the new job. So packing this extra gear on that early morning only made sense, better to have extra equipment, follow the safety standards established by the industry association of which his company was a charter member. Safety standard established by the industry to supplement the woefully inadequate federal standards of the Coast Guard and OSHA during the early days of the emerging industry.

This road with no impediments was meant for speed, and even with the full load, the young man pushed hard on the accelerator, enjoying the thrill of the open highway. Reaching across the freshly cleaned interior, he selected another CD. No music, it was time for a little Jeff Foxworthy. Listening to redneck stories was always a good way to pass that time, and it would also give more ammunition when confronted by some good old local boy intent on harassing this boy from the Northwest. Stories had become a way of life for Brian, learned from years of listening across the family dinner table. A table meant as much for sharing experiences as for the consumption of food. Brian relished a good story no matter how many times he heard it, and old Jeff Foxworthy could tell stories with the best of them. Listen to the stories, pulling out the best parts and then slip a few choice lines into conversation. It was a great way to get the goat of some unsuspecting cohort now that little brother and sister were not around much anymore.

Almost passing the exit, Brian pushed hard on the brake as he negotiated the curve meant to be traveled at twenty while traveling closer to sixty down the ramp and into the parking lot of the forever open Whataburger parking lot. There sitting patiently on a well-worn wooden bench, sipping some freshly brewed excuse for coffee sat Wiitala with his bags of clothes and personal equipment. Room was made for not only the new cargo among the already-overfilled bed of the little red truck but also a place hollowed out for dive helmet, which until now had ridden prominently on the only place a passenger might occupy. Once all was safely packed, arranged, and tied down, the old aluminum travel mug was retrieved from under the seat.

Up to the walk-up window, Brian presented the coffee-encrusted antique requesting a double tall latte with a little whip "and not too hot, please." Perhaps instructions that would have been understood by a barista in the North West, but here in South Eastern Texas, the words fell on the ears of a half-awake attendant more concerned in wiping away that stain on the counter that never seemed to want to disappear. Seeing that his request was not about to be honored or perhaps understood, Brian followed with "How about black coffee and a little room for cream?" as his eyes caught a glimpse of the sugar packets and individual plastic containers of creamlike stuff, covered with flies, sitting just there by the open window. Coffee was poured, Wiitala got his third refill, and the two men made their way back to the truck to continue the journey. As quickly as the highway had been left earlier, the little red truck containing the two men, equipment, clothes and their excuse for coffee, returned to the eastbound lanes of Highway 73.

With his coffee cup safely stowed, protected by the floating, ball-bearing filled gadget that Brian had installed between the seats, Wiitala was soon asleep. The driver continued east while attempting to shield his eyes from the rising sun while thinking of that afternoon spent the day before alone with his wife of eight months. A smile came to his face. Following the signs to Port Arthur, he left the highway and made his way south past the occasional farmhouse and open barrens of East Texas. Mile after mile of unkempt farms, outbuildings and equipment, once meant for plowing or harvesting, now were sitting idle, rusting and overgrown with dried vegetation. He turned off the paved road at the sign, reading, Cliffs Drilling, Port Arthur with the arrow pointing east. In the distance, great steel columns could be seen pointing skyward with the sun peering between all covered by that threatening sky above. The hard-packed red-dirt road quickly turned to little more than a pair of well-worn ruts coming to an abrupt halt by the remains of a once-proud dock, creosote-covered piles with rotten tops connected by sagging beams covered with wide, thick planks worn from use and abuse.

To the north stretched a muddy riverbank littered with bits and piece of rusting steel—some appearing to be discarded pieces of some previous greater importance, others of no recognizable use. Farther north those great steel columns seen from the paved road were now fully illuminated by the light of the now-blustery day. To the south lay a newly contracted marina, filled with boats intended for the harvesting of shrimp. Each well-worn craft-supporting booms, flying-tattered nets, cables, and lines. Some being made ready for the day's work, others looking like their last days work had come and gone forever. To the south of the first dock stood a sign Oil Field Equipment Dock, One mile. Continuing south along the banks of the Sabine River, the red truck, its cargo and two men, now late for the scheduled departure, sped past the hulks of steel littering the riverbank as they hurried looking for the right dock.

Once past the forest of unused steel, another dock with long thin slips and a fleet of steel crafts appeared. Each looking much like the other just of different size and in various states of repair. Some with decks covered with drums of unknown content, some filled with long pipes, fittings, and couplings; but all with cargo meant to supply the sea of offshore drilling rigs, production platforms, or exploration units so essential to supplying the oil needs of the hungry oil industry and oil-consuming American public.

There sitting among the drums of yet to be loaded supplies on dock B sat Kirk Austin, overnight bag at his side and a large plastic waterproof case. By now Wiitala had awakened from his one-hour nap perhaps by the rays of morning sun streaming through the truck window or the bumps of the heavily rutted road. He pointed to the man with the two cases and directed Brian to stop. Brian remained in the truck gathering up CDs to be packed while Wiitala joined the man on the dock. Pleasantries were exchanged and a hand pointed to the smallest of the crafts tied off at the end of the dock. Instructions followed, and Brian drove as close as possible to the waiting craft, unloaded and stowed as much of his cargo of dive equipment and personal gear as he could and then waited for the crane to do the rest. Austin and Wiitala had worked together before but could not seem to remember just where or when so as they continued in conversation. Brian unloaded and stowed the equipment the three of them would be requiring for the next three days. The others made their way aboard in search for coffee and a warm place to call home for the expected two-hour cruise down the Sabine and then the open crossing to the Cliffs 12.

All aboard and equipment stowed, Brian searched out his own personal space among the life jackets in that forward lazaret, a place to be found on all ships of commerce, a space he had first discovered on that ship years before while traveling with his father on that first cruise of adventure. Sleep came easy. It had already been a long day. And there were the thoughts of the day before that now turned to dreams.

His nap was cut short by the violent sudden change of course and Wiitala's fall to the deck alongside the stowed cargo. The once-calm waters of the river had now changed to the heavy swells of the open waters of the Gulf, and the threatening skies now unleashed torrents of cold-driven rain. The two men worked together, quickly securing the load and then headed for the protection of the craft's cabin: Wiitala thinking they were heading back for the missing members of the promised dive team; Brian, thinking he would ask the captain if he could get a double tall latte with a little whip (laughing to himself).

Back within the protection of the jetty, the craft slowed and continued north up the river to the point where the journey had begun. They were not returning for additional crew but rather the captain thought it unwise to proceed in the small craft electing, to return for one of the larger, heavier, and more seaworthy vessels. Tying up alongside a craft truly twice the size of the first, the young tender attended to the transfer of cargo as his two associates continued in animated and heated discussions of crew, equipment, and proper staffing for the task ahead.

Transfer completed, cargo secured, Brian found his way back to a pile of life jackets on the new craft—this time within the cabin, returning to his previously interrupted nap. Unnoticed by the man now attempting to build a nest among the cork-filled vests, a fourth passenger had boarded the craft to accompany them to the offshore drilling facility. Dressed in clothing to fend off the cold and protect him from the rain, he made his way to the cabin. He found a comfortable place to ride out the journey while pulling from his leather case a pile of documents to review and fill the time.

Everett was an employee of the American Bureau of Shipping, a private company based in Chicago with offices in Houston. They had just recently entered into a "Memorandum of Understanding" with the United States Coast Guard. In these days of budget cuts, reduced spending, and downsizing of government, this *understanding* was intended to last a period of eighteen months during which the feasibility of permitting the American Bureau of Shipping to conduct the required vessel inspection currently being done by the USCG. During this period of *understanding*, the Coast Guard would be present along with the ABS. Inspections would continue on as before, and if successful, ABS allowed to continue on in the future without USCG inspectors present. But this was to be a joint inspection. Five members of the Guard were reportedly already on the 12; it was only Everett and the underwater inspection team that was needed to complete the required underwater portion of the inspection.

The morning rains subsided and the craft continued south, southeast, passing beyond the United States coastal boundary. In the distance, the legs of a jack up rig could be seen on the southern horizon.

These mechanical bits of wizardry, half-ship, half-oil well dot the shores of the southern United States and truly are the front line of today's U.S. oil production. Made up of two-tanked hulls, one above the other connected by a series of steel columns. The Cliffs 12 had three such legs, each capable of being extended in order to reach the bottom of the shallow reaches of the gulf. This vessel would be towed to some predetermined location where by study or reckoning a pocket of sub sea oil was thought to be hiding. Then the lower of the two hulls would be intentionally scuttled and sent to rest on the soft sands or

Photo courtesy of John Carl Roat

silt below. The upper hull would then be *jacked up*, utilizing the columns firmly fastened to the now-submerged lower hull for support. And it was in this position the Cliffs 12 remained on this morning of March 4, 1996. Although some eleven miles off the coast the seafloor was only forty feet down, the lower hull rested firmly on the silty bottom while the upper hull was jacked some thirty feet above the water. There was no deposit of oil known to be at this location, but rather the 12 had been moved to this locality for the express purpose of doing the underwater portion of its reactivation survey.

The 12 had gone unused for two years, missing its last two required United States Coast Guard certifications. During those years of inactivity, the 12 had been beached along the banks of the Sabine River somewhere between the unused dock at the end of that dirt road and the piles of rusting steel of various descriptions seen by the dive team that morning. Fifteen days earlier, Cliffs Drilling Company had completed a contract to lease the 12 and, thus, the rush to certify and reactivate the aging vessel. On the previous Friday, the 12 was towed from the beach along the banks of the Sabine and moved to the shallow, clearer waters of the Gulf. On board was a crew of forty-seven men: some welders; some riggers; some oil field workers; others meant to do little more the clean, paint, or prepare the meals for the men that would be calling this floating island of commerce their home. Some stayed for just a few days, while others stayed till the rig was finally moved, drilling begun, and the black gold of the twentieth century uncovered and exploited. In addition, a team of Coast Guard inspectors had helicoptered in from their base in Port Arthur: four men, two officers, and two enlisted. They were there to check the fitness of the vessel, see that the fire-suppression systems functioned, hatches and water-tight doors worked, safety plans and evacuation plans were in order. Navigational lights, bilge pumps, cranes, blocks all the bits and pieces of this complex bit of part-ship, part-oil well function so as to provide not only a safe place to live and work but also one that would not endanger other ships or the environment.

The hour was approaching 11:00 AM as the supply boat hovered motionless below the starboard crane in anticipation of a crew basket to be lowered from the deck thirty feet above. Engines trust from slow ahead to slow astern, holding and waiting. Brian and Wiitala made ready their cargo for transfer. Everett secured his papers, Austin searched for the plastic box and his canvas bag. The crane above roared into action, sending a puff of black smoke into the gray sky. Swinging 180 degrees clockwise and lowering a pallet filled with equipment to the deck of the newly arrived ship. There were four high-pressure air bottles, two dive compressors, rolls of dive hoses complete with communication lines, safety lines, and harnesses—all emblazoned with the logo of American Oil Field Divers. With help from the crew the contents of the cargo contained on the pallet was switched with the gear that had begun the day in the warehouse of G&G along with Wiitala's and Brian's personal gear.

A hand signal sent the contents skyward followed by yet another puff of black smoke and the roar of an engine above. Moments later a woven rope crew basket with a wood platform dropped from above carrying seven men. All seven wearing blue coveralls embroidered with the same logo were seen on the equipment now lying on the deck of the boat.

A puzzled look came across Wiitala's face; the older of the men emerging from the basket looked annoyed. Brian boarded the basket knowing that a firm deck was now only moments away. Austin with black plastic case in tow followed. As Wiitala engaged the older man with the blue coveralls in conversation, Everett joined Brian and Austin. Shortly after Wiitala followed suit while looking down and mumbling to himself.

Once again the engine roared, and the four sojourners were propelled skyward, then gently lowered to the safety of the firmly anchored steel deck. Greeting them was a man in an orange jumpsuit, a company hard hat indicating he worked for Cliffs Drilling, and a name embroidered over his left pocket Buddy.

Buddy Horton was in charge of Cliffs's safety division. He had been sent out from the main office to oversee the reactivation of the 12. A task of paramount importance to Cliffs. Three months earlier in their annual stock holders report, the first page indicated that profits were down from the previous year "primarily due to the Cliffs 12 being dry stacked and not operating."[3] But this was to change, and Buddy was here to make it happen. Armed with twenty years of experience at Cliffs, a previous work experience with the Wriggles chewing gum company and a college degree in fine arts, he was here to make it all happen.

The United States Coast Guard had a policy that required certain procedures be followed to reactivate such vessels. Policies were made more restrictive if the owner elected to conduct the required inspections while in the water in lieu of dry

---

[3]   CLIFFS DRILLING ANNUAL REPORT TO INVESTORS 1995

docking.[4] Policies that included a ninety-day notice to the USCG so that they would have ample time to review previous dry-docked surveys, reference videos, and copies of diving procedures. Acceptability of the diving personnel. Pages of rules all meant to be followed to provide not only an accurate assessment of the vessel but also a safe inspection by those entrusted to do the inspection. From his posting in Venezuela, Buddy had sent a letter to Lt. Julio Martinez, United States Coast Guard, Port Arthur, requesting an immediate inspection and a variance from the norm. Now thirteen days later, Buddy was here from Venezuela, and Julio Martinez had choppered in from Port Arthur to complete the requested task.

Buddy wished a fond hello to his old friend Austin as he stepped out of the basket. These two had years of experience working with each other both here in the United States and on similar inspections at Cliffs' other bases of operation around the world. With arm draped over his old friend's shoulder, Buddy directed Austin to the onboard conference room, which until the completion of the survey would serve as Buddy's office. Brian and Wiitala set about establishing a dive station.

The inspection, like so many Wiitala had been on, would involve finding numerous key structural locations beneath the water. Points where welds-fastened columns to hull, or "mat" as they would refer to it, places where previous anomalies may have been noted or just random places, selected by either the ABS inspector or Coast Guard office in charge. At each location, it would be the diver's task to place a transducer, which had the ability to measure the current thickness of steel or weld to be compared with previous readings or original specifications and then sent that information back to the surface for continual monitoring and recording. In addition, United States Coast Guard regulation required that the entirety of the inspection be videotaped and observed from above. This would allow a surface-stationed inspector to oversee the diver's progress, direct the diver to points of interest, as well as create a permanent record for future reference. So it was to that end that the two men set out to set up for the inspection to come. First, there would need to be a dive station—a point of easy entry to the water below, a place where hoses and safety lines could be maintained and monitored. A place where communication gear providing verbal contact between diver below and tender above could be easily accessed. In addition, a place where a bank of valves and gauges could be located to monitor air pressure from the various air-supply systems and the all-important low-pressure air compressor, which would supply the bulk and, hopefully, only air supply that would be required. Next to the dive station would need to be the backup high-pressure reserve bottles. In the event of a mechanical problem with the compressor, the diver could be supplied life-sustaining air, once regulated down

---

4   http://www.uscg.mil/hq/cg5/nvic/pdf/1989/n1-89.pdf

to pressures required based on depth of diver and type of helmet in use. For this, as all commercial diving, was to be done with surface supplied air. The diver normally would also carry a small reserve air supply; usually containing only enough air to permit an emergency assent in the event all surface air supply was terminated for any reason.

In addition. to the voice communication equipment to be set up at the dive station, there would be space required for the color TV monitor and video-recording equipment. And then there was that black box brought by Austin. The electronic tools the divers would be transporting from place to place transmitting signals to be recorded and transcribed. The reason all the diving was to be done—a transducer, a bit of cabling and the receiving unit—all to measure and aid in evaluating the fitness of this aging offshore structure. Built at the Bethlehem steel yard in Beaumont, Texas, back in 1980, this 4,109-ton mobile offshore drilling unit was now two years out of service. By regulation, vessels over fifteen years old were required to be dry-docked and inspected, but this 220-foot-long, 185-foot-wide craft was scheduled to be inspected at sea without the aid of many of the other prerequisites required to undertake such a recertification.

With the dive station established the compressors need to be set up, the compressor was a Quincy 325 fixed in a rack alongside a diesel motor. A series of small belts parallel to one another connected the small power takeoff wheel mounted on the motors shaft to the larger wheel that drove the pistons of the compressor. A Quincy 325 was not intended to supply breathing air, but this one had been modified for the purpose.

The petroleum lubricants that would normally be utilized in such a compressor had been purged from the system, replaced with a nontoxic-vegetable-based lubricant, and fitted with an air-filtering system meant to clean the compressed air of any harmful impurities. By introducing a vegetable-based oil in the compressor side of the unit, any carryover of oil that might pass from the crankshaft to the compression chamber would be nontoxic and more easily removed by filters. In addition to the filters installed between the compressor and the dive station, there would also be a particulate filter that would remove impurities before they were allowed to enter the compressor. This filter was installed high above the compressor and upwind of the diesel engine to avoid the possibility of ingesting exhaust emissions. A location needed to be found near enough to the dive station for monitoring the compressor and its attached engine yet not so close as to interfere with communication.

The incessant running of the diesel motor would interfere with voice communication, so a balance of access and a respectful separation for sound was important. The dive station was set on the windward, starboard side of the deck, the compressor down wind and to port. Between would need to be an air storage tank or volume tank as it was called. The diesel motor would run continually. The compressor would engage when pressures in the storage tank dropped below predetermined minimums and then continued doing so until the high limit of pressure was achieved. Upon demand air in the storage tank would flow through the bank of gauges at the dive station through a hose and eventually to the diver's regulator mounted on his helmet. The pressure controlled at the dive station needed to be adjusted based on the depth of the diver and the individual requirements of the divers regulator. The regulator mounted on the divers helmet would account for the ambient pressure associated with the depth of the dive.

Additionally, it was the tender's responsibility to assist the diver in and out of the water, maintain hoses, manage the air rack, and keep the dive records. The diver in a surface-supplied dive would be connected to the surface by an "umbilical." Usually, this umbilical would consist of a primary air supply line, a safety line, a communication cable and a pneumohose used to monitor the depth of the dive. This pneumohose would be little more than an open-ended hose hooked to a pressure gage at the dive station. The pneumo could also be used in emergency. In the event the air line or regulator should stop functioning, a quick-thinking, well-trained tender could simply attach the dive station end of the pneumo to one of the standby bottles or the air rack itself while the diver insets the open end of the hose directly under the neck dam of the helmet. The result would be an unregulated flow of life-giving air, thus permitting the diver yet another source of air, but truly only if all else failed. In some cases, additional life-support systems can be added to the umbilical such as a warm water supply and return. Such a system would pump warm water down to the diver, circulate through the suit, and prolong the diver's ability to function in the cold, unforgiving underwater environment. This luxury would not be needed.

The two men spent the next several hours setting up the station, compressor, and storage tank, making all in order for the day's one scheduled dive. Wiitala remained silent continuing to be annoyed by his lack of staff and the conversation with the diving supervisor from American Oil Field Divers, who, by now, surely was safe onshore.

In addition to all the normal cables and hoses and safety line, this dive would also require a video link to the surface so that the entirety of the massive underwater portion of the vessel could be visually inspected, recorded, and added to the inspection records. In addition, the inspection requires inspection of the welds between the three legs and their individual connection to the now-submerged lower hull as well as thickness testing of the steel structure.

Together the diver and tender added yet another two cables to the umbilical—one for the video, the other for use with either the magnetic particle equipment or for the thickness gauging. With the aid of rings of electrical tape, the video cable supplied as part of G&G's contract, and the electronics cable supplied by Austin were added to the umbilical. Under such a structure, there would be more-than-enough locations to snag a line, by securing all the lines, communication, safety, air, electronics into a single umbilical the chances of a fouled line would be greatly diminished. Once the umbilical portion of the work was completed, the camera was attached to the lower end of the umbilical, the upper end attached to the monitor.

Attached to the monitor, there would need to be a VCR to capture the images transmitted from below. This video connection between the surface and the diver below would not only be what was required as part of the inspection record but also allow those topside to assist in directing the diver to the various points of interest as well as follow his progress. The recording of the visual inspection would also become a part of the permanent record as was required as part of the reactivation survey.

The scheduled first dive and only dive for Monday would put Kirk Austin in the water to conduct the magnetic particle inspections of the welds. Brian would tend the diver and Wiitala would man the communications and assure the video record was maintained. All was in order, but as all too often occurs when you are miles from home, one piece was missing.

The video cable supplied did not match the connection on the dive station end of the cable. Without this important component, neither the magnetic particle testing could be certified, nor could the underwater visual inspection be done and recorded. Wiitala quickly went in search for Austin. There would need to be a revision to the order of the work, or they would need to wait for a replacement cable. In addition, while establishing the dive station, it was discovered that there was but a single umbilical. Good practice required a second airline in the event the backup diver would need to enter the water to assist the primary diver. Although perhaps a prudent piece of gear to have, by USCG and OSHA regulation, it was not required. For that matter, a backup diver was not required to be at the ready or even available as this dive was to be taking place in less than 130 feet of water. Wiitala located Austin still in conversation with Buddy Horton in the warmth of Buddy's office. The situation was reviewed and a change in dive order agreed upon. The thickness testing would be done first as it did not require a video record. The other two inspections could be conducted on Tuesday and Wednesday. A call was placed to G&G Marine, and a request made to send out a replacement video cable.

Austin had originally asked to have a five-man inspection crew. Buddy had insisted that he do it with three. Austin wanted three divers, one to do the magnetic particle testing, one to do the video work, and yet another to do the thickness testing along with a tender to manage the above-water necessities. That would leave Austin to manage the record keeping and interpret the data being transmitted from below. Buddy wanted to control costs. Austin wanted to stay out of the water.

Austin had contacted Gilbert, G&G Marine late in the afternoon on Sunday, requesting two divers, the video equipment, and a backup shallow dive package. In turn, Gilbert called Wiitala to check on his last-minute availability. Initially, Wiitala refused the job, believing that with only him and a tender from G&G they would be understaffed. He would be in the water doing the bulk of the diving, and there was the issue of safety. Regulation did not require additional manpower, nor did it require additional equipment; but by practice, it was not prudent to proceed as Gilbert proposed. An hour later, Gilbert called Wiitala again and assured him there would be two additional divers accompanying Austin. He and Brian were there as backup and to supply the video equipment. Reluctantly Wiitala agreed and began preparing to meet for three days at sea.

Austin also wanted the two additional divers but for somewhat different reasons. He was certified to conduct the required tests, interpret the results of the test, and maintain the records. His only experience as a diver was limited to the skills he had obtained at the local YMCA five years before, and by observing divers, he had contracted with and supervised on previous projects. When he started up his inspection business years before, the intent was to inspect land-based equipment. Cliffs was pleased with the results Austin had provided in years, passed, and encouraged him to consider expanding to also do the underwater inspection work. Austin attempted to utilize other diving contractors, but few where willing to meet the restriction in personnel Austin often found his clients demanded. A call to Gilbert and the promises of proper staff would be all that was needed to get a bit of cash flow and perhaps save his struggling business. Horton would not agree to the added manpower; Gilbert did not need to know.

So that Sunday night after talking with Gilbert and a follow-up call to Buddy Horton, Austin dug out his seldom-used wet suit, the company-owned dive helmet, safety harness, and personal bail-out bottle. He had never used the bottle, which is little more than a small SCUBA bottle that a surface-supplied diver could elect to carry. Matted to the dive helmet, then strapped to the harness should there be a disruption of air from the surface, a simple turn of a valve would provide an adequate supply of life-giving air to allow a safe return to the surface. It was a prudent safeguard even though not required by regulation.

Austin, Horton, and Wiitala continued in conversation behind the closed door in the warmth and comfort of Buddy's temporary office aboard the Cliff's 12 as the hour approached noon on Monday.

The day was almost half-gone. For Wiitala, things had gone from bad to worse. First, the anticipated, promised divers were not there, the boat ride out had been a challenge, the video cable was missing, the backup umbilical was not there, the primary dive equipment was not on station. He did have his bail-out bottle as did Austin, and he did have two backup high-pressure air bottles, each capable of supporting a single diver at the planed dive depth for up to three hours. He was eleven miles at sea with a green tender, a dive supervisor with little or no diving experience, and a safety officer more intent on completing the reactivation of the aging vessel than what his title implied. The American Bureau of Shipping inspector was located, and the revised plan of inspection reviewed. Brian would be first in the water.

With the others meeting behind closed doors, Brian went in search for his camera. There was a bird perched on the newly assembled dive station. What a great photo that would make. The meeting now over Wiitala and Austin returned to the now-operational dive station chasing off the lone bird and reminding the young tender that they were there to conduct an underwater inspection, not photograph stray birds. Austin opened up his case filled with electronic gizmos, set up a monitor and connected it to the electronics cable on the umbilical. This one meant only to permit the electronic signals emanating from a handheld transducer the diver would carry from one predetermined location to another. A signal to be transmitted from the various underwater locations to the surface for evaluation and then recorded as part of the vessel's permanent inspection record.

Brian was sent to find his dive equipment, squeeze into that old farmer john wet suit and prep himself for this unexpected opportunity to "get wet." Wiitala fired up the compressor by starting the diesel engine as Austin adjusted the accuracy of the thickness gauging equipment.

With his suit on, Brian secured his helmet to the umbilical. Then adjusted the demand valve until the regulator began to free flow, then back off a turn so that air would only be allowed to enter on "demand" or when the diver inhaled. If the surface supplied air was allowed to freely flow, there would be a possibility the compressor would not be capable of maintaining proper pressure throughout the planned three-hour dive. In addition, a free-flowing helmet would make voice communication difficult as the sound of the continuing escaping air would mask any attempt at voice communication. And then the next setback for the day. The belt, the weights, his knife, and that quick-release buckle that had served him so well—where were they? Still on the deck at home where he left it drenched in WD40.

First, he attempted to borrow Austin's weights, but the reluctant-to-dive Austin had not planned to dive and had only brought his one-half-inch neoprene wet suit, a bail-out bottle and the company dive helmet. Without weight there would be no diving for Brian that Monday afternoon. Truly all dressed and no way to go, Brian reluctantly approached the already visibly upset Wiitala, who frustrated by the questionable dive station cobbled together from the leftover equipment supplied by Gilbert, the restriction on personnel by Horton, the half-truths or downright deception of Austin, the deteriorating weather, his conversation with the American Oilfield diving supervisor, and now the tender who not only brought out the wrong cable but also forgot his weight belt and knife. Fortunately, this was a shallow dive, what else could go wrong? Wiitala dug deep into his bag, located the weights and an old folding knife with a six-inch blade that had probably not seen the light of day in years.

Weight belt adjusted to fit the slimmer diver, neck dam snapped in place, and the dive helmet securely fastened as the hour approached 1330 hours. Brian had started his day at 4:00 AM, loaded his equipment—well, most of the equipment in his truck already, overflowing with company gear—drove the two hours picking up Wiitala along the way, loaded the equipment on the first boat, off-loaded the same equipment after the aborted first trip beyond the Sabine river, then reloaded the equipment on the second larger craft. Then two hours later, he loaded the equipment and personal gear onto the cargo basket alongside the Cliffs 12, set up the dive station, all while operating on those three cups of coffee, no whip. Wiitala would be the tender for this first dive; Austin would man the electronics. Horton would hold down his desk in the comfort of the heated office as a light afternoon rain began to fall.

They were ready.

There's one quick review of the blueprints of the near-football-sized underwater structure that would need to be inspected. American Oil Field Divers had been down the day before and had cleaned the predetermined spots in need of evaluation. They had left behind a down line tied to the ship's rail near the dive station leading down to the water level, along the submerged deck, and then to the bow leg of the vessel. Brian and Dan stepped into the man basket that earlier in the day had deposited the crew on the deck following their arrival from Sabine Pass. The crane's engine roared as the basket was lifted high enough to clear the rail, then slowly lowered to just above the two-foot seas. Austin played out the umbilical to assure it would not be fowled. Brian—with one hand on his face plate, the other holding the umbilical—took that giant step out of the basket, found the down line, and headed for the bottom. Wiitala rode the basket back to the deck and assumed his place at the communication center and checked the air gauges. Austin, still standing at the rail, looked down at the water thirty feet below, gathered up as much of the umbilical as he could lift, and threw it over the side. Then before returning to his station, he found a short piece of line and tied the umbilical to the rail.

This first dive of the day only lasted a few minutes. Brian had followed the down line to the first leg, but it configuration was not what he anticipated. He had reviewed the plan and what he was finding did not agree with the predive assessment. Perhaps he was disoriented, perhaps the poor visibility had restricted his ability to properly orient himself. Fortunately, he was in voice communication with Wiitala. They reviewed the situation, and it was decided to have Brian return to the surface and once again review the plan. The man basket was once again lowered to the water with Wiitala aboard, the diver retrieved, and both returned to the deck. Once again the blueprints were reviewed, and shortly, it was determined that the down line provided by the previous dive team was in fact leading to the stern of the vessel, not the bow. The plan that Brian had attempted to follow was backward. Another few moments of study, once again the two men entered the man basket for the trip to just above the waves.

Once back in the water, Brian found what appeared to be the first point of interest. He had been told that the previous dive crew had cleaned the spots to be inspected, but what he found was barnacle and oyster encrusted. They had anticipated some minor cleaning would be required as it was imperative that the transducer be placed on clean, bare metal to obtain an accurate reading. To that end, Brian, along with the old folding knife, had a roofing hatchet hanging from his harness attached by three feet of three-by-eight-inch nylon line. Confirming that this was the spot, he cleared away the growths and held the probe tight to the hull. Austin confirmed the positive reading above, and the diver was sent in search for the next of the forty places in need of inspection. For the next three hours, Brian systematically moved from one dark location to the next, cleaned the spots required, attached the probe, and then waited to be directed to the next.

In addition to the underwater inspection the United States Coast Guard in conjunction with the American Bureau of Shipping continued on with the above water inspection. This was a reactivation survey that would need to be completed before the aging vessel could be put back in service. As Brian reached the midpoint of his dive that afternoon, moving about in the chilly waters of the Gulf forty feet above, the two officers of the United States Coast Guard sat in the office of the ship's master, Ronald Townsend.

Townsend was a longtime employee of Cliffs and had been assigned to the drilling rig to manage the work aboard as the vessel passed from "dry stacking" on the shore of the Sabine until delivery to the client. The Coast Guard had been aboard reviewing systems, verifying compliance, checking fire systems, life boats, proper draft marking, hatch gaskets and all other life, safety, or navigational components, assuring that all would meet existing regulations as they applied to offshore drilling units. Townsend was ultimately the man in  charge and the one that would be held accountable for the life and well-being of all those aboard as well as for the vessel itself. On his desk was a list of corrections five pages long. Items that would need to be corrected before the Cliffs 12 would be allowed back in service. Some items were minor including the cleaning of soiled windows, repainting the name on the hull, properly numbering fire extinguishers, and some more serious.

Provide a Coast Guard—approved operations manual and provide an emergency evacuation plan. In addition, they would need to see the results of the tests currently under way fifty feet below their feet. The five pages were reviewed, the discrepancies explained, and as the meeting wound down, the sound of the helicopter could be heard as it began its approach to pick up the two officers and two enlisted men of the USCG. Their work on board was done until all corrections were complete. The American Bureau of Shipping inspector would remain on board. The Coast Guard was heading for shore, leaving the inspection of the below water work to the American Bureau of Shipping.

Now three hours into the three-hour-twenty-minute dive, Wiitala called Brian and suggested he dial down his free-flow valve. Often, a diver will allow the air supply to free-flow past the demand regulator. This would be done to evacuate water buildup in the helmet or clear a fogged face plate. The Quincy compressor had the capability to maintain pressure even with a free-flowing helmet, but this was an old compressor, the rings had been known to leak and the added strain on the unit was unnecessary. The compressor was bottoming out and was not able to maintain pressure. Brian responded that he was not free-flowing, the free-flow valve was closed. Several times earlier, during the dive, Wiitala was forced to leave the dive station and adjust the compressor. Each time he did so the compressor would respond and build pressure back to ninety pounds. Wiitala again headed to the compressor, attempted to adjust the pilot valve, the diesel engine was running normally. Pressure was low, 72 psi, but holding.

The workday was coming to an end. In addition to the United States Coast Guard inspection crew that had just departed by helicopter, there were other day workers attempting to leave by boat. By regulation, when a diver is in the water, there can be no other crafts permitted in the area, so the crew boat sent from Sabine Pass was asked to remain outside the exclusion area. On board was a young welder who had come out as part of a team to install a new piece of gear on the deck just above the temporary dive station. With his work done, equipment packed, the curious twenty-four-year-old welder, knowing that his trip to shore would be delayed, made his way down to the lower deck to watch the dive operations. He came up from behind Wiitala, who, by this time, had just returned from adjusting the compressor. Wiitala picked up the headset, talked a moment to the diver below while continuing to watch the monitor.

"Can I watch?" asked the curious man who had often fancied becoming a diver some day. "No problem," responded Wiitala.

There was little to see as the vague images on the monitor were difficult to see, obscured by the poor underwater visibility and inadequate lighting as the sun was almost totally behind threatening late-afternoon cloud cover. All he could hear was Wiitala's side of the conversation, which suddenly changed from calm although somewhat frustrated to frantic.

"Brian, calm down, we are going to bring you up."

Wiitala threw down the headset and headed back to the compressor, stopped a moment and then headed into the ship's galley. The curious welder continued to watch the monitor thinking it strange that the bubbles, which was all he could decipher on the darkened video monitor, appeared to be moving from the top of the screen to the bottom. Wiitala returned some five minutes later with a cup of coffee in a small white Styrofoam cup, behind him was Buddy Horton. Wiitala picked up the headset, mumbled a few words and then called out to Horton who now was standing at the rail gazing down at the water.

"Buddy, we have a situation here," Wiitala announced.

Buddy responded "Diver down" as he grabbed hold of the umbilical still tied to the rail and began pulling in the slack. The American Bureau of Shipping inspector seeing the sudden commotion joined Horton and together they pulled until the umbilical became taut. Wiitala threw down the headset and joined the two man at the rail but to no avail. The umbilical was fouled. Returning to the dive station now manned only by the curious welder Wiitala once again grabbed the headset and attempted to contact the diver. "Brian, you are going to need to un-foul your line, it is stuck, we cannot pull you up." There was no response. Wiitala once again threw down the headset, coffee cup still in hand, and headed back to the rail. Taking one last hit of coffee, he threw the cup into the water and directed the American Bureau of Shipping inspector to visually follow the cup. If the diver were able to release himself surely he would float to the surface, the cup would follow the current, and the diver should be close behind. Ron Everett did as directed and followed the cup as it floated under the platform and drifted to starboard.

Austin remained with his electronic gizmos continuing to transcribe the data that had been transmitted from below until Wiitala grabbed him by the shoulder and told him to suit up. "You need to go get him, the umbilical is fouled, and he is not responding." Austin went in search for his dive gear. Wiitala headed for the air rack and turned on the first of the two standby high-pressure air tanks. The gauges responded now showing 150 psi. Everett, after watching the cup float out of sight, returned to the dive station, picked up the headset, and began a one-sided conversation with the man he had only meet a few hours earlier just prior to the beginning of the inspection. He assured the diver that they were on the way, the secondary air supply was activated. All Brian needed to do was wait, help was on the way. All Everett heard was the sound of air rushing through the helmet of the now-fouled diver.

Austin worked at squeezing his portly body into the one-half-inch neoprene suit, a task that would take twenty minutes to complete. Horton asked if any of the men now assembling around the increasingly anxious situation site knew of a number to call for assistance, a number for the Coast Guard, perhaps a number for the helicopter service. Then he turned to the curious welder who continued his observation of the bubbles on the monitor and asked if he could quickly break out his oxygen, acetylene-cutting torch. They would need the hose, at least 250 feet, and the oxygen tank. By the time Austin had managed to slip into his suit, the first standby tank was empty. Wiitala quickly moved to set up the second. Turning it on line, the gauge indicated this tank too was already depleted.

The situation had turned from bad to worse, and Horton made his way back to the office. Armed with the number furnished by the ABS inspector, Horton called Air Logistics in Port Arthur. Once the dispatcher was on the line, Horton, in a nervous voice, asked that a helicopter be dispatched to pick up a diver from American Oil Field Divers and then bring him out to the Cliffs 12; they had a diver down and might need to transport him to the hospital. He gave his location as "South Cameron Block 38," then hung up, and called American Oil Field in search for a backup diver. The dispatcher thought it odd as the caller never identified himself and the location given did not exist.

While Horton continued looking for assistance, the welder continued to splice together oxygen, acetylene hoses, Everett continued talking over the communication system, and Austin completed his preparation to enter the water to retrieve the fouled diver. With the now-spliced-together hose connected to the oxygen, Wiitala hooked the other end to Austin's helmet as the crane on the deck above roared into action, lowering the man basket to their location. Wiitala, along with Austin, climbed aboard and was quickly sent to the wave tops. Austin was wearing his seldom-used suit and helmet, around his waist a length of rope extending to the deck and the hands of a recently enlisted member of the crew. Holding his face plate with one hand and the oxygen line in the other, Austin took that giant step he had seen so many divers do under his watchful supervision. In fact, he had overseen a diving operation done for Cliffs—again, with Buddy Horton as the safety officer, in Venezuela where all the diving was done using pure oxygen and the only air delivery system spliced together hoses.

He hit the water, found Brian's taut umbilical and attempted to pulling himself down. With no weight belt and a 1/2-inch neoprene suit the 220-pound, 5-foot-8-inch Austin managed less than a few feet before returning to the surface. Back in the basket they returned to the deck requesting someone find shackles, rigging anything that they could attach to assist getting Austin under water. Five minutes later, four large shackles had been located, attached to the rope around Austin's waist and the two men returned to just above the water for a second attempt to reach Brian. Once again Austin took that giant step but this time he shot straight down. Grabbing the rope he pulled hard and was quickly pulled to the surface by the newly enlisted tender standing on the deck thirty feet above. Wiitala pulled him back in the basket as Austin struggled to release his helmet. There was blood running from his ears and nose.

"I'm done with this, if I go back down there you will only be retrieving two dead bodies."

Wiitala grabbed the helmet still connected to the oxygen line, ripped the neck dam from the now-crying Austin and in seconds was in the water dressed only in his coveralls and the confiscated dive helmet. Pulling himself down the umbilical he found Brian. Suspended three feet above the lower deck, transducer cable floating free, air flowing out the discharge ports of his helmet and a three-by-eight-inch nylon rope stretched tight to a pipe running horizontal to the submerged deck. Brian's motionless body hung at a forty-five-degree angle, head up, safety harness partially released and his right arm pointing to the surface. As Wiitala approached, his air oxygen supply was interrupted. He pulled on the line giving the appropriate line pulls to signal those above of his situation. There was no one above trained in what the line pulls meant. He held his breath continuing until he could grab Brian by the arm with one hand and with the other reached down and cut the three-by-eight-inch nylon line, sending both rescuer and diver to the surface.

During the time Wiitala was in the water, Austin had been returned to the deck. Horton had return from attempting to contact emergency assistance and found his old friend Austin still bleeding from his nose and ears, crying, "He is dead, I could see him down there dead, I need to get to a hospital."

Fifteen nautical miles away, Walter Allan Linzy had just ended his shift at Air Logistics and was heading for his car at the end of a long day. He had been in the office just prior to 1700 that afternoon when a call had come in requesting a potential need for assistance from some unknown caller giving a nonexistent coordinate. He had waited for a call back. It was now 1730 and he was done for the day. As he approached his car, the dispatcher rushed to the parking lot telling him they had just received a call from a rig located at West Cam 83, not the previous nonexistent South Cam 38. They had a diver on the deck of the offshore rig, he was alive and required immediate medical evacuation. Linzy headed for his helicopter along with the dispatcher and prepared for flight.

Aboard the Cliffs 12, Brian and Wiitala had been lifted back to the safety of the deck, Brian's motionless body, weights, harness, and helmet still on. The curious welder attempted to remove the helmet to no avail, the mechanism was something he had never seen. He called for assistance. Austin was sitting slumped on the deck, surrounded by members of the crew, still attempting to regain his wits after his near brush with death. Wiitala removed his own helmet first, gasped for air, and then reached down releasing Brian's helmet. The curious welder now sprung into action along with a Cliffs crew member, and together, they took turns applying CPR. Brian's face was blue, and he remained motionless, a crew member showed up with a medical mask and oxygen. Chest compressions continued, and the color was returning to the face of the young man that had so loved his job working in the underwater world.

From the southwest, the air logistics helicopter was on final approach. Austin had made his way from the dive station to the helipad. The welder continued chest compressions, Horton was back in his office attempting to call his office. The master of the vessel, Ron Everett, was attempting to get his crew into the living units so as to "not be in the way." Wiitala sat motionless in his wet coveralls watching as the two young men worked attempting to maintain life in his young companion. Everett remained at the dive station with headphones still on.

Linzy brought the helicopter to rest on the helipad high above the deck where what crew remained watched to see if the young man would respond. Austin waited for the blades of the chopper to slow and then made his way to the starboard hatch and climbed aboard. Linzy handed Austin a headset so that they could communicate over the roar of the still-running turbine.

"He is dead," Austin announced. "I need medical attention."

This presented a dilemma for the man that had only twenty minutes ago been attempting to head home from work. Now he was eleven miles at sea with a man in the copilot's seat with a bloody nose. He was not authorized to transport a dead body, but then again, he was not about to leave transporting a man with nothing more than a bloody nose. Linzy called his dispatcher. The Coast Guard would need to make the pronouncement that the diver was dead, not an unqualified observer. The directive was if there was any hope he was to have the man brought aboard and returned to Port Arthur ASAP.

Looking out the starboard hatch, Linzy could see the man basket suspended from the crane, two men inside providing CPR—one doing chest compressions, the other holding a breathing bag over Brian's face. Linzy looked over to the man in the copilots seat and asked, "Are you sure the diver is dead?"

"Yes, he was without air for twenty minutes,"[5] responded Austin who sometime during the time he had left his aborted attempt at a rescue had fully dressed in dry work clothes.

Brian and the two men performing CPR were dropped on a lower deck below the helipad to avoid a confrontation between the crane and still turning blades of the helicopter. Quickly, with the aid of other members of the crew, Brian was transferred to a stretcher, carried up the ship's ladder, and slid into the rear compartment of the craft as Linzy prepared to lift off. The curious welder, now weary from twenty minutes of chest compressions, watched as the young man he had never met was loaded aboard accompanied by Wiitala, and the man who up until now had been entrusted with the oxygen and breathing bag. Wiitala, still dressed in his wet coveralls, grabbed the breathing bag to maintain a tight seal on Brian's face. His back seat partner took over the chest compressions. Austin stared directly forward oblivious to his surroundings, Linzy increased the RPM's and the craft lifted off turning north, north east for the return to Port Arthur.

---

[5]   Page 24, line 10, Deposition Walter Allen Linzy

Two decks below, Horton had just completed receiving his directions from the main office in Houston. Everett had left the dive station and found a seat in Horton's office. Townsend found his way there as well, letting Horton know the helicopter was bound for the hospital. Horton called Park Place Memorial, letting them know a drowning victim was incoming. Linzy piloted his craft to St. Mary's, the only hospital within range with a helipad.

Fifteen minutes later, the Air Logistics craft landed on the roof of the St Mary's. Linzy warned the crew as he slowed the rooter to keep their heads down, avoid the tail rooter. The sun was setting, Wiitala was shivering, still wearing his wet clothes and holding the oxygen bag, the Cliffs's deckhand continued the chest compressions. Austin stared forward. There was no one there to meet them. Wiitala, shouting over the roar of the winding down turbine, yelled at Austin directing him to get out and find help.

Austin removed the headset, opened the hatch, and ran to the only door available. Inside, there was an elevator and a gurney, still no personnel. He grabbed the gurney, pushed it through the still-open door, and with head down returned to the helicopter avoiding the tail rooter. Together the three passengers transferred Brian to the gurney, continued CPR, and went in search for the elevator.

Together the four men traveled down to the first floor and emerged in the hospital's main entry lobby. A surprised nurse quickly summoned assistance as two men dressed in hospital garb took over the life-sustaining CPR as a third man quickly pushed the gurney to the emergency area. Austin made his way to the waiting room, Wiitala went in search for a phone, the third member of the rescue team went in search for a ride home.

Aboard the Cliffs 12 Horton, the safety manager continued with phone calls, Townsend, master of the vessel, was assembling the crew and asking them to individually write up their observations. Everett, the ABS inspector, continued to sit in Horton's office waiting for some direction as to how they were to proceed. Horton placed a call to Gilbert at G&G Marine leaving a message that one of his "divers was down" and now were being transported to Park Place Memorial.

Wiitala eventually was able to locate Gilbert and appraised him of their situation. Brian, who had been fouled below water, was now in the emergency room and, from last report, his heart was beating on its own, color had returned; but he was still on a respirator as they were attempting to rewarm his hypothermic body. Gilbert, in turn, contacted Austin's wife, suggesting she find her way to Port Arthur to pick up her husband. Then a call to Kevin Lawdermilk. Kevin was a longtime employee of G&G—sometimes as a diver, sometimes as a supervisor, and sometimes as an equipment manager. Gilbert asked Kevin to head to Port Arthur to pick up Wiitala. Wiitala was there without transportation, was wet, and would need a friend. Then Gilbert placed a call to Julie.

Julie and Brian had been married now for eight months and was just returning home from work when her cell phone rang. Gilbert related the story as best he knew and suggested she find someone to take her the two hours from Houston to Port Arthur. She hung up, turned her car east in search for Interstate 10, and called her mother in faraway Washington State.

Chapter 5

BELLEVUE, WASHINGTON

The sun had just set and the ever-present March rain continued as I was driving north on 130th Avenue NW. To my right was my just-turned-nine-year-old daughter still dressed in the tights she had been wearing for the just-completed ballet lesson. The conversation was bright and bubbly as I was told about yet another new dance position and how well she had done. Suddenly, the only sound was that of the windshield wipers. Afton had grown quiet, stared straight ahead, and sat motionless. Then in a soft voice, still staring out through the rain-streaked windshield, proclaimed, "I never want to go in the water again, it's cold down there, it's so cold, you could run out of air, it's so cold." Then there's nothing more as the tears streaked her cheeks; and the child who, moments before was filled with passion, sat quietly not saying another word.

Ten blocks later, we arrived home—she headed for her room, I headed to the kitchen to start dinner. Karen was in the home office just off the family room attending to the mail and paying bills. I had no sooner started the pot of water boiling when there was a knock at the front door. It was Brian's mother-in-law, Eunice; Karen answered the door. I continued my appointed task, thinking what could Brian have done now to cause his mother-in-law to show up at the door unannounced. She had never approved of Brian or of his chosen profession. Brian had literally married the little girl down the street. They had met in middle school and been friends ever since. Brian grew to be six feet five inch tall while Julie never quite made it past five feet.

After a few moments, my wife of twenty-six years called out to me, requesting I join the two mothers in the office. There had been a call from Julie; she was driving from Houston to Port Arthur, Texas. Brian had been trapped underwater, but was now in a hospital, alive, but that was all she could tell. Julie was on her cell, driving alone and heading to join her husband.

I ran a construction business out of the house; there were multiple phone lines. I picked up the first line and called Julie. She was frantic, almost impossible to understand. I suggested she pull over; she refused. I turned that phone over to her mother. I picked up the second line and called information, thinking how many hospitals could be in Port Arthur, Texas? I called the first number and reached Park Place Memorial, but there was no one named Brian Pilkington there. Then a call to Saint Mary's. Yes, a young man had recently been admitted; no, they could not give me any information. I gave her my number and asked if she could pass it along to the doctor, to anyone who would call me back. I then picked up the fax line so as not to have all the lines tied up should someone call us back. Then a call to American Airlines. I would need two tickets to Houston. I explained the situation and then asked that they too call back with whatever they could find so that Karen and I could be in Houston as soon as possible.

Then the calls I truly had hoped to never need to make. The first to Brian's grandfather—my father, now seventy-four years old and living sixty miles to the north on Camano Island. There was silence at the end of the line, followed by "We are on our way, give us an hour, you do what you need to do." Finally, a call to the dorm at the University of Puget Sound. Jamie was a junior currently in the middle of his end of semester exams. He would need to know that his brother had been involved in an accident; he was alive but hospitalized. His roommate answered the phone and quickly found the younger brother. Jamie insisted we drive to the university on our way to the airport; he needed to come. I told him I would get back to him as the open phone line rang.

Julie had just reached the hospital and was still in conversation with her mother. Brian's mother listened in. I answered the phone. It was Father Dan Donahue, chaplin at Saint Mary's. The doctors were busy working on our son, and his heart was beating on its own. It would be another twenty-four hours before they would be able to truly know his condition. If we were to be there, we would need to leave now. Julie had just arrived and was heading to the ER. He continued on with words I did not hear about God and understanding when I heard the scream.

Julie had entered the room, took his hand and he died.

I too dropped the phone and went in search for the little sister that had left her room and was now sitting near the bottom of the staircase leading to the second floor, sitting and listening to every word. I sat and held her until Grandpa Fred and his wife, Mary, arrived. I never told them what had happened. There was no need to. No one was talking. Everyone knew.

I picked up the phone and placed a call to Jamie. "He did not make it, your Mother and I are heading to the airport." There was silence. Then an angry voice said,

"Come get me, I need to go."

"No," I replied, "I need to take care of this; your grandfather and Mary will look after Afton, you stay in school and I will call when we know more."

American Airlines had never gotten back to us, so we grabbed a change of clothes, and Karen and I headed to the airport. Leaving the car in short-term parking, we quickly made our way to the ticket counter. Karen in shock, things moving too quickly, the hour was late, and the airport winding down. American did have a direct flight to Houston, and there were no seats available. I explained the situation. Thirty minutes later, we were sitting all alone in the first-class section headed to Houston.

Chapter 6

HOUSTON

MARCH 5, 1996

With first light of day, we were on the ground in Houston. Road map in hand and a rental car to drive, we made our way to the apartment. Our son and his wife had called home for only the past four months. We had never been there, waiting for an invitation or at least giving the newlyweds the opportunity to have it in order before the old folks showed up for the first time. We found the complex, then the unit on the second floor. I knocked on the door, which was immediately opened by the little girl that had once lived down the street. Her eyes were red and swollen, the tears no longer possible. She was truly alone as the two Mrs. Pilkingtons embraced and together cried.

It might have been early March and the day was just beginning, but for a native of Washington, the weather was already too oppressive for me. I made my way to the balcony for fresh air, leaving the two women to commiserate. Out on the deck, there was a blue box that looked strangely similar to the one that had at one time been in my garage. Draped over the top was a weight belt, knife, and a quick release, looking very much like mine.

The hour was approaching 8:00 AM when the first call came in. I took the call. It was the medical examiner in Port Arthur. He explained how difficult a time this must be, but we needed to understand that time was of the essence. Could they harvest Brian's corneas, his eyes, kidneys, heart? He was a perfectly healthy individual; his organs could live on if they moved quickly. They had called earlier. Julie had hung up on them. I knew my son all too well; he would not have wanted his body disfigured, parted out like a used car; and so I thanked the gentleman for the opportunity, but no we would like to have him returned to us whole. It was then explained there would need to be an autopsy nonetheless. Any time a health person dies under questionable circumstances there would always need to be an autopsy. Today was Tuesday; it would be at least Thursday or Friday before the Coroner would release the body. I started with questions of my own, but was quickly silenced with "There is nothing I can tell you now, you will need to speak with the Coroner." I thanked the man for his time and followed my daughter-in-laws lead and hung up.

Moments later, the phone rang again. Again, I answered. This time it was a woman claiming to be an attorney representing G&G Marine. She gave me her number and name, Kenna Sellers, and then directed me not to contact her client but rather deal directly with her regarding anything pertaining to the accident. Her client was uninsured, and her office would be handling everything. She had no details; there was nothing she could tell me at that time. Perhaps in a few days they would have the facts and surely would pass them along to me.

I hung up the phone, suggested to the two Mrs. Pilkingtons that I head out and find some coffee, perhaps something to eat. Suggested they not answer the phone, take it off the hook; this was going to be a long day. I drove east a few blocks, found a motel, and checked in. Once in the room, I searched out the phone book and started making calls. It was too early. All I got was answering machines as most legal offices apparently do not open before nine. My own attorney in Washington would not be in for at least three hours. I found a doughnut shop, purchased a dozen of Houston's finest, three cups of black coffee, and headed back to rejoin the women.

We talked and cried for a while, tried to piece the story together as best we could. Julie told us that after she had left the ER the night before, Wiitala and Gilbert were sitting together in the hospital waiting room feverishly writing. A man claiming to be from the American Bureau of Shipping had come by to check on Brian; she did not remember his name. He was distraught when told the news. She had seen Kevin Lawdermilk bringing dry clothes for Wiitala and that the two of them left together. Gilbert had sat with her for a while, offered to pay to have Brian returned to Seattle. A chaplin had sat with her; she did not remember much if anything he had said. It was nice to have a calming voice. There was little else she knew. Our conversation was interrupted once again. This time a knock at the door. It was a friend of Julie from work with a gift of food. It would be the first offering of the day of nourishment that would never be eaten but welcome just the same. As each friend came, each wanted to know. Was it true? What happened? What could they do? As the containers wrapped in aluminum foil filled the kitchen, more questions came from concerned female friends and angry male friends. Each finding it inconceivable that Brian would not be coming home.

I had heard the same questions too many times and felt helpless that I could not answer. And then there were the comments from the attorney who had called. Do not contact her client. Her client was not insured? How could that be? Isn't every business required to be insured? Why was it important to tell me that? All I had wanted to know was what happened.

One more question from yet another friend bearing gifts that I could not answer. I had enough. With that, I left and headed back to the rental car. Armed with the address found in Julie's address book, ignoring the directive from the attorney claiming to represent G&G Marine, I headed north to the Woodlands and the office of Dan Gilbert, owner and operator of G&G Marine.

Twenty minutes later, after a few wrong turns, I found myself in a modest residential neighborhood filled with midcentury homes, manicured lawns, and a street lined with mature trees. Finding the numbers I had been searching for nailed to a tree adjacent to the street and at the end of long gravel drive, I stopped and readied myself. There had been no sleeping the night before as Karen and I sat alone in the first-class section of the red-eye from Seattle. Seats we had not requested, first-class seats we never paid for, but rather the ones the forewarned flight attendants thought best suited. It had been a long night with thoughts that truly there must have been some mistake, that we would land and find miraculously, through some medical intervention, our son was revived. How could such a vibrant young man have died? What happened the previous afternoon off the coast of Texas? Who else was there, what had he been doing, what caused the accident? Now I was sitting at the end of the long road leading to the office where the answers would surely be revealed.

Collecting my thoughts, I followed the gravel road and parked alongside the other cars already there. The office looked more like a temporary building, a job shack with a small warehouse close by. Without knocking I entered the office surprising those assembled.

There was a woman sitting behind a desk, a gaunt little man who looked like he had spent a bit too much time in the sun, another woman dressed in a three-piece business suit clinging to a yellow legal pad, and a man in his thirties sitting with his back to the wall who appeared to be the center of attention. The center of attention until I walked in. "Can we help you?" snapped the woman in the three-piece suit. "I'm Pete Pilkington, Brian's father."

There was a brief silence before the woman in the three-piece suit responded. "We are taking a statement from Mr. Wiitala, the man that attempted to rescue your son yesterday. This is something we need to do now while the events are still fresh in his mind. Here—" She paused for a moment as she wrote a name and number on the yellow tablet. Tearing off the sheet, she handed it to me with the words "We will get in touch with you in a few days."

"Can I listen, truly, I would like to know now?" I responded in disbelief. The only attorney I had ever met with no business card responded. "This is a client, attorney, privileged meeting, what we find out, whatever we discover will be made available in due course. Please let us continue, Mr. Wiitala has been up all night as has Mr. Gilbert. We need to get this information. We will be in touch in a few days."

With that I was directed back through the door. I had just moments before I entered with nothing more to show than a piece of paper, a name, and a phone number. That along with a vision of two men obviously anxious and in fear of what was to transpire.

There was obviously nothing to be learned here. Even the name and number I already had as earlier in the day, the attorney had given me the number over the phone just after advising me not to contact her client. Returning to the motel room I had rented earlier, I started calling one attorney, then another—all more than willing to discuss the case, all wanting me to head to their respective offices. Each confirmed that it was possible to operate in Texas with no insurance, and there was no requirement for business to have any insurance for their employees. This was, after all, a right-to-work state.

If there was nothing to be learned here in Houston, I needed to go to Port Arthur. Surely there would be an ongoing investigation, someone could tell us the facts, and that is where our son was. We would need to begin the process of returning him home. Leaving the motel, I made my way back to the apartment. The friends were all gone now, and the two Mrs. Pilkingtons were sitting together, looking at old photos, reading notes, sorting through memorabilia. I sat for a moment; no one was talking when yet another knock at the door. It was Julie's mother.

Eunice had taken the first flight on that Tuesday morning out of Seattle and was here to assist in any way she could to comfort her adopted daughter. There were arrangements to be made, and she was armed with the plan. First, we were to see that Brian was cremated, it only made sense. The strain on her daughter did not need to be increased with bills, funeral expenses, shipping . . . Before she could finish with her logical, well-thought-out plan, I interrupted.

"Our son is not to be returned home in a carry-on bag. Look after your daughter, I will see to my son."

Before there could be any further discussion, the phone rang and was answered by Julie. It was the Saint Mary's Hospital. Brian's remains had been released to a funeral home in Groves Texas, just outside of Port Arthur. We would need to contact them to make arrangements. With that a phone number and an address and the direction to assemble clothes. Clothes we would like him to be wearing.

Eunice and I retired to the living room, knowing it was pointless for either of us to speak. We each had our concept of what should be done, and we each knew that all the arguments either of us could muster would be unlikely to change the other's mind-set. Julie and Karen headed to the bedroom and began laying out the clothes for Brian's final trip home.

A blue blazer perhaps last worn while driving Hanna Storm down some one way street the wrong way in an attempt to get to the next sports venue. A white shirt with red-white-and-blue pinstripes in need of pressing. A blue tie, well-polished penny loafers, and two socks. One blue with white polka dots, the other blue-and-white striped. Just the way he would want it.

It had been long two days. Without eating, we agreed that Karen and I would stay at the motel, Eunice and Julie would try to find sleep in the apartment. We would all meet in the morning. Whoever was so disposed could head to Groves Texas.

Early the following morning, with little or no sleep, we met again at Julie's. A quick study of the road map, a cup of coffee in hand, I made my way back to the car. Karen would come, so would Julie and Eunice was not to be left behind. I drove with Julie to my right, the two mother-in-laws in the back. Between us, we had only Julie's phone, and it rang incessantly as shocked friends called to find if it was true. Calls to work to say she would not be coming in. We were an hour outside of Port Arthur when we left Interstate 10 at Winnie Texas. We would need to turn off here and follow Highway 73. There was a fast-food joint on the left, and none of us had eaten anything other the doughnuts and coffee earlier that morning.

The mothers headed to the counter of the Whataburger, I for a well-worn wooden bench to sit and be alone. Julie came and sat next to me, unable to think about food. She had her phone pressed hard against her ear so that she might hear every word over the roar of the highway we had just left. It was Holly at G&G marine, Brian's personal gear along with his truck had just been brought up to the company office. Would we like to come and pick it all up? They would understand if we were late, they would wait.

She had found her way to Saint Mary's two nights before in the dark; Groves was just north of there. We studied the map still numb from the ordeal of the last thirty-six hours. Brian had been pronounced dead just thirty-six hours ago and we were on our way to see to bringing him home.

An hour later we pulled up to the vacant parking lot at Clayton-Thompson. When I had talked to the Medical Examiner twenty-four hours ago who was interested in harvesting organs he had lead me to believe there would need to be an autopsy, the remains could not be released for forty-eight to seventy-two hours and only after approval from the Coroner. Now only twenty-four hours after Brian's death, we sat in a rented car in front of a funeral home, none of us wanting to be the first to go inside.

Together we left the car and made our way through the doors to be greeted by a somber-looking middle-aged women in a simple gray dress. We introduced ourselves; she followed suit along with the proper condolences. She did not expect us to be there so soon, asked us if we would care to come sit in a private room. She would let the director know we were there.

With respect and dignity, we were directed to a small room filled with overstuffed wing-backed chairs, dimmed lights, and soft music. Coffee quickly appeared, followed closely by a man in his late fifties, early sixties, dressed in a neat suit and carefully knotted tie.

"Mr. Pilkington, we did not expect you so soon. How was your trip from Washington? That was Washington State?"

"Yes, sir, we are all here from Washington State, we have come to see to our son," I replied for the four of us.

"Brian has just arrived with us last night. Would you like a moment, would you like to see him?" replied the man who had introduced himself, but by now already forgotten as he blended into the dimly lit room. "Perhaps you might consider giving us an hour, to get him ready. Did you bring his clothes? There are a few places close by where you could go have lunch, while . . . ," he continued.

Following his suggestion, we headed back for the lobby and out into the harsh light of the midday Texas sun. Two blocks down, we found some nondescript, all-you-can-eat cafeteria were I was scolded by the woman behind the counter for not ordering enough. "Hun, you need more to eat than that. You look like you haven't eaten in days, the food here is what you need, and you need to eat."

She was right, and she was not the first nor was she to be the last that day who would attempt to tell me what I needed to do. The four of us sat together with plates piled high with food we would never eat. Little was said as we waited the hour before returning to Clayton-Thompson.

Upon our return, we were directed to a larger room filled with metal-folding chairs. Much like the smaller room we had been directed to when we first arrived, this one too was dimly lit. We entered through the double doors; Brian's mother's eyes momentarily looked to the head of the room and, though as if she could make it go away, make it not real quickly looked down as she sat in the first folding chair there in the back of the room. There in a temporary casket, half-opened, was our son; eyes closed as though taking an afternoon nap. His mother screamed, holding her head and refused comfort as Julie and her mother proceeded forward. I sat next to my wife unable to aid or comfort, unable to bring myself to do much of anything but be angry.

Perhaps it was minutes, perhaps it was hours, we were once again directed to the small room with the overstuffed chairs. The mother, wife, and mother-in-law continued sobbing, unable to talk, each finding a chair, each with their own thoughts. After a few respectful moments, the director entered and asked if I could join him in his office; we would need to work out the details.

His desk was neat and tidy with comfortable chairs the room properly lit. He sat behind the desk and I in one of the two leather chairs directly in front. His previous somber demeanor now changed to one of anger as he began what I had suspected was a meeting to discuss arrangements, payment, the sort of things that needed to be addressed. "Mr. Pilkington," he began, "this is not right, twenty-three-year-old men in the prime of their lives should not be here in need of my services. You should not be here, your wife, your family should not have to go through this. You need an attorney, representation. These men that did this to your son, your family, they need to be held accountable. Twenty-three-year-old men do not just die. You need the truth. There needs to be justice."

Before I could respond, before I could tell him my frustration with the blocks to the truth I had already encountered, he leaned back in his chair and continued.

"See that picture?" he was pointing to an old photo of two young boys fishing on some nondescript river captured in an old black-and-white photo. "One of those boys is me the other. The other is the best damn Attorney in Texas, if you want answers, that's the man you need. Give me an hour and I bet I can have him here."

Twenty minutes later, a tall aging man dressed in cowboy boots, freshly ironed Carhartts with Stetson in hand walked through the door. We had just completed filling out the forms, selected the appropriate coffin, been assured that the travel arrangements would be made not only for Brian, but for us as well. None of us had tickets when we entered Clayton-Thompson, we now; all five of us had tickets home on the next day's flight. Karen, Julie, Eunice and I would be flying out of Houston on an American Eagle commuter flight to Dallas; Brian would need to be transported overland to Dallas. We would all then fly together on the evening American nonstop to Seattle. We would all be headed back to Seattle on Thursday.

Now our attention was focused on this man in the Carhartt. He was there at the request of his boyhood friend and fishing buddy. He had heard some of the details from his old friend and then there had been a call to Justice of the Peace John Borne. Something was amiss; we needed council if justice was to be served. He never introduced himself as though we already knew who he was. "This is somewhat unusual; I think we might all be more comfortable in my office. It's just twenty minutes north of here, let me arrange for a car to get y'all there, this all must be a great strain."

Within minutes the three parents from Washington and the wife from Houston were all in the back of a black limo heading north to Beaumont Texas and the offices of Walter Umphrey, attorney at law.

Downtown Beaumont looked more like a ghost town with boarded up storefronts, empty streets and the tell tale signs of decay caused by either urban flight or economic disaster, perhaps both. Sitting in the back of this elegant vehicle meant for luxurious transportation as we were now traveling down these barren streets of a once vibrant city made me feel a sense of guilt. But then this vehicle was most likely the one used to carry families and loved ones from funerals to cemeteries, perhaps we were in the correct ship of choice.

We pulled up in front of a multi leveled restored brick warehouse that filled half a city block, the other half devoted to parking. Under the cover of a brass supported Port Cochere our land yacht came to a stop and we were hurried inside. Past the elegant stairs, past the tall thin women standing ramrod straight alongside her desk of importance. Guided by a woman who had met us outside we were escorted directly to the outer office of Walter Umphrey. The walls were lined with framed news articles bestowing previous legal victories, stories of workers wronged and settlements achieved. But perhaps the most striking feature in this room of elegant wood detailing, wainscoting, crown molds and coffered ceilings was the life sized wooden effigy of the man we had meet just the hour before.

84

Through the open door to the inner office we could see the man we had met in the funeral home, standing beside his desk with hands raised in greeting, this time dressed in garb more fitting his stature. We all found a seat, a few minutes of small talk, tales of previous victories, the origin of the wooded statue in the outer office, where we were from, the tobacco suit he was currently arguing on behalf of the good folks of Texas and his previous land mark case against the asbestos industry. He would see that we received equal treatment and he had personally chosen the best man available, a man with maritime law experience, this would be a tough case, lots of jurisdictions. The Coast Guard, OSHA, the egregious act itself happening off the coast of Louisiana, possibly international waters, the death in Texas. We would need a young aggressive attorney with years of expertise and an organization to support the effort. With that we were ushered down the hall to an even larger room. Again with heavy wood detailing, wainscoting and moldings that must have kept a crew of carpenters busy for a year. In the center of the room was a long conference table with a top of green granite.

Sitting at the end of this green monolith with a small stack of papers neatly piled, dressed in a white shirt open tie, sleeves rolled up, a man in his late thirties perhaps early forties slowly left the papers he was diligently reviewing and brought himself to his feet. In a soft voice of compassion. "David Brandom, so very sorry to hear of your loss."

With that we were directed to all find a seat. More discussions of previous victories, the great injustice visited on our beloved son and Julie's husband. Contracts were presented, Julie had council. Karen and I had no standing but would be kept informed. As quickly as we had been brought to Beaumont we were returned to Groves and the parking lot of Clayton Thompson.

We drove the two hours back to Houston in silence. Once back at the apartment Eunice and Julie headed in for the security of the home, Karen and I continued on to the Woodlands. Finding the gravel drive that lead to G&G was not an issue this time. I had been there before. I pulled up next to the tree with the numbers affixed and directed Karen to wait. She would drive the rental car, I would go collect Brian's truck.

Down the gravel driveway past a solitary car and one shiny, clean red pickup with chrome wheels. Then through the door I had been asked to leave through the day before. Gilbert sitting behind the desk jumped to his feet and presented me with two keys attached to a blue metal key chain in the form of a shark with teeth meant for opening bottles.

"These are Brian's, for his truck, it's just outside," said the man that I had only seen the one time before. The slight little man who obviously had been subjected to too many hours of sun who I had seen in the office during the questioning of Wiitala.

"His personal gear is over on the deck by the warehouse," he continued "and I have a copy of Dan's statement for you to have and review." According to Dan, Brian disconnected his air connection during the dive, with all the confusion, his panic, he was able to tell Dan "I fucked up" as he attempted to right his misdeed.

With shock and disbelief I listened in silence. Brian may very well have made a mistake or two over the years. Brian would never have told anyone. Brian would have fixed the problem and surely not told anyone "I fucked up."

I took the keys and then went in search for Brian's personal gear. Sitting on the ground just outside the door to the warehouse there were two bags, a coil of hose, a metal rack containing a motor and compressor, other miscellaneous parts and pieces and a dive helmet.

I looked in disbelief and turned to the man following me across the parking area. "Is that Brain's dive helmet?"

All the other gear I recognized, the old school bag, my olive drab duffel; those were Brian's and I quickly snatched them up as I waited for a response from the little man. He eventually responded in the affirmative and, without asking permission, located the neoprene case neatly stored in the duffle and carefully sealed the helmet inside. With all loaded in the back of Brian's truck I turned looked down into the eyes of the little man and said, "Next time I see you, it will be in court, people like you should not be in business." With that I drove down the drive, turned on the paved road with Karen following close behind.

Another sleepless night. I awoke early and made a return trip to Beaumont, this time alone and in Brian's truck. Stopping once along the way at Whataburger for a cup of coffee, there was some sense of comfort as I sat on that well-worn bench, then continued east on Interstate 10. Back to the offices of Provost and Umphrey.

Depositing the helmet with the woman at the front desk, David had not yet arrived. She had a few details, there would be in inquest, it would be the following week at Justice John Borne's office. He was well know to the firm, a longtime judge and hunting companion of Walters. If there was to be a proper investigation he was the man to do it and he would certainly ask all the right questions. David would look after the civil end of things.

I thanked her for the first bits of information I could believe, returned to the red truck and drove the two hours back to Houston. My work was done here and now it was up to the capable hands of the men and women of Provost Umphrey and the old Judge.

Chapter 7

HOME

We had been in Houston three days. Now Brian's wife, my wife, Brian's mother-in-law and I sat at a bustling gate waiting for our flight to Dallas. Brian had left overland from Groves early that same morning in the care of Clayton-Thompson as the cargo compartment of this American Eagle commuter was not capable of holding anything larger than suit cases. Hobby airport was a busy place on a Thursday afternoon with commuter flights coming and going from all parts of the Midwest. The electronic board showed the progress of flights arriving and departing some on time some not, some delayed and some cancelled. There was talk of storms over Oklahoma and flight delays but we were not heading to Oklahoma; ours was a flight to Dallas, meet up with the direct flight to Seattle and home. It had been a long four days for all of us. The opportunity to sit and reflect welcomed as we waited.

A glance at the departure board and the status of our flight was changed from on time to cancelled. Looking to the others in my party who had not noticed the change and seeing the sudden convergence on the podium at the gate I left the comfort of my seat and headed quickly to the ticket area back in the main terminal.

Lines were forming, agitated passengers queued up in search for alternate flights. The storms over Oklahoma were causing chaos throughout the Midwest as the smaller commuters were unable to land, had been diverted or held on the ground waiting for a break in the weather.

Seeing the lines and realizing the possibility of finding a viable alternate flight I looked to a closed ticketing window still manned by a woman attending to some last minute task. I approached Maria Rodriquez and explained that I needed to get to Dallas, four of us needed to get to Dallas to meet our flight. She looked up for a moment, glanced at the forming lines and responded that those people were also in search for alternate flights, perhaps I should join them, her station was closed.

I went on to explain we need to get to Dallas to meet a connecting flight, to meet our son. He was already there and we all wanted to fly home to Seattle together. She looked up somewhat puzzled at the middle aged man standing in front of her and said. "Surely, your son is old enough to be traveling on his own."

I paused for a moment, looked down at her name tag, and responded, "Maria, he will be traveling in the baggage compartment, his mother and I would appreciate being able to make this last journey home with him."

Perhaps it was the gravity of my voice or perhaps the compassion of a mother, Maria picked up her phone and placed a call to the operations manager, American Airlines. Within mere moments a man appeared dressed in coat and tie and American Eagle emblem on the lapel. "What flight were you scheduled on, what flight do you need to meet up with in Dallas?" Nothing more other than a directive for me to rejoin my party at the gate.

At the gate frustrated passengers had surrounded the ticket agent, voices were raised, it was Thursday afternoon everyone was heading home. Karen, Julie and Eunice had remained where they had been when I left for the terminal. They told me of the cancellation of our flight, what were we to do? I told them of my experience back in the main terminal. Arrangements were under way.

The tarmac outside the gate was empty, no aircraft in sight other than large planes taking off and landing in the distance. The man who had briefly talked with me in the terminal arrived followed by several other men all dressed in coveralls. They stopped at the podium, talked with the agent as a small commuter plane pulled into the gate. He then turned to me and asked that I sit where I was, do nothing until he returned. With that his small army of men along with the gate agent descended on the arriving craft. Bags pulled from the belly of the craft, a tail ramp lowered and passengers disembarked. The whole operation completed with the precision of a well-oiled machine. The gate agent following the last of arriving passengers reassumed her place at the podium and announced the imminent departure of the previously cancelled flight to Dallas. On the tarmac the army of men dressed in American Airlines coveralls filled the plane with baggage with the help of the man with the suit and tie.

Departing passengers were filling up the rear gangway when we were approached and told that we would be the last to board. Our seats would be the four remaining at the back of the plane; Dallas had been called, so long as we were off the ground in twenty minutes we would make our connection.

When directed, we boarded, claimed the last four seats. A man reached from behind, place a hand on my shoulder and wished us luck. I thanked him, never knowing who he was but thinking someone must be looking after us.

The commuter set down in Dallas fifteen minutes after our scheduled departure time for Seattle. Once on the taxi way the plane came to a halt, ramp extended and we were directed to a car which whisked us across the field directly to a waiting American Airlines 737. We had made our connection, all five of us would return home together.

Chapter 8

MILE POSTS

It may have been clear and crisp it may have cold and raining. The stars may have been visible during these early hours before daylight or perhaps it was cold and dreary; I just do not remember. There are days in every person's existence that serve as markers along life's highway. Remembrances we use to register the passages of time. The occurrences that remind us of who we are and where we have been. Marriage, the birth of a child, an anniversary, a graduation, and the joyous memories along the path are things we all cherish. But we also use the passing of a leader, president, king, the beginning of some catastrophic event, the loss of a friend that will forever change our view of the world in which we live to mark the passage of time. Mileposts are not always friendly reminders of time gone by and this second Monday in March 1996 was to be just such a marker for the family of Brian Scott Pilkington.

I arose early from our sleepless night to begin the preparations for what was to be the most difficult day of our life together. It would be a day where I would have to be prepared to lend assistance to those around me, to comfort the members of our family who had gathered here from around the country; to express our appreciation to the friends and associates past and present who had been assembling to share with us in this moment of mourning and recollection. But the most over-riding consideration would be to console Brian's mother, my wife of twenty-six years. Today we were to lay to rest our son, the man she had nurtured through the twenty-four all too short years of his life, the man who had looked to me for direction and support while making life decisions; the man I had encouraged to chose a path that included finding a future doing what he enjoyed. His mother would need my support this day to view for the last time the mortal remains of her first son, to embrace and accept the condolences of the assembled mourners and to begin the realization that life would have to go on. I would need for her to forgive me for the part I perceived myself as having played in the passing of our son and confront an absolution I would not be able to accept.

During the flight from Dallas to Seattle three days earlier I had made an attempt to write a statement, an announcement condemning those persons I held most responsible for killing our son. It was a piece filled with venom and bile denouncing their cowardice and indifference. It was a statement I planned to present before the assembly of friends and family at Brian's funeral. I spent that evening as we flew from southeastern Texas to the Northwest in anger and denial knowing that just below my feet, somewhere in the cargo hold of that aircraft was my son making his last trip home with us. Surely these men who through their incompetence and greed must be held accountable for the action or lack of preparedness. That had caused the death of our son and to that end I would make all who would listen aware of the misdeeds. Of equal importance as I wrote that diatribe of hate and anger was the firm conviction that I had to enlighten anyone who would listen to my words that Brian was not responsible for his own death. There had been no error, no omission on his part that contributed to his death. Nothing under his control was amiss. This would have been of consequence to Brian; it was important to his mother and imperative to me.

The day following our return to Seattle, Karen, Julie and I were to meet with James Berkley, assistant minister of the First Presbyterian Church of Bellevue. As we grow older it is sometimes disconcerting to meet with someone whom we expect to have greater seniority and infinite wisdom; a person we expect to have gained great wisdom through extended life experience. Perhaps Jim was wiser than I but certainly not older and to me did not appear sufficiently aged to pontificate upon the greater meanings of our existence. Jim is a man short in stature with a well-trimmed beard surely meant to conceal a boyish face, an individual we had observed from the safety of our pew over the past few years as visitors to the church but had never actually engaged him in conversation. We had listened to his sermons and watched as he would extend his arms skyward spreading his pudgy fingers widely and evoking the benediction upon the assembled parishioners. This was a task he always seemed to relish as he would impart through those outstretched hands the blessing of his God upon those assembled. Although initially I thought him too young to preside over this all too solemn event, I had asked specifically for him. I had grown to appreciate his sincerity and his informal reverence expressed through those Sunday evening sermons which Brian's mother and I had experienced since first selecting First Presbyterian as our place of worship. He appeared equally comfortable whether standing in the official classic robe of the church, spreading the Word while dressed informally in an open shirt or sharing his bagpipe music while outfitted in his family kilt. Jim too, must have had someone advise him to find something he liked to do and then make that his calling or perhaps he had come upon this revelation on his own, but surely here was a man that reveled in what he did. It made little difference whether he was sharing the sacrament of the Lord's Table, explaining his interpretation of a passage or relating his personal view of a worldly event. Most of all, however, he seemed to luxuriate in those benedictions. Standing in front of his flock he would place the final punctuation on the spiritual message of the day with a vibrancy and sincerity that could only emanate from deep within a soul. Had Brian ever had the opportunity to meet this man of God I know he would have liked him and Jim certainly would have enjoyed our son. It was to this man that I would look this day to place the final punctuation on the mortal life of our son.

We arrived early for the prearranged meeting and wandered hopelessly lost through the back hallways of the church offices. Our previous visit to the building had always been confined to the sanctuary or Sunday school areas and this part of the facility was totally foreign to me. Turning a darkened corner we found ourselves confronted by an elderly gentleman with graying hair and wire rimmed glasses. A person much closer to my preconceived notion as to the proper appearance required of a person of elderly enlightenment. Dressed in a modest suit with a clean starched shirt and neatly knotted tie this obviously elder member of the church introduced himself and asked if he might assist in any way. I introduced Karen, then Julie and finally myself to the Reverend Harlow Willard and before I could ask for the assistance he had offered the semi-retired minister interjected. "You're here to see Jim. He has been expecting you and we are so terribly sorry to hear of Brian's accident and untimely death."

I was surprised by his knowledge of our situation but could not allow him to continue thinking that our son had fallen victim to some misfortunate of fate. "Our son was not involved in an accident, he was killed by his employer." And then I continued on with more angry details, as best I understood them at that time, as this man of the cloth stood and patiently listened to the ramblings of the agitated father he had encountered in his office hallway. Karen listened, as Julie stood by oblivious to the conversation not wanting to once again be subjected to the details of the horror she had lived through during the earlier part of that week. Willard placed a hand on my shoulder and passionately bestowed some words of biblical wisdom regarding forgiveness and God's plan and then leads us to Jim's open office door.

Pushing back from a busy desk, Jim sprang to his feet and grasped my single outstretched hand with both of his. He continued in turn greeting Karen and then Julie, directing us to be seated with a motion all too familiar to those accustomed to his expressive blessings. Reverend Willard remained for a respectful moment and then continued on his journey back down the darkened passage intent on completing whatever mission we had most certainly interrupted. Without being prompted or requested to do so the occurrences of the week were related to the intently listening younger minister before we explained the purpose for which we had requested the meeting. I had called from Houston the day after Brian's death and asked if it would not be possible to arrange for a funeral service. The time was allocated and the proper persons involved in such matters had been notified prior to our arrival home. But today we had asked for this meeting to discuss how we felt the service should be conducted. It was Karen's and my feeling that the family should, no, would play a major role in this final day of mortal remembrance. I asked to be allowed to present the eulogy and then upon my completion permit the pulpit to be made available to anyone who might wish to share a story, a thought, an expression of recollection of our friend who had been taken from us. Finally, we were to be permitted to present a brief video chronicling Brian's life. I am certain that the anger in my voice and the apparent pain expressed by all those presenting themselves before this man of the cloth promoted his negative response to our supplication. He continued, reminding us that this was Gods house and that this most solemn event should be conducted under God's direction. This was not a day to vent anger, express repugnance or create a forum for group therapy. This was to be a day to share in the Word of God done under a cleric's superintendence.

Perhaps he was correct and perhaps that would have been the easiest avenue for us to follow. Conceivably my place was best served by remaining at the side of my wife and permitting another individual to conduct and direct the service, permit him to bestow on the assembled friends and family the wisdom of the church, and have him explain the master plan we all follow as directed by an unseen Omnipotent Being. But we were not there to find the most expeditious means to proceed through the one day no parent should ever have to face. I had been responsible for helping in the direction of not only the course Brian had followed for the past twenty-four years but also had charted the direction of our family as a whole. This second Monday of March in the year nineteen hundred ninety-six, two days hence, could be no different. I went on to explain to the Reverend Berkley the importance to the family that we play a part in this most final day at whatever level we were capable. To some of us that might mean sitting in silent prayer. To others expressing treasured moments of remembrance and to others sharing personal insights and recollections. But to me I had a message to give and I, if not for myself but for my son, was determined to relate to all who would listen. Yes, we had come to him to ask for his guidance and assistance and would appreciate the scriptural reference and direction but we would need also, to participate. We would proceed under those conditions and nothing else would be acceptable. Reluctantly, I suspect, Jim agreed and the mechanics of the service were discussed.

Now, two days later the time had come. It was now six days and five hours since receiving the call from the unnamed priest in that faraway hospital in Texas who had delivered the message of Brian's passing. In these early-morning hours before the first light of day I arose from that sleepless bed and joined my collection of photographs in the home office to review alone the memories of a life now ended. The oak paneled walls and the soft leather chairs amid reminders of what was and what might have been. Pictures on the walls, memorabilia on every shelf. A military cover purchased in Red Square by a son now gone, a silver dhow forged from Maria Teresa coins by an Arab craftsman and a meager collection of classic novels intermixed with the colorful volumes of children's stories. Works of art, some produced by the more talented members of the family, some purchased, all carefully displayed on the boundaries of this my—personal sanctuary. But it is difficult if not impossible to surpass the value of the photographs and albums, those reminders of the past twenty-plus years of a family that once was complete and the promises that now would not be fulfilled. Emulsified remembrances of two small boys traveling the corners of the world growing up together but so different in many respects. Photos in brass frames of a maturing young lady sitting on the knee of jolly round man with a white beard and red cap, friends in tuxedoes and fine dress captured at a happier moment.

I stood there among this collection of physical reminiscence pondering the failures of a life now wasted and questioned why. There may have been so many chances to correct the course of events, to chart a bearing around the whirlpools of existence,; choices perhaps beyond the capability of the captain of this family ship. Old photos were spread in disarray with no order or even semblance on the desk and floor. Others were scattered on the leather chairs which were placed comfortably in the corner of the room where I would sit on occasion to read from my collection of books. Leather chairs in which Brian had spent many nights, as he would page through colorful text inventing stories to match the pictures as he related his imaginary accounts to his little sister. There were photos and slides, awards and memorabilia everywhere. My now-sleeping sisters had rummaged through every resource, every drawer and closet. The entirety of the Pilkington archive had been explored as they had searched for the perfect pictures to represent each stage of development in Brian's life. Pictures, after careful selection, which had been assembled and transferred to a format that could be displayed for all to see during the proceedings of this day. They had worked tirelessly over the previous four days; Aunt Beth with the mission of organizing and collating, checking for color and contrast, style and content; assembling the photographic remembrances of the man who had been more of a little brother than a nephew. Aunt Pat, with cloth handkerchief held tightly, thumbed through the photographic archive pondering each image, wiped a tear, then moved to the next.

Their task now done and safely stored on videotape, the castoffs of this labor of love were left in hopeless disarray scatted about the once orderly room. As I pick up a sufficient amount of this photographic permanence to provide a place to sit I too slowly examined each emulsified image as I attempted to prepare myself for the day to come. There were pictures of a boy with his dog, a man preparing for marriage, a baby receiving a bath, boys playing soccer and one special photo of a little man grasping tightly to the rusty rail of an almost forgotten ship sailing on some far off sea as he beamed with joy in the morning sun, his golden hair of youth blowing in the morning breeze, eyes beaming with the anticipation of what new wonder was to be experienced in that unexplored world just now visible on the horizon.

On the desk somewhere beneath the clutter lay the scraps of paper carried from Texas four days previously. Upon those fragmentary bits of yellow paper lay the words of condemnation I had prepared to deliver to the assembled that afternoon. As I looked at the memories surrounding me and thought of the words of wisdom imparted by Jim I searched for and found the diatribe and then destroyed it. My sisters were correct; this was a day to remember the good in a life gone by. Jim was correct, this was not a day to question why and condemn. This was not the place in which to lay blame and accuse; we should come to the house of the Lord prepared to accept and continue. To that end, I rewrote the eulogy including only as much as I felt I would be capable of reading. Enough so that all present who had known our son would remember him and those who had not had the privilege of knowing him would feel they had. Although I had heard the wisdom of Reverend Jim and had now accepted his counsel regarding forgiveness, I still found it necessary to insert a single sentence admonishing those responsible for the death of our son; a single statement that would signify to the assembled mourners that Brian was not at fault and that we as a family would not let his passing go unnoted. The words came slowly; there was so much to say. How to encapsulate a life in a few short paragraphs? How much easier it would be to accomplish this task had it been for an individual who had experienced a full life. The early morning faded as the first rays of morning sun penetrated the office window. The softly playing music emanating from the room's stereo masked the sounds of the awakening house. Aunt Beth stopped in for a moment, sat in one of the two leather chairs, cried over a picture or two and then left without a word.

Before the completion of my task I was called. The hour had come, and we must leave. The assembled members of the family had gathered in the kitchen, a kitchen piled high with offerings of food delivered by caring and compassionate members of the neighborhood over the course of the week. Neighbors, some of whom we barely knew, were endeavoring to help in whatever way they could to ease the mundane tasks of daily necessity. Hurrying past the living room crammed with flowers, cards, and letters delivered from all parts of the country expressing sympathy and condolence we made our way to the driveway. The front yard was covered by a huge shadow and the narrow lane that serviced the house was filled with a mobile crane towing a trailer filled with building components. There was no escape possible, no way to circumnavigate this collection of construction equipment hopelessly log-jammed in this all too narrow thoroughfare. There was no reason for this equipment to be there; no call for the beams and roof trusses to be delivered in this well-established neighborhood of long completed residences. I admonished the driver and directed him as best I could to move far enough to one side to allow us to pass leaving him with the unenviable task of backing his articulated rig back down the winding road subsequent to our escape.

Karen stood and watched as this mass of construction equipment slowly gyrated from side to side attempting to avoid the well-trimmed lawns and vegetation of our neighbors' yards. "Brian has done this. Only he would think to arrange such a practical joke, make us late for his funeral. He always liked a good prank." The first sign of a smile to grace her tired face in a week appeared as she entered the car to await the clearing of the road. This may not have been the mysterious working of some unknown power or it may have been the carelessness of a dispatcher reversing the shipping and billing address at the lumber yard from which I purchased supplies but in any case I was to discover soon that this would not be the last of the day's calamities.

Before the church service a small gathering of family and a few close friends had been invited to join with us at the funeral home where Brian had remained between the time of our return from Texas and the church service. Earlier that morning he had been moved to the main chapel from the small private room where Julie had remained for as long as permitted. At his mother's request the shiny black metal casket with the chrome trim was to be opened for one last time so that any who felt they must, could see him before he began that most final of all journeys. Dressed in his blue blazer with brass buttons and best white shirt with striped tie, one polka dot sock, one striped just the way he would have liked it. It was here that Afton would have the opportunity to return to her big brother the little brown teddy bear borrowed years ago; that a mother could place the tattered remnants of a blanket that had never been out of reach of her son as a toddler. Saved these many years so that she might pass along to his children at the appropriate time; a time that would now would never come. After a brief farewell she placed the blanket of security across his now perpetually folded hands, ran her fingers through his long brown hair, touched his cheek and the casket was closed and sealed for the final time.

As we made our way out of the chapel leaving only Julie behind for a few moments alone with her husband before accompanying him on the four miles to Bellevue First Presbyterian, we paused at the building's entry. Outside the open double doors of this most austere building a bright new Land Rover screeched to a stop beneath the canopied entry. Jumping from the driver's seat a neatly dressed man with shaved head and closely cropped white beard emerged and hurried around to complete the opening of the passenger door. Once opened, a tall thin woman, who until now had been concealed by the new car sticker prominently displayed in the window, swung her legs from the confines of the leather trimmed interior and joined her companion. The Nebels were unquestionably my most important clients at the time and had understandingly permitted my lack of attention to their project as I devoted my attentions to the needs of the family. They had come to share with us in our grief but first felt obligated to offer apologies for the lateness of their arrival. As I was introducing them to the others present we continued walking back into the funeral home when the alarm sounded. Sitting just outside the open doors of the building a well-locked Ranger Rover screamed for assistance. There was no intruder, no sign of violation, just a lone vehicle in plain view announcing for all to hear that its security system had been betrayed. An embarrassed owner scurried back to alleviate the interruption to no avail. The keys would not work, the doors would not open, some system unknown to the new owner had been initiated and there would be no way to alter the course save to await the appropriate interval for the system to reset.

Karen smiled for the second time that day and said over the blaring siren as she slowly shook her head "Brian" and then nothing more. Nothing more needed to be said except perhaps to the Nebels who had not been present earlier that morning and were now most assuredly embarrassed as the assembled mourners chuckled in understanding.

*   *   *

There would be no open shirt of informality this day as the Reverend James Berkley, dressed in his official robe met the arriving family at the sanctuary door. He assured us that all the details had been addressed, all was in order and how fortunate Brian was to have so many friends. The lower floor of the sanctuary was nearly filled to capacity with relatives, classmates, and friends past and present. A third grade teacher, now retired, who passed his idle hours searching for the names of old friends in local obituaries; how shocked this well-read educator was to find the name of an old pupil, fifty-six years his junior. Neighbors, business associates, past employers and family acquaintances were all there. Brian's music was already playing quietly throughout the structure; another little detail agreed to by Jim and arranged for with the help of Aunt Beth and Brother Jamie. Selections of Brian's favorite melodies that would be appreciated by him and appropriate for the situation played along with what I suspect may have been a selection or two specific to the younger brother. There would be no pipe organ music this day, no pianos or violins, unless played by Eric Clapton, Elton John, or Garth Brooks. This would be Brian's day and we would do as much as we could in a manner to his liking. Just inside the door waited Jim Humphrey—my sometime employee and longtime friend. He had been entrusted with arranging for the playing of the music and setting up the audio-visual equipment needed to display the photographic remembrance created by my sisters from the family archive. As the Reverend Jim had done so earlier, Jim too assured me all was in order. The music was playing on the buildings sound system, the three television monitors which were already wired, each to a single video recorder. Two copies of the tapes were available, all contingencies had been anticipated and I was not to worry. There were no problems; all the details had been addressed. Each looking after his individual avenues of responsibility the two Jims took good care of the Pilkington family that afternoon, each attending to our needs though certainly on somewhat different levels.

The two Mrs. Pilkingtons and I were directed to the seats closest to the pulpit, far from the safety of the pew we were more familiar with high in the balcony above our heads. Behind us sat Brian's grandfather with his wife and daughters, the two Aunts who had made the trip from New York to lend support and create the video now waiting to be displayed. Sunlight streamed through the stained glass windows accenting the colorful array of flowers carefully arranged about the focal point of the sanctuary.

Brian arrived on time encased in his black casket carried by his brother and two friends on one side; best man, Erick Leonard; Uncle Brian; and Jim on the opposite. Eric Clapton's rendition of "Tears from Heaven" continued as the assembled waited pensively for the first words of condolence and affirmation from the minister standing solemnly at the head of this unfamiliar flock. A space had been cleared where the piano normally rested to allow Brian a place of prominence among the carefully arranged flowers.

As the music faded our youthful minister began the service. His remarkably resonant voice intoned, "Jesus said, 'I am the resurrection and the life. Anyone who believes in me, even though he dies, shall live and whoever lives and believes in me shall never die.' He said, 'Come to me all yea who labor and are overburdened and I will give you rest.' "Reverend Jim continued, "We are gathered here today to worship God who in the time of life and in this time of death is worthy of our praise. And we have come to celebrate the life of Brian Pilkington. Some of you have come here today to share your remembrances. First, from Brian's father, Peter."

I had planned originally to stand next to my family and read what I felt must be said from that point of security as I hoped others among the assembled might also do when their time came. But the room seemed so large and the people so many. What I had to say I wanted to be heard and the pulpit had direct access to the amplified sound system and perhaps a closer connection to those about to receive our son. Ignoring my fear of public speaking I made my way replacing, for the moment, the Reverend Berkley at the head of the congregation. With one hand firmly placed on the left side of the pulpit I pulled from my pocket the words written earlier that morning and my newly acquired reading glasses. Years of use, many of them over bright white paper with a 4H pencil in hand had finally taken its toll all too familiar to persons approaching their fiftieth birthday. Attempting to focus on the written page through the now-moisture-stained lens proved impossible and as best I could I recited the passage I hoped never to have needed to write.

"We were first introduced to Brian almost twenty-four years ago in the maternity wing of Albany Medical Center, upstate New York. When he was first brought to me, I picked him up, counted his fingers and toes, and wondered at this perfect little person we had brought into this world. We returned him home and began our lives together.

His early years were filled with puppies, kittens, trucks, games of imagination, stories and fantasy. Toys were for taking apart; wheels were for removal and replacing. If an object of desire was not made available they would be created from whatever was handy, fashioned from some perfectly good something into the more wondrous creation of his imagination.

Seesaws from paint buckets and planks, cars from wood and tape, wire and string; wheels from bikes and baby carriages. There was always the task that needed to be completed, the job that was critical to the well-being of a friend or the family. Brian loved to create his imaginary world in a form that could be revered by others, enjoyed by all and shared with his friends.

He learned to swim in the waters of the Persian Gulf and Indian ocean while watching and studying with fascination the newfound world below the surface. There were fish of all colors, turtles and coral, crabs and mysterious creatures of the deep seen only by him. During that time Brian accompanied me on board a cargo ship we had chartered to deliver building material to a remote island off southern Iran. With fascination and delight, he explored this mechanical-floating marvel with all its pulleys, ladders, wheels, huge engines, and strange sounds. As night fell, we retreated to the safety of the wheelhouse with all the dials and gauges, lights, compasses, buttons, and strange gizmos of all description. But most intriguing to Brian was the unmanned green monitor with its revolving white stripe and the suddenly appearing and then fading white dots.

From sunset to first light, the four-year-old master of the ship protected us from all the passing blips as first they would appear and then fade to the protecting edges of the screen. At about 2:15 AM, an unseen object made its first presence known only to Brian. As our ship approached the white dot, Brian left his position of importance to report in person to Masude, captain of the vessel. Masude in patient cooperation studied the monitor with all the false images knowing our position to be miles off the nearest shipping lane and, after checking with both port and starboard watches, returned to his post at the helm. It was a clear night; the moon had already faded from the sky. The only sound was the constant roar of the engines below deck. That is, until Brian turned to Masude and said, "I told you so," as the sounds of splintering timbers and cracking beams shattered the calm of the night waters and sent a rumble through the entire length of our vessel. We had struck an unmarked Arab sailing dhow, traveling from Dubai to India with a cargo of smuggled TVs.

The following day, Brian returned home as copilot of the company helicopter. With even more gadgets and gizmos to watch and study, complete with headset and almost capable of reaching the controls our "copilot" was armed with the anticipation of landing his craft to the admiration of mother and friends on the beach which was his front yard. No one was home.

Toys and gadgets were soon replaced with more serious machines like bikes that were never meant to be ridden. Why ride when you could take apart and study why the individual parts did what they did and then reassemble them into something better than before—something of personal pride, another challenge? Bikes lead to remote control any things and then cars. It didn't matter what kind, so long as it was red, shiny, but most importantly, in need of customization.

Brian loved to tinker, fix and repair, work with his hands, but he found his greatest joy in sharing his accomplishments with others—returning to service and to its owner some forgotten, seemingly unfixable mechanical object.

His family was his friends, his friends were his family. He was kind and compassionate. When his young sister needed comforting and quieting only Brian, and sometimes his mother, would have the ability to accomplish the task. He would spend hours with little sister on his lap reading words that had never been written from the pages of colorful books, perhaps the same book but never the same story. But then there was the day when even big brother was not capable of accomplishing the task. Brian, in full view of this terrible two-year-old found a catalog of children's clothing, and after methodically examining each glossy page searching for the most pristine little girl in the most perfect dress he picked up the phone and placed an imaginary call to some unknown mail order house.
"Yes, this is Brian Pilkington."
"Yes, I would like to order model number R374129."
"Yes, the one with the red dress."
"Now are you sure this one will behave?"
"Are you sure this one will listen to her big brother, will she go to bed when told, pick up after herself and no whining right?"
"Okay, I'll take that one."

"Yes, I'll have the other one ready for return Wednesday."

Afton would not answer the front door for a week.

Brian's wit and humor were enjoyed by all, well perhaps not always by his sister. He surrounded himself with a family of friends, enjoyed hours of endless conversation across the nightly dinner table; grew into a man of loving compassion, a source of pride to his parents, a friend to his brother, a comfort to his sister and most recently the gentle base to a loving relationship with his wife.

Brian was a man who could not be angered; who saw only the best, never understood the worst. He would want us to forgive the men who were responsible for his death and look to us to find a way to prevent it from happening again.

Those twenty-three years ago when I first picked up my newborn son, after counting fingers and toes, I promised him a life filled with whatever I could provide, whatever he needed to allow him to be the best he could be. He grew to be my companion and friend. We are left knowing what he had become and guessing what he might have been. Our son is here with us today and will remain with his mother and me forever; he will not be forgotten.

I wish to thank all of you who were our sons friends for just being that and ask you, if you wish, to share with us a story, a remembrance of our friend Brian. Please share in your own way, here up front, or standing in your place, to your neighbor to yourself. But first from Brian's longtime friend and wife, Julie."

Making her way to the front Julie replaced me and began her recollections of their all too short time together. Stories from high school, New Orleans, personal reflections of private moments shared together; insights into the personal confidence displayed by her husband and finally a retrospection of how perfect it had been. Emotionally unable to continue her abbreviated remembrance she sought the comfort of her mother, sister and mother in-law seated in the front row.

The sanctuary remained silent, no one stood and nothing more was said. Nothing more until Aunt Beth slowly made her way to that most unfamiliar place of prominence. Tucked beneath her arm were the shabby remains of a little well-loved stuffed animal with tattered ears and a button nose. A woman closer in age to her now-departed nephew than to either of her siblings she had grown to know Brian more as a little brother. He became a brother she had played with, laughed with, cried with, as they matured together over the past years. This day would be as difficult for her as anyone but still she presented herself to this assembly of mourners to share a story. She told of Brian's sense of direction and purpose as manifested in the form of a little boy who would not let his grandmother travel down the wrong road saving her from the certain peril of being hopelessly lost. And then a poignant tale of a little boy who gave his favorite teddy bear to a weeping teenage Aunt to remember him by and ease the pain of separation before he left for three years in Arabia. She still had the stuffed reminder "But it doesn't make me feel good anymore" she wept, clinging to the furry gift of love given to her years ago. She hurried to the safety of her pew and the comfort of her father.

The silence that filled the room was broken by the steady cadence of leather soles striking the polished concrete floor of this most modern of sanctuaries. Robert Patton, a longtime family friend, confidante and adopted uncle to our children made his way with strident confidence to the head of the assemblage. Speaking to large groups was nothing unfamiliar to this man with thirty-plus years of experience with the Boeing Company. Whether articulating to a group at the Renton engineering center, presenting a dissertation to a group of colleagues in Moscow, or just addressing fellow coworkers concerning the mundane tasks of daily necessity in the aerodynamics department, Bob was always prepared. There would be no need for the listeners to fill in any detail not specifically mentioned as Bob had carefully crafted a document, thoughtfully choosing each word to most effectively express his feelings and those of his wife. From his pocket he pulled a prepared collection of thoughts and remembrances. He adjusted his glasses and presented his recollections of the young man he had watched grow from a gangly preteen full of mischief to a kind and caring adult. There were stories of gifts of clothing presented to a young boy, clothing that would be worn at the earliest opportunity in silent appreciation and recognition of their giving; remembrances of a high school graduation, thoughtful introductions to friends and classmates and the acceptance of Uncle Bob and Aunt Cindy as a part of Brian's family. They had witnessed the good times and the bad, shared in the joys, celebrated the accomplishments, and accepted the disappointments; all the things expected of members of a family, even if the relationship was one based on voluntary affiliation. Although Uncle Bob and Aunt Cindy had never had children of their own this day they too would be laying to rest a son, a friend, a man they had watched mature and evolve from that gangly preteen to the caring base of a marriage just six months earlier. Once his statement was complete the paper was neatly folded and then returned to the pocket from whence it had come, glasses were once more adjusted and he began to follow the same path traversed earlier, returning to his pew and the side of Aunt Cindy.

The fears of the family were realized as from immediately behind me the sounds of Grandpa Fred could be heard as he rose from his place next to Aunt Beth who was still clutching Brian's tattered stuffed bear. I had prewarned Reverend Jim to avoid any mention of God's will or divine intervention when addressing the family patriarch. To him there was no will of god that had caused the loss of his first grandchild, no divine intervention, it had been the incompetence of men, men who were either unable due to a lack of training or preparedness, compassion or greed to foresee what their actions or lack of action would manifest. For this man, Brian's only living grandparent, the teachings of the church in regard to plan and will were not to be answers for what had transpired. The mention of some master plan would only serve to further infuriate this man of compassion and believer in personal responsibility. Passing the returning Uncle Bob the two stopped, exchanged a gesture of support and then each continued to their predetermined destinations, Bob to his original seat and Grandpa Fred to the left and away from the now-vacant pulpit.

"My son has a sister whose husband once said that the Pilkington family crest should be emblazoned with the words, "Never let the truth get in the way of a good story." "Well, Uncle Brian, here's another one for you." All delivered with the commanding voice perfected while attempting to educate five generations of high school students and in such a convoluted manner as to challenge the thought processes of his current audience. There would be no need for the electronic amplification of the words he would project and each syllable would now require careful scrutiny for fear of being quizzed on content at a later date by this man who had served so admirably as a school administrator and teacher. Four years ago my wife and I accompanied my son and his family on a trip to New Zealand. For five weeks, we traveled the back roads and highways of that enchanting land down under, much of the time in the company of old friends who had worked with Karen and Peter while in the United Arab Emirates. They too had now returned to their homeland, and we were invited to join them on their Christmas holidays, middle of the summer in that hemisphere. On one of these excursions down a long, narrow gravel road through a sparse forest of tortured fir and rocky ledges accented with canyons and swift flowing rivers I spotted a bridge far up a side chasm with no apparent connecting road. "Look," I called out to my wife, "there is that bridge, you know the one those crazy New Zealanders jump off with great rubber bands attached to their legs, the one you see in the travelogues." Now you must understand that I am somewhat hard of hearing and at times treated as a slightly retarded adult by those around me and as a result I would sometimes find myself unaware of the purpose for many of these daily outings. "Fred," she said, "that's where we are going. But it will not only be crazy New Zealanders trusting in those rubber bands, your grandsons are also here for the test."

"Well, my son found a place along the canyon wall where he might best photograph for the family archive these leaps of faith; a place where the light would be right, composition acceptable and close enough to hear the screams of fear or exhilaration. Jamie went first. Jumping to the heavens with arms stretched wide, back arched and head looking up, looking up until the inevitable force of gravity sent him plummeting to the river below and the clutches of the those cold dark waters as increasing tension quickly filled the tendons of the great bundle of rubber fiber attached to his ankles. As quickly as his head and chest entered the water, that built-up tension reversed the fall projecting him once again toward that bridge far above. Three times he would rebound, followed by three more returns to just above the water. Each subsequent rebound less than the one before until he was lowered into a waiting rubber raft and returned to shore. One hundred and forty nine feet above, looking more like 190 miles to me, Brian readied himself to emulate his exuberant brother, now scampering up the trail from the river's edge. Staying as close as I could to the center of this antique span, I made my way to the point of departure and the side of my first grandchild. Two men were methodically adjusting the harness, now firmly affixed to his ankles, correcting for weight the length of the bungee cords so that the full effectiveness of these tendons of salvation would not take effect until a proper baptism in the cold waters or reality below had been achieved." At that point, Grandpa paused and looked to the ceiling of the sanctuary and, after a suitable pause, addressed an unseen listener above. "Please excuse the direct quote. Brian turned to me, then peered apprehensively over the edge to the ribbon of water below, then once again to me and said" 'Jesus Christ what am I doing here' "as he thrust himself, as his brother had before him, to the waters below."

Fortunately for those assembled that day, and the purity of the sanctuary, Grandpa Fred elected to go no further in quoting Brian either by choice or perhaps because he did not hear the completion of that sentence uttered four years before as Brian propelled himself to that inevitable union with the cold waters of the Shotover River.

Grandpa continued, "My wife and I, being retired, have occasion to travel often. As my son and his family live close to the airport we customarily leave a car at their home while away. Now I don't spend much time looking to the appearance of my vehicle but I could always be assured that upon my return from a trip it would be neatly washed, polished and vacuumed because that's the way Brian would want it to be. After one such excursion we returned to find our freshly detailed car covered with the remains of at least a dozen eggs. Down the street lived a little . . . miscreant whom Brian suspected of spoiling his previous day's labor. Brian turned to me and said, "I should have him arrested for treason; your vehicle has prisoner of war license plates." There may have been more to say and I'm sure there was but again a long pause from this man who had spent time in a German prisoner of war camp after being wounded and captured in that war so many years ago. He ended his story abruptly with, "That's all I have." Again, he looked to the ceiling briefly and then made his way back to his original seat.

To my left sat the six young men that had volunteered to assist Brian on his way in and out of the church that day. From among them, rising to his feet and replacing the now-seated grandfather came Brian's old high school friend. Eric Leonard is an exuberant young man, still filled with the naivety of young men and the vision of a future beyond the college classroom. Good looking, with wavy brown hair and a slender build he looked much the same as his now-departed cohort, even though somewhat shorter than the six foot five inch Brian. Finding his way to the pulpit he began. "Fred, not only was your car always freshly washed and polished, it also had at least 250 additional miles accumulated in your absences. Brian and I attended high school together. I was the best man at his wedding back in August. Brian would often call me asking for some plan, some new and ingenious method for turning back an odometer, conjuring up a prank or developing some scheme to delight a friend or aggravate a foe. I watched him develop into a man far ahead of what I was ready to accept. He always could find a way to make the most difficult task simple with some outrageous product of his imagination. I watched as he married, moved away and began his life as an adult. But I would always revel when, on occasion, the little boy with the childish notions and clever wit would re-emerge, if only for a moment. I will miss my friend and the world will miss the gadget or the invention that will never see the light of day."

Brian was laid to rest that afternoon on a grassy hillside overlooking the city. The sun was just passing between that slimmest of space between the marine cloud cover and the distant snow-covered Olympic Mountains. The gathered mourners huddled tightly together seeking protection from the late-afternoon chill and the refuge offered by the few umbrellas needed to shield off an unexpected shower. Julie had made this last earthly journey from the church to Sunset Hills with her husband of six months, her friend of ten years. The flowers, family, friends and the Reverend Berkeley followed close behind. Passages were read, thoughtful words expressed and then, as Brian was lowered to his final place of rest, the Reverend Jim raised his hands and pronounced that final benediction with an adoration and sincerity unique to him.

Brian's work on earth was done; his father's now only just begun.

The descending sun brightly illuminated the underside of the threatening clouds and the light rain turned to a steady downpour sending those assembled scurrying to the protection of their cars; all that is, save Brian's mother, who remained undeterred by the wet and the cold.

Chapter 9

SEARCHING FOR THE TRUTH

The week after the funeral was filled with phone calls. First to Willy Wilson, Divers Institute of Technology. Willy had worked for the commercial dive training school here in Seattle as an instructor and mentor since leaving the United States Navy twenty years before. As a younger man Willy had set a record of diving to 1,010 feet and truly was one of those old salts how could answer my questions, perhaps point me in the direction that only a man with years of experience could do.

I explained that according to the statements from Wiitala the compressor was only maintaining 90 psi, dropping to as little as 70 during the three-hour dive, that there was no backup equipment, Brian was in the water alone, was all this possible? I was a sport diver, you would never dive alone. 90 psi? Was that enough? I asked him about the Coast Guard. Did he have any connections? Surely he would know who I could contact?

He assured me that if the United States Coast Guard was given the opportunity to investigate they would be thorough. They were aggressive and would have the weight of the United States Government to back them up. If anyone would get the truth it would be those bull dogs. He questioned the air pressure but confirmed that on a shallow dive, less than 130 feet it was normal to have a single, tended diver in the water. He went on to ask me questions regarding equipment, personnel, location of the dive, all questions I could not answer. Then he passed along a name of a USCG captain in Washington D.C. who was in charge of investigations suggesting I give him a call.

Then I called Provost Umphrey to find the status of the inquest. Would someone from their office be present, would there be an opportunity to ask questions, could

I be present? Brandom was not available, the woman on the phone suggested I call Judge John Borne.

Then a call to the Judge; he was in court but the woman answering the phone let me know that the Judge had cancelled the inquest after receiving verbal statements from those on site during the incident and suggested I call my attorney for additional information.

A call to Willy's contact at the United States Coast Guard in Washington D.C. was polity and compassionately answered by Captain Kranz with a suggestion that I contact Captain William H. Fels, captain United States Coast Guard, officer in charge, marine inspections, Port Arthur, Texas.

So a call to the number in Port Arthur and a brief conversation with the captain. He suggested that I speak to Lt. J. G. Blake Wellborn, the investigator assigned to the marine casualty report. After being transferred to Wellborn a brief discussion ensued regarding information contained in the Wiitala statement, was still awaiting a statement from Austin. I told him of the compressor and dive equipment I had seen outside G&G and that I was somewhat puzzled that it was not in custody. He went on to explain that he had contacted Buddy Horton, the safety manager at Cliffs Drilling demanding that the equipment, compressor, hoses and helmet all be function tested as well as Austin and Wiitala would need to be drug tested. I then asked had the Coast Guard actually interviewed either Wiitala or Austin, had they visited the crime scene. What investigation was ongoing other then the written statement he had from Wiitala and the one they expected to get from Austin. Wellborn let me know he had been in the office of Judge John Borne and heard the verbal statements from Wiitala and Austin over the phone and he had taken notes. All would be included in the final report along with the test results on all the divers and the equipment. Again I reminded him where he might find the equipment and asked that he try to keep me informed.

I then called the Occupational and Safety Office in Houston. I was more familiar with how they conduct business. I explained the purpose of my call and was transferred to John Lawson—Area Director Occupational Safety and Health Administration, Houston North Area Office. I once again explained the situation and the run around I had been encountering. He suggested I contact the United States Coast Guard, they had a memorandum of understanding with OSHA.

G&G Marine was a member of the Association of Diving Contractors. Perhaps they would know how best to proceed. The Association of Diving Contractors was an industry group established to further the art and science of commercial diving as well as diving safety. They had created a "Consensus Standard" far more comprehensive then the out dated federal regulations and their three-hundred-plus member companies pledged to follow those more responsible guide lines. G&G was a member and as such the ADC would certainly be aware of the investigation if not conducting their own in depth review. Finding their number in Houston I called and was immediately passed along to their executive director, Dr. Ross Saxon.

Dr. Saxon had worked his way up through the ranks in the U.S. Navy. Starting as an enlisted sailor in the mid-1950s, he earned his way to becoming a deep sea diving and salvage officer as well as a qualified submarine as well as surface ship officer. After his retirement from the navy Dr. Saxon held various positions until finally becoming the executive director of The Association of Diving Contractors.

He not only took my call that day he first listened as I told him Brian's story as I knew it, the bureaucratic tread mill I had encountered, the finger pointing, the indifference. Surely the ADC would also be investigating?

Once given the opportunity Dr. Saxon attempted to bring me up to speed on the current regulations and the marked differences between their contemporary safety standards and the twenty-year out-of-date Federal Regulations. The Federal regulations did not require a backup umbilical but the ADC members had a consensus that they would not dive without a backup air supply system. The current Federal regulations did not require a backup diver and although he personally believed it to be prudent, there were many members who operated small companies and could not justify the added expense. He went on to tell me that the ADC was working with the Coast Guard to rework the out dated regulations, make them more like the ADC Consensus Standard. Possibly to just adopt their Consensus Standard as the new regulation. He had the capability to push his agenda, he was the only representative of the diving industry on the National of Shore Safety Committee. In fact he was the only representative that had ever served on this United States Coast Guard advisory committee.

Regarding the ADC investigating G&G Marine, he went on to explain that he knew G&G had a proper safety manual that complied with the more stringent ADC standard. He in fact had written it. But the ADC only had the authority to investigate member companies. Dan Gilbert had contacted the ADC and withdrawn his membership. And one more thing before our conversation was brought to an abrupt end. Dr. Ross Saxon, only after I told him all I knew and only after telling me of his extensive knowledge into diver safety, government regulations and assuring me of his commitment for the creation of a safer underwater work place, told me he was an owner of G&G Marine. I thanked him for his time and went in search for some more reliable source of information.

Two days later, I called Wellborn again to follow up on the equipment tests only to be told the Lieutenant JG was on vacation and would call me back when he returned. Using the direct line number supplied by Captain Kranz I dialed Captain Fels.

I called the captain and expressed my displeasure with the conduct of the investigation. Was the compressor in custody? Were they the only people within the legal system conducting an investigation? He immediately transferred me back to Wellborn who must have just returned from his momentary vacation.

Wellborn assured me that the investigation was moving ahead but cautioned me that he would not be at liberty to discuss the investigation, I would need to be patient, these things take time "diving fatalities are few and far between so we are kind of treading in new waters." I thanked him for his time and sat down to write the first of hundreds of letters. The first to Senator Slade Gorton.

If the USCG was just going through the motions, surely a U.S. senator could help move things along. As in any investigation it is the first few days that are most important. Brian had died almost two weeks before and all that had been done was to take two verbal statements over the phone. And of course the one written statement made with the help of an attorney with the company owner in the room.

The senator wrote back letting me know that he would not get involved so long as there was ongoing civil litigation. He would call the Coast Guard and request that they keep him informed and in kind he would pass to me any information that he was given.

Weeks later Com. John C. Miko, Congressional and Governmental Affairs, USCG, office of the commandant, responded to the Senator. In that letter to a United States senator the commander stated that "Diving casualties are few and far between as Coast Guard investigations go. Accordingly officers assigned theses cases must climb a steep learning curve and research dive operations from ground zero. This in turn tends to lengthen the duration of the investigation. This was, in fact, reflected in this investigation. Although this investigation has moved slowly, it has been through and complete. Sworn depositions have been taken from the divers involved in the operation along with sworn statements from other witnesses."

"The air compressor utilized in the dive operation has been tested. The results of the test are included in the final report." Apparently, the commander was not aware there had actually been 28 fatalities that year in United States Coast Guard jurisdiction.

Perhaps I had not reached out far enough. If the senator was unable to assist because of ongoing litigation and the road block throw up by the commandant's office perhaps I would need to look further.

Six months had passed since Brian's death and the only information forwarded to me was the note from the commander in Washington claiming that "Diving casualties are few and far between as Coast Guard investigations go" and a letter from the Department of Labor informing us that our son's wife would not be eligible to collect death benefits. I had written to my Congressmen, OSHA, my U.S. senator, the governor of Texas, the Jefferson County Texas District Attorney, the Local Justice of the Peace in Beaumont Texas, the president of the United States, pretty much anyone that I could find an address for that I thought might be able to assist in finding out what happened to our son. I did get responses from various low level officials or members of their staff, some reassuring, some helpful, none casting any information of what happened that fourth day of March 1996.

Then on the afternoon of October 18, 1996, I returned to my office and found on my desk a hand written envelope addressed to me from Conroe Texas. Inside a cryptic letter suggesting I call the author, there were things I should know, followed by a phone number.

It was late in Seattle even later in Texas but I placed the call never the less. A man with a young sounding voice then related a story from seven months before. He had been called on the evening of March 4, 1996, by Danny Gilbert. It was late but Danny need him to grab some dry clothes, drive to Port Arthur, Texas, pick up Dan Wiitala. There had been an accident. Brian was in intensive care, Wiitala was wet and need a ride home.

Kevin Lawdermilk then told me the story of meeting Wiitala late on the evening of March 4. Julie was in the waiting room, crying, he tried to talk to her but she did not respond. Wiitala was in conversation with Gilbert, both were angry. Gilbert snatched up some papers and Wiitala went in search for a place to change into the dry clothes.

The ride from the hospital back to the Whataburger where Wiitala had parked his car earlier that morning started out quiet. Kevin not knowing what to say, Wiitala appeared to be in shock. But then he related the story of how the compressor would not hold air, the pilot valve was in need of constant adjustment. Austin was useless, not a diver, no experience. Everything went wrong, no one knew what to do. The compressor would not make air, belts were slipping, smoking, the backup air bottles were empty. The rest of the trip was conducted in silence.

The next morning Gilbert arranged for Kevin to be taken back to the offshore docks on the Sabine river, pick up Brian's truck, load all the gear. There would be two HP tanks, the compressor, umbilical, gas can, oil, Brian's personal stuff. Bring it all back. the gear was in transit back from the oil rig, the keys would be in Brian's sea bag.

Kevin went on to explain that he picked up the gear and managed to return all to the warehouse in the Woodlands leaving the truck parked just outside the office. The gear placed by the warehouse door.

He went on to explain that he had worked on and off for Gilbert for years. Sometimes as a diver, sometimes as a dive supervisor and sometimes just maintaining equipment. Prior to 1992 when Ross Saxon worked there they had a full time equipment guy but shortly after Ross left, the day to day operations, Gilbert let the maintenance guy go. After that it was up to the divers to maintain equipment. There were no more air quality tests done and if they need filters either rags would be used or most often Kotex pads. They fit just fine in the canisters where the fresh air would be sucked into the air compressor. The rags were mostly used on the engine side of the rack.

The conversation lasted for hours with more questions, more stories of how Gilbert had a bit of a problem with the brown bottle. How Brian had most likely been given air bottles that were empty as G&G did not have an established policy on tagging the bottles. The compressor sent out that day had been sent back from another job after it malfunctioned. There was little reason to have it fixed, work was slow, cash flow was slower. Maintenance was a joke and how he realized that by telling me all this he too could be blackballed and never work as a diver again.

And then he told me the rest of the story. Gilbert had instructed him to load the compressor into his truck, deliver it to McKenzie Equipment in Houston. Gilbert would call ahead and let them know what needed to be done. A week later he was told to return to pick up the compressor. When he arrived the original Lister diesel engine was mounted in the original rack with a new compressor mounted along side. In addition, he was given a box containing the original compressor broken down into its components. The technician explained that Gilbert had sent a note to McKenzie indicating "this compressor has not been used in a while" and requesting it be repaired. The mechanic went on to explain that when the compressor arrived it was not able to make a single revolution. they disassembled the unit only to find burned bits of red rags in the pistons and valves. Gilbert had been notified that the compressor was beyond economic salvation. It would be cheaper to just replace it.

The following morning I called Lt. J. G. Blake Wellborn. He was on vacation. I typed up a summary of my conversation with Lawdermilk along with a suggestion that they might want to drop in and get a statement from McKenzie equipment.

I sent a copy of the same message to Julie's Attorney, David Brandom, at Provost Umphrey. Wellborn called me back moments later asking me if I knew where McKenzie equipment was located. I dialed information on the second line and supplied him with their number.

The next few months were filled with more letter to more bureaucrats most unanswered or passed along to subordinates. Five months passed before a Fax arrived from the Thirteenth Coast Guard District based in Seattle. It had been sent by Com. Ken Armstrong who I had been directed to months before by United States Senator Patty Murray. The senator had been most helpful as I negotiated the Federal mine field and her suggestion that I contact Armstrong had been a good one. The commander helped to explain the workings of the Coast Guard, their strengths as well as their short comings. He promised to follow the investigation being done in the Eighth District but went on to explain they were not as well connected as you might wish to believe with each district working somewhat independently.

It was March 20, 1997, Brian had died one year and sixteen days before and now here was the United States Coast Guards investigation report sitting on my Fax machine. The report indicated that the cause of death was that the diver had panicked, disconnected his own air line and drowned. The report was based on only the two statements. One from Austin, one from Wiitala. There was no mention of the compressor, the air hose, no other witnesses were questioned. The accident site had never been visited.

The only violations listed were; failure to maintain a log book with appropriate entries, failure to provide an operations manual for the dive evolution, failure to appoint a dive supervisor and no maintenance log for the compressor. Followed by

"LEGAL ACTION POSSIBLE [N]"

The narrative went on to explain, **"While dive industry safety standards specify the need for standby safety equipment, specific standby equipment is not required by regulation for surface supplied dives to depths less than 130 ft."** The report was concluded with **"Had it become evident to Cliff's that this information** (no operations manual, no appointment of a dive supervisor) **did not exist, it may have prompted the person in charge to preclude the dive from being conducted."**

How strange that last sentence is the all too brief account of the incident aboard the Cliffs 12. Was it not the responsibility of the person in charge to verify that the vessel under his command was being safely operated? By regulation it was his responsibility to assure the diving operations were being conducted per the letter of authorization issued by the USCG. And it was curious that there was no mention in this United States Coast Guard report that there were in fact four members of the Coast Guard on board during the dive evolution, two of them officers, one of them the man that had issued the approval to do the underwater inspection. Also no mention that the assumed dive supervisor was in fact not a diver at all.

Notably absent from the report was the results of the function tests on the air compressor that had been promised by Com. John C. Miko in his letter to United States Senator Slade Gorton. Perhaps in our current environment of expedience and half truths it has become acceptable to openly supply false information in the name of expedience. Or perhaps the Commander Miko had relied on information supplied to him by the author of the investigation report. In any case the compressor was not shown to have been a causal part of the fatality.

For me my next cause of action would be to get back in touch with Senator Gorton letting him know of the previous deception by members of the Coast Guard and asking his assistance in having the investigation reopened. Reopened in a different venue where the investigator would not be the one who had lost custody of the evidence, where the investigator would not be sharing an office with the inspector who was present during the dive evolution and by regulation was required to stop the dive. Opened in a venue where all the regulations that were violated would be explored.

Shortly after getting back with the Senator, shortly by USCG time, Com. Thomas K. Richey responded to Senator Gorton. "We apologize for any confusion or misunderstanding that our poor choice of words may have caused. As a result of Mr. Pilkington's concerns the entire matter is under review. Our letter of April 18, 1997, indicates that the compressor used in the dive operation that resulted in the death of Brian Pilkington was "tested." The letter also states that the results of the tests are included in the final investigative report. However, the air compressor was not tested to assure it was operating in accordance with the applicable regulations (46 CFR 197.462). In particular, the quality, the pressure and volume of output air was not tested. The air compressor was evaluated by a private business contracted by the operator and the report of the evaluation indicates that the air compressor was in need of overhaul. The report states that it would be too costly to repair the compressor and recommends that the purchase of a new air compressor. Additional issues regarding this matter also are presently under review by the commander,

Eighth District. Please know that we take Mr. Pilkington's comments and concerns very seriously."

In addition to the compressor there was also no mention of the hose being function tested or the dive helmet. The hose much like the compressor had been returned to the contractor and subsequently lost in obscurity. I Had found the helmet on the warehouse floor two days after Brian's death and it was in the custody of Julie's attorney. David Brandom rather then send it out for repairs before testing, as Gilbert had attempted to do with the compressor, sent Brain's helmet to the United States Navy Underwater research center in Panama City Florida.

Chapter 10

FORT EUSTIS, VIRGINIA

They had spent two days preparing for the test. The helmet had been shipped from the United States Navy Underwater Research Center in Panama City and was hooked up to a low pressure air line. Inside the five foot diameter steel decompression chamber Ric Walker was preparing for a twenty-minute test. Walker had learned to dive while training to be a United States Navy Seal in 68. Served on Seal team 1 in Vietnam continuing his diver training at the College of Oceaneering after leaving the navy. Then spent years working in the industry as a diver, saturation diver, diving supervisor and now as a consultant. According to his resume he had made saturation dives to over seven hundred feet, worked for numerous dive contractors both in the United States and abroad; but now most of his time was spent consulting with responsible oil companies in establishing safe diving practices.

Today he was hooked to electrodes to monitor his heart rate, gauges to follow his respiration and pulse rate as well as recording devices to monitor oxygen and carbon dioxide levels. Sitting on a fixed exercise bicycle inside the chamber dressed in shorts, a tee shirt, Brian's dive helmet and neck damn he was ready to start the test. To his left, hunched over in the confines of this steel cylinder was Dr. David Youngblood. Armed only with a flashlight in one hand a stop watch in the other and years of experience in hyperbaric medicine, he too was ready. The door to the chamber clanged shut, air was flowing to the dive helmet at the manufactures recommended 120 psi as the sound of hissing air entered the chamber.

Youngblood called out over the intercom. The sound off his voice echoed of the cold steel walls "Take us to twenty-eight feet, reduce the air pressure to the helmet to 80 psi. Ric start peddling."

Chapter 11

WHAT IS A MAN WORTH?

It was early May when Julie's attorney contacted us telling us we were to be deposed. There would be attorneys representing Cliffs Drilling, the American Bureau of Shipping and G&G Marine coming to Seattle to question Julie, Karen and me. It should all be able to be done in one day. He would arrange a place, be prepared to be there all day. We would be quizzed individually. Julie would be allowed to stay through it all, Brian's Mother and I would only be allowed in during our questioning but only individually. My only question was why depose Karen and Julie, they have no idea what happened more than a year before? Nothing other then what they may have heard over a dinner conversation or one side of an overheated conversation as I chastised some low level bureaucrat for his inattention or incompetence. Before I could ask the question David continued,

"We are getting together for one reason and only one reason and it has nothing to do with what happened on March 4, 1996."

Chapter 12

THE DEPOSITIONS

MAY 18, 1997

It was an unusually crisp morning for the last Wednesday before the advent of summer. The streets were still damp from the previous evening's rain and a chilling breeze made its way east up Pine Street from the Seattle harbor beyond. Karen, Julie and I made our way apprehensively to the left, down Post Alley to the entrance of the Market Inn and the 8:00 AM appointment that awaited us there. A tranquil fountain stood sentry amid the brick paved lane, surrounded with spring flowers and the smells of freshly brewed coffee emanating from the Starbucks we had just passed. All this did little to calm the fear of the unknown proceedings that waited beyond the revolving doors. Pausing momentarily to enjoy our last vestige of independence we pressed through to the marble tiled floor partially covered with oriental carpets. The walls were brightly adorned with milky white trim, embossed wall papers, paintings of tranquil city scenes and brass wall sconces still lit to supplement the meager morning sun light. Prominently placed stood a single, filigreed, gold plated easel supporting a framed cardboard notice.

Welcome
Provost and Umphrey
Jefferson Room
3rd floor

There would be no need to disturb the neatly attired attendants busily working behind the highly polished mahogany front desk. All we needed to know, to locate our destination, was there posted for all to see. No other notices for other conferences, no other meetings scheduled for this elegant oasis of a hotel nestled in the center of the Northwest's largest city. Up the elevator, down the hall and through the heavily painted wood doors to the only conference room, apparently, in this most elaborate if not diminutive inn. Centered in the room stood an arrangement of six smaller tables each covered with an individual linen cloth, encompassed by fourteen chairs neatly placed and ready. Stood what would be our table of inquisition. Squarely placed in front of each seat atop the starched linen cloth was a single pad with two number two pencils all clearly embossed with the name of the inn. Centered on the table was one of those multidirectional speakerphones found all too often when one or more participants are discourteous enough or unable to attend a conference in person. Pushed tightly against the north wall were two additional tables formed to look as one. On top of their starched covers stood six rows of cups, each row exactly four cups high and three cups deep with each cup placed on its separate saucer with a scalloped paper doily between. And to the left of the army of cups, stood waiting, four silver pots each appropriately labeled to indicate what sort of hot beverage would be contained within.

Along the western wall a brace of windows permitted a partial view of the harbor and alley below. A single attendant, dressed in hotel uniform, scurried about the room completing the last of the minor details assuring us that all would be in order for the scheduled 9:30 AM deposition. I couldn't help but think if only as much attention had been given to the preparation for the ill-fated dive the year before, we would not have needed to be here today. The three of us watched as the hotel orderly completed his appointed tasks and then proceed out the door through which we had just entered only to be stopped by a casually dressed man entering from the corridor. Turning to each other, ignoring the men at the door, we questioned the need for all the chairs and cups. Was it not only we three that were to be questioned today? Perhaps there would be others from the local area these men from Houston would need to interrogate; perhaps instructors from the dive school; other divers, friends, past employers, classmates? Surely they would want to know all there was to know about our son who was not here to represent himself?

The casually dressed man, upon completing his instructions to the hotel worker turned his attention to us. He walked in our direction with hand out-stretched and announced. "Hi, I'm David Brandom, Julie's attorney, we met in Beaumont." Before us, attired in a loose fitting open-collared shirt more appropriate for a humid Texas afternoon than a chilly Seattle morning stood the man who had summoned us here today. This was the same man who had instructed us in a written letter weeks before to present ourselves in a manner appropriate for court. Julie and Karen were dressed in conservative business suits and I in a newly purchased jacket and tie, acquired specifically for the occasion. We returned his greeting. We had all met previously for the only time, two days after Brian's death, at the Law offices of Provost and

Umphrey in Beaumont Texas. Individually selecting a cup of coffee from the neatly organized silver pots we listened as we received our first instructions on how to conduct ourselves and what we could expect to transpire over the next several hours.

David was a man in his mid thirties, slightly balding, athletically built with that ever-present drawl reminding us continually of his southern roots. Educated at Baylor University he had spent his entire working career with one firm, Provost and Umphrey. Now it was our turn to share in a portion of his wisdom and experience.

Depositions are meant to be fishing expeditions. Where the attorneys representing Brian's employer, Cliffs Drilling and the American Bureau of Shipping would be looking for anything that might help their case; any tidbit of knowledge that could be used against Brian; anything that could be twisted or turned to reflect a negative light on Brian or his now-widowed wife. Almost any question could be asked. Almost any subject could be explored. But we were instructed by David to keep our answers brief; one word if possible, no elaboration, no offering of additional information. Do nothing to hurt the case. David would object to any inappropriate questions. Be truthful; but briefly truthful. Do not tell them of Brian's mechanical aptitude. They would turn that against him. Do not offer insight into his work ethic. They would find fault with that too. Do not relate stories of past accomplishments. Keep it simple; be brief, get it over with, get out early—but most importantly, don't jeopardize the case. David explained all this to the three of us now seated across the starched tablecloths of the conference table. All the time he was staring directly at me, for he knew it was I that would be most likely to break the rules, most likely to divulge more than the opposition was entitled to know. I knew too much and from me they would have the most to learn.

There should be three attorneys representing the opposition: one from Cliffs Drilling, the prime contractor, one from the American Bureau of Shipping, the company entrusted with overseeing the oil well inspection, perhaps there would be one representing G&G Marine, Brian's employer, although that seemed doubtful as G&G's budget for legal representation was nearing exhaustion. Even if G&G were to lose the case there would be nothing to get, no assets, no monies, no bank accounts, no deep pockets. There was also Kirk Austin, but no one expected him to either show or be represented. There was already some rumor of a move afoot by this coward who was responsible for misrepresenting not only himself but his company's ability to complete the contract he personally had signed, to declare bankruptcy seeking the protection of the court. However, all that was of little interest to us. We were not here for the money; we were here for justice. At least the three of us were. and we hoped Julie's attorney would assist us in our quest for the truth.

119

Over the past months I had talked to him briefly by phone each time some new fact was brought to my attention. During the preceding fourteen months there had been a letter from divers who thought I should know the truth, contacts with the Coast Guard Investigations unit reportedly investigating the incident, information pertaining to the compressor and its location all passed along to this attorney from Beaumont. David had been the brunt of numerous phone calls and letters from me looking for either action or answers to the slow grinding of "the system." And we hoped he would have the same dedication to justice that we would like to think all officers of the court should possess. Interrupting David's legal lecture and returning my mind to the reality of the day a soft knock emanated from the direction of the entrance.

Once again the conference room door swung open, revealing a pleasant looking young woman. Dressed in a brightly colored, flowered yellow dress, she was hunched over in an attempt to navigate through the doorway her black leather case outfitted with tiny chrome wheels, a handle and an array of metal tubes all neatly attached. David immediately sprang to his feet to advise her that we were not as yet ready for her and that perhaps she could find a place in the lobby until we were in need of her reporting services. Pushing her burden back from where it had come, she left without a word.

Looking at the time it was already 9:00 AM. We had received one hour of legal advice on procedure, decorum, what to say, what not to say, who could be present, who could not. This was our first insight into the workings of the United States legal system; approximately one hour's more information than I cared to know. Only the defendants, the plaintiff and their respective attorneys would be allowed to be present during the entire period of questioning. Mother and father had no such special privilege and hence would be excluded until each would face his or her inquisition alone. I expressed my displeasure at the prospect of both my wife and daughter-in-law being grilled without the support of any other member of the family and thought that perhaps with me present at least some of the inquiries might be more civilized or tempered. Julie's attorney considered my concern and to our surprise suggested in his best south Texas drawl. "Perhaps "y'all" should join the case. If "y'all" were also plaintiffs not only could you remain for all the proceedings but (and again staring directly at me) you could claim as client attorney privilege whatever you know. That is what you know about the case that you have gotten through me. Now "y'all" did get everything you know from me? Now y'all did pay many of the expenses and as you know in a death on the high seas case the only thing you can sue for are lost wages, paid to dependents only and actual costs incurred.

Now his estate can also claim damages for any pain and suffering the deceased may have suffered and can be proven. Now Peter and Karen you have had expenses haven't yall?" Without so much as a response from either one of us our newly hired attorney made his way to the neat rows of coffee cups stacked on the table along the north wall. Behind the cups, tidily concealed, a hotel phone was quickly dialed and the information required transmitted to his Texas office.

Given the opportunity to take a break from the morning lecture those remaining at the table followed closely behind; each selecting a second cup and then filling it. Karen and Julie engaged each other in conversation. I moved to the window to gaze toward the harbor beyond and ponder what to expect.

When the door opened again, two men entered, paused and conversed between themselves momentarily. One was tall, thin and gaunt with little or no expression looking like the Iowa farmer in the Grant Wood painting "American Gothic"; the other short and round with a jolly expression beneath his dark closely cropped hair. Together they strode forward and introduced themselves. "Bijan Siahatgar, from Houston, representing Cliffs Drilling." and then nothing more from this man who had obviously never plowed an Iowa field—at least not in the two-hundred-dollar monogrammed shirt, which he wore this day without a tie. Then came "Dana Martin of Hill, Rivkins, Losberg, O'Brian, Mulroy, and Hayed," stated so that we might be impressed by the number of partners in what must certainly be an impressive firm. He added, "Representing the American Bureau of Shipping," following the lead established by his predecessor.

Dana Martin continued with small talk regarding the weather, which is always a predictable topic for any new arrival here in Seattle. Mr. Siahatgar remained respectfully aloof at an appropriate distance, listening but not participating. But it was in this man I was most interested. He represented the company I held most responsible for the death of our son, the company more interested in their bottom line than the safety of the work place. He, by his demeanor, would be the one from whom I expected the cruelest of questioning. It was to that end I engaged him in conversation. In the brief minutes that passed I was able to ascertain his mother's German heritage, father's Iranian roots, learned of his recent trip to Europe and his plan to extend his time here in Seattle after the depositions had concluded. Sort of a mini vacation lasting through the weekend. Seeking some common ground I told him of our travels through Iran and Europe; all in an attempt to show him we were more than the names included in the files contained within his leather briefcase. More than just another case to be disposed of clearing the deck for the next annoyance created by some other disgruntled employee or subcontract worker whose rights had been violated by his clients careless activities. David, having completed his instructions to his distant office, acknowledged the presence of the two recent arrivals and headed in search for the lady in the flowered dress as the two Mrs. Pilkingtons, the attorneys representing the opposition and I continued in insignificant small talk.

Once found the reporter made her way back through the door from which she had earlier been evicted and selected an unused, discreet corner of the conference table. She assembled the contents of the black leather bag mounting her strange typewriter atop the chrome stand, plugged in a 486 lap top computer perched on a second stand and set out a tape recording device so that nothing would go unnoticed. No words would go untranscribed, no verbalized thoughts missed. Everything was in order.

The appointed hour which had now arrived was interrupted by the electronic buzz of the multidirectional phone located midway between the assembled participants. It proved to be a long distant call from Kenna Sella, representing G&G Marine. Kenna Sella was the attorney I had met the day after Brian's death; the world's only attorney with no business cards. She would be unable to attend in person but could afford to listen in and participate via this electronic marvel of inconsiderateness. Some discussion between the attorneys actually in the room ensued involving who was to pay the phone charges incurred to keep G&G's distant attorney a part of the proceedings and then we were ready.

No one else would be here. Just, four attorneys, three in person, one on the phone, Karen, Julie, me and, of course, the court reporter. Looking about the room with its assemblage of tables and chairs, myriad of cup and amenities, all carefully orchestrated to be prepared for any eventuality, cater to our every need. How unnecessary, attorneys from Texas, reporter from some unknown service in Seattle, a mother, wife and father. Had the client these men from Houston claimed to represent spent as much time preparing and operating their respective business, paid as much attention to the details as the staff of this elegant Inn there would be have been no need for the events about to begin.

Although the proceedings were to be directed by the defense the first to speak was David. "Before we begin let me inform y'all that Mr. and Mrs. Peter Pilkington have joined our action."

The gaunt man in the expensive shirt, showing the first sign of emotion sat ramrod straight, glaring at our newly acquired counsel. "When did this happen? Were we notified? When was the filing?" And without a breath he continued. "Cliffs Drilling objects to this modification without proper notification."

Afraid to be left out, the dark haired man with the once jolly face joined in protest.

"I also, I mean the American Bureau of Shipping joins in that objection."

Faintly, an electronic voice could be heard originating from the multidirectional phone. "What's that? I can't hear, could y'all say that again?"

Displaying his electronic wizardry the attorney from Hill, Rivkins, Loesburg, O'Brian, Mulroy and Hayden reached forward adjusted the appropriate buttons until the attorney still in Texas could be heard.

Confirming that she could now also hear us Mr. Siahatgar repeated. "Mr. Brandom has just informed us that the Pilkingtons, that is Mr. and Mrs. Peter Pilkington have employed him as their counsel and will be joining the suit. We here have objected to the improper notification and have inquired as to when this all had taken place."

"We at G&G Marine also object." Came the loud, clear voice over the speaker.

A pleased look came across the once again jolly face of Mr. Dana Martin of Hill, Rivkins, Loesburg, O'Brian, Mulroy and Hayden, perhaps because of his displayed expertise in so competently adjusting the phone or perhaps because of their collective defensive solidarity. Now that all could hear, our lawyer from the little town of Beaumont, Texas regained control of the conversation. In his best southern Texas drawl he continued "Gentlemen I think y'all agree it is time we begin the day's proceedings." Nodding to the lady in the flowered dress he began. "The Pilkingtons contacted me this morning, asked if they too could be named in our action against your respective clients. I have considered their requests, contacted my office in Texas and had the appropriate paper prepared. As the hour in Houston now approaches 11:00 AM the filing should, by now, be complete. The Pilkingtons, all the Pilkingtons, as plaintiffs in this matter, will remain here throughout the proceedings."

Attempting to regain control of his scheduled confrontation, the man from the Grant Wood painting, stern and stoic, with a monotone voice only imagined by the observer of this now-famous painting of the Midwestern farmer, pitch fork and daughter, intoned, "The time is 9:30 and we are on the record. These proceeding will be conducted under the Texas Rules of Civil Procedure. Do we all agree?" Not waiting for confirmation he continued. "I am Bijan Siahatgar representing Cliffs Drilling, also present are Dana Martin, representing The American Bureau of Shipping, and Kenna Sellas, representing G&G Marine."

"Y'all still there aren't ya?" asked the man with the monogrammed shirt. "David Brandom, representing the plaintiffs, Mrs. Julie Pilkington, Mrs. Karen Pilkington and Peter Pilkington." Mr. Siahatgar continued, "Cliffs Drilling formally objects to the late notification and the addition of the Pilkingtons as plaintiffs to this action. And on behalf of Cliffs Drilling Company I'd like to object to the late notice with regards to the amendment of the petition, reserve the right to review the filings and may ask to reconvene the deposition of Karen and Peter Pilkington at a later date. I am objecting to the presence of Karen and Peter Pilkington in the deposition throughout Julie Pilkington's deposition, as I plan on invoking the rule. And I take it, Mr. Brandom, that you are going to insist that they remain here during the deposition?"

"Yes, Mr. Siahatgar, the Pilkingtons are here to stay," answered our man from Texas, not at all disturbed by the thought of having the "rule" invoked. Following suit, the little man to the right of our monotone moderator added.

"We at the American Bureau of Shipping also formally object to the late notification and the addition of the Pilkingtons to this action. We reserve the right to review the filings and may ask to reconvene the deposition of Karen and Peter Pilkington at a later date. We haven't seen a copy of the original petition as yet. It has, as I understand, maybe not been filed yet, it being about 10:00 AM., or before 10:00 AM. in Texas. And we, too, intend to invoke the rule, and we understand that we're being overridden on the point, and to that extent that may need to be raised at a later date with the court. We want to protect our position that the witnesses should be taken one at a time, without hearing each other's testimony. If the testimony of one witness is complete, we would be agreeable to allow them to sit throughout the rest of the depositions, but having them present before their deposition is given, we object to that."

Perhaps the established time difference between Seattle, Washington and Houston, Texas had been changed over the course of the day. But to the rest of us the time in Texas was still a lot closer to 11:00 AM than to 10:00 AM as stated by the learned attorney from Hill Rivkins Loesburg O'Brian Mulroy, and Hayden. Perhaps we too were supposed to be intimidated by the invoking of the "rule" a second time in so short a period but still our counsel remained firm on all of us remaining, even after the eloquent diatribe just delivered to us by Mr. Martin. The black box centered on the table crackled in electronic response. "G&G also joins in that objection."

Now that the defense team had once again confirmed their solidarity, Bijan Siahatgar began with a brief dissertation on how the proceedings were to be conducted so that the neophytes assembled might better understand the procedure. We would be allowed to answer any question regardless of objection. We should remain truthful and answer as completely as possible. Questioning would start with Julie and end with Karen, with me in-between. All that and much more was said before he reached below the table retrieving the black leather case stowed there earlier. Placing it on the white, starched cloth he opened the case and extracted a file. It was large, brown, with bellowed sides just barely able to contain its over-stuffed contents. With a thud he placed it on the table. Boldly emblazoned on the cover, printed with a bold black marker was

"CLIFFS # 12"

I looked on this folder with disdain. We had come here to discuss the death of our son. As far as I was concerned we were here to recount and recollect as best we could the all too short life and times of our now-departed friend. To bestow upon these men of the law whatever was required so that they too could understand the loss we all felt and perhaps along the way learn what had really happened fourteen months before. Here before us on the table was a file labeled "CLIFFS #12," not "Pilkington vs. Cliffs Drilling," not "Cliffs Drilling" not even just "Cliffs," but rather a reference to the inanimate object that had held our son squeezing the life from his body as the crew of Cliffs #12 stood by in ignorant acceptance.

Bijan Siahatgar, our inquisitor, would receive no quarter from me. This man of the law who apparently found more significance with his client's pile of weathered steel than with the lives it affected, began his fishing expedition.

"Let's start with Julie. Please raise your right hand. Do you solemnly swear to tell the truth, the whole truth, and nothing but the truth?"

"I do," responded the confident voice of our young son's bride.
"Please state your full name."
"Julie Pilkington."
And so went the questioning. Where did she attend school? Where did she live as a child? Where did she meet Brian? How long had they dated? Did they ever break up while dating? Did she ever visit him when he lived in New Orleans? Did the in-laws approve of her? What kinds of jobs had she held? What was her current employment? Was she a manager? In what store? How many people did she manage? Was there any place else to which they could have moved? And so on and so on. Endless inquires pertaining to her history, all which were answered with as few words as possible. Most answers required no more than a, "University of Idaho," "yes," "no," "eight years," "Bellevue Washington," "no," "yes," "I don't recall," and so on. Brief answers to brief, to the point, questions. Each question was phrased in such a manner that a single word would satisfactorily answer most. This, of course, was much to the delight of the lady in the flowered dress who had to hit only a single key or two to record the response.

I stared deeply into the bottom of the empty cup before me, pondering the dry residue of the last remainder of the once hot brew. So many questions about so little. Questions that had no relevance to the issue at hand. No insight into the death.

Nothing that could help anyone understand why. Of what consequence was Julie's employment or where she went to school? Why force her to recount how they met? How cold and impersonal were the questions; how cold and impersonal the answers. How difficult would it be for me to answer the same questions when my turn came? Questioning had drained Julie's emotional stability and a break was requested. Pushing back from the table Julie rushed for the doorway, with Karen close behind, seeking the refuge of the corridor that lay beyond. David and I followed slowly and remained at a respectful distance as the once stoic witness erupted in tears in the arms of her mother-in-law. David corralled me against the finely papered walls of the passageway, stared directly into my eyes and said,

"She was great. The perfect witness. Did nothing to hurt us, could not have done any better. Remember that when your turn comes." Then looking down the darkened hallway David paused as he observed the two Mrs. Pilkingtons comforting one another. "Think I need to give her a hug myself," and off he went. He walked down the corridor to join the ladies leaving me to ponder my second legal lecture of the day.

Our break now over the parties reassembled. The gaunt man representing Cliffs Drilling again prepared to cast his net on the barren waters. More simple questions more single word answers.

Where did she work, what did she drive, did they ever quarrel, did they have plans for the future? All answered with quick one word responses. Did she have a picture of Brian?

"Actually, I do," responded the stoic widow as she reached for her purse. "Don't we have thirty days to respond to that request?" interjected Mr. Brandom. "Of course," responded the counsel from Cliffs Drilling Company.

The photo was presented for inspection over the objection of counsel and then returned to its place of prominence among the young lady's other valuables. Then the questioning turned almost accusatory. He pointed directly at this young woman with less than eight months of married life experience and asked, if she was aware of how hazardous her husband's work was, did they ever discuss the dangers? Did she encourage him to do it?

The questioning continued regarding the motivation to leave the state of Washington and move to Texas in general, Houston in particular. Did she encourage him to work for a small company so that he might be able to dive and become more experienced? What were her spending habits? What were his? Who provided most of the income? Who paid the bills? Who filled out the income tax return? And then finally. "Did you decide who to file suit against or did your attorney?"

"Client attorney privileged information." Interjected the until now-silent attorney from Beaumont. There had been no need for him to intercede as his young pupil had performed admirably, with no misconduct in answering the senseless questions from the opposition save turning over the photo without proper notification.

The questions continued, "Are you making a claim for loss of consortium in this case? Let me ask this way. Your lawsuit says you're making a claim for loss of consortium. Do you know what that is?"

"I think I do," replied the puzzled witness.

"Can you describe for me the type of consortium that you're claiming for in your lawsuit?" snapped the attorney.

"I believe it's—well," began the even further puzzled young woman.

"Can you define it for her?" interjected Mr. Brandom." "I don't think she understands the term you're using."

"Do you have a good definition of 'loss of consortium' Mr. Brandom? I'm not sure that I do," quipped the attorney for Cliff's Drilling Company.

Without waiting for a definition, Julie said quietly, "It's everything that we would have had together, had he still been alive."

Not understanding that his question had already been completely answered the learned attorney in the expensive shirt found it necessary to complete the definition of the term that was the basis of the already answered question. "I think the loss of consortium is the care, comfort, support and relations that y'all generally had together. And the loss of consortium, therefore is a loss of those different things. Do you understand what consortium is?

"Yes," replied the reluctant witness.

"So then in your own words, if you can tell me what your loss of consortium is?"

"The companionship of my best friend, my husband, the future that we had planned and, you know, we had talked about buying a house, having kids, traveling, growing old together. All the things that married people do, people who are in love."

Seeing that this line of questioning had shown him little he moved on. "You're making a claim for mental anguish. Do you know what mental anguish is?"

"That night in the hospital, that will always be with me, that will forever be my nightmare."

Quickly changing tone the inquisitive attorney asked. "By the way, who was the best man at y'all's wedding?"

"Eric Leonard, he was Brian's best man, best friend."

"I think I've asked you enough questions, so I'm going to go ahead and pass, and let some of these other lawyers ask you some questions. Thank you." The man in the expensive shirt and solemn appearance referred to his notes carefully arranged between the covers of the folder marked Cliff's #12.

The attorney from Hill, Rivkins, Loesburg, O'Brian, Mulroy, and Hayden quickly seized the opportunity to display his judicial excellence by adding "Kenna would you like to go next? Kenna y'all still there aren't ya?"

Kenna lost no time in getting directly to the heart of her dynamic questioning. "Sure I just have a few questions. Can you tell in between the time y'all got married and the time of Brian's death did you take any vacations together?"

Now this was not the only question Kenna would ask but it was certainly the most insightful. Surely this woman of the law had not spent her employer's hard earned retainer just to ask questions about Brian and Julie's joint vacationing habits. But of the twenty-two questions she would pose that day, twenty-one involved vacations, entertainment or friends with whom they associated. The lone question that deviated from the rest was her last request from the now-tiring witness. "How would you describe your relationship with Brian during your marriage?"

"Very happy," was the immediate responses.
And as Bijan Siahatgar had before her, Kena Seiler passed the witness with a "I have no further questions."

"Okay. My name is Dana Martin, and I represent the American Bureau of Shipping." Was this to remind all of us present who might have forgotten who he was since he had introduced himself earlier? Then, apparently to remind all of us in the event we were either not listening or not awake earlier, he went on to ask basically the same questions asked by the man with the expensive shirt and stoic appearance. He did, however, insert a few original and more in-depth questions, such as what year was the Nissan Maxima Brian had given her for Christmas?

Just how far was it from Brian's grandfather's house to their apartment when they lived in Washington? What was the name of the church she attended? What was the name of the high school she attended? As the crow flies how close were the homes the two of them lived in while they were both in high school? On and on went the questions relating to her spending habits, athletic interests, summer vacations and Christmas parties; all the things that needed to be asked so as to better understand and determine the value that could eventually be applied to her dead husband.

For this was what was becoming, apparently, the reason for which we were requested to be here today. It was not to shed some new light on how our son was lost. It was to better understand the man who was killed because of an employer's indifference and incompetence. We were there to help these lawyers ascertain what that lost life was worth. It was their mission to mix up the ingredients of the information, simmer them down and come up with a dollar amount.

More follow-up questions came from Mr. Siahatgar and then similar follow-ups to the follow-ups by Mr. Martin. And then an unexpected "I think were done." This originated from the attorney representing Cliffs Drilling followed by total agreement from the man representing The American Bureau of Shipping.

"Cliffs Drilling has no further questions at this time. We pass the witness. Mr. Martin do you have any further questions?"

"The American Bureau of Shipping has no further questions at this time?" mimicked the now-not-so-jolly attorney from Hill, Rivkins, Losberg, O'Brian, Mulroy, and Hayded. Without a clue the forgotten electronic octopus centered on the table joined the chorus.

"G&G Marine has no further questions at this time."

Julie's work for the day was done as she pushed back from the table and headed quickly for the sanctuary of the corridor.

A startled inquisitor attempting to gain control before the exodus continued rose to his feet. "Perhaps we all need a break now. When we come back I like to begin with Mr. Pilkington. It's close to noon so why don't we extend long enough for lunch?" He was too late. Karen as before was close on Julie's heels. David, a step behind, attempted to avoid any suggestion of a long recess. Mr. Martin fumbled through his files; me staring, still seated, waiting for my turn.

The lunch break never happened. David Brandom did not want to make this an all-day affair This fishing expedition was of no benefit to him. If the questions to me were of no more substance than those to Julie, why waste any more time than necessary? Five minutes passed and all the players reassembled to their previously selected seats. That is, all except Julie and I who exchanged positions. The seat to the left of the lady with the yellow flowered dress was reserved for the person being questioned. It was reserved so that she might be able to hear every word, record every syllable, cast upon the record every emotionless "yes," "no," and "I have no personal knowledge." For me this would not be necessary. I would be able to be heard no matter where I might be seated. I had come to be heard.

To my surprise Mr. Hill, Rivkins, Losberg, O'Brian, Mulroy, and Hayded began the questioning.

"My name is Dana Martin. I represent the American Bureau of Shipping. Could you give us your full name?"

"Peter J. Pilkington," I replied.

"And what employment are you currently involved in?" asked the now-not-so-jolly-looking man I had met for the first time over coffee two hours before

"Self-employed, general contractor."

"How many children did you have as a result of any marriages, I guess, you've had? I don't know—what were their names?"

"Brian, the oldest, Jamie, and then Afton."

"How old are the younger ones?"

"Jamie is now twenty-two, and Afton is ten."

"Are they in college, the older one?"

"Jamie graduated from college a month ago."

"Which college?"

"University of Puget Sound."

"And Afton's in grade school?"

"Afton is in the fourth grade."

And then he continued asking about my education, where I had worked, professional positions I had held, when was I married, why had I moved the family to Arabia? Was I always married to the same woman? Was it true that my father, Brian's grandfather was a retired U.S. Army colonel ? Was he a POW at some point?

The questioning went on with more pointless questions about me, my family, my work. Why the questions about my father, his background, his military service? How could these bits of unrelated history shed any significance on why our son had been permitted to be violated by the clients of the attorneys sent here this day? All the trivial questions answered with as few words as possible, concisely and loud enough to have made Sergeant Brigands, my Marine Drill instructor from years gone by, proud.

"Could you give us Brian's birth date?"
At last a question about our son! Was that not what we were here to discuss?
"May 3, 1972. I'm sorry, the fourth." I answered somewhat puzzled. Surely they must know all that.
"May 4? Okay."
"May 4." I confirmed.
"What kind of education did he have that you remember?" The door had been left open to submit the standard answer of "I don't recall" which had been the response of the day until now.
"Elementary school" And before I could complete the response.

"Where, here in town?" interrupted the boyish attorney from Hill, Rivkins, Loesburg, O'Brian, Mulroy, and Hayden. In our opening discussions pertaining to decorum it was made clear that we not break in on each other's questions and answers. We needed to accommodate the court reporter and maintain order so that the record would correctly reflect what was transpiring. But I guess this rule of etiquette did not pertain to attorneys or perhaps he was not prepared for more than a one-word answer. So I answered louder and faster in order to preclude the opportunity of being interrupted again.
"He went to preschool when we lived in the United Arab Emirates. He then went to elementary school in Issaquah, Washington. Attended middle school in Issaquah. And then we moved in the middle of that period of time, he went to a middle school here in Bellevue. And then for high school, he went to a private school in Seattle."
"What was the name of the private school?" This surely was going to be a long day. Asking questions to which they already had the answers.
"University Preparatory Academy." I responded.
"Does that name have a special significance, or is it just given that name?"
"No, just a name."
"Okay. So it's not a direct beeline into any particular college because-"
"No." I responded before he could finish, he cut me off, I would return the gesture.
"It's named University Prep?"
"No, it's named University Preparatory Academy." I correct the attorney who may not have cared about accuracy, just filling in the blanks on his prepared list.
"Yes, you said that. Is there a special course at work because it's called University Prep as opposed to a vocational technical type?"
"No, University Preparatory Academy is strictly a private high school."
"Okay. So they offered the full gamut of vocational training." He replied, not understanding the correction to his first question. I thought it curious that this attorney would attempt to answer so many of his own questions and wondered if a judge would permit him the same latitude. Perhaps he had not yet realized that I

would actually answer his questions, answer his questions more fully than he was accustomed to. But this question required a simple. *"No."*

"What kind—did he have any voc-tech work that he did while he was there?" again asked by the attorney who obviously was not listening.

"No, not that I am aware of." Answered with a puzzled expression as perhaps this man just would not accept that the boy had not attended a vocational high school or perhaps he was still just reading from some unseen list of questions not bothering to actually listen to the answers being provided. Or perhaps he was laboring under some misconception that Brian educational track had been funneled toward the trades rather than the liberal arts education actually provided. Finally after what seemed to be an eternity of shallow questions regarding high school education, the questions turned to previous medical ailments. Questions about nonexistent broken fingers, possible lung and breathing problems all things surely having no foundation but then this was a fishing expedition so no telling what a loquacious father might say. Finding nothing I was willing to share and having no foundation on which to base questions of health other than a one page medical release form and a negative drug scan the focus turned back to high school.

"Did he participate in sports, at what was it University Prep?"

"Yes, he did distance running. He played tennis, and was a member of the soccer team."

"Okay. What was his specialty in track?"

"He ran distance." Answered to the man who obviously was still not paying attention to the answers already given.

"Oh, okay. He ran several different lengths?"

"Yes, but it was more social, he liked the camaraderie."

"Huh?" responded the Attorney who was most likely expecting a simple yes, so braking the rules I continued to expound

"It was more social for Brian. He enjoyed people and he enjoyed his friends."

"Did he letter in track?"

"No."

"Did he letter in soccer?"

"I believe so, yes." Answered with a tone of surprise. Perhaps he was actually listening.

"What about tennis?"

"Also, yes."

"What kind of friends did he have in high school that you remember? Did he have several neighborhood friends, school friends?"

"He had lots of friends. Some in the neighborhood, and then later when he went to the private school, it was a very small class. I think there were only 28 students in his senior class, and I would say that they were probably all his friends."

Seeing that there was nothing to gain by pursuing friends the questioning turned to driving habits, traffic tickets and drinking. All dead ends as the one infraction, a speeding ticket when 19, was certainly not enough to diminish his value significantly nor was it an indication of a misspent youth leading to a life of crime. For truly that's what they were searching for; some indication, some pattern that would have lead to a premature death with or without the aid of his client's inattention.

Then the questioning turned once again to carpentry skills, mechanical ability, and possible union memberships. One question after another as this attorney from Texas attempted to establish the earning patterns of a young man that had not been allowed to witness his twenty-fourth birthday.

"What were the ranges in pay?" How long had he been with each employer? Did he work well with others? Did he like his various jobs? But mostly questions relating to his earnings and then finally.
"So he did many things?"
"Yes, sir, he liked to work, mowed lawns, delivered pizzas, worked as a cook. Sometimes worked for me, for my construction company. Doing whatever needed to be done from construction clean-up to framing. When he was old enough drive the utility truck, pick up supplies, that sort of thing. Oh and some community service work."

Now with the look of a man that had just caught his first fish this man from Hill, Rivkins Losberg, O'Brian, Mulroy, and Hayded without hesitation asked.
"You said he did some community service work?"

Surely, he must have thought they had found the key to some indiscretion in the boy's past. Some misdeed that would have forced him to perform some act of community service. For what was this fishing expedition for if not to find some bit of dirt to discredit the deceased and diminish his market value?

"You mentioned that he had to perform community service?" asked a second time as I pondered an answer I knew that should never have be mentioned.

"Yes," answered reluctantly.
Now I had done it. Broken the rule. Volunteered information and opened a path that perhaps should not be traveled.

Pushing himself closer to the table so as not to miss a word the attorney fired back "and do you recall the circumstances for which Brian had to perform this community service?"

A simple yes would have answered the question. But I had already broken the first rule of answering questions in a deposition so I continued.

"Yes. In the summer of his junior year he was required to do forty-five hours of community service. Actually it did not have to be done during the summer, just needed to be complete by graduation. University Prep required that all students select, have approved by a member of the facility, perform and then write a report on some aspect of community service as a social studies credit."

"What sort of service did he perform?" was the immediate response from the now-somewhat-disappointed fisherman.

Now this presented a problem. I had been instructed to be brief, to the point, do not embellish. But this, this was my favorite, "I told you so" story. A story where for once, even in the eyes of an adolescent, a parent could be viewed as more than an unwitting fool whose only task in life was to interfere. They would all have to listen, these attorneys for the first time. Julie and Karen for the thousandth. I paused for a moment and recounted in my mind the events of the summer of 1990.

Brian had come to me just before the end of his junior year explaining the requirement. Knowing that I would be expecting him to work with me that summer he came seeking permission to pursue some sort of summer community service project. Knowing that Brian would most assuredly rather be doing anything but work for me on a construction site hauling gravel, packing lumber or some equally mundane task I was not surprised when asked would it be okay to do his community service project during the summer. Of course, he then went on to explain that by doing the work over the summer it would not interfere with his senior year's school work. I knew better. He went on to explain that lots of others at school would be doing the same. In fact the following day he and three of his friends had planned to head down to Seattle Center in an attempt to add their names to the growing list of hopeful volunteers for the biggest event to hit Seattle since the 62 world's fair.

That summer Seattle was hosting the 1990 Goodwill Games and Turner Enterprises was interviewing for volunteers. They would be requiring as many qualified people as possible to fill a myriad of tasks. There were extraordinary opportunities not only to fulfill that class requirement but also to partake in the grandeur of the spectacle. Athletes from the Soviet Union and the cream of the United States all competing for the first time against one another since the boycotts of the eighties. Pondering his request I responded that I realized that I was just an old man and didn't know much about anything, but the people that would be interviewing would be like me. Old and clueless. I advised him to get rid of the school sweatshirt, blue jeans and tennis shoes. Shave, shower, and put on your best white shirt, tie, pressed slacks and blue blazer. Then go in there tell them you can work whenever they need you. You can do whatever they need to be done. Stand straight. Speak with confidence and you can spend your summer with the ballerinas or be content to following the elephants. You decide. The next day after getting back from the barber, he donned his best shirt, blue blazer, tie and shined shoes and headed for the Seattle Center to apply.

Unlike his three friends who accompanied him in their tattered sweat shirts and tennis shoes he was not offered a job. The three would all spend their summer parking cars or directing traffic at the various sports venues. Instead Brian was asked to return for another interview. Then another and another each time he would wear his blue blazer, pressed slacks well-groomed hair and a smile. The only thing out of place would be his mismatched socks, one stripped the other polka dot that he always wore for luck. After a week of interviews he drove home in a white Cadillac Eldorado with the logo of the Goodwill Games emblazoned on each door, dashed into the house, asked to borrow a few dollars and then informed me he was on his way to the airport. When asked about the car and why the airport he simply said he had been given the task to drive some woman that would be working for Turner Broadcasting and that he would be doing so for the duration of the games.

So for the next five weeks Brian would get up at 8:00 AM, dress in his blue blazer, shined shoes and yet another pair of mismatched socks then rush to Seattle to pick up Hanna Storm, co-anchor for the TV broadcasts of the summer's events. Then spend his day transporting his newly acquired friend and celebrity from TV studio to sports venues, watch her work from behind the scene and then at the conclusion of each  day's work take her to the best restaurant in town. For at the end of each day's broadcast Hanna would say. "Brian, take me to the best place in town, it's time we ate" Each morning he would ask me which the best was. Each day I would give him a new one so that he might impress his new friend with the unlimited expense account. Each night he and Hanna along with unnamed others would partake in yet another of Seattle's finest eating establishments and each morning Brian would have another story to tell. I once asked him why he felt he had been given the job. His reply was that Larry King had requested that his driver be a middle aged woman and Nick Charles, the other co anchor, had asked for a younger woman to transport him about the unfamiliar city. Hanna Storm stood over six feet tall and he suspected that perhaps she had requested a young man closer to her stature who of course would know his way about town. I went on to ask how it was that he joined these people each night in establishments where most assuredly there were restrictions on those underage. His response was simple. He would just tell the truth when drinks where ordered. "I'm the designated driver" and then order water or some equally legal liquid. Although just 18 years old I would suspect that no one ever questioned that the 6'5," 210 pound mature looking young man with the pleasant smile was not where he should be.

Surrounded by the elite of the sports world, celebrities and stars what wait person would ever question? His days and nights that summer were filled with experiences that most of us will never know as he transported his charge the wrong way down one way streets with and without police escorts, to appointed events, to dinner parties, production meetings, TV studios and sporting venues that others were only wishing they might attend.

One morning as I was heading to the garage on my way to work I passed Brian on his way in. Curious as to where he had been and seeing the white Cadillac, sparkling clean in the morning sun and safely parked in what had once been my spot I asked what I suspect would be normal of any father. He went on to explain that the evening before Ted Turner had thrown a cast part to celebrate the end of the successful conclusion of the summer games. Hanna had invited Brian to attend. That year Turner had purchased MGM studios and along with the acquisition came the "Bounty" the very ship used in the film "Mutiny on the Bounty" which Ted had brought to the Lake Washington waterfront and opened for public viewing during the summer games. But this past night the ship was closed and available only to the invited guests of the farewell party. My normally quiet son continued on describing the events of the evening and telling me of the people he had met and shared the evening festivities. Of course, Larry King and Nick Charles were there, but he saw them every day at the studio or some sporting event. Ted and Jane attended along with Edwin Moses and Carl Lewis but there was one man who he did not recognize who most impressed my young son. He described him as being tall, really tall, a black man with hands, enormous hands, a white goatee and a deep friendly laugh. And when he sat his knees were as high as the top of the dinner table. I smiled for a moment and said: "I bet they called him Wilt?" and Brian replied "Yes, do you know who he is?"

He passed that summer pursuing a once in a lifetime dream while completing the required social studies credit. And his father would have the ultimate "Son I told you so story" and perhaps just a bit of credibility in the eyes of a teenage son not yet old enough to understand the wisdom of experience.

I looked to Karen and then to the men across the table and said *"He worked for Turner Enterprises at the 1990 Goodwill Games."* They would have no interest in detail, only boxes to fill on the preordained checklist.

The response from the man representing the American Bureau of shipping was slow and deliberate. "Did he get a grade for the effort?"
"Yes, I believe he received a C, apparently they did not think it was a very worthwhile effort," I responded attempting to avoid eye contact with my newly acquired council or my wife.

"Did he keep in contact with any of these people?" Responded the attorney searching for the next line of questioning to pursue.

"Only Hanna, Hanna Storm, they exchanged letters for a while and she sent him a logo jacket and some socks. He enjoyed that summer . . . ," answered a father who wanted to tell the rest of the story but knew these men would not be interested so cut himself off in midsentence.

And then more questions of where he worked, what kind of jobs how much he made all answered with more than a "yes" or a "no" or "I don't recall" All the time thinking I wonder just how much these men with the three hundred dollar shirts where earning when they were just a month short of their twenty-third birthdays. What value would they apply to themselves if that were the only benchmark they had available?

I could tell that there were a few unhappy souls in the room. I, as always, was talking too much. The inquisitor expected "yes" and "no" or "I have no personal knowledge." David wanted me to abide by his previously communicated rules. Karen tried in vain to kick me under the table. So I then permitted the next question.

But this time the questions were asked in such a manner that all could only be answered with a single word. Perhaps I was giving them more than they cared to know and now were more intent on completing the litany of questions. Questions pertaining to anything but the purpose for which I thought we had gathered. So on it went more questions were asked about things to which they already had the answer. All asked so they could be simply answered, each square checked off, each required box filled. For truly it was becoming apparent that this was little more than a charade. The real determination as to the amount of money their clients would pay would not be based on any findings here but rather determined at some other higher level. This was little more than a step to be taken to maintain the meter and keep the billable hours flowing.

And then finally a more thought-provoking question.
"All people have several things they talk about. What other things did you and your son discusses pertaining to his future plans?"

This was not a question I would need long to ponder. Over the past year, since Brian's death, I had thought over this question many a time. How much different things might have been if I had not imparted this little gem of wisdom to an adolescent son.

"Well, I guess I advised him to find something he really liked to do. Something he enjoyed doing more than anything else. Something he would like to be able to do for the rest of his life. Something he could be really good at. It didn't matter what it was, just so long as you could do it well, take pride in what you had done but most importantly that it was something you really liked to do. Then and only then go find someone willing to pay you to do it. Which I think convinced him to go into diving. Not just as a hobby but as a vocation."

And then the first compassionately asked question, "He enjoyed doing the scuba? When did he take up diving?"

"His first experiences underwater were with me and his mother while living in the Persian Gulf area. Of course, back then it was just swimming free among the fishes in unspoiled shallow bays filled with warm water. But his formal scuba education did not begin until high school. He took the first of three scuba certification classes, he passed all three. First one was alone at Silent World Diving in Bellevue. He took the second certification class some time later when Julie decided to get certified. He pretended to be a novice so she would not have to take her class alone and was certified a second time. And then, of course, he was certified again at the Divers Institute in Seattle."

"So he did the third time in a professional school, not a scuba school?" asked the inquisitor.

"Well, yes. They taught a separate class in conjunction with the professional diving."

Answered with no comment that the only certification you come out of the professional schooling was that recreational card as there was no professional certification program.
"So how long after you had the discussion on life choices did he did he decide to enroll at the diving school?"
"We had a discussion, and several days later he came back to me with a portfolio that he had obtained from the Diver's Institute of Technology. He explained the

curriculum, and had set up an appointment for the two of us go down for an interview and tour of their facility."

More questions regarding diving. First Brian's training and then mine. I thought it odd that there had been so many questions about high school and now so few regarding his training as a diver. But then perhaps he already knew that the educational standards for commercial divers in this country were at best substandard and not accepted or recognized as proper training anywhere else in the world. So the questioning then turned back to the recreational side of diving.

"So you and your son would dive recreationally together?"

"Yes, Brian, Jamie, and I dove together recreationally, primarily here in Puget Sound and up around the San Juan Islands. Brian liked to dive. It was noncompetitive and he was good at it." Again answered with more than the expected one word.

"Okay. So the younger son that's 23 now—or 22 now, he's a diver too?"

"Yes, Jamie, is also a recreational diver, but he did not have the interest that Brian had. Jamie is also a competent diver but he did not possess the love for it that Brian had."

"What kind of things are there to do diving recreationally in Puget Sound? What are you looking at?"

"Obviously fish, rock formations, in some cases, wreck diving, in some cases just purely the sensation to go diving. And then there's the comradey. A day of recreational diving might only involve two hours of in the water time, the rest of the day is spent relaxing, talking, and preparing for the next dive. Brian liked to sit around and listen to stories, tell stories of his own, fix a bit of gear of just enjoy a day on the water."

"I'll bet the water here is cool, though, isn't it?"

"Forty-eight degrees year round." I responded.

"Year-round! So there's never a time that he would actually be considered in warm water, like it would be in the Gulf of Mexico?" responded the man from South Texas.

"Correct. Brian use to call home and laugh about the boys from Texas who he would refer to as the warm water divers with the thin blood. For him diving in the Gulf was paradise."

"Did you talk to him much about his schooling here in Seattle while he was over there, where was it Divers Institute? I mean did he come home and give you reports, or was he a man of few words?"

"He told me about the—seemed to take great pride in his underwater welding abilities, his photography abilities, and also seemed to take particular pleasure in his cold water diving. He like snow on the deck, a cold rain above and the cold water in January, February and March. Strange but he always liked those blustery days when everyone else was heading for cover."

"So did he have, I guess, typical of a lot of kids that age, kind of a macho image of his abilities?"

"No. He was always very confident at anything he did, and didn't do things unless he was very confident of his ability to complete the task properly. Diving suited him well as there should be no reason for hasty decisions. Speed was not an essential criteria, only proper preparation and skill. Both areas in which excelled."

"Was diving sort of an outlet for him to express his personality?"

"It's a noncompetitive, athletic endeavor that he enjoyed. It suited him well."

"During the time he was at New Orleans—by the way, did he go straight from school to the New Orleans place?"

"He was hired the day after he graduated by a diving company based in New Orleans. I believe the job came through the placement office at Divers Institute. The school had actually sent out letters of recommendation and resumes for him prior to graduation."

"Was the plan for him to continue his career down there indefinitely, as far as you knew?"

"His plan was to generate as much experience as he possibly could in the Gulf area, as jobs down there were plentiful and there is very little diving activity here on the west coast of the United States. There are far more diving activities in the Gulf area, and thus better chance for advancement and experience. Basically here the Washington coast is restricted to oil drilling. There is no oil drilling permitted in the coastal areas of Washington. So as a result, it would be inspection work and/or working on ships in shipyards and that did not particularly appeal to him. But once he had the experience his plan was to return here or at least that's what he told his mother and me."

"Do you know what his income was while he was in New Orleans?"

"No idea." I responded sticking to the pre inquisition lecture.

"Did he call home and ask for money very often?"

"Never."

"So he supported himself in New Orleans?"

"Correct."

"Did he talk to you, write you about—phone calls, letters, about what the work was like at Professional Divers?"

"Phone calls, he never wrote much. But he would call his mother and me every week or so. Generally any discussion we had, again, was like previous discussions, where I would have to ask many questions to get few answers and generally I would get comments about places he'd been, things he'd seen, experience he's had, and what opportunities he'd had, what sort of jobs he'd been on. He was always excited about going in the water. I only remember, oh, a half a dozen different dives that he told me that he was actually in the water on. And he took photographs and sent home photographs."

"What kind of photographs did he send?"

"Primarily of just things that he had seen. It might even be only a bird, or an oil well, or a drilling platform, a sun set, a friend or some new piece of equipment

that had caught his eye. He noticed all the little things and had a good eye for photography."

"At what point did he start discussing getting married to Julie?"

"There was never any discussion until he had come home for his great-grandmother's hundredth birthday."

"Whoa." responded the attorney not wanting to know Brian came from a family with longevity in their genes.

"He announced it at the birthday party."

"What did he say about the time frame for getting married, when he announced it at the grandmother's hundredth birthday?"

"That they would be getting married the following summer at about the same time."

Apparently his marriage was of little or no interest or perhaps that was to be covered by one of the other attorneys so the attention was changed to the night of the accident.

"How did you hear about the accident which happened?"

"Julie's mother came to our home that evening. I was in the kitchen preparing dinner, the door bell rang, Karen answered, Eunice asked that I join them, she need to talk to both of us together, she told us that Julie had called and Brian had been sent to the hospital after a work site accident."

"And what did y'all do?"

"I immediately got on the telephone, contacted the hospital. Was in an extended conversation with the doctor. He related what he knew of the injuries and was hopeful that Brian would recover. Karen at the same time used our second phone to remain in contact with Julie. During the conversation with the doctor he turned the phone over to a Father Donahue. At that same moment I could hear a woman screaming in the background over the phone. The hospital priest explained that Julie had just arrived, took her husband's hand and he died."

"Did you eventually go to Texas?"

"My wife and I left that evening, and were there the following morning."

"What investigation did you do yourself, I guess, into what happened?" Asked the man that already had been made aware of my activities.

"My interest was not to investigate, but rather to try and sort out my son's affairs, look to his wife and then bring our son home. That is until we received a call the morning after his death while at Brian's apartment in Houston. A call from an attorney telling us that we were to have no contact with Brian's employer but rather should direct all communications through her. She had been asked by G&G for assistance as they were not insured and that she and she alone should be our only contact. At that point I made an excuse to leave both Karen and Julie at the apartment telling them I was going out for coffee. Instead I headed to the nearest motel, obtained a room and started making calls. Frankly I found it hard to believe if this was an accident as we had been told that an attorney would

have been so quickly brought in and the comment about no insurance seemed inconceivable."

"Who was it that told you not to contact the employer?" asked the seemingly puzzled attorney.

"The woman who is listening on the phone right now, representing G&G Marine.

"And as far as you remember, that was Kena Seiler?"

"Absolutely. I have her business card, which she gave to me that afternoon, which I shouldn't call a business card. It was her name written on a scrap of yellow legal paper, which I still have."

"Did you ever get interviewed by the Coast Guard for a report of any kind?"

"No."

"Did you ever talk to any public officials about getting a Coast Guard report or anything?"

"Yes."

What did that entail?

"Basically bureaucratic buck-passing letters."

"Oh, so you wrote some letters?"

"Many."

"Many! And who were they to?"

"To Slade Gorton."

"Who?"

"United States Senator Slade Gorton. To both the senators in Texas, to Senator Patty Murray, United States Senator from Washington, to Jennifer Dunn, United States Congresswoman from Washington."

"What kind of answer did you get?"

"I was given the name of Coast Guard officials to contact,. It was limited—very, very limited response initially."

"Did you ever get a Coast Guard report?"

"I did."

"How long did it take to get it?"

"Thirteen months."

"Did one of the congressmen have to get it for you, or did they deliver it to you personally from the Coast Guard?"

"It came from—it was faxed from the Seattle office of the Coast Guard with a cover letter from Slade Gorton."

"And Slade Gorton's the congressman?"

"No, he is still a United States Senator."

"Senator. Okay. Did anybody ever give you any other reason for his death, other than drowning?"

"No."

"Did you ever discuss, maybe even at the time, when you were talking to the doctor on the phone, anything concerning the hospital's view of the medical condition, or . . . his death cause?

"No."

"Did you ever get a copy of the coroner's report, or the autopsy?"

"Through my attorney, yes."

And with that he was done.

"Well, I think I've covered most of the factual stuff that I have. I pass the witness. I'll let Mr. Siahatgar ask some more questions."

Without reintroducing himself the man with the somber look of that Grant Wood painting picked up where the man from the grandiose sounding firm with all the partners left off.

"You mentioned when you contacted, I believe, various U.S. senators and congressman, that you got phone numbers and names of various members of the Coast Guard. Did you ever talk to anybody at the U.S. Coast Guard?"

"Yes."

"Who would those people have been?"

"Initially a Lieutenant Blake Wellborn in Port Arthur, Texas. Later his commanding officer, whose name escapes me. I talked to a—the commander of Coast Guard investigations in Washington, D.C., whose name I don't recall and I've talked to a Lieutenant Commander Armstrong here in the Seattle office."

"What was it that you discussed with either one or all these individuals?"

"Incompetence. Their incompetence."

"What—?" responded a puzzled attorney.

"Dereliction of duty and the fact that I wanted charges of dereliction of duty brought against, in particular, Lieutenant Blake Wellborn in Texas."

"And for what reason was that ?"

"Failure to complete an investigation and mission of the Coast Guard—a violation of their own mission statement."

"What was it that in your opinion was the reason why you felt that Blake Wellborn was in violation of the Coast Guard's duties, or in dereliction of his own duty?"

"His failure to properly collect evidence, his failure to maintain a proper chain of custody, his failure to take statements from the people involved and his failure to conduct any investigation of any kind what so ever. A task he had been entrusted with and was either too incompetent to perform or so poorly trained did not understand."

"What was your basis for your belief that—or for the knowledge that you derived for believing that?"

"Initially, two days after Brian's death, I stopped into the offices of G&G Marine, contrary to the directions of Ms. Sellers, to find what I would have thought to be

evidence in the custody of any reasonably competent investigative agency. The compressor, the air lines, all the equipment in use the day of the incident. But instead there it all was spread on a warehouse floor a hundred miles from the accident scene. Personally I collected what belonged to my son eventually turning it over to an attorney for safe keeping. I would have expected to have at least found an investigator asking questions but instead found an attorney representing one of the defendants here behind a closed door interviewing a witness. Then some weeks later, I contacted the officer in charge of the investigation furnishing him with information regarding the compressor. He never followed up."

"And once you saw that, what else was there in addition to that fact which led you to believe that the Coast Guard's investigation was less than you had hoped?"

"Because as of today, they have still yet to visit the accident site, interview a single witness or actually inspect any of the equipment in use the day my son was killed."

"You mentioned that you spoke with a commander at the Coast Guard in the Washington, D.C. office. What in particular did he have in response to your inquiries?"

"He was going to pass it down the chain of command and assist me in finding those who might be able to assist me. He contacted me, by the way. I did not make the initial contact with him."

"And was that in response to various telephone calls, or letters you wrote, or was it in response to various other outside inquiries that were made to them?"

"I have no way of knowing why he contacted me but I suspect it may have been as a result of a letter sent to Bill Clinton."

'Bill Clinton! And what was the nature of your letter to Bill Clinton?"

"It was a personal letter, basically one father to another, asking how he would have felt and what he would do in the same situation, with—after, I believe at that time, eight months, and no response. What would he do, where would he turn if his child was lost while working under the watchful eye of a United States Inspection team and another United States investigative unit had been entrusted with finding the truth, nothing was done."

"How long was it after your letter to Bill Clinton before you got a phone call from the commander in U.S. Coast Guard?"

"About eight days."

"When you contacted these other people lower down the chain of command, did you get any answers?"

"No. I have not gotten anything that I would consider to be an answer."

"What type of answer is it that you were looking for, or that you would have considered—well, I guess what you were looking for?"

"Simple, I just want to know what really happened."

"Have you ever spoken to an individual named Kevin Lawdermilk?"

"Yes."

"What was the nature of your discussion with Mr. Lawdermilk?"

"About six months ago Mr. Lawdermilk had written me a letter telling me that it was imperative that I get in contact with him. I did. He told me he was a diver, a dive supervisor working for G&G Marine. On the night of the incident he had driven to Port Arthur to pick up Dan Wiitala, the backup diver, and bring him home. In addition, two days later, he delivered the compressor that had been used the day of the dive to a machine shop in Houston. And then several days later told to pick the unit up, by Dan Gilbert, and make it into a million pieces."

"Was Kevin Lawdermilk employed by G&G Marine at that point, when he called you, or wrote you that letter?"

"I don't know, I didn't ask I just forwarded the information along to the investigating officer for the Coast Guard in Port Arthur?"

"Other than the matter with regard to the compressor, was there anything else that Kevin Lawdermilk discussed with you related to the incident in question?"

"He told me that a second diver on board the vessel that day was not a diver, and he told me that G&G Marine never serviced their equipment."

"Did you do any independent investigation to follow up on any of those comments?"

"I sent a fax the following day to the United States Coast Guard in Port Arthur, followed by a phone call to Lt. J. G. Blake Wellborn."

"Have you heard anything from the Coast Guard since then?"

"Wellborn claimed he could not find an address or phone number for McKenzie in Houston, the place Lawdermilk claimed to have taken the compressor for repair. Subsequently, I called information, found the number and passed it along."

"Have you learned anything from any source other than the Coast Guard, any information in response to that?"

"I have not."

"Have you ever attempted to contact the Association of Diving Contractors?"

"Yes."

"Who did you contact?"

"A few days after Brian's funeral, I contacted their executive director, a fellow by the name of Ross Saxon, sorry, Dr. Ross Saxon. As I was to find some weeks later, he was the only employee of the Association of Diving Contractors other than a secretary. I contacted him as my preliminary research had indicated G&G was a member of his association and that the association not only had standards all members agreed to follow but in the event of an incident such as this they would conduct their own independent investigation."

"And did you receive any other verbal information from the Association of Diving Contractors, or any of their employees or representatives when you contacted them?"

"Yes, and well actually some days after my initial contact Dr. Saxon informed me that he would be unable to discuss anything further with me, and turned

me over to a fellow in Rhode Island who was scheduled to conduct the supposed investigation. I called him, had a brief discussion and received a promises of a return phone call. He never did."

"Did Dr. Saxon tell you why he could not discuss the matter with you?"

"Actually he did. Apparently, Dr. Saxon was instrumental in writing G&G Marine's Safety manual while working for them as an employee. Something he had done prior to accepting his position with the Association of Diving Contractors. As a result he felt that might put him in a conflict of interest position, that and the fact he was a 30 percent owner of G&G. Something he had failed to mention initially. So I sent him $35 for the copy of the "Diving Consensus," the Association of Diving Contractors safety standard so to speak, which he sent. I then contacted—had the single discussion with the fellow in Rhode Island who was suppose to conduct the investigation and he was going to contact me. He never did."

"And you received the, what's it called Diving Consensus? The standard Association of Diving Contractors manual that you mentioned?

"I did."

"You don't consider yourself an expert on diving, do you?"

"Absolutely not."

"What did you glean from your review of this document, if anything?"

"Essentially their regulations that they ask to be followed by all members are essentially the same as the OSHA regulations and the United States Coast Guard regulations. They merely copied them. Inserting a few additional items but leaving out many of what you I might call just plain common sense things. Neither the Coast Guard, OSHA or the Diving Consensus require things as basic as a backup diver, backup air systems or for that matter any sort of standard of training or certification of divers. Something basic to the recreational community but overlooked for the working diver. I by no means am an expert but to me it is unconscionable that such basic safety is not addressed in the current standards."

"Have you ever been in contact with a McKenzie Company?"

"I have."

"When, about, was that?"

"The morning I—or the morning after—talked to Kevin Lawdermilk. He had given me the name of McKenzie. I had turned that over to the Coast Guard. The Coast Guard told me they had no knowledge or no way of contacting such a company unless I could get them additional information. This goes back to my incompetence theory. I picked up my phone, dialed information, asked for McKenzie's in Houston, and was immediately given the phone number. I called them, told them who I was, told them the information I was after, and that they would be contacted by the Coast Guard. And then I turned that information over to the Coast Guard the same day."

"Turning back to the Coast Guard briefly, in your various letters to the Coast Guard, to the president of the United States, and to your senators, have you ever—what

146

type of—strike that. With regard to the Coast Guard, what in particular did you want to have done either to the Coast Guard or with regard to the report that, in your opinion, was never done?"

"My primary interest was that they, in fact, conduct a proper investigation, that they level the proper fines and penalties that could be normally expected for the violations that to me were so apparent."

"Is it your opinion, sitting here today, still, that the Coast Guard did not conduct a proper investigation?"

"It is my opinion that the United States Coast Guard has not conducted any investigation at all. They have never interviewed a single witness, taken a single statement, never examined the crime site, never inspected or had the inspection of the equipment utilized the day of the incident or even questioned any of their own personnel that were on site at the time."

"Did you ever, at any time, threaten the Coast Guard, either directly or indirectly, or want to take any type of legal action against the Coast Guard?"

"I have not threatened legal action against the Coast Guard, no. I have asked for my Senator to turn the matter over to the Justice Department for their review."

"Did y'all ever try to discourage Brian from being a diver, in view of the fact that it's a dangerous profession?"

"Quite to the contrary. I'm a general contractor. The labor and industry rates here in the State of Washington for professional divers are, in fact, lower than that for a carpenter. It's a very safe profession when it's done properly and the rules are followed. Or at least that's the way I perceived it at the time Brian was alive."

"Do you feel that the job wasn't done properly when Brian's accident took place?"

"My personal opinion?"

"Yes." responded the man in the three hundred dollar shirt.

"Absolutely done wrong."

"What was your personal opinion of what was done wrong that day?"

"Failure to maintain safety records, failure to have a safety—or an evacuation plan, an emergency plan, all regulated by law. And I'm quoting from my own experience as a contractor, what I would be required to do here in Washington State. The simple posting of a Safety Plan. They did not even have an emergency phone number to call—no phone number for the nearest hospital. It was not until my son's near lifeless body was on the deck that afternoon that someone even thought of asking around if anyone knew who to call. An hour before Brian first called to the surface for assistance the U.S. Coast Guard had cited the vessel for not having a safety manual or evacuation plan. What the hell were they even doing out there twelve miles from shore with no plan? And why where they allowed to continue on with the work? If that had been here, in this State the job site would have been shut down, personnel removed to a safe location until and only until there was a functioning plan of safety and evacuation plan. Then there

was the simple matter of testing of equipment and the required record keeping. Perhaps had the compressor, you know that piece of equipment no one can now find, had been tested in accordance with United States regulations none of us would be here today."

"That's based on your personal review of the documents?"

"Yes, from what I have obtained so far."

"You've mentioned various documents right now. Have you kept a file of all these documents? Have you retained copies of all these letters you've gotten, and the letters that you've sent?"

"Of course, yes, I have."

And then finally a question directed to someone other than me. "David, I'd like to make a formal request now for copies of all these documents, a formal request for production. So—"

From my left came the slow and deliberate response. "Send me a letter and I'll respond."

"Well, I'm making a formal request on the record right now, which I guess is the equivalent."

"I'll consider any request in writing." retorted the man from Beaumont in an attempt to have whatever rules were still under his control adhered to. The men with the monogrammed three hundred dollar shirt rolled his eyes, noted the need to write yet another request for disclosure and continued his questioning.

"I understand now. Do you have any personal opinion as to acts or omissions that you believe my client, Cliff's Drilling Company, engaged in connection with your son's incident?

"Do I have an opinion?"

"Yes, your own personal opinion, What would that be?

"My opinion would be based on that of as an employer with twenty-five years experience who is responsible for the subcontractors and employees that I employ. Responsible to see that they are all properly insured, follow certain minimum standards of safety, possess a safety manual and conduct themselves in a safe, professional manner. It is my job as the employer, at least here in the State of Washington, to see that their work place is maintained in a manner which is in compliance with the laws and regulations governing my place of business. Further if I were to find an employee or subcontractor not following the standards as established it would be my responsibility to terminate their employment or invalidate their contract. It is the overall responsibility of the owner, the prime contractor to maintain a safe work place. Your client violated that trust and must be held accountable."

Possibly hearing all he needed to about responsibility, the subject was changed.

"Do you agree with Julie's assessment of Brian, that he was a relatively fiscally frugal individual?"

Without hesitation I continued *"He had little or no regard for how much money he had, or what he possessed, or what he owned, just so long as whatever he had was neat, tidy, clean, well maintained, and cared for—perhaps there was a personal touch he had added to make it better than it was before. It mattered little how much the car cost just so long as it was clean and freshly polished. He cared little how much he earned but rather cared that those around him thought he had done a good job. That's the way he was. He was never—I hate to expound, but you kept asking about the discussions we had about his employment. We would never discuss his employment. We would discuss things he had done, not how he felt about the people he worked with, but what he had done and what he had experienced. That's the way he was. Money was not important to him. It was his experiences which were important to him. He would never tell me how much he was making but rather tell me how he had made something better than it had been."*

"So basically having fun?" said the attorney while looking for another question on the list.

"I don't know that it's having fun—not a matter of having fun at all. To him having fun might be having a shiny car. To Brian, having a good time might be having a well-pressed shirt and a neat tie."

"Whose idea was it to seek representation in this matter? responded the attorney finding his next question.

"Mine." I replied slipping back to the one word response rule.

"And what are you suing for?" asked the Attorney in search for a bottom line.

There was no question that he was asking how much money were we seeking for our loss for from his perspective this was obviously what this was all about. We were not here to right some wrong or find a way to prevent similar tragedies we were here to see how much this was going to cost their respective clients. But my thoughts were not of monitory compensation.

"What are we suing for? We are suing for the son we will never see grow older, the grandchildren we will never know, the Thanksgivings that will never be the same, for that place at the family table that can never be filled. We are suing on behalf of the man that can no longer represent himself in an effort to prevent your collective clients from continuing to operate an unsafe work place"

And with that my questioning for the day was over. Karen would be next, Brian's mother did not need to be here and she certainly would have nothing that would be of value to these men from Texas except contribute to Brian's value. For truly that's what this was all about. How much was he worth? How much would their clients have to pay?

Karen's inquisition was stated by Bijan Siahatgar representing Cliffs Drilling with all the normal formalities. Name, place of residence, employment whether she understood that she could take a break at anytime but could not talk to anyone during her questioning. This was followed by questions about her relationship with her son. How many times did they talk while he was not living at home. Did she call him? Did he call her? Questions about his employment at Professional Divers of New Orleans. Did he like it there? Did he like his job? All answered with as few words as possible.

"What were your thoughts when he moved to Louisiana?"

"I didn't like it, he was my oldest child, the first one to leave the nest and Brian loved being home. but he liked working at Professional Divers, they were good to him."

"Did you ever have any conversations with him about why he moved home in 1995."

"Because he wanted to come home and make wedding arrangements with Julie for their wedding in August."

"We have already talked to your husband at length about how you heard of the accident and what happened and you didn't do anything differently than your husband?

When you were in Houston did you go out to G&G Marine?"

"No."

"I take it that you personally did not do any of the type of investigation or the type of inquiries that your husband engaged in, or did you do any of that type of stuff on your own?"

"No, I didn't do anything on my own he did it all."

"When you were in Houston, do you remember what you and Julie talked about?"

"No, not really, it was all a blur; we talked about the accident, the night in the hospital, we just sat. We just cried together, that's all."

"You have two other children how has this effected them."

"Afton was in the third grade when Brian died, she lost that whole year, retained nothing—"

"—and your middle son?"

"Jamie, he is a strong young man he would tell you he's fine."

"What do you think?"

"I think there are things Jamie cannot handle and he doesn't want to face. For instance he drives Brian's truck with Louisiana licenses plates. He has the Washington plates, he can't bring himself to change them. Jamie's Birthday is Christmas eve, he did not want to celebrate either this year. I mean does that give you some sort of clue as to his ability to deal with his brother's death?"

"Has he graduated from college yet?"

"He has with a bachelor's degree in biology from the University of Puget Sound, in the fall he will be starting his graduate work at New York Medical College."

Now the attorney quickly changed from the over achieving brother that would do little to diminish Brian's value and turned to a series of question regarding what

Brian's plans for the future had been. All answered appropriately with no or I have no knowledge.

Then more questions about his wedding, relationships with friends, money problems and again all appropriately answered with "**I don't know,**" or just "**no.**"

And then the question from the man in the expensive shirt. "What type of relationship did Brian have with his siblings?"

Without a pause Karen, responded, "**With Jamie, they were becoming very good friends. They were two and a half years apart, so they did everything that young boys separated by two and a half years do. They argued, they fought, they competed. They were two totally different people, Jamie and Brian, but they were in Brian**'s **own words 'I'm the good looking one, Jamie is the smart one and I guess we will just have to learn to live with that.' And as they got older they spent more and more time together. Brian would go to Jamie's college football games, carrying his sister on his shoulders. They spent their last summer together building an addition on their grandfather**'s **house during the day and enjoying each other**'s **company at night after work. They finally had become more than brothers. They were friends.**

And as far as Afton goes, Brain was the one she would seek out when she need to be consoled, Brian was the one that could talk to her, read to her. He enjoyed doing things with her. Afton had two brothers and two different relationships but Brian was the one she was closest to."

Yet another dead end, so the attorney tried a new line of questioning. "Your husband has some opinion as to what the various parties may or may not, or did or did not do wrong. Do you have any personal opinions of that sort?"

Not a smart question but answered as best a mother could.

"**The only opinion I have is that they let my son die. They did not do all that they could have done to help him. They put my son in the water with equipment that was—that we found out malfunctioned, despite the best efforts to conceal the facts. That's my opinion, I have nothing else.**"

"Mrs. Pilkington, I also asked your husband earlier about what he's claiming for in the lawsuit, the damages you have suffered in this case as a result of the incident?"

Again he was asking about monetary damage, a dollar figure, a bottom line but then referred to the death of her son as an incident. Karen answered:

"The damages I suffered, I can't explain the damage I suffered. There isn't a day that goes by I don't think about my son, the things we should have had that we now never will, the things my children should have had and never will. I have lost a lot of people in my life and there is nothing, nothing worse than losing a child."

And with that the attorney from Texas with the expensive shirt and the expression of the father in the Grant Wood painting said, "I pass the witness."

With that the deposition was concluded. Certain rules of decorum were followed, closing technicalities observed.

The lady with the flowered dress, as efficiently as she had begun the day, set to dismantling her array of mechanical tools. Each component returned to its specified compartment or case, each tape and cassette dutifully inserted into an appropriate sleeve. The lawyers from Houston stuffed their individual leather briefcases with the file they had brought along with the few bits of paper containing the fruits of a day questionably spent. David and I engaged in conversation, Julie and Karen again headed for the safety of the companionway.

Once all was packed each participant that had not already done so headed for the conference room doors. The man from the Grant Wood painting paused momentarily, looked to me and said. "Let me express my condolences, for the lost of your son." And then turned to complete his escape. "Bijan!" I called as he turned the knob, "Thank you, and enjoy the balance of your stay here in Seattle."

He turned back, opening a passage for the court reporter who now had made her way to the exit armed with her neatly assembled tools in tow, and said "Mr. Pilkington, I'll not be staying. I'm going directly to the airport, home and spending some time with my family." All said as he pulled open the door to permit the woman and her burden to pass. As the until now-silent women passed through the portal she turned to these men from Texas and said, "Nice worken for y'all and thanks for the new word for my spell checker." All said with a smile as she turned and completed her exit.

Bijan turned to his associate from Hill, Rivkins, Losberg, O'Brian, Mulroy, and Hayded and exchanged a puzzled look. David laughed.

Chapter 13

SETTLEMENT HEARING

It was just before Thanksgiving 1997 when the call came in from Provost Umphrey. We should begin making plans to return to Beaumont. The system required that we submit to a nonbinding mediation. Both sides would present their case in the presence of a court appointed mediator. It would then be his job to sort through the arguments each side would render and try to get all parties to agree avoiding what could be a long and costly trial.

Two weeks later Julie, Karen and I traveled back to Texas, meeting Aunt Beth in the Houston airport. Beth was my youngest sister closer in age to my son than to me and had she flown in from her home in New York. Aunt Beth was eight years old when Brian was born and had grown up with him more as a big sister then his aunt. She was here armed only with a copy of the video she had made from old family photos she had assembled while Karen and I had been in Texas eighteen months before arranging to bring Brian home that last time. Armed with that video and a sense that she would need to be there to comfort her sister-in-law as well as the wife of her "little brother." She needed to know what had happened, why had Brian's life been cut so short, who were these men who allowed this to happen? Karen knew little, Julie less, Beth next to nothing of what had transpired on March 4, 1996. I had attempted to keep them all protected from the speculation, the half truths, the pain of the ongoing investigations both civil and United States Coast Guard. Two investigations: one centered on rendering money from those responsible the other on finding the truth.

Together we drove to Beaumont finding a hotel close to the offices of Provost Umphrey. David Brandom had cautioned us that the next day would be a long one, starting with all parties assembling early the following morning to present their respective cases. Then each side would be sequestered away in individual rooms.

Those representing Cliffs Drilling, The American Bureau of Shipping and G&G Marine would go to one room. The Pilkington Family would go to another. Kirk Austin would not be there nor would he have any representation. He had refused to participate instead electing to seek protection from his obligations. This time he would declare bankruptcy rather than just saying, "I'm done with this" as he did twenty months before while serving as the "backup diver" or was he the dive supervisor?

As the appointed hour neared Julie, Karen, Beth, David Brandom and I filed into that conference room in the offices of Provost Umphrey where Julie had signed the papers two days after Brian's passing. Already at their seats were the two men that had been in Seattle to take our depositions five months earlier; Dana Martian, representing the American Bureau of Shipping and Bijan Siahatgar, Cliffs Drilling. Joining them would be Ruben Hope replacing the woman with no business card that had also been at the depositions but only by phone, representing Dan Gilbert of G&G Marine and a local attorney who looked strangely like Ed Bradley from *60 Minutes* who had been hired in the event a jury would need to be selected. A local attorney whose job it would be to see that only the correct individuals would be allowed to serve.

Sitting across from us, each attorney was dressed in a dark suit, all armed with their individual leather bound day timer with cell phone carefully perched atop. They presented a formidable front.

At the head of the table sat M. A. "Mickey" Mills who had been in the pool of court provided mediators from which the two sides were to make their selection. Mickey had made the cut and as we were finding our seats he continued searching through the documents spread about the green monolith table in front of him. Beth claimed the seat to his right, I sat to her right, Karen to my right with Julie between Karen and David.

At the appointed hour, 9:30, Mickey looked up, gathered the documents in a neat pile and start explaining to all of us his part in of this. This mediation was not binding but it would be our last chance to settle. We should all consider each other's positions, weigh the value of our own and attempt to reach an agreement. Only 2 percent of civil actions ever make it to court, most are settled here in mediation. This would be our only opportunity to avoid a trial and then his sage advice; settle this here today, move on with your lives.

The men seated across from us had heard the lecture before, many times before, along with David. Julie, Karen, Beth and I were hearing this for the first time. As I listened I watched the men across the table, all appeared to be listening, preparing for their opportunity to speak, all that is but "Ed Bradley" the local hired gun who was pushed back from the table reading the newspaper.

David would go first. He started by laying out the facts in a soft yet firm voice. Standing at the head of the table opposite Mickey, David laid out his case on a twenty-four-by-thirty-six-inch sheet of news print suspended from a three legged easel for all to see. He started with the events of March 4 and as he unfolded his story his voice increased filling with anger and commitment. He related how it was not just one incident that lead to Brian's killing it was a series of events as most accidents are. There was the weather, the missing equipment, faulty equipment, empty air tanks, no prudent backup safety equipment, a safety manager more concerned with a bottom line then the task he had been assigned. There was no safety plan, no evacuation plan, no plan of any kind. The cowardly and incompetent Kirk Austin not only misrepresented his ability but was uninsured. And then there were the questions still unanswered. Just why was American Oilfield Divers with their six man crew, two compressors, three umbilicals and four standby tanks sent to shore on the day of the ill fated job. Why if it only took Wiitala two or three minutes to get to Brian did they wait almost forty five? Why was the compressor never function tested? Where is the compressor? Dan Gilbert had not only falsified documentation, he had destroyed evidence. Gilbert had committed perjury. As David continued he became more and more angry as he laid out the short coming, the indifference, the lack of compassion. Finally he stated "This case is not about money, it is about justice."

With that he presenting Aunt Beth's video on a monitor standing next to the easel, Aunt Beth's video depicting Brian's life from birth to just before his passing, a video that had been condensed from its original thirty-five minutes to nine minutes ten seconds. All the time "Ed Bradley" continued reading the newspaper.

Then in turn each of the attorneys representing the defendants presented their case. Brian was responsible not their clients. No one made him go in the water: he knew the risk. He knew there was no backup equipment, no one held him under water. He, Brian, was the person who had the best chance to save himself. The American Bureau of Shipping was there to inspect the vessel not oversee the safety of the diving operation. G&G Marine was working as a subcontractor to Kirk Austin, G&G had been misled, they believed Austin would be supplying additional divers. Cliffs Drilling had relied on Austin to provide the proper personnel and equipment, they had done their part as required, participating in the rescue attempt. They too had been misled by Kirk Austin. It was Kirk Austin that had signed a contract verifying he was properly insured when in fact he had no insurance at all. It was Brian that was responsible to save himself. Surely a jury would see it that way.

With that, "Ed Bradley" folded his newspaper, pulled himself back to the table and presented the facts as he perceived them. First he had been hired by the defense to assist in jury selection. He knew the good people of Jefferson County, of Beaumont Texas. They are all good hardworking people, all had their own lives, their own hardships. They would not be moved by a video depicting the life of a middle-class boy growing up in an affluent community in faraway Washington State. Brian was a young strong man perfectly capable of swimming twenty-eight feet and saving himself. These men that had hired him to help select a jury were here to settle this today. Listen to what they have to offer and go home, go home to Washington State and get on with your lives. With that he returned to his seat and the news of the day.

The four of us guided by David left the grandiose conference room and moved to a smaller room with no windows. A small table, the appropriate number of comfortable chairs, a row of coffee cups complete with saucers, and a thermos of freshly brewed coffee awaited. We were there for the day at it would prove to be a long one.

Mickey would come and go four times. Each time with an offer or financial remuneration higher than the previous. The first three offers in turn accepted by Julie, then rejected by me. After each rejection Mickey would sit and discuss some other case he had mediated, most involving some horrific oil patch fatality, some maiming of an otherwise healthy oil field worker or some birth defect inflicted on some child who's only guilt was the proximity of the parents home to some oil processing facility. Each story told so that an appropriate amount of time would be allowed to pass before returning for the next offer of settlement. The first offer was half of the average paid to other commercial diver's dependents or sixty-six thousand dollars. Not only half the standard as the men in the other room believed Brian was at fault and a jury would certainly see it that way but the amount was divisible by three. That would make it easier for everyone. One third to the attorney, two thirds to the plaintiffs.

The second offer was twice the first, again accepted by Julie, rejected by me. This was a Jones's Act case, a death on the high seas. The dependent or dependents of a seaman that dies at sea are entitled to an amount equal to his or her earning potential for the rest of what could have been an expected life. Brian was young, his earning potential for the next forty-two years had been calculated to be over two million dollars, the offer of 132 thousand although more than the standard price paid to the dependents of divers that had the misfortune to die at work would not be accepted. More stories of horrific accidents before Mickey made his way back to tell stories to the other side for the appropriate length of time.

Lunch was delivered, no one ate. A third offer came and a third offer rejected. This time with an explanation from me to deliver to those men in the other room. It was not their money that we wanted it, it was their assistance in the creation of a safer workplace, a commitment to assisting in the creation of new diver standards. Help us to convince federal regulators that there need to be requirements for backup divers, backup equipment, diver training. kept the Kirk Austins of the world on the beach, the Dan Gilberts of the world unemployable, help us to achieve the goal that I had committed the family to in our son's eulogy. "Prevent this from happening to another."

Mickey looked puzzled. "You don't understand, this is about money."

There were more stories before Mickey returned to the four attorneys sequestered down the hall. The day was growing old, the sandwiches still wrapped in waxed paper were beginning to stain the conference table top when Mickey returned with the last and final offer: 1.2 million. That was their final offer and that was the maximum the boys in the other room were authorized to go.

Julie did not have the opportunity to reject this one. Quiet until that moment Brian's mother rose to her feet. Looked down at the little man with all the stories. *"Perhaps you have not been paying attention. We are not here for the money we are here to make a difference. If this is just to be about the money then give us enough to make the difference without the help of the boys in the other room. If that is the best they are authorized to do perhaps they should have sent the men who could have."*

With that Karen headed for the door, the rest of us followed. The chance to settle in Beaumont was over.

A week later David Brandom called me at my Bellevue, Washington office. The final offer was now the maximum amount that the Jones Act would allow. An amount equal to Brian's potential earnings for the rest of his projected life. Projected life if he had never worked for Dan Gilbert and had Brian been allowed to work for the next forty two years.

Chapter 14

PROVOST UMPHREY

JANUARY 21, 1998

Karen and I sat together in the lobby of Provost Umphrey for what we had hoped might be our last reason to ever have to be there. David Brandom had asked us to come to the office to pick up three checks and to sign releases. The releases would protect Cliffs Drilling, The American Bureau of Shipping and Dan Gilbert from any further legal action as it pertained to the events of March 4, 1996, and the death of our son. We would also need to sign away Jamie and Afton's rights to do the same. In addition, we would need to sign an agreement not to divulge the amount of the settlement. Once all was properly signed, notarized and recorded the three checks would be released to us. A fourth check had been made out to Julie who was not with us. We had not seen Julie since the night after the settlement amount had been agreed to; in fact, we would never see her again.

Sitting in the all too elegant office there was an overweight man with a rumpled sport coat who also appeared to be waiting to be admitted to the inner offices. After a reasonable time had passed he had made another enquiry of the woman at the desk and then returned to a seat close to mine. There were just the three of us waiting and the woman far across the room attending to her duties in the early-morning hours as the office had just opened. Karen and I were early; David Brandom had not arrived yet. The inquisitive man turned to me, "Are you here about the Tobacco Settlement?" I responded that we were not, but interested in passing the time explained that I knew nothing of a tobacco suit perhaps he could explain. For the next twenty minutes he told me that just the day before Walter Umphrey, Provost Umphrey, had along with four other Texas firms successfully negotiated fourteen billion dollar settlement with the tobacco industry on behalf of the people of Texas. The lawyers share would be one point two billion and he was there in an attempt to interview Walter. He did not have an appointment, but as a reporter for the largest paper in Texas surely someone other than me would be willing to grant him an interview.

I assured him there was nothing in my power that would get him past that front desk; but if he were interested in a story of far less monetary significance and had lots of time, I had a story for him. We talked for a few moment, filled him in on a few details of what had happened and why we were waiting with him that morning. With that the woman who been sitting at the front desk approached letting me know David could see us now. I turned to the impatient man who now would be alone in the lobby, handed him my business card. "Call me if you need a story and have a few hours to listen." You can reach me at the cell number or at the Holiday Inn, Port Arthur, across from the Marine Safety Office.

Our meeting with David was brief, they were still waiting for documents from Cliffs that we would need to sign. Perhaps we could return tomorrow; he would call.

Just after 5:00 that afternoon the hotel room phone rang. It was Richard Steward, the reporter from the *Houston Chronicle*, the man that had not been able to get by the front desk at Provost Humphrey earlier that morning. He was down at the hotel bar, would I care to join him.

Together we sat at a small table away from the noise of the normally busy lounge. I related the story of a young man growing up, his family, his experience, my desire to see that he would not be remembered only as a statistic. He should not be remembered as an inexperienced boy who through his own carelessness lost his life. In the morning my wife and I would be entering the office of an attorney and would be required to sign a nondisclosure statement in order to assure that funds would be available to pay for our son's siblings to complete their college educations. This discussion would be my last opportunity to share the facts of the events aboard the Cliffs 12.

We talked for hours and for the first time someone actually listened. He took notes, I talked, the crowd in the lounge thinned until there were just the three of us remaining. The reporter, a father relating a story and the man behind the bar polishing the last of the glasses before closing up for the night.

Outside a storm was raging. Hail pounded the metal roof of the building. I raised my voice to be heard. The power went out. I continued to speak oblivious that we were now in a darkened room illuminated only by the backup battery lantern that had been activated over the entry door. The bartender approached with a candle and another round of drinks. I continued Brian's story in the half-light, and Richard Steward listened to every word.

The following morning Karen and I returned to Provost Umphrey, the agreements were there ready to be signed. David had made a few revisions. There were also three checks. One made out in trust to Brian's sister in an amount that would, if properly invested, pay for her college studies. The second made out to Brian's brother in an amount equal to the sister's meant to pay for his graduate school education. The third made out to Karen in an amount equal to our expenses to date. We had mortgaged the house to pay the costs we had incurred over the past twenty-two months. This check would make us financially whole, nothing would ever make us emotionally the same, nothing would bring back our son.

Together we drove in silence from Beaumont to Hobby field just north of Houston. Karen would be returning to Seattle, I was heading back to Port Arthur and the United States Coast Guard Marine Safety office.

With no appointment I asked to speak with Lieutenant Plagge, the investigating officer that had written the narrative of the events aboard the Cliffs 12. The officer who had determined that Brian had died after disconnecting his air hose, panicking and then drowning. The man who had determined that the only culpability of anyone else were the three paperwork violations involving improper record keeping. Capable of determining all the facts in the case without ever interviewing a single witness, without visiting the accident site, without collecting any evidence and without any diving or industry knowledge.

He granted me twenty minutes of his time. I pointed out a few facts that might have gone unnoticed along with several USCG regulations far more serious that should have been considered. There was the requirement that compressors supplying breathing air be tested as required by CFR 197.450-197.340. Gilbert had admitted he never had the compressors tested. Perhaps that was overlooked because his predecessor, Lt. J. G. Blake Wellborn had failed to maintain custody of the compressor. Had the lieutenant considered the actions or lack of action by the person in charge as described in CFR 197.450-197.402?

There was mention in the official USCG report that it was a three man dive team. In fact had the Lieutenant asked a few questions it would have soon been evident that the third member of the team, the dive supervisor was in fact not a diver at all. In addition, the written statements supplied to the USCG indicated that Brian was receiving air at 80 PSI. Basic industry knowledge or a bit of research would have shown that it would require a minimum of 120 PSI for the helmet to function properly, ventilating the diver.

After my twenty minutes were expired, he suggested that perhaps I should speak to his superior, Captain Fels. If I had information that they had not been privileged to perhaps he, the captain in charge, could order a second investigation or at least a review.

The captain listened intently. I left him with depositions that had been taken under oath to supplement the statements that had originally been given to Justice John Borne over the phone. Expert testimony that had been assembled for the civil trial that was now no longer necessary. I suggested that even though it was approaching two years since the "incident" that they might consider actually interviewing witnesses. Interview not just the two people with the most to conceal but witnesses that were not involved. After all there were forty seven men out there, surely someone else saw what happened. He thanked me for my concern and wished me a safe return to Washington.

I left the Marine safety office knowing that at least two officers of the United States Coast Guard had clean desks and that most assuredly they would stay that way. Driving south I found my way to the offshore service docks, then to the Cliffs staging area along the Sabine River. There were mammoth jack up rigs under repair. Some being dismantled others being assembled. I sat and watched the men working, burning and welding, bolting and fastening, making yet another tool of commerce so important in our oil dependent economy. I paused for a while and watched. It had been a long few days. As I watched I feel asleep and remained sitting behind the wheel until the sun came up the following morning.

I then found my way to Saint Mary's Hospital just a few miles South West. Walking with no direction up one hallway and then down another feeling some comfort that at last I had come to the place where Brian had spent his last hour of life. Looking for a place to sit and be alone I found my way to the chapel, choosing a seat near the back of the empty room. There were the mandatory statues you would expect to see and candles, lots of candles in this solemn, dimly lit room. While I sat, one person after another would walk in from the door to my right, kneel for a moment, continue to the front of the space, light a candle, pause for a few moments and then exit through the door they had just entered. No one stayed long.

I remained alone sometimes watching the comings and goings but mostly reflecting on the occurrences of the past twenty-two months. A man dressed in black entered, kneeled for a moment, made the sign of the cross and chose a seat next to mine.

Introducing himself as Father Don Donahue, chaplin for Saint Mary's, was there anything that I needed, someone to talk to perhaps. I responded, we had talked once before almost two years before. He had been on the phone with me the night Brian passed away. He remembered the night. I talked and again someone listened. I told him of the night almost two years before and what I now believed to have happened. He told me of his remembrances of the night and how there had been so many nights like that here at Saint Mary's. He was pleased that I had shared Brian's story. "I see so many come in never to leave and almost never know why."

Leaving the chapel I made my way back to the Holiday Inn at Port Arthur finding a seat at the empty bar. It was a Saturday night. The businessman had all returned to their homes, no one vacations in Port Arthur. The bartender made his way over to his only client to inquire about my drink of choice.

"Beer, what do you have on tap?" I asked. "Budweiser and then we have Budweiser or Budweiser," he responded with a chuckle. Now for a man from the Northwest where every town, every village has its own special brew, it's own micro brewed beer with a distinctive character and flavor unique to itself, it caused me to pause. "How about a Budweiser?"

As he poured the first of many he asked if I had been one of the two men that had been sitting over at the corner table two nights before when the light went out. I confirmed I was. Than questions of what was keeping me in this little backwater town on a Saturday night. I explained that I was there on Coast Guard business or at least attempting to get the USCG to pay attention to my plea for assistance. The man I had been talking with was with the Chronicle, perhaps if the Coast Guard would not hear the story his readers would.

The friendly man with control of the intoxicating liquid smiled a half smile and replied, "The Coast Guard, you mean the big dog with no teeth. You are not the first to be sitting in that seat and I suspect you will not be the last that has come in here with a tale about those boys." Said as he surveyed the empty room seeing we were still alone. Apparently not only were the beer selections different in Washington but also the rules pertaining to bartenders. He reached into the cooler and pulled out a frosty glass, drew a beer while telling me stories that had been related to him over the years. Together we worked at draining his remaining keg of Budweiser as I told him stories of a boy growing up, his adventures, the man that he had become, my challenges with the men in the Marine Safety Office while he told me stories of injustices, inaction and incompetence by the boys across the street or the "puddle pirates" as he called them. Their officers moved from one posting to another. Posted eighteen months here, eighteen months there; never allowed to gain expertise and armed only with regulations so poorly conceived they were all but unenforceable. The old salts would also sit at his bar and relate stories of how easy it was to avoid inspections and investigations by simply answering what was asked, volunteer nothing. "You can't find what you don't know," Industry writes the rules, the boys across the street just follow them.

We talked for hours, more stories, more frustrations. Talked until the lights went out but this time because Jim would turn them off. It was closing time, time for us to go home.

The following morning February 1, 1998, I was back at Hobby Field waiting for the morning flight back to Seattle and home. It had been a few long days and a very rough night.

Next to me on an unoccupied seat at the gate was a copy of the Sunday edition of the *Houston Chronicle*. There on the front page was an all too familiar picture. A picture of my son, taken on the day of his wedding three years before. Followed by a story entitled "Troubled Waters."[1] Perhaps the United States Coast Guard was not listening but Richard Steward had. This was one story that had now escaped Jim's bar at the Holiday Inn.

I read the story, devoured every word. Most of it was accurate, some of it disturbing. Richard had interviewed Lieutenant Plagge. The Lieutenant was quoted as saying, "Coast Guard dive experts told him divers are trained to notice the warning signs of carbon dioxide problems or contaminated air. You'll taste it."

Strange as the Coast Guard did not have any diving experts, they use the navy experts, so who was he referring to? Who was it that had the ability to "taste" carbon dioxide. Perhaps the Lieutenant had been out sick for that class in sixth-grade science.

As I read, I thought back to that young man who twenty-one years before had pulled out a box of onions. Pushed it up against that electronic gizmo; used that box filled with onions to gain a perch from which he could obtain the stature required to protect us that night. Protect us from the hazards none of the men of authority that surround him could see.

Brian knew nothing of ships, navigation, rules of the sea, he only knew someone need to care. He was a novice, but he could see someone had to make a difference that night twenty-one years before. Like my son before me I had found my box of onions. If the Coast Guard would not listen, if the legal system needed to conceal the facts, I would need some other way to attain the stature required to make Brian's story heard. And here it was sitting on that vacated seat next to me that Sunday morning in Houston's airport. Take the story to the media.

Chapter 15

PORT ARTHUR, TEXAS

Two months had passed since my unscheduled meetings at the Marine safety office. Captain Fels had not reopened the investigation. In the eyes of the United States Government Brian was the cause of his own death. Just another statistic except to the Association of Diving Contractors. They failed to show him on their yearly report of diving fatalities. Failed to include him because although he had died while working as a commercial diver he was not working for a member company of the ADC. G&G Marine had dropped their membership. Lieutenant Plagge had been interviewed by the press regarding Brian's "accident." The lieutenant was quoted in the *Houston Chronicle* as saying "Coast Guard dive experts told him divers are trained to know the warning signs of carbon dioxide "You'll taste it." Apparently, the Coast Guard experts had some ability that none of the rest of us posses. The ability to taste an odorless, tasteless gas.

But changes were coming about that would affect the diving community. The United States Coast Guard lifted their "Memorandum of Understanding" with the American Bureau of Shipping and replaced it with an authorization to allow The American Bureau of Shipping to conduct ship inspections without Coast Guard Supervision. [II]

When an ABS surveyor attends a ship while acting as the representative of the U.S. Government, he will use the full range of his professional skill and judgment in assessing the manner in which that vessel meets the relevant statutory regulations.

Followed a few months later with an Alternative Compliance Program under which the U.S. Coast Guard extended the authorization given to the American Bureau of Shipping to include mobile offshore drilling units.[III] Weeks later the American Bureau of shipping would issue yet another press release. "Robert D.

164

Somerville, president and chief operating officer of ABS, is pleased to announce the appointment of Admiral Robert E. Kramek, recently retired commandant of the United States Coast Guard, as president of ABS Americas Division.[IV]

At the request of Senator Slade Gorton the Center for Disease Control would run a statistical analyses with the assistance of the National Institute for Occupational Safety and Health on commercial diving fatalities. The CDC would later conclude in the June 1998 edition of the MMWR (Morbidity and Mortality Weekly Report)

Of the 116 occupational diving fatalities reported by OSHA for 1989-1997 (13 deaths per year), 49 (five per year) occurred among an estimated 3,000 full-time commercial divers (OSHA, unpublished data, 1998). The average of five deaths per year corresponds to a rate of 180 deaths per 100,000 employed divers per year, which is 40 times the national average death rate for all workers. This group, which accounts for most of the commercial dive time underwater, includes divers involved in construction, maintenance, and inspection of vessels and structures such as oil rigs, bridges, and dams. This report did not include divers that died while working under United States Coast Guard jurisdiction. In 1998, the USCG did not have a data base that included commercial diving fatalities.

And then finally the United States Coast Guard announced that they would be seeking public comment on revisions to the outdated commercial diving regulations. There would be an opportunity for the public to review the proposed changes that the Association of Diving Contractors had submitted. All comments should be in writing there would be no public hearings planed.

If ever there would be an example of a need for reform, a review of the incident aboard the Cliffs 12 could prove to be just what would be needed to make a difference. The proposed rule making should not, could not be allowed to only include input from the diving industry. There needed to be a voice representing the men and women that make their living at the end of a hose. Although Brian was no longer able to defend himself he would be heard, the truth needed to be heard. I would need to return to the Marine safety office in Port Arthur and start again. This time I would not return alone.

Colonel Frederick A Pilkington had lost his hearing while fighting with the Allied Forces during a German advance in the last days of World War II. The Ardennes forest of Southern Belgium were considered a "quiet sector" when the then twenty-two-year-old Sergeant Pilkington was leading an advance patrol between his unit, the 422nd of the 106th Infantry Division, and the 423 to their right flank. On December 15, 1944, the young Sergeant spotted a group of white camouflaged soldiers advancing toward his position. Knowing that none of the Allied Forces utilized white camouflage he reported what he perceived as a German advance patrol; he radioed his superiors. He was told he was mistaken, there were no Germans in the Ardennes.

The following day December 16, 1944, the sergeant's observation would prove to be correct as the Forces of Germany would make their last great offensive of the war. Over the next month and a half the U.S. Army would be involved in the single largest and bloodiest battle that American forces would fight in World War II. The 19,000 Americans would be killed

T. Wayne Black, George Herring, Fred Pilkington, Ebenezer Love, Presley Williams, Dave Dennis

during the Battle of the Bulge. Tens of thousands more would be wounded and Sergeant Pilkington would be left behind enemy lines, legs riddled with shrapnel unable to be moved.

Days before Christmas, Sergeant Pilkington would have his first go at international diplomacy as a German field surgeon stood over him suggesting that he bite down hard on the wool cap that had been placed between his teeth. "We have no anesthetic, your legs will need to be amputated."[v]

Fifty-three years later this veteran of World War II, standing on two good legs, was ready to march inside the Marine Safety Office with his son in an attempt to clear the name of his grandson. If ever there was a man that understood that superiors were not infallible he would be the one. At twenty-two years old the young Sergeant Pilkington had thought himself to be "bullet proof," all young men do, today he knew better. If the captain responsible for marine safety was not willing to listen to the ramblings of a father perhaps out of some military courtesy the now-retired colonel of the United States Army might garner attention.

Once again, I had an audience with Captain Fels, this time with an appointment and this time with the support of an officer of equal rank to the head of Marine Safety. Once again I laid out the facts as I knew them, turned over more sworn statements and pleaded that he reconsider and reinvestigate. Captain Fels agreed to assign a new investigator and he would personally review the findings.

Our next stop would be in the Court of Justice of the Peace John Borne. Armed with copies of the same documents given to the captain we were there to ask that the Judge revise the cause of death on Brian's death certificate to anything but accidental. Not wanting to miss a word and caring less what the laws of Texas would allow I entered the court room with a recording device in my suit pocket.

Once again we laid out our case. This was no accident and the documentation we had submitted would attest to that. Brian, contrary to the information on his death certificate, had not drown, there was a blood gas report found in the files showing that Brian was subjected to a lethal dose of carbon monoxide. And that report was in the judge's file, a copy we had purchased from his secretary under a freedom of information request for fifteen dollars.

Judge Borne suggested I leave my documentation and he might reconsider his decision. It would take a year or two, but he said he might consider our request. I reminded the servant of the good people of Jefferson County that he was able to determine the cause of death two years before in less than a day. And that was the same day he made the decision to send our son's lifeless body to his old friends funeral home. His old friend and hunting partner, Walter Umphrey. Would it not be possible to obtain the correction within a similar time frame?

With that, the judge stood behind the safety of his bench and said, "Son, perhaps you need to be shown what Texas justice is all about." And before he could finish, I replied, "Judge, let's remember this is not the only court, we will see you in the Court of Public opinion." And with that, Colonel Pilkington and I headed for the safety of the parking lot with a vow to never again enter the jurisdiction of the old judge. Best we return home while we could.

I was in my office attempting to complete the drawings for a new home client when my office manager came in telling me Captain Fels was on line one. Two months had gone by since our meeting in Port Arthur. The captain, was calling to personally read his conclusion of the second investigation. A copy was also being faxed to my office. His new team of investigators were unable to determine. "The definitive reason your son experienced insufficient breathing air remains unclear." He went on to say, "I do not believe from the evidence available that the compressor experienced a catastrophic failure. Unfortunately the opportunity to determine the truth about the compressor no longer exists." He went on to make a reference to my complaint that Lieutenant Commander Miko, Coast Guard office of Congressional affairs, had made an intentional misleading statement to Senator Slade Gorton regarding the testing of the compressor. "I cannot comment on this issue as it is not within my purview."

He went on to assure me they were to "redouble our internal training program efforts to ensure my inspectors are familiar with the diving regulations. Also, the lessons learned from this casualty investigation have been incorporated into the training of all my Investigating Officers as well."

There was no proof that Brian was not the cause of his own death. The compressor had been destroyed; the Coast Guard had lost custody. The second report only supported the first. I thanked him for the call and sat in disbelief. I was up against the system, my resources had been depleted, the system won. It was over.

It was the middle of June 1998 and the spring day outside was glorious but inside my office there was only gloom. For the first time since the night of March 4 more than two years before I just sat there and cried. The office manager came to my closed office door, knocked, then slowly opened and peered in. "You have another call, this one is from Christen Woodworking" she said.

My response was fast and filled with emotion. "I have no time for a sales call, take a message, I'll call them back."

"I don't think he's a salesman, He says he a former commercial diver who lives in Louisiana."

I took the call.

Fort the next two hours, Eric Hofsommer would tell me his story of the industry in which he had spent eleven years working. He was a saturation diver which is about as close to space travel as a man can come without leaving this planet. A saturation diver must live and work in a pressurized environment breathing mixed gases, never permitted to leave without decompressing. This in some cases can take days. He had been accustomed to spending as much as a month living in a chamber on board ship; then being transferred to a dive bell through an airlock to a diving bell of equal pressure, for the trip to a work station far below. Normally there would be four men working in pairs. Two in the water at work far below the vessel, two in the chamber eating, reading, sleeping or just resting between work assignments. All the time being kept at a pressure equal to the working depth. The year before, Eric and his partner were working at three hundred feet when he was notified by the ship board tender that they would need to cut the operation short and return to the ship. Once hoisted to the deck the diving bell was mated to the chamber they joined the two men already inside.

The internal lighting was running on battery backup, air scrubbers were overloading and there were four zip lock bags in the medical locker. This compartment would allow for food, reading materials, any item of importance to be transferred from the outside world to the pressurized chamber. But this day there were just the four bags each containing a pad, pen and a note suggesting they fill out a last will, a note to a loved one. The boat was on fire and they would not be able to evacuate with the others.

As fortune would have it the fire raging around the four men trapped in their personal pressurized coffin was eventually suppressed and all four saturation divers survived. Eric, the dive supervisor, took it upon himself to challenge the Coast Guard regulations that had allowed the grandfathering of the dive boat to operate without a fire suppression system. A fire suppression system was required on new crafts but not on the one owned and operated by a member company of the Association of Diving Contractors.

Eric's protest earned him a black ball and effectively ended his diving career. Undaunted he continued his one man crusade for reform spending many hours in that same Marine Safety office that had been entrusted with the investigation of the events aboard the Cliffs 12. On one of Eric's visits a Lieutenant Plagge had asked the experienced dive supervisor for insight into diving procedures, air quality, compressor operation. Lieutenant Plagge had asked that Eric review a previously issued Marine Casualty report looking for inconsistencies, anything the Coast Guard Investigators might have overlooked. "The divers father is stirring things up a bit and we fear this one will not go away easily" Eric was told.

Eric gave what advice he could based on the limited information that was available but then also took down the name of the man who had lost his life while working at the end of hose. It would take Eric three weeks of calls to Pilkingtons all over the United States before he found the right father. The father that had been causing all the fuss in Port Arthur.

Eric was a wealth of knowledge. He was also working to supply the requested information the United States Coast Guard was seeking in their proposed rule making. He was after changes far more sophisticate than the simple things I thought need inclusion; a diver certification program, a dive supervisor licensing program, backup air supply systems, backup diver requirements. Eric wanted improved fire and smoke detection on any boat involved in diving operations, restrictions on underwater burning, synchronization of time keeping devices, double wall integrity for chambers, proper designation of dive supervisors, tougher standards for closed bell operations, proper record keeping. And then there were a few items we both had included in our suggestions to the Coast Guard for inclusion in the revised regulation; accountability of the person in charge, the tracking of breathing gas tests and pre dive checklists and perhaps most importantly, any reference to the accountability of the diving supervisor without also holding the dive contractor accountable.

But most interesting to me, Eric related a story of a lunch time break conversation. He had been discussing his exploits as a commercial diver when a welder among the land based construction crew told a story of a diving fatality he had witnessed years before. The welder had been waiting for the supply boat to come and was passing the time watching the diver working below on a closed circuit TV monitor. The images appeared to be coming from a camera mounted somewhere on the diver. He thought it strange that the bubbles were moving from the top of the screen to the bottom. There had been some sort of equipment malfunction and a company man had demanded the use of the welders oxygen acetylene equipment. They would need the oxygen tank and hose, there was no other breathing gas available to reach the stranded diver.

Two days later I was in the living room of Steve Champagne in Morgan City, Louisiana. I asked no questions but rather invited him to tell me what he witnessed on March 4 while waiting for that crew boat. With every word recorded I got back in my rental car and headed for the Hale Boggs Federal Building. 501 Magazine Street in New Orleans, home of the United States Coast Guard Eighth District.

The next afternoon I was allowed an hour to present my case for a reopening of the investigation. Pleading my case in front of Lt. Com. Jim Wilson, Lt. Com. Rod Walker, Com. William Baumgartner and Capt. Walter J. Brawand. I was prepared with much the same information as the Marine Safety Office had been given supplemented only by the statement from Steve Champagne and its inconsistencies with the two witness statements the previous two Marine Casualty reports had relied on. My argument was based on the facts that no witnesses had yet been actually interviewed by anyone within the Coast Guard, the failure of the Coast Guard to have maintained custody of the compressor, the numerous regulations that had been violated as well as the loopholes in the existing regulations. The one hour meeting started promptly at 8:00 AM lasting until 3:30 PM with no break. The meeting was concluded when the until then silent Captain Brawand pushed back from his seat at the head of the table and said, "They killed him, let's reopen the investigation."

Two days later I sat in the Washington D.C. office of United States Congressman Jay Inslee. If there was to be yet another investigation I wanted to be a part of it. Once again I explained the events of March 4 aboard the Cliffs 12. My believe that the root cause of the fatality was the failure of the compressor, a fact that the Coast Guard was attempting to disregard as they had lost custody of the compressor early on. There were also a series of out dated regulations that were in dire need of reform. The best if not only way for me to get a seat at the table, to represent the man that was now no longer able to represent himself was to request my right as a citizen, to be a party in interest. Under federal regulation it is possible for any citizen who can show cause why they should be included. My son's conduct was under investigation. I had significant information to contribute. Through my participation I could focus the investigation not only on what had caused the fatality but what needed to be done to prevent future fatalities. As a party in interest I would have the ability to have witnesses called and the ability to question them, under oath.

Two weeks and several letters later I had my designation. The next step was to request a formal investigation open to the public. It was time to make a change and this could not happen behind closed doors.

10 May 1999
BY FAX AND MAIL
Commander
U.S. Coast Guard
District 8
Hale Boggs Federal Building
501 Magazine Street
New Orleans, La
70130-3396

Request for the convening of a Marine Board

Dear Sir,
Brian Pilkington—Killed 4 March 1996

I refer to the previous Marine Casualty Investigations and the current investigation into my son's death.

Information and facts gathered by the current Investigating Officer indicate that, in accordance with 46 CFR 4.031 and the Marine Safety Manual, vol. 5 ch. 3, the death should have been classified either as a serious casualty or a significant marine casualty.

The Marine Safety Manual reports that the International Maritime Organization (IMO) defines a "serious casualty" as;

"An occurrence involving vessels of 1,600 GT or more that results in the total loss (including constructive total loss) of one or more vessels or a loss of life on vessels of 500 GT or more."

Brian was fatally injured while engaged on a commercial dive from a MODU vessel with a gross tonnage of 4,190 metric tonnes. Consequently his death falls within the meaning of the 'serious casualty' category.

In addition,

The Marine Safety Manual vol. 5 ch. 3 refers to a 'Significant Marine Casualty' and defines that category of casualty as *"those casualties that involve important safety issues or cause substantial media interest. Significant marine casualties generally involve the following:*

(a) *Multiple deaths or a single death caused by unusual circumstances;*

(b) *Hazard to life, property, or the marine environment (e.g., sinking of a chlorine barge); or*

(c) *Loss of any inspected vessel."*

Brian's death involved important safety issues, some singled out in the Marine Safety Manual vol. 5 ch. 3 (I) "Investigations Of Commercial Diving Casualties."

Brian's death was caused by unusual circumstances.

The causes of Brian's death, events, acts and omissions—culpable or otherwise, negligence, recklessness, lack of training, ignorance, ineffective regulations, failure to enforce existing regulations, in whole or in part, represent an immediate and ongoing potential for hazard to life and property.

Further, the Marine Safety Manual vol. 5, ch. 3 (C) "Marine Boards Of Investigation" defines the designation of a Marine Board as the following:

*If, as a result of preliminary evidence, recommendation of a district commander, or **information from any other source**, it appears that a **marine casualty is of such** magnitude or **significance that a detailed formal investigation will promote safety of life** and property at sea and serve the public interest, the commandant may designate a marine board of investigation to look into the casualty. The authority for this process is found in 46 CFR 4.091. **The decision to convene a marine board is influenced primarily by the lessons to be derived from the casualty. If the information to be derived has considerable significance,** or indicates vessel class problems or areas of technical importance, convening of a marine board ensures that every aspect of the case is probed.*

Information and facts uncovered thus far by your investigating officer have revealed serious errors, omissions, and conflicts in CFR 46, thereby representing a serious and immediate impediment to the safety of seamen and others engaged today in commercial diving activities from vessels.

There are many lessons to be learned from my son's death; many are common sense and others are technical in nature. The lack of implementation of the lessons represents a serious and immediate hazard to all commercial divers.

Many current federal commercial diving statutes are outdated
Diving contractors must comply with the relevant federal statues
Vessel owners and masters must adhere to federal statutes
USCG training programs must be amended to include effective training for IOs and MSO personnel.
A Marine Board would provide a platform to probe every aspect of my son's death and obviate other senseless and needless commercial diving fatalities.

If a Marine Board had been convened and its recommendations implemented prior to March 1996 then certain safety provisions would have been in place and my son would be alive today.

As a party in interest I recommend that a Marine Board be convened as soon as possible. To expedite the Investigation replies may be sent to me in e-mail format, addressed to me at divesafe@msn.com.

Yours sincerely,
Peter J Pilkington

The Marine Board of Inquiry was set for mid-June. Brian would finally have opportunity to be heard.

Chapter 16

GETTING READY

During the months and years leading up to what I saw now as our last opportunity not to only clear Brian of the sole culpability in his own death but as an opportunity for me to fulfill that promises I had made in eulogy three years before. *"Brian was a man who could not be angered, who saw only the best, never understood the worst. He would want us to forgive the men who were responsible for his death and look to us to find a way to prevent it from happening again."*

We would finally have that forum not to punish those that allowed the incident aboard the Cliffs 12 to take place but rather to highlight the failure of the system that remained in place. Young men will forever believe that they are invincible and it is the responsibility of us older men to assure, as best we can, that those invincible young men live to understand that they are not.

During the intervening three years I had learned a great deal of the underwater construction industry, had input from divers, contractors and inspectors. Most divers were eager to discuss what they perceived to be the short comings of the industry but reluctant to participate in reform as it could jeopardize their employment as it had Eric Hofsommer's. Contractors were eager to see an industry made safer through reform but were concerned that by following tougher standards it would push business to those willing to work outside the regulation. Inspectors also wanted reform but were bound to regulations so filled with legal loopholes that their hands were affectively tied. And then the resources made available to those inspectors were so archaic that their ability to enforce was as impotent as the regulations they were entrusted to enforce.

Among those not afraid to speak out and make a difference was Joe Walker and his associate Tom Mosele. Joe had worked as a commercial diver graduating from the same dive school as Brian only twenty years before. Joe had worked his way up as a tender, diver, dive supervisor and saturation diver, certified with a North Sea bell card. He then moved to management, eventually working his way up to vice president and managing director of Asia Pacific/Middle East Region, Oceaneering International Inc. With work assignments in South America, Columbia, Mexico, Ecuador, Venezuela, Trinidad, Peru, Brazil, Yemen, Oman, Qatar, Iran, Egypt, Malta, Israel, Australia, Dubai, Saudi Arabia, Taiwan, Brunei, Malaysia, Indonesia, Singapore, and Thailand. Joe knew the industry and he knew it well. But today his work as an industry insider was over. He had left diving and returned to school earning a law degree from the South Texas College of Law. And by the summer of 1999 was a partner in the law firm of Franklin Mosele and Walker. Joes name had been passed along to me by a United States Navy Seal who was now working within the commercial diving industry as a consultant; he suggested I seek out Joe Walker. Joe was a man I needed to talk with.

One of Joes associates was Tom Mosele. Like Joe, Tom started his career working in the trades. First as an equipment operator working his way up to superintendent. He had worked in pile driving, tunnel boring, heavy foundations, submerged pipelines, port facilities, bridge construction; he knew the heavy construction industry well. Like his current business partner he returned to school and earned a law degree from Southern Texas College of Law in 1992 to complement his degree in Civil Engineering from Tulane. Together these men not only knew the industry, they knew the law.

Joe would spend hours telling stories of industry shortfalls, carelessness, incompetence and cover-ups. Tom would usually start a calm conversation about the legal systems that allowed industry to circumnavigate their moral responsibility but his demeanor would always change to an angry indignation of the system and what it would mean to those adversely effected.

Now the Coast Guard was about to reopen the investigation. And truly I was the dog that had finally caught the car, now what? With less than two weeks to prepare and no resources left to employ council I reached out to Joe and Tom.

> June 5, 1999
> Dear Joe and Tom,
>
> This might not be as significant as a day in front of the Supreme Court but could be the next best. Last month I was given the designation of a party in interest per the attached letter. Yesterday the United States Coast Guard Agreed to a Formal Investigation into the events aboard the Cliffs 12.

We cannot make a difference until the Coast Guard acknowledges their responsibility when granting variances, for permitting violations to be ongoing, for disregarding established policies for inspections and investigations for failing to issue citations for violations exposed.

Last weekend I read volume 5 of the Coast Guard Manual. Years ago someone laid down the policies for not only the conduct of an underwater inspection but also how to conduct an investigation in the event of a dive fatality. Apparently the captain of the port elected to disregard those policies. Now this is our opportunity not to only hold him responsible, but also send a message that the granting of variance, the disregarding of regulations can have consequences. We can also use this forum to point out the need for more comprehensive, enforceable regulation. Regulations written not by the industry but by the people those regulations are meant to protect.

My interest in all this was to first clear my son's name; and secondly to make a difference, send a message, leave a better situation then the one we found. But here lies the problem. I am a house builder not a lawyer. I may have opened the door but now that I am inside I fear that I may not be capable of finishing the job. Will you help?

Peter J. Pilkington
Divesafe@msn.com

Two weeks later Joe Walker and Tom Mosele joined me in my temporary Texas office in the Holiday Inn across the street from the Port Arthur Marine Safety Headquarters.

Chapter 17

U.S. COAST GUARD-MARINE SAFETY OFFICE

Operator: Thank you for patiently holding, everyone. Welcome to the recorded call. The reference number on today's call is ATB1588. That's ATB1588. Our number, in case for further assistance, is needed during this call is 1-800/232-1234. That's 800/232-1234. I'd like to take a brief roll call, please. Respond when you hear your name. Mike Wilson? (Yes), Kirk Austin? (Yes), Kena Seiler? (Yes), Joe Walker? (Yes), Bijan Siahatgar? (Yes), Tom Marion? (Yes), Houston? (Yes). Thank you. All parties are on.

Houston: **Hey, ma'am?**

Operator: Yes.

Lt. Com. Tom Beistle: **Were you able to contact a Mr. Joe Walker?**

Joe Walker: I'm here.

Lt. Com. Tom Beistle: **Oh, okay. I'm sorry, Joe. I—**

Joe Walker: The person I'm waiting for is Mr. Pilkington and he hasn't arrived.

Lt. Com. Tom Beistle: **Mr. Pilkington is here with me at the Coast Guard Marine Safety Office.**

Joe Walker: Okay, good.

Lt. Com. Tom Beistle: **Okay, everybody. That takes care of the introductions, so we just saved ten minutes. Let me ask, did everybody get my last-minute e-mail yesterday with the agenda and the other items? It sounds like it from the silence, we are all good. I tell you what, if we run through this, if you run into anything that you don't have available, let me know, and we'll punt. Okay. I tell you what, if we run into—because I'll be going over virtually every page here, so if we run into something that you obviously don't have, let me know and we'll fix it.**

Tom? Tom Marion?

Tom Marion: Yes. I received everything.

Lt. Com. Tom Beistle: **And for those of you who don't know, I guess I haven't introduced you. Tom Marion is an attorney with the Eighth Coast Guard District Legal Office up in New Orleans. He'll be assisting me. He'll be advising me on this hearing. Does everybody else know? I'm assuming maybe from the civil litigation that everybody knows who's serving in what role? Anybody doesn't know? Anybody not know someone? No one speaking up, so it sounds like everybody knows who's filling what role.**

Just one other thing that I should let you know. I know that the operator did say this at the beginning. This conversation is being recorded by AT&T, and I'm going to get a transcript of it, so hopefully any decisions we make and the process that we decide to implement will be documented so that we'll all know what the heck's going on.

Okay. Let's get started. Have we covered the introductions part of this agenda? I'm assuming by the fact that nobody spoke up that everybody does know who's doing what. Is that right? Do I have a consensus to move on to discussions of the time and date and the location of this hearing?

Mike Wilson: No problem here.

Lt. Com. Tom Beistle: **Great. I'm going to make a proposal. I talked to most of you except I think you, Ms. Seiler, and I apologize for not being able to get to you sooner. I'm proposing that we get started next week. My mandate from the district commander, my implementing order, says that we should do this on or about the fifteenth, and obviously, I sure didn't make that, but there's still a pretty rigorous timeline, and I'd like to meet it as much as possible.**

I'm proposing that we get together early next week as soon as we can round up witnesses and get everybody there. I'm proposing that we not start on Monday because there are a lot of people who are driving in and flying in from all over creation. My understanding is that we'll have people coming in from New Orleans, New York, Houston, and pretty much everywhere in between, so I'm suggesting that we use Monday as a—Monday morning at least as a travel day and that we hold—that everybody come in on Monday or sooner if they want to—that we hold a get-together to walk through the spaces and lay down the ground rules and all that sort of thing Monday afternoon at about 2:00 or so. That will give everybody chances to check into hotels and so forth. We'll be able to go through the physical spaces, look at how the set-up, how we've arranged the tables and that sort of thing, and make sure that we know how we're going to conduct this hearing at about 2:00 on Monday afternoon, and then I propose that we get started on Tuesday morning at about 8:00. What do people think about that? Time and location, and we'll work on getting you folks directions on how to get here.

This is Kirk Austin. I cannot make the Monday preliminaries.
Well, just looking at the table arrangements and things of that nature, I'll be there Tuesday morning at 8:00. I'll drive in early Tuesday morning.

Lt. Com. Tom Beistle: **Okay. How about this? I will make a point not to get started on Tuesday morning until we give you—until I specifically give you a run-through of what we're going to do and how we're going to do it and listen to any objections you might have. Will that work?**

Kirk Austin: That's fine. Thank you.
Just so you know—this is Kena Seiler—I'm not going to be there. Ruben Hope from my office will be there.

Lt. Com. Tom Beistle: **Mr. Siahatgar, is that schedule okay with you?**

Bijan Siahatgar: Absolutely.

Lt. Com. Tom Beistle: Great. Mr. Wilson?

Mike Wilson: That's fine.

Tom Marion: I'll be there.

Pete Pilkington: That's fine.

Lt. Com. Tom Beistle: **Yes. Mr. Pilkington's here, so I'm assuming he'll be ready to go. Okay. Then I think we've at least discussed when we're going to start. Let me propose something. I know that this is really navel gazing or crystal ball gazing, but I'm going to suggest to you that I'd like to—obviously the purpose of this thing is to develop all the information necessary in order to do a good investigation. Having said that, I would like to at least propose that on the days that we hold the hearing we go for as long as our guts and adrenaline will let us go, so basically 8:00 in the morning until we can't see straight. If it means 8:00 at night, that's fine. I'd like to get this done in about two days, Tuesday and Wednesday, if that's possible. Anybody have any thoughts on that?**

This is Joe Walker—My only problem is, I have a court scheduled deposition on another diving injury in Morgan City on Wednesday.

Lt. Com. Tom Beistle: **Yes, sir. On Wednesday**.

Joe Walker: Now, Mr. Mozel, my co counsel, will substitute for me on Wednesday if necessary.

Lt. Com. Tom Beistle: **Okay, sir. Nobody here—I don't hear anybody objecting if we could do this in one day. If we could do it all in one day, that would be great with everyone. Okay, good. So I'm going to propose, or at least give us a target that says let's try and get this done, except Mr. Walker, obviously, who if he's not going to be here, then Mr. Mozel will stand in for him. And, also, I'm not going to try and stick to any ordinary workday. I'm going to try and do this for as long as this needs to be done. So if that means going until whatever time of the night, then that's okay. Any objections?**

Tuesday morning we'll meet at the Texas Air National Guard Armory where the hearing's going to be held. But, hopefully, everybody except Mr. Austin—and Mr. Austin, we're still working on getting you directions, by the way. We will get those out to you and to everyone else. But, we'll meet at the Air National Guard Armory, but we should see those spaces Monday afternoon when we go there to look through them. Everybody should know how to get there. Is that okay? Okay. I propose we move on to agenda item number three. We're five minutes ahead of schedule. Good for us. Now we're into the meat of it. I have, for no particular reason whatsoever, just listed—and I'm not even sure I've attributed—I've said who's asked for these various witnesses. I'm sure that'll become evident as we go along. But I've got a grouping of the witnesses and the documents that everyone has asked for so far. So what I'd like to do is I'd like to just start.

If you folks could turn to appendix one, which is listed as "The Witness and Document List for the Parties and Interests." I should say, "The Requested Witness and Documents List." Has everybody got appendix one?

Okay. No one said no, so I'm assuming you do. Let me start off by saying that there was a clerical error here, and that's my fault. That's my fault. The first—well, no. As a matter of fact, these are listed according to who asked for them. The first item up there is listed ABS, and it says Ron Everett, and the way Ron Everett's name is featured, it may give the appearance that he's been named as a party in interest. He has not been. That was an administrative oversight on my part or a clerical error. Ron Everett is simply associated with ABS, and he's been requested to be a witness only. He's not named as a party in interest.

So now can we start off just with—as a matter of fact, it's even a little bit awkward because ABS isn't even asking for Ron Everett. Other people are. But we can start off with Mr. Wilson?

Mike Wilson: Sure. You list four witnesses here that I assume that obviously these people will be necessary. But just for the record, ABS did not request these or any other witnesses.

Lt. Com. Tom Beistle: **You know, you're right. Your letter, as a matter of fact, said will provide Ron Everett. And I synthesized this. Your letter, in fact said, will provide Ron Everett in words to the effect of, or I think Ms. Adams' letter said words to the effect of, "Since you're calling these other people, we'll provide Ron Everett. We really don't feel there's a need to call any other witnesses," or words to that effect. Is that correct?**

Mike Wilson: Yes. That's right.

Lt. Com. Tom Beistle: **Okay. Having said that, I guess I'd like your opinion on these witnesses—Kirk Austin, Dan Wiitala, Ron Townsend, and Buddy Horton. Is your sense that these folks are people who are necessary and appropriate for this hearing?**

Okay. These are the same—I hate to sort of put you on the spot because all these witnesses have been asked for by other people. Nevertheless, I would like some cogent discussion about the necessity of these individuals. Would you like to sort that, or would you sort of like to check to the dealer and let other people discuss it? It's up to you.

Mike Wilson: ABS would prefer to take a back seat on that point.

Yes. This is Bijan Siahatgar. I was intimately involved in the litigation. I'd be happy to field that issue.

From the standpoint of the necessity of these first four witnesses listed on page one of appendix one, certainly we're going to provide Buddy Horton and Ron Townsend, so I don't really think it's necessarily an issue whether or not they're going to be required or not. It's my understanding that you have requested Buddy Horton one way or another, so I don't really think that's going to be an issue. Ron Townsend is a party in interest, so he's going to appear. So I don't really think he's going to be someone that we necessarily need to discuss whether or not he's going to be necessary or not. With regard to Dan Wiitala and Kirk Austin, Kirk Austin, I believe, has also been made a party in interest and Dan Wiitala certainly, I believe, is a highly relevant individual, since he was involved in the diving operation.

Lt. Com. Tom Beistle: **Right. I think two points that you make there are particularly important. You're quite correct. Mr. Austin and Mr. Townsend have both been named as parties in interest as well as obviously as witnesses in this thing. So I think that their presence is almost a given. Let me ask, when we're getting to Dan Wiitala and Buddy Horton, can you tell me specifically? You just told me that you're going to provide Mr. Horton. How is he going to be available? Is he going to be available in person or for telephonic testimony?**

This is Bijan Siahatgar: By telephone. He is either now or certainly is going to be by Monday in Venezuela on other business, and I believe he's already down there at this point in time. He will be available by telephone at whatever given time we deem is necessary. So I think what we need for him is we can get one hour lee time to him, we can have him on the telephone for as long as we need.

Lt. Com. Tom Beistle: **Thank you very much.**

Okay, now we talked about your providing Mr. Horton, but I would like some discussion here at the outset about his necessity. I just want to get it on the record. Now, my understanding is that Mr. Horton was the safety manager on board the Cliffs 12 at the time and was an employee of Cliffs. Is that correct?

Bijan Siahatgar: That's correct.

Lt. Com. Tom Beistle: **Can somebody, because a lot of people have raised his name—anybody who'd like to, I'm not asking for an offer of proof, but I would like just a short discussion of what value he might add? Does anybody want to take up that challenge? Mr. Pilkington?**

Pete Pilkington: Well, Buddy Horton obviously was the safety manager. This was certainly a safety issue. He was also responsible for filling out the necessary paperwork for the Coast Guard inspection and the contact with the ABS. In addition, Buddy Horton took witness statements at the time of the incidents. His testimony is crucial.

If I may add—this is Joe Walker—I'm going to defer generally to Mr. Pilkington on the facts. But it's my understanding he's actually a material fact witness to the rescue attempt and also had prior working experience with Mr. Austin.

Lt. Com. Tom Beistle: **I think you're right, Mr. Walker. I think that's correct.**

Joe Walker: I think any fact witness, frankly any fact witness to the actual incident, with the exception of Mr. Horton, should be physically present if we can.

Lt. Com. Tom Beistle: **I agree. I agree in principle. Again, I'm going to err on the side of getting as many people as we possibly can. If we can only get them—you know, frankly, I'm saying this, but Mr. Horton is outside my jurisdiction.**

Joe Walker: Yes, because I think you need these fact witnesses, or frankly, if we can get them physically, your hearing will go a lot faster.

Lt. Com. Tom Beistle: **I agree. I agree. But I agree that Mr. Horton is—I mean, it's my sense that he's very necessary. I just wanted to kind of get it on the record, get other people to kind of buy into that. Kirk Austin certainly. And now how about Mr. Wiitala? He's the other—he's the other person who's not a party in interest that's listed here. I certainly have my own feelings, but would anybody like to weigh in on—I guess the same thing would apply. He was a fact witness as much as anything else. Anybody care to comment?**

This is Kena Seiler. He was an employee of G&G Marine. He was out there with Brian Pilkington and he was involved in the rescue attempt. He knows more about this than probably anybody.

Lt. Com. Tom Beistle: **I agree.**

Joe Walker: Obviously, for the record, he would have knowledge of the violations of various safe diving practices and other regulations committed by the diving company.

Lt. Com. Tom Beistle: **I agree. So I think we're in agreement. Mr. Austin is a party in interest and is also a fact witness just as Mr. Wiitala is. Mr. Wiitala was**

there on the scene at the time and is also an employee of G&G. Mr. Townsend is a party in interest and was also, for my purposes I'd like to add, was licensed by the Coast Guard. He was the offshore installation manager of the Cliffs 12, and Mr. Horton was the safety manager and was also on the scene at the time and was involved in the rescue attempt. So I think we're generally in agreement that those four people are vital to this fact-finding hearing, or this hearing.

That's correct with—you know, this is Mr. Walker again. I'd certainly like as many fact witnesses present that can make it just because these telephone depositions of all these parties could be a real nightmare.

Lt. Com. Tom Beistle: I agree. **We're going to do our best, Mr. Walker. But otherwise, you agree on these four witnesses?**

Joe Walker: Absolutely.

Lt. Com. Tom Beistle: Mr. Pilkington?

Pete Pilkington: Yes.

Lt. Com. Tom Beistle: **Mr. Townsend, do you agree? Or, I'm sorry, Mr. Siahatgar?**

Bijan Siahatgar: Yes, I do.

Lt. Com. Tom Beistle: **Okay, let's move on. Mr. Gilbert will be present?**

Kena Seiler: Yes.

Lt. Com. Tom Beistle: **next, Jerry Lare. Who is he**?

Bijan Siahatgar: Right. He was—again, he is someone who I do not believe needs to be subpoenaed for this at this time. He is someone who was—and I honestly can't remember if he is the individual or if somebody else was the individual who participated in the CPR of Brian Pilkington or not. Both—all three, Jerry Lare, Ed Tatum, and Fred King is not anybody who I think necessarily needs to be subpoenaed at this time. They may be people whose testimony may become relevant along the way in this investigation. And let me tell you why. The only reason I listed them was because I received some correspondence from Col. Fred Pilkington as well as read some, I guess, something in the Beaumont Enterprise that made me think some additional testimony might be necessary to rebut some of the information that I had read there. And these three gentlemen, I think can do it if necessary. Again, they probably may not be necessary, and I think it's going to be something I'm going to leave up to you at a later point, whether you think it's necessary or not.

Lt. Com. Tom Beistle: **Well, I hear what you're saying, but let me get sort of specific. When you say there's no need for a subpoena, does that mean that they'll show up willingly, or do you think it's problematic as to whether they're even going to be necessary? I'm not sure what you mean.**

Bijan Siahatgar: Probably the latter. I don't think they're going to be necessary. Jerry Lare—I'm flipping through some documents right now. He was the medic who flew on the helicopter with Brian Pilkington to the hospital.

Lt. Com. Tom Beistle: Okay. **I thought that was Fred King**.

Bijan Siahatgar: That's what I thought as well until this morning.

Lt. Com. Tom Beistle: **Okay. Jerry Lare was the medic who flew on the helo.**

Bijan Siahatgar: Correct.

Lt. Com. Tom Beistle: **You know, the helo pilot, or excuse me, the medic—I really am interested in his testimony if I can get it. I think it would add value. I don't think it would take very long to talk to him. I'd just like to hear his story first hand. Does anybody know, was he deposed in the civil litigation?**

Bijan Siahatgar: He was.

Lt. Com. Tom Beistle: Okay. **And then as for the other two, Fred King and Ed Tatum—**

Bijan Siahatgar: Yes. I'm looking at Fred King. Fred King was who I thought was the medic. He was only roustabout out there. I don't see if there's any relevance to anything he's done or his knowledge of that's anything more than anything else.

Lt. Com. Tom Beistle: **But for the fact that he's a fact witness like one hundred other people on board.**

Bijan Siahatgar: Right. Same as Ed Tatum.

Lt. Com. Tom Beistle: **And the same. Okay. I tend to agree with Mr. Walker that generally the more fact witnesses we can get, the better chance we have of developing the facts, but for the fact that at some point it's going to become** redundant. Let's just table that discussion and see if you can find out their status. It could be that both of these guys live a block and a half from the meeting room, the hearing room, and so it wouldn't be a problem. Let's just defer a decision until we find out what their status is.

Bijan Siahatgar: Okay.

Lt. Com. Tom Beistle: **Now, let's talk about Mr. Everett. Whose list is this? This is yours, Mr. Siahatgar.**

Bijan Siahatgar: Yes.

Lt. Com. Tom Beistle: **Would you please give me some sort of sense of what you think he'll add to the party?**

Bijan Siahatgar: I don't—as you know, Everett was, I guess, the ABS man on the rig at the time. He might be able to give us some information with regards to ABS inspections in general, what the rig was doing, how the rigs worked to get back to ABS certification or ABS approval, what was going on in that regard. He may or may not be able to add information to that extent.

Joe Walker: I believe, from what I understand, he participated in possibly the rescue and recovery. He is a fact witness.

Well, I guess—this is Bijan Siahatgar again. From that standpoint, you have about 60 people who are fact witnesses because, as in any emergency situation, when you have something like this arise, basically everyone on deck tries to do a little bit to participate in the emergency situation to do whatever they could to help the situation out. So I mean I understand that Ron Everett was on deck and he did somewhat participate. But I think from that standpoint, I think that's kind of an overboard definition of people that we would want to have at this hearing next week.

This is Joe Walker again. Let me respond to that. I mean, I understand he was on deck at the inspection site. He's a neutral, or I assume a neutral third-party witness, and he's not like some roustabout sitting in the cafeteria having a cup of coffee. I assume he has a lot of observations that he saw during this incident.

Yes. This is Pete Pilkington. In addition to that, Mr. Everett needs to be interviewed in regards to what his function was out there on that given date. The purpose of the Coast Guard investigation is more than just to determine more than what the cause of the death was. The purpose of this investigation is to determine what rules and regulations are in need of change. Mr. Everett was fully aware of, or should have been, and we need to discuss that with him, the conditions of NAVIC 1-89. He should have intimate knowledge and be able to explain to us why this inspection was being undertaken to begin with.

Lt. Com. Tom Beistle: **I think that makes a lot of sense to me. I think he's probably a good witness in this case and could probably develop this discussion. We're now under the witnesses listed as requested by Peter Pilkington. I don't hear any objections, so everybody must be on the same page. Okay. Let's move down to Captain Fels. Has everybody been able to read the—I hate to call it a justification—but I don't know whether it's justification or offer of proof. It's just . . . Mr. Pilkington, this is yours. Would you like to comment?**

Pete Pilkington again: Well, we were asking to call the captain. He was, in the first place, responsible for issuing the permission to have this vessel inspected to begin with, and secondly was responsible for the investigation of the casualty, and he can bring pertinent information in regards to the casualty investigation.

Lt. Com. Tom Beistle: **Let's break that up. Let's talk about responsible for issuing permission. Could you give me some sense of what you expect to—**

Pete Pilkington: What I'm looking for, is in order for a vessel to undergo an underwater inspection, according to Coast Guard regulation, there has to be a 90-day period of notification which was never done. The question for the captain is, why was this done without submission of all the necessary documents under NAVIC 1-89? One-eighty-nine required that there be notification of the diving contract or notification of who the diving personnel were going to be. There had to be submission of a safety plan and all that had to go through Captain Fels' office.

Lt. Com. Tom Beistle: **Well, I'm not so sure about that, but—by the way, for everybody's information, I've done some preliminary legwork on this, and I have talked to Captain Fels. I've talked to most of the witnesses that have been listed here that I could get my hands on unless they're somebody specific like Mr. Gaetti or somebody who's unique to one party of interest. So I've done a fair amount of talking to a fair number of people. Okay, so specifically with respect to Captain Fels, you're interested—oh, by the way, I have talked to Captain Fels. He will be available for telephonic testimony on Tuesday or Wednesday, so I mean, I guess the point is that he is available. And, as I understand it, your concern or your area of interest there is his interpretation of or understanding NAVIC 1-89 and the processes for permitting underwater inspections in lieu of dry docking on—.**

Pete Pilkington: Correct.

Okay. And I think he's also—this is Joe Walker again—I think he's also interested in the information that he was able to attain during the investigation of the accident, death, and the lack thereof or whatever information was not given to him. Did he have all the information?

This is Bijan Siahatgar. What exactly is **NAVIC 1-89?** I'm seeing a bunch of documents and I've actually done a little digging around.

Lt. Com. Tom Beistle: **I actually have it, and I can either e-mail it to you or I think we pulled if off the Coast Guard website. I think we can tell you how to—somebody smarter than I am can tell you how to pull that down. Okay, but what it is generally is it is a—NAVIC is an acronym for Navigation and Vessel Inspection Circular. Generally they are sort of like an open letter, I think is the best way to put it—an open letter to the industry that tells the industry how, in a general fashion, we the Coast Guard expect to sort of do our business to enforce the regulations. NAVIC 1-89 has to do with underwater inspections in lieu of dry docking and how the Coast Guard anticipates that it will do business with industry on these—when these underwater exams are done. So it's half policy, half open letter and comment. It's more informational than anything else. And this one deals specifically with under waters in lieu.**

If it would make it easier for everyone—this is Pete Pilkington—I have it in an e-mail attachment. I'll send it to all the parties in interest.

Lt. Com. Tom Beistle: **I tell you what, if you don't mind, I want to defer making a—I hate to say a decision, but I want to hold off on talking about Captain Fels until I talk about the next really four witnesses, all of whom are Coasties. Let's talk about Lt. J. G. Wellborn. It says here, let me just read it. I think everybody can read it, but I want to say it out loud anyway. As the U.S. Coast Guard Office first assigned to investigate the fatality, he would have intimate knowledge as to the procedures regarding custody of physical evidence and policy regarding conduct of investigations. Would you kind of elaborate, Mr. Pilkington?**

Pete Pilkington: Basically what I'm looking for here, Lieutenant Wellborn, Lieutenant J. G. Wellborn, who elected not to take into custody the evidence and returned the evidence to the dive contractor, subsequently that evidence became not available, which has been at best a costly venture to reproduce the evidence or to find it.

Yes, this is Joe Walker again. I think it's a two-pronged issue. Number one, I think we have the actual cause or problems that occurred at the accident itself. Then in a general sense, what information did he receive? What information or lack thereof did he receive in order for him to conduct a proper investigation? What experience did he have in investigating this type of action? I think it's more than just a custody issue, but in a general sense, a follow-up or the follow-up or procedures that were followed following the death.

Pete Pilkington: And, in addition to that, there's the Coast Guard regulation which specifically requires than in a diving fatality that someone trained in diving accidents investigate. I'd like to be able to question Lieutenant JG and see if he in fact is knowledgeable. If he's not, then again, I've got another question for Captain Fels. Why was he assigned?

This is Bijan Siahatgar, and I guess I'm going to address this more to, I guess, to the whole group. The question is, what is the whole purpose of this next couple day investigation? I mean, if we start going into all these different details, there's no way we'll get done in two days. My feeling is we need to decide what the scope of this investigation's going to be, the three-day hearing's going to be, and then decide which witnesses to go, because now that we're talking about all these—Mr. Beistle, as you put them, Coasties, I mean, I think we're starting to go way far afield here in some of the different areas that we're addressing. A lot of these issues are post-incident issues which may or may not be what you're looking at for this investigation in this hearing next week. So I'm, just going to throw that out there.

I'd like to make a comment on that. This is Joe Walker. I think, and my feeling is, and don't get me wrong, I think maybe these post-accident investigations are actually a very important part because it's my experience if the Coast Guard is not getting the information or all the facts to enable them to do a proper investigation, then I think it's important to explore what facts these guys were given by the diving company relating to the cause of death. I see this time and time again where the Coast Guard issues a report, and number one, they're diving contractors. They are trained to be diving contractors. They are trained to be commercial divers, so they have to rely on the information that they receive in order to come up with a casualty report. Unfortunately, the casualty reports are not accurate sometimes and often times due to the fact that they're not getting the information. So I think the follow-up or the investigation to the accident is probably very critical to this whole process.

If I could just interrupt here for a second—this is Pete Pilkington—let me just read a paragraph from the Marine Casualties Investigations Manual. It says, *"Objective of a Marine Casualty Investigation. An important purpose of a Marine Casualty Investigation is to obtain information for the prevention of a similar casualty as far as is practical. It is necessary for the cause of the casualty to be determined as precisely as possible so the factual information will be available for program*

review and statistical studies. It is not sufficient to know only how a casualty occurred. It must also be clear why it happened."
I can read the rest of it, or I can send that all out to you as an e-mail, because I also have that as an attachment. That's the purpose of a Marine investigation. It's not only to find out what happened to Brian Pilkington. It's to find out what you need to do to make sure it doesn't happen again.

Well, this is Bijan Siahatgar again. It seems like we're putting the cart in front of the horse. I mean, the question is, is this investigation tailored more toward whether the Coast Guard investigation was done properly or is this investigation tailored more toward what happened at this incident and what happened to Brian Pilkington?

Pete Pilkington: I don't think you can separate the two. I think the initial part of this hearing should be determined. And, as I said before, the fact witnesses should be taken in order as to the actual incident. Then I think the fact witnesses, or the next fact witness should be those that investigated the incident. I don't think you can separate the two. I think it should be a two-pronged process.

This is Lieutenant Commander Beistle again I've had some discussions with my district legal office and also done a fair amount of research. As a matter of fact, can I give you folks a site please? It's 46 USC 6301, and that's really in pamphlet. Are you folks familiar with the pamphlet? Obviously it's U.S. 46 USC 6301, and F6301 essentially sets out the—it sets out the mandate for congressional mandate for doing Coast Guard investigations. And one of the things I'm a little troubled by in going down this path—and I don't want you to think that I'm ruling this out at all—but one of the things that I'm a little troubled by is the fact that 6301, just as Mr. Siahatgar indicated, is fairly narrowly focused on investigating a casualty and the events that contributed to the casualty. So one of the problems, I think, about going too far down this path is that essentially—I mean, it's almost analogous to being sort of an ultra—sort of issue. I'm not saying that the Coast Guard can't investigate itself. In point of fact, I'm sure it can, and that's part of our process of getting better. But to the degree that we go down that road, I think that we lose focus. We start to lose focus at some point and really my congressional mandate which is to investigate the casualty and what events contributed to the casualty.

This is Joe Walker again. I'm not trying to belabor this thing, but that particular section, 46 USC 6301, looks at two issues. The first issue is the cause of the casualty, including the cause of any death, which there's no doubt with anybody in this room that that should be the first day of this hearing.

A fact witness that deals with—that knew, that was there, that knows, that was in charge of the diving. They should be first guys out of the chute. But section 2 of 6301 looks at a willful act of misconduct in confidence, negligence,—violation of law, and so forth, and part of that should be at least a determination as to what facts these Coast Guard investigators were given by this diving company. What information was given to them? What information was not given to them? It's important for them, I think, to see whether they—and I hate to use this word—whether they were hoodwinked.

This is Mike Wilson. Well, I think if I could—the section 2 that you just cited, in fact, are there any willful act, confidences, etc, that has contributed to the cause of the accident? So I think the focus of this should be on the incident and not on investigating the investigation, which appears to me it's a valuable undertaking, but it's probably an internal Coast Guard matter that probably should not concern any of us.

Lt. Com. Tom Beistle: **Thank you, Mr. Wilson. Actually you kind of touch on another issue that sort of troubles me here. And that is that when—I just recently received a tasking letter and an appointing letter from my district commander, Admiral Pluta, to convene this formal investigation. I don't know how much of this is just splitting hairs, but I really am troubled by this issue. I feel that when Admiral Pluta appointed me to do a formal investigation, he essentially rendered a lot of the work that was done before, a lot of the investigation that was done before to be almost—the preparatory work, to what's being done now. I'm not going to suggest that everything that was done before is mute or irrelevant. It certainly isn't, but at most it became the preparatory or legwork to the hearing that we're going to do next week. I'm just sort of troubled by the concept of going back essentially in mid-investigation and investigating how we got to this point in the investigation.**

This is Tom Marion out of New Orleans. Tom, let me jump in at this point. There's a separate administrative process by which individual or individuals or corporations can in fact comment on investigations that were done properly or improperly, hence one of the reasons why we're here in the first place. And again, by virtue of the fact that a separate investigating officer has been assigned, that you have this level of form. Because one does not necessarily have this level of form mandates that the focus should be on the facts and circumstances surrounding the casualty itself and not in fact questioning or delving into the Coast Guard's prior investigation.

Now I will be quick to add that the current regulations that exist in 46 CFR 197 and the guides that exist in the Marine Safety Manual, vis-à-vis these type of casualties, could be commented on if there are problems or situations whereby the current regulations are deficient. That is the safety issue. But the last one I want to throw in is—and this was touched on earlier by Mr. Pilkington—he said that there are Coast Guard guidance or regulations that require an investigating officer to have diving experience. Hence, Mr. Wellborn was listed. Well, that in fact was not the case. The Marine Safety Manual clearly states that, "Due to the specialized nature of diving, it is helpful though not mandatory for diving casualties to be investigated by investigating officer with diving experience." Now, given that suggestive writing and it's not mandatory, that is why it's good for Mr. Beistle to have experts in this field in order to supplement his knowledge so that he can conduct a thorough investigation. Mr. Beistle does not have diving experience, which would consist of navy training on Level 2, resident professional training courses or commercial diving expertise.

However, he will be armed with witnesses, which allow him to apply their knowledge to the case at hand. Clearly, having said all that, my advice to him is going to be not to go that route as to second guessing what previous investigating officers have done or not done.

Lt. Com. Tom Beistle: **Thank you, Tom. By the way, that's a little footnote I should add there that in looking around for witnesses for myself, witnesses that I want, you'll notice that I stacked the deck in the sense that I didn't list the witnesses that I want. I'm working on bringing over—I believe he's a dive physiologist—anyway, an expert from the navy's experimental dive unit in Panama City, Florida, actually looking to bring over a dive master and a dive physiologist who can shed some light and give me some perspective on what we hear during the hearing. And, as a matter of fact, I expect that they'll testify. So I guess for lack of a better word, I guess I'm telling you that I hope to be armed with people that will sort of withstand scrutiny and be qualified as experts to give us sort of a fair, unbiased, and impartial perspective on what's going on.**

This is Joe Walker. I'd just like to make a comment again. I think if you're investigating a diving injury—and I do have the experience of being a formal commercial diver and an officer of Oceaneering International—if you're going to investigate an accident—and one of the things in 6301 looks at is the act of misconduct and confidence, negligence and skillfulness, and willful violation of law, I think it's imperative that at least these Coast Guard investigators address the willful, if there was any, mission of things that happened out there. Because I think it goes to the—well, I hate to use a criminal term, but it goes to the men's—.

Lt. Com. Tom Beistle: **No, and I do. I think that you're absolutely right about that. But as to any information that they have first-hand knowledge of or that they were witnesses to or that they have direct knowledge of, my concern with Blake Wellborn is that he came into this way after the fact. I would agree wholeheartedly that if he has first-hand knowledge of any of this stuff that isn't going to be brought up by other witnesses that we're bringing, then he clearly should be—he should testify**.

Pete Pilkington: In response to Blake Wellborn, Blake Wellborn was made aware of the fact, where the compressor was, that the compressor was in bits and pieces at McKenzie's Equipment. He had the ability to go see that compressor, at least maintain custody of it. He chose not to. I think he needs to answer exactly why.

This is Mike Wilson. So is the purpose of doing this to bring him on so we can punish him?

Pete Pilkington: No, not to punish him but to find out what his mindset is. What operational order is he under that he doesn't conduct a proper investigation? And I will remind the United States Coast Guard that it was three years and four days before anybody from the United States Coast Guard ever interviewed anyone in regards to this case, including Mr. Wellborn.

Mike Wilson: Well, let me just reiterate that. Under 6301, the investigation is to look at acts or failure to acts that contributed to the cause of the casualty. It would appear to me that if any witness does not have anything to add to this investigation, finding out the cause of the casualty, that they're really irrelevant to the investigation.

Joe Walker: Because I think one of the things that is very important is if a 6301 investigation of a casualty, it's not just what caused it but what these diving companies are telling the Coast Guard. And I think it's very important to determine what was told to these people, because the Coast Guard may have decided to act or not to act based on the lack of information given to them.

Lt. Com. Tom Beistle: **Now, I hear what you're saying, Mr. Walker, and I like the idea. I'm a little bit concerned about robbing the scope to making this a wholesale investigation of the industry. But other than that, I'm generally receptive to what you** . . .

Joe Walker: What if we find out that there's been a deliberate obstruction . . . these Coast Guard investigators?

Lt. Com. Tom Beistle: **Yes. That will be fertile territory if we find that out**.

Mike Wilson: I would submit that that would then lead to a different investigation, not this one. This one, I thought, is limited to the cause of this incident.

Lt. Com. Tom Beistle: **And I think you're right. I think you're absolutely right. I'm not going to do any criminal investigation. I'm frightened that if we go down this road too much, people are—we're sort of going to sabotage the spirit of cooperativeness that's sort of pervaded this process so far. I want you to know that, again, my purpose generally is—my purpose specifically is set out in 6301. By the way I'm approaching this, is I'm trying to find out all the facts that I can about the cause of this casualty, and then after that—that's the purpose of this hearing. And then after that, as part of the deliberative process, I'll decide what the—who to refer what to and when and why. But this is just a fact-finding process right now, please. I'm not prosecuting anybody, I promise. It's not my job.**
Okay, let's move on to Lieutenant Martinez. Mr. Pilkington, would you—?

Pete Pilkington: Well, Lieutenant Martinez was there on site prior to the commencement of the dive, again referring back to the NAVIC 1-89. It specifically states in that NAVIC that prior to the dive the Coast Guard Inspector is to interview the dive team, review the guide procedures, the operations, that he is not to proceed unless it is deemed to be in a safe manner. We know that the compressor that was used that day was four years out of compliance. We know that there was no safety manual, and we have a written statement from—or written work order stating that they didn't have an operations manual. Why did he permit the operation to proceed?

This is Joe Walker In support of that statement he's obviously a fact witness.

This is Tom Beistle. **Anybody else care to comment? I tend to agree. I think that he would add value. I think that in some sense he's a fact witness, although I don't think he was on board at the time of Brian Pilkington's casualty or fatality or accident, death. He was not on board at the time. I think he will add value though, so I'm very receptive to the idea of calling him. I'll tell you that he is in Puerto Rico, and I don't intend to call him in. I think I can make him available through telephonic testimony, so I think we'll call him. How about Lieutenant Thompson?**

Pete Pilkington: Lieutenant was also there at the time. The NAVIC also requires that the inspector witness the test.

Lt. Com. Tom Beistle: **Is he redundant or repetitive to Lieutenant Martinez?**

Pete Pilkington: Very well could be. But is he not currently in this office or has he also been transferred out of your jurisdiction?

Lt. Com. Tom Beistle: **No. Well, in a manner of speaking. He's in the area and he is available, and I can have him here.**

Pete Pilkington: He also would be able to testify as an independent as to the condition of the dive site and the condition of the vessel at the time, which apparently was 12 miles offshore without an operations manual.

Bijan Siahatgar: Again, I just think I don't see why this investigation's relevant to the investigation of the actual incident itself. I agree with what you said earlier.

Pete Pilkington: I disagree with that totally. The man was on station with a duty assignment and he violated it. And had he done his job, the diving wouldn't have proceeded. The diving operation was in violation before they went in the water. He was there at that time.

Lt. Com. Tom Beistle: **Okay. Mr. Austin?**

Kirk Austin: I have no opinion on this.

Lt. Com. Tom Beistle: **Tom Marion, what do you think?**

Tom Marion: Well, with regards to Mr. Martinez, I guess my only—what gives me pause here is that, again, and you touched on this, that NAVIC 1-89, as is the case for all NAVICs, they're not regulatory in nature. That is, they don't have the same force and effect of 46 CRF Part 197. It is guidance given to the field to the commercial entities out there, sort of as the Coast Guard saying, "Look. FYI. This is out there." So typically, if you have an inspector out there, especially one that is not tasked with overseeing or specifically tasked with overseeing underwater testing, he is not going to be out there with a NAVIC checklist or with the contractor or subcontractor saying, "Oh, you've got to do this, this, and that." That's not his role. That's nowhere on his list of responsibilities. But, having said that, if there are facts that he is privy to that could add to probing the casualty at hand, then the course is relevant.

Lt. Com. Tom Beistle: **Okay. Yes, I think that's what we're going to do. I think we're going to put—I think Lieutenant Martinez, I'd like to hear from him as much as anything else. So I think we're definitely going to call him. And now we're going to go back. I want to go back and talk about Captain Fels again. Here's what I am proposing. I'm not substituting my judgment for anybody** else's on somebody's credibility, but I have talked to Captain Fels. I mean, I'll be honest with you. He's not reluctant to be called. He's happy to weigh in. I can tell you that he's going to—with respect to Captain Fels, he's not going to add much value because he did not have any particular—or specific input on the breakout of the Cliffs 12. Based on that, I'm reluctant more than anything else to waste the hearing's time with somebody who really doesn't have very much information to add. What I'm going to do is I'm going to suggest that we table that, we talk to Lieutenant Martinez, develop whatever information he has to develop, and if there appears to be a reason to call Captain Fels, we'll get him on the phone. It's not a big deal.

This is Joe Walker. I think what Mr. Pilkington wants to explore and it may be that NAVIC 1-89 is not even followed. But I think those questions need to be asked as to whether from Captain Fels' point of view of whether they're just a memo or whether they have any force or authority at all. At least at that stage, after the hearing, I'll be more than happy to write a brief on that issue.

Lt. Com. Tom Beistle: **That's great, and I don't have any problem with that. Well, first of all, let's look at the justification of Captain Fels. It says, "As the Senior U.S. Coast Guard Officer, he had overall responsibility for the activities on Cliffs 12 on 4 March 1996. I think if you ask Captain Fels that, and I'm certainly not speaking for him, I'm just speculating, but he would probably give some sort of an answer that said, "Yes." I mean, insofar as the Coast Guard had authority over anything, yes. So now we've confirmed the obvious. And then the next thing it says, "He was the Senior Office in charge and responsible for the two investigations and the Marine Casualty Reports, I guess, into Brian Pilkington's death, issued by personnel at Marine Safety Office Port Arthur." And again, I think he would answer, yes, and I'm not sure what value we've gotten, you know, where we've added value in going back to my mandate in 6301 into looking into the cause of, casualty cause of Brian Pilkington's death. So again, I'm not ruling him out at all. We will—him online in a heartbeat as long as we can do it on Tuesday or Wednesday. He's got obligations on Thursday out of his office, but frankly, just administrative efficiency suggests that we explore what we can with Lieutenant Martinez before we decide whether it's even worthwhile to call Captain Fels.**

Joe Walker: Okay. We can table these. We can look at these other—Martinez, Wellborn, and Fels on Wednesday.

Lt. Com. Tom Beistle: **That's a great idea. Okay, moving on. Dan Gilbert, G&G. That's a non-issue. That's a repeat. Now let's go to Steve Champagne. Mr. Pilkington?**

Pete Pilkington: Steve Champagne was a witness, uninvolved third party who witnessed the on goings on the Cliffs 12, recently furnished a statement to the Coast Guard in regards to that.

Lt. Com. Tom Beistle: **Now, I've distributed that to the people that I could preliminarily by e-mail. I only compiled a contact list yesterday, late yesterday. I'll distribute that statement. Believe me. It's not an affidavit. I did not pretend to make it. Well, I think I may have used that word just to—probably inadvertently—I probably should have used the word "statement," but I will provide that statement to everybody else here very quickly. Now, here's the deal. I have no problem with calling him. I want to provide his statement to everybody and certainly take a look at it. Logistically there may be a problem in the sense that I've got to get out there and serve him, and he may or may not be working offshore right now. I've got to get to that as quickly as possible. Let me ask a key question. Does anybody think that he is a vital witness; without him we can't go forward? I mean, if I make good faith efforts to get him here, is he a vital witness that we can't go forward without? Anybody care to comment?**

This is Joe Walker. I'll defer that to Mr. Pilkington on that issue.

Pete Pilkington: I think it's absolutely vital. He is the only individual, or he was the first of the individuals that was interviewed that was not either a party to the incident itself—in other words, was not a diver, was not a member of the Cliffs' crew. He's the only party that had absolutely, didn't have an ax to grind, had no position to protect. He was just standing there, watching it. He saw it, and wrote down not only recently what he saw, but he wrote down on the day of the incident, and that information was supplied to Cliffs' Drilling at that time.

Joe Walker: So if this was a trial setting, I consider him a pretty key witness.

Lt. Com. Tom Beistle: **Well, I tell you what, before we go there, let me ask a question. I'd like—it's not a trick question. I'm just curious as to Mr. Pilkington's emphasis or appreciation of the importance of this witness, particularly in light of the fact that we do have a statement.**

Joe Walker: Well, I want to interject again. I think that we're cutting out a lot of the posts. It appears that we're going to be tabling the post investigation. It appears that we're going to limit or have some disagreements on the NAVIC 1-89. So we're going back to the 46 CFR 6301. Under that mandate, I think he's absolutely critical.

Lt. Com. Tom Beistle: **No, I—please, I don't want to give you the impression. I agree with you. He was a witness. I talked to him. Mr. Champagne—you**

know, I spent five hours in his kitchen talking to him. I think he has value, so I'm certainly not trying to eliminate him at all. I'm just saying that logistically I couldn't send out a subpoena until as soon as we get done. In other words, I couldn't send out a subpoena until today. Today will be the first time, and I have no concept of his status, so I'm really almost lumping too many issues together. I'm trying to get an assessment of people's sense of his value and his importance to this thing, whether he's worth calling at all. Anybody has any sense other than Mr. Pilkington, especially in light of the fact that we do have his statement, and then based on that I want to sorely get a consensus as to what happens if we can't get in touch with him.

I want to—this is Mike Wilson. I've got the statement in front of me, and clearly this guy knows a lot of the facts, but I wonder whether any of these facts are in dispute by anybody.

Lt. Com. Tom Beistle: **That's an interesting question.**

This is Bijan Siahatgar speaking, and I'm reading the statement for Steve Champagne again, and one of the questions you had is whether or not anybody disputes it? And I think Steve Champagne is confusing two different days of diving, number one. And, number two, if he ever did provide a statement, it wasn't to Cliffs' Drilling Company, so I'd have that. So at least there are certain parts of his testimony that we disagree with.

Pete Pilkington: Well, Bijan, let me just respond to that. He got not only a telephone call two weeks later from Cliffs' Drilling. He also got a letter from Cliffs' Drilling confirming his role in all this. Cliffs Drilling may not have seen his statement, but the people out on the rig that asked him to write it up certainly did.

This is Joe Walker. It sounds to me like we've got some objections, so I think we ought to bring him live.

Bijan Siahatgar: I mean, I'd just like to see that statement. I mean, if in fact there is a statement like that, and if there's in fact a letter that he did receive from Cliffs', I'd like to see it.

Lt. Com. Tom Beistle: Okay. **I'm almost there fellas, ma'am. I'm also going to try and send you one from a fellow named Donny Henrie.**

This is Joe Walker, I think it's imperative that Donny Henrie be at the hearing. I mean, the issue about the oxygen hoses is absolutely—

Joe, this is Bijan. With all due respect, I don't think anything that Donny Henrie says is necessarily in dispute. The whole deal with the oxygen hoses is well documented through the deposition testimony. I don't see why Donny Henrie would be a necessary witness.

Pete Pilkington: Well, I object to that because I think Donny Henrie is critical. Donny Henrie directly disputes Mr. Austin's testimony that he went in the water.

Bijan Siahatgar: Well, I think there are probably five or six witnesses who've all testified that Kirk Austin went in the water. I don't think that necessarily is in dispute.

Joe Walker: Well, obviously this guy disputes it.

Bijan Siahatgar: Well, Kirk, why don't you tell us whether you went in the water or not.

Kirk Austin: I went in the water a number of times.

Bijan Siahatgar: All right.

Tom Marion: That makes it easy.

Pete Pilkington: I wasn't aware that this was a hearing.

Joe Walker: Well, I think you've got—to be frank here, you don't have that many on-site fact witnesses. You have Kirk Austin, a party in interest. You have Wiitala, who may or may not be. We have some bias in his testimony.

Joe let me interrupt, this is Pete Pilkington Wiitala has also testified that he can't remember if Kirk Austin ever went under the water apparently there is some question as to Mr. Austin's involvement in the recovery attempt.

Joe Walker: We have Lawdermilk?

Bijan Siahatgar: Lawdermilk wasn't on site.

Joe Walker: Wasn't on site. So you have Champagne and Henrie. That's really about it.

Bijan Siahatgar: Well, Joe, again with all due respect, for example, the three individuals from Hercules that I listed that we decided we would perhaps subpoena for Thursday, I mean, all three of them were on site also, for example, and there's probably another half dozen or so Hercules hands who were on deck who assisted in splicing the other oxygen, assembling oxygen torch hoses that I don't have in front of me, but I'd have to pull out of my discover responses that were all on site as well.

Joe Walker: Sure. Then why—if we're bringing Henrie, why wouldn't he solve that problem? Why not bring him live? Then you don't have to have all 25 witnesses?

Bijan Siahatgar: I don't think there's anything in Henrie that's inconsistent with anything anybody else has testified to.

Lt. Com. Tom Beistle: **Mr. Walker, I have one of my guys faxing this stuff over to you right now. Okay, listen folks, it seems to me that it's worthwhile. What I'm going to do is I'm going to do my dead-level best to get both Mr. Champagne and Mr. Henrie there to the hearing. Now, what that's going to mean is that I'm going to wind up issuing a subpoena as soon as this hearing is over and trying to get it over to the Morgan City office and get them to serve this thing. I will keep you apprised. It's going to be—I'll believe it when I see it. I'm not saying it's impossible. I found both of these guys. I'm sure that somebody else can. It's just a matter of whether they're home. But I'll work on that today.**

Lt. Com. Tom Beistle, this is Bijan Siahatgar again. If you're going to try to subpoena Steve Champagne and Donny Henrie, I personally don't have a problem with anything Donny Henrie says in his affidavit. I think it's consistent with everything else that's out there. But Steve Champagne, I think some of the materials that he may talk about, some of the matters he may talk about are inconsistent. I think in that case the Fred King individual I listed may be a necessary party or may be a good fact witness to have as well.

Lt. Com. Tom Beistle: **Okay. You know, I may have made too sweeping a statement there. Let me tell you frankly that I sat down and talked to both of these guys, Steve Champagne and Donny Henrie. And frankly, I'm going to tell you that my personal opinion is that Mr. Henrie isn't going to bring much to the dance. I certainly don't think I heard anything new, original, or different from him. You know, honestly, he doesn't remember it that much. I mean, I was sitting in his living room, drinking coffee with him. I don't think he had any reason to, or he certainly didn't appear to be doing the two-step on me. I'm just not sure if we're bringing them all the way over from Lockport, Louisiana, how much value he's going to add. He's probably—you know, I spent an hour and a half with him or closer to two hours of which about 90 percent of that was trying to get my computer to print on my portable printer. Is there some** discussion here? Does anybody think that we need both Steve Champagne and Donny Henrie? Or if we can get Steve Champagne, can we look for efficiency so we can try to get this thing rolled through? Can we just accept Mr. Henrie's statement?

Joe Walker: I'll defer to Mr. Pilkington on that. This is Joe Walker.

Pete Pilkington: As long as there is no objection to admitting his statement.

Joe Walker: Okay. That sounds reasonable.

Lt. Com. Tom Beistle: **Good. So maybe we can just get Mr. Champagne and we can just submit Mr. Henrie's statement. Okay, moving on down the line Marty Husband from McKenzie Equipment. I've talked to Marty Husband at length. He has reasonably good information. I don't have a witness statement from him. Okay, does anybody have any comments one way or another?**

Joe Walker: My comment is that he should be there. Certainly he should be there to testify.

Lt. Com. Tom Beistle: **Does anybody else have any feelings? Okay. We'll try and get him, which raises another issue that I'm going to bring up after we're done here. But I think we are stroking along pretty good. Guy Kirby. Guy Kirby also from McKenzie's, I think this is a valuable witness because he did dismantle the compressor. The only problem is that I've yet to be able to track him down. To my knowledge he is out of pocket unless he has just recently moved back into the state and is living with his mother or sister, one of his—with his family again. I've been completely unsuccessful at tracking him down. Does anybody have any ideas about how to track him down? I take from the loud silence that nobody has any good ideas.**

Pete Pilkington: The only good idea I can give is the U.S. government, with all its resources. We've got the man's Social Security number. He should be relatively easy to locate.

Joe Walker: Get a hold of the IRS. They know how to track him down.

Lt. Com. Tom Beistle: **Well, I will tell you that in my experience in the past, CGI does not activate that—as a matter of fact is not allowed to tap into that for administrative kinds of investigations. It has to be truly, truly criminally related and I have to be able to prove it ahead of time. So they typically don't tap into that resource unless I can prove that it's an absolute criminal investigation and**

I can show them that warrants are about to issue or something. And frankly, I couldn't put together any kind of a justification to issue warrants for Mr. Kirby's arrest. I don't think anybody's suggesting that he's done anything criminal. So having said that, I think my resources are more limited than you might expect.

Pete Pilkington: Well, I might suggest then, if you can't contact Mr. Kirby that we contact Mr. Husband one more time. There were three other technicians that worked on that compressor.

Lt. Com. Tom Beistle: **There are, and they're all connected with McKenzie, and that's going to be an issue that I want to raise a little bit later. I've got that tabled. Let me make a commitment. I will talk to CGI and see whether there's anything that they can do to contact Mr. Kirby. I will tell you that I've made reasonably strong efforts in the past and have had no success. And frankly, unless it's—it's just by dumb luck that he's moved back into the state and is living with someone that we know he's connected to, I have very little expectation we'll be able to contact him. So we'll try. That's the best I can do. I think he's a good witness. I think he's an excellent witness. I'd like to hear from him. I'm just not sure I can manage it. Kevin Todd Lawdermilk. Anybody care to comment?**

Kena Seiler: I don't know how much he has to add. I mean, he was not present beforehand. He was present and I think drove Dan Wiitala home from Port Arthur. I know he's got an ax to grind with Dan Gilbert. I mean, we can take care of that if you guys think he's really necessary. I don't know how much he adds as to the actual cause.

Lt. Com. Tom Beistle: **I also have a statement by him that Mr. Pilkington produced awhile back that Mr. Lawdermilk signed. I talked to him at length awhile back and I talked to him several times. He sort of confirms the content of the statement. I don't have it as readily accessible. It's in my files. I understand what you're saying, Ms. Seiler. I know that he has one point of view and Dan Gilbert has another point of view, so at some point it could just be a swearing match.**

This is Pete Pilkington: I asked for him to be called for three reasons. First of all immediately after the incident Wiitala spent two hours with Lawdermilk driving from Port Arthur to Houston. Wiitala had just witnessed a man being killed while working under his supervision. During that drive Lawdermilk and Wiitala had a lengthy conversation. That conversation certainly, if it were presented, I believe, before Mr. Wiitala, that Mr. Wiitala might very well confirm it. Secondly, Kevin

Lawdermilk also had custody of the compressor. He delivered it to McKenzie's, and he picked up the new compressor and returned it to Dan Gilbert. In addition, and this is probably the most salient reason to bring him, is that he was in some respect responsible for the maintenance of the compressor.

This is Joe Walker, That's pretty pertinent to me.

Pete Pilkington: That was prior to the accident. In other words, he can go into the maintenance practices at G&G Marine. It is the maintenance practice at G&G Marine that was directly attributable to the death of Brian Pilkington.

Joe Walker: And that certainly would be relevant under 6301.

Lt. Com. Tom Beistle: **I tend to agree. The burden's going to be on me. I'm going to have to try and reach out and touch him, so I'll try. Or I think we can do that. Okay, Ross Saxon. Comment?**

Joe Walker: I understand he was a part owner of that company?

Lt. Com. Tom Beistle: **Certainly not at the time. About three years before I think he might have been.**

Pete Pilkington: Incorrect. Ross Saxon divested his interests in G&G Marine in 1996 after the incident. I have a copy of their minutes of their meeting when they bought his interests out. He was an owner of G&G. He owned two hundred of the one thousand shares that were outstanding at the time. He also wrote the safety manual that G&G operated under. He also advised Dan Gilbert that it was not necessary to maintain records and that the records could be destroyed on paydays, all diving records.

Joe Walker: Well, they can subpoena him. He's the president of the Association of Diving Contractors. Certainly he can talk. If he was an owner of G&G Marine, or involved in their safety manual, he certainly should be able to help the Coast Guard understand proper diving safety procedures.

Bijan Siahatgar: Ross Saxon. Yes, we're starting to go a little bit far afield again in my opinion.

Joe Walker: For what reason?

Lt. Com. Tom Beistle: **Yes. Listen. Here's the deal. Anybody who can add value, the problem—you're right, Mr. Walker. Let me ask this just as a** hypothetical—and I'm not asking you to take a position. I'd really appreciate sort of an unbiased instant analysis. How's that for putting you on the spot? I've really gone over in my own mind the question of—and I've tried to analyze this—of whether we'd be able to support a subpoena if we issued one. In other words, if we issued a subpoena to Mr. Saxon and he challenged it, which is at least potential or at least a likelihood, do you think I'd be able to go into the U.S. attorney's office and give him enough bullets in his gun to go to a federal district judge or a magistrate and get him to support that subpoena, enforce the subpoena?

Joe Walker: Well, if he wrote the diving regulations and safety manual and he had an ownership in the companies, then he should be able to address whether G&G Marine violated their own safety regulations that he wrote. Wasn't G&G Marine also a member of the Association of Diving Contractors?

Lt. Com. Tom Beistle: **As a matter of fact, I think he's the executive director. Is that right?**

Joe Walker: Yes. Were they a member of the Association of Diving Contractors at the time of the incident?

Lt. Com. Tom Beistle**: I think that's a good question**.

Joe Walker: And if they were, the Association of Diving Contractors may offer some very interesting information as to whether they independently investigated the accident since they do indicate that they do those types of things.

Lt. Com. Tom Beistle**: I do like that idea. As a matter of fact, I believe that G&G was a member of ADC at the time of the casualty, though I think they left soon thereafter.**

Joe Walker: Or maybe they were thrown out soon thereafter. I'm not sure.

Lt. Com. Tom Beistle: **Well—**

Kena Seiler: Soon thereafter they were not.

Joe Walker: They were not?

Kena Seiler: They were not thrown out of the Association of Diving Contractors. They withdrew their membership.

Lt. Com. Tom Beistle: **Okay. Let me ask a question here. I kind of do like the idea because I like the idea of, if for no other reason than the fact that G&G was a member of ADC, ADC does have consensus standards, and so I think Mr. Saxon can add some value in the sense that he can talk about what ADC's expectations are for members to comply with the consensus standard. Now, having said that, I am also aware, and I think a few of you are aware, of a sort of brewing sort of tangential issue. That is the fact that the Coast Guard is—or is reexamining its regulations, its commercial dive regulations, and is going through the rule-making process and taking public comments. I know that ADC has their submission in, and I know that Mr. Pilkington has his submission in. I don't mean to talk down to this and know that I'm talking to you, Mr. Pilkington. Sorry, that's just my mode. One of the issues I'd like to avoid, only because I think it would cause delay and I feel that it would blur the focus of this investigation, is I would like not to get in a debate at this hearing with Mr. Saxon about present-day rule making on commercial dive regulations. In other words, I believe that there's another venue, another forum to that. They're holding public hearings on that and I'd like to, if we can get Mr. Saxon to show up, I'd like to do it in such a way that we discuss the events of the day and not fast forward to what's going on present day in another forum, a rule-making to create new regulations. Anybody care to comment on that issue?**

This is Joe Walker. I think that he should be obviously limited to the relevancy of the testimony he has to offer regarding the application of ADC standards to the accident that occurred and the death that occurred or the lack of application nor the non-use of ADC regulations if obviously Gilbert was a member of the Association of Diving Contractors at the time. I agree with you. I don't think you want to get bogged down in present hearings that are subsequent to all this.

Lt. Com. Tom Beistle: **I appreciate that. I agree. Does anybody care to comment? I mean, this is not some sort of tacit assumption that we're going to call him. That's still an open question. Maybe I'm putting the cart before the horse here. Anybody have any sense of—I guess I'm proposing—or where I see him adding value to this is to the limited issue of discussing ADC policy and the consensus standards at the time of the casualty and when G&G was a member of ADC. Does anybody care to comment?**

This is Joe Walker again, I just want to make a comment. As the—regarding Mr. Saxon's role with the Association of Diving Contractors and the fact that he did put the regulations, or apparently write the regulations for G&G Marine, I think his testimony would be very valuable if he indeed can testify that G&G did not comply with both his safety manual and the regulations, the consensus standards.

This is Pete Pilkington. In addition to that, let me add that Ross Saxon not only wrote the safety manual, but up until 1992 Ross Saxon was responsible for the air quality testing, the testing that was required by the 46 CFR that were done on the G&G compressors and they were routinely done until 1992, until Ross Saxon's departure.

Lt. Com. Tom Beistle: **Yes, but I think that's a fact—candidly, I think that's a fact that we can establish just by documentation.**

Pete Pilkington: But he must have established a policy at G&G by which they determined that it was necessary to follow federal regulations.

Lt. Com. Tom Beistle: **My only concern is, I mean, if you look at the road we're going down here, what we're talking about doing essentially is saying, "Okay, Mr. Saxon, thanks for coming to the hearing. Did you help write this safety manual?" And he'll say, "Yes." Then we'll say, "Did you expect that G&G would comply with the safety manual while you were there?" "Yes." "When did you—I don't know about divorcing yourself from any ownership of this—but when did you leave G&G and stop having anything to do with the operations?" And my expectation is he's going to say, "Two or three years prior to the casualty," and then we'll say, "Did you have any impact or any influence or have any expectations about what was going to happen with G&G after you left?" And he's going to say, "No." And there we go. Now we've got our witness. We've heard what we expected to hear, and we're going to move along. Did anybody expect to hear anything different than that?**

Joe Walker: Well, yes, I do. I expect him to comment on what happened out there and comment as to whether as a prior manager of G&G, just like you would on any other diving accident. If you're going against Cal-Dive or American Oil Divers or any other one, you often times will call a prior safety manager to testify to establish in his mind and in his opinion the egregiousness of this violation. And remember, 6301 is looking at misconduct, incompetence, negligence, and willful violations. And his testimony could certainly appease the former founder of G&G Marine or owner and stockholder of G&G Marine.

Lt. Com. Tom Beistle: **Was he—is Mr. Saxon a diver?**

Joe Walker: Apparently, he was a navy diver with no commercial diving experience.

Bijan Siahatgar: I believe that's incorrect. I don't think Mr. Saxon has any diving experience.

Let me interrupt if I can, this is Pete Pilkington, I don't know if Dr. Ross Saxon has any diving experience or not. I do know that Mr. Saxon does not have a legitimate PHD, for that matter I doubt he has ever set foot on a college campus. But Mr. Saxon has been the only representative of the diving industry to ever be a member of the United States Coast Guard Of Shore Safety Advisory committee. A position he still holds today. Let's have him here in that capacity. After all this is about offshore safety.

Lt. Com. Tom Beistle: **But I'm going to have a crusty master diver from the United States Navy Experimental Diving Unit and also a dive physiologist who's going to be sitting there listening to this whole thing.**

Joe Walker: Well, I understand that, but I think it's—and I will say, with all due respect to the navy, that often times the navy experience is different than the commercial diving experience—but Mr. Saxon, as head of the ADC, if he indeed testifies that his company's violations—or the company that he helped start and write the safety manual—their violations were incompetent and willful and grossly negligent and everything else.

Lt. Com. Tom Beistle: **But how is he going to know that three years after the fact?**

Joe Walker: Because he's the president of the Association of Diving Contractors and he may have discussed this incident with Mr. Gilbert. I'm sure he didn't just look at this injury and not have any discussions with G&G Marine. In fact, the Association of Diving Contractors regularly investigates these types of accidents, so he may be able to shed light on what he found out.

Kena Seiler: I had the understanding that the ADC did no investigation of this accident because there was a lawsuit pending.

Pete Pilkington: Ross Saxon told me that the Association of Diving Contractors did no investigation because Dan Gilbert withdrew his membership from the ADC and the ADC only had the authority to investigate member companies.
Bijan Siahatgar: I have no problem with anything Ross Saxon is going to say.

Lt. Com. Tom Beistle: **Yeah, and you know, frankly neither do I—I mean, obviously, I don't. I don't have a dog in this fight. Mr. Pilkington, can you get him? Can you round him up for me?**

Pete Pilkington: I would suspect that if I were to write him or contact him, he would elect not to show up at the last moment, making it too late to subpoena him. I think it would be better off if you issue a subpoena.

Lt. Com. Tom Beistle: Okay. Here's what I'm going to do. I'm going to call Ross Saxon or at least the ADC and try and talk to him immediately after this, and I'm going to feel this out. My sense is that I'd like to have him—I'd like to have him on the issue that I've discussed, which is G&G's compliance with the consensus standards at the time of the casualty. If I can get him—and I expect to get him—I'm not going to hesitate to get him. But, candidly, if he gives me his word that he'll show up, I'm not going to issue the subpoena. I'm going to trust him on it. And if I wind up regretting that later, I'll just regret it. But I'm going to try and get him to show up on that limited issue, but I'm going to tell everybody right now that I'm going not to go into this whole issue of the present day rule making and what's going on there. How about Howie Doyle? Anyone care to comment?

Bijan Siahatgar: Howie Doyle. I think we can withdraw him from the list if we're not going to be concerned with affecting future regulation. That's the only thing that Howie Doyle could effectively address. He wrote "Bridge Over Troubled Waters" and . . .

Lt. Com. Tom Beistle: Right. It would be interesting to have him submit something—if he wants to write it and submit it as part of a hearing for me to include as an enclosure, I'd be happy to do that. "Bridge Over Troubled Waters"
is an article in a magazine called Underwater—what I'll do is I'll attach that in an e-mail that I'm sending everyone—and what it is Howie Doyle's response to an article where I had requested that the Coast Guard rewrite their regulations. Howie Doyle countered that and published it in his magazine, saying that there was no need for new regulation, there was only need for the Coast Guard to enforce the regulations they already have. I'll e-mail that to everyone.

Next, Senior officers of Cliffs Drilling, anyone care to comment?

Bijan Siahatgar: The comment I can make is that some of the information that Mr. Pilkington is trying to elicit, certainly Buddy Horton can provide one part of that information. I'm trying to dig up a lot of the other information relative to the agreement between Cliffs' and Hercules, which I'm going to redact appropriately, but I'm going to try to produce that by Monday at the latest. Yes. So certainly, I think both Mr. Horton and Mr. Townsend can provide certain types of information in that regard, but more importantly I just don't see how 46CFR33 or the two NAVICs are really relevant from the standpoint of this incident . . .

Pete Pilkington: Our interest is strictly, we don't need the people. All we need is a copy of the contract. Time had to be of the essence. We've got a paper trail which shows that the vessel 30 days prior to the incident didn't have a COI. We have evidence that there was a rush to get the vessel back into the water and get it certified and as a result, certain timeframes were violated. And what I'm looking for specifically is I'm looking for the performance clause—there must be a performance clause in that contract. Why was it such an urgency to get that rig up and running?

Lt. Com. Tom Beistle: **So if I understand what you said, Mr. Pilkington, what you really need is the charter party? With the dates? And whoever would have given Buddy Horton the authority or the direction to; one on that short timeframe, and two to move the vessel without a Certificate of Inspection.**

Right. I'd appreciate that. And that'll pretty much address that issue. Great, so if we can get that then that'll keep one witness out. Okay Next on Mr. Pilkington's list is an OSHA representative. Were you expecting him to be a witness?

Pete Pilkington: We would like to call the OSHA representative who investigated G&G Marine and their record keeping. Their record keeping or lack of record keeping is directly responsible for the cause of the violation.

Lt. Com. Tom Beistle: **I will tell everybody. I talked to the OSHA office this morning, and I will tell you that I'm not going to go there because there's an ongoing investigation. At least I've been told that there's an ongoing investigation. OSHA, I expect, will be in attendance, but they will not, to my knowledge, be participating as a board member. We certainly don't have any arrangements for doing that, but I am not going to subpoena an OSHA representative to discuss an ongoing investigation. So that's no.**

Pete Pilkington: Well, we made that request before there was not an ongoing investigation.

Lt. Com. Tom Beistle: **Okay. Documents. This is a fairly long discussion of documents Mr. Pilkington is asking for. I will be candid with you that there may be nuggets of good stuff in here, but there's a fair amount of stuff that I don't see a good showing of how they're relevant—how they're relevant to the narrowly focused issue that we're trying to get to next week. Perhaps that's not the best way to start this, but can I have some discussion about this next page?**

Pete Pilkington: What we are looking for here is entirely involving G&G Marine. If you want to see proof that they in fact they bought oil, that they bought ware parts, that they bought filters and the likes of the compressors. The compressors not only—well, I guess if we're limiting ourselves prior to 1996, we want any evidence that they have that they ever bought wear parts for those compressors, proprietary parts, air filters anything. Something more than just Kotex pads and red shop rags.

Mike Wilson: Okay. You're seeing nothing from ABS.

Pete Pilkington: Nothing that I can see here from ABS. No. Other than copies of the submission for the Cliffs 12 into the underwater inspection program.

Lt. Com. Tom Beistle: **Don't you already have that?**

Pete Pilkington: We do not. We have no evidence that the Cliffs 12 was ever admitted into the underwater inspection program.

Lt. Com. Tom Beistle**: Is that something you can get your hands on, Mr. Wilson?**

Mike Wilson: I can find out.

Pete Pilkington: That's all outlined in that NAVIC 1-89 that I'll send you. It describes the videotapes that are required, the documentation that's required. It may be in the NAVIC, but it refers back to the 46 CFR.

Mike Wilson: Yes. Our role as class—we don't do something called an underwater inspection program. Obviously we were conducting this under ABS rules. It may be much the same material, but I know of nothing called an underwater inspection program.

Pete Pilkington: Well, I have a copy of your program. I'll send it to you on American Bureau of Shipping stationery. I can't e-mail that, but I can hand deliver it to you Monday. Or perhaps you might consider contacting your office, it is your program after all.

Ms. Seiler, this is Tom Beistle. It sounds like most of the documents that he's looking for are coming from your client. Do you have any comment on that?

Kena Seiler: Well, it's an awful lot of documents for me to get together in just a couple of days. I don't know how many of these documents exist. I mean, quite honestly, I'm going to have to talk to my client and see whether it's even possible to get these documents together. Like everyone else.

Lt. Com. Tom Beistle: **Let me suggest to you that I think that, if I understand where Mr. Pilkington is going, he is essentially trying to develop evidence of**

any kind of documentary evidence in the form of receipts or what-have-you to show what kind of maintenance practices were conducted or maintenance was done on the compressors.

Kena Seiler: Right, but we're talking about something that happened over three years ago and I don't know that those documents are still even in existence.

This is Joe Walker. Wouldn't that document, those documents have been made as part of the original litigation file? Most of this stuff should have been produced.

Bijan Siahatgar: I don't even know if it was requested, to tell you the truth.

Kena Seiler: This type of stuff was not requested—purchase orders, documents for maintenance. I mean, there were some very limited requests for the Coast Guard, but in terms of receipts for oil and that kind of stuff, no one ever requested that.

Joe Walker: What about maintenance records for that particular compressor? I'm sure that wasn't asked in the underlying litigation?

Kena Seiler: Well, if you tell me specifically what you're looking for within—

Pete Pilkington: I'll tell you what I'm specifically looking for. Specifically, the compressor failed when it ingested a rag and was jammed and burned. What I'm looking for is proof that Mr. Gilbert ever purchased a filter, a proprietary filter for a Quincy compressor, what I am looking for is proof that Mr. Gilbert ever installed anything other than a shop rag or a ladies panty liner as a primary filter on the air intakes of his compressors.

Kena Seiler: Okay. Anything else?

Pete Pilkington: Yes, whether or not he bought—well, I guess since we don't have the OSHA records and OSHA won't be testifying, as we believe there might be an ongoing investigation. So I'm looking for any proof that filters have been bought for those compressors from 1994 to 1999.

Joe Walker: And those are—let me interject. Those aren't oil filters. They're very specific air filters for diving compressors. The Filters used to assure the air delivered to the diver was clear of particulates. Obviously, if there were maintenance records kept for that compressor, that's a record that Gilbert should have. So there were there any maintenance or any information regarding purchase of these air filters.

Kena Seiler: I don't know. I will have to ask him. That's never been asked before.

Well, if you give me a specific description, I will—

Pete Pilkington: All right. I'll give you the specific description. Proprietary air filter.

Lt. Com. Tom Beistle: **Let me give her the specific description. I'm looking for any receipts that Mr. Gilbert has prior to the fourth of March 1996 or receipts, or rather for parts to be used to maintenance or to maintain any of the compressors that he used in his diving operations, specifically the Quincy 325s that he has, and that's specifically what I want.**

Kena Seiler: So that I understand. I am going to have him go through his records, find any receipts prior to March 4, 1996, for parts to maintain any of the compressors used in his diving operations and also receipts from 1994 through 1999 for air filters for Quincy compressors, and I can bring any other document.

Lt. Com. Tom Beistle: Hold on. **I'm not sure about the 1994 to 1999. I'm not going to go there because frankly that may interfere with somebody else's investigation. So I'm not seeking any receipts for anything after March of 1996.**

Joe Walker: Can I interject here? Make sure—you know the Quincy compressor has two air filters. One is just a general air filter like you have on your car, the diving air filter, air purity filters, we need to see them both.

Lt. Com. Tom Beistle: **Well, we run into a problem there. I understand what you're saying, but I'd like to know about any maintenance that was done on them. Unless—now here's the thing, Ms. Seiler. If that turns out to be over broad, if you go back to your client and talk to him and he says, "Hell, I've got thousands and thousands of receipts for thousands and thousands of parts," then you need to let me know and we'll narrow it to just the air filters. But as it stands right now, if he has receipts prior to March of 1996 for parts that were purchased to maintenance the Quincy 325s, then I'd like to see them if it's not too large a group? Understood?**

Kena Seiler: Absolutely.

Lt. Com. Tom Beistle: **Okay. Now, as I understand—now if I could have that back. As I understand, this request for documents, this first request here is only directed towards G&G, Mr. Gilbert, Ms. Seiler. There's no requirement for ABS, at least as part of this request to produce anything. Wait a minute. There was a discussion.**

Joe Walker: The admission into the underwater inspection program.

Lt. Com. Tom Beistle: **Oh. Any documentation that you have about your underwater inspection program. Not any, but whatever the procedures are—**

Joe Walker: The manual is specific for the Cliffs 12.

Lt. Com. Tom Beistle: **And anything that's specifically for the Cliffs 12.**

Pete Pilkington: In order for that inspection to have taken place, Cliffs 12 had to be admitted into the underwater inspection program.

Lt. Com. Tom Beistle: **Okay. We understand. Okay.**

Pete Pilkington: Now that's a 46 CFR. Not the NAVIC.

Lt. Com. Tom Beistle: **Okay. Now as I understand, this request is not targeted towards anyone else, not targeted towards Ron Townsend, not targeted towards Kirk Austin, not targeted towards ABS other than that specific issue of the underwater exam program. So nobody else has any duties or responsibilities. Now, the next issue is that I talked to Marty Husband and he's a pretty good witness. He's got a decent recollection of what went on and his discussions with Guy Kirby. Guy Kirby would clearly be the best witness, but again, I just haven't been able to lay my hands on him. Does anybody—and I'm asking you, Mr. Pilkington here as well. Does anybody have a sense of anybody other than Marty Husband, anybody who's with McKenzie's right now that can add any more value than Marty Husband himself?**

This is Pete Pilkington. Marty Husband has indicated that there were three other technicians that worked on the compressor. The problem with Marty Husband is that he himself never physically worked on it.

Lt. Com. Tom Beistle: **And I'm not sure that I agree with you. Having talked to Mr. Husband, he indicated there was a shop supervisor and there were other technicians at McKenzie's. He didn't suggest to me that there was anybody who had nearly as intimate a knowledge of or connection with the compressor other than Guy Kirby. In other words, it wasn't passed around hand to hand. There were other people in that area who might be able to add value.**

Pete Pilkington: Might be able to add value, but it was Kirby who actually took it apart, worked on it, and told everybody else. So everyone else just got hearsay information . . . Guy Kirby, including Kevin Lawdermilk because Guy Kirby also related this same story to Lawdermilk.

Lt. Com. Tom Beistle: **And here's the issue. Marty Husband has a reason to ask. Now admittedly, I know that we're talking about hearsay and everybody has to understand up front that the only rules of evidence that apply in these relaxed administrative proceedings are privilege and relevancy. So as long as it's relevant and as long as it's not privileged and as long as I want to hear it, it's coming in, whether it's hearsay or not. Everybody knew that, didn't they? Marty Husband, I think, has value because he had a reason to talk to Guy Kirby about this specifically because he started to get calls from everybody about the condition of this compressor. So he went and asked Guy Kirby. So I think as a consequence, he had a better reason to pay attention, to remember, to synthesize the information . . . the other guys in the shop who were basically just kind of sitting around shooting shit with him. So I think that Guy Kirby is a more credible witness from that perspective, and the problem is, it's not like I'm trying to rule out different opinions. But I have a strong hunch that the more people we pull in, the more different opinions we're go to get, the cloudier the issue is going to get, and we're going to wind up defocusing rather than focusing this issue. I don't know. Anybody have any thoughts on that?**

Kena Seiler: I want to say there was someone else at McKenzie who may be able to provide testimony. I think his name was Eugene who worked on the compressor, but that's all the information I have.

Lt. Com. Tom Beistle: **Eugene. Do you think he's worthwhile? Do you think that's fertile territory?**

Kena Seiler: Probably.

Lt. Com. Tom Beistle: **Any chance you can find out who this guy is?**

Kena Seiler: Yes. I'll see what I can find out.

The phone conference was then ended with the understanding that Ms. Seiler would once again attempt to retrieve any record, produce and evidence that G&G Marine had actually purchased filters for their Quincy compressors, not just the compressor in use that day but any breathing gas filters for any life-support system that Dan Gilbert owned. And she agreed that they would be made available at the hearing. Of course, Ruben Hope would have to bring the records, she was off on vacation.

Two days later, Sunday June 20, 1999, Fathers Day, the front page of the largest circulated paper in Texas read,

FATHER DIVES DEEP FOR ANSWERS IN SON'S DEATH

Private campaign spurs Coast Guard to reopen inquiry into 1996 offshore oil rig fatality

JAMES PINKERTON Staff
SUN 06/20/1999 *Houston Chronicle*, Section A, page 1, 4 STAR Edition

At a U.S. Coast Guard station on Tuesday, Peter Pilkington will begin to get the answers he has sought since his son died more than three years ago while working for a small Houston dive contractor.

He wants to know why Brian Pilkington, a healthy, 23-year-old commercial diver, suddenly died in March 1996 off Sabine Pass while inspecting an offshore oil rig in 28 feet of water.

He wants to know why the Coast Guard, the federal agency in charge of marine safety, conducted what he considers a shoddy investigation into his son's death. It was an inquiry in which no witnesses were interviewed or any piece of diving equipment examined or retained by officials, Pilkington said.

And he wants to know why two Coast Guard officers let the dive take place, even though they had cited the Cliff's Number 12 offshore rig, operated by a Houston-based drilling firm, for safety violations that day because a required predive safety inspection had not been completed. [VI]

Chapter 18

U.S. Coast Guard Investigation

into the Events Aboard the Mobile Offshore Drilling Unit (MODU) Cliffs Drilling Rig #12 on 4 March 1996

THE INVESTIGATING OFFICER LT. Lt. Com. Tom Beistle: *This hearing will come to order. The record will show that the hearing was called to order at 8:15 on the twenty-second of June 1999, and is being held at the Texas Air National Guard Armory in Beaumont, Texas.*

Good morning, ladies and gentlemen. My name is Lt. Com. Tom Beistle of the U.S. Coast Guard Marine Safety Office in Port Arthur, Texas. I've been directed to serve as the investigating officer of this formal investigation which has been convened by the commander, Eighth Coast Guard District, under the authority of Title 46, United States Code, Section 6301, and 46 Code of Federal Regulations Part IV.

I'm here to investigate the circumstances surrounding the death of Brian Pilkington on March 4, 1996. I, as the investigating officer, will report my findings, conclusions, and recommendations to the commander, Eighth Coast Guard District, and to the commandant of the Coast Guard.

Present at this investigation are Mr. Michael Wilson, Mr. Kirk Austin, Mr. Dan Gilbert, Mr. Ruben Hope, Mr. Peter Pilkington, Mr. Joe Walker, Mr. Ronald Townsend—there we go—and Mr. Bijan Siahatgar.

Did I get everyone? I didn't overlook anyone?

Mr. Joe Walker: *Do you have Mr. Tom Mosele here?*

Lt. Com. Tom Beistle: *How do you spell your name, Mr. Mosele?*

Mr. Mosele: *M-o-s-e-l-e.*

Lt. Com. Tom Beistle: *Thank you.*

This investigation is intended to determine the causes of this casualty and the responsibility, therefore, to the fullest extent possible, subject to final review and approval by the commandant of the Coast Guard. And it is intended to obtain information for the purposes of preventing and reducing the effects of similar casualties in the future. It is also intended to determine if any incompetence, misconduct, or willful violation of the law on the part of any licensed officer, pilot, seaman, employee, owner or agent of such owner of any vessel involved, any officer of the Coast Guard, or any officer or employee of the U.S. or any other person caused or contributed to the cause of this casualty or if there is evidence that any act was committed in violation of any provision of the U.S. Code or the regulations issued there under.

This investigation is also empowered to recognize any commendable actions by persons involved and to make appropriate recommendations in this regard.

All witnesses, for your information, will be examined under oath or affirmation. When testifying, witnesses are subject to federal laws such as 18 U.S.C. 1001 for perjury or making false statements under oath. All parties in interest have a statutory right to employ counsel to represent them, to cross examine witnesses, and to have witnesses called on their behalf. Witnesses who are not parties in interest may be advised by their counsel concerning their rights. However, such counsel may not examine or cross examine other witnesses or otherwise participate.

A party in interest is an individual, an organization, or other entity that under the existing evidence or because of his or her position, may contribute significantly to the completeness of the investigation, may have a direct interest in the case at hand, or otherwise enhance the safety of life and property at sea through a participation as a party in interest.

The following individuals and firms have been designated as parties in interest: The American Bureau of Shipping, G&G Marine, Mr. Peter J. Pilkington, Mr. Kirk Austin, and Mr. Ronald Townsend.

Will the parties in interest and their representatives please introduce themselves for the record? And I think we'll just go ahead and start in order, if you would.

Good morning. My name is Thomas Mosele. I'm here today and I'm an attorney assisting Mr. Pilkington.

My name is Joe Walker. I'm here today, also an attorney assisting Mr. Pilkington.

I'm Peter J. Pilkington. I'm here representing my son.

Lt. Com. Tom Beistle: *Mr. Austin?*

Kirk Austin: I'm Kirk Austin. I'm a party in interest.

My name is Ronald Townsend. I'm a party in interest.

My name is Bijan Siahatgar. I'm counsel for Mr. Townsend.

I'm Ruben Hope, and I'm counsel for G&G Marine.

: I'm Danny Gilbert, party in interest.

Michael Wilson, I represent the American Bureau of Shipping.

Lt. Com. Tom Beistle: *Thank you, everyone.*

I would like to request the cooperation of all persons present to minimize any disruptive influence on these proceedings in general and on the witnesses in particular.

Smoking is not permitted during the hearing.

The news media may question witnesses concerning the testimony they have given but only after those witnesses have been released by me. Such interviews will be conducted outside of this room.

In addition, I would like to say that for all those of you in the audience, you're welcome to be here. I'm glad you're here, and I appreciate your participation. If you would, please, as a courtesy to this hearing, please turn off your beepers or at least put them on buzz and/or vibrate and please don't talk on cell phones or take cell phone calls in this room. I would appreciate that. I appreciate that.

This concludes my opening statement. Thank you for your attention. Could I ask just by a showing of hands—I know that there are a couple of media folk here. Would you please just let me know where you are, who you are?

(PARTIES NOD IN AGREEMENT)

Lt. Com. Tom Beistle: *Thank you. Great. Okay. This hearing will come to order.*

Now, let me take a minute just to introduce you folks to all the people up here at the front of the room. At my right is Lt. Com. Thomas Marian who will be acting as my counsel. He's with the Eighth Coast Guard District legal office out of New Orleans.

To my left is Lieutenant J. G. Greg Crettol, and Greg has been my able assistant on this and is responsible for all the good logistics that have occurred here so far. I'm responsible for everything that has been overlooked.

Again, to my left is Petty Officer Jeremy Henn, who is going to be assisting us throughout this investigation. He's going to be helping us with the technical issues, helping us with the cell phone—or rather with the telephone conference—telephone interviews and so forth.

And then to my far left is Chief Warrant Officer John LaFlamme, who is attached to the Coast Guard Marine Safety Office in Port Arthur and is a very knowledgeable member of our inspections department. He's going to be helping me. He's going to be listening and being an extra set of ears and an extra brain to help me formulate questions and analyze testimony here.

In addition, tomorrow my expectations are that we're going to be joined by Lieutenant Josh Peters. He's on leave today, but he should be back for the duration of the hearing starting tomorrow.

I'm going to list briefly the witnesses that I know that we expect to be able to call: Steve Champagne—by the way, has anyone seen Mr. Champagne? Is he—he's here, Mr. Steve Champagne. And I'm not going to give any explanation right now of what we expect to adduce or what role these folks play. I expect that will play out during the questioning.

Mr. Steve Champagne, Mr. Jerry Lehr, Mr. Walter Linzy, Mr. Dan Wiitala, Mr. Buddy Horton, Mr. Ronald Townsend, Mr. Kirk Austin, Mr. Marty Husband, Mr. Guy Kirby, Mr. Fred King possibly, Mr. Kevin Lawdermilk, Mr. Dan Gilbert—who is also a party in interest—Mr. Ron Townsend and Kirk Austin are, as well—excuse me—Mr. Ross Saxon, Mr. Dennis Jahde, Mr. Ronald Everett, and Lieutenant Julio Martinez.

In addition to that we have a number of other witnesses. Let me say I also expect to call Dr. John Clark, who is from the Naval Experimental Dive Unit, and I believe Dr. Clark is in the audience now. And also—is it master chief?

Master Chief Brick Bradford: *Yes, it is.*

Lt. Com. Tom Beistle: *Master Chief Brick Bradford, who is with the Navy Dive School, who is also in the audience.*

For the record, do any of the parties in interest have any comments or objections to the witnesses who will testify at this hearing or the order of their presentation?

Joe Walker: *I have one comment. I believe we discussed a Mr. Ric Walker.*

Lt. Com. Tom Beistle: *Mr. Ric Walker. Thank you, Mr. Walker. Mr. Ric Walker I'm going to add to the witness list.*

The emphasis on this formal investigation is to evaluate the facts and circumstances surrounding the death of Brian Pilkington, not to second guess prior investigatory efforts by the U.S. Coast Guard. Now, this is consonant with everything that we talked about in our prehearing conference, but I wanted to get that on the record and make that known to the public, as well.

Let's start with Steve Champagne, Jr.

Lt. Com. Tom Beistle: *And what do you do today? What's your job?*

Steve Champagne, *I'm a welder/fitter at Conrad Industries in Marksville.*

Lt. Com. Tom Beistle: *Mr. Champagne where did you work—or rather—yeah, where did you work or what did you do back in March of 1996?*

Steve Champagne: *I was an officer or supervisor for SMB Fabricators in Berwick.*

Lt. Com. Tom Beistle: *Were you on board the Cliffs 12 on March 4 of 1996?*

Steve Champagne: *Yes, I was.*

Lt. Com. Tom Beistle: *First off, we might as well draw a little bit of a picture. Can you tell me a little bit about what the Cliffs 12 was?*

Steve Champagne: *It was—it was a jack-up rig. They was doing some work on the cantilever and we was installing the BJ unit on the top deck of it.*

Lt. Com. Tom Beistle: *How long had you been out on the Cliffs 12, or when did you go out on the Cliffs 12?*

Steve Champagne: *I got on the—on the rig on the third, and we left on the fifth. We arrived at the rig and cut the Halliburton beams clean from the deck and set the engine package, pulled in place, set the pump package, beams and made up the unit.*

Lt. Com. Tom Beistle: *Okay. 'Made up the unit', what does that mean?*

Steve Champagne: *Well, the cement unit comes in three different pieces. You've got an engine unit, you got a package unit, and you've got a ram tub on the back end of it. And we had to set it all together. Then we pull it together, bolt it together, and start fab'ing up our pipe, welding the unit down to the deck, et cetera.*

Lt. Com. Tom Beistle: *Great. Okay. Now, on the fourth—are you familiar with the casualty that occurred, the diving casualty that occurred on board the Cliffs 12 on the fourth of March?*

Steve Champagne: *Very much so.*

Lt. Com. Tom Beistle: *Can you tell me how you became aware of it? When did you first become aware of it?*

Steve Champagne: *We was ready to leave, but the crew boat couldn't approach the rig because they had a diver in the water. So we was just on standby, waiting for the diver to come out of the water so we could get on the crew boat. While we was standing around, I had noticed a gentleman to the left from where I was standing, looking at a monitor, I approached him and asked him if he would mind if I watched, then that's when I realized, you know, the diver was down in the water, I believe at the time he was inspecting. I don't know exactly what he was doing.*

when I approached the man at the monitor he had a headset on and he was just looking at the monitor, asked if he would mind if I watched, he told me, "Not at all." I asked him, you know, what he was watching and he said, "I have a diver in the water." I was looking at the screen, I couldn't make it out, but he was pointing to the screen and telling me what's this and what he was doing. Telling me, you know, it was a leg, "This is the leg of the rig. This is what he's inspecting." I said okay, you know, just sat there and watched.

Lt. Com. Tom Beistle: *Okay. Did you actually look at the monitor? Were you able to look at the monitor that he was looking at?*

Steve Champagne: *Yeah, it was just a little—it looks like maybe six inches or so, just a little bitty old monitor he was looking at. I mean, I couldn't make nothing out of what he was looking at. I mean, it was dark. But I mean, he seemed to know what he was pointing at and explaining what it was.*

Lt. Com. Tom Beistle: *Okay. Did he explain anything of what was going on there?*

Steve Champagne: *He just told me, you know, the diver was down there inspecting the leg, and he showed me an image that he seen that, I guess, assumed that it was the leg of the rig.*

Lt. Com. Tom Beistle: *Okay. Well, what happened—oh, let me ask you: The headset, the headphones that he had on, could you tell, were they—I mean, what was their purpose? Could you tell?*

Steve Champagne: *I didn't know—I assumed, you know, he was having communications with the diver, you know. That was my assumption.*

I was watching him for—you know, it was a while—and then as time went on, when I actually heard him talking to the diver, something went wrong. Something happened. All I could hear was, you know, "Calm down, Brian, calm down." So my assumption, you know, something was wrong. Brian was panicking or something. The man at the monitor just kept on saying, "Brian, calm down."

It went on for a little while, and then it was like "Brian, are you okay? Brian, are you okay?" And then he, the guy that was at the monitor, he got up, and he walked away.

So you know, I stayed there looking at the monitor to see, you know, what was going on. I couldn't see nothing. I couldn't make out anything, heads or tails of it.

Then the guy walked around to the back of the rig to the galley area, and he come back, and he had a cup of coffee or something and when he come back to the monitor, you know, he sat down and he put the headphones back on and it was like "Brian," he kept on saying, "Brian, are you there? Brian?"

He looked at the monitor, and when he looked up, there was an older gentleman standing by the handrails, looking down over the water where Brian's hoses were going in the water and he looked from the monitor at the gentleman and he said, "We have a situation."

So the man at the monitor—him and the gentleman at the rail got together, and the older gentleman said, you know, "We have an emergency situation now. We've got a diver down." And then after that, I mean, pandemonium broke out in the rig. People was running all different directions, trying to get stuff hooked up or whatever, to get—to help the diver that was in the water. And as time went on—they was running around all over the place. A gentleman looked at me and I'm pretty sure he was a tool pusher, he looked at my welding shirt and asked me, "Are you a welder?"

And I said, "Yes, sir. I'm working with BJ."

And he said, "Do you have a torch, oxygen, acetylene hoses?"

I said, "Yes, sir, I do."

And he said, "What kind of psi can your hoses withstand?"

And I said, "Well, we put one hundred pounds on it, you know, every day."

And he turned to the man at the monitor and said, "Do you think that will work?"

And he said, "It will have to."

So me and my helper went to our toolbox at the top deck, grabbed the torch hoses, come down, and gave it to the gentleman, and the other guy gave it to another guy, and he took off with the hoses, and he went and hooked them up wherever he hooked them up at. I don't know.

Then one diver went down first in the basket. They had two different divers. One diver went down. And I mean, it wasn't long, he come right back up in the basket. When he come up in the basket, and he pulled the helmet off, he was bleeding from the nose and the ear area. So all attention went to him to find out what happened to him, what was wrong with him. I was checking his pulse and his heart rate.

Then the other guy, the guy that had been watching at the monitor, he put on the helmet and asked for some shackles. So me and the helper had to go back to our box, grab some shackles, come back down, gave it to them, And then he hooked it to some kind of belt or something he had on, hooked some shackles to it. Then he got in the basket with, I believe, two other gentlemen. The crane lowered them down to the water. I was helping the other guy that was bleeding from the nose.

And after he was okay, you know, he kept on telling me, "I'm fine. I'm fine, you know. Don't worry about me." I made my way to the handrails to see if they was getting the other diver down. I can recall when the diver finally got them, they was pulling Brian into the basket and Brian fell back in the water and the diver grabbed his hoses and he was able to pull Brian back into the basket and the other two gentlemen pulled him into the basket and the crane lifted them up to the top deck.

When they got to the top deck, we laid him down on the deck and I tried to get his helmet off, but I couldn't because he had some kind of—some kind of lock ring or something. So the guy that actually got him out of the water come and pulled his helmet off and we tried to get another—a neck ring or something, and I couldn't get it off either. And so, the other guy had a—we had to turn his head and tilt it or something and we just ripped it off. As soon as we got everything cleared, we—he had a wet suit on, we had to undo his wet suit and everything; as soon as all that was clear, we started CPR immediately on him.

Lt. Com. Tom Beistle: *Okay. Now, when the man standing at the monitor got up and went to get the cup of coffee—or at least he got up and left, as you described it. And when he came back, he had a cup of coffee. How long was he gone?*

Steve Champagne: *Two minutes at the most. I mean, he wasn't gone that long because, I mean, where we was set up at, the galley is maybe ten, fifteen feet from us on the—it was the backside of the galley. You know, they had drinks and everything set up on the backside. Or you can go in the galley and get you something to drink. I mean, you just walked over there, and you know, he come right back after that.*

Lt. Com. Tom Beistle: *How long was that span of talking to the diver, saying, "Are you okay? Calm down"?*

Steve Champagne: *He said it, I guess four or five times. Then he got up and walked away, when he walked away, I assumed the diver was okay because, to my recollection, if something was wrong, he would have never got up and walked away.*

And when he come right back, he asked, "Brian, are you all right? Are you there?" And there was no—I assume there was no response—"Brian, Brian." And then he looked at the monitor and that's when he popped up, and he looked at the gentleman by the rail and said, "We've got a situation."

And that's when the older gentleman walked over, and they talked whatever they talked about and then they said, "We've got a diver down."

Lt. Com. Tom Beistle: *What was his tone when he said, "We've got a situation"?*

Steve Champagne: *Scared, a scared tone. It was like he was shocked, you know. He couldn't believe what happened or whatever. Everybody that was around. They had a lot of people on the deck because they had, you know, my crew and another crew was all ready to leave and then they had all the diving crew there and then they had a bunch of hoses and stuff rolled up all over on the deck. I mean, it was a mad house. I mean they had people all over the place. he just hollered, "We've got an emergency situation now."*

Right after that, the tool pusher come down and then that's when he noticed me, well, wearing my welding shirt and asked me, "Do you got any oxygen acetylene hoses?"

Lt. Com. Tom Beistle: *And he said, "Do you have any oxygen acetylene hoses?"*

Steve Champagne: *"Yes, sir," and then he asked, "Do you think it would help to put oxygen to—to get oxygen to the other diver to retrieve him?"*

I said, "I don't know. I'm not a diver." so he turned to the guy at the monitor and said, "Do you think it would work?"

The other guy says, "How many pounds of pressure can your hoses withstand?"

And I said, "We put one hundred pounds on it every day."

And he was like "Well, that will have to do," so me and the helper went up there to grab our hoses.

Lt. Com. Tom Beistle: *Okay. Now, the man—the first diver, you said that there was one—the first diver who went into the water to try and rescue Brian—or rescue the diver who was down, can you describe that in more detail? You said he went into the water. What did you actually see?*

Steve Champagne: *I really didn't see anything because I stayed back because I really didn't know at the time that he was going down in the water. All I seen was the basket going down, and as soon as the basket got down, it come right back up, and when it come right back up, he was there and when they pulled him out of the basket and pulled his bell off, then he had blood from the nose and ears.*

Lt. Com. Tom Beistle: *You say as soon as he went down, he came right back up. How long do you think it took before—can you tell me that duration of time?*

Steve Champagne: *Thirty seconds to a minute. I mean, we wasn't high off the water at all. We maybe had a ten-foot air gap and whatever the length of the rig was. I mean, it was like he got in the basket, went down, and then he was coming right back up after that.*

Lt. Com. Tom Beistle: *Was he using anything other than the helmet? In other words, did he have a wet suit or anything else on?*

Steve Champagne: *Yeah, he had a wet suit on.*

Lt. Com. Tom Beistle: *Okay. And how much—when you say he was bleeding from the—from what did you say, the nose and ears?*

Steve Champagne: *Nose and ears, It wasn't much, just a little trickle. His nose, it just bled for a little while, and it stopped. His ears, once he wiped his ears, I mean, the blood was gone.*

Lt. Com. Tom Beistle: *What was your—did he appear—how did he appear to you, other than bleeding?*

Steve Champagne: *Shortness of breath, complaining that, you know, his head sounded like it snapped. That's what he told me. He just said—a lot of pressure. He said, "I had a lot of pressure. I'm fine. Don't worry about me" and you know—so I got up and walked away, and I went to the handrails and that's when we watched the other diver go down.*

Lt. Com. Tom Beistle: *And do you—did you know either of these divers? In other words, did you know the first guy who went down, or did you know the second man who went down?*

Steve Champagne: *No, sir. The only way I know the second guy was he was the guy at the monitor I was standing with.*

Lt. Com. Tom Beistle: *Okay. You said that the second man attached some shackles to his—to his belt. And then he—and then what did he do? He got in the basket?*

Steve Champagne: *Yes, sir.*

Lt. Com. Tom Beistle: *And he was lowered to the water, or at least did you—did you actually see him go into the water?*

Steve Champagne: *No, I didn't see him go in the water because I was helping the other guy. But when I got to the handrail area, his—I seen my torch hose and stuff go in the water. So but I did see him go into the basket, but I did not see him go into the water. When I got to the handrail area, it wasn't long after I was at the handrails, I seen him come up holding onto Brian.*

Lt. Com. Tom Beistle: *So now, describe what happened when he brought Brian back up.*

Steve Champagne: *When I was standing over the handrails, you know, and I seen him come up and he had Brian around the waist area and it was—the two guys that was in the basket was trying to pull Brian into the basket and at the same time, a wave or something came and knocked him loose. Well, when Brian was falling to the water, the other diver just grabbed and he grabbed the hoses and he pulled Brian back up with the hoses. And at the same time he was climbing into the basket, and then the other two gentlemen grabbed around his waist and leg area and pulled him into the basket.*

Lt. Com. Tom Beistle: *When he grabbed those hoses, could you tell where the hoses were attached to on Brian? In other words, where were they attached?*

Steve Champagne: *From where I was looking down, you know, I couldn't tell where the hoses were attached to until he got up on deck. Then I seen—*

Lt. Com. Tom Beistle: *What did you see then?*

Steve Champagne: *The hoses run to the—to his back area, and it come and looped up on top of his bell, and it looked like some quick connects or something snapped right into the back of his hood.*

Lt. Com. Tom Beistle: *Okay. Were you able to see—did you look for any reason that—whether they were connected to his helmet or not?*

Steve Champagne: *Yeah, the hoses were connected to his helmet.*

Lt. Com. Tom Beistle: *And when did you see that?*

Steve Champagne: *When I was trying to take his helmet off.*

Lt. Com. Tom Beistle: *And how did you know that they were connected? In other words, did—*

Steve Champagne: *They was running to the back of his helmet.*

Lt. Com. Tom Beistle: *Did they—I mean, when you were trying to get that helmet off, could you see the—I mean, did the hoses move? Did they—did you see any effect on the hoses when you were—*

Steve Champagne: *Not to my recollection.*

Lt. Com. Tom Beistle: *Okay. By the way, what was the weather that day? What was the weather in sea state as you remember it?*

Steve Champagne: *We was right outside the jetties. So always in the jetties, it's always choppy. So I mean, you know, two-foot seas. I mean, just choppy. It wasn't no white-caps or anything like that, but it was choppy.*

Lt. Com. Tom Beistle: *Were you able to look at the hoses? You know, what was their appearance? Did they—did you even notice the hoses by any chance?*

Steve Champagne: *No. I mean, I wasn't concerned about the hoses or anything. My concern was trying to get the helmet off of Brian so we could start helping him.*

Lt. Com. Tom Beistle: *Okay. How much time—from the time when you first heard the man at the video screen say, "We've got a situation," how much time between then and when the first diver went in the water to attempt to help Brian?*

Steve Champagne: *About twenty minutes. It was a while.*

Lt. Com. Tom Beistle: *And then once the first diver came back up, got back on board, how—what was the time duration between that—if you know, between when he came back up and the second rescue diver?—*

Steve Champagne: *Well, it was—it was kind of like right away, you know. Once they seen the other guy was okay, everybody tried to help the other guy get everything he needed. Then he needed some shackles. He needed some weight or something to help him go down. So my man had to run all the way to the top of the rig to get shackles, run down, give it to them. So about five, ten minutes, you know, five minutes or so.*

Lt. Com. Tom Beistle: *How much time—this is not asking the same question three different ways, I promise, or at least I'm not trying to do that. But how much time from when you first heard that "We have a situation" or "We've got a diver down," to when they first started administering CPR, at a guess, your best estimate?*

Steve Champagne: *That—that was a while. When they first said they had a situation and until Brian actually came up on deck, to me, my opinion, it felt a good thirty, forty minutes, you know. I mean, I didn't sit there with a watch or anything, timing it, but it was a good while before Brian got on the deck, before we started CPR.*

Lt. Com. Tom Beistle: *Did you see on the—when you were wrestling with the helmet, did you see a camera or anything attached to the helmet? Did you see anything attached to the bell?*

Steve Champagne: *To me, what I thought was a camera, you know. I really didn't pay no attention to it because I was trying to get the helmet off and I was frustrated because I couldn't get it off. But right on top of the helmet or something, they had something taped to a handle and to my knowledge, yeah, I assumed that was a camera, you know, but I really didn't pay no attention to it.*

Lt. Com. Tom Beistle: *How long would you say between when you first started helping with CPR, administering CPR, and when the helicopter arrived?*

Steve Champagne: *Ten minutes. Five, ten minutes, I would say. It wasn't long after we got Brian on the deck that the chopper showed up.*

Lt. Com. Tom Beistle: *And so, after the helicopter left, what did you do?*

Steve Champagne: *Some other guy came and asked me, I was with my crew, we was all down in the hall and everything and he asked the crew, "Who was the one who was helping do CPR?" And I said, "It was me." And he come and got me, and he said, "I need you to come with me." So I went into his office. It was the medic office. They had a desk, with a bed and a first-aid station and stuff like that, he asked me, "What did you do?" I told him, I said, "I was the one that did the CPR on him. I tried helping him." And he said, "Okay." So he was writing it down in a logbook, and he read it back to me and said, "This is what you did?" And I said, "Yes, sir, this is what I did." He said, "Okay. Sign here." And he asked me, he said, "What company are you working for?" I said, "I work for SMB Fabricators." He said, "What's the address?" I gave him the address, the phone number, you know, everything he asked for, then he said, "Okay. So sign this." And so, I signed this, and he said, "Okay. You can go back with your crew."*

Lt. Com. Tom Beistle: *And you said that—now, did you make the entry? Did you write something in the log, or did he write something in the log?*

Steve Champagne: *He wrote what I did in the log, and all I did was sign it.*

Lt. Com. Tom Beistle: *Did you see the logs? Did you see what they looked like?*

Steve Champagne: *The cover of the log was green, and you know, it had Log written on it, and he opened it to whatever the pages he wanted to, and he put the dates and my name, what I did, and then I signed it. And then I believe he wrote in a tablet also. He had a little, tablet and he wrote it in a tablet, and in the tablet is where he asked me my company name, address, phone number.*

Lt. Com. Tom Beistle: *And I think when we talked about this before, you said you actually got a follow-up letter?*

Steve Champagne: *Yeah. About a week later my company received a letter in the mail. It was a thank you letter for participating in trying to save a life and it was just, you know, a gratitude, saying thank you and my company was very proud of it and we hung it up on the billboard for a while, you know, showing the clients and stuff, you know, our crew is CPR trained and—*

Lt. Com. Tom Beistle: *Thank you Mr. Champagne, I pass the witness to Mr. Joe Walker*

My name is Joe Walker, and I'm going to ask you a few questions to try and maybe fill in some things. Do you recall what activity was going on near the dive station in terms of rig activity?

Steve Champagne: *There was no rig activity going on at all. The rig was shut down. We was repairing it. All I know is ABS came out there that morning, gave an inspection, and they failed the inspection. So they was doing repairs and whatever they had to do to pass the inspection.*

Joe Walker: *You mentioned something about watching the video monitor. When you looked at this monitor, was it like a TV screen?*

Steve Champagne: *Yeah, it looked like a TV screen. It was just, you know, a real small monitor.*

Joe Walker: *Were you able to see part of the platform or the leg or anything?*

Steve Champagne: *The guy that was at the monitor, he pointed out a leg to me, but I didn't know what it was.*

Joe Walker: *What did you see when he pointed out a leg?*

Steve Champagne: *Just an image of something. I mean, it was dark. The screen was real dark.*

Joe Walker: *On the screen did you see any other things like, you know, little spiking readings and stuff like that?*

Steve Champagne: *No.*

Joe Walker: *Okay. When you were looking at this monitor, did you see him taking notes?*

Steve Champagne: *Not to my knowledge, no. I don't recall him taking any notes.*

Joe Walker: *Did you see anybody else in the dive station doing anything?*

Steve Champagne: *They had so many people around, I really wouldn't know who was doing what.*

Joe Walker: *Okay. Just to clarify, according to your earlier testimony the man at the monitor was the diver that eventually brought up Brian?*

Steve Champagne: *Yes, sir, he was the one that went in after the first diver got the bloody nose and ears.*

Joe Walker: Okay, *so the guy who had the bloody nose and blood coming out his ears, did you ever see him at the dive station?*

Steve Champagne: *No, sir, the first time I saw him was when they were getting him ready to go in the basket.*

Joe Walker: *Now, when he got to the surface—and you're used to working with whips and stuff like that, are you? You're a welder, right?*

Steve Champagne: *Welder, yes, sir.*

Joe Walker: *And you're familiar with hearing—if you would hear a leak or something coming out of a hose, you would notice that, wouldn't you?*

Steve Champagne: *Yes, sir.*

Joe Walker: *Do you mind if I stand up? And I'm going to represent to you, sir, this is the helmet that Brian wore, and this is a Kirby Morgan SuperLite.*

Joe Walker: *And this is also—let the record reflect that's called a neck dam that connects to the—slips over his neck.*

Joe Walker: *And do you recall when the driver got out of water whether he had this harness, a harness around him?*

Steve Champagne: *I don't remember.*

Joe Walker: *As you previously testified, that the hose was connected to him and came into this—into the side of the helmet?*

Steve Champagne: *Yeah, it came up his—like up his back and looped around and came in.*

Joe Walker: *Does this look like where it was connected?*

Steve Champagne: *Yes, sir.*

Joe Walker: *Now, when it was on the deck, did you hear any air coming out of it?*

Steve Champagne: *No, sir.*

Joe Walker: *Did you hear like, you know, the sounds you hear if you've got a leaky hose?*

Steve Champagne: *I didn't hear nothing.*

Joe Walker: *And being a welder, if you've got a leaking O_2 hose, you're used to that sound, right?*

Steve Champagne: *Yes, sir.*

Joe Walker: *That's something you're used to noticing, isn't it?*

Steve Champagne: *Yes, sir.*

Joe Walker: *And did you notice any air coming out of the side of the vents here (indicating)? Did you hear any air coming out of there?*

Steve Champagne: *No, sir.*

Joe Walker: *Did you hear any air coming out of this hat at all?*

Steve Champagne: *No, sir.*

Lt. Com. Tom Beistle *Let me—and during this pause, let me mention that Mr. Walker is pointing to—when he said that a hose was connected, he's pointing to, if you're facing the helmet, a hose connection on the left of the helmet. Is that correct, Mr. Walker?*

Joe Walker: *That's correct.*

Lt. Com. Tom Beistle *And there is no connection—there's no sort of opposite but equal connection on what would be facing the helmet on the right side. So it's literally the only connection.*

Joe Walker: *That's correct. And let the record reflect apparently when—when this helmet was brought here, there was another valve up here connected (indicating). That's strictly for the bail-out. So according to his testimony, at least, there was no bail-out with—or bail-out attached. So that was actually broken.*

Joe Walker: *Now, when he got to the surface, did you see a bunch of people playing with the valves?*

Steve Champagne: *No.*

Joe Walker: *When you took the hat—were you there when the hat came off?*

Steve Champagne: *I was the one trying to get the hat off.*

Joe Walker: *Was there a lot of water in the hat?*

Steve Champagne: *No.*

Joe Walker: *When the hat came off, did you see any water?*

Steve Champagne: *Very little. It had some water in the hat, but very little.*

Joe Walker: *What color was his face?*

Steve Champagne: *Blue.*

Joe Walker: *When you started CPR and they gave him oxygen, did his color—or at least his color return?*

Steve Champagne: *No, sir.*

Joe Walker: *So he stayed blue?*

Steve Champagne: *Yes, sir.*

Joe Walker: *Did you notice any water come out of his mouth?*

Steve Champagne: *Yes, sir.*

Joe Walker: *What did that look like?*

Steve Champagne: *Just a mucus color.*

Joe Walker: *But you were the one that first took that helmet off or helped get it off, right?*

Steve Champagne: *I tried to get it off. I couldn't get it off. The diver that actually retrieved him was the one that got it off. The man that I first saw watching the monitor.*

Joe Walker: *Okay. And you also noticed a little camera—and let me go back to this helmet. Did you see where I picked the helmet up by the handle?*

Steve Champagne: *Yes, sir.*

Joe Walker: *There was something attached here (indicating)?*

Steve Champagne: *Attached there.*

Joe Walker: *Was it two inches, three inches?*

Steve Champagne: *An inch and a half—I mean, an inch, inch and a half. It was real small.*

Joe Walker: *What color was it?*

Steve Champagne: *Black.*

Joe Walker: *Was there like a cord coming from it?*

Steve Champagne: *Yes, sir.*

Joe Walker: *Like you would for a coax cable?*

Steve Champagne: *Yes, sir.*

Joe Walker: *Okay. So that was attached to the top of the helmet?*

Steve Champagne: *Yes, sir.*

Joe Walker: *Now, did that line come to the surface in a separate line, or was it wrapped around the—*

Steve Champagne: *It was taped through his air hose and everything.*

Joe Walker: *And when he took the helmet off, you saw some water coming out of the helmet?*

Steve Champagne: *I mean, very little. I mean, when he pulled it off—*

Joe Walker: *When you tried to get it off, did any water come out?*

Steve Champagne: *I couldn't pull it. I couldn't get it off at all.*

Joe Walker: *Now, you talked about three lines being taped together. Tell me a little bit more about that if you would, please, sir.*

Steve Champagne: *I really don't know what they were. To my knowledge, you know, it was his air hoses. It was all—two big lines and just one real small line. The small line was running to the top of his helmet, to whatever they had taped to the top of his helmet. To my knowledge, it was a camera.*

Joe Walker: *Could it have been a light?*

Steve Champagne: *No, because it didn't have a bulb or nothing in it.*

Joe Walker: *Why do you think it was a camera?*

Steve Champagne: *Because I—that's what we was watching from the screen.*

Joe Walker: *How do you know that's what you were watching from the screen?*

Steve Champagne: *Because they didn't have nothing else hooked up to his helmet.*

Joe Walker: *So you think that there was a video camera on his helmet, and it was producing an image on the screen?*

Steve Champagne: *Yes, sir. My opinion, yes, sir.*

Joe Walker: *Did you ever give an interview to any one after other then the crew member on the Cliffs 12 after March 4, 1996 regarding what you did or witnessed that day?*

Steve Champagne: *Yes, sir.*

Joe Walker: *Okay. Who did you give that to?*

Steve Champagne: *Lieutenant Commander Beistle two weeks ago.*

Joe Walker: *How about before that, any time before that?*

Steve Champagne: *I talked to Mr. Pilkington over the phone and he come to my house and visited me and we talked there a little while.*

With that the welder/fitter from Louisiana was passed along to the others parties for cross examination. Questions to clarify his account that had varied from the statements that had been given to Judge Borne years before and raised more questions.

Where did the man watching the monitor go after learning Brian was in need of assistance? Why was the man watching the monitor not compelled to mount an immediate rescue attempt? Was all this contained on a video tape?

Perhaps most concerning to the lawyer, Bijan Siahatgar, who this day was representing the Master of the Vessel, Ronald Townsend. Where was the witness statement Steve Champagne reported to have dictate and signed that afternoon aboard the Cliffs 12? Was his client withholding evidence, or perhaps was it just never asked for? Were there other statements taken that had not been released?

Perhaps the next witness might be able to answer at least some of those questions. After being properly sworn and the normal questions about the spelling of the name, address, education and work experience Dan Wiitala was ready for his questioning by Lieutenant Commander Beistle. But first a few question to establish foundation starting with an understanding of what the duties of a dive tender might be?

Being duly sworn Wiitala answered. *"I think it's understood that the new guys have to do the jobs that the senior guys don't want to do: Haul fuel, set up, this and that. That's the way it is. And with that, I accepted the responsibilities of taping hose, setting up, hauling fuel and, in turn, did my dive during the day."*

Lt. Com. Tom Beistle: *Okay. Then let's step back. Let's take a hypothetical shallow water dive. So you show up at the shop. This is one where you're going to go into G&G and participate in getting ready. What are your—what was the normal routine?*

Dan Wiitala: *Well, normally most of the gear is already ready to transport. I mean, you spend so much time taking gear back and forth that you keep a lot of it on racks or on trailers or things like that, you know. The majority of the big gear is already ready to transport. The small stuff, making sure you have fuel cans, duct tape, things like that.*

Lt. Com. Tom Beistle: *Did you ever get any direction from anybody at G&G specifically about how to put together a dive package or what G&G's dive package consists of?*

Dan Wiitala: *I'm sure I did. I just—I mean, there's always people that have been there longer than you, and you just fall in line and—*

Lt. Com. Tom Beistle: *Yeah. Any written direction on it anywhere?*

Dan Wiitala: *No.*

Lt. Com. Tom Beistle: *Any checklists?*

Dan Wiitala: *You know, I don't know.*

Lt. Com. Tom Beistle: *Well, I'm kind of—I mean, I hear what you're saying, but I really would like a better—I mean, this is fundamental. This is the issue of how you're getting your equipment out to the job so that you can do your job. I mean, I've heard somebody say one time you don't get paid for blowing bubbles. You get paid for doing a job. So you've got to have the right tools to go out there and do it.*

Dan Wiitala: *Yes, sir.*

Lt. Com. Tom Beistle: *I mean, was there—how did you learn to get the right tools, the right equipment out there so that you could do your job?*

Dan Wiitala: *There may have been—at that time, a diving supervisor may have had a written checklist. Being new, I didn't know it. We just kind of went down the list: Okay. Do you have this? Do you have that? Yes, we do. Do you have the radio? Do you have the batteries? Make sure it's on there. Okay. We got it. Can you think of anything else? What do we got? Two fuel cans, that's fine.*

Lt. Com. Tom Beistle: *Yeah. Okay. So in your—in the thirteen years you worked there at G&G, did you ever use a list? Did you ever use some sort of a checklist to get yourself squared away before you went on a dive?*

Dan Wiitala: *Yes.*

Lt. Com. Tom Beistle: *What did you use?*

Dan Wiitala: *I would make one up at home the night before if I was running the job, just a handwritten thing, and then when we get there, just check them off as we load them and make sure we have them.*

Lt. Com. Tom Beistle: *Had you ever shown up without two air hoses?*

Dan Wiitala: *Yes.*

Lt. Com. Tom Beistle: *What had you done? What did you do?*

Dan Wiitala: *Depending on the job, went ahead and did it or went and got another one.*

Lt. Com. Tom Beistle: *And so, you have done other jobs—you've done jobs where you showed up without two hoses, let's say, and you went ahead and did the job anyway?*

Dan Wiitala: *Yes.*

Lt. Com. Tom Beistle: *I'm not going to put words in your mouth. What was your reasoning? Why would you go ahead and do it?*

Dan Wiitala: *Well, it just seemed silly not to. If it's—if it's that—I mean, people go down on SCUBA, there's no hoses involved there. There's no radio system involved there. I mean, if you could feasibly drop down with a bottle on your back and do a job, I think you could do it on one hose.*

Lt. Com. Tom Beistle: *Okay. One hose necessarily means no standby diver?*

Dan Wiitala: *That's correct.*

Lt. Com. Tom Beistle: *So what I hear you telling me—tell me if I'm off base—you're saying that if it was a shallow dive, then the—it was an acceptable risk not to have a standby diver?*

Dan Wiitala: *Maybe not acceptable, but I've taken that risk myself.*

Lt. Com. Tom Beistle: *Okay. So let's go back to when you worked for G&G. Do I understand that there are essentially sort of three jobs on any dive site? There's essentially a dive tender, a dive supervisor, and a diver. And then you have multiple divers, a standby diver, what have you?*

Dan Wiitala: *That's correct.*

Lt. Com. Tom Beistle: *Those are the three titles: Tender, diver, and dive supervisor?*

Dan Wiitala: *Yes.*

Lt. Com. Tom Beistle: *Was there any qualification process to get yourself called up for any of those positions at G&G?*

Dan Wiitala: *I'm not sure I understand what you're asking me. You mean a set of black-and-white guidelines—*

Lt. Com. Tom Beistle: *Right.*

Dan Wiitala: *That says you fill in here or there?*

Lt. Com. Tom Beistle: *Right.*

Dan Wiitala: *No.*

Lt. Com. Tom Beistle: *So how did you know that you were ready, let's say, to be—let me ask you this, let's start at the bottom: Did you feel like you were ready to be a dive tender when you went to work for G&G?*

Dan Wiitala: *Yes.*

Lt. Com. Tom Beistle: *Based on what?*

Dan Wiitala: *School. I mean, I had gone to school for it. I feel like if you went to school to learn how to fly a plane, when you get out, you fly a plane.*

Lt. Com. Tom Beistle: *Did you feel like you were qualified to be a dive supervisor when you went to work for G&G?*

Dan Wiitala: *No.*

Lt. Com. Tom Beistle: *When did you first—were you asked to work as a dive supervisor when you went to work for G&G? Did you fill that position?*

Dan Wiitala: *At what point? You mean when I first worked there?*

Lt. Com. Tom Beistle: *Right.*

Dan Wiitala: *No.*

Lt. Com. Tom Beistle: *When did you first act as a dive supervisor for G&G?*

Dan Wiitala: *That, I couldn't tell you. Several years.*

Lt. Com. Tom Beistle: *And what had you done in that process to become qualified to be a dive supervisor?*

Dan Wiitala: *I don't know. I wish I knew, or I would have not done it.*

Lt. Com. Tom Beistle: *When did you know you were ready to be a dive supervisor? I mean, did you say, "Okay, I'm ready to do it," or did somebody—did Mr. Gilbert or somebody else say,"*

Okay, you're going to be a supervisor?"

Dan Wiitala: *I more or less got crowded into it. I never wanted to be.*

Lt. Com. Tom Beistle: *And was there any process, anything whatsoever, even the most unofficial, just some process that was acknowledged by anyone for you to actually work your way or progress towards becoming a dive supervisor?*

Dan Wiitala: *Well, you learn on the job. It's on-the-job training. There was no written test, is that what you're asking.*

Lt. Com. Tom Beistle: *Okay. Let's go over what in your estimation is a shallow dive package. Earlier you said you would have one or two compressors. Is it one or two?*

Dan Wiitala: *Well, depending on the duration of the job. Sometimes we would go with one, sometimes with two.*

Lt. Com. Tom Beistle: *So the decision to go with one or two was based on how long the job was going to take?*

Dan Wiitala: *Usually.*

Lt. Com. Tom Beistle: *Why would the length of the job have anything to do with the number of compressors?*

Dan Wiitala: *A compressor is just a machine. Sometimes it dies.*

Lt. Com. Tom Beistle: *Had you had compressors die on you before with G&G?*

Dan Wiitala: *Yes.*

Lt. Com. Tom Beistle: *How often?*

Dan Wiitala: *That's like asking me how often my car breaks down. I mean, I don't really know how to answer that.*

Lt. Com. Tom Beistle: *Okay. How often would you say in the—let's say in the 13 years you worked for G&G, how often would you say you were on a job and one of their compressors broke down?*

Dan Wiitala: *Probably once a year.*

Lt. Com. Tom Beistle: *Once a year. So in thirteen years, probably thirteen times you had a compressor die on you on a job?*

Dan Wiitala: *Yes.*

Lt. Com. Tom Beistle: *What are your options? Assuming you're on a shallow water, surface supplied—well, in some of the instances that you had, what did you do when your compressor died?*

Dan Wiitala: *Shut it down and fix it. Send for another one.*

Lt. Com. Tom Beistle: *Did you always have a backup air supply?*

Dan Wiitala: *No.*

Lt. Com. Tom Beistle: *Why not?*

Dan Wiitala: *I don't know.*

Lt. Com. Tom Beistle: *Were you aware of any kind of maintenance schedule? Was there any requirement for equipment to be maintained in any particular routine fashion?*

Dan Wiitala: *At first, no, but—there was a time when things got fixed as they needed to be fixed, and then there was a time period when—I guess you already know—Ross Saxon came aboard. And things got a little more structured, and he implemented the safety manual, maintenance schedule, things like that. And at that point we had a regular shop man, a regular maintenance man. I was kind of out of the maintenance at that—*

Lt. Com. Tom Beistle: *Who was the shop man?*

Dan Wiitala: *Al May.*

Lt. Com. Tom Beistle: *And then you had—you said you had a shop man and a maintenance man or equipment man? What did you call the other one?*

Dan Wiitala: *One and the same. I meant the same person.*

Lt. Com. Tom Beistle: *Okay. And what was that person's responsibility?*

Dan Wiitala: *Inventory, maintenance, just keep things in good order for the next job. When we would bring stuff in and it was tore up, he would make sure it was up to par to go back out on the next one.*

Lt. Com. Tom Beistle: *How long was Mr. May affiliated with G&G?*

Dan Wiitala: *I'm going to say a year.*

Lt. Com. Tom Beistle: *Was it while Mr. Saxon was with the company?*

Dan Wiitala: *Yes.*

Lt. Com. Tom Beistle: *Okay. When he left, was there any kind of a maintenance schedule maintained on equipment?*

Dan Wiitala: *I don't know.*

Lt. Com. Tom Beistle: *Was there—to your knowledge, was there—did anybody ever take Mr. May's place when he left? In other words, somebody was responsible for maintaining equipment?*

Dan Wiitala: *I don't think so. I think whoever was available, whoever wanted the extra money to do shop work.*

Lt. Com. Tom Beistle: *To your knowledge, was there any requirement for any kind of scheduled preventative maintenance that had to be done on a piece of equipment before it could be taken out?*

Dan Wiitala: *I don't know.*

Lt. Com. Tom Beistle: *Well, now, you've mentioned air bottles but you have said that there was at least some practice that air bottles weren't supposed to go out unless they were at least three quarters full—is that right?*

Dan Wiitala: *That's right.*

Lt. Com. Tom Beistle: *So that's at least one standard. What about for anything else, compressors?*

Dan Wiitala: *Well, I know that there was oil changes and things like that done. I mean, we always checked the oil on them and, you know . . .*

Lt. Com. Tom Beistle: *What do you mean by 'always'?*

Dan Wiitala: *On the job.*

Lt. Com. Tom Beistle: *What would you do—what would you do when you checked the oil?*

Dan Wiitala: *Just pull the stick to see if it was up to the proper levels, see if it was dirty.*

Lt. Com. Tom Beistle: *Did you ever find a time when it wasn't up to the proper level or it was dirty?*

Dan Wiitala: *Yes.*

Lt. Com. Tom Beistle: *You've been appointed by Dan Gilbert as a dive supervisor?*

Dan Wiitala: *Yes.*

Lt. Com. Tom Beistle: *So what were your jobs when you were acting as dive supervisor?*

Dan Wiitala: *Make sure everybody is okay, make sure all the equipment is good, make sure the job is getting done, make sure that everybody is happy. Make sure the paperwork is getting done, everybody's fed, slept, not griping. It's kind of like I'm sure your responsibilities over—anytime you get a gang of guys together and you're in charge of them, you've got a lot on your shoulders.*

Lt. Com. Tom Beistle: *If you folks will hold on just a moment. I've got a—for the parties here, I've got something I'm going to show Mr. Wiitala that was produced in the civil litigation. I suspect you folks almost all probably have it.*

Let the record reflect that I am showing Mr. Wiitala a piece of paper with a handwritten note on it that says at the top: Job No. 1—Job No. 1138, Texas NDE, and it's dated 3/4/96.

Lt. Com. Tom Beistle: *Mr. Wiitala, would you look at that and tell me, is that document anything—I mean, have you ever seen that before?*

Dan Wiitala: *No.*

Lt. Com. Tom Beistle: *Did you see that prior to going out—did you see that list or that document prior to going out on your job on March 4?*

Dan Wiitala: *No.*

Lt. Com. Tom Beistle: *Does it look—have you ever seen anything like that—seen a document like that prior to going out on a job? Have you ever gotten a piece of paper or anything like that from Mr. Gilbert or from G&G prior to going on a dive?*

Dan Wiitala: *This is typical to something I would write up prior to a job.*

Lt. Com. Tom Beistle: *Okay. Have you—do you recognize that handwriting?*

Dan Wiitala: *It looks like Mr. Gilbert's.*

Lt. Com. Tom Beistle: *Okay. Has he ever given you a list like that before on other jobs?*

Dan Wiitala: *Probably.*

Lt. Com. Tom Beistle: *Okay. What were the—what do you think is the minimum acceptable pressure down there?*

Dan Wiitala: *Well, you figure you need 60 pounds to operate the hat and another 14 pounds to overcome the depth. So you've got—75 pounds will probably do you, if you—you know, I wouldn't want it, but you know—*

Lt. Com. Tom Beistle: *Is that—can you work at those pressures? In other words, can you do physical work?*

Dan Wiitala: *I have. I just dial the hat out.*

Lt. Com. Tom Beistle: *Are you special? I mean, are you tougher than most?*

Dan Wiitala: *No, no, not at all. No, I think anybody could.*

Lt. Com. Tom Beistle: *On March 4, how many standby bottles did you have?*

Dan Wiitala: *Two.*

Lt. Com. Tom Beistle: *And you had blown through one, and the other one was empty?*

Dan Wiitala: *Yes.*

Lt. Com. Tom Beistle: *Is it a standard practice to bring empty bottles out on dives?*

Dan Wiitala: *No.*

Lt. Com. Tom Beistle: *Had you ever been out on a dive and had an empty bottle before?*

Dan Wiitala: *I couldn't say for sure. It's the only one I remember.*

Lt. Com. Tom Beistle: *So—okay. So you didn't have—you had blow through one bottle. The other bottle was empty. So you used one of the oxygen bottles from the welder?*

Dan Wiitala: *Uh-huh.*

Lt. Com. Tom Beistle: *Was it straight O_2?*

Dan Wiitala: *Straight O_2.*

Lt. Com. Tom Beistle: *And was it regulated?*

Dan Wiitala: *Yes.*

Lt. Com. Tom Beistle: *How was it regulated?*

Dan Wiitala: *Had an oxygen regulator on the bottle.*

Lt. Com. Tom Beistle: *What happened next?*

Dan Wiitala: *Well, we attempted to dive Kirk to go get Brian.*

Lt. Com. Tom Beistle: *What happened to Kirk?*

Dan Wiitala: *He made a couple of attempts to go down and after the second attempt, pretty much told me he wasn't going. So I put on his hat and went.*

Lt. Com. Tom Beistle: *Could you see anything that indicated why Kirk didn't want to go?*

Dan Wiitala: *He was visibly upset.*

Lt. Com. Tom Beistle: *Why?*

Dan Wiitala: *I don't know.*

Lt. Com. Tom Beistle: *What was your guess?*

Dan Wiitala: *Scared.*

Lt. Com. Tom Beistle: *Do you know how deep he went? Did he get in the water?*

Dan Wiitala: *He got out of the basket, into the water.*

Lt. Com. Tom Beistle: *How deep did he go?*

Dan Wiitala: *I don't know, I don't remember.*

Lt. Com. Tom Beistle: *So what happened next? Did you dive over the side, or what did you do?*

Dan Wiitala: *No. I was—I was just in my boots and my Levi's and put on Kirk's hat and went down.*

Lt. Com. Tom Beistle: *Did you have the O_2 coming to the helmet?*

Dan Wiitala: *Yeah.*

Lt. Com. Tom Beistle: *Could you breathe?*

Dan Wiitala: *Well, I got about halfway down and I don't know if it pinched off or what happened, but the O_2 just quit coming.*

Lt. Com. Tom Beistle: *By the way, when you went down to Brian, did you see any bubbles coming from the helmet?*

Dan Wiitala: *Yeah, I did, out of the whiskers, which is the—if nobody's familiar with the hat, it's a black plastic piece that's on the side of—on both sides of the face. And bubbles were kind of trailing out of the whiskers.*

Lt. Com. Tom Beistle: *Did you happen to see whether the—whether the umbilical or at least the air hose was connected to his helmet or not?*

Dan Wiitala: *I didn't, and I—I still can't remember, to this day, whether it was or not. I've been trying to, but—*

Lt. Com. Tom Beistle: *Yeah. Educate me because I'm certainly a novice at this. If he had air bubbles coming out of the whiskers, does that imply anything to you?*

Dan Wiitala: *To me, it surprised me when I first saw it because my first thought when I got to him was: I hope he's still alive. And I shook him, you know, and I grabbed his hands. Like I'm here (indicating), you know—*

Lt. Com. Tom Beistle: *Right.*

Dan Wiitala: *And then when I saw the air traveling out, I was wondering what the problem was because if there was air there, there's sure no reason to be—*

Lt. Com. Tom Beistle: *You didn't check his air supply to see whether he had air?*

Dan Wiitala: *No.*

Lt. Com. Tom Beistle: *Did you attempt to maintain any airway while you were ascending; in other words, did you try to make sure the hose was—*

Dan Wiitala: *No. If what you're asking me, did I make any rescue attempts on him, no. I grabbed him and took off to the surface. He had a hatchet, like a roofer would use. He took it down to clean the spots to be tested. It was tied to his weight belt with a three-by eight-inch line. It was snagged around a pipe. I just cut him loose and took off.*

Lt. Com. Tom Beistle: *Okay. When you got back up, as a matter of fact, did you by any chance happen to check the compressor?*

Dan Wiitala: *I think I was the one that turned it off.*

Lt. Com. Tom Beistle: *You did turn it off?*

Dan Wiitala: *I believe I did. When everybody was on deck, I think I went over there and shut it off because it was still hammering away.*

Lt. Com. Tom Beistle: *And did you happen to check the gauge?*

Dan Wiitala: *No.*

Lt. Com. Tom Beistle: *Were you able to identify that as a compressor that you had worked with before?*

Dan Wiitala: *Oh yeah. I'm positive I've worked with it before.*

Lt. Com. Tom Beistle: *Ever had any problems with it?*

Dan Wiitala: *It's a machine. I mean—*

Lt. Com. Tom Beistle: *What kind of problems did you have with it?*

Dan Wiitala: *Breaking down, not starting. I mean, any time you get a piece of machinery that runs, it's going to break down, and there's no way around that.*

Lt. Com. Tom Beistle: *Okay. Where was the intake located?*

Dan Wiitala: *Of the engine or the compressor side?*

Lt. Com. Tom Beistle: *For the compressor, for the air intake.*

Dan Wiitala: *We just situated it over on the stern and just turned it upwind.*

Lt. Com. Tom Beistle: *Had you ever done any maintenance on that particular compressor or on any of the compressors?*

Dan Wiitala: *On that particular one, I don't know. On any compressor, yes.*

Lt. Com. Tom Beistle: *Ever swapped out any filters on them?*

Dan Wiitala: *No.*

Lt. Com. Tom Beistle: *No. Did you check the filter on that Quincy 325 before it—before you used it?*

Dan Wiitala: *No.*

Lt. Com. Tom Beistle: *You know, you've mentioned—you mentioned, I think, that you had—you had adjusted the flow on the—from the compressor, I think. Is there a way to adjust the flow from the compressor, or is it just what it is?*

Dan Wiitala: *Just turn it wide open.*

Lt. Com. Tom Beistle: *Turn it wide open?*

Dan Wiitala: *It's set. It's preset. There's a—what they call a VD pilot valve, which stands for variable differential, and that's what we were discussing earlier. When it starts loading, when it quits loading, that 130, 150, you can set that anywhere from zero to—until it pegs out. But they were all set at around 150.*

Lt. Com. Tom Beistle: *Do you know whether the compressor intake filter was installed on this one?*

Dan Wiitala: *No, I don't.*

Lt. Com. Tom Beistle: *Okay, folks. I'm going to call a halt to my part of this and I'll turn it over to Mr. Walker.*

My name is Joe Walker, and I'm going to kind of bounce around since he's covered a lot of ground, so I may be skipping to different places. So just kind of bear with me.

One of the first things, most of your experience that I can—that I understand, prior to this dive, was strictly working for G&G Marine—is that correct?

249

Dan Wiitala: *That's correct.*

Joe Walker: *So any policies or procedures or types or methodology of diving was strictly the experience you got working for G&G?*

Dan Wiitala: *Yes.*

Joe Walker: *And that's really—that really was the sum total of your experience other than diving school, is that correct?*

Dan Wiitala: *Well, I had freelanced for Underwater. I had done some work for Taylor Diving.*

Joe Walker: *When you worked for G&G Marine, I take it the manual that you used was the G&G operations manual, which was shown to you—is that correct?*

Dan Wiitala: *That's correct.*

Joe Walker: *And also that manual adopts the ADC consensus standards?*

Dan Wiitala: *Yes.*

Joe Walker: *And I take it you were very familiar with those standards?*

Dan Wiitala: *Yes.*

Joe Walker: *Had you read the standards?*

Dan Wiitala: *Yes.*

Joe Walker: *Had you read your manual?*

Dan Wiitala: *Yes.*

Joe Walker: *Okay. And you went offshore on the Cliffs 12—and you mentioned that you had just two other divers with you, isn't that correct?*
Dan Wiitala: *Yes.*

Joe Walker: *Okay. You mentioned that—we talked earlier about tender's responsibilities. Once Brian was suited up, I take it when he suited up, as a tender, you were then taking over the tender's job, right?*

Dan Wiitala: *Yes.*

Joe Walker: *Because you helped him get suited up, isn't that correct?*

Dan Wiitala: *Yes.*

Joe Walker: *And you checked his gear?*

Dan Wiitala: *Yes.*

Joe Walker: *Isn't that part of a tender's responsibility?*

Dan Wiitala: *Yes.*

Joe Walker: *The diver puts his hat on-line, but isn't it kind of like jumping out on the airplane? The next guy in line checks the stag line before he goes in the water—jumps out of the plane, right?*

Dan Wiitala: *Yes.*

Joe Walker: *So before Brian went in the water, I take it you checked his comms, right?*

Dan Wiitala: *Yes.*

Joe Walker: *You checked the fitting on the hat, isn't that correct?*

Dan Wiitala: *No.*

Joe Walker: *You didn't?*

Dan Wiitala: *I did not.*

Joe Walker: *Did you check to see what kind of equipment he had?*

Dan Wiitala: *Well, I made sure he had his hatchet for cleaning and that he had his probe.*

Joe Walker: *Okay.*

Dan Wiitala: *And he came without a weight belt. So I made sure he had mine.*

251

Joe Walker: *And you didn't check the—check to see whether that fitting was secure?*

Dan Wiitala: *No.*

Joe Walker: *But that is part of the tender's responsibility, isn't it?*

Dan Wiitala: *Yes.*

Joe Walker: *So if you didn't do that, you didn't carry out your full responsibilities as a tender, isn't that correct?*

Dan Wiitala: *Yes.*

Joe Walker: *Okay. Now, when he went in the water, at that stage, you went from the tender to the supervisor, isn't that correct? In other words, you went to the rack, then, right, to the radio?*

Dan Wiitala: *Well, we only had three guys out there.*

Joe Walker: *I understand that.*

Dan Wiitala: *I mean, you can't label them. I was wearing whatever hat I was wearing at the time.*

Joe Walker: *I understand. I'm just trying to figure out who's on first and who's on second here. He goes in the water, and the next thing you do is go to the radio, isn't that right?*

Dan Wiitala: *That's correct.*

Joe Walker: *Now, when he went in the water, what did you do, give him enough diving hose to let him move around freely?*

Dan Wiitala: *Yes.*

Joe Walker: *And then what did you do, tie the diving hose off?*

Dan Wiitala: *I don't recall if I was standing on it with one foot or had somebody else holding it for me, one of the rig hands. Someone may have been asking if I needed any help, and I may have said, "Yeah, would you hold that hose for me?"*

Joe Walker: *But you don't know whether a rig hand was holding the hose or not?*

Dan Wiitala: *No, I don't. I just don't recall.*

Joe Walker: *But there was no trained diver tending his hose, is that correct? When you're on the rack or the radio, there was nobody tending that hose that is a qualified diver, isn't that correct?*

Dan Wiitala: *Well, there's a lot of times I'm tending and running the radio. I mean, I might have been holding his hoses in my hand and running the radio.*

Joe Walker: *So you were holding his hoses the whole time and running the radio?*

Dan Wiitala: *I don't know. I doubt it.*

Joe Walker: *And you are aware that the ADC regulations and the Coast Guard regulations and your safety manual requires that a diver's hose be tended at all times?*

Dan Wiitala: *Yes.*

Joe Walker: *And that's just not stepping on it, is it? That's not proper tending, is it?*

Dan Wiitala: *No.*

Joe Walker: *And, in fact, that's what you learn in dive school? When you tend a diver, you feel that diver, don't you?*

Dan Wiitala: *Yes.*

Joe Walker: *And the guy tending the other line of the diver should be feeling that other line too, shouldn't he?*

Dan Wiitala: *Yes.*

Joe Walker: *Because if not, you can get a whole bunch of line down there and a diver can get disoriented, isn't that correct?*

Dan Wiitala: *Yes.*

Joe Walker: *Okay. Now, so I'm just kind of figuring out this dive crew. When you're on the radio, what was Mr. Austin doing?*

Dan Wiitala: *Monitoring the scope and looking at the plans of rig and taking the thickness readings, I assume.*

Joe Walker: *So when you were on the radio, then really Mr. Austin was not acting in the capacity as a diver, was he?*

Dan Wiitala: *Well, if he's not in the water, he's not a diver.*

Joe Walker: *Well, he's not tending either, is he?*

Dan Wiitala: *No.*

Joe Walker: *He's not running the radio, is he?*

Dan Wiitala: *No.*

Joe Walker: *He's not checking the compressor, is he?*

Dan Wiitala: *No.*

Joe Walker: *He's just operating that little NDT machine, that thickness thing, right?*

Dan Wiitala: *That's correct.*

Joe Walker: *So he's not operating in any capacity as part of the diving crew at that stage.*

Dan Wiitala: *I hope he is, or I was out there alone.*

Joe Walker: *But he wasn't doing any diving activities, was he?*

Dan Wiitala: *Well, neither was I. I was just—I don't understand what you're asking me.*

Joe Walker: *Well, what was he doing that was related to diving activities? Because you just said all he was doing was looking at that little machine.*

Dan Wiitala: *Well, he was standing right beside me.*

Joe Walker: *I understand that, but what does that machine have to do with—does it have anything to do with tending the hose?*

Dan Wiitala: *No.*

Joe Walker: *Does it have anything to do with running the dive?*

Dan Wiitala: *No.*

Joe Walker: *And you initially said that you were concerned about going out there with three divers, weren't you?*

Dan Wiitala: *Yes.*

Joe Walker: *And yet, when you found out there weren't three divers, you decided to go anyway, isn't that correct?*

Dan Wiitala: *Yes.*

Joe Walker: *So in terms of Brian's diving activities, you were really his diving supervisor, weren't you?*

Dan Wiitala: *No.*

Joe Walker: *Well, then, who was?*

Dan Wiitala: *Kirk.*

Joe Walker: *How could Kirk have any authority over Brian's diving activities?*

Dan Wiitala: *I got delegated to the rack. Brian got delegated to the water.*

Joe Walker: *Is there anything in G&G's manual that allows or states that somebody that is not a G&G employee could run your diving activities?*

Dan Wiitala: *I don't know.*

Joe Walker: *Do you know any section of the G&G manual that states that if the person—or they're not sure of that person's training, they will ensure that they run through a training course?*

Dan Wiitala: *No, I don't know.*

Joe Walker: *Wouldn't you want to make sure that you were aware of somebody's experience before you had them supervise your diving crew?*

Dan Wiitala: *Yes.*

Joe Walker: *And was it your understanding, talking to Mr. Gilbert, that he told you were going to have five divers?*

Dan Wiitala: *That's correct.*

Joe Walker: *Now, when you were setting up the dive station, did anybody check the air pressure on the HP bottles?*

Dan Wiitala: *I don't know.*

Joe Walker: *You didn't?*

Dan Wiitala: *I don't remember.*

Joe Walker: *When you put the dive station together, is it at that time you discovered you didn't have a diving umbilical, is that correct?*

Dan Wiitala: *I don't know.*

Joe Walker: *Well, you knew sometime before the diver went in the water that there was not a second diving umbilical, isn't that correct?*

Dan Wiitala: *Yes.*

Joe Walker: *What kind of contingency plan did you all work out before you put the diver in the water without a second diving umbilical?*

Dan Wiitala: *None.*

Joe Walker: *What kind of plan did you have—if the diver got fouled—how were you going to rescue him?*
Dan Wiitala: *We didn't have one.*

Joe Walker: *Is that a safe diving practice?*

Dan Wiitala: *No.*

Joe Walker: *Now, if Kirk Austin—you previously testified that you weren't the supervisor and that Mr. Austin was the supervisor—did you ask to see his diving manual?*

Dan Wiitala: *No.*

Joe Walker: *Do you know what kind of diving manual he was operating under?*

Dan Wiitala: *No.*

Joe Walker: *And you never saw him to go the—identify himself as the supervisor to anybody on the drilling rig, did you?*

Dan Wiitala: *Well, to the rig superintendent, yes.*

Joe Walker: *He said, "I am the diving supervisor"?*

Dan Wiitala: *Well, I mean, I left him there to discuss what we were going to do.*

Joe Walker: *Do you recall when you went out on site whether there were any people from the U.S. Coast Guard on board the vessel?*

Dan Wiitala: *I don't know. I don't recall.*

Joe Walker: *So you don't recall whether anybody there asked to see—from the Coast Guard—asked to see your dive manual or any other manuals that might be on board?*

Dan Wiitala: *I don't know. I was outside helping Brian with the gear. Kirk was talking to the rig superintendent. I wouldn't have been involved in that anyway.*

Joe Walker: *You did kind of a handwritten dive sheet, didn't you? Didn't you write something like this (indicating)? I've written some red markings on it, but didn't you write a synopsis of this?*

Dan Wiitala: *At the hospital, yes.*

Joe Walker: *And that was at the hospital?*

Dan Wiitala: *Yes.*

Joe Walker: *Did you have a dive sheet offshore?*
Dan Wiitala: *Yeah. I had a log saying what time he went in, what time he came up, that kind of thing.*

Joe Walker: *Did Mr. Austin write that log or you?*

257

Dan Wiitala: *All I had was a scrap of paper so I could log the time he went into the water.*

Joe Walker: *Okay. Did you see whether Mr. Austin might be using a dive sheet since he was the supervisor?*

Dan Wiitala: *I'm sure he was. I was going to give this to him when I was done.*

Joe Walker: *During the beginning of the dive, you noticed the pressure dropped to 80 psi, didn't you?*

Dan Wiitala: *80 or 90, yes.*

Joe Walker: *And it wasn't just at the end of the dive, was it?*

Dan Wiitala: *No.*

Joe Walker: *Now, when the dive went down to 80 psi, at that stage you didn't make the decision nor Mr. Austin didn't make the decision to abort the dive?*

Dan Wiitala: *No.*

Joe Walker: *How many times did it have—and then it went down to 80 psi again before he got in trouble, didn't it? It happened more than once, didn't it?*

Dan Wiitala: *Yes.*

Joe Walker: *And you still didn't make the decision to abort the dive?*

Dan Wiitala: *No.*

Joe Walker: *And, in fact, I think—and I don't want to go back over old testimony because we could be here all day, but I think you previously testified when you went to recover Brian, that the fitting was on the helmet, isn't that correct?*

Dan Wiitala: *I don't know.*

Joe Walker: *But you would have no reason to disagree to what you previously testified to?*

Dan Wiitala: *I wouldn't have any reason to disagree with what I've already said, but I don't recall.*

Joe Walker: *Okay. And, in fact, when you went down there, you didn't see bubbles coming out of the fitting connected to the helmet, did you?*

Dan Wiitala: *I don't remember.*

Joe Walker: *That's something you would have noticed, right?*

Dan Wiitala: *I'm sure.*

Joe Walker: *Because you saw bubbles coming out of the whiskers, right?*

Dan Wiitala: *Yes.*

Joe Walker: *But you didn't see any coming out of the hose fitting, did you?*

Dan Wiitala: *I don't remember.*

Joe Walker: *Now, at least from this statement here, it took approximately fifteen to twenty minutes to jump the standby diver from the time you realized he was in trouble, is that correct?*

Dan Wiitala: *I don't remember specific times. If I testified to that, then I'm sure that's—I have no reason to dispute it.*

Joe Walker: *Okay. Assuming from your report here, it says you started bringing the diver at 1632 and at 1645 you jumped a standby diver. So that would have been approximately what, how many minutes—thirteen minutes?*

Dan Wiitala: *What were the times again?*

Joe Walker: *1632 to 1645.*

Dan Wiitala: *Yes.*

Joe Walker: *And even after you jumped the standby diver, all the way up to 1700, you state Brian was still talking and gasping at this time. And then at 1700, he stopped responding. So between 1632 when you felt the need to jump a standby diver and to 1700, we have twenty-eight minutes where the diver was still responding, isn't that correct?*

Dan Wiitala: *Yes.*

Joe Walker: *And at that stage, you still hadn't gone in the water, is that correct?*

Dan Wiitala: *No, I had not.*

Joe Walker: *And, in fact, it took another fifteen minutes to get him to the deck, didn't it?*

Dan Wiitala: *From the time I went in the water?*

Joe Walker: *No. From the time he stopped responding, it took another fifteen minutes, according to your recollection, from this log?*

Dan Wiitala: *Yes.*

Joe Walker: *In fact, it only took you about two minutes to rescue him, didn't it?*

Dan Wiitala: *That's correct. Less than that, I believe.*

Joe Walker: *So if it only took two minutes, if it's 1632 when the diver started having trouble, if he had had a standby hose out there with a helmet, even without an additional diver, he probably would have been out of that water by 1635, isn't that correct? You certainly would have gone and gotten him, isn't that correct?*

Dan Wiitala: *Yes.*

Joe Walker: *If he had that standby hose and a helmet, he probably would be alive today, wouldn't he?*

Dan Wiitala: *I don't know.*

Joe Walker: *What do you think?*

Dan Wiitala: *Well, if there's no air—not sufficient air to go to Brian, there sure wouldn't be sufficient air to tax on another hose. I don't know.*

Joe Walker: *So you don't know—since you just said there was not sufficient air going to Brian, what makes you know—who told you that there wasn't sufficient air going to him?*

Dan Wiitala: *Well, I mean, that's what I keep hearing.*

Joe Walker: *Who did you hear that from?*

Dan Wiitala: *Just—I don't know.*

Joe Walker: *You know there was something wrong with that compressor; you found out later, didn't you?*

Dan Wiitala: *I don't know.*

Joe Walker: *Now, if there was sufficient air going to Brian and we had had a standby hose and a helmet, then he would be alive today, wouldn't he?*

Dan Wiitala: *In my best guess, more than likely.*

Joe Walker: *Okay. Do you know how often the compressor—do you know what the regulations are regarding the checking of these compressors for air quality?*

Dan Wiitala: *No.*

Joe Walker: *Do you know whether Mr. Gilbert had any procedure to check the compressors for air quality?*

Dan Wiitala: *No.*

Joe Walker: *Did you ever see any certificates on that compressor to indicate it might have been checked for—to show when it was checked or when it was maintained?*

Dan Wiitala: *No.*

Joe Walker: *Did you ever see a compressor log on that compressor?*

Dan Wiitala: *No.*

Joe Walker: *You never saw a compressor log here that said the compressor was removed from service the next day after this injury—after this death?*

Dan Wiitala: *No.*

Joe Walker: *Who would be able to tell me about that?*

Dan Wiitala: *I don't know.*

Joe Walker: *Do you know who would have the most knowledge about this equipment maintenance log, any idea?*

Joe Walker: *Who wrote it?*

Dan Wiitala: *I don't know.*

Joe Walker: *Now, when Mr. Austin tried to go and rescue him, you indicated that his demeanor appeared to be scared?*

Dan Wiitala: *It appeared to me.*

Joe Walker: *Why don't you elaborate on that a little bit?*

Dan Wiitala: *I don't pretend to know how he felt.*

Joe Walker: *Did he appear to be panicking or—*

Dan Wiitala: *He didn't want to go.*

Joe Walker: *He didn't want to go in the water, is that correct?*

Dan Wiitala: *That's correct.*

Joe Walker: *Did he tell you that before he went in the water the first time?*

A No.

Joe Walker: *Only after the second attempt?*

Dan Wiitala: *That's correct.*

Joe Walker: *Is that the hose (indicating the hose submitted by G&G Marine) that he actually—that was actually used on the dive?*

Dan Wiitala: *I don't believe it is.*

Lt. Com. Tom Beistle: *What makes you think it's not?*

Dan Wiitala: I don't recall it being red, the red pneumo.

Joe Walker: *So you don't think this is the hose?*

Dan Wiitala: *I don't think it is.*

Joe Walker: *Because I'm just trying to figure out, if this is the hose, why the pneumo's been cut. Do you have any idea?*

Dan Wiitala: *No.*

Joe Walker: *Did you instruct him to try to use the pneumo, stick it in his helmet?*

Dan Wiitala: *I don't remember.*

Joe Walker: *Do you know what kind of policy Mr. Gilbert had regarding—or Gilbert Marine had regarding changing of diving filters?*

Dan Wiitala: *No.*

Joe Walker: *There should be one filter in the compressor itself, is that correct?*

Dan Wiitala: *Yes.*

Joe Walker: *And there's a filter on the air intake to the compressor?*

Dan Wiitala: *Right.*

Joe Walker: *Not to the motor side, to the—the compressor side?*

Dan Wiitala: *That's right.*

Joe Walker: *Do you know whether occasionally—what kind of—what do they use for filters in those air intakes? Do you know?*

Dan Wiitala: *Usually paper elements with wire screen around them.*

Joe Walker: *Did they ever use non—no specified filters?*

Dan Wiitala: *I'm not sure what you're asking me.*

Joe Walker: *Did they ever use—for the air intake for the compressor, did they ever use rags or maybe a Kotex or something like that?*

Dan Wiitala: *On the compressor? No.*

Joe Walker: *Okay. And you were not involved in periodically checking those filters?*

Dan Wiitala: *No.*

Joe Walker: *Were you concerned that if you had turned this job around without the number of divers and without a backup hose, you might have gotten run off?*

Dan Wiitala: *Sure.*

Joe Walker: *Did Brian have a bail-out bottle?*

Dan Wiitala: *No.*

Joe Walker: *Did he have a bail-out bottle available, to your knowledge?*

Dan Wiitala: *Well, I had mine there, I know that, but it was plumbed up to my hat.*

Joe Walker: *Did you discuss using it?*

Dan Wiitala: *Actually I think we did.*

Joe Walker: *Could you have used—could Brian have used your bail-out bottle? In other words, would—mechanically would it have worked? Could you have hooked up your bail-out bottle to his equipment?*

Dan Wiitala: *Yes.*

Joe Walker: *You said something interesting. You said that when you went down, you went down with the expectation that he had drowned. Am I right about that?*

Dan Wiitala: *I think so, yes.*

Joe Walker: *And then you were surprised when you saw air coming—bubbles coming from the whiskers of his helmet?*

Dan Wiitala: *That's correct.*

Joe Walker: *This is a surface-supplied air dive. How—why would you expect that he had drowned?*

Dan Wiitala: *I thought he had fiddled with his hose, unscrewed it trying to screw it back on tight. I thought he had turned it the wrong way, blew the hose off the hat.*

Joe Walker: *Is there any kind of a valve in there or would that be a free—*

Dan Wiitala: *No, the hose would have been wide open.*

Joe Walker: *Well, but what about his hat, would his hat have been wide open?*

Dan Wiitala: *No, it's sealed up. I mean, you're not getting any air, but you're—you're not being supplied with enough air to breathe, but you're not going to flood up. Are you following me?*

Joe Walker: *No, I'm not.*

Dan Wiitala: *Okay. It's not like just having a bucket over your head. You're sealed off around the neck, and as long as that hose is pumping air through the hat, you've got enough air to breathe. If that hose comes off, you wouldn't be able to really breathe, but you wouldn't—your hat wouldn't flood up immediately, in other words.*

Joe Walker: *Well, okay. So suppose, for the sake of argument, that your expectation had come true, the hose was gone from his helmet.*

Dan Wiitala: *Uh-huh.*

Joe Walker: *How was he—how was that going to affect or cause water to get into his helmet?*

Dan Wiitala: *Well, the truth of the matter is, is I thought that with the pressure dropping—the hose was wide open. Since we went through that bail-out bottle so fast, the standby air, I just assumed that hose was wide open.*

Joe Walker: *I understand what you're saying about that. I'm saying I understand that you—your expectation was that that hose was no longer connected to his helmet, is that right?*

Dan Wiitala: *That's correct.*

Joe Walker: *Okay. So I—*

Dan Wiitala: *Oh, I see where you're going. I expected to find him without a helmet on, drowned.*

Joe Walker: *Yeah. And that was my question to you. How were you expecting him to have drowned in that situation?*

Dan Wiitala: *I expected him to be out of the hat. If it would have been me and I wasn't getting—I probably would have just took the hose and poked it underneath my neck dam, and everything would have been all right.*

Joe Walker: *Now, which hose?*

Dan Wiitala: *The dive hose, the one that came unscrewed, whatever.*

Joe Walker: *Okay.*

Dan Wiitala: *I would have just put it underneath my neck dam. In hindsight, in that depth, I probably would have just dropped the weight belt, dumped the hat, and floated away, swam back over to the basket, and say, "Hey, you know—"*

Joe Walker: *Yeah, I see your point. So when you went down, your expectations were that a series of events had occurred?*

Dan Wiitala: *Exactly. I fully expected that maybe he forgot to dump his belt, maybe he forgot to cut the line or something and then dumped his hat, swam for the surface, and wasn't getting anywhere. And that's why I thought he would be drowned. I don't know what I was thinking. It just surprised me to see him in his hat with air.*

Joe Walker: *With air coming through?*

Dan Wiitala: *And I thought to myself: What could possibly have gone wrong?*

Joe Walker: *And you said that you were—you said that you had helped Brian set up the dive station, set up the equipment.*

Dan Wiitala: *Yeah. I hooked up the radio and the battery.*

Joe Walker: *Did you hook up the bottles?*

Dan Wiitala: *Probably, yeah.*

Joe Walker: *So I guess my question is, if you have one—I mean, there's still some ambiguity here because you said you put a gauge on that second bottle that you were trying to use; and the gauge read empty.*

Dan Wiitala: *That's correct.*

Joe Walker: *And I'm just saying when you were moving those bottles around, did you notice—did you have an opportunity to notice whether there was any difference in the weight between the two bottles?*

Dan Wiitala: *No.*

Lt. Com. Tom Beistle: *Okay. For the record, I've put in front of Mr. Wiitala an umbilical that was provided, pursuant to subpoena, by Mr. Gilbert of G&G Marine.*

Lt. Com. Tom Beistle: *And I wanted to ask you: Do you—is there any way to look at this and tell whether this was or was not the umbilical that was used on your dive?*

Dan Wiitala: *For sure, I couldn't say, but I—no, I couldn't say for sure.*

Lt. Com. Tom Beistle: *Well, how long did you work at G&G?*

Dan Wiitala: *13 years.*

Lt. Com. Tom Beistle: *How many hoses—how many umbilicals over there do you know that had red pneumohoses as part of them?*

Dan Wiitala: *Two.*

Lt. Com. Tom Beistle: *Two of them?*

Dan Wiitala: *Yes. One about this length and a real short one, just a shallow water quick-jump hose, like one hundred foot long.*

Lt. Com. Tom Beistle: *How long would you say this one is?*

Dan Wiitala: *Well, you got deck equipment in here too. Guessing 175-200 feet.*

Lt. Com. Tom Beistle: *And how many umbilicals did G&G have while you were working there?*

Dan Wiitala: *Four that I knew of.*

Lt. Com. Tom Beistle: *Let me turn you back to Mr. Walker.*

Joe Walker: *One question on the panic, just out of curiosity. That seems to be a word thrown around. You can panic, but you can survive all day long as long as you've got an air supply, right?*

Dan Wiitala: *That's correct.*

Joe Walker: *Have you ever smelled—do you know whether—when you went to diving school, did they ever teach you the dangers of carbon dioxide or CO_2?*

Dan Wiitala: *Sure.*

Joe Walker: *Do you know whether you can smell CO_2?*

Dan Wiitala: *I know you can't.*

Joe Walker: *Do you know what the symptoms or what people exhibit when they get under a CO_2 hit?*

Dan Wiitala: *You mean unconsciousness?*

Joe Walker: *Do you know whether a CO_2 hit is similar to being asphyxiated? Do you remember what they taught you at diving school?*

Dan Wiitala: *Asphyxiated? You mean choked, physically choked? I don't know what you're asking me.*

Joe Walker: *Unconsciousness, suffocate?*

Dan Wiitala: *Unconsciousness, yes.*

Joe Walker: *Suffocate. Similar?*

Dan Wiitala: *Yes.*

Joe Walker: *And just one question. There was a discussion regarding—I went back earlier, regarding, you know, if we had the hat and the standby hose, would Brian be here today? And the question was—well, not if he had enough air supply. But certainly we had a—we had an HP air supply hooked up to the rack, isn't that correct?*

Dan Wiitala: *That's correct.*

Joe Walker: *And I believe you thought it was almost a full bottle, isn't that correct?*

Dan Wiitala: *Yes.*

Joe Walker: *So we could have at least given high-pressure air through the manifold to a standby diver, isn't that correct?*

Dan Wiitala: *If I wanted to isolate the two, I would have just hooked the standby hose right up to the bottle.*

Joe Walker: *You could have done that, but essentially you had enough HP air to last, from what you testified to, for fifteen minutes, isn't that correct?*

Dan Wiitala: *That's correct.*

Joe Walker: *So you certainly had enough HP air to run two divers off that rack, isn't that correct?*

Dan Wiitala: *With that hose wide open, that would be pretty—that would be pretty sketchy. I mean, you never know when he's going to run out.*

Joe Walker: *With what hose wide open?*

Dan Wiitala: *With Brian's hose wide open like that, sucking air down so fast.*

Joe Walker: *But when you got down there, you didn't see any massive bubbles coming out of his helmet, did you?*

Dan Wiitala: *No.*

Joe Walker: *So how do you know whether his hose was wide open?*

Dan Wiitala: *I don't.*

Joe Walker: *If his hose wasn't wide open, couldn't you run two divers off an HP air rack?*

Dan Wiitala: *Yes.*

Joe Walker: *Particularly when it only took you two minutes to rescue him, right?*

Dan Wiitala: *Right.*

Joe Walker: *One of the things you mentioned, when you got out on the boat, you said you were kind of mad at Brian, is that correct?*

You were mad when you found out he didn't have his dive belt, right?

Dan Wiitala: *Mad—I was disgusted, is a good word.*

Joe Walker: *Just another question. Everybody's talking about releasing the belt to bring the diver to the surface. Just out of curiosity, when you got down there, why didn't you just go ahead and dump his belt?*

Dan Wiitala: *I don't recall.*

With that Joe Walker passed the questioning to Kirk Austin. Austin would proceed down a line of questioning in an attempt to establish that G&G routinely allowed their divers to work as subcontractors. Once that task was complete he would pass the witness to Bijan Siahatgar who would be representing Ronald Townsend.

Bijan Siahatgar: *Mr. Wiitala, I've just got a couple of questions. It's my understanding that this was a three man dive crew, is there any reason you could think of that a three man crew could not have successfully completed this job.*

Dan Wiitala: *No.*
Bijan Siahatgar: *Are you aware of any regulations that would have required additional personnel?*

Dan Wiitala: *No, not that I am aware of.*

Followed by more questions clarifying that the members of the crew assisted in the rescue attempt, that no one aboard interfered. Once confirmed he too passed the witness.

Ruben Hope representing Dan Gilbert would continue by asking questions regarding Wiitala's dive school education, dealing with entrapment situations, the length of the dive on March 4. Establishing that surely the cause was panic on the part of the diver. Establishing that all systems on the deck were operating as expected. Once it had been established that Brian and not his clients equipment was at fault he passed the witness to the Mr. Wilson representing the American Bureau of Shipping.

The American Bureau of Shipping would ask but a single question. *"Was Brian wearing a knife."*
Answered by Dan Wiitala with a simple *yes.*

With that Dan Wiitala's questioning was ended with a thanks from the court and a question as to whether he would be back to view the balance of the testimony. Dan replied, *"I hadn't planned on it, no."*

With that the next witness was called and sworn in followed by establishing the correct spelling of his name, where he lived, his reason for being aboard the Cliffs 12 on March 4, 1996. Jerry Lehr confirmed that he was the chief mechanic for Parker Drilling and had been sent out there that day as part of the crew that would eventually take over operations. Once the Cliffs 12 was issued a Certificate of Inspection.

He confirmed his participation in the rescue, assisting in the splicing of hoses, coordinating with the crane. Assisting Austin into and then out of the crane basket. Then assisting with the CPR once Brian was on deck. Remaining with Brian all the way to Saint Mary's Hospital.

The only major new information he would supply was his recollection that when Brian was pulled from the water his umbilical was no longer attached. With that revelation the witness was passed to Joe Walker.

My name is Joe Walker, and on behalf of the Pilkington's, they want to thank you for the attempts that you made, sir, to rescue their son.

When you were grabbing this hose, was anybody else—were you the first one to the hose?

Jerry Lehr: *There was another man helping, but I don't recall his name. There was two of us.*

Joe Walker: *Was he there before you, or did y'all run to the hose and start pulling it?*

Jerry Lehr: *I can't recall that.*

Joe Walker: *Okay. And when you pulled this hose and you said it came off the helmet, what did you see?*

Jerry Lehr: *I was surprised it came off. What did I see? It just came off.*

Joe Walker: *And what did the hose do?*

Jerry Lehr: *It swung out here, and we pulled it on up.*

Joe Walker: *Okay. What did you hear?*

Jerry Lehr: *I didn't.*

Joe Walker: *Did you hear any air coming out of the hose?*

Jerry Lehr: *I don't remember hearing air coming out. Not a lot. I don't remember hearing air coming out.*

Joe Walker: *And that's something you would be careful of since it was a hose, right?*

Jerry Lehr: *Yes. If it was excessive air coming out, it would be whipping around. It's got a metal end. It would hurt you.*

Joe Walker: *And the hose didn't whip around, did it?*

Jerry Lehr: *No, sir.*

Joe Walker: *In fact, did you see any bubbles coming out of the hose when it came loose?*

Jerry Lehr: *I don't remember it going back in the water.*

Joe Walker: *Okay. But you pulled it up hand over hand until it was near y-all?*

Jerry Lehr: *Right.*

Joe Walker: *And you were obviously making sure that that thing didn't whip around and hurt you, right?*

Jerry Lehr: *Well, we just pulled it up. We were probably more concerned—I don't remember.*

Joe Walker: *But you didn't hear any air—*

Jerry Lehr: *I didn't hear any air coming out of the hose.*

Joe Walker: *Okay. Have you been around busted hoses before?*

Jerry Lehr: *Yes, sir.*

Joe Walker: *You know what that sounds like?*

Jerry Lehr: *Yes, sir.*

Joe Walker: *You didn't hear any of that noise?*

Jerry Lehr: *No, sir.*

Joe Walker: *When you took the hose off that helmet, do you recall whether the diving compressor was still running? Did you hear any noise?*

Jerry Lehr: *I don't recall. I'm sorry, sir. I'm sure it was running.*

Joe Walker: *But you don't know for sure?*

Jerry Lehr: *No, sir. But, I mean, we would never shut that hose off as long as the man—off as long as the man's on the other end of that hose. That's his lifeline.*

Joe Walker: *Were you part of the diving station?*

Jerry Lehr: *No, sir.*

Joe Walker: *Had you ever seen a diving job where someone had to run around and get an oxygen acetylene hose—*

Jerry Lehr: *No, sir.*

Joe Walker: *And use that for a backup diver?*

Jerry Lehr: *No, sir. I didn't know you could attach it to that helmet. I didn't know it was the same fitting.*

Joe Walker: *That was kind of a first for you to see that?*

Jerry Lehr: *Yes, sir.*

Joe Walker: *You've been around a lot of diving operations, right?*

Jerry Lehr: *I've been around a few.*

Joe Walker: *You normally see a standby hose sitting there, right?*

Jerry Lehr: *Yes, sir.*

With that the witness was passed with no significant cross examination questions then thanked by the court for his participation and excused.

After a short recess Mr. Marty Husband was called

Lieutenant Commander Beistle: *Mr. Husband, if you will, please stand and let the court reporter swear you in.*

Lieutenant Commander Beistle would lay the foundation that Marty Husband was an employee at McKenzie Equipment in Houston Texas and in 1996 had acted as Service manager. Lieutenant Commander Beistle started his questioning.

Sometime in the March time frame in 1996, did you have reason to become aware that G&G had sent a compressor over to McKenzie's?

Marty Husband: *Not so much then, but probably within a month afterwards, yeah. I mean, I knew that they had one in the shop that we put a new compressor on, yes.*

Lieutenant Commander Beistle: *Okay. And what did you find—did you have any reason—did you wind up going to look into that whole issue?*

Marty Husband: *Only that Mary Ann McKenzie asked me to look into it so I enquired into the history with Guy Kirby. He turned over his notes.*

Lieutenant Commander Beistle: *Why Guy Kirby?*

Marty Husband: *He was the sole guy that did the compressor repair.*

Lieutenant Commander Beistle: *So what does this piece of paper represent that Guy turned over?*

Marty Husband: *Just notes basically on what he found when he tore the compressor apart.*

Lieutenant Commander Beistle: *And to your knowledge, did he make those notes—*

Marty Husband: *Yes.*

Lieutenant Commander Beistle: *Yes. And so, based on those two things, his notes and your discussion, what did Mr. Kirby find when he tore the compressor down?*

Marty Husband: *Basically, what's stated here: That it was carboned over, valves weren't holding. I mean, this is what we normally do when a compressor comes in, or McKenzie did at the time, is they put it on a test standard run. They try and pump up pressure and maintain pressure with the compressor.*

Lieutenant Commander Beistle: *Do you know whether he did that?*

Marty Husband: *Yes. It's done on every unit. And if it doesn't hold, then they start to disassemble it, which is usually the head section comes off first. So that's what I say, basically what he found were the heads—the seats and the heads were bad. They had a lot of oil carryover and bad rings. So based on the cost of the parts versus the cost of a new one, it exceeded 50 percent, which we would normally recommend a replacement.*

Lieutenant Commander Beistle: *As a matter of fact, didn't he estimate—how much did he estimate it would cost to repair it?*

Marty Husband: *$900 would cost to repair it, and a new unit would cost $1,100.*

Lieutenant Commander Beistle: *And so, what was the recommendation? Did he have a recommendation?*

Marty Husband: *Our recommendation was to buy a new unit.*

Lieutenant Commander Beistle: *Okay. you indicated bad carbon buildup. Is that carbon buildup—where was the carbon buildup?*

Marty Husband: *Well, the carbon buildup would have been more likely in the top section of the cylinder around the valves and the discharge port.*

Lieutenant Commander Beistle: *Now, was that on the compressor side, or is that on the prime mover's side?*

Marty Husband: *That would be on the compressor side, the compressed air side.*

Lieutenant Commander Beistle: *How would a compressor—did you say pistons, is that right?*

Marty Husband: *Yeah. It's at the top of the cylinder.*

Lieutenant Commander Beistle: *How would you get carbon buildup there?*

Marty Husband: *Oil carryover past the piston and heat.*

Lieutenant Commander Beistle: *Okay. We've heard testimony in this case that the oil used on the compressor side was like a vegetable oil or a monolithic oil. Is that right, monolithic (pronouncing)?*

Marty Husband: *Monolec.*

Lieutenant Commander Beistle: *Monolec oil which, as I understand it, is not a carbon—it's not a—*

Marty Husband: *Not a hydrocarbon, no, sir.*
Lieutenant Commander Beistle: *Hydrocarbon-based oil. So how would you—can you speculate, how would you get a carbon buildup on the compressor side if you weren't using carbon-based oil?*

Marty Husband: *Well, in Guy's case here, it would be called a carbon buildup. It's possible that you can get the vegetable oil hot enough that it would still leave a residue which would be black from heat and burn. So in his sense, he was thinking it was carbon.*

Lieutenant Commander Beistle: *Okay. Did he indicate—do you happen to remember offhand whether he found a filter in the filter housing on the compressor side, the intake side?*

Marty Husband: *No. I mean, this was something—I mean, I didn't really ask Guy a lot of questions, more or less what I heard just from people in the shop.*

Lieutenant Commander Beistle: *What did you hear from people in the shop?*

Marty Husband: *Some of the guys in the shop were saying that they found particles of a rag in the suction.*

Lieutenant Commander Beistle: *Is it possible to overheat a compressor that doesn't have any unloading device?*

Marty Husband: *If you block the inlet.*

Lieutenant Commander Beistle: *Which inlet, the air inlet?*

Marty Husband: *The suction.*

Lieutenant Commander Beistle: *The suction on the compressor?*

Marty Husband: *Yeah.*

Lieutenant Commander Beistle: *And would that lead to any of the—*

Marty Husband: *It would lead to all of that. With no air movement through there, it's—it's trying to pump and it has no way to expel it out the inlet side.*

Lieutenant Commander Beistle: *And so—*

Marty Husband: *So it's just sitting there pumping and creating heat.*

Lieutenant Commander Beistle: *And that might be consistent with the idea of a rag in the inlet?*

Marty Husband: *Right, some type of blockage in there could cause enough heat to burn the pistons.*

Lieutenant Commander Beistle: *Do you recall whether this mechanic told you that the compressor would not even turn a revolution?*

Marty Husband: *I really don't remember.*

Lieutenant Commander Beistle: *Does it say anything about the rings? Do you know?*

Marty Husband: *Just needs new rings.*

Lieutenant Commander Beistle: *So there really wasn't anything on that compressor worth saving, I take it?*

Marty Husband: *No, not without major rework on it.*

Lieutenant Commander Beistle: *You have a note here saying something about the 325 should not be used for breathing air.*

Marty Husband: *Well, it specifically states that on the compressor.*

Lieutenant Commander Beistle: *Do you know what compressors are recommended for diving use?*

Marty Husband: *Bauer and Eagle are two that I know of.*

Lieutenant Commander Beistle: *Just a couple of questions. Actually, what are the mechanical differences between the Bauer and the Eagle and the Quincy to make one suitable for diving, and the Quincy not?*

Marty Husband: *The filter system.*

Lieutenant Commander Beistle: *Are they more expensive, Bauers?*

Marty Husband: *Considerably.*

Lieutenant Commander Beistle: *Did you—when the person described bits and pieces of the rag, you overheard that, is that correct?*

Marty Husband: *Overheard that.*

Lieutenant Commander Beistle: *They said it was a red rag?*

Marty Husband: *Yeah.*

Lieutenant Commander Beistle: *Did you hear them say anything else?*

Marty Husband: *To be honest, it's been awhile since all this happened.
You know, it's just things that I heard in passing that was two years or three years ago. If it had been a few months ago I may have remembered better, but at this time, I don't.*

Joe Walker: *Did any of the mechanics know why the compressor had been brought to the shop to look at?*

Marty Husband: *No. Just basically that it was—you know, was not pumping air, I guess. I mean that would be their normal speculation if it would not hold pressure.*

Lieutenant Commander Beistle: *Just a quick question, sir. If—you said that there's a disclaimer on the Quincy 325 that says, don't use for breathing air.*

Marty Husband: *Yeah. It states not to be used for breathing air.*

Lieutenant Commander Beistle: *And McKenzie's knew what kind of business G&G was in, weren't they—didn't they?*

Marty Husband: *I would imagine.*

Lieutenant Commander Beistle: *They knew it was a diving company, didn't they?*

Marty Husband: *I would imagine they probably did.*

Lieutenant Commander Beistle: *Then why would they sell them a compressor that—it was likely to be used for diving operations that says, "Not to be used to supply breathing gas"?*

Marty Husband *That, I can't say. That's would by something you would need to ask inside sales at McKenzie.*

Joe Walker: *There's a couple of other documents here. You've got a work order here, also: Run and check unit for proper operation. It states: Hasn't been run in a while. And that was 3/7/96. Can I ask a question on this work order?*

Lieutenant Commander Beistle: *Sure. Let me finish this up.*

Lieutenant Commander Beistle: *And I note on here that there is a statement that says, "Run and check unit for proper operation, dash, hasn't been run in a while." Where—how would that notation have wound up on this particular piece of paper, this work order?*

Marty Husband: *It would have been—that would have been what—service had a secretary. She took all incoming calls and information. She would then write up the work order and put in what the customer basically told her.*

Lieutenant Commander Beistle: *And so, did she—I mean, to your knowledge, did she sort of transcribe whatever the customer told her?*

Marty Husband: *Right.*

Lieutenant Commander Beistle: *And I notice that the purchase order was verbal, and is says Mr. Danny Gilbert in the upper left-hand—*

Marty Husband: *Yeah.*

Lieutenant Commander Beistle: *On the question of that work order, there's a—the one you're looking at and that is dated 3/7/96, that you just referred to, regarding the "run and check unit," there's a notation there or an indication that two belts were used. Do you know why they were used?*

Marty Husband: *No. They probably would have been used to put—you know, to replace the belts for some reason. Or it's possible that the belts were in bad condition?*

With that the questing continued with the other parties in interest quizzing the service manager on the diesel engine, were other diving companies utilizing the same compressors for diving operations, how the un loaders worked.

The Attorney for G&G attempted to discredit the written reports from Guy Kirby as Guy Kirby he was not available to verify.

And then perhaps the most curious question from Bijan Siahatgar. *"You indicated that McKenzie's returned the compressor assembly to G&G Marine with a new compressor. What kind of oil was in the unit?"*

Marty Husband responded. *"Hydrocarbon-based oil, all our compressors are sent out that way, G&G sent it back and had us flush it out, replacing the oil with Monolec."*

Then one last question before the court was to thank him for his participation from Mr. Joe Walker. *"Do you remember ever telling anyone that the belts on the compressor were so badly damaged when the unit came in that they need to be replace?"*

Mr. Husband thought a moment and responded. It's been a longtime, *I just don't remember if I said that or not.*

With that the service manage was released with the thanks of the court.

The hour was late. A suggestion was made that a brief recess and then one more witness to finish out the day. After a ten-minute break and ten hours since the day's questioning had begun Kevin Todd Lawdermilk was duly sworn

The still fresh lieutenant commander began the questioning, *"Good to see you again, Mr. Lawdermilk."*

Mr. Lawdermilk: *You, too, sir.*

The lieutenant commander would continued by laying the foundation that Kevin had attended a dive school worked for several years for various employers before accepting a position at G&G.

Lieutenant Commander Beistle: *So could you tell me when you worked for G&G Marine as a diving supervisor—can you tell me what that job—give me sort of a job description for that job?*

Kevin Lawdermilk: *Well, the commercial dive supervisor is the one that carries out the duties of the job, the particular job at hand, makes sure that all the operations go the way they're supposed to go. He's the one that sets up—you know, goes—when he's on the job site, he's the one that controls the job.*

Lieutenant Commander Beistle: *You said you worked for G&G for about seven years?*

Kevin Lawdermilk: *Approximately, yeah.*

Lieutenant Commander Beistle: *And did you start with G&G as a diver supervisor?*

Kevin Lawdermilk: *No, I didn't.*

Lieutenant Commander Beistle: *What was your job when you started?*

Kevin Lawdermilk: *I was just hired on as a diver.*

Lieutenant Commander Beistle: *Okay. And so, then you went to work out of school for American Oilfield Divers—is that right?*

Kevin Lawdermilk: *Uh-huh.*

Lieutenant Commander Beistle: *When you went to work for AOD, in what capacity did you go to work for them?*

Kevin Lawdermilk: *I was just a tender.*

Lieutenant Commander Beistle: *And tell me, if you would, give me a job description for what a tender does.*

Kevin Lawdermilk: *A tender is the one that basically on a job does most of the—sets up the dive site, tenders while the diver is in the water. That's basically why—it's kind of self-explanatory. He tends the diver while he's in the water, brings him up and down, gets tools basically.*

Lieutenant Commander Beistle: *Can you describe that process for me a little bit? Can you describe how you sort of worked through the system, matriculated through the system from tender to breakout diver?*

Kevin Lawdermilk: *Well, yeah, as a tender, like I said, you start out—you don't really ever get in the water. The more jobs you go on, they mainly let you do small or shallow dives. You can do something very simple. The more dives you accumulate, you know, the more the supervisor's going to know you. They're going to let you build up a little bit, you know. It's a steady process that you have to go through. You don't just jump into it as a diver.*

Lieutenant Commander Beistle: *Was—did AOD have any program to—formal program to get you qualified to move up the ladder?*

Kevin Lawdermilk: *At that time it wasn't really a formal program, but it—breakout time was probably—the normal was about two years. Like I said, it wasn't formal.*

Lieutenant Commander Beistle: *Now, how do you—now, you've used a term here that I understand is pretty common in the industry, and I kind of want to get your—get a sense of what your understanding of it is. You've used the word breakout or breakout diver? What's a breakout diver in your estimate?*

Kevin Lawdermilk: *A breakout diver is someone that has just come from tender position into a diver/tender position. So he's just broken out into a diver.*

Lieutenant Commander Beistle: *Okay. And so, while you were with AOD, what kind of work did you do both as a tender and then as a breakout diver?*

Kevin Lawdermilk: *All kinds of different work. Anywhere—anything from working on jack-up rigs to working on barges, you know, and laying pipeline.*

Lieutenant Commander Beistle: *And so, when you say "working on," what were you doing specifically? What kind of work are you talking about was necessary for a commercial diver?*

Kevin Lawdermilk: *Well, there's thousands of different jobs, you know, a diver can do. Anything under the water basically.*

Lieutenant Commander Beistle: *Yeah. I know that's a big question. Let me ask it another way. I'm assuming you're talking about doing things like doing underwater welding? Were you welder qualified?*

Kevin Lawdermilk: *Yeah. I did get qualified as a welder, diver welder, yes, but as a breakout diver, you're going to stick to simple stuff.*

Lieutenant Commander Beistle: *Like what?*

Kevin Lawdermilk: *Turning shackles, go down—you know, put a—anything from putting, you know, a skid on a pipeline to jetting, a lot of jetting. A lot of the physical work basically.*

Lieutenant Commander Beistle: *Less the technical, more of the physical work?*

Kevin Lawdermilk: *Exactly.*

Lieutenant Commander Beistle: *And so, once you—you were with AOD for three years—once you left AOD, where did you go?*

Kevin Lawdermilk: *I went to G&G Marine.*

Lieutenant Commander Beistle: *And what was your job with G&G?*

Kevin Lawdermilk: *I was a diver. At G&G, everybody did diving and tending. I wasn't, you know, just a diver.*

Lieutenant Commander Beistle: *Or just a tender?*

Kevin Lawdermilk: *Right.*

Lieutenant Commander Beistle: *Nobody was just a tender?*

Kevin Lawdermilk: *Exactly.*

Lieutenant Commander Beistle: *And in your experience, was anybody ever hired to just do tender work, dive tender work?*

Kevin Lawdermilk: *Not that I recall, no.*

Lieutenant Commander Beistle: *Okay. So now, you came to G&G with a fair amount of experience?*

Kevin Lawdermilk: *Right.*

Lieutenant Commander Beistle: *School and then three years with AOD?*

Kevin Lawdermilk: *That's right.*

Lieutenant Commander Beistle: *In your experience with G&G, was that common, did people come with that level of experience?*

Kevin Lawdermilk: *No. That was actually the first time I had ever seen it, but G&G didn't just do oil field work. They were basically a ship husbandry company, you know. So you know, the guidelines were a little different there.*

Lieutenant Commander Beistle: *What do you mean?*

Kevin Lawdermilk: *Well, we—it wasn't—I don't know how to explain this. They didn't do just simply oil field work. Their main line of work, which was ship husbandry, was new to me anyway. I had never done any of that type of work before. So—*

Lieutenant Commander Beistle: *And what would you call ship husbandry?*

Kevin Lawdermilk: *Maintenance to large vessels, cleaning, working on propellers, just basic ship maintenance on a vessel on the outside skin under the water.*

Lieutenant Commander Beistle: *In the seven years or so you were with G&G, how many divers would you say that you—how many divers did G&G employ when you went to work for them?*

Kevin Lawdermilk: *Probably eight to ten.*

Lieutenant Commander Beistle: *And in the time that you were there, how many divers did they hire, are you—that you're aware of?*

Kevin Lawdermilk: *Probably 35 to 50, somewhere around in there.*

Lieutenant Commander Beistle: *Are there any accurate, sort of characterizations that you can make? Were they generally experienced divers or inexperienced divers, any way to—*

Kevin Lawdermilk: *Both. No. Basically there, you know, it was all types, guys right out of school and guys that had been in the business a while.*

Lieutenant Commander Beistle: *Did G&G have any program to assess the—you know, the skill level of these divers?*

Kevin Lawdermilk: *No, no, nothing.*

Lieutenant Commander Beistle: *Did G&G have any way to sort of test these divers and see what they were qualified to do?*

Kevin Lawdermilk: *No more than just bring them on a job and find out. That's about all you can do.*

Lieutenant Commander Beistle: *Who was responsible for maintaining equipment at G&G?*

Kevin Lawdermilk: *Nobody. There was a gentleman, when I very first went to work for G&G, that he was in charge of it, but after he left, there wasn't anybody from then on out.*

Lieutenant Commander Beistle: *And he was there when you first went to work at G&G?*

Kevin Lawdermilk: *Yes.*

Lieutenant Commander Beistle: *And he was—did he have a title?*

Kevin Lawdermilk: *I don't know that he had a title. He was an older gentleman that basically just worked in the shop and maintained the equipment.*

Lieutenant Commander Beistle: *How long was he there when you—while you were there? How long was he there, to your knowledge?*

Kevin Lawdermilk: *About a month after I went to work there.*

Lieutenant Commander Beistle: *He left?*

Kevin Lawdermilk: *Yes.*

Lieutenant Commander Beistle: *After he left, was there anybody who was responsible for upkeep and maintenance on equipment?*

Kevin Lawdermilk: *No.*

Lieutenant Commander Beistle: *Well, then, how did equipment get maintained?*

Kevin Lawdermilk: *Basically on the job, by the dive team.*

Lieutenant Commander Beistle: *Can you elaborate on that a little bit?*

Kevin Lawdermilk: *Well, if something went wrong, I mean, on the job, you know, whoever was on the job, they would fix the equipment to get the job done. I mean, every now and then, you know, if something—if a compressor or even a power unit or something on a job was having problems, yeah, when it went back to the shop, you know, it might get fixed and it might not.*

Lieutenant Commander Beistle: *You went to work for G&G. How long did it take you to qualify or to become a dive supervisor?*

Kevin Lawdermilk: *Six months. I don't know exactly, approximately six months.*

Lieutenant Commander Beistle: *And how did you know when you were a supervisor?*

Kevin Lawdermilk: *I didn't. There was a particular job that we were on that I had to—our dive supervisor—we were out of state. He had to come home, so I was the next man in line. There was basically three of us at G&G that did most of the dive supervisory. You know, we all three were on jobs before, and one of us might go on a job as a supervisor on one job and the next job may not be.*

Lieutenant Commander Beistle: *So when you—aside from these situations where the dive supervisor left on a job that you got fleeted up, like your first time, when you went out as a dive supervisor, did you normally know when you were going out that you were going to be the supervisor?*

Kevin Lawdermilk: *Yes, normally.*

Lieutenant Commander Beistle: *How did you know that?*

Kevin Lawdermilk: *You were sent a book and you were basically—on that book you were told that you were the dive supervisor and it would have had your crew members listed on there, also, or your dive team.*

Lieutenant Commander Beistle: *When you were at G&G, were you aware of—or were—were the compressors, air compressors being tested, or was the—was their output being tested for purity and so forth?*

Kevin Lawdermilk: *Tested as far as the O_2 level or just if it was maintaining pressure?*

Lieutenant Commander Beistle: *Well, both, for the O_2 level—*

Kevin Lawdermilk: *Well, I don't mean the O_2 level. They have a chemical test that they do on—that the compressors go through every so often. I don't know what the schedule is of them.*

Lieutenant Commander Beistle: *Were those tests being done, to your knowledge?*

Kevin Lawdermilk: *No, not to my knowledge. No.*

Lieutenant Commander Beistle: *Did you ever see anything—anything on the compressors that indicated that they had been tested?*

Kevin Lawdermilk: *When I very first started working there, yeah.*

Lieutenant Commander Beistle: *And what was it? What showed you that they were being tested?*

Kevin Lawdermilk: *There was actually a certificate that come back—it was actually in that book. There was a sheet that was kept in the book. It was usually kept at the back end of the book.*

Lieutenant Commander Beistle: *And was that—was that continued while you were there?*

Kevin Lawdermilk: *No.*

Lieutenant Commander Beistle: *When did it stop?*

Kevin Lawdermilk: *Probably a year after I went to work there. I mean, I don't know that it just stopped.*

Kevin Lawdermilk: *Right.*

Lieutenant Commander Beistle: *And how many—how many compressors were there at G&G? Let me be specific. How many Quincy 325 compressors were there, over the time that you were there.*

Kevin Lawdermilk: *Four or five.*

Lieutenant Commander Beistle: *Four or five. Okay. I understand you were not on the Cliffs 12 on March 4 of 1996, were you?*

Kevin Lawdermilk: *No.*

Lieutenant Commander Beistle: *Do you happen to know offhand which compressor—are you familiar with the compressor that went out on the Cliffs 12 job on the fourth of March?*

Kevin Lawdermilk: *Yes.*

Lieutenant Commander Beistle: *Had you worked with that compressor before?*

Kevin Lawdermilk: *Yes, I had.*

Lieutenant Commander Beistle: *What was your sense of the compressor usability, I guess?*

Kevin Lawdermilk: *It had basically been sitting on another trailer because it had had problems loading and unloading.*

Lieutenant Commander Beistle: *What do you mean by that?*

Kevin Lawdermilk: *Building up pressure and maintaining it and holding it.*

Lieutenant Commander Beistle: *What kind or problems? Had you experienced those problems yourself?*

Kevin Lawdermilk: *Yes. I was on a job several months prior to that, that I had had a lot of problems with the pilot valve.*

Lieutenant Commander Beistle: *Did you tell Mr. Gilbert about the problem with this compressor?*

Kevin Lawdermilk: *I had at that particular job where I had first had problems with it, yeah.*

Lieutenant Commander Beistle: *To your knowledge, had he done anything to fix or repair it?*

Kevin Lawdermilk: *Not that I know of. No, not that I know of.*

Lieutenant Commander Beistle: *I mean, had it been set aside purposefully or was it just—in other words, because it was not working right or was it just because there wasn't a need for it at that time or do you know?*

Kevin Lawdermilk: *Probably both. There wasn't a need for it at that time probably. We had other compressors that we used as our main compressors.*

Lieutenant Commander Beistle: *To your knowledge, was any work done on the—on the 325, on that particular compressor, between when you found out that it was bad and told Dan Gilbert and when it went out on the fourth?*

Kevin Lawdermilk: *No.*

Lieutenant Commander Beistle: *Would you—would you have known if any work had been done on it?*

Kevin Lawdermilk: *Yeah. Yes.*

Lieutenant Commander Beistle: *Why?*

Kevin Lawdermilk: *At that particular time frame, in that—round about that month, year, I pretty much—I wasn't in charge of the shop, but I knew quite a bit—I knew all the work that was done to anything that was done in the shop. It wasn't my responsibility, but I did work in the shop loading out jobs, getting jobs ready.*

Lieutenant Commander Beistle: *How did you first find out that there was a problem with the loader on that particular compressor?*

Kevin Lawdermilk: *How did I first find out?*

Lieutenant Commander Beistle: *Yeah. You were on a job, you were working it, and you had found out that there was a problem with it. How did that problem manifest itself?*

Kevin Lawdermilk: *The gauge on the volume tank would slowly bleed down and it wouldn't build back up and we would have to go over and adjust it, get it to build back up.*

Lieutenant Commander Beistle: *How would you adjust it?*

Kevin Lawdermilk: *You basically—well, I can't really explain it. It's got two nuts on it that you use to make the pilot go in and out, to adjust it to where it loads and unloads. Well, that's the problem. It would—you would go over there and adjust the pilot valve and it might work—thirty minutes to an hour, it may work correctly. And then as you're watching, you notice it bleeding back off, the gauge on the volume tank. So you would have to manually go back over and readjust the compressor. But you would have to actually manually go over with the crescent wrenches, adjust the valve, get it working properly.*

Lieutenant Commander Beistle: *Okay. Now, here's the dumb question of the world, but is that a problem?*

Kevin Lawdermilk: *Well, it's—if—it's a problem if you get all the way to the end of the pilot valve and you can't adjust it any more. Yeah, it's a problem.*

Lieutenant Commander Beistle: *And in doing this, if you had to go over there and adjust the pilot valve on this thing, would that require you to leave the dive station?*

Kevin Lawdermilk: *If—if whoever was running the dive station had to do it, if he was the only one that knew how to adjust it, yeah.*

Lieutenant Commander Beistle: *So now, how do you know that that particular compressor was the same compressor that was used on the Cliffs 12 a few months later?*

Kevin Lawdermilk: *Because we only had three working compressors at that time, that was one of them, and the two main compressors.*

Lieutenant Commander Beistle: *And so, did you go pick this compressor up from the—from the Cliffs 12 job on the fourth?*

Kevin Lawdermilk: *No. It would have been the fifth. I picked it up when it came in on the crew boat.*

Lieutenant Commander Beistle: *Okay. So you're certain—you're fairly certain, within your ability to put it together, that the one that you had problems with a few months before—*

Kevin Lawdermilk: *Yeah, it was the same compressor.*

Lieutenant Commander Beistle: *And you're certain that you told Dan Gilbert when he came out on the day that you were having trouble with it, that that compressor was having problems?*

Kevin Lawdermilk: *100 percent.*

Lieutenant Commander Beistle: *What maintenance did you see being done on this equipment? What kind of routine maintenance was being done?*

Kevin Lawdermilk: *There wasn't any routine maintenance. If it had a problem, you know, we would try to either get it fixed while we were out on the job or get it—whatever problem it had, before we went out on the next job.*

Lieutenant Commander Beistle: *Did you ever see—did you ever change any filters, or are you aware of any filters being changed on any compressors?*

Kevin Lawdermilk: *Not routinely, no.*
Lieutenant Commander Beistle: *When they were changed, that you're aware of?*

Kevin Lawdermilk: *Basically if we divers felt that the air was getting bad in some of the compressors, yeah, we do whatever we could to get something changed out.*

Lieutenant Commander Beistle: *So what would you do?*

Kevin Lawdermilk: *We—if we could get a filter, we would put a new filter in.*

Lieutenant Commander Beistle: *Did you ever put anything in other than a filter?*

Kevin Lawdermilk: *A couple of times, yeah.*

Lieutenant Commander Beistle: *What did you use?*

Kevin Lawdermilk: *Sometimes we used Kotex. A couple of times we used rags—towels, I mean. Not rags.*

Lieutenant Commander Beistle: *What kind of towels?*

Kevin Lawdermilk: *Just a terrycloth towel, put some marbles in it and Kotex.*

Lieutenant Commander Beistle: *The main intake. Do you have any idea what kind—whether there was a filter in this compressor with the aluminum frame?*

Kevin Lawdermilk: *There wasn't a filter in it, no.*

Lieutenant Commander Beistle: *How do you know?*

Kevin Lawdermilk: *Because it had—I knew what it had in it. It had some rags in it.*

Lieutenant Commander Beistle: *Why were the rags in the compressor?*

Kevin Lawdermilk: *Because it didn't have a filter, and actually, the filter canister on that compressor was either lost or had broken off or something. It didn't have the proper canister that the filter would fit down into.*

Lieutenant Commander Beistle: *Did—are you familiar with or did you know which—are you familiar enough with the equipment that G&G had to know which bottles they used, which bottles went out on that job?*

Kevin Lawdermilk: *No. We had a lot of bottles sitting around the shop, you know, probably 10 or 12 at one time. So no, I mean, they get exchanged out all the time.*

Lieutenant Commander Beistle: *Okay. Did you—what about the—what about after, on the next day when you went to pick them up—did you pick up the bottles?*

Kevin Lawdermilk: *Yes.*

Lieutenant Commander Beistle: *Did G&G keep its bottles full or ready to go?*

Kevin Lawdermilk: *Well, like I said, at any one time, you know, in the shop, there might be five full ones and five half-full ones and, you know, five empty ones. They were marked if—typically if they were empty, they were marked with some duct tape and marked "empty." Typically, I mean, it wasn't—*

Lieutenant Commander Beistle: *Do you have any knowledge about the two bottles that went out on that job?*

Kevin Lawdermilk: *Dan Wiitala told me one of them—both of them that was sent out, one of them was empty, and the other one, I think was half-empty, half-full, not even enough air to fill the bail outs.*

Lieutenant Commander Beistle: *And when did he tell you that?*

Kevin Lawdermilk: *On our trip back home, that night, the night that the accident occurred.*

Lieutenant Commander Beistle: *Had that ever happened before? Had an empty bottle ever gone out on a job before?*

Kevin Lawdermilk: *Yeah.*

Lieutenant Commander Beistle: *So that was a common practice for Gilbert to send divers out there without a backup dive hose?*

Kevin Lawdermilk: *I don't know that it was a common practice, but it was done. we had three compressors and four hoses. If all the compressors were on different jobs, only one job would have an extra hose.*

Lieutenant Commander Beistle: *So if the diver got fouled or troubled, there would be no way to get him out?*

Kevin Lawdermilk: *Well, like I said, it would depend on the job, I guess. But yeah, if a diver got hung and fouled, yeah, he would be on his own, I guess.*

Lieutenant Commander Beistle: *Did he say anything about the compressor?*

Kevin Lawdermilk: *Yeah. He said that he had had trouble with it and told—got on the radio and told Brian. He had to switch over to a bottle and get off-line, off the compressor.*
Lieutenant Commander Beistle: *Let's get back to the compressor, did you deliver the compressor used on the Cliffs 12 job to McKenzie?*

Kevin Lawdermilk: *Two days after the incident Danny Gilbert told me to take the compressor to McKenzie's and then a week or so later sent me back to pick it up. When I got there the compressor unit had been replaced with a new unit. I asked were the original unit was. They took me over behind the shop and it was in a box laying on the ground in pieces.*

Lieutenant Commander Beistle: *Did he tell you what was wrong with the original compressor?*

Kevin Lawdermilk: *Yeah. Well, it had several problems. The main problem was that it—he picked up a rag—a rag and said that this had been sucked through the cylinders, and the valves were wore out, stuff like that. They pointed out that there was a rag jammed in the valves and cylinder.*

Lieutenant Commander Beistle: *Did he pick a rag out of the box?*

Kevin Lawdermilk: *Uh-huh.*

Lieutenant Commander Beistle: *It was actually in the box?*

Kevin Lawdermilk: *It was in the box.*

Lieutenant Commander Beistle: *But he actually physically reached in the box and picked this rag up and said, "This is what I found in there"?*

Kevin Lawdermilk: *I don't know that he actually picked it up and said, "Here, here you go. This is what"—he pointed it out.*

Lieutenant Commander Beistle: *And he basically said that caused the compressor to what?*

Kevin Lawdermilk: *Well, he didn't say—he just said that this, you know, had been sucked through there, and then some of the rings and stuff were wore out of the compressor. It was an old compressor. It was already wore out even though it wasn't—not from the rag itself. It was already wore out.*

Lieutenant Commander Beistle: *But he indicated that the rag had probably finished the job?*

Kevin Lawdermilk: *That's right.*

Lieutenant Commander Beistle: *Okay. Now, what were they going to do with these compressor parts? Were they going to throw them away, or did they tell you what they were going to do with them?*

Kevin Lawdermilk: *No. I picked them up and brought them back to the shop, picked up the box and brought it back to the shop.*

Lieutenant Commander Beistle: *And what did you do with it when you got it to the shop?*

Kevin Lawdermilk: *Set it on the floor in the shop.*

With that the questioning for the day was suspended. Joe Walker, Tom Mozel and I return to my temporary office at the Holiday Inn to prepare for day two.

Chapter 19

DAY 2

Lt. Com. Thomas Beistle: *Okay. Folks, welcome back for day 2, and I understand that we're ready to go. We've got Buddy Horton on the line and ready to go, is that right, Bijan?*

Mr. Bijan Siahatgar: *Yes. Buddy, can you hear me?*

Mr. Horton: *Yes, I can hear you. Everyone else will have to be quiet, though.*

Having been first duly sworn, testified as follows via telephone:

Lt. Com. Thomas Beistle: *Mr. Horton, for the record, would you tell us where you are, please?*

Mr. Horton: *"I am in Maturin, Venezuela."*

Lt. Com. Thomas Beistle: *Well, what were your duties? If you would be kind of specific, what were your duties aboard the Cliffs 12?*

Buddy Horton: *I was assisting in reactivating the rig. At that particular time, the—all of the certifications had been dropped. The rig had been stacked in the river for approximately a year and a half and we had let the COI expire. So we were getting the—all the surveys redone and, you know, preparing it to go to work.*

Lt. Com. Thomas Beistle: Okay. *Let's go to the facts of the fourth of March. You, of course, remember—remember the commercial diving casualty that occurred on board or beside the Cliffs 12 on that day?*

Buddy Horton: *Yes.*

Lt. Com. Thomas Beistle: *Well, tell me when you—when did you first hear that there was any—that there was a problem?*

Buddy Horton: *If I remember correctly, I was—I think I was in the office at the time and there was some running in the hall of the quarters and, you know, I asked what was going on and they said that there was a problem with one of the divers.*

Lt. Com. Thomas Beistle: *Do you remember about what time that was?*

Buddy Horton: *Offhand, no, sir, I don't. It was in the late afternoon. I remember that.*

Lt. Com. Thomas Beistle: *Okay. And who did you—who did you first talk to that could actually give you some specific details about what was going on?*

Buddy Horton: *I went outside and—to see what was happening, and I don't remember specifically who it was, you know. I mean, there was a lot of guys out there right then in that area. And I asked what was happening and they said that the—the diver was in the water and in trouble and they were trying to get him out.*

Lt. Com. Thomas Beistle: *And so, what did you do?*

Buddy Horton: *At that particular time, I think Ronald Townsend—I think it was Ronald that was in a personnel basket and they were getting ready to go over the side of the rail and Kirk Austin was being suited up and they were putting the personnel basket overboard. So—I think someone said, "Get some life jackets," or either I thought to get some life jackets, and that's what I did. I went to get some life jackets and gave it to the—gave it to the other guys on the personnel basket.*

Then we—then I stood by to wait and see for a few minutes, and someone said, "Let's get a chopper out here," I believe. So I went back inside and started trying to contact the helicopter company to get a chopper out there. And from that point it was decided that—I think they were having some difficulties getting him out. So we decided to get another dive team to come out and we started to try to locate one in the Sabine Pass area or the Port Arthur area and have them go to the heliport so we can—you know, bring them on out and assist in the rescue.

And then I'm pretty sure it was Ron Everett came into the office and said, "Get us another dive team out here." So I called them right back and I said, "Don't leave. Stay there. We're going to get a dive team to come to the heliport. I'll call you back." And then I hung up, and I called the—we started looking for a dive team. I think it was Ron that knew of a local dive team that was very close to the heliport area, and so we called them and—trying to get them lined up to head out there. The next thing that happened was they came running back into the office and said, "We've got him. Get the helicopter." So I called the heliport back and told them, "Don't wait for the dive team. Leave now," you know, "Get out here as soon as you can."

Lt. Com. Thomas Beistle: *Okay. So did you—did you see—what did you do, if anything, during the—during the rescue out on the deck, aside from making these phone calls?*

Buddy Horton: *I didn't do anything. I would go out just very briefly, just stick my head out the door to see, you know, what was going on. Everyone—everyone was outside.*

Lt. Com. Thomas Beistle: *Was there a designated person in charge, in writing, on board the Cliffs 12?*

Buddy Horton: *There was a designated person in charge as far as the vessel, yes. Ronald Townsend's letter of designation was on board.*

Lt. Com. Thomas Beistle: *As a matter—he was the officer installation manager, is that right?*

Buddy Horton: *That's correct.*

Lt. Com. Thomas Beistle: *For Cliffs 12. Did you know who the dive supervisor was on this particular dive?*

Buddy Horton: *Yes. It was Kirk Austin.*

Lt. Com. Thomas Beistle: *Did you meet with Mr. Austin?*

Buddy Horton: *Yes, I did.*

Lt. Com. Thomas Beistle: *Did you—do you know offhand, did they have their safety manual, their operations manual with them?*

Buddy Horton: *I—I don't know. They didn't give one to me, no.*

Lt. Com. Thomas Beistle: *Did you ask?*

Buddy Horton: *No, I didn't.*

Lt. Com. Thomas Beistle: *Did Mr. Townsend ask?*

Buddy Horton: *I have no idea.*

Lt. Com. Thomas Beistle: *Did the Cliffs 12 have something like a ship's log or something like that? Did you have one where you logged—logged who came on board and why they came on board?*

Buddy Horton: *Well, usually, yes. You know, during our operations, we have a log like that, yes, sir.*

Lt. Com. Thomas Beistle: *Were you maintaining one at the time?*

Buddy Horton: *I don't remember.*

Lt. Com. Thomas Beistle: *Was it your responsibility to maintain one?*

Buddy Horton: *No, sir.*

Lt. Com. Thomas Beistle: *Whose would it have been?*

Buddy Horton: *Well, it would have been the vessel's responsibility. You know, the catering crew would also keep a log of personnel coming on board, and they may have had one.*

Lt. Com. Thomas Beistle: *The catering crew?*

Buddy Horton: *Yes, sir.*

Lt. Com. Thomas Beistle: *So the ship's cook was in charge of tracking who was on board and who wasn't?*

Buddy Horton: Yes, sir. *He would do that for his meal counts, and they also—a lot of times, you know, they're the guys who are responsible for assigning beds, as well.*

Lt. Com. Thomas Beistle: *What if you had to evacuate? How would you have known whether you had everybody evacuated? Would you have just done it up in your head as you were getting on board the—getting on board the work boat, just tallied it up?*

Buddy Horton: *Probably so at that point.*

Lt. Com. Thomas Beistle: *You know, Mr. Horton, just about every platform and every rig I've ever been on, as soon as I got on board, they trotted me to a shack someplace and made me listen to a—to a safety lecture, and then they made me sign in. Are you saying that you didn't have any kind of a procedure for people signing on board? That's all I'm trying to get to is, I want to know—and so, if it was the cook, that's fine. I just want to know.*

I just find it a little bit strange that there was nobody, other than the cook, who was in charge of keeping a count of who was on board for all of those different reasons, for evacuation purposes and for making sure that the safety—that the safety lecture had been given. Are you saying that there was nobody who was responsible for that?

Come on, Mr. Horton. You're the safety manager. You should be able to tell me that.

Did you log these people on board when they came on board? Did you log it anywhere?

Buddy Horton: *No, sir, I didn't.*

Lt. Com. Thomas Beistle: *So you never logged anywhere who came on board and who was in charge of—who was in charge of this team that came on board?*

Lt. Com. Thomas Beistle: *Mr. Horton, you're in charge of regulatory compliance, aren't you?*

Buddy Horton: *Yes, sir.*

Lt. Com. Thomas Beistle: *Didn't you just tell me that Mr. Townsend was the person in charge on board the Cliffs 12?*

Buddy Horton: *That's correct.*

Lt. Com. Thomas Beistle: *I want to read—and this is a little unfair and I'm going to admit that and sort of apologize up front, but you're the one who told me that you were in charge of regulatory compliance. I'm going to read just a little bit here from Title 46 of the Code of Federal Regulations, Part 197. It says—197.400 says, Diving operations may only be conducted from a vessel or facility subject to this subpart if the regulation of this subpart are met. And then it says, 197.402 Responsibilities of the person in charge. It says the person in charge shall, one, be fully cognizant of the provisions of this subpart; shall, prior to permitting any commercial diving operations to commence, have, one, the designation of the diving supervisor for each diving operation as required by 197.210; shall also have a report on the nature and planned times of the planned diving operations; the planned involvement of the vessel or facility, its equipment, and its personnel in the diving operation; a means of rapid communication with the diving supervisor while the diver is entering in or leaving the water as established; and a boat and crew for diver pickup in the event an emergency is provided.*

And then it goes on. Are you telling me that Ron Townsend didn't have any reason to talk to the dive supervisor?

Buddy Horton: *No. What I think I said was that I didn't know if they had spoken.*

Lt. Com. Thomas Beistle: *No. You told me—and I remember this distinctly because I thought it was odd. You told me that you didn't think that there was any reason for Ronald Townsend to talk to the dive supervisor. Now, I'm asking you, as the man in charge of regulatory compliance for Cliffs, after I just read that to you, do you still stick with that statement?*

Buddy Horton: *Well, I think maybe I misstated myself or maybe you misunderstood what I was meaning. What I meant was, during this meeting of what we were trying to set up to be accomplished, there was no reason for Ronald to be involved in that part of it. Now, as far as these regulations are concerned, then obviously there is some responsibility there. Now, whether it occurred, I don't know. They may have had conversations that I wasn't witness to.*

Lt. Com. Thomas Beistle: *But didn't you tell me that you were in charge of this inspection, you were the one who was leading them, showing them what to do? Or did you just let them wander around the MODU?*

Buddy Horton: *I was coordinating the survey. Once we accomplished the meeting with the ABS and once we accomplished what we wanted to—what the ABS wanted to do to accomplish the survey, then I showed them the area that they could set up. I gave them the supper times and found out if they wanted to go eat dinner before they started their work. I don't even know at that particular point—not know, but I don't remember—if they started immediately. If I remember correctly, it was a couple of hours before they even started. I'm not sure. I'm not sure of the timing of it.*

Lt. Com. Thomas Beistle: *Mr. Horton, here's my problem: You've told me that you're the safety manager for Cliffs and you've told me that you're in charge of regulatory compliance for Cliffs, and yet when you tell me what you did with—interacting with this dive team, it sounds an awful lot like you were in charge of the hull inspection. Are you a marine inspector, are you an ABS surveyor, or are you the safety manager?*

Buddy Horton: *I'm the safety manager.*

Lt. Com. Thomas Beistle: *And so, let me ask you specifically what acts, if anything, did you do—when you were on board the Cliffs 12. Did you have any safety-related functions or job descriptions?*

Buddy Horton: *I'm not sure I understand what you're saying. Did I have any safety-related job?*

Lt. Com. Thomas Beistle: *Let me ask it more directly. When you were on board the Cliffs 12 on the fourth of March 1996, what if anything did you do—what activity did you do that was related to or directly under—within the scope of your safety and regulatory compliance job description?*

Buddy Horton: *When I was on the Rig 12, you know, I was working with Ronald, trying to get the rig reactivated, which includes working with the Coast Guard on getting our COI reactivated. Part of that is to have our underwater survey done, and at that particular point, I was coordinating that effort. There was a lot of other things that I was doing as well. You know, we had crane inspections to do. We had fire equipment inspections to do. We had—you know, we had repairs to do on the rig. I did a walk-around on the rig looking for safety hazards. I gave a work list to Ronald to get accomplished in preparation for the inspections. A lot of things—you know, there was a lot of things. This—the underwater survey was just one part of it.*

Lt. Com. Thomas Beistle: *Okay. Let me ask you specifically then: On the fourth of March 1996, on board the Cliffs 12, what if anything did you do in relation to the diving operation that was safety oriented?*

Buddy Horton: *Not very much.*

Lt. Com. Thomas Beistle: *You're not an expert—you don't claim to be an expert in diving operations, is that right?*

Buddy Horton: *That's correct.*

Lt. Com. Thomas Beistle: *Do you claim to be an expert in regulations?*

Buddy Horton: *No, sir.*

Lt. Com. Thomas Beistle: *But that's kind of your job, isn't it?*

Buddy Horton: *It's part my job, yes.*

Lt. Com. Thomas Beistle: *It sounded like it was the majority of your job.*

Buddy Horton: *No, sir, it's not.*

Lt. Com. Thomas Beistle: *I thought you said that you were the safety manager and the regs. compliance manager for Cliffs Drilling?*

Buddy Horton: *I am, but you know, we have—we have a lot of different kind of rigs that aren't marine. Well, my attention was focused on that project. I was focused on that effort, you know, pretty intently.*

Lt. Com. Thomas Beistle: *You mean activating the rig, right?*

Buddy Horton: *Yes, sir.*

Lt. Com. Thomas Beistle: *In your mind, on the fourth of March 1996, on the Cliffs 12, what—what safety-related responsibilities towards this dive operation did you have, if any?*

Buddy Horton: *In my mind, at that particular point, very little.*

Lt. Com. Thomas Beistle: *Who was responsible—*

Buddy Horton: *The dive supervisor.*

Lt. Com. Thomas Beistle: *And who was the dive supervisor?*

Buddy Horton: *Kirk Austin.*

Lt. Com. Thomas Beistle: *And that understanding that it was Kirk Austin is based on your discussions with Kirk Austin on that day?*

Buddy Horton: *Well, on that day and the previous work. He had always served in the capacity of dive supervisor. I had worked with him on two or three other occasions, I don't remember exactly. They were down in Venezuela on some of our other rigs.*

Lt. Com. Thomas Beistle: *Had he ever given you a—or had you ever seen a letter or any piece of paper that indicated that he was the dive supervisor or anything appointing him as dive supervisor?*

Buddy Horton: *No, sir. but then the regulations do not require that I see the letter, only that there is a letter.*

Lt. Com. Thomas Beistle: *So as I understand what you're saying, he was a dive supervisor because he acted like a dive supervisor and talked like a supervisor, and you assumed he was a supervisor?*

Buddy Horton: *I didn't assume it. On the initial time that we hired them, it was recommended from another division within our company. They had worked with them before and told me that they had done good work.*

With that Lieutenant Commander Beistle turned the questioning over to Tom Mosele.

Mr. Horton, this is Tom Mosele. I'm here today assisting Mr. Pete Pilkington. Can you give me a brief explanation of your educational experience?

Buddy Horton: *Most of it is seminars in the field of safety. My previous education is high school graduate with three years of college, and then I dropped out of school and went to work, you know, for a living.*

Tom Mosele: *Okay. Do you have any formal certification in any safety areas?*

Buddy Horton: *No, I don't.*

Tom Mosele: *Okay. Were there any other employers that you worked for?*

Buddy Horton: *Yes. I worked for Wrigley Gum Company.*

Tom Mosele: *Okay. And when did you first become involved with vessel certification issues?*

Buddy Horton: *Somewhere in the Nineties—1992, I think, somewhere in that range.*

Tom Mosele: *Okay. Did somebody mentor you on the methodology that was to be employed in dealing with MODUs?*

Buddy Horton: *No. Pretty well what I did was—is gather up all the old files of the rigs and started going through them and reading the reports out of them. Got me a set of CFRs, which I already—you know, I already had some of them, but I got some more so I would have a reference point. And then pretty well just kind of jumped into it.*

Tom Mosele: *Did you review any CFRs in the course of your looking over these MODU inspections?*

Buddy Horton: *Some of them, yes. You know, there were—in the old records, there would be references to CFRs and sometimes I wouldn't understand what was being said in the 835. So I would look up the—the actual listing of it to try to understand it better.*

Tom Mosele: *Did you also look at the sections of the CFRs that dealt with diving operations?*

Buddy Horton: *I don't remember specifically, you know, doing that. You know, it was over—over a long period of time. I tried to cover as much of it as I could. I went out and bought a set of books, CFR books, you know, from the Government Bookstore in Houston.*

Tom Mosele: *Okay. Did anybody ever provide you with NVIC 1-89?*

Buddy Horton: *I don't know offhand what that refers to.*

Tom Mosele: Okay. *That specifically refers to navigation and investigation—pardon me—Navigation and Vessel Inspection Circular. It's for underwater survey guidance, and the purpose is to provide vessel owners and operators, underwater survey diving contractors, and other interested persons guidance for conducting underwater surveys. Are you familiar with that document?*

Buddy Horton: *You're talking about 1970's Is that—*

Tom Mosele: *No, no, sir. I'm actually referring to NVIC 1-89 and it's about a nine-page document that's specifically providing underwater survey guidance.*

Buddy Horton: *I don't think I ever seen that.*

This is Lieutenant Commander Beistle, Mr. Mosele, I'm interested in this area too. I don't want to block it off, but here's my point: I don't think you're going to be able to make much hay with someone who doesn't know what you're talking about.

Tom Mosele: *I'm on to a different subject already. Okay. Mr. Horton You previously worked with Mr. Austin and Texas NDT, is that correct, sir?*

Buddy Horton: *That's correct.*

Tom Mosele: *And on what occasions did you work—what type of activity was that?*

Buddy Horton: *We were doing underwater surveys in Venezuela.*

Tom Mosele: Okay. *And you said that they brought equipment with them, is that correct?*

Buddy Horton: *Well, they brought their personal dive gear with them, yes.*

Tom Mosele: *Okay. And you also said they were able to overcome some adverse situations, is that correct?*

Buddy Horton: *Well, it was a different situation. It was in much deeper water. It was rougher seas. It was in open—more adverse meaning that it was—on the day of the incident in question, it was relatively calm versus some of the—the weather that I observed and worked in before.*

Tom Mosele: *Okay. What type of air supply did Texas NDE use in Venezuela?*

Buddy Horton: *They used compressors.*

Tom Mosele: *Didn't they also use oxygen bottles from acetylene units as well?*

Buddy Horton: *Yes, sir they did.*

Tom Mosele: *They were using pure oxygen for breathing gas?*

Buddy Horton: *Yes, sir they were.*

Tom Mosele: *Are you still the safety manager for Cliffs?*

Buddy Horton: *Yes, sir, the only one.*

Tom Mosele: *Okay. Back to the events on the Cliffs 12. Did you attempt to investigate the accident in any way, shape, or form?*

Buddy Horton: *Yes. We—you know, I tried to—since I wasn't involved in most of it, you know, I needed to find out what happened and so we got together as a group and, you know, started talking about what had occurred. And, you know, I would imagine—I don't remember right now, but I had quite a few questions and was trying to get it laid out in my mind, you know, exactly what had happened and why it had happened. And, you know, I knew that I was going to be responsible for making a Coast Guard report on it, I think by that time I had already reported it to them, I'm sure.*

Tom Mosele: *Okay. So it would have been part of your responsibility as a safety manager to fill out an accident report, is that correct?*

Buddy Horton: *Well, not necessarily to fill out the accident report; it's not my responsibility, but it's somebody's, you know. It has to be done. I was taking on the responsibility of reporting it to the Coast Guard. And I think that the rig manager—or Ronald, in this case—would probably have filled out the accident report.*

Tom Mosele: *Okay. You said you had a meeting with various people. Do you know the names of the people in that meeting?*

Buddy Horton: *Well, I think—I'm pretty sure it was—Ronald Townsend was there. I remember speaking with him. Ron Everett was there. I'm pretty sure of that. Who else was in the room, I'm not sure. I mean, you know, this was when we were in the office. Now, later on we had all the crew members, we got everybody gathered up in the TV room and, you know, had a meeting in there. But, you know, we—I don't remember asking opinions of anybody in there. The object of that was to get everybody settled down and calmed down on it, you know, see if anybody needed any assistance.*

Tom Mosele: *Okay. Did you take any statements of people regarding this accident?*

Buddy Horton: *I didn't take any direct statements. We asked everyone to write down what they knew of the incident, you know, without any speculation or whatever. Just specifically what they saw and put that in writing and sign it, and I collected them and put them in the office.*

Tom Mosele: *Okay. And what happened with these statements that people wrote and signed?*

Bijan Siahatgar: *I've got to lodge an objection. I've got to make sure, Buddy, that you don't talk about anything that you and I talked about. I have to raise a privilege objection.*

Tom Mosele: *Okay. Well, I can ask what happened to them. I think that's appropriate. Where did those statements go, sir?*

Buddy Horton: *I think at that point the Houston office sent our attorney out, and once he got there I believe I gave them to him.*

Tom Mosele: *Okay. But you took those statements before you talked with the attorney, is that correct, sir?*

Buddy Horton: *That's correct.*

Tom Mosele: *Were any of those statements taken of people who were not direct employees underneath your supervision?*

Buddy Horton: *I don't even really consider it a statement, if you really want to know what I think. I mean, we just asked them to write down what happened. I didn't—the only direction I gave them on it was: Try not to speculate, try not to put down what you don't positively know. Just put down what you know, and that's it. Don't put down what other people have told you, and everybody just write down what they know.*

Mr. Horton, this is Lieutenant Commander Beistle. *I don't want to quibble about what a statement is or isn't. Let's just call it a statement. When you took those statements—and I'm going to call them that—were they done in anticipation of preparing them for your—for a safety investigation, or were they done because you expected to turn them over to the attorney?*

Buddy Horton: *Yes, for our own internal investigation.*

Lt. Com. Tom Beistle: *Are you—are you familiar with that procedure?*

Buddy Horton: *Yes.*

Lt. Com. Tom Beistle: *Under the circumstances, under whatever circumstances you had there, did you follow that procedure?*

Buddy Horton: *Pretty much, yes.*

Lt. Com. Tom Beistle: *Does that procedure include turning your work product over to the company's attorneys?*

Buddy Horton: *Yes.*

Lt. Com. Tom Beistle: *Was it—was this investigation done in anticipation of litigation, future litigation?*

Buddy Horton: *Yes. That was part of it. That wasn't the main focus of it, but that was definitely part of it.*

Tom Mosele interrupted. *"Who did you speak with before you started taking these statements? Who did you speak with at the home office? Did you call the shore after the accident?"*

Bijan Siahatgar: *I think we might go into some kind of privilege here also. It's certainly some type of party communications that would attach that also. I don't have a problem with him saying who he spoke to, but as to the nature of it, I would have to object.*

Lt. Com. Tom Beistle: *I agree. He can talk about who he talked to, but as to the nature or the content, I don't think—I think that's roped off.*

Tom Mosele acknowledged the objection and continued. *Did you ever make any of these statements available to the Coast Guard, Mr. Horton?*

Buddy Horton: *I don't remember that. I don't remember if I brought copies or not. I don't think I did.*

Tom Mosele: *I have a handwritten report. It appears to have your signature on the bottom of it. It was titled "Section 3, Personnel Accident Information." Do you remember filling out a handwritten form of this nature? I see that at the bottom it's dated March 6, 1996.*

Buddy Horton, *"Is that the Coast Guard form? Yes, I filled that out."*

Tom Mosele: *Are there matters in the statements that you gathered that give information that is additional to what is reported here to the Coast Guard?*

Bijan Siahatgar: *I think we're treading a fine line here.*

Lt. Com. Tom Beistle: *Yeah. That question is okay.*

Buddy Horton: *Would you repeat the question, please? I'm sorry.*

Tom Mosele: *Did those statements have information in them that is not reflected in the Coast Guard report you filled out?*

Lt. Com. Tom Beistle: *Mr. Mosele, I'm—I understand what you're saying. My expectation is that there's no way you can get everything that they may have collected into a 2692. I mean, if your suggestion is that he—that he somehow violated some Coast Guard regulation by not filling out everything into a 2692, I don't think that that holds water because that 2692 is not obligatory. They have to give us a written statement. That's simply the form that we use to ask them to give us the written statement.*

Tom Mosele: *But the point I'm getting to is that is there information that was inadvertently left out of what was told because it had ramifications that were unknown at the time.*

Lt. Com. Tom Beistle: *Yeah. And I hear where you're going and I'm interested in this, although, you know, at some point we're getting away from the casualty here. But the problem is that the witness doesn't have that in front of him.*

Tom Mosele: *Mr. Horton, who were the persons that you actually took statements from? Do you recall their names?*

Buddy Horton: *I have no idea. It was the—most of the Hercules personnel that were on board.*

Tom Mosele: *Okay. So the Hercules personnel, though, they were not your employees; they worked for Hercules, is that correct, sir?*

Buddy Horton: *That's correct.*

Tom Mosele: *What about the service hands such as the B. J. Construction people or the SOS welders?*

Buddy Horton: *If they were on board, they were in that room, and we asked them all to do the same thing. It wasn't a requirement. We didn't make them do it. We didn't even count, I don't believe. We just—when, you know, as they finished, they came up and handed them to us and, you know, there may even have been some guys in there that didn't fill out one, you know. I don't have any idea.*

Tom Mosele: *From a list that I have here, I see that the people that were direct employees of Cliffs were only four people on board: Ronald Townsend, Clint Bryant, Doug Reed, and yourself. From the list provided by the "catering crew" there were forty-seven people out there. I believe that is who you said kept track of the people on board. How many witness statements did you actually receive?*

Buddy Horton: *I don't know.*

Tom Mosele: *Was it more than half a dozen?*

Buddy Horton: *I remember—trying to remember. To be honest with you, I don't know. I really don't know. I would say somewhere in that range.*

Tom Mosele: *Okay. Did you receive reports from people other than Mr. Townsend, Bryant, and Reed?*

Buddy Horton: *Yes.*

Tom Mosele: *And I'm going to object to their nonproduction.*

Buddy Horton: *And I don't even know if they wrote one down, to tell you the truth.*

Lt. Com. Tom Beistle: *Stand by, Mr. Horton. I'm sorry.*

Tom Mosele: *Okay. I'm going to object to the nonproduction of those reports because this is clearly a third party. They're disclaiming their association with Hercules. They're saying they're a separate entity. And how anybody is employed by a separate entity can somehow create a privilege of investigation in anticipation of litigation on behalf of a separate autonomous company is completely foreign to my whole line of thinking here.*

Lt. Com. Tom Beistle: *Okay. Yeah. I see what you're saying, but are you objecting to them not producing that? Oh, you're not talking about civil litigation. You're saying here, he should be able to talk about what his conversations with Hercules employees were?*

Tom Mosele: *There should be no privilege to that and I object to him posing a privilege on it.*

Bijan Siahatgar: *Well, let me respond to that real quick. Number one, I don't think there was any request for us to produce any documents. Whatever documents I have been requested to produce, I am producing. The Coast Guard certificate that he has, the Hercules/Cliffs master service contract, I have that. I think there was one other thing that you asked me to produce. I produced all of those.*

Lt. Com. Tom Beistle: *I agree.*

Bijan Siahatgar: *With regard to the civil litigation, that's a completely separate issue, and just to address that right now, just to let you know, I identified everyone I took a statement from in the civil litigation and gave them the identity of these people. Their lawyer never asked for those, and I don't think that's relevant to this situation here right now.*

Lt. Com. Tom Beistle: *I completely agree. I think what Mr. Mosele was saying is that Mr. Horton should be able to, to the ability that he has any—to his ability to recollect at all, he should be able to discuss what, if anything, he did or heard or whatever, in talking with the—with the Hercules employees and that that shouldn't fall under the privilege. Is that what—*

Tom Mosele: *I think it's a bigger issue than that even.*

Lt. Com. Tom Beistle: *And let's also take into account here that the civil litigation is over. Let's consider—*

Without letting the lieutenant commander complete his thought Tom Mosele continued,

"We understand that, but the bigger issue happens to be; There's obviously some conflicting fact issues and the fact that this was very near-term recollection made by, in many cases, disinterested parties, objective observers in the situation that if that information has been withheld, not just from a civil litigation but from a Coast Guard investigation apparently, is improper and there ought to be adverse inferences for despoliation of these documents.

I think that if the Coast Guard had been made aware of this information, it certainly would have influenced their investigation as to how they dealt with this situation and what were apparently some significant equipment failures and deficiency in procedure.

Mr. Horton, this is Tom Mosele again. Why did the dive crew from American Oilfield Divers leave the vessel the same day that this accident occurred?

Buddy Horton: *They had completed their assignment.*

Tom Mosele: *Do you know if they were certified by ABS for performing underwater NDT?*

Buddy Horton: *I believe they were, yes.*

Tom Mosele: *What size was their dive crew?*

Buddy Horton: *I don't remember the exact number.*

Tom Mosele: *A little—about half a dozen, maybe a couple of more?*

Buddy Horton: *That would be about right.*

Tom Mosele: *Okay. Was there—did you consider that they had an adequate spread for performing the underwater work on the Cliffs 12?*

Buddy Horton: *For the job assignment, yes, probably so. They would require several more divers and, you know, more personnel for what they were doing.*

Tom Mosele: *Mr. Horton, is it your understanding that AOD was cleaning the very spots where this NDE inspection was going to take place on the mat?*

Buddy Horton: *Yes. That was their job assignment, was to clean the mat areas so we could do the mag. part of the testing and the gauging.*

Tom Mosele: *So they were intimately familiar with the exact location where this testing had to take place, isn't that correct, sir?*

Buddy Horton: *Yes.*

Tom Mosele: *Why didn't you have them do the NDE work while they were out there?*

Buddy Horton: *Because my confidence was in Texas NDE. That's who I had worked with on all of my previous jobs and I knew those people and that's who I wanted to do that testing.*

Tom Mosele: *Was the price from Texas NDE significantly less than what AOD would have charged?*

Buddy Horton: *I have no idea.*

Tom Mosele: *One last thing before we let you go. Earlier you mentioned you had worked with Kirk Austin in Venezuela. Was Mr. Austin diving in a wet suit?*

Buddy Horton: *No, sir they were all just wearing coveralls and tee shirt.*

Tom Mosele: *Sounds like pretty adverse conditions to me. I'll pass the witness.*

With that the examination of Cliffs Drillings only safety manager was concluded.

Lieutenant Commander Beistle: *Okay, folks, here's the restraint. It's now 10:41 and Dr. Clark has a plane to catch at 12:00 and a rental car that needs to be filled with gas. So I'm guessing we have until 11:20. Let's get started.*

Dr. John R. Clark being duly sworn in by the court reported began his testimony with a question from Lieutenant Commander Beistle: *Where do you work, Dr. Clark?*

Dr. Clark: *At the Navy Experimental Diving Unit in Panama City.*

Lieutenant Commander Beistle: *Dr. Clark, what do you do there?*

Dr. Clark: *I'm the scientific director.*

Lieutenant Commander Beistle*: And has everyone had a chance to—Mr. Austin, I'm not sure you've seen his curriculum—his CV. Has everybody else seen his CV?*

Bijan Siahatgar: *We'll stipulate to his expertise.*

Lieutenant Commander Beistle: *Will everybody stipulate?*

Mr. Wilson: *I had to put sunglasses on to read his CV. I will certainly stipulate to it.*

Lieutenant Commander Beistle: *Have you had a chance to listen to the witnesses that have talked—that have given testimony?*

Dr. Clark: *Yes.*

Lieutenant Commander Beistle: *Okay. Dr. Clark, you have had a chance to listen to the witnesses testify. What other material have you reviewed?*

Dr. Clark: *I have reviewed an autopsy report. I've reviewed a summary report from Dr. David Youngblood, whose credentials I'm aware of and respect. I've also reviewed an EDU report which was written summarizing experimental diving unit testing that was done on the accident rig back in 1997.*

Lieutenant Commander Beistle: Okay. *Dr. Clark, based on all the material you've reviewed and the witnesses you've heard, tell us what conclusion you've reached, please.*

Dr. Clark: *Well, from our initial findings of the performance of the helmet, we at EDU were surprised that the helmet would perform reasonably well at low pressures. The*

U.S. Navy uses a very similar helmet. We certainly do not operate in that manner nor does the company, Diving Systems International, recommend it being operated at that manner.

We did discover that based on the way the regulator was adjusted it had appeared to be operating in that manner for some time, in that it basically was supplied with the proper intermediate pressure with overflow or free-flow very strongly. That would not be the case unless that regulator had been adjusted to operate at a low pressure.

So assuming that helmet had been used before at low pressure, it was probably to just about the optimal performance we could expect. We would hope we never find one of our helmets adjusted in such a manner. It did supply and it could supply a sufficient gas to keep the diver alive if the diver was barely working. In some cases, if he were a very experienced diver who had learned to move efficiently underwater without consuming an awful lot of oxygen and producing an awful lot of CO_2, then that diver could get by all right in that helmet.

However, what is very obvious in my experience and from the reports that I've read is that if a diver ever overexerts himself, starts generating more respiratory demand than the helmet is going to supply, then the diver results in what we call hypoventilation or under breathing. SCUBA divers sometimes call it skip breathing. It simply means the diver is not breathing as much as he normally would. The result is that CO_2 in the bloodstream and arterial blood begins to increase. This can be an ever-escalating process unless something happens to restore the gas flow or unless that diver were to stop working.

Most divers, if they're working hard and begin to sense a buildup of CO_2, will ventilate, as this diver did, with a steady flow valve. Then if this happens more than once or twice, typically the diver would stop work, take more of a breather, and once he's caught his breath again and things are back under control, continue working.

From what I heard in the testimony yesterday, apparently the diver was operating a steady flow valve repeatedly and only closed the steady flow valve when somebody topside explained to him that he was going to lose gas pressure unless he did that. That situation undoubtedly crests to a point of panic. To me, the cause of panic would be the realization that he did not have enough gas perhaps, also if he could not make an escape to the top, but that's purely conjecture.

Obviously the diver was not getting the gas he needed, whether it was from low ops from a compressor or due to the leakage of the gas umbilical. I certainly have no evidence to suggest that it's one or the other. I cannot tell. I don't see any evidence of that.

Looking at the autopsy results, we have an indication that the diver, while being ventilated on a ventilator—and I'm assuming he did attain sinus rhythm again once he's in the hospital, otherwise he probably would not have been on the ventilator. In other words, the CPR was effective in sustaining him to get his heart going. There is marked evidence of a lot of CO_2 retention in that diver.

Now, the question is that CO_2 retention due to the fact that he was—in other words, his arterial pH was very low and the amount of CO_2 in his bloodstream, arterial blood, was very high. Now, we have no real indication what his arterial oxygen levels were because he was right away put on oxygen. The first blood gas indicates that his O_2 was very high, which indicates that his heart was beating, he was essentially resuscitated, and then over a period of time the CO_2 began washing out. And it washed out fairly quickly because of the efforts of the emergency room crew and the fact that he was on a ventilator. That ventilator was really pushing a lot of gas into him.

The rationale or reason for the high CO_2 is very difficult to say. Was it due to the fact that, perhaps, he had accumulated a lot of CO_2 in the dive, in fact enough to knock himself out? We don't know.

The fact that he became panicky and did become unconscious indicates to me that there had to be a cause. That cause could either be due to the very high CO_2 within him or due to an inadequate gas supply. But why we would have a high CO_2 hours later when he was receiving medical treatment is difficult to say because, after all, he had apparently not been breathing well when he was in the helmet. Supposedly he had become unconscious. There was some evidence of water in the helmet, and there's a possibility—certain signs that water had been ingested into the lungs. It doesn't take a lot of water to cause problems with gas exchange in the lungs. A little bit of lung fluid can result in edema, and the edema was obviously evidenced when the diver surfaced.

Whenever you have froth coming out of the mouth it indicates that you have fluid which belongs in your lung capillaries that has been pulled out of those lung capillaries and are not in your air sacs or the alveolar spaces. That can come from two reasons. One, it can come from damage caused by salt water ingestion, or it can come from strenuous labored efforts to take a breath. Either one is quite plausible. I would not be at all surprised if Brian felt that he was not getting enough gas, that he was tugging very vigorously on his oral nasal strap, trying to pull some gas out of that second-stage regulator.

You can generate such high negative intrathoracic[6] pressure that, in fact, you can pull fluid—serum—directly out of your bloodstream through your alveolar wall, and that can result in pulmonary edema.

Also, if you have a person who has gas trapped in his lungs and he's brought rapidly to the surface, as he was, and the airway is not kept patent and that gas is not allowed to escape normally, then you have a possibility of overexpansion of the lungs, and once again, you can result with fluid in the lungs.

So we know what the results were. We had somebody who's unconscious from a lack of gas—whether it be to gas leakage or just inadequate gas supply, we don't know. We do know that another diver in different circumstances, who perhaps was used to a lower gas supply, might have been able to tolerate the situation unless something acute happened to exacerbate the situation. And, of course, we heard speculation that the compressor may have quit putting out gas at all.

I suspect that Brian was getting some gas, although an inadequate amount, because he survived. If he was getting no gas supply at all, he definitely would not have survived for as long underwater as I understand that he was. I heard the rescue efforts lasted perhaps thirty minutes or more.

I think it's important to point out that, although some divers can work with a helmet that's putting out a low gas supply, other divers—and not necessarily do I mean inexperienced divers, but just other divers—prefer to work with higher flow levels for their gas. Some divers will tolerate a large amount of CO_2 in their bloodstream and get along just fine. I personally have worked with divers who have exercised very vigorously under hyperbaric conditions and claim that they're very comfortable, and then suddenly go unconscious because, in fact, they were comfortable because they weren't breathing hard, but at the same time their arterial CO_2 was steadily climbing, steadily climbing, and finally reached a point where unconsciousness snuck up on them and they were totally unaware and boom, they were out like that.

And the other divers, what I basically consider to be safer divers, are those who do not like the feeling of having their gas restricted, who like keeping their arterial CO_2 levels down, and want a lot of gas. Eventually they'll reach a point when they feel they're not getting enough gas and they'll stop. "I'm not doing this anymore" or "I'm going to stop and take a breather, catch my breath, ventilate"—whatever.

---

[6]   within the thorax

I suspect all these things were going through Brian's mind at the time and he undoubtedly did stop and ventilate himself. However, in spite of those efforts, if his gas supply was still wanting, his mental confusion would get progressively worse, and at some point he might have started taking actions that were not in his best interest.

It is possible—again, solely conjecture—that in the confusion he may have reached back and started releasing something he shouldn't have. I have no idea. But what we do know is that in the course of sustaining a large carbon dioxide insult, you become very anxious. It sounds like Brian was becoming anxious. Of course, if somebody cut off your air supply, anybody would become anxious, but CO_2 alone can do that.

And then you begin to be increasingly confused, mentally, and not able to think straight and not able to—at one point eventually—to not even be able to respond to what is being said by topside. You're not aware of anybody else talking to you. You're totally involved in yourself. It's a strange and very dangerous state that you end up in, and if the situation is not remedied immediately, then eventually CO_2 can reach such high levels that you can convulse and become unconscious. Of course, at that point, if you have one in a helmet, then partial drowning is more or less inevitable. It will happen.

And there seems to be evidence in the autopsy reports and the reports we were getting. Once Brian was brought to the surface then, yes, there was water in the helmet. One question is how would water get into the helmet? That, to me, makes me believe that, perhaps, the umbilical was connected because in the course of making large respiratory efforts, it's quite possible to create negative pressures inside the helmet, enough negative pressure to balloon the neck dam backward and actually pull water up past the neck dam.

It's also possible to pull water in through the exhaust valves. It's one of the concerns we have about using a helmet like this, as it is, for contaminated water diving. If you're making large respiratory motions, you will get water coming backwards through the exhaust valve.

So the fact that he had some water in the helmet, whereas otherwise he would not have, makes me speculate that he was creating very high negative pressures. If he was creating high negative pressures and the umbilical was connected, I would have thought he would have pulled a lot of water in through the umbilical. How much, I don't know. We're really getting into the area of speculation at this point.

But it's not at all surprising with a diver making desperate respiratory efforts to find some water in the helmet. Of course, when he passes out, especially if he's in a poor position, that water would be inhaled. If it was not inhaled when he was underwater, it could very easily have been inhaled during the rescue efforts when he was brought up to the surface.

Dr. Youngblood's account I do not disagree with. I do not have any information on the water temperature, although since the dive was in March, in this area I would expect the water to be fairly cold. I would estimate somewhere in the sixties, perhaps. I don't know what the water temperature was.

Dr. David Youngblood made some notes of hypothermia. Hypothermia could be contributing certainly to the confusion. I don't think in this case hypothermia would have been necessary to have the results that we had, but it certainly would have been contributing.

That's basically it in a nutshell.

Lieutenant Commander Beistle; *Terrific nutshell, sir. Thank you. Let me ask you, just very quickly, what are the outward signs, the effects, the symptoms of CO_2 toxicity?*

Dr. Clark: *Well, the inward sign is probably the most important in that the diver himself would feel very flush. His face would feel hot. He would feel like he's not getting enough gas and to a dive supervisor, for instance, the only way he could suspect that the diver is not getting enough gas, he would have to presume that he's getting a CO_2 depth simply because of the fact that he's perhaps opened his steady flow valve more than would be expected or that he's becoming a little less responsive or slowing his response.*

In that case a diving supervisor would say, "Ventilate, give yourself more gas." This diver was doing that on his own. So as soon as you hear the accounts of what the diver was doing, it was very obvious that this fellow was not getting enough gas.

Lieutenant Commander Beistle: *When Brian was brought up, the testimony was that his face was blue. Can you tell me why his face turned blue?*

Dr. Clark: *His face would have been blue if he was not getting proper gas exchange because of water that would have been inhaled in his helmet. It's my best guess.*

It's also possible that the CO_2 narcosis could have reached such a high point that he became very narcotic, in fact, stopped breathing. That would obviously cause a blue face. I have no idea when he was brought to the surface if he had any ventilatory efforts on his own or not, but that would be one of the end-stage signs of CO_2 narcosis.

Lieutenant Commander Beistle: *You heard here last night, testimony by Mr. Marty Husband, who used to work for McKenzie's Equipment Company, about the compressor and you also heard testimony from Kevin Lawdermilk talking about at least the potential—people who had looked at the compressor, the potential for a rag to have been ingested and conceivably that a rag or perhaps the oil or something else could have burned in this compressor.*

Is there any—based on that, do you have any opinions at all about the possibility of carbon monoxide poisoning rather than carbon dioxide? What would you call an access of carbon dioxide?

Dr. Clark: *I think carbon monoxide would have been more assiduous. I don't think it would have adduced the panic. I don't think he would have been aware of it. I think he would have quietly gone to sleep if that would have been the problem.*

I think what would be more likely in a case like that, if you're talking about a frank failure of the compressor, that you get sudden reduction in gas flow and, all of a sudden, a bad situation would turn much worse.

The carbon monoxide itself, it's a possibility; but it's one I don't think we would be able to run down. I'm not sure. I'll have to go back and look at the blood gas analyses to see what the CO levels were. I need to do that.

Lieutenant Commander Beistle: *Dr. Clark, you heard the testimony from Mr. Wiitala earlier about how he turned on the HP air bottle, the secondary air bottle after the compressor—after he was having trouble with the compressor, and he said that that bottle dumped in about fifteen minutes or so, if I remember his testimony. I mean, is there kind of a connect-the-dots relationship there? Is it possible—I'm just asking you to speculate, but is it possible that with the HP air bottle, it could actually produce conceivably the right levels of air, you know, between 115 and 200 psi that you're suggesting the thing needed? Would that have tripped Brian's helmet regulator so that it would free flow and actually use up that bottle faster?*

Dr. Clark: *Very likely, now that you say it. I haven't thought of that, but that's exactly what we would predict. If that regulator was set up the way it was when we received it, the result would have been free flow.*

Lieutenant Commander Beistle: *Now, my question that comes out a little bit later is—I know that there's going to be additional testimony that when he came up out of the water, that the air hose either came off or was not connected to the helmet. Did you take that into consideration?*

Dr. Clark: *I did. And again, the way I would interpret that is if the hose was not connected, Brian would have been dead by the time he reached the surface. So he must have been getting gas.*

Lieutenant Commander Beistle: *At some level?*

Dr. Clark: *Right, at some level, enough to support life. Not enough to support consciousness, but enough to support life.*

Lieutenant Commander Beistle: *Did you also remember Mr. Wiitala testifying that he was hyperventilating for a period and then he settled down to a more calm breathing? Do you remember that?*

Dr. Clark: *That's exactly what I would expect if he became unconscious.*

Tom Mosele: *Dr. Clarke, could you explain, at least in dive physiology, the differences that, let's say, a large athletic person such as Brian—who was 6 feet 5 inch, 210 pounds—what their air demands and how they might differ from say, a smaller person, or is there a wide variance in people and their air needs?*

Dr. Clark: *Yes, there is. Oxygen consumption and CO_2 production is based on A per mass. It's per kilogram typically or per pound, if you will. The more poundage you have, the more oxygen you typically consume when engaging in various activities. So typically, if you have somebody who is large and especially very muscular, they would, on an average, have a greater requirement for oxygen than somebody who—on an absolute basis—is smaller.*

However, it becomes more difficult when you're talking about ventilation being supplied by a breathing apparatus. It's really the ventilation which is controlling and not oxygen there that is much less dependent on size. A small person may need as much gas flowing in through their lungs and back out, again in order to accomplish the same amount of work as a large person. So when you're looking at the ventilation requirements, that is not nearly as clear as the amount of oxygen in a person's body.

Lieutenant Commander Beistle: *Okay folks, thank you. We are going to have to call a halt to this. The Dr. has a plane to catch, thank you for your assistance here today. Sir you are released, have a good trip back to Panama City.*

If we are going to call Lieutenant Julio Martinez, who is in Puerto Rico, which is two hours ahead of us or call Captain Fels in Florida, one hour ahead of us. Perhaps we should start with the Lieutenant. Let's go on the record. For the record, it's five minutes until noon on the twenty-third of June 1999. We're going to call Lieutenant Martinez, Julio Martinez.

Lieutenant Commander Beistle: Okay. *You understand, Lieutenant Martinez, that your testimony today is—even though it's telephonic, it's just as important as testimony would be if you were here with us in this hearing room?*

Lieutenant Martinez: *Yes, sir.*

Lieutenant Commander Beistle: *Thank you. And where are you—where are you stationed right now, Mr. Martinez?*

Lieutenant Martinez: *Currently stationed at the Marine Safety Office, San Juan, Puerto Rico.*

Lieutenant Commander Beistle: *Okay. Were you qualified to conduct the inspection of a Mobile offshore Drilling unit in March of 1996.*

Lieutenant Martinez: *Yes, sir.*

Lieutenant Commander Beistle: *Okay. Oh, by the way, Lieutenant Thomson, Lieutenant J. G. Thomson then, was he with you on this, on the inspection of the Cliffs 12 in March of 1996?*

Lieutenant Martinez: *I believe so, yes. There was more than one inspector.*

Lieutenant Commander Beistle: *Okay. What was his status at the time? Was he a qualified MODU inspector?*

Lieutenant Martinez: *To be honest, I can't recall.*

Lieutenant Commander Beistle: *I'm going to tell the board. I threw that one out there. I probably shouldn't have. I'll tell you from my preliminary investigation that I found out that he was not a qualified MODU inspector at the time. Okay. If you would, kind of look through this five-page work list and just give me a sense, from what you can remember and what you see here, of how that inspection went?*

Lieutenant Martinez: *Okay. What I can recall is that we were on board the vessel, and she needed a lot of work. In other words, there was a lot of requirements that needed to be taken care of. She was, again, in what we call a stacked status. Just close it up, shut it down, and she was left there. And they had numerous items to correct. She needed to be cleaned up and what I meant by that is physically needed to be cleaned up. They had just put it there, stacked it, and didn't do any housekeeping.*

Lieutenant Commander Beistle: *Okay. So what was the status of that MODU? In other words, did you consider it to be an inspected vessel or an uninspected vessel? How did you treat it when you went on board?*

Lieutenant Martinez: *I treat the vessel as an inspected vessel, even though it didn't have a current certificate. We treat it because the company requested to get the vessel recertified. We use all our policies, NVICs, regulations, whatever pertains to that particular vessel to be recertified if they meet the minimum standards.*

At the time they were still doing ongoing work, repairs on the vessel. The list of our items that we gave them, they were in the process of repairs and she was also going through an inspection with the Class Society to get her documents up to speed also. I believe the vessel was classed by ABS. So she was going through that portion of the phase also. There was also a lot of construction work, if you will, ongoing.

Lieutenant Commander Beistle: *according to our records you issued a work order on March 4, 1996 with some 21 items that would need to be addressed.*

The lieutenant commander started at the top of the list asking the lieutenant the importance of each item and whether it could have been deferred or need to be completed prior to the issuance of a certificate of inspection. Replace a broken lens cover, replace a navigation light, blank off a sprinkler, replace a jumper hose, the list continued each given a value of importance until item seven.

Item number Seven, provide Coast Guard approved operations manual. Was this an item they would need to provide before the Certificate of Inspection could be issued?

Lieutenant Martinez: *That could be deferred until later.*

Lieutenant Commander Beistle: *When later?*

Lieutenant Martinez: (no response)

Lieutenant Commander Beistle: *Did you hear me?*

Lieutenant Martinez: *I'm sorry, sir. What was that?*

Lieutenant Commander Beistle: *When? You say it could be deferred until later. When?*

Lieutenant Martinez: *Normally we give them about 30 days.*

Lieutenant Commander Beistle: *To produce the manual?*

Lieutenant Martinez: *Yes, sir.*

The balance of the items in need of attention were reviewed and the witness passed for cross examination.

Lieutenant Martinez, my name is Pete Pilkington.
Earlier you indicated that you were qualified to conduct MODU inspections, I believe your record show you had three years of experience prior to the inspection on the Cliffs 12. Can you explain to us what that's all about?

Lieutenant Martinez: *As far as what, sir?*

Pete Pilkington: *How do you get qualified, what sort of training you go through?*

Lieutenant Martinez: *I go through a—what we call a PQS book or a personal qualification book. In it is several pages listing different items pertaining to machinery, lifesaving, fuel systems, fire extinguishing systems. Of all that, you have to physically research it through the regulations, documentations, policies, and NVICs and then on-the-job training with other qualified inspectors. And we also have to go through an outer continental shelf inspection course.*

Pete Pilkington: *So then you would be familiar with the 46 CFR as it pertains to vessel inspections?*

Lieutenant Martinez: *Yeah.*

Pete Pilkington: *How about the 46 CRF in regards to commercial diving operations?*

Lieutenant Martinez: *Yeah, I'm familiar with that.*

Lieutenant Commander Beistle: *Could you be a little more specific? Are you talking about 46 CFR 197?*

Pete Pilkington: *Correct. Would you normally review these before you go out to a rig where you know there are going to be diving operations under way?*

Lieutenant Martinez: *Yes. Sometimes I do, just to refresh my memory.*

Pete Pilkington: *Would you also review the NVICs?*

Lieutenant Martinez: *When the situation arises pertaining to the inspection.*

Pete Pilkington: *Okay. Would it be reasonable for you to inspect the Safety and Operations manual when you arrive on a vessel?*

Lieutenant Martinez: *Yes.*

Pete Pilkington: *And you indicated earlier that you wouldn't require an operations manual while you were there?*

Lieutenant Martinez: *No. I stated that they have to have an operations manual, but what the write-up was for a Coast Guard approved. Many times, through their own misplacement of the documents, they don't have the staff letterhead for the manual and sometimes have misplaced the approved manual, but they have their other manual. Sometimes they'll have two manuals, but only one of them has been stamped approved by the Coast Guard. And sometimes they'll remove a page and file it instead of keeping it attached to the manual, but they are required to have the actual manual on board.*

Pete Pilkington: *What about in an emergency evacuation plan, would you expect to see that?*

Lieutenant Martinez: *Yeah.*

Pete Pilkington: *Did you see one on the Cliffs 12 on March 4 when you inspected?*

Lieutenant Martinez: *I'm sorry. Could you repeat that again?*

Pete Pilkington: *On March 4, 1996, when you inspected the Cliffs 12 did you see an emergency evacuation plan?*

Lieutenant Commander Beistle: *Have we established that he was on board on the fourth?*

Lieutenant Martinez: *Actually I don't recall if I was there on March 4. I know I was there on the third and again on the eighth, but I don't recall being there on the day of the casualty.*

Pete Pilkington: *In that case, we reserve the right to call Tuan Thomson. Tuan Thomson signed the work order on March 4. He so he must have been there.*

Lieutenant Commander Beistle: *It may be necessary. Okay. But go ahead.*

Pete Pilkington: *If he's telling us he wasn't there, we'll just—*

Lieutenant Commander Beistle: *No. He's not saying he wasn't there, Mr. Pilkington. He's saying he doesn't remember being there.*

Pete Pilkington: *Doesn't remember being there, fine. I'm just saying I can't go down the line—lead the question regarding the dive manual or the dive operations because he doesn't remember seeing the divers. So we've got to bring in Tuan. Let's try this first. Lieutenant Martinez you've indicated already that you're familiar with the 46 CFR regarding diving operations and with vessel inspections, and you indicated that you're familiar with the NVICs.*

Lieutenant Commander Beistle: *Well, let me see—before we go down this road, let me ask you a question, Mr. Pilkington. Are you suggesting that Mr. Thomson is a better witness? Therefore, is there any purpose in talking to this witness?*

Pete Pilkington: *Only in regards to the application for entry into the underwater inspection program as required by NVIC. Lieutenant Martinez signed the documentation indicating that he would be out there for these inspections, or that the Coast Guard was going to do the inspection. So he must have been involved in the pre application process. I would just like to go through a series of questions to know whether or not the pre application process was ever completed.*

Lieutenant Commander Beistle: *That makes sense to me.*

Pete Pilkington: *Did you ever review an underwater or a dry-docked video of the vessel prior to the inspection of the Cliffs 12?*

Lieutenant Martinez: *Which inspection, COI or the—*

Pete Pilkington: *NVIC—and I'm going to refer to NVIC 1-89. It requires that a reference video be made in dry dock and that you have to review that reference video before you can approve the vessel for an underwater survey. Was that ever done?*

Lieutenant Martinez: *I—I don't recall.*

Pete Pilkington: *Were you notified as to the identity of a diving contractor that was going to be doing the underwater diving? That, by NVIC, is supposed to be supplied to you 90 days before the survey.*

Lieutenant Martinez: *I don't recall if the company submitted the company that was going to do the actual diving operations.*

Pete Pilkington: *Do you recall if you got a copy of a dive operating manual, as required by 46 CFR 197.420, 90 days before the diving operations proceeded?*

Lieutenant Commander Beistle: *Wait a minute. Hold on, Mr. Pilkington. Let's not bust through these. This is important. So let's try this a little bit slower. Okay. Would you ask that question again?*

Pete Pilkington: *Did you receive a copy of a diving operations manual from the diving contractor prior to 4 March 1996?*

Lieutenant Commander Beistle: *Wait a minute. Wait a minute. You've jumped—you've jumped ahead here. First you were asking whether they had received an application 90 days before, and now you're asking had they received a manual 90 days before.*

Pete Pilkington: *Correct.*

Lieutenant Commander Beistle: *Did he get a chance to answer the original question?*

Pete Pilkington: *I believe his answer was "I don't recall."*

Lieutenant Commander Beistle: *Okay.*

Pete Pilkington: *That's why I went to the next question.*

Lieutenant Commander Beistle: *Okay. Go ahead.*

Pete Pilkington: *So the next question was, did you receive a copy of the dive operations manual?*

Lieutenant Martinez: *I don't recall.*

Pete Pilkington: *Did you receive a letter from the vessel master or the chief engineer stating the general condition of the vessel?*

Lieutenant Martinez: *I don't remember.*

Pete Pilkington: *Did you receive an application for continued participation in the underwater survey program?*

Lieutenant Martinez: *One moment. Hold on for a second. Okay. Could you repeat that question again and refer to where that question—where you're directing that question from?*

Pete Pilkington: *I'm pulling this from paragraph 3 of NVIC 1-89.*

Lieutenant Martinez: *Okay.*

Pete Pilkington: *Paragraph 3 starts out with application for continued participation in the underwater survey program by vessels 15 years of age or older.*

Lieutenant Commander Beistle: *Does everybody have—have we made enough copies?*

Lieutenant Martinez: *Now, let me answer that, that that particular application pertains to vessels other than MODUs. It does not apply to MODUs.*

Pete Pilkington: *You said that does not—referring you back to Paragraph 2, Page 1. It specifically says, Structures of large mobile offshore drilling units. Those are MODUs, aren't they?*

MR. WILSON: *I'm sorry. Where?*

Pete Pilkington: *Go to Page 1, Paragraph 2, background.*

Lieutenant Martinez: *Oh, okay.*

Pete Pilkington: *Seven lines down and eight lines down: Acceptability of the structure, of large mobile offshore drilling units, MODUs, since 1969.*

Lieutenant Martinez: *Right.*

Pete Pilkington: *So this does apply to MODUs, does it not?*

Mr. Wilson: *Objection.*

Lieutenant Martinez: *A portion of it does. If you will read further, this NVIC was promulgated for the Military Sealift Command for repositioning their forces. And it also states that these regulations provide the option of alternating dry dock examination with underwater surveys to owners, operations of tank vessels, cargo and miscellaneous vessels, and oceanographic research vessels that are less than 15 years old.*

Pete Pilkington: *Can you tell us how old the Cliffs 12 was on 4 March 1996?*

Lieutenant Martinez: *I have no idea.*

Lieutenant Commander Beistle: *We can get that out of MSIS. Can you tell us what you think it is?*

Pete Pilkington: *It was built in 1980. It was 16 years old.*

Lieutenant Commander Beistle: *Lieutenant Martinez, can you elaborate? Can you tell me what your understanding of the application of NVIC 1-89 or how NVIC 1-89 is to be applied?*

Lieutenant Martinez: *Okay. NVIC 1-98—excuse me—1-89, it's really applying to tank vessels.*

Pete Pilkington: *Before I go on to the CFR, just a few things on your inspection on—or the inspection that you mentioned or that you went down a list earlier, which I believe was done on the fourth, where you referred to certain items that were not in need for some period of time. I believe you said thirty days?*

Lieutenant Martinez: *Depending on the requirement and conditions, we can grant up to 30 days for the requirements to be corrected.*

Pete Pilkington: *And on that list you included safety—I'm sorry—an operations manual?*

Lieutenant Martinez: *A Coast Guard approved manual.*

Pete Pilkington: *And a fire emergency plan?*

Lieutenant Martinez: *Yes.*

Pete Pilkington: *The eyewash cups?*

Lieutenant Martinez: *Yes.*

Pete Pilkington: *Just a question, what if there was a fire on board during that 30-day period of time?*

Lieutenant Martinez: *And your question is, sir?*

Pete Pilkington: *Wouldn't it be reasonable to have a plan?*

Lieutenant Martinez: *They may have had one, but it needed to be revised. In other words, the inspector saw certain additional items that needed to be added to the fire control plan. What those items are, I don't recall.*

Pete Pilkington: *What about the operations manual?*

Lieutenant Martinez: *They may have had one, but apparently it was, probably outdated and needed to be resubmitted with—in addition to maybe additional equipment or what have you. I don't remember the specifics for the requirement of the update.*

Pete Pilkington: *What about an emergency evacuation plan?*

Lieutenant Martinez: *Again, they probably had one, but it would have to be revised. The vessel was not operating for a long period of time.*

Pete Pilkington: *There were forty-six people on this vessel or forty-eight, depending on who's counting and at that time of the day, and at some part of the day there were four Coast Guard personnel on board as well. Wouldn't it be reasonable to expect there to be an emergency evacuation plan in place? Remember, we're twelve mi to sea.*

Lieutenant Martinez: *Yeah. And like I said, I don't recall exactly but I'm sure they had one, but it probably had to be revised.*

Pete Pilkington: *Earlier you stated they would have thirty days to produce a plan is that correct?*

Lieutenant Martinez: *Yes, sir.*

Pete Pilkington: *Earlier you mentioned that before the vessel could be towed, the navigation light had to have been repaired.*

Lieutenant Martinez: *Uh-huh.*

Pete Pilkington: *How did the vessel get twelve miles out?*

Lieutenant Martinez: *Could you be more specific with the question?*

Pete Pilkington: *Well, you indicated earlier that on March 3, 1996, the vessel was in Sabine Pass. On March 4, it's cited for not having a proper navigation light. Now, it's twelve miles from where it was the day before. How did it get there without a COI?*

Lieutenant Commander Beistle: *Well, it was towed there.*

Pete Pilkington: *It was towed there, but I'm just going back to the lieutenant who said that you can't tow it without the navigation light.*

Lieutenant Commander Beistle: *Right. I agree with you. I would just like to see some nexus between this and the casualty is all.*

Pete Pilkington: *Well, my direction on all of this is that the vessel was improperly inspected to begin with. It should not have been there.*

Lieutenant Commander Beistle: *Why not?*

Pete Pilkington: *It should not have been inspected. It was not entered into the underwater inspection program. I can now go through the same exercise in the CFR, if you would like. The CFR is record. The lieutenant doesn't indicate—or is indicating that he doesn't understand it applies. I believe it does.*

Lieutenant Commander Beistle: *Well, okay. And you're entitled to have a difference of opinion here, but let me ask—what I'm saying is, ask questions—because I'm interested in this too. Ask questions that get to—and let me just offer a suggestion. For example, how about asking-Lieutenant Martinez, the Cliffs 12—actually we did the—I actually asked one of my guys to do a plot on it and I think it was about 10.1 miles off the beach on the Louisiana side of the Sabine Pass channel.*

Lieutenant Martinez: *Uh-huh.*

Lieutenant Commander Beistle: *So if you will just take that as a given, obviously it had to be towed there, right?*

Lieutenant Martinez: *That's correct.*

Lieutenant Commander Beistle: *So let me just ask you a general question, which is that is there any problem, to your knowledge and in your experience at MSO Port Arthur, with the—well, let me step back and ask a preliminary question. Did they ask you whether they could—did Cliffs or anyone else ask you if they could tow it there?*

Lieutenant Martinez: *Normally the company does request permission. For this particular vessel, I don't recall. I don't remember if they asked. But normally we do get calls requesting to move the rig from their present location, in this case Sabine Pass, to offshore so they can commence other work on the vessel to get it ready.*

Lieutenant Commander Beistle: *Okay. And what's the purpose of that phone call, that request? In other words, why are they asking you for permission?*

Lieutenant Martinez: *Usually—sometimes they're not very familiar with the Coast Guard requirements. Also, they would like to take the rig to deeper water where the clarity is better so that they can conduct their underwater inspection.*

Lieutenant Commander Beistle: *Okay. And are they—to your knowledge, are they required to ask you for that permission?*

Lieutenant Martinez: *No.*

Lieutenant Commander Beistle: *So if they—if they moved it without calling you first, what would you think?*

Lieutenant Martinez: *What would I say, sir?*

Lieutenant Commander Beistle: *Yeah. What's your impression of that? Is that bad, good, or indifferent?*

Lieutenant Martinez: *To me, I would think that it's bad.*

Lieutenant Commander Beistle: *Why?*

Lieutenant Martinez: *Generally it would be just good general courtesy to let us know that they're conducting this so we're familiar with the location and where it's going, so we're not surprised.*

Pete Pilkington: *Are you aware if the Cliffs 12 was ever cited for failure to have a designated person in charge?*

Lieutenant Martinez: *No.*

Pete Pilkington: *Now, about how many MODU inspections have you done?*

Lieutenant Martinez: *Quite a few. I don't have the number figure.*

Pete Pilkington: *More than one-hundred?*

Lieutenant Martinez: *Again, I don't have the number figure, but it's quite a few.*

Pete Pilkington: *On any of these MODU inspections, have there been dive teams present?*

Lieutenant Martinez: *Not all of them, but at times, yes.*

Pete Pilkington: *Well, when you have been on an inspection and there has been a dive team present, have you inspected the dive station?*

Lieutenant Martinez: *Yes.*

Pete Pilkington: *What is it that you generally look for?*

Lieutenant Martinez: *General safety requirements; the diver supervisor, their certification; operations manual; location of their equipment, visually generally looking at the equipment to see if it appears to be in satisfactory condition; their records of maintenance repairs; their hoses, air hoses when they've been tested; their emergency procedures; the other divers' certifications; things of that nature.*

Pete Pilkington: *What kind of diver certifications would you look for?*

Lieutenant Martinez: *See if they're certified divers for that particular—for the type of diving operations.*

Pete Pilkington: *Certified by whom?*

Lieutenant Martinez: *Whoever certifies the divers. They have to go through a training course to be a certified diver.*

Pete Pilkington: *I guess that's a question that I would like to pursue. What sort of certification have you ever seen for a commercial diver, that they've brought out to you and visually shown you on a site?*

Lieutenant Martinez: *What I can recall is their documents and certificates.*

Pete Pilkington: *So they bring their diplomas from whatever school they graduated from?*

Lieutenant Martinez: *Yeah. Some of them—as a matter of fact, some of them have placed it in their—what could be considered an approval package beforehand, listing all the names, their copies of their certificates in these books. And some of them address how long they've been conducting these operations and what their qualifications are, if they can conduct nondestructive testing, what kind of nondestructive testing, underwater welding operations, things of that nature.*

Pete Pilkington: *You indicated earlier, in your last statement here, that you would look at the documentation that they supplied to you before the dive?*

Lieutenant Martinez: *Usually, yes.*

Pete Pilkington: *All right. Is that a requirement of the NVIC, that they submit that information to you prior to the dive, in fact prior to even going to the dive site?*

Lieutenant Martinez: *We try to do it prior to the dive so there will be no problems later on down the road if we happen to be on board and there are some difficulties with the diving operation.*

Pete Pilkington: *So do you verify that the divers that are on site the day of the dive are, in fact, the ones that the diving contractor said were, in fact, going to be used?*

Lieutenant Martinez: *Usually, yes.*

Pete Pilkington: *You indicated earlier, in your last statement here, that you would look at the documentation that they supplied to you before the dive?*

Lieutenant Martinez: *Usually, yes.*

Pete Pilkington: *So you do have some sort of a checklist?*

Lieutenant Martinez: *No checklist, just go by our references of forty-six and any other information we have.*

Pete Pilkington: *And do you check their prior experience or training?*

Lieutenant Martinez: *Yes.*

Pete Pilkington: *Would you evaluate the professional approach and the attitude evidenced by the organization of the dive plan?*

Lieutenant Martinez: *Yes.*

Pete Pilkington: *Would you expect to review a reference video with the dive team prior to putting them in the water, showing them the underwater conditions or showing the vessel?*

Lieutenant Martinez: *Showing the vessel's underwater conditions?*

Pete Pilkington: *NVIC requires that a reference video be taken and that a predive survey be viewed. Do you normally do that?*

Lieutenant Commander Beistle: *And let me say here. I don't mind you asking the question. That's fine. Let's recognize that there's a general disagreement here. And you're suggesting—and I'm certainly going to—I certainly understand what you're saying, but you're suggesting that NVIC 1-89 applies to this operation and Lieutenant Martinez in on the record as saying he believes that NVIC 1-89 does not apply. So there's kind of a disconnect here when you say the NVIC requires it. Do you demand it?*

And let me—if I could, just as a point of illustration—and I'm not—we're fine with time here. But as a way of illustrating this, I just want to make a point as to the difference here between what a NVIC says and how it's applied. I'll agree with you that NVIC 1-89 does, in fact, say—and I'm going—and we're going to introduce this for the record. We're going to introduce this at the end of this discussion.

But I'll agree with you that it does say, in pertinent part, in enclosure 1, section 2, alpha, it says, Applications for underwater surveys, as required by—and then it gives the string cite here—should be submitted at least ninety days before the requested survey, to the OCMI who will conduct the underwater survey.

But you will notice two things. It says, "should," and should is not the same as shall. In other words, it doesn't say that it's obligatory. And then let me also point out to you, I want to call your attention to 46 Code of Federal Regulations, Section 107.265(e). Now, I'm not—I'm sorry. I'm not trying to blindside you with this, but I want to point this out. This is the section that applies to U.S.—inspection of U.S. flag MODUs, and it says there only—and I'm going to quote this: 'The master person in charge, owner, or agent of a certificated unit must notify the appropriate officer in charge of inspection before the unit is dry-docked or specifically examined.'

And you'll notice the operative word there, the timing word just says "before." Now, I'm not quibbling about whether—I mean, I agree that NVIC is—you know, if we get notification ninety days ahead of time, that's better. That gives us a better chance to do things better. But what I'm saying is that legally, as I understand the mandate, it simply says—according to the Federal regulations there, it simply says that the application has to be made before—to the OCMI before the dry dock is done. It doesn't give a time requirement.

And my understanding is that the regulations are obligatory and mandatory, and NVIC is merely advisory. I just wanted to cover that. So that's not to say that guidance in NVICs aren't good, good guidance, but I'm not sure that they're obligatory or mandatory.

Pete Pilkington: *Well, can we refer to CFR 31.10, inspections, which requires, in part, that vessels undergo a dry docking every two and a half years?*

Lieutenant Commander Beistle: *Which one is that?*

Pete Pilkington: *This is 31.10, Inspections, 46 CFR, Shipping.*

Lieutenant Commander Beistle: *Yeah. But I think the more applicable regulation is 107.267. Yeah, 46 CFR 107.267. Special exam in lieu of dry-docking for self-elevating units is the section that specifically applies to MODUs.*

I think—I'm not sure Mr. Pilkington, but I think the section that you referred to has to do with tankers, deep draft tankers. Subchapter 1, 107, deals with MODUs.

Pete Pilkington: **So in other words, you are telling me that's NVIC 1-89 which specifically says large offshore drilling units, MODUs, does not apply to large offshore drilling units?**

Lieutenant Commander Beistle: *I'm not sure that that's what it says, sir.[7]*

Pete Pilkington: **What I'm saying is that NVIC, in detail, lays out a nice comprehensive safety program which, if followed, there wouldn't have been a fatality or a casualty on the Cliffs 12. Well, the problem with most of my questions, the remaining questions all have to do with what actually happened out there and the lieutenant apparently—am I correct in this, Lieutenant, you don't recall being out there on the fourth?**

---

[7]   In Jan 2000 the office of the Commandant would agree that NVIC 1-89 did apply.

Lieutenant Martinez: *That's correct. I don't recall being out there on the fourth.*

Pete Pilkington: *Then we reserve the right to ask the questions of the officer that was there. Can I just ask a few more questions?*

Lieutenant Commander Beistle: *Sure. Yes, sir.*

Pete Pilkington: *When you do an inspection, what sort of compressors and air supply tests are normally given to you on site, you know, at the dive station?*

Lieutenant Martinez: *We don't conduct any actual tests. I would look at their records and may request to see that the machinery—to start it, and sometimes the machinery is already running just so—the diver—excuse me—and the diving supervisor is already doing their pretest to make sure everything is functioning normally. So I would view that and see if there's any general hazards, safety guards, properly—in other words, they're not—the unit is a properly self-contained fueling system, not something that's been jerry-rigged, things of that nature.*

Pete Pilkington: *Would you normally look to see if, say, for instance, a compressor had been tested for air quality?*

Lieutenant Martinez: *No.*

Pete Pilkington: *Do you know how often a compressor needs to be tested for air quality?*

Lieutenant Martinez: *I don't recall, no.*

Pete Pilkington: *Would you normally inspect the compressor to see if it had proprietary air filters in it or proprietary filters of any kind?*

Lieutenant Martinez: *Proprietary air filters?*

Pete Pilkington: *Filters that are meant to be used by that particular manufactured unit. In other words, something that fits in it, the proper air filters for either the intake of the air or the outtake of the air in a diving compressor.*

Lieutenant Martinez: *There's no way for a marine inspector to know that.*

Pete Pilkington: Okay. *Would you normally require that the diving contractors display to you an operations manual?*

Lieutenant Martinez: *Yes.*

Pete Pilkington: *How many divers would you expect to find on a dive site?*

Lieutenant Martinez: *It depends on the diving operation and how long the diving operation is going to be, and that's all governed by the diver supervisor on site.*

Pete Pilkington: *Would you normally expect to see more than one source of breathing gas for a diving operation?*

Lieutenant Martinez: *Yes.*

Pete Pilkington: *Would you expect to see more than one umbilical?*

Lieutenant Martinez: *Yes.*

Pete Pilkington: *Would you expect to have a backup diver?*

Lieutenant Martinez: *Yes.*

Pete Pilkington: *Would you require any of those things?*

Lieutenant Martinez: *Yes.*

Pete Pilkington: *If you found that there was not a backup umbilical, would you cancel a dive?*

Lieutenant Martinez: *I'm sorry. Repeat that again. I couldn't hear you.*

Pete Pilkington: *If in your inspection on a dive operation, if you found that they did not have either the backup air supply or a backup umbilical or a backup diver would you—would you cancel the dive? Would you stop the dive operation?*

Lieutenant Martinez: *Yes, sir, I would.*

Pete Pilkington: *You would cancel the operation even though none of those items are required by regulation, interesting.*

Would you have reason to check the air in the high-pressure systems; in other words, in the high-pressure air bottles?

Lieutenant Martinez: *I would verify with the diving supervisor, I would question him and request that he show it to me.*

Pete Pilkington: *Would it be normal to see some sort of a tag-out system on the bottles; in other words, an indication that the bottle is empty or full?*

Lieutenant Martinez: *He should have some kind of tag-out system, yeah. I would expect that.*

Pete Pilkington: *One more question here: Would it have been reasonable for Lieutenant J. G. Thomson to have gone out on the first day of the inspection offshore on a MODU? I thought he was in training?*

Lieutenant Martinez: *Again, I don't know what his training status was at that time.*

Pete Pilkington: *Interesting I believe Lieutenant Commander Beistle indicted that the USCG records should that Lt. J. G. Thompson was still in training. Thank you. I have no other questions at this time.*

Lieutenant Commander Beistle: *Lieutenant Martinez, Are you familiar with a small red book? It's an 840 book, typically referred to as an 840. And this one happens to be titled: MODU Dry Dock Inspection or Special Examination in Lieu of Dry Dock Inspection.*

Lieutenant Martinez: *Yes, sir.*

Lieutenant Commander Beistle: *Do you carry those with you when you go off on—do you carry those with you when you go off and do an inspection?*

Lieutenant Martinez: *Yes, sir.*

Lieutenant Commander Beistle: *Do you carry them with you routinely?*

Lieutenant Martinez: *Usually.*

Lieutenant Commander Beistle: *And what do you use this book for?*

Lieutenant Martinez: *It's a little bit of a checklist and it lists any items that we may have found deficient or a certain uniqueness or that we might have—something different or that might be a little strange to us, we would annotate that.*

Lieutenant Commander Beistle: So *essentially it's a job aid and a memory jogger, is that right?*

Lieutenant Martinez: *Exactly.*

Lieutenant Commander Beistle: *Do you typically follow that checklist?*

Lieutenant Martinez: *Usually, yes.*

Lieutenant Commander Beistle: *Okay. Any reason—do you have any recollection, did you use one of those 840 books on the Cliffs 12?*

Lieutenant Martinez: *I don't recall using it for the Cliffs 12.*

Lieutenant Commander Beistle: *Just for the record, I've searched the file and we don't have one in the record. Do you typically include those in the record?*

Lieutenant Martinez: *Yes.*

Pete Pilkington: *Just a couple of quick follow-up questions.*

Lieutenant Martinez: *Yes, sir.*

Pete Pilkington: *Do you know if the Cliffs 12 was ever inspected underwater before March 4, 1996?*

Lieutenant Martinez: *No. I don't know if she was inspected before.*

Pete Pilkington: *On any other inspection where you were there, present, or where you would be present for an underwater inspection, would you normally expect that the inspection would be videoed?*

Lieutenant Martinez: *For the underwater exam, yes.*

Pete Pilkington: *The underwater portion. What portion of the inspection should be videoed?*

Lieutenant Martinez: *Depending on the style of the mobile offshore drilling unit, all the critical connections, in the essence of a mat support unit, as this one is, a video of the—and a swim-by of the diver of the top, sides, and bottom of the mat once it's been elevated.*

Pete Pilkington: *So in other words, as far as the underwater portion is concerned, you would expect to see a video of them conducting the inspection or just a swim-by after they had completed the inspection?*

Lieutenant Martinez: *The inspection is done in concurrence. It's an ongoing process that while they're examining the critical connections, conducting the nondestructive testing, and then they do the swim-bys monitoring the different structures of the hull. It's all done during that phase.*

Pete Pilkington: *So am I correct, then, in assuming that during the entire inspection process, there's a video being taken?*

Lieutenant Martinez: *Yes.*

Pete Pilkington: *Whether it be mag particle testing, would that be videoed?*

Lieutenant Martinez: *Yes.*

Pete Pilkington: *If it is thickness testing, would that be videoed?*

Lieutenant Martinez: *I'm sorry. Could you repeat the last again?*

Pete Pilkington: *Thickness testing, when the thickness testing is done.*

Lieutenant Martinez: *Oh, you mean the gauging?*

Pete Pilkington: *The gauging.*

Lieutenant Martinez: *Only if it's required.*

Pete Pilkington: *Well, the CFR requires that you know—and I hesitate to quote it because I don't have it right in front of me, but I believe it states that you're supposed to know the position of the diver. How would you know where he was if you weren't videotaping him?*

Lieutenant Martinez: *Well, the diver is videotaping what he is doing. There is audio communication to the topside. That's also tied into the video. He's giving his location and position, where he's at. If he finds something, he annotates it verbally and possibly marking it, what it is, how big it is, and location.*

Pete Pilkington: *And when he does this, you can see it on the monitor topside, is that correct?*

Lieutenant Martinez: *Yes.*

Pete Pilkington: *So that the diver in some fashion has to have a video camera or somebody else has to be down there videoing what he's doing, is that correct?*

Lieutenant Martinez: *Correct. Usually the diver has a helmet-mounted video cam.*

Pete Pilkington: *Would you permit a vessel that was undergoing an underwater inspection in lieu of dry-docking, to be commenced without the diver having a video record of what he was doing?*

Lieutenant Martinez: *You're asking would I allow it?*

Pete Pilkington: *Yeah. Would you allow it? Would you permit it to continue if the divers show up and they don't have a video camera? Would you let the inspection continue?*

Lieutenant Martinez: *I could not accept the results of that diving operation.*

Pete Pilkington: *So in other words, it would be good exercise, then, but you wouldn't accept it?*

Lieutenant Martinez: *No. We want a video of the operation and then to that, a written report.*

Pete Pilkington: *So the written report—*

Lieutenant Martinez: *A visual documentation with audio and a written documentation.*

Pete Pilkington: *And anything less than that would not be acceptable?*

Lieutenant Martinez: *I would not accept it.*

This is Lieutenant Commander Beistle again. I need to interject. I need you to be clear on that, Lieutenant.

Lieutenant Martinez: *Yes, sir.*

Lieutenant Commander Beistle: *When you say you would not accept it, what is "it"? What do you mean by "it"? You would not accept what?*

341

Lieutenant Martinez: *If the divers were to go down below and conduct their inspection without a video and audio attached to it, I have no way of knowing what they are actually doing.*

Lieutenant Commander Beistle: *So what you're saying is that if they were to go down without a video, then you would not accept—if they didn't—if they didn't produce a video, you would not accept the results of the exam, is that right?*

Lieutenant Martinez: *That is correct.*

Pete Pilkington: *Lieutenant Martinez, normally who would witness the videos besides the dive contractor?*

Lieutenant Martinez: *Coast Guard, if they're present, or the Class Society surveyor.*

Pete Pilkington: *Okay. So you would expect to be someone from the Class Society or from the Coast Guard present during the videoing?*

Lieutenant Martinez: *It depends on the circumstances. Sometimes either party is available, and sometimes none of the parties are available.*

Pete Pilkington: *Well, let's specifically refer back to the Cliffs 12. And I understand you don't remember if you were there or not for the underwater portion. Would you have—had you gone out there, would you have expected to see a color video monitor when you showed up?*

Lieutenant Martinez: *Yes.*

Pete Pilkington *Now, who would you have expected to be watching that video monitor, someone from the Class Society or someone from the Coast Guard?*

Lieutenant Martinez: *Well, first off, the diving supervisor would be there monitoring the operations through the monitor and communications. And the Class Society is—well, again, depending on the circumstances, they're there when they can. These surveys could be done for either class requirement or Coast Guard or both, or for the company if the company has a—a known problem or they need to monitor something or something has just occurred to the vessel. They can contract the divers to go ahead and go below and examine the structure of the MODU.*

Pete Pilkington: *Let me be more specific.*

Lieutenant Martinez: *Okay.*

Pete Pilkington: *In a special exam in lieu of dry docking, who would be witnessing the video?*

Lieutenant Martinez: *Coast Guard, usually.*

Pete Pilkington: *Who is ultimately responsible for an inspection of an offshore vessel?*

Lieutenant Martinez: *Inspection of the vessel itself is the Coast Guard.*

Pete Pilkington: *I'm going to refer back to your letter of February 26, 1996, and I realize this is going to be difficult, but I believe it was supplied to you.*

Lieutenant Commander Beistle: *I think he has a copy. Lieutenant, do you have a copy of that?*

Lieutenant Martinez: *I'm searching for it now. Okay. Is it the—*

Pete Pilkington: *It's dated 16 February 1996. It's attention to Buddy Horton, Cliffs Drilling Company. Would you have expected, based on that letter, that there would be a dive video taken and that dive video would have included all of the underwater inspection done, as a requirement in that letter?*

Lieutenant Martinez: *Yes. Sir that's what I would have required.*

Pete Pilkington: *Thank you. I have no more questions. Tom, I have no need to call Lieutenant J. G. Thomson.*

Lieutenant Commander Beistle: *Mr. Austin?*

Mr. Austin: *I have no questions.*

Mr. Wilson: *I have no questions.*

Lieutenant Commander Beistle: *Folks I have no more questions for Lieutenant Martinez and I don't have any expectations of needing to call him back.*

Lieutenant Martinez you are released from this hearing, thank you for your help.

Kirk Austin as a party in interest was in the room as was Ron Townsend. Captain Fels was in Miami but available by phone, Lieutenant J. G. Tuan Thompson was available if needed and Mr. Everett was in the holding area outside the court room.

Lieutenant Commander Beistle: *My expectation would be to go back to our list, I think Mr. Townsend and Mr. Austin are next up in the batting order. For now let's skip over Captain Fels unless someone has an objection. Mr. Austin do you have a preference? Are you ready to go?*

With that Kirk Austin slowly made his way from the safety of his seat behind the table provided him as a party in interest and claimed the witness stand to the right of Lieutenant Commander Beistle and was sworn in by the court reporter.

Lieutenant Commander Beistle began the questioning by confirming that Austin was a party in interest, that he understood his rights, that he had been present during all the previously provided testimony. Then questions regarding his qualifications, previous work experience, his ownership in the now-defunct Texas NDE. Then The lieutenant commander continued with. *So Mr. Austin what did you do to get yourself qualified by whatever standards? I mean, what did you feel you needed to do in order to be qualified to go do the diving portion of that?*

Kirk Austin: *After I made the first dive, I would—it was down in Brownsville with American Oilfield Divers. After I did that—I had no training at all. I just took some instruction and got in the water. It was ten feet or so, and I figured if I had any problems, I could stand up just about and be out.*

And after that I went and I took a SCUBA class. I thought that would be a starting point. It seems to me like the regulators on the dive hat work the same and the depth that we were thinking about trying to work in were going to be very shallow. So I did that, and then after that, it was just on the job training.

Lieutenant Commander Beistle: *Where did you take the SCUBA class?*

Kirk Austin: *At the YMCA in Houston.*

Lieutenant Commander Beistle: *How much—what are the—was it typical recreational SCUBA training?*

Kirk Austin: *Yes.*

Lieutenant Commander Beistle: *You took the SCUBA class at the Y in the early nineties. And then between when you took that and when you went out on March 4 of 1996, you had done five or six different dives?*

Kirk Austin: *Right.*

Lieutenant Commander Beistle: *No more than that?*

Kirk Austin: *No more than that.*

Lieutenant Commander Beistle: *Ever had any formalized commercial dive training?*

Kirk Austin: *No.*

Lieutenant Commander Beistle: *Ever had any training on how to be a dive tender?*

Kirk Austin: *No.*

Lieutenant Commander Beistle: *Ever had any training on how to be a dive supervisor?*

Kirk Austin: *No.*

Lieutenant Commander Beistle: *Ever been told—ever been trained on what the responsibilities of a dive supervisor are?*

Kirk Austin: *No.*

Lieutenant Commander Beistle: *Do you think you can tell me now what the responsibilities of a dive supervisor are?*

Kirk Austin: *I can tell you some things, but I could not—*

Lieutenant Commander Beistle: *If you told me, what would you be basing that information on?*

Kirk Austin *Well, I've watched a number of dives throughout my career, and I've also learned a lot over the last four years.*

Lieutenant Commander Beistle: *Sure. I can imagine. Okay. Can you tell me what your expectations are or what your understanding of the responsibilities of a dive supervisor are?*

Kirk Austin: *The dive supervisor is in control of the diving portion of the job. He designates the order that people dive. He monitors the amount of time that they're in the water. He monitors the depth that they're working at so—to determine the time he's in there. And he oversees the dive operations. He looks after keeping his people safe and keeping the job moving.*

Lieutenant Commander Beistle: *Were you familiar with the term dive supervisor?*

Kirk Austin: *Dive supervisor. Dan was the senior man. So I would—I guess I worked on the assumption that he would handle those duties.*

Lieutenant Commander Beistle: *You heard his testimony up here. He was operating on the assumption, he says, that you were the dive supervisor. Is that a surprise to you?*

Tom Mosele: *Actually I think Mr. Pilkington wants to do this questioning.*

Mr. Hope: *You guys are going to have to talk up.*

Pete Pilkington: **I'll do my best.**

Let's just go over a few things which I think we've already covered and I'm going to bounce around a little bit because so many of these questions have already been asked, but can you tell me, in your experience, what you consider to be a qualified commercial diver?

Kirk Austin: *In my experience, the qualified commercial divers I've seen are divers that are capable of making a dive and completing their tasks and returning to the surface.*

Pete Pilkington: *Do you know of any test of skill or ability that is required under Coast Guard regulations?*

Kirk Austin: *I'm not aware of any.*

Pete Pilkington: *Do you know of any required training under Coast Guard regulations?*

Kirk Austin: *I'm not aware of any.*

Pete Pilkington: *How about any under OSHA regulations?*

Kirk Austin: *I'm not aware.*

Pete Pilkington: *Any—no level of skill, ability, or knowledge?*

Kirk Austin: *Not that I'm aware of.*

Pete Pilkington: *To be a qualified diving supervisor, are you aware of any test of competency?*

Kirk Austin: *No.*

Pete Pilkington: *Any level of skill?*

Kirk Austin: *No.*

Pete Pilkington: *Any level of ability or knowledge?*

Kirk Austin: *No.*

Pete Pilkington: *Would—could you be qualified as a commercial diving supervisor?*

Kirk Austin: *I don't know if I could or not.*

Pete Pilkington: *But you did, on March 4, 1996, consider yourself to be a commercial diver?*

Kirk Austin: *I considered myself to be an NDE technician that had to dive to get the job done.*

Pete Pilkington: *Well, let me just ask you a question. If you were down in twenty-eight feet of water, could you have held your breath and returned to the surface?*

Kirk Austin: *I believe I could have.*

Pete Pilkington: *Would that have done any damage to you if you had done that?*

Kirk Austin: *I don't think it would have.*

Pete Pilkington: *So in your opinion, there is nothing in the United States Coast Guard regulations that would have prevented you from being a commercial diver on the fourth of March 1996?*

Kirk Austin: *Not that I'm aware of.*

Pete Pilkington: *Could you have passed the dive physical?*

Kirk Austin: *I don't know.*

Pete Pilkington: *Do you know if a dive physical is required—*

Kirk Austin: *I don't know.*

Pete Pilkington: *Under the current regulations?*

Kirk Austin: *I don't know.*

Pete Pilkington: *On March 4, 1996, did you hold a predive conference on board the Cliffs 12?*

Kirk Austin: *I spoke with ABS and the other—the divers that were out there, to get things lined out, what the jobs—what job we were going to do. If that constitutes a conference, yes.*

Pete Pilkington: *Did you review a video record of the vessel?*

Kirk Austin: *No.*

Pete Pilkington: *Did you review plans of the vessel?*

Kirk Austin: *We reviewed some plans, yes.*

Pete Pilkington: *Did you supply, prior to the dive, a dive operations manual to the Coast Guard?*

Kirk Austin: *No.*

Pete Pilkington: *To ABS?*

Kirk Austin: *No.*

Pete Pilkington: *Did you provide a list of divers to the Coast Guard?*

Kirk Austin: *No.*

Pete Pilkington: *Did you provide a list of divers to ABS?*

Kirk Austin: *No.*

Pete Pilkington: *Did you provide a list of equipment to ABS?*

Kirk Austin: *No.*

Pete Pilkington: *Did you require—did you supply a list of equipment to the United States Coast Guard that you were planning to use on the dive for that day?*

Kirk Austin: *No.*

Pete Pilkington: *You indicated earlier that Brian was calling for assistance at the—just prior to you going into the water.*

Kirk Austin: *I never heard Brian on the radio. Everything was relayed to me through Dan.*

Pete Pilkington: *That's what I'm trying to confirm. So at no time did you ever hear any of the conversations between Brian and the person on the communication system?*

Kirk Austin: *No.*

Pete Pilkington: *So you were not on the communication systems at the time?*

Kirk Austin: *No.*

Pete Pilkington: *How were you directing the diver doing the thickness testing?*

Kirk Austin: *I was looking at the scope and I would turn over and talk to Dan on what I needed and then I would turn back and watch to see the—you know, I was expecting the signal to change and then I would watch for that signal change.*

Pete Pilkington: *Was there anybody witnessing this exam?*

Kirk Austin: *There could have been some folks standing around on the deck. ABS could have wandered by at that time. I'm uncertain.*

Pete Pilkington: *It's not required, then, that ABS be there to witness an exam, an underwater exam, to the best of your knowledge?*

Kirk Austin: *I don't know what the requirements are.*

Lieutenant Commander Beistle: *Well, in your past experience, has ABS—*

Kirk Austin: *ABS comes by and checks, and you shown them what—what you've done so far, the thickness—if we're doing gauges, the thickness measurements that we've obtained in these locations, and, you know, they look at that and see if they're reasonable looking and go on.*

Lieutenant Commander Beistle: *So they don't make a practice of standing next to your shoulder and watching you as you make notations?*

Kirk Austin: *No. They might stand there for a few minutes and they go and do something else.*

Lieutenant Commander Beistle: *Sorry. Go ahead.*

Pete Pilkington: *I'm going to jump around here a little bit. But the first time you went into the water on this recovery attempt, how deep did you go?*

Kirk Austin: *I don't know. It wasn't far. I ran out of air hose and got pulled back out.*

Pete Pilkington: *You said you had a half-inch suit on?*

Kirk Austin: *Yeah.*

Pete Pilkington: *And you were able to get yourself under the water with a half-inch suit?*

Kirk Austin: *Not very well, no.*

Pete Pilkington: *How far would you say, an inch, two inches, five inches?*

Kirk Austin: *About two or three hand pulls and that was it. I mean, I don't know how far I traveled.*

Pete Pilkington: *Let me get this straight. You had a half-inch wet suit on. Were you much thinner then than you are now?*

Kirk Austin: *No. I was just as fat then as I am now.*

Pete Pilkington: *And you were able to get under the water with a half-inch wet suit on?*

Kirk Austin: *I got into the water. I don't know how far I got.*

Pete Pilkington: *Did you get your head under the water?*

Kirk Austin: *I believe I did, yes.*

Pete Pilkington: *When you came back up, how much weight did they put on you to get you down?*

Kirk Austin: *I don't know what the amount was. There's a—they brought a bunch of large shackles and put them on me.*

Pete Pilkington: *Ten pounds?*

Kirk Austin: *I don't know.*

Pete Pilkington: *Well, would it be more or less than ten pounds?*

Kirk Austin: *I can't even—I don't know the weight of one of the shackles. I had a weight belt on, we added some shackles to it, and we went and tried again.*

Pete Pilkington: *Do you have any idea how much weight it would take to get a man of your size, with a half-inch wet suit, down twenty-eight feet?*

Kirk Austin: *No, I don't. It would take a lot because it was a struggle.*

Pete Pilkington: *Had you worn that wet suit before?*

Kirk Austin: *No. The first time.*

Pete Pilkington: *Whose wet suit was it?*

Kirk Austin: *It was Texas NDE's wet suit.*

Pete Pilkington: *So Texas NDE has another employee the same shape and build and so forth as you?*

Kirk Austin: *Very close, yes.*

Pete Pilkington: *I see. Was it Mark Wright's wet suit?*

Kirk Austin: *It was Texas NDE's wet suit. Mark wore it before, though, yes.*

Pete Pilkington: *Was it Mark Wright's helmet?*

Kirk Austin: *It was Texas NDE's helmet.*

Pete Pilkington: *How many helmets does Texas NDE own?*

Kirk Austin: *At that time they owned one.*

Pete Pilkington: *How many wet suits did they own at the time?*

Kirk Austin: *One.*

Pete Pilkington: *Where was Mark Wright?*

Kirk Austin: *He was on another inspection job.*

Pete Pilkington: *Was it an underwater job?*

Kirk Austin: *No.*

Pete Pilkington: *So you're telling us that you went to the underwater job and you sent the diver to the above-water job, is that correct?*

Kirk Austin: *Well, at that time the customer called for Mark and I was the next one available.*

Pete Pilkington: *How many jobs have you done in Venezuela?*

Kirk Austin: *Two for Cliffs.*

Pete Pilkington: *Have you ever seen diving operations take place anywhere where oxygen and acetylene torch hoses were used for breathing gas, besides the day of March 4, 1996?*

Kirk Austin: *Yes.*

Pete Pilkington: *Where?*

Kirk Austin: *In Venezuela.*

Pete Pilkington: *And who would the contractor have been on that job?*

Kirk Austin: *A Venezuelan diving company. I don't know the name of them.*

Pete Pilkington: *And on what vessel would you have been diving?*

Kirk Austin: *I don't remember the vessel. We did two jobs, and I don't remember the name of them.*

Pete Pilkington: *Who would have owned the vessel?*

Kirk Austin: *I don't know who the owner was. We were working for Cliffs.*

Pete Pilkington: *You were working for Cliffs. Who was the safety manager on that job?*

Kirk Austin: *I don't know who the safety manager was.*

Pete Pilkington: *Does Cliffs have more than one safety manager?*

Kirk Austin: *I don't know.*

Pete Pilkington: *So your testimony, then, is that you dove in Venezuela where they were using oxygen and acetylene cutting-torch hoses for breathing gas?*

Kirk Austin: *They were using the hoses attached to a compressor.*

Pete Pilkington: *Well, that brings up an interesting question. If down in Venezuela you were using oxygen and acetylene cutting-torch hoses to supply air to divers, why is it that on March 4 you elected to take oxygen and acetylene cutting-torch hoses and hook them to the oxygen bottle rather than the high-pressure bottles or the—or the gas rack?*

Kirk Austin: *I didn't make that election. It was the—it was just handed to me. I didn't know where that air was coming from until afterwards.*

Pete Pilkington: *So you had nothing to do with splicing these hoses together?*

Kirk Austin: *No.*

Pete Pilkington: *Had nothing to do with—are you aware of the toxic effects of oxygen, breathing under pressure?*

Kirk Austin: *After the fact, yes.*

Pete Pilkington: *On March 4, 1996, while you were diving on the Cliffs 12—or while you were supervising the diving on the Cliffs 12, was there another boat in the water during the diving operations?*

Kirk Austin: *I don't recall one.*

Pete Pilkington: *So you don't recall if there was a boat either in or around or near the vessel, or was there a boat available on the deck?*

Kirk Austin: *I don't recall.*

Pete Pilkington: *What would you have done if you had to retrieve a diver from the water?*

Kirk Austin: *Repeat that, please.*

Pete Pilkington: *What would you have done if you would have had to retrieve a diver from the water?*

Kirk Austin: *What would I have done if I had to—*

Pete Pilkington: *Retrieve a diver who, for whatever reason, you had to get out of the water? Your only access was via the crane basket, correct?*

Kirk Austin: *That's correct.*

Pete Pilkington: *What if the diver had gotten caught in the current and floated away, did you have a contingency plan for that?*

Kirk Austin: *Didn't even think of that.*

Pete Pilkington: *Were you an ABS certified—or at that time were you an ABS certified vendor?*

Kirk Austin: *We were on ABS list of approved external specialists.*

Pete Pilkington: *How did you get on that list?*

Kirk Austin: *We submitted our certifications for the personnel of our company, our quality manual to them. They reviewed that paperwork and then they came out and audited our shop.*

Pete Pilkington: *Did they come out just the one time, or were there subsequent visits?*

Kirk Austin: *One visit.*

Pete Pilkington: *How long were you in their inspection program?*

Kirk Austin: *Probably between three and five years. I'm not certain exactly when we entered.*

Pete Pilkington: *So during three and five years, your employee lists remained the same?*

Kirk Austin: *No. When employees changed, you had to send the certifications in, send them a letter, who to take off and who to add to the list.*

Pete Pilkington: *How about equipment, did they certify you—what equipment you were using?*

Kirk Austin: *They didn't—they didn't certify equipment. Initially we gave them our equipment list and they came out and looked at that, but I don't remember ever sending them any updates on equipment.*

Pete Pilkington: *So how would they know, based on what you could supply them, that your—say, for instance, your thickness testing equipment was properly gauged and calibrated and was in working order?*

Kirk Austin: *When we were on the site, our equipment had to be calibrated, had to have stickers on it and—that we could show to whoever the surveyor was on site.*

Pete Pilkington: *So there are stickers that are available to show the quality of the testing equipment that you used?*

Kirk Austin: *Yes, sir.*

Pete Pilkington: *There are stickers that show that the electronics in the equipment are calibrated on an annual basis.*

Pete Pilkington: *Do you know if there are stickers that are available that you can put on a compressor to show that the compressor is in certification?*

Kirk Austin: *I don't know.*

Pete Pilkington: *How about a gauge or an air hose that would be used for life-support?*

Kirk Austin: *I don't know.*

Pete Pilkington: *Have you ever seen a—say, for instance, a tag like that (indicating) on an air hose that would indicate that it was certified?*

Kirk Austin: *From this distance?*

Lieutenant Commander Beistle: *For the record, I'm going to retrieve this orange tag and hand it to Mr. Austin (tendering).*

Pete Pilkington: *No. I do not recall ever seeing any of these on an air hose.*

MR. WILSON: Let me see that.

Pete Pilkington: *For the record, you probably never have seen that on a commercial diving operation.*

MR. WILSON: Is there a representation as to what this is?

Pete Pilkington: *What that is, is that's a recreational sticker that goes on a recreational hose to prove that it's in certification. Why isn't there something in the commercial industry? Recreational divers do it.*

Pete Pilkington: *Does ABS ever come in and inspect your records during a five-year period of time?*

Kirk Austin: *The only time was that initial audit.*

Pete Pilkington: *So basically you get certified by ABS and just go on forever and ever and ever?*

Kirk Austin: *I don't know about forever and ever. While we were in it, it was that one audit.*

Pete Pilkington: *What did ABS certify you to do on their list, on their vendor list?*

Kirk Austin: *Our letter said we were external specialists for nondestructive testing and diving.*

Pete Pilkington: *And for diving?*

Kirk Austin: *Yes.*

Pete Pilkington: *Were they aware of the extent of your diving arsenal?*

Kirk Austin: *From the paperwork we gave them, that's where they issued the letter from. So I guess that they must have been aware somewhat.*

Pete Pilkington: *And what information did you supply to them as far as the amount of diving equipment that you had?*

Kirk Austin: *No diving equipment.*

Pete Pilkington: *So they approved you as a diving contractor based on what?*

Kirk Austin: *I don't know.*

Pete Pilkington: *Or I shouldn't say diving contractor. As a supplier of diving services?*

Kirk Austin: *I don't know what their criteria was.*

Pete Pilkington: *How many pages was this form that you filled out to get on their certified list?*

Kirk Austin: *It seems like they sent a letter that asked us to supply a number of documents. I don't know that there was a—a form that we filled out.*

Pete Pilkington: *On March 4, 1996, I believe earlier you indicated you didn't have a dive manual?*

Kirk Austin: *Yes, sir.*
That's correct.

Pete Pilkington: *Do you have any feeling as to what dive manual you would be subjected to if you didn't have a dive manual?*

Kirk Austin: *No.*

Pete Pilkington: *Earlier you indicated that you didn't review any videos before you went into the water or before you commenced diving operations on 4 March 1996. Do you normally video all your mag particle testing?*

Kirk Austin: *Not all of it. There's sometimes that it's been—the video on it's been waived.*

Pete Pilkington: *On what kind of an inspection?*

Kirk Austin: *I don't recall if it was just for the customer or if it was for a classification society.*

Pete Pilkington: *If you were doing an inspection for ABS, would you videotape the inspection?*

Kirk Austin: *Yes.*

Pete Pilkington: *On all of them?*

Kirk Austin: *I'm not sure if we did it on all of them or not, no.*

Pete Pilkington: *So your testimony here is that you might not have done a video on all mag particle testing—*

Kirk Austin: *That's correct.*

Pete Pilkington: *For ABS?*

Kirk Austin: *That's correct.*

Pete Pilkington: *How would the ABS surveyor know that you had done the examination?*

Kirk Austin: *I don't know.*

Pete Pilkington: *Would you normally videotape the thickness testing?*

Kirk Austin: *No.*

Pete Pilkington: *Did you ever videotape the thickness testing?*

Kirk Austin: *There might have been times that the diver had the video in his hat and it was taped.*

Pete Pilkington: *Did ABS ever certify—or ever require that you do the videotaping of thickness testing?*

Kirk Austin: *They might have.*

Pete Pilkington: *Might have?*

Kirk Austin: *Yes.*

Pete Pilkington: *You don't know if they if they ever did?*

Kirk Austin: *Well, I've taken a lot of gauges over my career and I cannot define a specific time where I remember them saying, "Yes, videotape this" or "No, don't videotape that."*

Pete Pilkington: *Well, I guess I'm just curious. How does the surveyor know that the diver hasn't just gone down and sat on the bottom in one spot, cleaned a little spot and just sat there all day taking readings? You can't see his air hose from the surface, can you?*

Kirk Austin: *Well, in most cases you can't see the diver from . . .*

Pete Pilkington: *Preceding the dive on March 4, 1996, who determined how many divers would be required?*

Kirk Austin: *You know I don't remember, probably Texas TDE.*

Pete Pilkington: *Do you remember back on—I know I'm asking you to go back a longtime, but on November 5, 1996 you were asked in a deposition: Who determined how many people were supposed to be at the Cliffs 12 to do the diving services? Do you remember that deposition?*

Kirk Austin: *I remember giving a deposition, yes.*

Pete Pilkington: *And may I refresh your memory with your answers on that date?*

Kirk Austin: *Sure.*

Lieutenant Commander Beistle: *Let me just jump in here. That's fine, but if we're going to quote from it, will you make me a copy real quick afterwards so I can get it in the record?*

Pete Pilkington: *Yes, sir, not a problem, we have multiple copies available.*

Lieutenant Commander Beistle: *Thanks. Go ahead.*

Pete Pilkington: *I'm reading from page 25, Kirk Austin deposition done on November 5, 1996*

"Who at Cliffs told you that you were limited to three people?"
ANSWER: "Buddy Horton." QUESTION: "He didn't explain why. ANSWER; He alluded he was trying to hold the cost down."

Pete Pilkington: *Mr. Austin do you remember that testimony?*

Kirk Austin: *I have a vague remembrance of it, yes.*

Pete Pilkington: *Can you expound on that at all?*

Kirk Austin: *Today—today I can't. That's a longtime ago and I don't remember that conversation very clearly.*

Pete Pilkington: *You mentioned earlier that there was a market niche that you were trying to fill.*

Kirk Austin: *Uh-huh.*

Pete Pilkington: *By doing shallow water underwater nondestructive testing, right?*

Kirk Austin: *Right.*

Pete Pilkington: *Is this how you filled that market niche?*

Kirk Austin: *We considered that, yeah. There was a lot of work that was, you know, in very shallow water. We never were successful in capturing that.*

Pete Pilkington: *So you were able to capture it—let me lead you a little bit. You were able to capture that by cutting corners in the numbers of people that you would utilize, is that correct?*

No response.

Pete Pilkington: *But that's what you were doing, is you were supplying fewer divers?*

Kirk Austin: *For the area that we needed to work, we were supplying an adequate number of people.*

Pete Pilkington: *By whose standards were you supplying an adequate number of people?*

Kirk Austin: *I guess by our standards, by Texas NDE's.*

Pete Pilkington: *Did Texas NDE have a dive safety manual?*

Kirk Austin: *No, they did not.*

Pete Pilkington: *If they didn't have a dive safety manual, what were they operating under? You didn't have your own operations manual. I don't believe that that would be correct.*

Pete Pilkington: *When Dan Wiitala went in the water, did he put on a half-inch wet suit?*

Kirk Austin: *No.*

Pete Pilkington: *Would it be reasonable to believe that had Dan Wiitala put your hat on and jumped in the water the first time that we wouldn't be here today?*

Kirk Austin: *Probably reasonable, yeah.*

Pete Pilkington: *This half-inch wet suit you had to put on before you jumped in the water—*

Lieutenant Commander Beistle: *Can I follow up? I just want to get something on the record. And I know this is pure speculation, but I just want to get it on the record.*

Is it fair to say that if the dive team had had another member and had had a standby diver who was rigged up and ready to go or able to get a suit on and—or get his helmet on in short order, that there's a good likelihood that Brian would be alive today?

Kirk Austin: *Yeah, there probably is.*

Lieutenant Commander Beistle: *I just wanted to get that in somewhere. Thank you.*

Pete Pilkington: *Thanks, Tom. that would have been difficult for me to ask.*

Pete Pilkington: *Had you ever had this half-inch wet suit on before?*

Kirk Austin: *I had put it on and got in my swimming pool with it.*

Pete Pilkington: *You had never worn it in salt water. So you had never done a buoyancy test. You had no idea how much weight you were going to need?*

Kirk Austin: *No.*

Pete Pilkington: *You were the standby diver?*

Kirk Austin: *I was the NDE guy out. There was no designation that I—that we had here: You're the diver. You're the standby diver. I'm running the rack. There was none of that designation made.*

Pete Pilkington: *Mr. Austin, based on your ABS certification, would any vessel owner reasonably expect that you were a diving contractor?*

Kirk Austin: *I don't know about a vessel owner.*

Pete Pilkington: *Your ABS certification was that you were a diving contractor, wasn't it?*

Kirk Austin: *We're an external specialist that could do NDE gauging and diving.*

Pete Pilkington: *What does ABS stand for?*

Kirk Austin: *American Bureau of Shipping.*

Pete Pilkington: *So the American Bureau of Shipping certified you as a diving contractor with one diving hat, one half-inch wet suit, and a weight belt?*

Kirk Austin: *Yes.*

Pete Pilkington: *You mentioned earlier that you were certified to dive at the YMCA?*

Kirk Austin: *Yes.*

Pete Pilkington: *Do you have a card that indicates that?*

Kirk Austin: *Yes.*

Pete Pilkington: *Can you show it to me?*

Kirk Austin: *Maybe.*

Mr. Wilson: *Can I ask the relevance? Are we bringing the YMCA in here too?*

Pete Pilkington: ***No, we're not bringing the YMCA into this. This is also—this hearing, I believe, has to do with the need for new regulation.***

Have you ever been on a commercial diving operation where the commercial divers had a certification card?

Kirk Austin: *I don't know.*

Pete Pilkington: *In other words, a card that would indicate that they were, in fact, a commercial diver?*

Kirk Austin: *I don't know.*

Pete Pilkington: *Would it be a hindrance to have to carry something like this around?*

Kirk Austin: *I don't know.*

Pete Pilkington: *Would it be any more burdensome then say a driver's license? I've carried my recreational diver certification card around for thirty years. I still have it and I have got a new one that actually has my medical records imbedded in it along with a photo appropriately aged. Nothing like that in the commercial world, is there?*

Lieutenant Commander Beistle: *And your point is that it wouldn't be very hard to have—*

Pete Pilkington: *It wouldn't be very hard for a commercial diver—*

Lieutenant Commander Beistle: *I agree.*

Pete Pilkington: *to have a card that, in fact, shows what level of training.*

Lieutenant Commander Beistle: *I agree.*

Pete Pilkington: *You could bury a microfiche in it with your medical records. Would that all be possible?*

Lieutenant Commander Beistle: *Yes, sir. I think we can accept that.*

Pete Pilkington: *Earlier—*

Lieutenant Commander Beistle: *Stand by just a moment, sir. I'm going to hang on to this for a moment because we're going to have to get a picture of it as an exhibit, and then I'll make sure that I give it back to you.*

Pete Pilkington: *Another quick question. If you had a bail-out bottle and you had a helmet, why did we go through the exercise with the oxygen bottles and the hoses? Why didn't you just put the bail-out bottle on the hat and jump in the water?*

Kirk Austin: *The bail out was empty. I had planned on filling it out there.*

Pete Pilkington: *Where is it customarily—or do you fill the bail-out bottles?*

Kirk Austin: *We've always filled them on the site.*

Pete Pilkington: *You use the compressor to fill them?*

Kirk Austin: *Use a high-pressure bottle.*

Pete Pilkington: *All right. Why didn't you fill them from the high-pressure bottles?*

Kirk Austin: *There was no facility to do that.*

Pete Pilkington: *Was there any air in the high-pressure bottles?*

Kirk Austin: *I don't know.*

Pete Pilkington: *Wouldn't it have made far more sense to put air into the—into the bail-out bottle from the high-pressure bottle and jump into the water rather than spend twenty minutes stringing together oxygen and acetylene hoses?*

Kirk Austin: *That makes—*

Pete Pilkington: *Isn't it, in fact, true that neither one of the bail-out bottles that were out there that day had air in them?*

Kirk Austin: *Mine did not have air. I don't know about the other one.*

Pete Pilkington: *I think you testified earlier that you knew that his didn't have air.*

Kirk Austin: *I don't recall doing that.*

Pete Pilkington: *One last comment off the record Mr. Austin. Earlier I asked you if you were down in twenty-eight feet of water, could you have held your breath and returned to the surface? And I believe your answer was "Yes." I suspect that you might believe that but actually if you did hold your breath and attempt to swim to the surface, you would be dead by the time you got there.*

Kirk Austen would be subjected to cross examination by the other parties about his lack of diving skills, his business practices and his association with the American Bureau of Shipping. By the end of his testimony it was becoming clear that the intent of the hearing was not to punish those involved on March 4, but rather to demonstrate the short comings of the system that allowed the conditions to exist on the Cliffs 12. Short comings that were not confined to the events aboard the Cliffs 12 but pandemic throughout the industry.

The next witness would be Ronald Everett who until being called had been outside the court room. Lieutenant Commander Beistle would lay the foundation that the witness had inspected some 100 to 150 mobile offshore drilling units during his nine years of employment with the American Bureau of Shipping. He had arrived on the same crew boat as the dive team, that his qualification to be an inspector was gained by accompanying more senior employee as they conducted inspections and then signing a document that they had read all the rules and regulations.

He would go on to testify that during much of the day of March 4 he had been attending to other duties aboard the Cliffs 12. He did not inspect the dive station nor did he verify the qualifications of those conducting the testing; that was not his area of expertise. The American Bureau of Shipping was there to view the results and compile the information. They were not responsible to inspect the equipment the dive gear or the qualifications of the divers.

He would testify that the first time he was aware there may have been a problem with the dive evolution was around 5:00 PM when he saw Austin at the ship's rail attempting to pull the diver in using the umbilical. *I think he told me(Austin) that it was—he had the line in his hands; and I think—if I remember it correctly, he asked me to help pull to see if we can pull it loose. It was after that they really indicated that there was a situation. I think it was then when Mr. Wiitala came up said that he (Brian) had quit talking.* Mr. Everett continued to describe the recovery attempt as best he could but explained that for much of the initial effort Wiitala had asked that he watch the water on the far side of the rig in the event the diver was able to release himself and float to the surface. To assist him Wiitala had thrown a white Styrofoam cup in the water that followed the current passing under the rig and emerged out the other side. Once the divers were lowered to the water he had returned to the dive station. He did not see the divers in the water. With that the witness was passed for cross examination to Tom Mosele.

Tom Mosele: *Now, you've testified earlier that somebody asked you for telephone numbers.*

Ron Everett: *Yes, sir.*

Tom Mosele: *Did anybody indicate that they had no local emergency contact list or that they were just—why did they need that?*

Ron Everett: *The first thing they wanted was the local Coast Guard office to—to notify them, as I think is required. I'm not sure. But then they wanted support that they could get in the most rapid manner. I even think they called the boat on the radio, the crew boat, to tell it to turn around and come back because it was there shortly afterwards, but I'm just assuming that. But they wanted some sort of support, and helicopter's the fastest method.*

Tom Mosele: *Do you know—as part of your activity with ABS, have you ever required, prior to the inspection commencing, that a dive supervisor be appointed?*

Ron Everett: *ABS, as far as I know, doesn't require that. They just—they bring out the crew, and they do what they have to do.*

Tom Mosele: *And ABS doesn't require an operations manual of any type?*

Ron Everett: *No, sir.*

Tom Mosele: *They don't require any type of diving plan?*

Ron Everett: *No, sir.*

Tom Mosele: *Do they have any specific requirements for following certain CFRs—NAVICs, any Governmental regulations?*

Ron Everett: *No, sir.*

Tom Mosele: *Diving operations?*

Ron Everett: *No, sir.*

Tom Mosele: *Does anybody at ABS specifically qualify companies that might present themselves as diving contractors?*

Ron Everett: *Does anyone at ABS? I don't follow the question.*

Tom Mosele: *Okay. Is there any leg of ABS that would, when you're looking at these certifications, actually takes and looks at the qualifications, equipment, personnel of a diving company?*

Ron Everett: *I've never done that myself, so I don't—I've never had any reason to follow that. So I don't know. They obviously do something because they produce the paper.*

Tom Mosele: *Today I understand that ABS has the authority to actually do these inspections without the Coast Guard being present, is that correct, sir? Is there some recent authority given ABS—*

Ron Everett: *Not on MODUs.*

Tom Mosele: *Are you aware of some kind of understanding or something in progress to that would allow the American Bureau of Shipping to do these inspections without the Coast Guard?*

Tom Mosele: *To allow ABS to do these inspections absent of the Coast Guard?*

Ron Everett: *No, sir, not for MODUs.*

Tom Mosele: *Okay. I have a press release here that was issued by the American Bureau of Shipping on September 11, 1998, that states that the American Bureau of Shipping in fact was granted the authority to perform MODU inspections without the USCG being present. Are you familiar with that?*

Ron Everett: *No, sir.*

Tom Mosele: *Here let's see, I think we have it here let me read the first few lines.*

In a major development underscoring the success of the Alternative Compliance Program the United States Coast Guard has extended the authorization given to American Bureau of Shipping to include mobile offshore drilling units (MODUs) that adhere to the Code for the Construction and Equipment of Mobile Offshore Drilling Units.

At the same time the Coast Guard has also authorized ABS to conduct surveys and issue certificates in accordance with the '89 MODU Code. The Coast Guard has previously granted ABS other statutory recognitions including various surveys and certifications in accordance with the Load line, SOLAS, and MARPOL international maritime conventions.

Under the terms of the Alternative Compliance Program ABS surveyors had been empowered to act as agents of the Coast Guard in issuing certificates to U.S. flag ships in support of the USCG Certificates of Inspection.

Mr. Everett, were you aware of this?

Ron Everett: *No, sir.*

Tom Mosele: *And this was something that I was asking about. I think if it's recognized by the Coast Guard that, in fact, there's autonomous authority now for ABS to act, I think it's important that we understand what guidelines they're now issuing for dive activities. If the United States Coast Guard has granted the American Bureau of Shipping the authority to do the inspections without USCG oversight who is responsible to see that the inspections are done safely and in compliance with current regulations? United States Regulations?*

Lieutenant Commander Beistle: *Can we go off the record for a moment?*

Mr. Mosele, after talking with brain trust up here I'm told there is a new NVIC that is about to be published that addresses that issue. We will attempt to produce it tomorrow.

Tom Mosele: *I'm trying to keep in the spirit and mission of what this hearing is partially about, it is looking at how things are approved. There's an authority that's being transferred beyond the realm of the Coast Guard, dealing with the safety of the personnel doing the inspections and apparently they don't, the American Bureau of Shipping, know what their own regulations for controlling these types of diving activities are.*

Lieutenant Commander Beistle: *Mr. Mosel, I agree with you, to a degree, let me produce the new NVIC tomorrow.*

After a short discussion off the record the witness was passed to the other parties in interest; none asked a question and the witness was excused with the thanks of the court.

It was 8:00 PM we had been at it for eleven and a half hours on the second day of the investigation when Lieutenant Commander Beistle suggested a ten-minute break before calling the next witness.

Lieutenant Commander Beistle: *Okay, we are back on the record. It's ten minutes past 8:00 on the twenty-third. The next witness, I-I think we've agreed during the break, that it's going to Mr. Gilbert.*

Now let me make sure I can get this on the record, if I can have everybody's attention. I distributed to all the Parties in Interest a copy of the transcript of Mr. Gilberts testimony when I asked him some questions on May 19, 1999, last month. What I'm proposing to do is to ask probably a dozen questions I've developed since then: but otherwise, I'm not going to develop any background information or anything else with Mr. Gilbert because I feel like I did that during this conversation back on May 19. Mr. Gilbert now that you have been sworn in can you tell me how many diving jobs has your company performed since our deposition on May 19?

Mr. Gilbert: *Maybe six.*

Lieutenant Commander Beistle: *How many diving jobs from May 1 to May 19, 1999*

Mr. Gilbert: *Maybe two or three.*

With that the Lieutenant Commander asked for the names of the employees who had worked on the jobs, the locations of the jobs and the equipment utilized. Before Gilbert could answer his attorney, Mr. Hope raised an objection, *What's the materiality?*

Lieutenant Commander Beistle: *Just to see pattern and practice.*

Mr. Hope: *You've got his deposition and you didn't figure that out?*

Lieutenant Commander Beistle: *Mr. Gilbert could you please answer the question? the names of the employees and the locations of the dives please.*

With that Danny Gilbert pulled from his briefcase a list and began reading of the details of the previous months diving projects including the names of the employees, the company equipment utilized and the dive locations. All the dives had taken place in areas under OSHA jurisdiction, not offshore. Sitting in the front row of the court room was the Houston area director for OSHA.

Lieutenant Commander Beistle: *And you were utilizing the Quincy 325s for breathing gas supply?*

Danny Gilbert: *Yes, sir, on some of them, others we used high pressure air bottles or SCUBA.*

Lieutenant Commander Beistle: *Have you had the required air tests done on any of your compressors since May 19 since your May 19, 1999 deposition?*

Mr. Gilbert: *Not yet. We've ordered the test kits and they should be here in a week or so.*

Lieutenant Commander Beistle: *When did you first order theses air quality kits?*

Mr. Gilbert: *Last Friday, I think.*

Lieutenant Commander Beistle: *Mr. Gilbert do you know the minimum manifold pressure required to properly ventilate a Kirby superlight in twenty-eight feet of sea water?*

Mr. Gilbert: *Yes, sir, sixty pounds at ambient.*

Lieutenant Commander Beistle: *What did you base that number on?*

Mr. Gilbert: *I've heard that figure somewhere and that kind of just stuck in my mind.*

Lieutenant Commander Beistle: *When you are on site do you ever work as the diving supervisor?*

Mr. Gilbert: *Sometimes.*

Lieutenant Commander Beistle: *Have you had any of your compressors tested since May 19 when your deposition was taken. Any of the compressors that you supplied to your employees for air supply, have any of them been tested?*

Mr. Gilbert: *No, sir, but we plan to do so.*

Lieutenant Commander Beistle: *When was the last time you did an air quality check on your compressors, can you remember what year that was?*

Mr. Gilbert: *Probably 1993*

Lieutenant Commander Beistle *Are the volume tanks you utilize specifically made for breathing gas, or are they made for air driven tools?*

Mr. Gilbert: *I don't know. I do know they have an ASME stamp on them. I bought them at Granger supply, I think.*

The questioning would continue into maintenance schedules, testing of air hoses, who was in charge of the testing all answered essentially the same. It was up to the dive supervisors to maintain the equipment, on the job. Mr. Gilbert continued to explain his none maintenance program until the Lieutenant Commander asked, *"We heard testimony from Kevin Lawdermilk that one of your compressors failed during a job. It died I think he said."*

Mr. Hope: *Objection, I think you are misquoting Mr. Lawdermilk, I think he said the compressor—*

Lieutenant Commander Beistle: *I have the transcript, he said, "It died."*

Then more questions on safe diving practice, inspections, equipment maintenance, why Monolec oil should be used, the number of employees that had worked for G&G the past year followed up with one last question from Lieutenant Commander Beistle. *Has any dive supervisor working for you ever been fired for performing an unsafe dive or for using equipment not properly set up?*

Answered by Mr. Gilbert. *To my knowledge there has never been a dive performed with unsafe equipment.*

With that, the witness was passed.

Pete Pilkington: *Just a general question. Do you consider yourself to be a safe diving contractor?*

Danny Gilbert*: I see where we could be safer, yes, sir.*

Pete Pilkington: *You indicated earlier that you were on a classification dive this week or sometime in the last month for Lloyd's?*

Danny Gilbert: *I believe so, yes.*

Pete Pilkington: *Are you on some sort of an approved list with Lloyd's?*

Danny Gilbert: *Yes, sir.*

Pete Pilkington: *You indicated earlier that you bought some kind of air quality testing equipment. Can you tell us what that is?*

Danny Gilbert: *No, we ordered it. We didn't buy it. We got on a program with a company out of Austin called Texas Researching Institute, and they're going to send us a test package every six months where we test the quality of the air, send it back to them to be analyzed, and they'll give us a certificate or let us know what the quality of the air is.*

Pete Pilkington: *And this is the first package that you're gotten from this research company since 1992, is that correct?*

Danny Gilbert: *About then, yes, sir.*

Pete Pilkington: *So between 1992 and today, all of the compressors that you've been using have not been tested, is that correct?*

Danny Gilbert: *That's correct.*

Pete Pilkington: *So every compressor that you've used in every dive that you've conducted since 1992 until today, has been conducted with a compressor out of Federal Reregulation, is that correct?*

Mr. Hope: *Excuse me. If that's the question, then I'm going to suggest that he not answer on the Fifth Amendment.*

Lieutenant Commander Beistle: *On what grounds?*

Mr. Hope: *The Fifth Amendment.*

Lieutenant Commander Beistle: *Is he invoking the Fifth Amendment privilege, is that what you're saying?*

Mr. Hope: *Is this for publicity purposes or what?*

Lieutenant Commander Beistle: *As far as I know, I'm not aware of any potential criminal violations involved in this.*

Pete Pilkington: *I'm not an officer of the Court.*

Lieutenant Commander Beistle: *Yeah. I'm going to interpret this broadly. If I were to try to compel him to testify, you know, my next phone call is to the U.S. attorney and then to the magistrate, and then we're talking about—we're talking about hauling people into court.*

You've made your point. If you want to stand pat on this issue, then we're suddenly talking about next month before anything gets done, so—

Mr. Mosele: *Can we take a quick break, two minutes?*

Lieutenant Commander Beistle: *We can.*

Pete Pilkington: *Can I make one request before we take the break?*

Lieutenant Commander Beistle: *Yes, sir.*

Pete Pilkington: *We requested under discovery to have a proof of purchase of proprietary air filters for the Quincy 325.*

Lieutenant Commander Beistle: *Oh, that is a good point. That's right.*

Pete Pilkington: *While we're taking a break, perhaps those could be delivered to us.*

Lieutenant Commander Beistle: *Mr. Pilkington has just raised a good point and I appreciate you reminding me of it. Mr. Gilbert do you have those record, receipts, any documentation that G&G has ever purchased air filters or any other maintenance parts for the Quincy 325s compressors your company normally utilizes for breathing gas? Any documentation that G&G Marine has on record for any parts that G&G had purchased for the Quincy 325. Any maintenance—routine maintenance parts?*

Mr. Hope: *The records are not available today.*

Lieutenant Commander Beistle: *So what I would hope is that, Mr. Gilbert, could you check your records this evening. Could you check your records and see if you can—if you can produce that stuff for us before this hearing—this hearing adjourns tomorrow?*

Mr. Hope: *I think he's staying here. Are you going back home?*

Mr. Gilbert: *I was going to stay here tonight because I think it's going to be late.*

Mr. Hope: *We will look and supply you with that information as soon as possible.*

Are you looking for all repairs, or are you looking for filters in particular?

Lieutenant Commander Beistle: *The way the prehearing conference went, as I understood it, what we're looking for is receipts for parts or pieces that were purchased for Quincy 325 compressors prior to March 4, 1996, as well as after March 4th 1996 to today.*

Mr. Hope: *Let me ask the question—and I'll do it on the record—what's the materiality of this, something that occurred after 1996?*

Lt. Com Beistle*: I'm just curious about it because my understanding—*

Mr. Hope: *Well, but curiosity is not a reason to ask and obtain this information.*

Lt. Com Beistle*: The reason that it's material is because my understanding is that having talked to McKenzie's and having talked to Marty Husband, as well, I thought that they were out of the dive compressor business, and I thought that they were out of the business of dealing with anybody that did diving operations.*

Mr. Hope: *I don't mind for that purpose, if that's the reason you're asking it.*

Lt. Com Beistle*: Yeah. So, I guess it goes, frankly, to the credibility of the witness because I have got opposing stories. I have one piece of information from one witness, Marty Husband, that says that they don't do anything to dive compressors and then Mr. Gilbert who says he still does business with McKenzie.*

I've asked Mr. Gilbert to produce any evidence that back in November—and I have checked my notes, and in fact he did indicate that he had had equipment serviced at McKenzie's back in November of 1998. So, I asked for any evidence that he was still doing business with McKenzie's.

Okay. Mr. Gilbert we will wait for your submission—I think Mr. Pilkington had the floor.

Pete Pilkington: *Mr. Gilbert how many compressors do you own?*

Danny Gilbert: *Three.*

Pete Pilkington: *And how many umbilicals?*

Mr. Hope*: Again, what's the materiality of it?*

Danny Gilbert: *Four.*

Tom Mosele: *I think it goes to material.*

Pete Pilkington: *I Think it goes to practice.*

Mr. Hope: *Yeah. What's the materiality of this investigation, what he owns now, three years later?*

Pete Pilkington: *OK let's do it your way, In 1996, how many compressors did you own on March 4th?*

Mr. Hope: *Asked and answered.*

Pete Pilkington: *OK, let me try it this way. Previously you testified that you owned three compressors and previously you testified you owned four umbilicals in 1996. Is that your testimony?.*

Mr. Hope: *I think that's been asked and answered.*

Tom Mosele: *Can we get an answer?*

Pete Pilkington: *Am I to understand that I can't ask the question of how many umbilicals he owned in 1996? Let's try this on page 83 of the transcript. Question from Mr. Pilkington: 'Earlier you mentioned that G&G had three compressors and four umbilicals.' and Mr. Gilberts answer was 'Yes, sir.' Then I asked "In a standard operation, how many umbilicals would you send out with each compressor?' and Mr. Gilbert Answered 'Two.'*

So basically what I am attempting to get at is that we have established that G&G Marine owned three compressors. We have established that on March 4th all three were on jobs including the compressor Kevin Lawdermilk described as being defective. The one sent out to the Cliffs 12.

We have established that G&G owned four umbilicals.

If Mr. Gilbert had all three compressors out and owned four umbilical's my question is how could he have sent two umbilicals out with each compressor? I'm a house builder not a math wizard or a lawyer but I am the father of a man who stands accused of not bring out that second umbilical. That second umbilical that had it been there on March 4th 1996 would have made it unnecessary for us to be here today.

375

Well, basically all the questions that I wanted to ask, I asked four weeks ago when we deposed Mr. Gilbert. Since those questions and answers have been admitted into the record, I guess I've only got one more question to ask. **Mr. Gilbert is it your personal belief that it was as a result of your failure to properly maintain your compressors in accordance with the 46 CFR, that was a direct cause of the death of Brian Pilkington in 1996?**

Mr. Hope: *I object. This is asking him to draw a conclusion that he has no basis to draw, and it's already been beat around the bush a thousand times.*

Lt. Com Beistle: *It hasn't been beat around the bush here.*

Mr. Gilbert: *I can answer that.*

Lt. Com Beistle: *Hold on, Mr. Gilbert.*

Pete Pilkington: *Let me rephrase it.*

Pete Pilkington: *Do you believe that the equipment maintenance problems led to problems on the job in March of 1996?*

Pete Pilkington: *Do you believe the equipment to be poorly maintained?*

Danny Gilbert: *No, sir.*

Pete Pilkington: *Previously in testimony you admitted that the equipment had not been—had air quality tests done from 1992 to 1996, is that correct?*

Mr. Hope: *Excuse me. That has nothing to do with what he's been trying to drive at.*

Lt. Com Beistle: *Well, that may be a foundational question. I'm going to let him go. Go ahead. Go ahead, sir. Answer the question, Mr. Gilbert.*

Danny Gilbert: *I'm sorry, Mr. Pilkington. Would you repeat?*

Lt. Com Beistle: *You previously testified that the compressors had not been—had not been—the air quality had not been tested from 1992 to 19—*

Pete Pilkington: *1996.*

Lt. Com Beistle: *1996, is that right?*

Danny Gilbert: *That's correct.*

Pete Pilkington: *Do you believe that that failure to maintain the compressors or to have air quality tests done on the compressors, in any way led to the malfunction of the compressor?*

Danny Gilbert: *No, sir, I do not.*

Pete Pilkington: *Did you have the compressor used during the dive evolution of March 4, 1996 on the Cliffs 12 function tested?*

Danny Gilbert: *Mr. Horton contacted me—Buddy Horton contacted me two or three times wanting to know if we had had the air compressor in question function tested and I told him no, that I had not. And he said, 'Well, you need to do it because the Coast Guard's going to require it be done.' I told him, to the best of my recollection, that, 'Okay. When they require it, then we will have it done.' In another conversation, Mr. Horton called and asked me if I had had it function tested, and I said, 'No, sir. I have not been directed to by the Coast Guard yet.'*

Pete Pilkington: *In fact, I think he called you twice even before he talked to the Coast Guard, telling you to get it function tested?*

Danny Gilbert: *I don't think he was telling me to. The way I remember, he was asking me.*

Pete Pilkington: *Asking you to?*

Danny Gilbert: *Yes, sir.*

Pete Pilkington: *And then apparently he got a call from the Coast Guard, which I believe he was probably predicting and at that point he called you again and asked you to get it function tested?*

Danny Gilbert: *Correct.*

Pete Pilkington: *A couple of follow-up questions. You indicated that you told McKenzie's that you wanted the compressor function tested.*

Danny Gilbert: *Yes, sir.*

Pete Pilkington: *Is that what it says on the work order? That you wanted it function tested?*

Mr. Hope: *He just indicated that he told them specifically to function test it.*

Pete Pilkington: *I did not asking him what he thought he said I asked him what the work order said. What does the document say Mr. Gilbert?*

Mr. Hope: *What it says: Run and check unit for proper operation,—*

Lt. Com Beistle: *Mr. Hope. Let's have the witness answer the question. We're talking about I.O. Exhibit No. 20, page 0009. Mr. Gilbert, if you will, just read what it says.*

Danny Gilbert: *Run and check unit for proper operation.*

Pete Pilkington: *: Excuse me. That's not what is says, please read the whole thing.*

Danny Gilbert: *(Reading) Run and check for proper operation. Hasn't been run in a while.*

Pete Pilkington: *Does it indicate on there who said that or who placed the order?*

Danny Gilbert: *Purchase order, as he just said, verbal, Dan Gilbert.*

Pete Pilkington: *Per Danny Gilbert. Do you remember your testimony in the deposition you gave during the civil procedure which is already in record? Did you admit that that's what you said?*

Danny Gilbert*: Yes, sir.*

With that Mr. Mosele made a motion that the court adjourn for the evening. It was just after 10:00 *p.m.*, we had been at it for just under 12 hours. There were no objections.

Chapter 20

PROCEEDINGS DAY THREE

JUNE 24, 1999

Lt. Com. Tom Beistle: *If you will, just take a seat. Okay, folks. We're back on the record. It's 8:45 on the 24ᵗʰ. Mr. Gilbert is on the stand again. Mr. Gilbert, I remind you that you're still under oath.*

Good morning, Mr. Gilbert. My name is Thomas Mosele, and I, on behalf of Mr. Pilkington, will be continuing the questioning from yesterday. Mr. Gilbert you previously testified that you left the ADC for personal reasons, is that correct, sir?

Danny Gilbert: *That's correct.*

Thomas Mosele: *What were those reasons?*

Mr. Hope: *Excuse me. What's the materiality of him leaving a volunteer organization to this investigation? I understood that what we were going to do was do some follow up on whether or not we had any rebuttal, I didn't know that we were going to do a complete new deposition here today. Now if that's what we are trying to do here, then I object to Mr. Mosele going into it; and I would like Mr. Pilkington to finish the questioning. This morning, before we went on the record I was assured that if Tom Mosele took over for Mr. Pilkington it would be shorter, this doesn't seem shorter to me.*

Joe Walker: *If you have a problem I'm sure Mr. Pilkington would be more than willing to take over the questioning.*

Mr. Hope: *I have a problem with completely going into new material. Yesterday we quit to do one thing and that was to go over receipts that we had from our files. That was my understanding.*

Lt. Com. Tom Beistle: *Mr. Pilkington still had questions he was going into, but frankly Mr. Pilkington raised a legitimate issue last night. At the pre hearing conference last week as well as when Mr. Gilbert was deposed prior to these proceedings Mr. Gilbert was requested to produce any evidence that he had ever purchased proprietary air filters for any of the compressors G&G used to supply breathing air to its employees. Any evidence that G&G ever purchased any maintenance parts for the compressors. Mr. Gilbert has been asked now three times, Ms Seiler, who is not here today, was asked once and you sir were here last night when we asked yet again.*

And the point in fact is none of that information has ever been made available. So that's where the whole issue of receipts came up: but it was raised as part of Mr. Pilkington's question and was not meant to end his questioning. I will grant you that this is Mr. Pilkington's second bite at the apple with Mr. Gilbert, but we didn't establish any protocol at the outset that said you can only cross someone or only examine someone one time. And so far throughout this hearing that hasn't been a problem.

Mr. Hope: *Fine.*

Lt. Com. Tom Beistle: *Mr. Mosele, I believe you have the floor.*

Thomas Mosele: *Mr. Gilbert you previously testified that you left the ADC for personal reasons, is that correct, sir?*

Mr. Hope: *Excuse me. What's the materiality of him leaving a volunteer organization to this investigation?*

Lt. Com. Tom Beistle: *The materiality—if I can answer that because I'm interested in this too. The one thing that I would say is that Mr. Mosele, if you would, check the Gilbert deposition. Because I think he went into that on your questions, Mr. Pilkington. Did he or did he not?*

Mr. Pilkington: *the question was asked during the previous deposition but if you read his response he never completed the answer. We would just like to hear a complete answer if that is possible.*

Lt. Com. Tom Beistle: *I'm interested in that as well.*

Mr. Hope: *Fine. Let's go.*

Lt. Com. Tom Beistle: *Let me explain why.*

Mr. Hope: *You don't have to explain. Let's just do it.*

Lieutenant Commander Tom Beistle: *Well, no. You've asked for an explanation. I'm going to give you an explanation. Mr. Gilbert, or G&G anyway, was a member of ADC, at least as I understand it, at the time that this casualty occurred. And I'm interested in this less because of Mr. Gilbert and more because I'm interested in how the diving industry interacts with ADC. As a matter of fact, I've asked Mr. Ross Saxon, a representative of ADC, to appear here today because I want to go into that very issue. I'm interested in how the ADC manages, if you will, its membership and I'm interested in that whole dynamic of what kind of controls are put on the commercial diving industry. So to that degree, I'm interested in the answer.*

Mr. Hope: *I know what his answer's going to be, so I'm not worried about his answer. What I am worried about is this continuing on and on with stuff that's not material. Let's go.*

Lt. Com. Tom Beistle: *I'll tell you what. Your point is well taken, and I'll ask Mr. Mosele to focus this.*

Joe Walker: *I would just like to respond to the objection. The ADC Consensus Standards are part of their safety manual and it's probably an integral part of their manual, so his interaction with the ADC is very important because it's probably still in their manual. I think he has a right to ask.*

Thomas Mosele: *In addition to the ADC consensus standards, it's being proposed as a guideline for regulation in the dive industry on a national basis.*

Lt. Com. Tom Beistle: *I understand, but I don't think we have to go there to get there, Mr. Mosele, because we didn't rope off the new regs in our prehearing conference. Go ahead.*

Thomas Mosele: *Okay. Mr. Gilbert, what were your personal reasons for leaving the ADC?*

Danny Gilbert: *There were several reasons. In my opinion, the ADC did not have any regulatory ability. I guess what I'm trying to say is this: They didn't have any bite in their rules and regulations in order to enforce their rules and regulations with diving companies. I was familiar with other diving companies diving in less than safe conditions and I knew that this had been reported to the ADC and nothing was done. Nothing could be done at the time because they didn't—they didn't have any powers to do so. At the time of this—when this accident occurred, then I started getting inquiries from the ADC and was told that they were going to launch an investigation and they wanted the facts and I told them at that time, "I'm sorry, it's under litigation," and if they wanted anything, talk to the attorney, that I couldn't start giving out information to the ADC. I was—already had made up my mind prior to that, that—I don't know if I had renewed my membership fees prior to that or not. I may have. I'm not real sure on that. But I was—prior to this accident, I was leaning towards not participating in the ADC itself.*

Thomas Mosele: *Okay. So basically one of the reasons was that you didn't want to have an investigation on your firm performed by the ADC, is that correct, sir?*

Danny Gilbert: *That is not correct, no.*

Thomas Mosele: *What is your understanding of ADC's duties for oversight of the dive industry?*

Danny Gilbert: *To promote diver safety and to assist in teaching divers and dive contractors safe diving practices and we could do that without the ADC oversight.*

Lt. Com. Tom Beistle: *Mr. Gilbert, you previously testified that you are aware that the—your compressors that are used on dive operations, the quality of the air has to be tested every six months. Do you remember that?*

Danny Gilbert: *That's correct, yes, sir.*

Lt. Com. Tom Beistle: *Was that something the ADC would oversee?*

Danny Gilbert: *No, sir, not that I am aware of.*

Lt. Com. Tom Beistle: *Okay. Did you send your divers to ADC type training courses?*

Danny Gilbert: *I was unaware of any ADC type training courses.*

Lt. Com. Tom Beistle: *Well, did you run any training courses for your divers at G&G?*

Danny Gilbert: *The only training courses we do at G&G is for ship husbandry, and we let them practice on underwater burning and welding in the shop.*

Thomas Mosele: *There is previous testimony that there aren't dive logs because G&G threw the dive logs away, is that your understanding?*

Danny Gilbert: *I don't believe so. I think they're a matter of record, if I remember correctly, sir.*

Thomas Mosele: *Well, wasn't it a practice for G&G to dispose of the dive logs after the pay period?*

Danny Gilbert: *Yes.*

Thomas Mosele: *You also remember testimony that G&G would dive sometimes without a standby umbilical, is that correct, sir?*

Danny Gilbert: *Oh, I've heard that, yes, sir.*

Thomas Mosele: *And also there was prior testimony that indicates that the actual bail-out bottles on this job site on March 4, 1996, were empty. Do you remember that testimony?*

Danny Gilbert: *I heard that one was full and one may have been empty.*

Thomas Mosele: *Okay. Do you think that any of these items that I just listed were a violation of safe diving practices?*

Danny Gilbert: *Any of the items you just listed?*

Thomas Mosele: *Yes, sir.*

Danny Gilbert: *It wouldn't be in violation of the ADC diving standards if—I'm not aware that there is a X amount of bottles you have to have for backup air.*

Lt. Com. Tom Beistle: *That wasn't the question, Mr. Gilbert. The question was: Were these violations of safe diving practices in your opinion? You've testified that you've been diving for some twenty years or more. Based on your experience, are any of these problems, problems that would have compromised safety on a diving operation?*

Danny Gilbert: *If they were true, some of them would be—would compromise safety, yes.*

Thomas Mosele: *Is it true there was not a standby umbilical on the job on March 4, 1996?*

Danny Gilbert: *That's my understanding.*

Thomas Mosele: *Is it true that you didn't check your compressors prior—the compressor prior to this job on March 4, 1996?*

Mr. Hope: *I object, I mean, you've got three people over there feeding questions, we could go on for days.*

Tom Mosele: *Mr. Gilbert, could you answer the question?*

Danny Gilbert: *I can't remember if it was started before it was loaded out or not, sir.*

Thomas Mosele: *Is it true that you didn't do air quality tests on the compressor?*

Danny Gilbert: *Yes, sir. I think that has been established.*

Tom Mosele: *Are you aware that the hose used by G&G on the dive during March 4, 1996, was not in compliance with federal regulations?*

Danny Gilbert: *No, sir.*

Lt. Com. Tom Beistle: *Do you know that to be true, Mr. Mosele?*

Thomas Mosele: *We've requested those records. In fact, at this time we also were expecting receipts for the spare parts for that compressor.*

Lt. Com. Tom Beistle: *Right. I didn't mention that. I talked to Mr. Gilbert. He indicated—prior to the hearing convening—he indicated to me that he contacted his office this morning and his office is searching their records.*

Mr. Mosele: *Well, we will pass the witness in anticipation of actually receiving the documentation.*

Mr. Siahatgar representing Ronald Townsend, Mr. Hope representing Danny Gilbert, Mr. Wilson representing the American Bureau of Shipping and Mr. Kirk Austin representing himself all passed the witness and with the thanks of the court Danny Gilbert left his seat of interrogation and rejoined Mr. Hope.

Lieutenant Commander Beistle: *Our next witness will be Mr. Ric Walker, Mr. Walker if you would stand and raise your right hand.*

With that Ric Walker, who had already assumed the chair that had so quickly been vacated by Danny Gilbert, stood for a moment while taking the obligatory oath, answered the standard questions about the spelling of his name and gave his current address.

Mr. Joe Walker would start the questioning. *Can you give a brief background as to your training as a diver?*

Ric Walker: *I started—and years will be approximate as I get into this—but in 1968, I went into the navy and went into the Navy SEAL program, served with SEAL team 1 in Vietnam where I—besides the SEAL basically swimmer's school, self-contained breathing apparatus and closed and semiclosed circuit breathing apparatus, I also attended second-class diver school which gets into, I guess the navy version of commercial diving.*

In 1973, after I got out of the navy, I went to Commercial Dive Center, now the College of Oceaneering, took their commercial diving course and went to work that year, in 1973, for Ocean Systems in Morgan City, Louisiana. I worked for them for five years and then for International Oilfield Divers. This was all surface-supplied air, mixed gas diving, saturation diving to—in the range of 740 feet, and then did similar work for International Oilfield Divers in 1978.

In 1979, I went to work for a company out of the UK called Odberg where I got back into saturation diving more actively, working in Mexico on the IXTOC UNO blowout and various welding programs. There was a big pipe-laying agenda down there at the time for a few years.

In 1980, I went to Brunei for four and a half years as a consultant for Brunei Shell Petroleum where we ran a diving program with Oceaneering of about 110 divers, doing all of the work in that Brunei-Shell Petroleum field.

Throughout the eighties, I came back to the states and worked for some other companies here, Gulf States Diving in Pasadena and Cal Dive and whatever, but jumped back and forth between consulting and actively diving. I've done that ever since. I've been a consultant now since 1987 full-time for a company called Wet Solutions out of Morgan City.

Now I primarily am working as a diving consultant on behalf of the oil companies that I represent, doing all of the—I've done everything from writing specifications for jobs to writing diving specifications for Trinidad and whatever, to going out and getting the work done. So a wide range of—

Joe Walker: *And you recently came back from overseas, is that correct?*

Ric Walker: *I just spent most of the last six months in Gabon, West Africa, for Marathon Oil Company, installing ten and a half miles of ten-inch pipeline and an umbilical over the same length.*

Joe Walker: *And what type of diving is that?*

Ric Walker: *We did a lot of ROV work, remotely operated vehicles. We had the Dynamic Installer dynamically position our dive support vessel with full sat capability, eight divers in sat and, of course, we had surface diving in support of that, and also did some various surface diving in addition to that on the Ocean Constructor and off of the ETPM lay barge CT 101.*

Joe Walker: *One of the things I wanted to ask you, did you ever try to do a simulation of the conditions that occurred to Brian?*

Ric Walker: *Yes, I did. And if I may state the circumstances of why we did that: There was some speculation as to the hat that Brian Pilkington was wearing not having functioned correctly or, perhaps, not having been designed to handle the air pressures that we heard quoted in depositions, sworn depositions, and we decided to take the hat to test in Fort Eustis, Virginia, I believe. We set up a test there with Dr. David Youngblood—and I don't recall the other doctor's name—but the two doctors are long experienced in the diving physics and physiology and tables and everything else. I've known Dr. Youngblood for a long time. He was very supportive of my opinion that we should test this hat. They set the test up and we did some dry runs in the chamber and then took the hat in the chamber to a depth of twenty-eight feet, I believe it was.*

Joe Walker: *And I'm going to hold you right there for a second. And the hat you're referring to is this hat here (indicating) that was worn by Brian?*

Ric Walker: *I haven't checked any numbers or anything, but I believe that's the same hat. It's at least the same color.*

Joe Walker: *But you did ensure that you used this hat?*

Ric Walker: *Yes, we did.*

Joe Walker: *What happened then? You went down to twenty-eight feet—*

Ric Walker: *Twenty-eight feet.*

Joe Walker: *In a chamber.*

Ric Walker: *Ultimately we made several dry runs over the course of two days to make sure that all of the monitors and various equipment—test equipment were working, that they were getting the pulse rate, analyzing the oxygen and CO_2 properly. Then on the second day, we took it to the twenty-eight feet, and I was to reconstruct the exertion levels that we were—that we anticipated that Brian might have been under during his stress. I was on a bicycle—what is it—an ergonomically—anyway, a bicycle in the chamber with the hat on and pedaling this bicycle with my legs to simulate the exertion.*

Joe Walker: *Now, what kind of pressure did you have going to the hat?*

Ric Walker: *We started off with normal operating pressures, and if I remember correctly, this hat's designed to function with a minimum pressure of either 115 or 125 psi, and I don't recall—*

Lt. Com. Tom Beistle: *If it will help, from looking at the operations manual for that helmet, it says 115 psi.*

Ric Walker: *Okay. That's what I thought. So anyway, we lowered the supply pressure to get 80 psi, if I remember correctly. Again, I was sucking on the hat instead of watching the pressures but—*

Joe Walker: *Okay. Let me hold you right there for a second. Why did you lower the supply pressure to 80 psi?*

Ric Walker: *It was my understanding, again from testimony of witnesses at the scene of the accident that the pressure output of the compressor had reduced for one reason or another to approximately 80 psi.*

Joe Walker: *Okay. And so, then what happened?*

Ric Walker: *All this time, the breathing resistance, CO_2, heart rate and everything are being charted automatically and they were watching those results as I pushed this hat basically to the limits at that time because it was—and I believe we proved that it was not designed to work at that pressure. It was very difficult to breathe in this hat.*

Joe Walker: *And when you say 'very difficult to breathe', describe what happened to you in the space of twenty-eight minutes.*

387

Ric Walker: *The best description I can give, and I have some pretty serious feelings about this because I think that I—you know, we all can speculate about what Brian—you know, what went on in those last minutes down there—and I apologize for jumping ahead to this. But I think, more than anybody else, I'm the one who—if anybody saw what Brian, what Brian Pilkington saw in the last minutes of his life—I saw it because I—and I'll describe what happened with this hat. As they lowered the pressure, we got—I believe that the pressure—the test was run finally—the ultimate test that we tried to—you know, that we worked toward and ultimately achieved was for me to pedal this bicycle, create that exertion level at the same pressure level that we had heard quoted, 80 psi, and somewhere along the line in the vicinity of thirteen to fifteen minutes, I believe was what was estimated that Brian had after he made everyone know that he was in trouble.*

In any event, again, I can only state what I saw. I started pedaling this bicycle and I remember looking through the faceplate of the mask at Dr. Youngblood standing in the opposite end of the chamber—and I say 'standing', but the chamber is only five feet in diameter. So you can imagine he's all bent over and bracing himself up in the chamber. He looks at his watch and he says, "Two minutes." He announces this to the speaker in the hat, inside the chamber.

And in my mind I'm thinking—I'm feeling my legs burning and everything else, thinking, you know, "Fifteen minutes to go? I don't think I can do this." I mean, that's what immediately went into my mind. I was so rapidly fatigued at that time with this strong demand to pull air out of this hat, that my thighs were burning like they were on fire. And at some point I just stopped pedaling and went limp and went relaxed in the chamber, just tried to breathe and I remember Dr. Youngblood looking at his watch again and saying, "Twenty-three minutes."

I only recall one thing that occurred apparently several times during that period of time and that was Dr. Youngblood shining a flashlight in through the fog on the faceplate on the inside of the mask.

Joe Walker: *Let me ask you this: After you went limp, how long did it take you to actually recover your senses?*

Ric Walker: *Well, I stayed on the hat—they wanted to monitor the recovery in the hat because that was the only way we had to monitor the respiration, the negative pressure and everything to draw on the hat. So to keep the chart going, I stayed in the hat. I don't know the amount of time.*

Joe Walker: *Let me ask you this—*

Lt. Com. Tom Beistle: *Let me ask a question. You don't know the time because you don't remember it now or because—*

Ric Walker: *I was not monitoring the time, and I could have—I could say, "Well, it seemed like ten minutes" or "It seemed like X number of minutes," but I was not, you know, I was concentrating on every breath at that time. I do remember that.*

Lt. Com. Tom Beistle: *After you did regain consciousness, I mean, how—what was your*

Ric Walker: *Perception?*

Lt. Com. Tom Beistle: *Your state of mind, your ability to perceive?*

Ric Walker: *I don't know if I would have been a good judge of that, quite frankly, but I felt I knew what was going on around me. I was ambulatory. Just tired, extremely tired.*

Lt. Com. Tom Beistle: *Were you able to carry on a conversation with Dr. Youngblood?*

Ric Walker: *Oh yes, I was. They were asking me, how I was feeling. I recall Dr. Youngblood telling me—because I asked why he was shining the light in my eyes—he said he was trying to see my pupils and I took that at first that he was trying to recognize if my pupils were dilated or whatever and I don't even know the implications of which way they would have been or anything. But that's what I was anticipating in answer and he said, "No, I couldn't see your pupils" because my eyes were crossed. So I don't know. And again, I don't know the implications of that.*

Joe Walker: *Of the, during that period of time, how much of that actual test do you remember?*

Ric Walker: *About two minutes and then I remember—from the end I remember sitting there and—I remember on the rise and fall of my chest and I couldn't hold the helmet up anymore. I was just—every time I would inhale, I would have to rise and raise the hat up to give my chest room to expand, and then I would just collapse on the exhalation. I remember doing that for who knows how long, several minutes for sure.*

Joe Walker: *Did Dr. Youngblood relate to you in his opinion what would happen if you continued in that helmet with the same pressure?*

Ric Walker: *Well, he—all I remember is his discussion of the redness of my face and the symptoms or signs, I guess, of CO_2 buildup, but I don't recall anything specific other than that.*

Joe Walker: *Did you—during the time that you collapsed, do you think you would have been capable of doing any major tasks?*

Ric Walker: *I had one task. I mean, I was pedaling that bicycle, but I had one thing I was concentrating on. Well, say, pedaling the bicycle. The other thing I was concentrating on was breathing because every time I would inhale, the regulator—and anyone who is a diver here knows this—the regulator, if you over breathe it, it more or less bottoms out. And I could feel it bottom out. Dr. Youngblood commented on this, too, that he could hear it because I was inhaling like with two stages of inhalation. I would inhale with a big surge and then it would like reach a point where there was nothing else there and then I would inhale—you know, try to force the inhalation a little harder, trying to get more air to fill my lungs, but it would not come any faster than that.*

Joe Walker: *Do you feel that you could have performed tasks underwater in that condition such as unfouling yourself or unfouling your umbilical or—*

Ric Walker: *I remember very vividly that I—I had no other concern except my next breath.*

Joe Walker would continue with questions regarding industry standards, existing regulations, contractor responsibilities and common sense. Once all the questions had been fully and competently answered the witness was passed to Mr. Austin.

Austin's questions all revolved around diving supervisors; their qualifications, whether a supervisor could be a nonmember of the dive team, supplied by a different company. All asked from the point of view of a diver that had received his training at the YMCA.

Mr. Siahatgar representing the ship's Master, Mr. Townsend, continued down that same line of questioning. *How unusual is it for a group of divers to come out from one company to be supervised by someone from a different company?*

Ric Walker: *I haven't been in that situation, I don't know that I have ever seen that in all my years of diving.*

Followed by more questions regarding the actual test that had been conducted in the hyperbaric chamber. Why had they not run the test at 90 psi? Why use a bicycle in the chamber. The questioning went on to Ric Walker's understanding of the Association of Diving Contractors diving standards. And then a question regarding diver certification. *As far as you know in the United States is there any form of commercial diving license?*

Ric Walker: *No, sir, nothing that I am aware of.*

Bijan Siahatgar: *Do the Coast Guard regulations have any type of minimum requirements to be a dive tender?*

Ric Walker: *No, sir, nothing that I am aware of. The Coast Guard regulations primarily are focused on equipment.*

Bijan Siahatgar: *And finally, if there is a dive operation that takes place anywhere, the ultimate responsibility is the dive supervisor?*

Ric Walkers: *Yes, sir, ultimately the dive supervisor is the one that is held accountable.*

Bijan Siahatgar: *Do the Coast Guard regulations have any type of minimum requirements to be a dive supervisor?*

Ric Walker: *Only that he be named in writing, nothing else.*

With that Bijan would pass the witness. The other parties in interest or the attorneys that represented them would continue the questioning, each more concerned with protecting their individual concerns. It was only Bijan, who through his questioning, seemed to realize that the purpose of this hearing was not to punish. It was to find the truth and to use that truth to finally make a difference.

Once Kirk Austin had verified that, by regulation, he had done nothing outside existing convention, Mr. Hope had supplied yet another smoke screen for his client to hide behind and Mr. Wilson representing the American Bureau of shipping made a veiled attempt at discrediting the witness as lacking experience. Ric Walker was released with the thanks of the court.

After a short break the master of the Cliff's 12 on March 4, 1996, and party in interest, Ronald Townsend was duly sworn in. After the obligatory questions he was asked to present a brief résumé of his work experience, how he had risen from the ranks of a roustabout to licensed Master in charge of a jack up oil drilling platform. Then his recollection of the day of March 4.

Ron Townsend: *The Coast Guard showed up at 10:00 AM—and after the office paper work sort of deal was complete, we divided up into two teams. Lt. J. G. Thompson and Doug Reed went to the life boat area of the rig and started the life boat and evacuation inspection. Clint and Lieutenant Julio Martinez went down in the hull and started inspecting the machinery. I was floating around between the two inspection groups, when they would find a problem I was called over the PA system.*

Mr. Tom Mosele: Lieutenant Julio Martinez, he was there?

Ron Townsend: *Yes, sir, he was on board from 10:00 until the Coast Guard left at 1630.*

Mr. Townsend then was asked to recount what he could remember about the incident as it unfolded starting at 1700. His account was fairly consistent with all the other witnesses until it came to the air line. Townsend recollected that not only had the airline not been connected to the helmet, the harness the air line was connected to had also come free as Brian was being pulled from the water. Contrary to every other witness had reported. Mr. Townsend did not recall if the airline he recalled as being hanging loose had air coming out of it but was certain it was not connected to the helmet. He also contended that the helmet was removed while they were in the basket at water level, contrary to every other witness that reported that they were unable to remove the helmet until Wiitala did so on the deck.

Lt. Com. Tom Beistle: *Mr. Townsend do you remember Mr. Champagne's testimony, Mr. Lehr, Mr. Everett, Mr. Wiitala, as well as the sworn statement from Donnie Henry that the helmet was not taken off, could not be taken off until Wiitala undid the mechanism on the deck of the Cliffs 12?*

Ron Townsend: *I can't reconcile the difference, I just know in my mind when the hat came off.*

Lt. Com. Tom Beistle: *You testified that the hose was not connected to the helmet, did you hear air escaping, was the hose moving?*

Ron Townsend: *No, sir, not that I recall. I was not listening. I was in the basket attempting to get my Pilkington out of the water, There was about a three foot sea and I was knee deep in the water.*

Lt. Com. Tom Beistle: *Let's move on to the regulations. And I'm referring to 46 CFR 197.402. On March 4, 1996 as the designated person in charge, were you fully cognizant of the Subpart B of Title 46CFR 197?*

Ron Townsend: *I would say no.*

Lt. Com. Tom Beistle: *What I'm talking about is Subpart B which is the commercial diving operation regs. What I'm asking you specifically: As the person in charge, were you fully cognizant of the provisions of this Subpart B?*

Ron Townsend: *I would say no, I wasn't fully cognizant.*

Lt. Com. Tom Beistle: *Okay. Secondly, as the person in charge, prior to permitting commercial diving operations to commence, did you have—did you demand or require that the designation of the diving supervisor for the diving operations be presented to you or given to you?*

Ron Townsend: *No, I did not.*

Lt. Com. Tom Beistle: *let me pass the witness, Mr. Walker?*

Joe Walker: *Just a couple of things. In—one thing I'm curious about. You have all these AOD divers on the rig and they had done the cleaning and all the hard work prior to this inspection. You only had about a day of inspection—isn't that correct—about a day job, full day?*

Ron Townsend: *Yeah, give or take.*

Joe Walker: *Did it kind of surprise you that those guys were being sent off the job and you were having to remobilize another group of divers?*

Ron Townsend: *I wouldn't say it surprised me, no, sir. I wouldn't say it surprised me, no.*

Joe Walker: *All right. Would it cost more money to do that?*

Ron Townsend: *I don't know. I don't have that knowledge. I mean, I don't know. I don't know the cost of one crew in relation to the other crew.*

Joe Walker: *How many divers—*

Ron Townsend: *But just out of here, mobilization cost, I'm sure, yes, it would cost more money.*

Joe Walker: *How many divers were on the AOD job before Mr. Austin's group was brought out?*

Ron Townsend: *Clearly numbers, I don't know, but estimate, I would say six or seven.* Joe Walker: *When they came back to finish the inspection job, there were about at least six or seven, weren't there?*

Ron Townsend: *Yes, there was. I think probably six at that point.*

Joe Walker: *So when AOD came back out on the job, they had about twice as many divers as Mr. Austin's group, isn't that correct?*

Ron Townsend: *Yes, that's correct.*

Joe Walker: *You cannot tell us why Kirk's group was brought out on March 4 to replace the AOD divers.*

Ron Townsend: *No, sir, I can only speculate.*

Joe Walker: Why don't you go ahead and speculate?

Ron Townsend: I believe it was for consistency of records. Basically they had tested before in Venezuela for Cliffs, kind of like getting all your eggs in one basket. There's no need to try to use this inspection company, this job and go to a different company on the next. Soon you would have records scattered all over the Gulf of Mexico. We have preferred vendors that we do business with—we have one certain company just for example that inspects our BOPs.

Lt. Com. Tom Beistle: *BOPs?*

Ron Townsend: Blow out preventers, we like to remain consistent so use the same vendors whenever possible.

More questions from the various parties. Questions about the dive equipment American Oil Field Divers had brought out, did they designate a dive supervisor, did they have the proper manuals? All answered as best Mr. Townsend could recall after two and a half years had passed. Mr. Townsend's day as a witness was over and he returned to his seat alongside his lawyer, Bijan Siahatgar

Throughout the hearing Master Chief Brick Bradford was either sitting behind the two representatives from OSHA in the audience or, during the interview of divers, to the right of Lieutenant Commander Beistle. The master chief had been assigned to the hearing to lend technical support to the Coast Guard as the USCG did not have a diver training facility but rather was dependent on the U.S. Navy for support and training. The U.S. Navy had moved diving and diving safety into the twentieth century establishing decompression tables, safety programs and extensive rules and regulations many used as the basis for industry standards. The master chief had assisted in formulating questions from the expert divers point of reference to supplement the legal expertise of the Lieutenant Commander. Now as most of the evidence had been presented, the testimony transcribed, it was the Master Chief's opportunity to share his understanding of the proceedings.

Lt. Com. Tom Beistle: *It is ten minutes past two o'clock on the twenty-fourth. All members who were present before are present now. At the stand is Master Chief Brick Bradford.*

Master Chief, will you please stand to be sworn. Please take a seat.

Lt. Com. Tom Beistle: *Where are you currently assigned?*

Master Chief Brick Bradford: *The Naval Diving and Salvage Training Center in Panama City, Florida.*

Lt. Com. Tom Beistle: *And what do you do there, Master Chief?*

Master Chief Brick Bradford: *I am a master diver assigned to a specialized diving division. I have thirty-eight instructors; we train the explosive ordnance disposal students in diving operations and we train Marine Corps combat divers.*

I enlisted in 1976, and I worked in the fleet for about four and a half years. Then to dive school, the Navy Dive School, in 1980; working as a second-class diver for about three years. I went to first-class diving school which is training conducted to become a diving supervisor. I worked in that capacity until 1990 when I went back for a master diving evaluation. I qualified as a master diver in 1990 and I have been assigned to approximately six commands since that time.

Lt. Com. Tom Beistle: *You said that your original training was—I think you made reference to like a second-class dive school, is that right?*

Master Chief Brick Bradford: *That's right.*

Lt. Com. Tom Beistle: *And what is—what kind of training—what are you qualified to do when you go through a second-class dive course?*

Master Chief Brick Bradford: *You begin by learning physics, diving physics—or physics as they apply to diving, the formulas, diving medicine, physiology. Then you go into the SCUBA phase. Then you go into the lightweight surface-supplied phase.*

Lightweight, the Mark 27 here (indicating) is a—or the SuperLite 27 is an example of lightweight diving equipment. Then you go into deep sea hard hat. And then deep sea in the Mark V as a final phase of training.

Lt. Com. Tom Beistle: *Okay. So how long did you work as a diver before you went back to first-class diver?*

Master Chief Brick Bradford: *Approximately three years.*

Lt. Com. Tom Beistle: *Okay. And what kind of work did you do?*

Master Chief Brick Bradford: *Underwater ship husbandry, some salvage. I—my average bottle time annually consisted of approximately forty-five days during that period.*

Lt. Com. Tom Beistle: *And then you went to first-class dive school? And what did that training consist of?*

Master Chief Brick Bradford: *The initial phase—that training consisted of eighteen weeks. The initial phase consisted of a reinforcement of diving physics, followed again by formulas, into medicine, up to the point where you could plan and—plan your diving operation and then supervise the diving operations. From there we went into salvage, and from salvage we went into mixed gas diving. We reinforce cut—I did not mention cutting and welding in the second-class dive school, but that was part of it. Again, we did cutting and welding in first-class dive school. We did salvage demolition in first-class dive school, and that's pretty much it.*

Lt. Com. Tom Beistle: *Now, I understand from our discussions earlier off the record that essentially one aspect of first-class dive school was that that's where you learned to be, at least, a navy dive supervisor, is that right?*

Master Chief Brick Bradford: *Yes, it is.*

Lt. Com. Tom Beistle: *And so, do you come out as a qualified dive supervisor after first-class dive school?*

Master Chief Brick Bradford: *You come out with the tools to be a diving supervisor. You don't actually qualify as diving supervisor until you go to the command and you learn that system, you learn the operational parameters and the characteristics, you become familiar with the equipment that they use and the type of work being done, and that is a formal qualification process. Once you've completed that process, you normally take an exam, followed by an oral board. And then lastly, there will be an on-station evaluation by the senior supervisor there and you are finally formally qualified by the commanding officer.*

Lt. Com. Tom Beistle: *And so, did you qualify as a dive supervisor?*

Master Chief Brick Bradford: *At every command.*

Lt. Com. Tom Beistle: *Did you have to re-qualify at every command?*

Master Chief Brick Bradford: *Yes, because every command is unique. You'll have different diving systems at each command. You may have a different mission, scope of responsibilities, or diving activities at each command, and therefore you do have to re-qualify.*

Lt. Com. Tom Beistle: *Did you qualify as a dive supervisor on surface-supplied air diving operations?*

Master Chief Brick Bradford: *Surface-supplied air, surface-supplied mixed gas diving, and SCUBA operations, as well as chamber. I didn't mention that either. We also trained in recompression chamber operations.*

Lt. Com. Tom Beistle: *Then you went back to—I think what you called master dive school, is that right?*

Master Chief Brick Bradford: *Master diver evaluation.*

Lt. Com. Tom Beistle: *Master diver evaluation. What was that training about?*

Master Chief Brick Bradford: *That was six weeks of intense hell. It really is an evaluation process. We had four weeks of classroom. Every day was—you were faced with either an oral board or a written exam. There was zero tolerance for failure. In either case, if you failed, you were gone. After the fourth week, you went to sea for an entire week. That was called a free week and during that time you ran one dive a day in each rig available—that was currently used by the navy. And then the following week they flew in master divers and senior diving officers from the fleet and they came in and they evaluated you formally. Again, you dove each rig one day throughout that week and there was—the scenario—it was a structured scenario where you may have guys dying on the bottom, planes crashing, ships sinking, and those types of things, and it was your responsibility to recover successfully without injuring or harming the diver.*

Lt. Com. Tom Beistle: *Folks, I'm going to offer Master Chief Bradford for the limited purpose of being an expert on diving and safe diving. I'm not suggesting that he's a commercial dive expert, but I'm suggesting that he's an extraordinarily knowledgeable person about diving operations.*

Master Chief, you've obviously been up here, everybody has seen you, and you've sat in on these proceedings from the very beginning. I'm just going to ask you some questions about what you've heard. I'm going to ask these just because these are a series of questions. I'm not in any particular order. Don't hesitate to just sort of give us your opinion as long as it's on the point and don't necessarily feel compelled to stick to the question.

Well, these are pretty specific questions. That's okay. Do you think—well, let me start out this way: do you think you've heard enough from the witnesses to give—are you confident enough to be able to give any kind of a cogent discussion about what you feel happened on the fourth of March on the Cliffs 12?

Master Chief Brick Bradford: *I do.*

Lt. Com. Tom Beistle: *Okay. Getting back to what you heard, can you give us just a general overview of the most important parts of what you've noted, using the dive manual if you need to?*

Master Chief Brick Bradford: *I can. I would like to begin by citing the responsibilities of the diving supervisor and standby diver.*

"The diving supervisor is in charge of the actual diving operation for a particular dive or series of dives. No diving operations shall be conducted without the presence of a Diving Supervisor."

"The diving supervisor must consider all possible contingencies, determine equipment requirements, recommend diving assignments, and establish backup requirements for the operation. The diving supervisor shall be familiar with all divers on the team and be able to evaluate the qualifications and physical fitness of the divers selected for a particular job. The diving supervisor inspects all equipment and conducts predive briefings of the personnel. While the operation is under way, the diving supervisor monitors progress."

"The diving supervisor must verify the fitness of each diver immediately before a dive. Any symptoms such as cough, nasal congestion, apparent fatigue, emotional stress, inner ear infection is reason for placing the diver on the binnacle list until

the problem is corrected. A diver, for any reason, does not want to make a dive, should not be forced."

The standby diver: "A standby diver with a tender is required for all diving operations but must have equivalent depth and operational capabilities."

What I'm saying there is. The diver's umbilical must be as long or longer than the diver's umbilical so they can at least get out as far as that diver to rescue them, and they must have the same air supply requirements and the same depth characteristics as the rig being employed for the evolution progress.

"A standby diver is a fully qualified diver assigned for backup or to provide emergency assistance and is ready to enter the water immediately. For surface-supplied diving operations the standby diver must be dressed to the following points:

"In the Mark 21 or SuperLite 17, he will have the strain relief attached to his harness"—and that's attaching the umbilical to the harness with the neck dam on his head.

"The standby diver receives the same briefings and instruction as the working diver." And "the standby diver is to monitor the progress of the dive and be fully prepared to respond if called upon for assistance."

I have the manning requirements by the navy. For putting one surface-supplied diver in the water, the navy requires that you have six as a minimum.

Lt. Com. Tom Beistle: *What would those rules be, six?*

Master Chief Brick Bradford: *Yes, sir, at a minimum six people each qualified for their specific assignment.*

Lt. Com. Tom Beistle: *I understand that Mr. Austin, if I remember correctly, testified that he did take the YMCA SCUBA course and then he, if I remember correctly, said that he had had about five or six excursions as a commercial diver, hard hat diver. In your estimation, based on that, do you think that qualifies a person to be a dive supervisor?*

Master Chief Brick Bradford: *No, I do not.*

Lt. Com. Tom Beistle: *Why not?*

Master Chief Brick Bradford: *And I would like to expand and say I don't believe that qualifies you to be a commercial diver either. The issue of a commercial diver, first: He has no formal training in the rig that he's using. He knows nothing of the operational—it's possible that he knows nothing of the operational characteristics of the equipment, how to maintain that equipment, how to set that equipment up for use, how to properly use that equipment, how to recover from a possible emergency relating to that equipment. If he's doing—and it's obvious surface-supplied diving is the intended purpose of the SuperLite 27, may not be familiar with decompression procedures and those kind of things.*

Lt. Com. Tom Beistle: *Okay. Let's go to Mr. Wiitala. You've heard his testimony. Do you think Mr. Wiitala was qualified to be a dive supervisor?*

Master Chief Brick Bradford: *I do not. And if I may—I'll use myself as an example. I told you I graduated from second-class diving school and that annually I logged approximately forty-five days on the bottom doing a variety of tasks over a three-year period. At that point in time, had I been asked to supervise a job, a diving job, I would have supervised a job, but it was not until I went to first-class diving school to specifically qualify as diving supervisor that I became aware of the responsibility involved in supervising a diving evolution. And, therefore, I would have been operating out of ignorance because I was not formally qualified or trained.*

We've had three commercial divers who claimed to be dive supervisors testify here over the past three days. There was a question asked of all three: If they knew what the minimum manifold pressure was—the requirements were for the depth of the dive and for the equipment being used. And nobody knew, or at least could answer the question correctly. Mr. Wiitala answered 75 psi, Mr. Lawdermilk answered 115 and Mr. Gilbert answered 60 psi. If we look at the manual for the Kirby Morgan Superlight. The manufacturer requires 115 psi over bottom pressure for the helmet to properly ventilate . . . it would take 128 pounds of pressure, air pressure, at the 28 feet that everybody agrees that Brian Pilkington was working, just to—just to get—just to make the helmet function properly. Just to give him the air that he needed to exist. 128 psi to prevent CO_2 poisoning from occurring.

Through training and experience diving supervisors and divers alike learn to handle a wide range of actual and potential emergency situations. They must be able to separate the important from the trivial, while recognizing that a seemingly minor symptom or event may foreshadow an emergency. They must be able to identify or react appropriately to the warning signals of various physiological disorders affecting either themselves or other divers. They must have a working knowledge of the most effective methods for handling physical emergencies, such as diver entrapment or equipment malfunction, as well as the basic knowledge of the correct steps to take in treating medical emergencies. Most importantly, they must be able to handle an emergency while under emotional and physical stress. To answer your question was Mr. Wiitala qualified to be a dive supervisor. No

Lt. Com. Tom Beistle: *Great answer but it raised kind of an interesting point for me. You heard Mr. Wiitala's testimony here about his interaction with Brian. One of the things that's kind of pinged on me or triggered my interest ever since he discussed this, was the fact that he had to tell Brian at least three—or felt compelled to tell Brian at least three times, I think, perhaps more, to shut down his free flow valve because, according to Mr. Wiitala, the pressure—the compressor pressure was falling and he attributed that to the free flow valve being open. And, in point of fact, as I understand it, every time Brian did shut down his free flow valve, apparently the pressure went back up. Is there anything about that situation that you would deem to be something that would alert you if you were out on a dive or supervising a dive?*

Master Chief Brick Bradford: *Absolutely. You're looking at a gauge, and the gauge is dropping substantially below the minimum ample requirements. Therefore, that is immediate cause for aborting a dive and returning the diver to the surface. I would, prior to that or in the process, an immediate action would include shifting to my secondary air source and isolating the primary bank or the primary air source. The problem here is Mr. Wiitala apparently was working with the belief that 80 or 90 psi was adequate. Mr. Pilkington was slowly being poisoned by an inadequate air supply system and the ignorance of his tender.*

Lt. Com. Tom Beistle: *So you've got a period—you've got a period of three hours that he's down there, which indicates that either something happened conceivably catastrophically in the last few minutes or something happened over a period of the entire three hours. Can you sort of give me what the scenario would be if it played out over that three-hour period?*

Master Chief Brick Bradford: *It's hard for me to conceptualize any scenario that would have allowed the umbilical to discontent. The fact that it was secured at the harness, the diver would literally have to do 360-degree maneuvers to unthread the umbilical; I just don't see that as reasonable. I think that this would be more related to the compressor efficiency and the minimum manifold requirements—again this is a demand rig with no dead air space. You inspire, the body metabolizes it, you expire and you wash out all of the metabolic wastes, which is your CO_2 by product of respiration, if you are getting marginal performance or less than designed performance, you will get a going to begin building up a CO_2 debt and that's, that will cause a chronic fatigue. Was there a catastrophic failure at the end of the dive there is no way to know as the evidence was destroyed. But that would have*

401

been secondary; once the dive supervisor, had there been one, realized there was a problem he should have switched to a secondary air supply and aborted the dive. That should have been done at the first indication.

Lt. Com. Tom Beistle: *Can you tell me what the symptoms of CO_2 poisoning are?*

Master Chief Brick Bradford*: Confusion, inability to concentrate, drowsiness, loss of consciences, convulsions as well as a slightly euphoric feeling.*

The master chief would continue to explain the need to follow checklists, the need for redundant equipment, standby divers, bail-out bottles, training standards for both divers and supervisors. He would go on to comment that two of the dive supervisors that had testified if they did not have a piece of equipment *"You would have to suck it up and get the job done"* and how that attitude can lead to complacency.

The other parties in interest in turn would ask questions of the master chief proposing scenarios that would absolve their individual clients of any wrong doing, or cast a negative light on the need for tougher navy-style regulations that could provide noting more than an economic burden.

To that end Mr. Hope asked. *Now you told us that you would check the checklist on compressor maintenance while preparing for a dive operation. What the next thing you would do?*

Master Chief Brick Bradford: *I'd go about doing—perform the procedures, the predive procedures outlined in the maintenance package—*

Mr. Hope: *Tell me what you would do without looking at your book.*

Master Chief Brick Bradford: *Well, there you go, sir, the fundamental flaw. I would not proceed without having a checklist in hand.*

With that Master Chief Bradford was thanked by the court for his expert assistance and released. As he stood to shake the lieutenant commanders hand he turned to the audience and said.

I want to just bring something out. The rescue divers that jumped in the water, jumped in the water breathing 100 percent oxygen—and that is—and that is most significant in that that, in itself, I am—I am surprised that we're not sitting here talking about two fatalities because 100 percent oxygen at twenty-eight feet of water in a nervous, panicked, excited state would most likely cause central nervous system oxygen toxicity and would have put this man into immediate convulsions to which he most likely would not have recovered from. And I think that that was a very heroic attempt. He may not even realize the implications of it, but I wanted to make that—I wanted to make that known.

After a short recess Lieutenant Commander Beistle returned to his seat at the head of the court.

It's was now ten minutes to five on the third day of what was originally planned to be a one day hearing. We had received testimony from three of the Parties in Interest, diving experts, an equipment supplier, a U.S. Coast Guard inspector, the safety manager for Cliffs Drilling, a United States Navy seal and fact witnesses. All had been called by the court or at the request of those of us representing the one man that was not capable of being there to defending himself. There were now two men left to testify, the next would be called at the request of Bijan Siahatgar.

Lieutenant Commander Beistle looked up from his ever expanding stack of exhibits and began. *Okay as we discussed in our preliminary meeting, Mr. Dennis Jahde, who is present now has been called by Mr. Siahatgar, So I am going to let Mr. Siahatgar direct the witness and then I will ask a few questions. So, Mr. Jahde, if you would please take the stand and be sworn in.*

Bijan Siahatgar would start by asking questions qualifying Mr. Jahde as a long-time, well-qualified expert in the commercial diving industry. A man who after his service in the navy attended college earning a degree in marine diving technology followed by employment as a commercial diver, working his way from tender to operations manager for a multinational diving company. After authoring one of the first commercial dive safety manuals Mr. Jahde while continuing as an officer of a diving company also served as chairman of the Association of Diving Contractors Safety, Medical, and Education Committee. And it was during his time, while serving as a director of the ADC, in the mid to late 1980s that much of the ADC's Consensus Standard was written. The same Consensus Standard that remains in effect today. Once Mr. Jahde was duly shown to be knowledgeable in the field of diving safety, Bijan Siahatgar started his questioning. *One thing of note on your résumé here is that you led the efforts to increase industry manning requirements for shallow water diving, can you tell us a little bit about that?*

Mr. Jahde: *The industry standards at the particular time, especially in water depths less than sixty feet, was one diver and one tender, shallow water system. All the major diving companies and especially the small diving companies engaged in using a single diver and single tender offshore. I myself as a diver was in—through many occasions—was offshore in that capacity. I didn't feel like if you got hung up that the tender could do a whole lot of good regardless of whether you're in thirty feet of water or three hundred feet of water. The manning requirements needed to be increased. So as the chairman of the Safety, Medical, and Education Committee, I crusaded to increase the manning requirements for shallow water diving, even though you can interpret the Coast Guard regulation and get by with Coast Guard and OSHA regulations with one diver and one tender, I felt like it was not an adequate approved manning requirement. I preferred two divers and two tenders, but we ended up compromising on two divers and one tender to a minimum crew.*

Bijan Siahatgar: *You mentioned the Coast Guard diving regulations. Are you familiar with what their general requirements are?*

Mr. Jahde: *Any diving that takes place in less than 130 feet of water, any diving that has no compression element to it, and I believe the diving has to have—it can't be in a restricted area. It can't be diving inside of a tube or something like that.*

Bijan Siahatgar: *Now, the dive that Brian Pilkington's fatality took place on was what would be considered a shallow dive.*

Mr. Jahde: *Yes, it would.*

Bijan Siahatgar: *And I would like to go through a list of things that the Coast Guard regulations, as they presently stand, do not require for this type of dive, First of all, for a shallow dive, the type that Brian was performing, is a standby diver required by the Coast Guard regulations?*

Mr. Jahde: *No, it is not.*

Bijan Siahatgar: *Is a bail-out bottle required by the Coast Guard regulations?*

Mr. Jahde: *No, it is not.*

Bijan Siahatgar: *Is there a requirement even for a second dive hose per the Coast Guard regulations.*

Mr. Jahde: *No, there is not.*

Bijan Siahatgar: *Is there any limitation on the dive supervisor's ability to perform more than one job under the Coast Guard regulations as they presently stand?*

Mr. Jahde: *No, there is not.*

Bijan Siahatgar: *And I guess that goes back to what you're saying, that even under the present Coast Guard regulations, you can interpret it to mean that you can still have a two-men dive crew for a dive up to 130 feet, assuming you were staying away from the decompression tables?*

Mr. Jahde: *That's correct.*

Bijan Siahatgar: *Is there any requirement for a written report to the person in charge on a vessel for a shallow dive?*

Mr. Jahde: *There's a requirement for a report, but it doesn't specify that it needs to be written.*

Bijan Siahatgar: *Is there a requirement for a secondary air supply?*

Mr. Jahde: *No, there is not.*

Bijan Siahatgar: *How about as a diver under the Coast Guard regulations?*

Mr. Jahde: *Well, because they don't mention any kind of experience requirements or training requirements or aptitudes, then, yes, he would qualify as a diver, as well.*

Bijan Siahatgar: *How about a dive supervisor? Would he qualify as a dive supervisor under the Coast Guard regulations?*

Bijan Siahatgar: *There's been some talk today about certified divers. There's no such thing as a certified diver in the United States, is there?*

Mr. Jahde: *There is no such thing as a certified commercial diver. There's certified recreational divers.*

Mr. Jahde: *There's a requirement to have records. It doesn't require you to bring them out with you to the job site.*

Lieutenant Commander Beistle: *Are you talking specifically about the air-testing, quality-testing records?*

Bijan Siahatgar: *I'm talking about any piece of equipment out there, whether it was a compressor, whether a hose, or anything else.*

Bijan Siahatgar: *And that's the question I want to ask. As we go back to these Coast Guard regulations—and what I'm hearing is that there's a problem because you've got the regulations, which kind of set a minimum standard and they're somewhat vague and then you have the diving companies trying to figure out, well, if you're a bigger company, you know, there's kind of a problem because you may have a small company trying to just interpret those standards as tight as they can and the bigger company has a hard time competing on the same job—is that correct?*

Mr. Jahde: *Yes.*

Bijan Siahatgar: *And you would like to see a four-men—a minimum four-man crew, wouldn't you?*

Mr. Jahde: *Personally, yes.*

Bijan Siahatgar: *And, in fact, you think that these regulations should be changed and the diving industry would benefit if they had a four-men crew, don't you?*

Mr. Jahde: *I think there's things in these regulations that could be a lot clearer, and yes, I think there's some things that need to be changed.*

Bijan Siahatgar would continue to question his own expert witness verifying that his clients, Cliffs Drilling in the civil suit and today Ronald Townsend, were working within established regulations. And at the same time driving home the purpose of this whole exercise we, those representing Brian Pilkington and all the other men that make their living at the end of a hose, had come to Texas to reveal. The existing regulations needed reform. The existing regulations need to be enforced. Mr. Jahde demonstrated his own frustration with the association that he could not get the industry to support more stringent regulation. Regulations so vague and filled with loopholes they were all but unenforceable.

To put a final exclamation point on Mr. Jahde's testimony, Mr. Joe Walker asked the last question. *You would like to see a four man—a minimum four man crew, wouldn't you?*

Mr. Jahde: *A personally, yes.*

Joe Walker: *And in fact, you think these regulations should be changed and the diving industry would benefit if they had a four-men crew, don't you?*

Mr. Jahde: *I think there's many things in the regulations that could be a lot clearer, and yes, I think there is a need for change.*

The questioning of Mr. Jahde would continue until each of the parties was satisfied. After that the former director of the ADC safety committee was excused with the thanks of the court.

One final witness before adjourning. The current executive director of the Association of Diving Contractors. Dr. Saxon would be quizzed; on the purpose of the ADC, his involvement with Dan Gilbert, the need for new standard, the application of the existing standards. Dr. Saxon would go on the record, agreeing that there needed to be tougher regulations, the ADC was committed to see that it would come to pass, but cautioned that it was a long and laborious process that he had been working at for years. And then there was the issue of establishing a consensus, getting all the members to agree.

Bijan Siahatgar had suggested in the preliminary phone conference that there was not much that Ross Saxon could add to the investigation. As it would become evident, Bijan was correct. The man with the mail order degrees and the title of executive director of the Association of Diving Contractors brought little of value. His questioning went quickly, and he was excused with the thanks of the court.

One more request was made for any evidence Danny Gilbert could produce to verify that he had ever purchased an air filter for any compressor he owned. Nothing was presented.

Lieutenant Commander Beistle explained that all the parties would have an opportunity to submit their individual summaries for his review. He would be reviewing the testimony, exhibits, and any information the party in interest would like to submit to supplement the record or add as their personal finding of facts, conclusions, and recommendations.

With that Lt. commander Thomas Beistle concluded: *Thank you for your participation and assistance. Let the record* reflect that this hearing is adjourned, taking the foregoing conversation into account at 8:15 on 24 June 1999. Thank you all very, very much.

Chapter 21

FINDINGS IN FACT

Bellevue, Washington
May 4, 2001

It would have been Brian's twenty-ninth birthday on this first Friday of May 2001. The formal investigation into his death and the need for new regulation had concluded twenty-three months before. There was no final report, the proposed rule making into the revisions to the Federal code of Regulations was at an impasse. I had done everything my resources would allow. On the way home from work the sunny spring day, I stopped to place flowers alongside the ones brought by others earlier in the day to that small plot of land overlooking the city. Someone else had placed a small red car with chrome wheels. There was a freshly potted plant and someone had trimmed away the grass and wiped the polished granite marker. I paused a few moments to read the inscriptions that had been carved in the stone five years before and thought of that promise I had made that had never been fulfilled.

I do not remember the rest of the journey home that afternoon, but as I pulled in the driveway, there was a white car with official plates already there. Sitting on the front steps to the house was a man dressed in the blue uniform of a United States Coast Guard Captain. I slowly pulled next to the car already there taking a moment to compose myself before leaving the safety of my truck.

With an out stretched hand the man that had moments before been sitting on the step approached and introduced himself. *I'm John Veentjer, the Commandant has asked that I personally deliver this letter along with the United States Coast Guard's final findings of facts into the incident aboard the Cliffs 12. Perhaps we could go somewhere, get a cup of coffee or something. I would like to review the report with you. Answer any questions. Most importantly I would like to thank you for your persistence in all of this.* All said while handing me an official looking ten-inch-by-fourteen-inch white envelope with one hand and shaking my hand with the other.

He directed me to the passenger's seat of his car as I carefully opened this so long awaited document. As the captain drove I read. There was a cover letter signed by Admiral James M. Loy, Commandant.[VII] Then seventy-five pages of findings.[VIII] A far cry from the original four pages of neatly filled-out forms that had been the marine casualty report sent to me by fax four years before.

The captain drove as I read through the recommendations.

1. Require bail-out bottles for all commercial diving operations.
2. Require a backup air supply system for all commercial dives
3. Require a standby diver dressed out and at the ready
4. Require increased manning for all commercial dives
5. Require site specific rescue plans
6. Require Hazard Analysis plans
7. Require diving stages at the water entry point
8. Require pre dive checklists
9. Change the USCG regulations to hold diving contractors accountable
10. Change the reference from "The diving supervisor shall ensure" to "The diving contractor shall ensure" throughout the CFR
11. Require that the master or designated person in charge review diving plans.
12. Require that the revised CFR define a dive tender including the words "the person tending the diver shall have no other duties while the diver is under the water."
13. Require a diver certification program
14. Require a diving supervisor certification program
15. Require that the revised CFR define a diver
16. Require log books
17. Require operations manuals be on site and include maintenance records
18. Require operations manuals be on site and include compressor air quality reports
19. Require that the diving contractor maintain testing records for a period of not less than three years
20. Require that the Dive Supervisor and the Master or person in Charge execute a declaration of Inspection prior to the beginning of the dive evolution.
21. Require that USCG not designate dive safety enforcement to any classification society.

22. Require that dive casualty investigations be conducted by trained marine safety inspectors
23. Require that Coast Guard divers assist in any dive related fatality investigation
24. Require that the Coast Guard seek an agreement with the U.S. Navy experimental diving unit to provide assistance in all diving casualty investigations

The list of suggested revisions to the existing Federal Code of Regulations continued for six carefully thought out pages. Lieutenant Commander Beistle truly had taken the plight of the commercial diver to task and as he had told me before the formal investigation he "would do the right thing."

By the time we reached the coffee shop the recommendations had been read. I continued to read the findings in fact as the captain ordered the coffee.

Some of the most interesting findings were the admission that, clearly, the commercial diving regulations were not followed or enforced. Many people failed in their responsibilities, including the senior Coast Guard inspector.

The senior inspector I had to assume referred to the Lieutenant that had authorized the ill fated inspection in violation of the Coast Guard's own established policies. This was the same inspector who was unable to attend the Formal Investigation and for reasons unknown was unable to remember being on the Cliffs 12 on March 4. Even though official Coast Guard reports showed he was there as did on site witnesses. The question still remained was the Lieutenant ignorant of the regulations he was there to enforce, or did he have some other motive to push through the inspection and issue a certificate of inspection?

The captain and I sat and reviewed the entirety of the document. He commented that the investigator, Lieutenant Commander Beistle, gave little weight to Wiitala's testimony and clearly, through Wiitala's actions, he knew that the compressor had catastrophically failed. Why else would he have turned on the backup air supply. Why turn on backup air if the hose had come undone? Wiitala was the only person who testified that he heard Brian say the fitting was loose. Why would Wiitala have not attempted to hook the oxygen acetylene hoses to the air rack? Surely as a trained, educated diver he had to know that breathing pure oxygen at depth can be fatal. That coupled with the lack of urgency, there never was a rescue attempt it, was a recovery attempt.

I told the captain of my interviews with Wiitala and Lawdermilk. Wiitala knew the compressor had failed; he had admitted that to Lawdermilk the night of the incident, and he would not deny it when I asked him. Lawdermilk knew the compressor would not turn a single revolution, the belts connecting it to the engine had burned and were broken. Guy Kirby also knew that. One would not testify to it; the other could not be found. The Coast Guard had lost custody of the compressor and had to dance around the compressor issue as a result. The entirety of the investigation would not had been necessary had that compressor only been held as evidence.

The report went on to recommend that Lt. Julio Martinez be investigated, and that Danny Gilbert be charged with manslaughter. But most importantly to me, the report exonerated Brian of any culpability in his own death; any culpability other than being twenty-three years old and like most young men believing it would never happen to me.

Most importantly to the men that make a living at the end of a hose, if the recommendations contained within the body of the report were included in the revised Federal Code of Regulations, and if they were enforced, there would be a new safer underwater work place. A new professionalism.

I had made a commitment five years before in eulogy to find a way to prevent this from happening to another. I thanked the captain for the coffee, for bring me the report, for spending the time to review and for his insight as we returned to his car and the ride home knowing that I had done what I needed to do but not alone.

Joe Walker, Tom Mosele, and I had entered that formal investigation, now almost two years before, with two goals: present an argument that the existing Federal Regulations as they pertain to underwater construction and inspection work were out-of-date and in need of revision and argue that with vivid examples of what could happen, what did happen—all within the letter of the current regulation and clear the name of the man who was no longer capable of defending himself. The report cleared his name. Now all that was left was to have the commandant's recommendations contained in this final report included within the regulatory reform.

The captain dropped me off in front of the house. I thanked him for the coffee, the review and for the document that validated our efforts. He promised to keep in touch and let me know how the proposed rule making was progressing. After he left, I returned to my truck and headed back to that little plot of land overlooking the city. There I read the report one more time; this time allowed, this time for that boy who years ago had climbed atop a box of onions and stood watch as those men of authority that surrounded him ignored his council. Perhaps this time they will pay attention.

For Brian.

Epilogue

In the United States today, under existing United States Coast Guard regulations, there is no requirement for backup divers for commercial diving in less than 130 feet of water.

Under existing United States Coast Guard regulations, there is no requirement for backup breathing gas supplies for commercial diving in less than 130 feet of water.

Under existing United States Coast Guard regulations, there is no requirement for backup equipment for commercial diving in less than 130 feet of water.

Under existing United States Coast Guard regulations, there is no requirement for the testing of skills, or knowledge, or for ability for commercial divers.

Under United States Coast Guard regulations, there is no requirement for the licensing or testing for competency for commercial diving supervisors.

The Federal Code of Regulations, as they pertain to underwater construction work done under United States Coast Guard, remain unchanged since they were conceived in 1972.

The proposed rule-making procedures as they pertain to commercial diving are still under review.

A commercial diver is still forty times more likely to die at work than all other employees.

G&G Marine continues doing business as a diving contractor, was never reinstated as a member of the Association of Diving Contractors, and was never able to produce any evidence that they had ever purchased an air filter to any of the compressors they were utilizing for breathing gas supply; nor were they ever capable of providing any evidence that they have conducted the required air quality testing.

Danny Gilbert, despite admitting he was utilizing noncompliant life-support equipment from 1992 to 1999, was never cited nor was the recommendation that he be charged with manslaughter ever followed up.

Judge John Borne continued to refuse to change the cause of death from an accidental drowning despite a blood gas report found in the Judge's own file showing that Brian Pilkington's blood had a lethal level of carbon MONOXIDE in his system at the time of death.

Joe Walker and Tom Mosele continue to fight for the rights of the commercial diver.

Appendix

ɪ. **TROUBLED WATERS**

Since losing a son in a diving accident, Peter Pilkington has been crusading to spare others his family's anguish. He won a settlement, but wants more: Tougher regulations

RICHARD STEWART, Houston Chronicle East Texas Bureau Staff
SUN 02/01/1998 Houston Chronicle, Section State, Page 1, 2 STAR Edition

BEAUMONT—It was already past dark in the Seattle suburb of Bellevue as Peter Pilkington drove his 9-year-old daughter home from dance class on that Monday almost two years ago.

The little girl grew quiet and then made an odd announcement, particularly for someone who was growing up with two older brothers and a father who all scuba dived, a little girl who could swim like a fish herself.

"I don't ever want to go under the water again," said young Afton. "It's cold and it's dark and you can die down there."

At that moment, Pilkington's oldest child, 23-year-old Brian, was across the country following his dream of working as a commercial diver. Unknown to his father, he was in the cold, dark water of the Gulf of Mexico at a drilling rig 10 miles southeast of Sabine Pass.

And he was dying.

After spending thousands of dollars of his own money and virtually abandoning his home construction business on a crusade to spare other families his anguish, Peter

Pilkington earned a little satisfaction three weeks ago with a multimillion-dollar settlement of a lawsuit he filed on behalf of his daughter-in-law.

But he wants much more. Pilkington has trekked back and forth from Washington to Texas, written letters to the president and congressmen and pounded on the doors of regulatory agencies in a drive to make conditions safer for divers who work in the busy offshore petroleum industry.

He's seeking industry wide standards that would require every commercial diver to be certified to ensure that he has the training and experience needed to do the job at hand. He wants backup divers ready to help out the instant any diver gets into trouble. And he wants tougher standards to ensure the equipment divers use is safe.

Such improvements, Pilkington is convinced, would have saved his son.

Brian Pilkington moved to Texas to follow his dream. Ever since he'd learned to swim in the Indian Ocean as a youngster while his family was living in the United Arab Emirates, he had loved diving. He, his father and his younger brother, Jamie, had been frequent recreational diving companions. After high school he had gone to commercial diving school and was certified as a commercial diver. He then headed for the Gulf Coast to learn the trade.

In New Orleans, he married his high school sweetheart and the couple moved to Houston, where Pilkington worked primarily as a backup diver, building up experience before moving to more difficult jobs and maybe someday owning his own company.

He had about two years under his belt on the day he died, March 6, 1996. He wound up the lead diver instead of a backup, however, when not enough qualified divers had shown up.

So he was asked to slip into the murky waters alone to inspect the three legs of an offshore drilling rig called Cliffs Number 12. The rig, owned by Houston-based Cliffs Drilling Co., had been "stacked"—sitting unused—near the mouth of the Sabine River, but had been moved about 10 miles offshore so it could be surveyed before being put back into service.

Brian was about 28 feet under, using a helmet and air supplied from above. After three hours under water, with less than 20 minutes to go, those on deck realized he was in trouble.

Talking to the people on deck via a connection that was part of his tether to the rig, he said he was experiencing a loss of air pressure. A diver at the scene told U.S. Coast Guard investigators that those on deck thought the pressure loss was from a blower used to keep fog off the inside of the helmet.

According to the Coast Guard's report on the incident, Pilkington "reported he heard the sound of air escaping, and realized his air line connection to his dive helmet was loose." He told a diver on the deck that he had forgotten to properly tighten his air line to the dive helmet before the dive.

"That caused Pilkington to start to panic," the report says.

Divers Dan Wiitala and Kirk Austin told investigators they tried to pull Pilkington out of the water, but found he was stuck. A hatchet attached to him by a lanyard had gotten entangled in the rig structure. In his panic, Pilkington didn't cut the lanyard or release himself from the harness that was holding him under.

"Attempts to rescue Pilkington were delayed by 15 or 20 minutes due to the lack of standby equipment being readily available," the report states. "While dive industry safety standards specify the need for standby safety equipment, specific standby equipment is not required by regulation for surface-supplied air dives to depths less than 130 feet."

The two other divers on deck didn't have air lines to allow them to reach the man trapped below. They didn't have scuba gear. They tried fashioning a makeshift air line from hoses used for welding. Finally, one of the divers simply held his breath and went to try to free Pilkington.

"After about 10 more minutes, and three unsuccessful dive attempts by Austin, Wiitala stated he dove to Pilkington, and found him floating motionless, face down in a near horizontal position, with the hatchet stuck underneath a pipe," the report says.

Wiitala cut the lanyard and pulled Pilkington to the surface. He was hoisted up to the deck. A worker there said in a deposition that Pilkington's face and feet looked blue. Workers started resuscitation and within 10 minutes a helicopter arrived to take him to the hospital.

Back in Bellevue, Wash., the Pilkingtons were just sitting down to dinner when they got news of the accident. Brian was being taken by helicopter to a Port Arthur hospital.

"I got on the phone to the hospital and was on the phone with them until he died," Peter Pilkington said. His son had never regained consciousness. Doctors had put him on a respirator, but he died that night.

Wiitala later told investigators that Pilkington's helmet was a quarter filled with water when he reached him, although air was still coming out of the helmet's exhaust ports.

"It is likely that Pilkington inhaled the water in his panic while breathing rapidly," the Coast Guard report says. "It is possible the water entered Pilkington's helmet through a combination of lower air pressure in the helmet due to the loose air line connection, and Pilkington's actions once he became panicked."

But Peter Pilkington discounts the idea that the air line was loose. The problem, he contends, was with the air compressor.

There were allegations by a former equipment shop manager for G&G Marine, Pilkington's employer at the time, that the air compressor would not hold air pressure, according to the Coast Guard report.

Peter Pilkington contends that because not enough air was reaching his son, he began to breathe his own carbon dioxide and gradually became disoriented.

A medical expert he hired conducted tests on a diver simulating the reported air pressure and other conditions—though without a loose helmet connection. That diver became confused and passed out, too, Pilkington said.

But Lt. Casey Plagge, the Coast Guard officer who completed the investigation, said Coast Guard dive experts told him divers are trained to notice the warning signs of carbon dioxide problems or contaminated air. "You'll taste it," he said.

Like pilots, who are trained to act on instinct the moment anything goes wrong, the young diver should have known what to do, he said. The standard procedure was to simply slip out of his diving harness and climb the umbilical to the surface.

In any case, the air compressor was never tested by Coast Guard investigators. After the fatal incident, G&G Marine sent the machine to a repair facility, where it was dismantled after a checkup revealed it needed a costly overhaul.

"No further examination was conducted," the Coast Guard report states.

Peter Pilkington contends the Coast Guard should have treated the scene much like police at the location of a crime, carefully protecting evidence for future investigation. But the Coast Guard never considered the area a crime scene, Plagge said.

"We considered it an accident scene," he said.

Two Coast Guardsmen had been on Cliffs Number 12 the day of the incident, but left before the dive started, Plagge said. They were observing the overall survey, not the diving, Plagge said. Neither noticed, or particularly looked for, violations of safety standards associated with the dive.

The Coast Guard report found that G&G Marine failed to maintain a dive log book or provide an operations manual for the dive that day or designate a diving supervisor. Plagge said the company was fined $1,500 in a civil penalty.

Dan Gilbert, operator of G&G Marine, could not be reached for comment for this article. Kirk Austin, who operated a diving subcontractor called Texas NDE Technologies Inc., declared bankruptcy before the lawsuit settlement and also could not be reached. Officials of Cliffs Drilling did not return telephone calls about the case.

All three companies, as well as Gilbert, Austin and the American Bureau of Shipping, a nonprofit organization that certifies vessels, were defendants in the lawsuit.

Under the terms of the settlement, none of the defendants acknowledged negligence or responsibility. The exact amount of money paid to Brian Pilkington's widow, Julie, was not revealed.

The Coast Guard and the U.S. Occupational Safety and Health Administration have separate, though similar, regulations covering dive operations. But Peter Pilkington contends neither set of rules goes far enough and he believes the rules should be standardized by the two agencies.

Under an agreement between OSHA and the Coast Guard, the Coast Guard enforces its regulations at sea and OSHA has jurisdiction over inland operations. As one OSHA official said, "We don't have boats."

Pilkington wants a uniform method of certifying divers. OSHA regulations call for a minimum level of competence, for example, but the Coast Guard doesn't. Pilkington contends that associations of commercial divers could issue proper credentials showing that divers are trained and proficient enough to do certain kinds of dives. At least, he argues, his relatively inexperienced son should not have been the lead diver the day he died.

Under current regulations, supervisors in charge of dives such as the one in which Brian Pilkington are not required to be divers themselves or be ready to go into the water to save a diver who is in trouble.

Pilkington wants a requirement in both OSHA and Coast Guard regulations that would require a standby diver who is suited up and capable of entering the water in a timely manner during all dives.

Dissatisfied with the Coast Guard investigation, he also is seeking the ability to appeal to another investigating agency. Currently, the Coast Guard is the only agency that investigates fatal accidents at sea.

Plagge said he understands how Pilkington could be upset about the death of his son, but said Coast Guard officers did a good investigation. Although commercial dive operations are common on the many offshore platforms and vessels along the Texas-Louisiana coast, Brian Pilkington's death is the only commercial dive fatality he has investigated in two years of being stationed at Port Arthur, Plagge said.

Pilkington is asking the Coast Guard's district office in New Orleans to review the investigation. He's also asking his home state's two U.S. senators and his congresswoman, U.S. Rep. Jennifer Dunn, R-Washington, to push for tougher regulations. He is at work on a book about his son, the accident and his efforts to get the regulations changed.

Finally, he is planning to start scuba diving again. His wife, Karen, had urged him not to dive after the accident, but Pilkington said he has been an avid and safe diver for more than 30 years and he thinks his son would have wanted him to continue.

II. ABS IS FIRST TO RECEIVE
USCG ISM AUTHORIZATION
FEBRUARY 9, 1998

ABS is the first classification society to receive formal authorization from the U.S. Coast Guard to issue International Safety Management (ISM) Code Safety Management Certificates and Documents of Compliance on behalf of the government agency. "This acknowledgment of the professionalism and expertise of ABS by the Coast Guard builds upon the long standing relationship which has been fostered between our two organizations," says Robert D. Somerville, president of ABS. "It is indicative of the trust the U.S. Government places in the services we have provided as their statutory agent, and is a validation of the quality system to which ABS itself adheres." The new responsibilities which have been accorded ABS are in addition to those contained in the 1995 joint Memorandum of Understanding relative to SOLAS and other statutory responsibilities entrusted to ABS. The new authorization is valid for a period of five years.

When necessary, Coast Guard observers may accompany exclusive ABS auditors conducting audits of either a vessel or a company. However, evidence of the seriousness which the U.S. Government agency has attached to the proper implementation of the ISM Code, is the specific provision within the agreement that no certificates are to be issued to companies which in any way impede the participation of the Coast Guard observers. In the same vein, the delegation of authority to ABS also carries a clear requirement that the classification society promptly report to the Coast Guard the discovery of "any deficiency that directly or indirectly affects the validity of any aspect of any certificate issued by another classification society." "ABS applauds the commitment the U.S. Coast Guard has made to the creation of a culture of compliance within maritime safety," says Somerville. "We take this delegation of authority very seriously indeed. When an ABS surveyor attends a ship while acting as the representative of the U.S. Government, he will use the full range of his professional skill and judgment in assessing the manner in which that vessel meets the relevant statutory regulations.

"We believe that the ISM Code is a major step towards meeting the goal of a safety compliant industry. We are pleased to partner the Coast Guard on this issue as we firmly believe that the safety of life, property, and the protection of the marine environment will be enhanced through adherence to the spirit and provisions of the ISM Code."

III. ABS APPROVED FOR MODU INSPECTION
ALTERNATIVE COMPLIANCE PROGRAM
CERTIFICATION
SEPTEMBER 11, 1998

In a major development underscoring the success of the Alternative Compliance Program (ACP), the U.S. Coast Guard has extended the authorization given to ABS to include mobile offshore drilling units (MODUs) that adhere to the IMO "Code for the Construction and Equipment of Mobile Offshore Drilling Units—1989" ('89MODU Code).

At the same time the Coast Guard has also authorized ABS to conduct surveys and issue certificates in accordance with the '89 MODU Code. The Coast Guard has previously granted ABS other statutory recognitions including various surveys and certifications in accordance with the Loadline, SOLAS, and MARPOL international maritime conventions.

Under the terms of the ACP, ABS surveyors had been empowered to act as agents of the Coast Guard in issuing SOLAS and MARPOL certificates to U.S.-flag ships in support of the USCG Certificates of Inspection (COI). This voluntary program has now been extended to include owners of new and existing U.S.-flag MODUs, subject to the '89 MODU code, who may wish to enroll.

ABS President Robert Somerville said, "This dual recognition from the Coast Guard is a significant achievement for ABS as it demonstrates the confidence this leading flag state agency has in our capabilities. This is a confidence that was fostered and has grown during the years we have worked together developing the ACP."

Mr. Somerville credited the recent reorganization of ABS offshore activities as a factor in gaining the two new authorizations. "No doubt the Coast Guard viewed our enhanced internal engineering and technical support services as sharpening our practice and reinforcing our leading position within the offshore sector," he said.

He also noted that work is in progress to extend the Coast Guard's authorizations to include existing MODUs that are subject to the IMO "Code for the Construction and Equipment of Mobile Offshore Drilling Units—1979."

ABS has maintained a dominant position within the MODU and other offshore sectors. "ABS offers the most advanced technology and the most comprehensive Rules and Guidelines to meet the sophisticated needs of this progressive industry," Mr. Somerville said. As evidence, the ABS President cited market share figures within the MODU sector alone which show that 83% of existing jack-up units, 50% of existing semisubmersible units, and 87% of existing drillships are in ABS class, a total of 542 units. More than a dozen of the most advanced drill ships and semisubmersible units now being converted or building are also to ABS class.

United States Coast Guard Rear Admiral Robert C. North, Assistant Commandant for Marine Safety and Environmental Protection, explained that, "This authorization given to ABS to incorporate MODUs into the ACP is an extension of the mutual efforts undertaken by ABS and the Coast Guard to streamline the Coast Guard's inspection activities while maintaining adherence to our common missions of protecting life and property at sea."

He also indicated that, "By incorporating the resources of ABS into our flag-state inspection efforts, a great deal of duplication has been eliminated resulting in significant potential savings for MODU owners with no reduction in the level of safety standards." For U.S.-flag MODU owners a significant benefit is the harmonization of USCG requirements with international convention standards, particularly those contained within SOLAS, MARPOL, and the ABS Rules. A guide to the enrollment in the ACP is available to owners of both new and existing MODUs. It advises users on the simple procedures of enlisting and participating in the program.

The clear operational and financial savings of the ACP that have been identified by shipowners and operators during the pilot phase and the year since are now expected to encourage participation from owners and operators of MODUs as well.

IV. ADMIRAL ROBERT E. KRAMEK APPOINTED PRESIDENT, ABS AMERICAS JUNE 1, 1998

Robert D. Somerville, President and Chief Operating Officer of ABS, is pleased to announce the appointment of Admiral Robert E. Kramek, recently retired Commandant of the United States Coast Guard, as President of ABS Americas Division. "Bob Kramek is one of the most distinguished leaders of American and international maritime policy," says Mr. Somerville. "We are fortunate to have him join the senior management team at ABS. He brings a wealth of administrative, management, and technical experience to his new position and to our organization." Admiral Kramek served as USCG Commandant from 1994 to 1998. During this period he also led the U.S. delegation to the International Maritime Organization (IMO) and chaired the Safety of Life at Sea Subcommittee within the Department of State and the SOLAS Committee of the National Safety Council.

"Bob Kramek's career has been remarkable for the emphasis it has placed on maritime safety, quality management systems, and environmental policy," says Mr. Somerville. "It is these three elements—safety, quality, and the environment—which are at the heart of everything that we do at ABS. When these skills are coupled with the tremendous managerial experience which Bob Kramek has amassed as Commandant, and as the former Chief of Staff of the Coast Guard when he had direct responsibility for all budget, administrative, and management programs of the government agency, it is hard to imagine anyone better qualified to help lead ABS into the 21st century." As President of ABS Americas, Kramek will be located at the divisional headquarters in Houston. He will be responsible for the administration of more than 600 ABS surveyors, engineers, and support staff located in offices throughout North, Central, and South America.

Admiral Kramek served in the U.S. Coast Guard for a total of 36 years. He holds Masters degrees in naval architecture and marine engineering, mechanical engineering, and engineering management. He also holds a Military Masters degree in strategy, policy and international affairs. Coast Guard posts held over the years include Senior Repair Superintendent, Chief of Construction, Assistant Chief of Design, Chief of Naval Engineering and Engineering Maintenance, Commanding Officer of a Coast Guard vessel, and District Commander.

Other postings include U.S. Interdiction Coordinator for the National Drug Control Program, Head of the Haitian Migration Task Force, Chairman of the Environmental Summit with external environmental groups, and Director of the USCG's Total Quality Management program.

Admiral Kramek is a member of the American Bureau of Shipping and the ABS Council in addition to more than 20 other prominent maritime organization memberships. "ABS is currently enjoying record earnings and the strongest book of new construction classification contracts since the 1970s," Mr. Somerville points out. "Yet the challenges which are confronting the leading classification societies have never been greater as we seek to develop and implement sensible, practical safety standards and to harness the most modern technology in support of those standards. The recent success of ABS is a tribute to the strength of our senior management. Bob Kramek is an outstanding addition to that team."

Bob Kramek will join ABS on or about 15 August 1998. He will replace Bud Roth, the current President of ABS Americas, who has been promoted to Corporate Chief of Staff.

V. STANWOOD/CAMANO NEWS
TUESDAY, NOVEMBER 9, 1999
"LUCKY" WORLD WAR II VET LIVED THROUGH LAND MINE BLAST AND CAPTURE

By Patrick Moody
Special to the NEWS

Most people have an easily understandable definition of luck. Generally a person considers himself lucky if he finds a parking space close to the mall entrance on a rainy day, or if he hits his tee shot into the woods and it caroms off a tree back onto the fairway, or if his car is the last one to board a ferry on a busy holiday weekend. A person considers himself really lucky if he wins the lottery, or best of all, if he's lucky in love.

Camano Island resident Fred Pilkington's definition of luck is more expansive than average. During World War II, Pilkington stepped on a land mine, badly injuring his legs. Shortly thereafter he was taken prisoner by the Germans. A few days later, forced to endure indescribable pain, he had shrapnel removed from his legs without the benefit of anesthetic.

Then for four months he was held in a German prisoner-of-war camp, in terribly cold, spartan and unsanitary conditions, where he lost nearly 65 pounds.

When Pilkington describes his wartime ordeal, he repeatedly mentions how lucky he was, causing one to wonder: Just what would have to happen to Pilkington to make him consider himself unlucky?

Fred Pilkington is a bear of a man at six feet, four inches tall. He speaks in a deep gravely voice that commands respect. It's easy to imagine Pilkington giving orders and his subordinates quickly obeying.

Pilkington grew up in the Bronx, New York. Though not raised a Catholic, he was educated through the eighth grade at St. Rita's Elementary School in the Bronx. (Pilkington's mother prevailed on the parish pastor to enroll Pilkington in the school because the nearest public elementary school was a considerable distance from their home. During his eight years at the school, Pilkington was the only non-Catholic student.)

In 1939 Pilkington enrolled in Hartwick College, a small liberal arts college in Oneonta, New York, where he had been awarded a football scholarship. Hardly

426

a gridiron powerhouse, Pilkington spent autumn Saturday afternoons getting his "brains beat out," but nonetheless, he looks back fondly on his days there.

In January of 1942, shortly after the Japanese attack on Pearl Harbor, Pilkington and three friends tried to join the Marines. Due to poor eyesight in one eye, Pilkington was not allowed to join, so the following September he enrolled in the Enlisted Reserve Corps, which is the equivalent of today's Army Reserves.

Enlisting in the reserves offered one advantage for Pilkington. It allowed him to continue playing football—and getting his brains beat out for Hartwick College on Saturday afternoons. He wasn't called to active duty until the following March, in 1943.

Pilkington trained at Fort Jackson, South Carolina and was eventually assigned to Camp Atterbury, Indiana. During this time, he was promoted to corporal and then to platoon sergeant. He was assigned to an intelligence and reconnaissance platoon in the 106th Infantry Division. He loved the training—the long marches and rigorous exercise, and he even remembers the food fondly!

After a brief detour in which the Army unsuccessfully endeavored to assign him to a map-making battalion in Wisconsin, an assignment which Pilkington fought (he had his heart set on being an infantryman), Pilkington's unit was shipped out to England in November of 1944. He spent a short time there before he was sent to the Belgium-German border on Dec. 10.

Pilkington's regiment, the 422nd, was stationed on the front lines. The 423rd Regiment was stationed to the immediate right of the 422nd, but to the left of the 422nd there was a one-and-a-half-mile gap between Pilkington's regiment and the next American troops. It was the job of Pilkington's platoon to patrol the gap, checking for incursions by German troops.

Pilkington was excited to be on the front. "When you're 20 years old, you think you're bulletproof," he said. "I didn't feel any fear. I was excited.

"We were bivouacked in a stone farmhouse located on a hill. Underneath the house there were chickens, two cows, and a bull. We took good care of the animals because we knew Christmas was coming and we planned to have a nice Christmas dinner."

Patrolling the gap

On Dec. 15th, Pilkington's unit was patrolling the gap when he saw a group of soldiers dressed in white camouflage. To the best of Pilkington's knowledge, none of the Allied troops possessed white camouflage, so he assumed he had spotted a German reconnaissance unit. However, when he reported this sighting to his superiors, he was told that he must be mistaken—the unit he spotted must have been an Allied one. "Perhaps you were overexcited," Pilkington's superiors told him.

Pilkington was unconvinced, and the next day's events would unfortunately prove him correct, because on Dec. 16, the Battle of the Bulge began. (The Battle of the Bulge started when the Germans made one last attempt to turn back the Allies by launching an offensive in which they endeavored to drive a wedge, or bulge, between the Allied troops.)

On the morning of Dec. 16, Pilkington's regimental commander decided to send some men back to division headquarters to deliver some information. "In those days, radio communication was not the best," Pilkington recalls. On this day, radio communication had broken down completely, so communication with division headquarters had to be done by messenger.

Pilkington volunteered to make the drive to deliver the information, but his platoon leader, Lieutenant Krol, volunteered to go in Pilkington's place. Pilkington stayed at the farmhouse while Krol departed with a driver and a radio operator.

In the morning the farmhouse started to come under light artillery fire, but by the afternoon the fire began to intensify. Pilkington was ordered to patrol the one-and-a-half mile gap. He took a squad of eight men with him, and the mission went well until the unit came under Allied artillery fire. After a number of failed attempts, one of Pilkington's men was able to get a radio to work, and the radio operator convinced the unit firing the shells to cease firing.

"It took some time until the firing finally stopped," Pilkington said. "Fortunately, despite falling tree limbs, no one was wounded or injured."

On the way back to the farmhouse, on a route that took his unit through a heavily wooded area broken up by some relatively broad fields, Pilkington suddenly spotted a group of men digging foxholes. Above the men who were digging was another group of 15 to 20 men huddled on a hill.

Using binoculars, Pilkington was able to discern that the foxhole diggers were German soldiers, and the men above them on the hill were captured Americans.

"I was flabbergasted!" Pilkington recalls. "The Germans were behind our lines."

Rescue attempt
Pilkington, though his unit was lightly armed and had only a small supply of ammunition, decided to take a stab at liberating the American prisoners. There was

an open field between his men and the Germans, but because Pilkington's unit was hidden in the trees, the Germans had not spotted it.

Pilkington took four men and started to walk across the open field. His plan was to get as close to the Germans as possible, and then when the Germans spotted them, Pilkington and the four others would shout to the prisoners to break free. Meanwhile, the other four men in Pilkington's unit would provide covering fire.

"The idea was to try to bluff the Germans into thinking we were a larger force than we actually were," Pilkington said.

"To a certain extent, the plan worked," he said. "We got to within 100-150 yards before the Germans saw us and started firing. Then I started waving wildly and shouting, 'Break free! Break free!'"

Before long the Germans began to suspect that Pilkington's force wasn't very large. Off to his right, Pilkington saw two German soldiers. He surmised that the Germans would try to surround his small force.

Pilkington started firing at the two Germans, and soon they surrendered to him!

Unfortunately, none of the American prisoners had tried to break away. Pilkington took the two German prisoners, and because he was badly outnumbered, he and his men began to retreat when suddenly a single American prisoner started running toward them.

"He ran directly to me, and I was amazed to recognize Don Johnson, the radio operator who had accompanied Lieutenant Krol on the early morning trip (to Division Headquarters)," Pilkington said.

Johnson later explained that he, Krol, and the driver, Lex Schoonover, had made it to Division Headquarters without incident but were captured as they tried to return to the farmhouse.

Later that night Schoonover also managed to escape. Krol, a popular and much-loved officer, never escaped and was killed, probably by American artillery fire. He left behind his wife and unborn daughter.

The following morning, Dec. 17, Pilkington and another officer were instructed to climb up into the hayloft of a partially destroyed barn to help direct American artillery fire against the Germans. From the hayloft, Pilkington could see thousands of German troops streaming over the hills and through the gap he had spent the previous days patrolling.

Included in the German columns were tanks, trucks, and horse-drawn wagons.

The situation becomes desperate

The next day, Dec. 18, "our situation had become critical," Pilkington said. His regiment was under near-continuous artillery fire and intermittent small arms and machine gun fire. To make matters worse, the regiment was running out of ammunition. Officers decided to evacuate the area and make an effort to join a nearby regiment. They began marching.

It was bitterly cold. Darkness soon feel and the convoy stopped for the night. "It was a night of almost total confusion," Pilkington recalls. "Everyone was tired, hungry, and cold." During the night, Pilkington's unit made brief contact with a couple passing units, and occasionally small arms fire erupted. It was impossible to tell if the passing units were Allies or Germans.

The next day it became apparent that Pilkington's unit was surrounded by Germans. The officers in charge decided that the convoy would press on. They hoped to join other American units who they thought were holding a nearby town.

Pilkington was ordered to organize a jeep patrol and investigate the route his regiment planned to take to the town. Unfortunately, an overeager first lieutenant with little experience and poor map-reading abilities decided he wanted to lead the three-jeep patrol. He hopped into the lead jeep and ordered the driver to "head out," whereupon the driver commenced driving at a high rate of speed.

Generally there are strict procedures to follow for this kind of reconnaissance mission, Pilkington explained, and the eager Lieutenant followed none of them. It was considered foolhardy, to say the last, to travel at a high rate of speed.

"It was like something out of the Keystone Cops," marvels Pilkington.

The lead jeep was traveling so fast that, less than a mile into its journey, it flew right past two German soldiers who were standing near the road. Pilkington and the men in his jeep engaged these two Germans in a brief firefight and took them prisoner, then continued their pursuit of the first jeep.

Soon all three jeeps drove into an area that was completely under German control. The lead jeep drove into a ditch. A German tank was coming down the road toward the jeeps. Pilkington and his comrades were lightly armed, and their only chance was to make a run for it. Accompanied by their two German prisoners, the men ran up a hill, only to be stopped by a booby-trapped barbed wire fence.

One of the men, directed by Pilkington, crawled through the fence and made it to the crest of the hill, only to see scores more German troops. Pilkington directed his men to try to run back down the hill and escape by another route. By this time, they were under fire from both machine guns and small arms.

Injured and captured

Pilkington took a couple of steps down the hill and then stepped on a land mine. "The next thing I remember, I was lying on my back, afraid to look down to see what happened. I discovered that my pants and the tops of my boots had blown off. My belt buckle and two back pockets were still on."

Pilkington's first thought was to check to see if "certain personal bodily items," were still attached to his body.

He lifted his belt buckle, "even though it was not necessary to do so," to conduct an investigation. "Great was my relief when everything seemed to be intact," Pilkington recalls.

In the meantime, several of Pilkington's comrades crawled back to help him. He ordered them to leave him and try to escape. They refused. They carried Pilkington to a small depression.

"I recognized that it was time to face facts," Pilkington said. "We were out of ammunition and we were under sustained fire. Back down on the road, I could see the few Allied troops we had left behind coming in column, led by a soldier carrying a white flag. That scene etched itself into my mind. I still recall it, a crystal-clear picture."

It was time to surrender. Pilkington ordered the two German prisoners, who miraculously were still with them, to crawl out of the hill and tell the German troops to stop firing because the Americans were surrendering. Frightened, the two Germans refused to go.

At this point, Pilkington pointed his gun at the Germans and threatened to shoot them if they didn't go. What the prisoners didn't realize is that Pilkington didn't have any ammunition. They went, and soon the shooting stopped. "I was glad the bluff worked," Pilkington said.

"Those who were with me were marched off at gunpoint," Pilkington said. "I was placed on a stretcher and carried away, not knowing that after nightfall of that day, I would never see another member of my division until after the end of hostilities and my return to the United States."

Life as a prisoner

Pilkington was taken to an aid station. By this time, night had arrived. There were American and German wounded soldiers there. "I received some first-aid treatment and then was put in a panel truck with five or six others," Pilkington said. "The truck drove off, and late at night, it came to a farmhouse. The driver and guard got out of the truck and spent the night in the farmhouse. They left us in the truck. We had no food or water."

"The next day we spent the better part of the day driving around before we were taken to a hotel," Pilkington said. The hotel had been converted into a military hospital. Once again, "we were mixed in with German wounded," Pilkington recalls. "There was a German soldier right next to me."

Two days later, Pilkington and other Allied prisoners were taken to a local movie theater. The seats had been removed in the audience area, and up on the stage were a number of operating tables. Pilkington could hear a lot of screaming as amputations were being performed without anesthetic.

When Pilkington's turn came there were no tables available, so Pilkington was examined while lying on the floor. The examining doctor asked Pilkington if he had ever been to New York City. Pilkington responded with his name, rank, and serial number.

"I know that," the doctor said. Then he repeated the question.

"I thought about his question and figured that I wouldn't be divulging any great military secrets by giving an answer," Pilkington said.

When Pilkington answered that he had been to New York City, the doctor seemed pleased and asked if Pilkington knew where Riverside Drive was. Again, Pilkington decided that he would not be hurting the Allied effort by answering the question, so he said yes.

At this point, the doctor, who seemed pleased at Pilkington's answers, stopped his examination and told Pilkington that he had lived on Riverside Drive in New York City for 10 years while he received his medical training.

The doctor then apologized to Pilkington for not having any anesthetic, removed Pilkington's wool cap from his head, handed it to him, and suggested he chew on it during the operation.

When the operation was over, the doctor told Pilkington that "he got all the big pieces." Later in the afternoon, Pilkington was returned to his bed in the hotel lobby.

A day or two later, Pilkington was nudged by the German soldier whose bunk was next to Pilkington's. The soldier could speak some English. He wanted to know why the Americans were fighting the Germans.

"It was evident he was sincere in his perplexity," Pilkington recalls. "Our discussion was not heated, but rather a calm examination of the problem. It ended in a stalemate, but without animosity."

It was Christmas Eve, 1944. Earlier that day, local civilians had brought gift baskets containing fruit, cookies, and wine for the German soldiers. The Americans received nothing. Shortly after the lights were turned out, Pilkington heard a soft clinking noise against his bunk. He turned to see the German soldier holding out a bottle of wine. "Have some," he said.

On Christmas Day, the American prisoners cum patients were put on a moving van and transported downtown to a two-story schoolhouse. It was bitterly cold, and snow had fallen overnight.

"There were German medics in the building, but they were not allowed to assist us," Pilkington said. "German SS troops were in charge until we got to the door of the schoolhouse."

The German soldiers forced the badly injured men to make their own way from the truck to the schoolhouse door. The prisoners were forced to roll off the tailgate and walk, roll, crawl, or somehow drag themselves in the snow between two lines of SS troops who taunted them, until the prisoners got to the schoolhouse door and the medics could assist them.

The prisoners were taken to the second floor where they stayed for a week. They received no medical attention and their bandages remained unchanged. In addition, the unmarked building was regularly strafed by Allied planes, so the men had to hunker down when they heard the planes approaching. They managed to avoid injury, even though it was not uncommon for bullets to go in one window and out another.

A week later, Pilkington was transported to a prison hospital. At this hospital, medical care consisted of a one-day-per-week visit to a room in which attendants removed his bandages and a portly Polish physician conducted a cursory examination.

The doctor examined scores of men every day in an assembly line fashion. "We called him Henry Ford," Pilkington said. "His claim to fame was that he liked to amputate. Outside the examination room, there were piles of feet, hands, and legs. They were taken out every day and burned.

Pilkington was getting worried. His legs, especially his right one, were getting worse. There were large holes in the leg, and they were emitting pus. "Our bandages were similar to crepe paper. Every time they were removed, my wounds would be torn open," Pilkington said.

One day the Polish surgeon told Pilkington that his leg would have to be amputated below the knee if it did not improve by the following week's examination.

"I was lucky," Pilkington said. Shortly after he received the amputation warning, Allied forces crossed the Rhine, and Pilkington and other prisoners were taken out of the prison hospital and transported to a standard prison camp.

Once again, one is struck by Pilkington's definition of luck. Just about 36 hours after he left the prison hospital, it was liberated by the Allies. He barely missed being freed. Instead of freedom, more hardship awaited.

The train ride to the prison camp was not without incident. The prisoners were piled in boxcars. The conditions were horribly crowded and unsanitary. Worse, the train was unmarked, so it made a tempting target for Allied warplanes. During one attack, the train was forced to take refuge in a tunnel. The Allied planes then bombed both ends of the tunnel, sealing the train inside. It remained trapped for 24 hours before the Germans got one end of the tunnel opened.

The train took the prisoners to a huge prison camp near Hanover, Germany. Men of various nationalities were housed here, separated by nationality. Injured prisoners were mixed in with the non-injured. Pilkington declined to ask for medical care because he surmised he would be better off without it. Furthermore, he was able to ameliorate his leg infections slightly by using two small packets of sulfanilamide powder he was able to obtain while in prison.

Conditions at Pilkington's new camp were similar to those at the prison hospital—dirty, unsanitary, and bitterly cold. Men slept two to a bed so they could share blankets and body heat. They spent parts of their days picking lice off their bodies and burning lice eggs out of the seams of their clothing. Their diets consisted of a morning ration of a liquid that was generously called coffee, followed in the afternoon by one loaf of bread for every seven men, and a bowl of potato or cabbage soup for each man.

Pilkington and his colleagues spent a great deal of time thinking about food. They would construct elaborate and detailed fantasy meals, consisting of all kinds of food. "My own special desire was steaming hot muffins dripping with real butter and jelly," Pilkington said. "I had recurring dreams of muffins, trays filled with them being drawn from an oven."

Though the prison conditions were horrible, the prisoners were not without hope. A particularly resourceful prisoner had managed to build a working radio, so every night the prisoners could listen to the BBC radio network. "We had a pretty good idea that liberation must be coming soon," Pilkington said.

Liberation
On April 11, the German guards and administrators fled the camp. The prisoners were left under the guardianship of Polish soldiers, who, in Pilkington's view, weren't very interested in working as prison guards for the Germans.

"The guards remained in their guard towers and didn't bother us," Pilkington recalled. "An unwritten truce prevailed. They left us alone and we ignored them."

On April 16 the camp was liberated by British troops. Pilkington, who had weighed a strapping 220 pounds at the time of his capture, now weighed 156 pounds. "It's easy to lose weight when you don't eat," Pilkington quipped.

Almost immediately, the Allied prisoners broke into storehouses and commandeered whatever they could get their hands on, including large bags of oatmeal. The men in Pilkington's barrack cooked up a giant pot, served it, and then "everyone got sick," Pilkington laughed. The tasty oatmeal was too much of a shock to their systems after the months of deprivation.

Food continued to be a problem for Pilkington and his fellow prisoners even after they were taken out of the camp and transported to a prison hospital outside of Oxford, England.

"We were one of the first prisoner units to come back," Pilkington said. "Everyone was scrawny. They didn't know what to do with us.

"They left the mess hall open 24 hours a day. We could eat whatever we wanted whenever we wanted.

"The medical personnel didn't know that such a sudden change in diet could cause yellow jaundice. We all got it. Part of the treatment was to put us on a bland diet!"

Pilkington and the others got over their jaundice, and though it took some time, Pilkington's legs recovered as well. He returned to the States in August, and promptly volunteered to go to Japan. His plans were thwarted when the Japanese surrendered on Aug. 15, 1945.

So Pilkington never made it to Japan. He probably considers himself unlucky.

Fred Pilkington returned to the States and graduated from Hartwick College. He worked in public education for nearly 40 years before moving to Camano Island in 1986. He has three children seven grandchildren and two great grandchildren. He lives on Camano Island, Washington with his wife Mary.

VI. FATHER DIVES DEEP FOR ANSWERS IN SON'S DEATH

Private campaign spurs Coast Guard to reopen inquiry into 1996 offshore oil rig fatality

JAMES PINKERTON Staff
SUN 06/20/1999 Houston Chronicle, Section A, Page 1, 4 STAR Edition

At a U.S. Coast Guard station on Tuesday, Peter Pilkington will begin to get the answers he has sought since his son died more than three years ago while working for a small Houston dive contractor.

He wants to know why Brian Pilkington, a healthy, 23-year-old commercial diver, suddenly died in March 1996 off Sabine Pass while inspecting an offshore oil rig in 28 feet of water.

He wants to know why the Coast Guard, the federal agency in charge of marine safety, conducted what he considers a shoddy investigation into his son's death. It was an inquiry in which no witnesses were interviewed or any piece of diving equipment examined or retained by officials, Pilkington said.

And he wants to know why two Coast Guard officers let the dive take place, even though they had cited the Cliff's Number 12 offshore rig, operated by a Houston-based drilling firm, for safety violations that day because a required predive safety inspection had not been completed.

"We have fought to get this hearing for the last three years," said Pilkington, a 51-year-old architect and building contractor from the Seattle suburb of Bellevue, Wash. "It was unconscionable to me that . . . after this young man died . . . there was no investigation.

"Not a single witness was ever interviewed by the U.S. Coast Guard until three years and four days after the accident," said Pilkington, referring to interviews taken in advance of Tuesday's hearing.

Testimony from 10 to 15 witnesses is expected to begin Tuesday morning in Beaumont, where the U.S. Coast Guard is convening a formal board of investigation, revisiting the initial inquiry conducted after the young diver died on March 4, 1996.

Coast Guard officials say the decision to reopen the inquiry was the result of information provided by Pilkington, who has conducted a costly three-year campaign to find out what happened to his son.

Coast Guard officers in Port Arthur had determined, in a report issued 13 months after the accident, that Brian Pilkington had improperly attached an air hose, allowing water into his diving helmet, and that he panicked and drowned after becoming entangled on the rig.

But Pilkington said a poorly maintained air compressor failed near the end of his son's three-hour dive, cutting off his air supply.

Coast Guard officials did not examine the compressor, allowing the dive contractor to remove it. Employees of a Houston equipment dealer who examined the compressor told Pilkington it failed because a shop rag being used as an air filter was sucked into the machine.

Pilkington has filed complaints with state bar officials against the lawyers for the rig owner, Cliff's Drilling Co. of Houston, claiming they concealed evidence and made up the story about his son disconnecting his air supply to limit their client's liability.

The attorneys did not return a call from the Chronicle.

In January 1998, his son's widow accepted a multimillion-dollar settlement in a civil suit she brought against the company and the contractor.

"We certainly will be looking into the Coast Guard's conduct as well," said Lt. Commander Tom Beistle, the Coast Guard officer who will conduct the proceedings.

"The purpose of the hearing is to investigate the facts underlying the casualty, to determine if any Coast Guard regulations were violated," said Beistle, adding that the inquiry will also determine "if Coast Guard (diving) regulations are appropriate and need to be amended to better promote marine safety."

During his private three-year inquiry, Pilkington said he not only learned the tragic and preventable circumstances of his son's death but the often hazardous working conditions facing commercial divers across the country.

He and others, including a nationwide commercial diver's trade group, say the Coast Guard has done a poor job of protecting divers despite having the legal tools—in two sets of federal safety regulations—to do so.

438

"They're not enforcing the regulations," said Frances Stepp, president of the National Association of Commercial Divers in Charlottesville, Va. "All the players in the industry agree on one thing—the enforcement is not being done. The Coast Guard is not going out and investigating these casualties and accidents like they ought to."

Critics charge the Coast Guard rarely takes action against commercial diving firms found to have violated federal safety regulations.

"My point is not to put anyone in jail," explained Pilkington. "But if the Coast Guard continues to let them violate the law without punishing them, what's to keep them from continuing to violate the law? Nothing! . . . They (divers) refer to the Coast Guard as the big dog with no teeth.

"The regulations are there. We're only asking them to enforce the existing regulations," he said. "We also think there ought to be a few more for backup divers, backup equipment and certification" of commercial divers.

Backup equipment is currently not required for commercial diving in less than 130 feet of water, but maybe could have saved Brian Pilkington's life.

Since the dive team did not have a scuba tank or extra air hose with them, those on board the rig spent a futile 20 minutes trying to splice together welding hoses to use in a rescue attempt, which failed.

In the end, a fellow diver simply held his breath, dived down and found Brian Pilkington's lifeless body. He was airlifted to a Port Arthur hospital, where he was pronounced dead.

Pilkington contends that the Coast Guard's investigating officers never visited the accident scene, did not question any witnesses in person or take any sworn statements and refused to examine or secure any evidence. And when U.S. Sen. Slade Gorton of Washington inquired about the investigation, the Coast Guard claimed the compressor had been tested—and later issued a letter of apology about the mistake.

And it was only Monday that OSHA inspectors visited the offices of G&G Marine—the Houston dive company Brian Pilkington worked for—to examine the records on required maintenance and testing of the company's three air compressors currently being used.

In a sworn statement taken on May 19, conducted in Houston by Lt. Cdm. Beistle, company owner Danny Gilbert acknowledged he has never sent his three diving compressors for air quality testing, as required every six months by federal dive regulations.

Gilbert said he couldn't remember if the air compressor Brian Pilkington was using the day he died had been sent in for required testing.

"How about the three (compressors) that you've got now? Do you have air tests done on them routinely?" Beistle asked.

"No sir, we haven't had," Gilbert replied, explaining later his practice is to test compressors by sniffing the air ". . . If it smells foul, you don't use it . . . if the air compressor is putting out pressure and the air smells good, I'll dive it," Gilbert said.

Asking if that was a suitable substitute to the required testing, Gilbert replied, "I don't know."

Gilbert did not return a call from the Chronicle.

The events of Brian Pilkington's case are all the more important because diving deaths are not isolated events.

"Of the 116 occupational diving fatalities reported to OSHA for 1989-1997 (13 per year), 49 (five per year) occurred among an estimated 3,000 full-time commercial divers," according to a June 1998 weekly mortality report from the U.S. Centers for Disease Control and Prevention. "The average of five deaths per year corresponds to a rate of 180 deaths per 100,000 employed divers per year, which is 40 times the national average death rate for all workers."

Coast Guard officials in New Orleans said Tuesday that 27 divers had been killed and 28 had been injured from 1992 to December 1997 in the 8th Coast Guard District, which covers most of the Gulf of Mexico from Texas to the Florida panhandle and extends north to the Canadian border.

However, after first saying the casualties were the result of commercial diving, Coast Guard officials on Wednesday said they include both recreational and commercial diving accidents. And, Coast Guard officials in New Orleans said they could not readily determine from their own records how many of the 55 incidents, if any, resulted in sanctions against commercial diving contractors.

"The Coast Guard can't tell you about (commercial) diving deaths, they keep no statistical information, they have no idea about how many accidents have occurred. They have nothing, and OSHA doesn't either," said Stepp, the head of the commercial divers group.

Besides Brian Pilkington's death, there have been other young commercial divers killed, according to accident records obtained by Stepp.

In October 1997, 31-year-old Troy Elwood died two minutes into his first commercial dive 15 feet beneath a dive boat operated by Cal Dive International Inc., a large Houston-based commercial diving firm.

Coast Guard officials later found a company employee had fabricated records showing that maintenance had been performed on faulty valves on the dive boat's air compressors that allowed Elwood to breath a fatal amount of pure helium instead of compressed air, according to Coast Guard documents.

No action was taken against the company, Stepp said.

"This was blatant neglect," he said. "Somebody should be up on murder charges for this."

In November 1997, Pattison resident Jerry McHazlett, a 35-year-old commercial diver who was married with one son and expecting another, had a heart attack and died shortly after making a 200-foot-plus dive below an oil rig in waters offshore of Louisiana for Cal Dive.

Joe Walker, a Houston attorney who filed suit against the diving contractor, alleges that McHazlett was not medically fit to dive, that an inoperative hatch on the diving bell prevented co-workers from reaching him during the first crucial 20 minutes of the emergency, and that Cal Dive had no procedures to deal with this type of emergency.

"I think if the divers down there had a procedure, a plan, this guy's life could have been saved," Walker said. "But they didn't know what to do."

McHazlett's sudden death occurred when his wife, Tami, was expecting the couple's second child, John Jerry McHazlett III, born a year ago.

"I have two sons who will not know their dad, and he was a terrific person," Tami McHazlett said. "He had a lot to contribute, a lot more things to do in life, and I feel that he was just ripped away from us."

The young widow is angry, and said Cal Dive officials were not candid with her about the circumstances of her husband's death. She had to hire a lawyer to collect the supplemental life insurance purchased by her husband after Cal Dive refused to pay, claiming her husband had not filled out an eligibility form.

"The feeling I got from the company was just basically 'how is this going to impact our bottom line,'" said McHazlett, referring to a meeting with company executives a month after her husband's death.

"There was no remorse, there was no 'This is not going to happen again.' They didn't take responsibility for anything."

New Orleans attorney Patrick Baynham, who is defending Cal Dive, called the suit frivolous and said McHazlett's autopsy indicated "he had 100 percent blockage in one artery and 95 percent blockage in the other."

"To say this is somehow related to Cal Dive procedures is absolutely ridiculous," said Baynham. The attorney said CPR was begun immediately on McHazlett by his co-diver, with only brief interruptions as the co-diver cleaned debris from the hatch so it would seal properly before the diving bell was brought to the surface.

Baynham, who has handled the majority of Cal Dive's legal work over the last five years, said the Houston diving firm is one of the world's largest and safest.

"Like all these diving companies, they have an extensive safety program. (And) Cal Dive has extensive training, both prior to going offshore and once someone is offshore," Baynham said.

Another fatal diving accident occurred in May 1997 when Brent Lewis, a 24-year-old diver, died after his air hose was severed as he blew silt from beneath the Lady of the Isle casino boat near Bossier City, La.

OSHA investigators found the water intakes on the underwater pump Lewis was operating were fitted with a makeshift rope guard, allowing his air hose to be sucked in and cut. The diving company, Cal Dive, contested OSHA's proposed $4,500 fine and paid a $2,250 penalty, according to Stepp's inquiry into the case.

"If you call the industry . . . and ask them can they tell how many deaths there have been in the last 10 years, they tell you they have one death a year. But we have documents that stipulate that is not so," said Stepp, who said she had obtained records from the Coast Guard of five commercial diving deaths in 1997 and two in 1996.

She was referring to the Association of Diving Contractors International, a Houston-based industry group formed in 1968 and representing 360 dive companies, the majority headquartered in the United States.

"We have a safe industry," insists Ross Saxon, the ADC's executive director since 1992. "We are going to have accidents and fatalities, but all we can do is do our damnedest to continue to reduce them. I think we have a hell of an excellent track record and it will get better."

Saxon said that in the 1960s and 1970s, 10 commercial divers were killed each year and others seriously injured, prompting the Coast Guard and OSHA to draft safety regulations with help from the ADC.

In the last decade, Saxon said, there were an average of 1.5 diving deaths per year among commercial divers working for ADC members.

"I can say in the last 14 months, as far as member companies of our association subject to U.S. regulation are concerned, we've not had a serious injury or a fatality that's been reported," Saxon said.

But Saxon said the Coast Guard's task of overseeing commercial diving operations is huge, and estimated there are perhaps 50 or 60 taking place each day in U.S. waters.

"Could the Coast Guard enforce better? Yes. Are they properly equipped to do so? Most probably not," Saxon said. "They are an agency of the government with a tremendously large area of responsibility, with budget restrictions and they are not trained in commercial diving.

"I think the Coast Guard must look to the industry to be self-regulating."

Houston attorney Walker, a commercial diver for 10 years before he went to law school, said the complexity of the commercial diving industry exceeds the Coast Guard's expertise.

"It's a very high burden to place on the Coast Guard, which does not have a deep diving division; they really don't have the facilities or the manpower," said Walker, who advocates the use of independent diving experts to investigate diving accidents.

Walker said he is preparing for an August trial in a negligence case where commercial diver Todd Baldridge, then 28, lost consciousness and suffered disabilities in a May 1996 accident during a 258-foot dive from an oil platform in Louisiana.

An open bottom diving bell, required by federal regulations on dives of this type, was not in place, said Walker, adding that Coast Guard investigators did not cite the violation in their report.

"I keep seeing the same kind of accidents, over and over," Walker said. "Maybe the only thing that will change that is making the insurance premiums go up enough where the company will be forced not to be dangerous."

Pilkington said he hopes the Coast Guard inquiry into his son's death will result in changes that will prevent more tragic deaths.

"It took me three years and probably $300,000 to get where we are right now," he said. "Initially, it was to try and clear my son's name—now it's to try and make a difference."

VII. FINAL REPORT COVER LETTER

U.S. Department
of Transportation

United States
Coast Guard

Commandant
United States Coast Guard

2100 Second Street, SW
Washington, DC 20593-0001
Staff Symbol: G-M
Phone: (202) 267-2200

16732

APR 9 2001

Mr. Peter Pilkington
Commercial Dive Safety Organization
2795 152ⁿᵈ Ave. NE
Redmond, WA 98052

Dear Mr. Pilkington:

It is with heartfelt sympathy that I am forwarding to you the enclosed copy of the investigative report regarding the tragic death of your son, Brian.

Because of your strong personal interest in preventing a reoccurrence of an accident like this, and as a result of your dissatisfaction with our original investigative report, we reopened the casualty investigation and convened extensive formal hearings into the numerous causal factors contributing to this accident. This investigation involved an extensive examination of the immediate events surrounding your son's death as well as the commercial diving regulations, commercial diving operations, and the Coast Guard commercial diving regulatory program. The subsequent report and casualty analysis clearly documents areas for improvement and makes substantive recommendations to prevent a reoccurrence of such an accident.

As you will note in the report, we have taken a number of actions to address those areas for improvement. We are conducting a technical review of our commercial diving regulations and policies. We have developed a commercial diving orientation course and we are developing a performance qualification standards workbook for diving operations for our personnel. Additional actions that we are taking are discussed in the "Action on Recommendations" section of the report beginning on page one.

I truly appreciate your persistence. Without it, we certainly would not have taken the closer look this casualty deserved and we could not begin to make the changes that clearly need to be made. I hope that this investigative report and the recommendations it makes for improving safety in the commercial diving industry, in some small way, eases the pain you have endured. If we can be of further assistance, please do not hesitate to contact us.

Sincerely,

JAMES M. LOY
Admiral, U.S. Coast Guard
Commandant

Encl: (1) Cliff's Drilling Rig No. 12 Investigative Report

VIII. THE FINAL REPORT

U.S. Department
of Transportation

United States
Coast Guard

Commandant
United States Coast Guard

2100 Second Street, S.W.
Washington, DC 20593-0001
Staff Symbol: G-MOA
Phone: (202) 267-1430
FAX: (202) 267-1416

16732/ MC00011781
MAR 1·5 2001

COMMANDANT'S ACTION
ON THE FORMAL INVESTIGATION INTO THE
CIRCUMSTANCES SURROUNDING THE

COMMERCIAL DIVING ACCIDENT

ONBOARD THE MOBILE OFFSHORE DRILLING UNIT
CLIFF'S DRILLING RIG NO. 12 ON MARCH 4, 1996
WITH THE LOSS OF LIFE

ACTION BY THE COMMANDANT

The report of the Investigation into the subject casualty has been reviewed. The investigative report, including the findings of fact, conclusions, and recommendations, is approved.

ACTION ON RECOMMENDATIONS

Recommendation #1: Commandant should require bailout bottles for all commercial diving operations, regardless of depth. The bailout bottles should have sufficient capacity to supply a diver with an appropriate volume of air at the deepest depth being worked. The facts of this case do not strongly support a recommendation for bailout bottles. Nevertheless, all diving experts consulted by the Investigating Officer agreed that bailout bottles come in so many sizes and configurations, and are so inexpensive that every dive should begin with the presumption that a bailout bottle will be used.

Recommendation #2: Commandant should require all unused auxiliary gas ports on diver worn life support equipment to be capped or blanked during all commercial diving operations. This will remove the possibility of water entering a diver's helmet if he inadvertently opens an emergency valve.

Recommendation #3: Commandant should require a standby diver dressed out and with a separate air supply, ready to quickly deploy for all commercial diving operations regardless of depth.

Recommendation #4: Commandant should require diving stages for all commercial diving operations regardless of depth, except where they would be impractical. This will speed entry to the water for divers and rescue divers and remove the need for rescue operations to work from personnel baskets. In this casualty, the rescue operation was itself so slow that using a crane operated Billy Pugh basket, as rescue platform did not significantly add to the delay. Nevertheless, there is no question that a diving stage at water level would have speeded up the rescue.

Recommendation #5: Commandant should require the Diving Supervisor and the Master or Person-in-Charge to develop a site-specific rescue plan designating the equipment and personnel that will be used for a rescue or removal of an injured diver from the water for all commercial diving operations.

Recommendation #6: Commandant should require that, prior to any commercial diving operation, the Diving Supervisor describe the rescue plan to all members of the diving team.

Recommendation #7: Commandant should require the Diving Supervisor to complete a Job Hazard Analysis before every commercial diving operation. See IO Exhibit 57, ADC Consensus Standards, pg. 3-9 to 3-10b.

Recommendation #8: Commandant should require Diving Supervisors to complete a pre-dive safety checklist suitable to the type of diving equipment and procedures to be used, prior to all commercial dive operations. See IO Exhibit 53, Navy Dive Manual, pg. 4-37 to 4-49.

Recommendation #9: Commandant should consider changing Coast Guard regulations to ensure accountability of commercial diving contractors for maintaining records and logs for their diving equipment. Commandant should also make minor changes to Coast Guard regulations in addition to those described above to ensure Offshore Installation Managers play a more active role in pre-dive safety preparations. Present Coast Guard diving regulations place record keeping responsibilities on diving supervisors. Diving supervisors are appointed on a job to job basis and their designation ends when the diving job they supervise ends. Many of the record keeping responsibilities, however, are continuous and must be completed between diving jobs, away from the dive site. The following recommended regulation changes illustrate how the commercial diving contractor and Offshore Installation Manager could be given a more responsible role in the record keeping and pre-dive safety processes.

a) At 46 CFR 197.204 [Definitions], Commandant should add a definition "Commercial Diving Contractor" to describe the person or business that provides commercial diving services.

b) At 46 CFR 197.484 (a) [Notice of casualty], after the words "person-in-charge", Commandant should include the words "Diving Supervisor or Commercial Diving Contractor."

c) At 46 CFR 197.486 [Written report of casualty], after the words "person-in-charge of a vessel or facility" Commandant should include the words "or Diving Supervisor or Commercial Diving Contractor."

d) Commandant should change 46 CFR 197.210 [Designation of diving Supervisor] as follows:

2

"The Commercial Diving Contractor shall designate in writing a Diving Supervisor for each commercial diving operation. The Diving Supervisor shall present the written designation to the Master or Person-in-Charge."

e) Commandant should change 46 CFR 197.402 (2) (i) [Responsibilities of the person-in-charge] as follows:

"Prior to permitting any commercial diving operation to commence, the Master or Person-in-charge shall examine the Diving Supervisor's written designation to ensure it is complete as required by Section 197.210."

f) Commandant should cross-reference 46 CFR 109.109 [Responsibilities of master or person-in-charge] with 46 CFR 197.402 [Responsibilities of person-in-charge].

g) Commandant should change 46 CFR 197.480(c) [Logbooks] as follows:

(c) The Diving Contractor and the Diving Supervisor conducting commercial diving operations from a vessel or facility subject to this subpart shall maintain a logbook for making the entries required by this subpart.

(d) The logbook required to be maintained by this subpart shall be taken to the jobsite for every commercial diving operation and shall be available for inspection by the Master or Person-in-charge, the United States Coast Guard or any other cognizant agency.

(e) The Diving Contractor shall retain the logbook required to be maintained by this subpart for a period of not less than three years.

h) Commandant should change 46 CFR 197.482 (d) [Logbook entries] as follows:

(d) The Diving Contractor and the Diving Supervisor shall insure that a record of the following is maintained:...

(e) The Diving Contractor and the Diving Supervisor shall insure copies of each of the records required under paragraph (d) are included in the operations manual required by 46 CFR 197.420. The records required under paragraph (d) must be maintained by the Diving Contractor for a period of not less than three years.

i) At 46 CFR 197.420 [Operations manual], Commandant should add the following:

(e) The operations manual must contain copies of the records required to be maintained by 46 CFR 197.482 (d) and (e).

j) At 46 CFR 197.450 [Breathing gas tests], Commandant should change the words " The diving supervisor shall ensure that" – to

"The Diving Contractor shall ensure that -

k) At 46 CFR 197.450 [Breathing gas tests], Commandant should add the following:

3

448

(d) <u>The Diving Contractor shall maintain the above stated test records for a period of not less than 3 years.</u>

Recommendation #10: Commandant should require the Dive Supervisor and Master or Person-in-Charge to execute a Declaration of Inspection verifying their respective duties have been competed before any commercial dive operation begins. See 46 CFR 35.35-30 for an example of the concept as it is applied to oil transfers.

Recommendation #11: At 46 CFR 197.204 [Definitions], Commandant should include a definition of "Diving Tender." Commandant should consider adopting the description of Diver Tender set out in the Navy Dive Manual. See IO Exhibit 53, Part 4-8.5.3.

Recommendation #12: At 46 CFR 197.204 [Definitions], Commandant should include a definition of "Dive Tending" or Tending.

Recommendation #13: Commandant should consider limiting the duties of a dive tender to only tending the dive umbilical during a commercial diving operation, as illustrated by the following wording.
At 46 CFR 197.432(c) [Surface-supplied air diving], Commandant should add the words:

<u>; the person tending the diver shall have no other duties while the diver is under water;</u>

Recommendation #14: At 46 CFR 197.204 [Definitions], Commandant should consider consolidating the definitions "*Commercial diver*" and "*Diver*" into one inclusive definition.

Recommendation #15: Commandant should establish minimum manning standards for all diving operations. Commandant should consider adopting the standards set out in the ADC Consensus Standards. See IO Exhibit 57, pg. 3-24 to 3-29.

Recommendation #16: Commandant should establish commercial diving qualification standards for Commercial Divers, Commercial Diving Tenders, and Commercial Diving Supervisors. Commandant should consider adopting the standards set out in the ADC Consensus Standards. See IO Exhibit 57, pg. 2-3 to 2-8.

Recommendation #17: In the absence of a diver qualification program, Commandant should publish criteria for OCMI's to use when reviewing SEILOD (Special Examination in Lieu of Drydocking) applications to evaluate qualifications of divers to safely conduct diving operations.

Commandant's Action on Recommendations #1 through #17: We concur with the intent of these recommendations. We are currently conducting a technical review of the Commercial Diving Operation regulations at 46 CFR 197. Upon completion of the review, the changes recommended in recommendations 1 through 17, will be included in an upcoming Notice of Proposed Rulemaking (NPRM) to the extent that they are warranted, feasible, and allowed by existing legislative authority. If necessary, we also may seek additional legislative authority.

Recommendation #18: Commandant should examine NVIC 12-69 and NVIC 1-89 to determine whether the older one should be cancelled and incorporated into the newer.

4

Commandant's Action on Recommendation #18: We concur with the intent of this recommendation. Both documents are being examined in conjunction with the review of the current requirements for commercial diving operations. Once the regulatory update is complete, a determination on whether one or both NVICs should be cancelled or combined will be made and up-to-date policy guidance will be provided.

Recommendation #19: Commandant should require dive operation inspection training for all marine inspectors.

Commandant's Action on Recommendation #19: We concur with the intent of this recommendation. Training on commercial diving operations will better prepare our marine inspectors and investigators to prevent and respond to incidents involving this sector of the marine industry. A Commercial Diving Orientation Course curriculum has already been developed. This new course will be formally incorporated into the Marine Safety training program for marine inspectors and investigators.

Recommendation #20: Commandant should remove the diving component from the MODU Inspector PQS workbook and establish a separate Performance Qualification Standards workbook for diving operations.

Commandant's Action on Recommendation #20: We concur with this recommendation. A separate Performance Qualification Standards (PQS) workbook for commercial diving operations is being developed in conjunction with the recently completed Commercial Diving Orientation Course curriculum.

Recommendation #21: Commandant should evaluate the adequacy of the MODU/SEILOD (Mobile Offshore Drilling Unit/Special Examination in Lieu of Drydocking) job aid, CG-840H-1 (9-92), to determine whether additional inspection items should be added to the diving checklist (pg. 20-22). See IO Exhibit 31.

Commandant's Action on Recommendation #21: We concur with this recommendation. An evaluation of the MODU/SEILOD job aid, CG-840H-1, is currently underway. The job aid's adequacy is being evaluated in conjunction with the commercial diving orientation training curriculum and the development of a performance qualification standards workbook (PQS) for diving operations. Appropriate modifications will be made when the evaluation is completed.

Recommendation #22: Commandant should publish guidance emphasizing that Coast Guard marine inspectors should not attempt to delegate dive safety enforcement duties to any third party, including classification society surveyors.

Commandant's Action on Recommendation #22: We concur with the intent of this recommendation. All guidance associated with dive safety enforcement duties is currently being evaluated in conjunction with the technical review of the Commercial Diving Operation regulations. When the regulatory update is complete, appropriate policy guidance, including clear delineation as to what duties may and may not be delegated to third parties, will be provided.

5

Recommendation #23: Commandant should require dive casualty investigation training for all marine safety casualty investigators.

Commandant's Action on Recommendation #23: We concur with the intent of this recommendation. We agree that it would be desirable for marine safety casualty investigators to have formal dive casualty investigation training in the event they were called upon to do such an investigation. However, diving casualties accounted for less than 4% of the total Coast Guard casualty investigation workload from 1995 to 2000. Given the limited training resources available to the Coast Guard, this level of frequency does not warrant formal training of all casualty investigators in this area at this time. However, several initiatives have been undertaken to improve the knowledge level of investigators in this area, including the development of a Commercial Diving Orientation Course for marine inspectors and investigators. Regarding investigations specifically, this diving casualty investigation was included as a case study at the 2000 Senior Investigating Officers (SIO) Conference. The case study was also included on a CD-ROM given to each attendee at the conference to be used at their field units for reference and local training on this topic.

Recommendation #24: Commandant should consider tasking Coast Guard divers to assist in the investigation of diving casualties. In this case, the IO was assisted by a former Coast Guard diver and a U.S. Navy Master Diver, both with exceptional insight. However, previous investigators to this casualty did not have those valuable resources. The Marine Safety Manual recommends that an IO investigating diving casualties have diving experience, but there are few IO's available with that background.

Commandant's Action on Recommendation #24: We concur with the intent of this recommendation. The Officer in Charge, Marine Inspection (OCMI) has the authority to use Coast Guard divers or U.S. Navy Divers to assist in any type of Coast Guard casualty investigation. The Office of Investigations and Analysis will encourage the use of these resources and will provide updated guidance to investigating officers in the Marine Safety Manual.

Recommendation #25: Commandant should consider seeking an agreement with the Navy Experimental Diving Unit and the U.S. Navy Diving School to provide assistance in Coast Guard diving casualty investigations.

Commandant's Action on Recommendation #25: We concur with this recommendation. The Coast Guard currently has a liaison at the Navy Diving School who has provided assistance to the Coast Guard in the past on investigations and we will continue to use our liaison. The Office of Investigations and Analysis will discuss the need for a Memorandum of Undertaking (MOU) with the U.S. Navy Diving program. Additional guidance on diving investigations will be provided in the Marine Safety Manual.

Recommendation #26: Commandant should establish a working group of industry experts to examine ways to improve safety practices in the commercial diving industry. The working group should consider whether the Coast Guard should adopt by reference the ADC Consensus Standards for commercial diving operations where they do not conflict with Coast Guard

6

UNITED STATES COAST GUARD

INVESTIGATION INTO THE CIRCUMSTANCES
SURROUNDING THE

COMMERCIAL DIVING ACCIDENT

ONBOARD THE MOBILE OFFSHORE DRILLING UNIT
CLIFF'S DRILLING RIG NO. 12 ON MARCH 4, 1996
WITH THE LOSS OF LIFE

moa
16732
30 August 2000

SECOND ENDORSEMENT on report of formal investigation of commercial diver fatality on CLIFF'S DRILLING RIG NO. 12 on 4 March 1996

From: Commander, Eighth Coast Guard District
To: Commandant (G-MOA)

Subj: FORMAL INVESTIGATION INTO THE COMMERCIAL DIVING ACCIDENT ABOARD THE MOBILE OFFSHORE DRILLING UNIT CLIFF'S DRILLING RIG NO.12 ON 4 MARCH1996, WITH LOSS OF LIFE.

1. Forwarded recommending approval. I concur with the conclusions and recommendations.

2. This formal investigation was convened to determine why a diver needlessly lost his life. What the investigation uncovered was that the current dive regulations- coupled with the Coast Guard's inadequate experience in diving operations & casualty investigations- allow sub-par commercial diving operators to thrive. This investigation clearly and painfully outlined shortfalls in the commercial diving regulations, commercial diving operations, and Coast Guard marine inspections & investigations experience. The Investigating Officer's report thoroughly reflects the myriad of contributing causes to this casualty and purposefully outlines the numerous solutions to assist in preventing future needless deaths. The IO is commended for his outstanding efforts during the investigation and for this exceptionally comprehensive report.

3. Recommendations 5-8, which require specific dive supervisor responsibilities, should be implemented immediately. There were at least three diving casualty deaths in D8, since March 1996, that resulted directly from the person in charge or the dive supervisor's poor supervision & management. The Coast Guard's biggest impact on safe diving operations will be through effective regulations (incorporating ADC Consensus Standards), comprehensive training and interactive partnership with marine industry. Adoption of the recommendations spelled out in this report should be the first step toward the Coast Guard assuming its leadership role in commercial diving safety.

4. The Eighth District has forwarded a request for criminal referral to Commandant (G-MOA) against G&G Marine and Dan Gilbert. It is quite clear from this investigation that G&G Marine has continued to operate with little regard to diver safety. In the four years since the casualty occurred, G&G Marine has not implemented safety practices or equipment maintenance procedures, yet they are still conducting commercial diving jobs.

moa
16732
30 August 2000

SECOND ENDORSEMENT on report of formal investigation of commercial diver fatality on CLIFF'S DRILLING RIG NO. 12 on 4 March 1996

5. While this investigation discusses the marine inspector's failure to conduct an inspection of the dive station, numerous other obvious factors were missed that showed a lack of consistent guidance and leadership. The fact that the trainee thought that American Bureau of Shipping surveyor would handle the underwater portion including diving operations highlights the inconsistent training and misunderstood guidance that is prevalent for commercial diving operations in the marine inspection program. The fact that NVIC 1-89 is not applicable to this vessel yet was the standard guidance to be used by inspectors also highlights systemic problems in written guidance to field inspectors. Lastly, the fact that an IO did not initially go to the site of the casualty to secure the compressor & dive helmet and gather witness statements & evidence in a timely manner clearly proved that diving casualty investigations expertise was non-existent. This formal report is likely the first opportunity for the Coast Guard to establish a basis for improving our training and expertise in commercial diving inspections and diving casualty investigations. Recommendations 17-25 appropriately address steps for implementation that would hopefully prevent future recurrence of the problems noted. The solution to the vast problem is not to hold one marine inspector accountable; the solution is to take proactive steps to educate the field and institute value-added and timely training.

R. J. MORRIS
By direction

Copy: CO, MSO Port Arthur

16732
5 June 2000

FIRST ENDORSEMENT on report of formal investigation of commercial diver fatality on
CLIFF'S DRILLING RIG NO. 12 on 4 March 1996

From: Commanding Officer, Marine Safety Office Port Arthur
To: Commandant (G-MOA)
Via: Commander, Eighth Coast Guard District

Subj: FORMAL INVESTIGATION INTO THE COMMERCIAL DIVING ACCIDENT
      ABOARD THE MOBILE OFFSHORE DRILLING UNIT CLIFF'S DRILLING RIG
      NO. 12 ON 4 MARCH 1996, WITH LOSS OF LIFE.

1. Forwarded recommending approval and closing of this casualty case.

2. Due to the time between the casualty and the taking of formal testimony and due to the
inability to question the deceased, many facts cannot be determined with confidence. They do
not all need to be known for this investigation to serve its purpose of improving safety.
However, the investigator has developed the most likely scenario based on the few hard facts
available. We will never be able to determine conclusively the details of what happened when
Pilkington developed breathing difficulties 28 feet from the observation of other humans.

3. Clearly, the commercial diving regulations in 46 CFR 197 were not followed or enforced.
Many people failed in their responsibilities, including the senior Coast Guard inspector. Only
one or two differences in a myriad of contributing causes would likely have prevented this most
unfortunate death. Regardless, there is room for improvement in 46 CFR 197 and having an
active project in place to update those regulations should allow expedient changes.

4. I do not intend to pursue further investigation into the possible violation of regulations. First,
more than four years have passed since the casualty, meaning timely enforcement is no longer
possible. Second, there is no evidence of intentional violation of regulations. Third, the
challenge to demonstrate accountability under the regulation is great, in that many of the
apparent violations would be pursued against the dive supervisor. There was no designated dive
supervisor and involved parties testify they thought someone else had that responsibility. Fourth,
a number of the potentially responsible parties are no longer in business. Fifth, civil litigation
cases were concluded more than a year ago. The businesses involved have learned their
responsibility through the numerous investigation and litigation activities. In short, the time and
effort to pursue further investigation and civil penalties is not worthwhile or in the best interests
of safety.

G. W. ANDERSON

455

**U.S. Department
of Transportation

United States
Coast Guard**

Commanding Officer
U.S. Coast Guard
Marine Safety Office

Federal Building
2875 Jimmy Johnson Blvd.
Port Arthur, TX 77640-2099
Phone: (409) 723-6509
FAX: (409) 723-6541

16732
2 June 2000

From: LCDR Thomas Beistle, USCG
To: Commandant (G-MOA)
Via: (1) Commanding Officer, Marine Safety Office Port Arthur
        (2) Commander, Eighth Coast Guard District

Subj: FORMAL INVESTIGATION INTO THE COMMERCIAL DIVING ACCIDENT
ABOARD THE MOBILE OFFSHORE DRILLING UNIT CLIFF'S DRILLING
RIG NO. 12 ON 4 MARCH 1996, WITH LOSS OF LIFE.

Summary:

On the afternoon of 4 March 1996, Brian Pilkington, a commercial diver, began an underwater
inspection of the mat of the Mobile Offshore Drilling Unit (MODU) CLIFFS DRILLING RIG
NO. 12 (Rig 12). Pilkington's dive lasted about three hours with him moving around the mat
under the direction of two members of an inspection team on the deck of Rig 12 (See figure 1).
At about 1645 hours, Pilkington indicated that he was having trouble breathing and soon
thereafter quit communicating with the surface. A rescue operation was quickly initiated, but
was unable to reach Pilkington for nearly 35 minutes. At about 1720 hours, Dan Wiitala, one of
the inspection team members, reached Pilkington about 28 feet below the surface. Wiitala found
Pilkington unconscious, floating face down at about a 45 degree angle to a horizontal plane.
Pilkington's body could not float free because a hand axe attached to his diving belt was fouled
on a pipe on the rig's mat. Wiitala cut the lanyard and brought Pilkington to the surface where
he was lifted to the deck of Rig 12 in a personnel basket. Members of the crew began
cardiopulmonary resuscitation (CPR) and then loaded him onto a helicopter for transport to St.
Mary's Hospital in Port Arthur, Texas. The helicopter arrived at St. Mary's at 1820 hours.
Brian Pilkington was pronounced dead at 2230 hours.

16732
2 June 2000

FORMAL INVESTIGATION INTO THE COMMERCIAL DIVING ACCIDENT ABOARD THE MOBILE OFFSHORE DRILLING UNIT CLIFF'S DRILLING RIG NO. 12 ON 4 MARCH 1996, WITH LOSS OF LIFE

Vessel Data:

Name:	CLIFFS DRILLING RIG NO. 12
O.N.:	D622669
Service:	Mobile Offshore Drilling Unit
Propulsion:	None
Gross Tons:	4109
Net Tons:	4109
Length:	220.00 feet
Breadth:	185.00 feet
Depth:	27.50 feet
Built:	30 June 1980, Bethlehem Steel Corp., Beaumont, TX
Owner/Operator:	Cliffs Drilling Co.
Manager:	Ronald Wayne Townsend
Manager's License:	Offshore Installation Manager (OIM)

Deceased:	Age:	Next of Kin:
Brian Pilkington	23	
		Wife

Parties In Interest:[1]

Peter J. Pilkington
Commercial Dive Safety Organization
2795 152nd Ave. NE
Redmond, WA 98052

Ronald Townsend

American Bureau of Shipping
Two World Trade Center, 106th Floor
New York, NY 10048

Counsel:

Joe Walker and
Thomas Mosele
4200 Westheimer, Ste 130
Houston, TX 77027

Bijan Siahatgar
Griggs & Harrison, P.C.
1301 McKinney, Ste 3200
Houston, TX 77010-3001

Michael Wilson
Kirlin, Campbell & Keating
5 Hanover Square
New York, NY 10004

---

[1] Cliffs Drilling Co. and Dan Wiitala were named as Parties In Interest but declined to exercise their rights at the Hearing. USCG Investigation, Vol. 1, pg. 3-5 and 128-132.

- 2 -

16732
2 June 2000

FORMAL INVESTIGATION INTO THE COMMERCIAL DIVING ACCIDENT ABOARD
THE MOBILE OFFSHORE DRILLING UNIT CLIFF'S DRILLING RIG NO. 12 ON
4 MARCH 1996, WITH LOSS OF LIFE

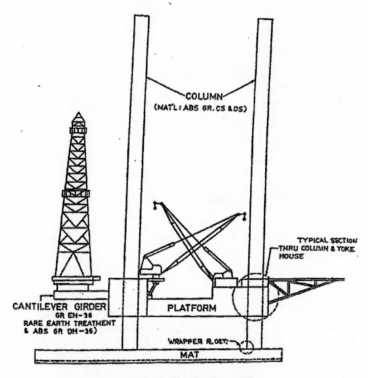

Figure 1: Mobil Offshore Drilling Unit

Inspection (OCMI).[6] Typically, if all the requirements set out in the regulations are met, the
plan is approved. Cliffs' SEILOD proposal addressed all but two of the required items.[7] The
proposal did not specify the inspection location or the name of the diving company to be
used. SEILOD proposals often do not contain those two items because diver availability is
often not known 60 days in advance and the need to find water clear enough to conduct an
underwater inspection may cause the location to change. These items are usually identified

---

[6] Marine Safety Manual, Vol. II, Ch. 35.C.16 - Special Underwater Inspection in Lieu of Drydocking
[7] USCG Investigation, Vol. 4, IO exhibit 33 (Cliffs Drilling Co., Proposal to Conduct Inspection)

- 4 -

16732
2 June 2000

FORMAL INVESTIGATION INTO THE COMMERCIAL DIVING ACCIDENT ABOARD
THE MOBILE OFFSHORE DRILLING UNIT CLIFF'S DRILLING RIG NO. 12 ON
4 MARCH 1996, WITH LOSS OF LIFE

as the inspection date approaches, and the omission of these items is not normally cause to disapprove a proposal. Cliffs' proposal also did not meet the 60-day notice requirement. The short notice was caused by Cliffs' need to reactivate Rig 12 quickly to meet their charter agreement with Hercules. This too is common and would not normally be cause for disapproval.

4. In its application, Cliffs requested a waiver of a liveboating prohibition against diving from one hour after sunset to one hour before sunrise.[8] The Commandant may grant variances from the regulations, but OCMIs have not been delegated that authority.[9] Nevertheless, Marine Safety Office Port Arthur waived the sunset to sunrise restriction based on Cliffs' promise to take precautions to ensure diver safety. Cliffs took the promised precautions.[10]

5. The Coast Guard conducts SEILODs on MODUs according to Navigation and Vessel Inspection Circular (NVIC) 12-69. The Commandant, Office of Merchant Marine Safety (G-MVI-2) promulgated NVIC 12-69 on 12 December 1969. The SEILOD procedures were established because drydocks were not able to accommodate the large MODUs being built. Rather than exempt MODUs from drydock requirements, G-MVI-2 developed special examination methods not requiring drydocking. NVIC 12-69 imposes no requirements on OCMIs to evaluate divers, diving companies, or diving safety on SEILODs. NVIC 12-69 has not been canceled and remains an effective circular.

6. NVIC 1-89 was drafted almost 20 years after NVIC 12-69 to expand the SEILOD program to other classes of vessels.[11] Both NVICs addressed the SEILOD process and the latter is an outgrowth of the former. NVIC 1-89 clearly envisions a proactive OCMI role ensuring the safety of commercial diving operations related to SEILODs.

> Divers, Diving Equipment, and Operations: The underwater survey should not be conducted unless the inspector is satisfied that the equipment and procedures being used by the divers will provide a safe and meaningful examination of the ship. Safety must be foremost on the minds of all those working together on the actual diving operation. While matters in this regard are best left to the experienced, professional individuals normally found conducting this type of work, everyone involved in the survey should be alert to these needs and ensure that any requirements regarding this inspection can be safely accomplished. As required by 46 CFR 197.202, commercial diving operations

---

[8] USCG Investigation, Vol. 4, IO exhibit 33 (Cliffs Drilling Co., Proposal to Conduct Inspection)
  See 46 CFR 197 et. seq. Commercial Diving Operations; *Liveboating* means the support of a surface-supplied diver from a vessel underway. 46 CFR 197.204, 46 CFR 197.436(a)(2)
[9] 46 CFR 197.206
[10] Champagne, testimony, Vol 1, pg. 21
[11] Tank Vessels, Cargo Vessels, other miscellaneous vessels, and Oceanographic Research Vessels less than 15 years old. 46 CFR 31.10-21(e) and 46 CFR 189.40-3(e) also permit continued participation in the underwater survey program for vessels 15 years old and older. Vessels more than 15 years old that have not previously participated in the underwater survey program are ineligible.

- 5 -

16732
2 June 2000

FORMAL INVESTIGATION INTO THE COMMERCIAL DIVING ACCIDENT ABOARD
THE MOBILE OFFSHORE DRILLING UNIT CLIFF'S DRILLING RIG NO. 12 ON
4 MARCH 1996, WITH LOSS OF LIFE

taking place from vessels required to have Certificates of Inspection issued by the Coast
Guard, regardless of geographical location, must comply with the provisions of 46 CFR
Part 197 Subpart B – Commercial Diving Operations.

Acceptability of Diving Personnel and Equipment: A professional commercial
diving firm should be employed by the owner. While specific approval is not
required by the Coast Guard, a subjective evaluation by the OCMI or the
attending inspector will be conducted. Such an evaluation may consider:

(a) Prior experience or training;

(b) Qualifications of dive team members in photography, nondestructive
testing (NDT), underwater damage repair, and other training and
experience;

(c) The degree of professional approach/attitude, as evidenced by an
organized dive plan, personnel assignments, standby and backups,
compliance with appropriate safety regulations (Coast Guard,
Occupational Safety and Health Administration (OSHA), various
states), etc.[12]

7. Circulars are not usually meant to be binding on either the OCMI or industry. Generally, the
Commandant promulgates them as advice to industry, which was clearly the case with NVIC
1-89.[13] However, circulars also are strong advice on marine inspection issues to OCMIs.
NVIC 1-89 clearly established a Commandant expectation that OCMIs examine commercial
diving operations associated with SEILODs on vessels other than MODUs to determine
whether the diving company is capable of conducting SEILODs safely.[14]

8. Two Memoranda of Understanding (MOU) between the Coast Guard and OSHA enabled the
Coast Guard to act on behalf of OSHA for activities occurring on the Outer Continental
Shelf, including commercial diving operations.[15] The MOUs enable Coast Guard marine
inspectors to conduct periodic onsite inspections to ensure compliance with health and safety
regulations. To accomplish this, the Marine Safety Manual establishes a Commandant

---

[12] U.S. Coast Guard Investigation, Vol. 4, IO Exhibit 30, (NVIC 1-89, encl. 1, para. 5.f.)

[13] "Underwater survey diving contractors *are encouraged* to use the guidance in enclosure (1) when preparing to
conduct an underwater survey." NVIC 1-89, para. 4.b. (emphasis added)

[14] None of this, however, indicates intent by Commandant to relieve the vessel owner or diving contractor of
responsibility for safety. Especially since many SEILOD dives are conducted when Coast Guard personnel are
not present. "It must be stressed that the underwater survey program is an option that the ship's
owners/operators have elected to use. Responsibility for the management of the vessel, its personnel, and
maintenance of necessary safety and service systems remains at all times with the master and his
representatives." See NVIC 1-89, encl. 1, para. 5.a.

[15] Memorandum of Understanding between the Coast Guard and OSHA dated December 19, 1979
Memorandum of Understanding between the Coast Guard and OSHA dated March 8, 1983

- 6 -

16732
2 June 2000

FORMAL INVESTIGATION INTO THE COMMERCIAL DIVING ACCIDENT ABOARD
THE MOBILE OFFSHORE DRILLING UNIT CLIFF'S DRILLING RIG NO. 12 ON
4 MARCH 1996, WITH LOSS OF LIFE

expectation that marine inspectors verify compliance with commercial diving regulations
coincident with other inspection activities.[16]

9. At the time of the casualty, Rig 12 was undergoing a Classification Society (Class) survey in
addition to a Coast Guard SEILOD. Class for Rig 12 was the American Bureau of Shipping
(ABS). A classification society is an organization, other than a flag state, that issues
Certificates of Class and/or International Convention Certificates.[17] The Coast Guard is
statutorily responsible for safety of life and property at sea.[18] But the Coast Guard may rely
on ABS reports, documents, and certificates to complete its inspection duties.[19] To complete
Rig 12's inspection for certification and SEILOD, Coast Guard marine inspectors attended
the vessel at least three times, on 1, 4, and 8 March 1996. During the inspection, they noted
37 deficiencies and worked with Cliffs' Director of Safety and Personnel, Buddy Horton; and
Rig 12's Offshore Installation Manager (OIM), Ronald Townsend, to ensure that the
deficiencies were resolved. By March 8, Cliffs had cleared a majority of the deficiencies and
Rig 12 was deemed by the marine inspectors to be fit for its intended route and service. The
inspectors issued a new COI and endorsed the vessel's International Oil Pollution Prevention
certificate and record of inspection card. The marine inspectors also issued a CG Form 835
as a worklist of 21 additional items to be fixed aboard Rig 12.[20] While Rig 12 was laid up,
its operations manual, like all other inspection requirements, had been allowed to lapse. On 4
March, a copy of the manual was on board Rig 12 under review by the Coast Guard. The
manual had not been approved as of 4 March.[21]

10. To satisfy the inspection requirements of Class and the SEILOD requirements of the Coast
Guard, Horton contacted Texas NDE, a company specializing in nondestructive testing. One
of Texas NDE's owners, Kirk Austin, had worked for Cliffs on at least two other MODU
inspections. Cliffs hired Texas NDE to do two types of nondestructive testing on Rig 12: (1)
magnetic particle testing to detect cracks and welding discontinuities in the metal of the legs
and mat and (2) ultrasonic testing (gauging) to determine hull thickness. Gauging was to be
done at 40 spots selected by Class and Cliffs on the legs and mat of Rig 12. Typically,
magnetic particle inspections are video taped for ABS and then submitted to the Coast Guard
for review.

---

[16] Marine Safety Manual, Vol. II, Chapter 16.E.1
[17] Marine Safety Manual, Vol. II, Chapter 23.B.3.a
[18] 46 USC Part B
[19] 46 USC 3316
[20] U. S. Coast Guard Investigation, Vol. 6, IO Exhibit 65 (USCG Inspection Case # MI96008514); U.S. Coast Guard
Investigation, Vol. 4, IO exhibit 29 (Inspection Worklist, 835 dated March 4, 1996)
[21] Martinez, testimony, Vol. 2, pg. 150-151.

16732
2 June 2000

FORMAL INVESTIGATION INTO THE COMMERCIAL DIVING ACCIDENT ABOARD
THE MOBILE OFFSHORE DRILLING UNIT CLIFF'S DRILLING RIG NO. 12 ON
4 MARCH 1996, WITH LOSS OF LIFE

Texas NDE

11. In 1996, Austin was Texas NDE's President and Operations Manager and had 15 years of
NDT experience. Austin handled sales, hiring, payroll, and marketing in addition to doing
much of the company's NDT work. Austin was certified by the American Society for
Nondestructive Testing with Level II technical proficiency in ultrasonic, eddy current, and
liquid penetrant testing. He also was Level III qualified in magnetic particle testing.[22] Texas
NDE also employed Mark Wright, Dale McInnis, and Henry Hodge. Texas NDE began as a
NDT company working on those portions of MODUs above the waterline. The company did
not plan to do diving or underwater testing when it was formed. The company found though,
that diving companies were reluctant to accept low paying shallow water jobs (defined by
Austin as 30 feet or less) and Texas NDE saw potential for more work if the company
included shallow water diving as part of its service. Of the four company employees, only
Wright had prior diving experience. He had been a Marine Corps diver trained by the U.S.
Navy. According to Austin, "[h]e was the one who kind of guided us on what we needed to
think about."[23] By 1996, McInnis and Hodge had each made; at most, two or three shallow
water surface supplied air dives for the company.[24] Austin's first surface supplied air dive
was in 10 feet of water while working with a large diving company. Austin then took a
YMCA SCUBA[25] class as a "starting point" to become proficient in commercial diving. The
class met two nights a week for one or two months.[26] Aside from the 10-foot dive and the
YMCA course, by 1996 Austin's total diving experience consisted of five or six shallow
water commercial dives made over the span of about five years.[27] Prior to 4 March, Austin
had dived on two shallow-water NDT inspections for Cliffs similar to the Rig 12 job.[28]
When Horton hired Austin to do NDT of Rig 12, Texas NDE did not have enough personnel
available to do the job and Austin subcontracted with G&G Marine to provide divers.[29]

G&G Marine

12. In 1996, Dan Gilbert was the owner, operator, and sole manager of G&G Marine (G&G).[30]
Gilbert began sport diving in the 1960's while in the military and after leaving the service in
1970, he went to work as a commercial diver for International Marine Technology in
Houston, Texas. Two years later, Gilbert left to work for Underwater Technology, Inc., also

---

[22] Austin, testimony, Vol. 2, pg. 204-206
[23] Austin, testimony, Vol. 2, pg. 216, 233
[24] Surface supplied air diving means the diver is supplied with compressed breathing air from the dive location. See
46 CFR 197.204 (Definitions)
[25] Self Contained Underwater Breathing Apparatus means the diver is supplied with compressed breathing air from
diver carried equipment. See 46 CFR 197.204 (Definitions)
[26] U.S. Coast Guard Investigation, Vol. 4, IO exhibit 39 (YMCA card)
[27] Austin, testimony, Vol. 2, 213-216
[28] Austin, testimony, Vol. 2, pg. 217, 235
[29] Austin, testimony, Vol. 2, pg. 223
[30] USCG Investigation, Vol. 4, IO exhibit 40, (Danny R. Gilbert, "Sworn Statement", Houston, May 19, 1999, pg.
23); Mr. Gilbert was still the owner/operator of G&G at the time of this writing.

- 8 -

16732
2 June 2000

FORMAL INVESTIGATION INTO THE COMMERCIAL DIVING ACCIDENT ABOARD THE MOBILE OFFSHORE DRILLING UNIT CLIFF'S DRILLING RIG NO. 12 ON 4 MARCH 1996, WITH LOSS OF LIFE

based in Houston. Gilbert learned his trade "on the job" by watching other, more experienced divers and made over 100 surface supplied air dives every year for those companies. In that time, Gilbert conducted hull surveys, damage inspections, and cleaned ships' hulls. He worked in the Gulf of Mexico, Central and South America, and the Caribbean. In 1974, Gilbert started his own company, Gilbert Marine, and twelve years later merged with Taylor Diving & Salvage.[31] Gilbert worked at Taylor for 18 months as manager of ship diving. In that capacity, he solicited work cleaning ship hulls and conducting ship surveys. Gilbert bid jobs and assigned dive teams from a pool of 200 divers. One of his responsibilities was to assign and designate, in writing, dive supervisors for every job. In 1988, Gilbert left Taylor to start G&G Marine in Houston, Texas.[32]

13. At G&G, Gilbert hired workers, scheduled jobs, and directed field operations. G&G's practice for equipping its dive operations appears to be consistent with industry practice. "[The diver is] responsible for his -- what we call personal dive gear, which is your wet suit (if required), coveralls, booties, fins, weight belt, harness, knife, hand tools (i.e., crescent wrenches, a pair of pliers), gloves, a bailout bottle, if they want one. They are not required to supply their own diving helmet. We have one that's available."[33] Pilkington, Wiitala, and Austin all used their own helmets for the Rig 12 diving job.[34] Aside from the personal dive gear, "G&G supplied everything from the end of the hose back."[35] This meant that when G&G sent divers into the field, the company supplied air compressors, hoses, gauges, video equipment, and cables – the larger, more expensive equipment. G&G had once been a member of the Association of Diving Contractors (ADC), but by 1996 Gilbert had withdrawn G&G's membership for "personal reasons".[36] Nevertheless, in 1996 G&G's operations manual claimed that G&G still complied with all ADC standards. Both ADC and G&G's standards called for two divers and one tender on a dive like the Rig 12 inspection.[37]

14. G&G's procedures for outfitting a dive operation were not set out in the company's operations manual or any company policy.[38] When G&G sent divers to a job, diving equipment was selected and loaded at the direction of any one of several people. Gilbert

[31] USCG Investigation, Vol. 4, IO exhibit 40, (Gilbert statement, pg. 16)
[32] USCG Investigation, Vol. 4, IO exhibit 40, (Gilbert statement, pg. 20)
[33] USCG Investigation, Vol. 4, IO exhibit 40, (Gilbert statement, pg. 106)
[34] Wiitala, testimony; Vol. 1, pg. 315-317.
[35] Wiitala, testimony, Vol. 1, pg. 169
[36] USCG Investigation, Vol. 4, IO exhibit 40, (Gilbert statement, pg. 87)
[37] "There is no standard size dive crew. Each individual job will dictate the number of persons detailed for conduct of the dive operations. The dive crew composition will be dictated by physical and environmental conditions and, by regulatory requirements published by the various agencies under which the operations will be conducted. However; in no case shall G&G Marine operate with fewer persons than as set forth in the Diving Consensus Standards of the Association of Diving Contractors."; USCG Investigation, Vol. 4, IO exhibit 16, (G&G's Safe Practices and Operation Manual, pg. 1-4); Wiitala, testimony, Vol. 1, pg. 258-259; USCG Investigation, Vol. 4, IO exhibit 57, (ADC Consensus Standards, pg. 3-24(D))
[38] USCG Investigation, Vol. 4, IO exhibit 16, (G&G Safe Practices and Operation Manual)

-9-

16732
2 June 2000

FORMAL INVESTIGATION INTO THE COMMERCIAL DIVING ACCIDENT ABOARD THE MOBILE OFFSHORE DRILLING UNIT CLIFF'S DRILLING RIG NO. 12 ON 4 MARCH 1996, WITH LOSS OF LIFE

apparently made equipment lists.[39] So, too, did the dive personnel.[40] Dan Wiitala, a G&G employee, testified that several years after he began working at G&G, one of the employees "raised a fuss" about needing a secondary air supply when diving.[41] Thereafter, it became company policy to send a secondary air supply on dives, though insufficient evidence was found to determine whether the policy was ever put into writing.[42] G&G did not require divers to use bailout bottles as a tertiary air supply, nor were bailout bottles discussed in G&G's safety manual.[43] G&G did maintain dive logs, but had a policy of throwing them away at the end of each pay period.[44]

15. In 1996, G&G did not have a shop manager or anyone charged specifically with routine equipment maintenance. At one time, for about a year in 1989 or 1990, G&G employed Mr. Al May strictly to maintain equipment. Mr. May also may have been responsible for ensuring that air quality testing on G&G's compressors was completed. When May left in about 1990, he was not replaced and no one else was designated as the equipment maintenance person. Nevertheless, for about a year after May left the company, G&G's maintenance program was efficient enough to ensure that air quality testing continued.[45]

16. Gilbert said that he was responsible for shop maintenance, but that all G&G employees would identify equipment problems and bring them to his attention.[46] From time to time, Gilbert also paid divers to work in the shop maintaining equipment.[47] Starting in about 1993, the maintenance program, at least for the Quincy 325 compressor used on Rig 12 (Compressor 2)[48] consisted of periodically changing the engine oil, compressor oil, and filters (See figures 2 & 3). Between February 1993 and March 1996, Compressor 2's engine oil was changed eight times, the compressor oil three times, and air intake filters four times. The compressor maintenance log required by 46 CFR 197.480, and 197.482(d) does not indicate that any other repairs or modifications were made to Compressor 2 during that period.[49] Gilbert indicated that routine maintenance like checking compressor oil levels, was done as equipment was loaded for shipping to dive sites. However, during his equipment

---

[39] USCG Investigation, Vol. 4, IO exhibit 15, (G&G equipment list)
[40] Wiitala, testimony, Vol. 1, pg. 136-138
[41] Wiitala, testimony, Vol. 1, pg. 152
[42] USCG Investigation, Vol. 4, IO exhibit 16, (G&G's Safe Practices and Operation Manual)
[43] USCG Investigation, Vol. 4, IO exhibit 40, (Gilbert statement, pg. 92)
[44] USCG Investigation, Vol. 4, IO exhibit 40, (Gilbert statement, pg. 91)
[45] Lawdermilk, testimony, Vol. 1, pg. 441-442, 447; 46 CFR 197.340 (Breathing gas supply) and 46 CFR 197.450 (Breathing gas tests)
[46] USCG Investigation, Vol. 4, IO exhibit 40, (Gilbert statement, pg. 44)
[47] USCG Investigation, Vol. 4, IO exhibit 40, (Gilbert statement, pg. 51)
[48] Generally referred to as Compressor 2 by G&G employees. USCG Investigation, Vol. 4, IO exhibit 40, (Gilbert statement, pg. 41)
[49] USCG Investigation, Vol. 4, IO exhibit 40, (Gilbert statement, Exhibit 1); Wiitala, testimony, pg. 164-166; Lawdermilk, testimony, Vol. 1, pg. 442

- 10 -

16732
2 June 2000

FORMAL INVESTIGATION INTO THE COMMERCIAL DIVING ACCIDENT ABOARD
THE MOBILE OFFSHORE DRILLING UNIT CLIFF'S DRILLING RIG NO. 12 ON
4 MARCH 1996, WITH LOSS OF LIFE

loadout on 3 March 1996, Gilbert did not check Compressor 2 before it went out for the Rig 12 job.[50]

17. One employee working for G&G on 4 March 1996 was Kevin Todd Lawdermilk. He worked for G&G for seven years as a diver and occasionally as an in-house maintenance person.[51] Lawdermilk was familiar with all four compressors G&G owned in 1996, and had worked on each. Lawdermilk testified that G&G often would not buy replacement parts to do ordinary equipment upkeep. As an example, Lawdermilk testified that G&G employees would put red shop rags or Kotex pads in a supply side air intake filter housing when factory specified air filters were not available. Lawdermilk indicated that, before 4 March, there was a strong likelihood that a red shop rag weighted down by marbles had been put in the air intake filter housing of Compressor 2 in lieu of an ordinary filter. Lawdermilk did not know whether the rag had been removed or replaced by 4 March.[52] Lawdermilk also testified that Compressor 2 had malfunctioned on a diving job several months before the Rig 12 job and had been set aside so it would not be used on other jobs. To Lawdermilk's knowledge, Compressor 2 had not been repaired before the Rig 12 job. Wiitala also did not know whether Compressor 2 had a factory specified filter on 4 March since he did not check the air filter housing before using the compressor.[53]

18. When asked (three years after the casualty) to produce receipts for purchases of routine maintenance and parts for G&G's compressors, Gilbert produced four receipts, three dated in 1993 and one in 1998.[54] None of the receipts indicated purchases of an air filter for Compressor 2.

---

[50] USCG Investigation, Vol. 4, IO exhibit 40, (Gilbert statement, pg. 48)
[51] USCG Investigation, Vol. 4, IO exhibit 40, (Gilbert statement, pg. 50-51); Lawdermilk, testimony, Vol. 1, pg. 443.
[52] Lawdermilk, testimony, Vol. 1, pg. 459-465, 510
[53] Wiitala, testimony, Vol. 1, pg. 513-514
[54] USCG Investigation, Vol. 4, IO exhibit 41, (McKenzie work order dated September 11, 1998) and U.S.Coast Guard Investigation, Vol. 5, IO exhibit 56, (McKenzie receipts for G&G Marine); Gilbert, testimony, Vol. 2, pg. 399

- 11 -

16732
2 June 2000

FORMAL INVESTIGATION INTO THE COMMERCIAL DIVING ACCIDENT ABOARD
THE MOBILE OFFSHORE DRILLING UNIT CLIFF'S DRILLING RIG NO. 12 ON
4 MARCH 1996, WITH LOSS OF LIFE

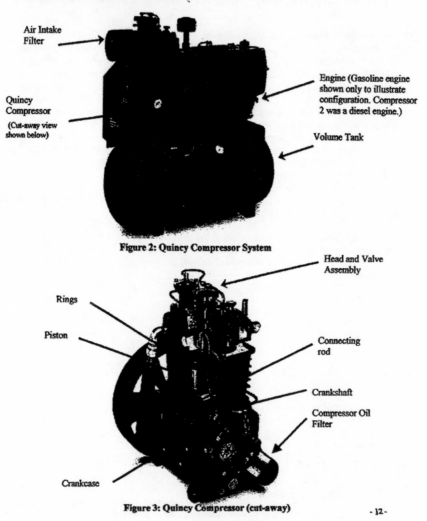

Figure 2: Quincy Compressor System

Figure 3: Quincy Compressor (cut-away)

- 12 -

466

16732
2 June 2000

FORMAL INVESTIGATION INTO THE COMMERCIAL DIVING ACCIDENT ABOARD THE MOBILE OFFSHORE DRILLING UNIT CLIFF'S DRILLING RIG NO. 12 ON 4 MARCH 1996, WITH LOSS OF LIFE

19. G&G's diver training program focused on ship maintenance rather than diving fundamentals.[55] Gilbert believed that when a diver graduated from dive school he was fully qualified to dive on any company job.[56] This was not consistent with training and qualification programs at other, larger, diving companies or in the military. One large diving company operating in the Gulf of Mexico, Oceaneering, expects a prospective diver to begin his career by working two or three years as a dive tender, with the majority of his time spent assisting dive operations and doing light to moderate diving under close supervision. The employee then graduates from tender to diver and will spend one or two years learning his trade to become fully qualified. A diver can, but is not guaranteed to, progress over time to dive supervisor after more training.

20. G&G's practice, by comparison, was to use a prospective diver as a tender for two or three months during which time he might carry out five or six dives under the supervision of a more experienced diver. Depending on workload demands, G&G then would deem him to be a fully qualified diver. Training at G&G was on the job. "We don't hire just divers and we don't hire just tenders. We found over the years that our best people are people that we hire straight out of commercial diving school and we teach them how to dive the way we want them to dive. And we give them the opportunity to get in the water quicker than they would with Cal Dive or American Oil Field Divers or Oceaneering – somebody like that."[57]

Dan Wiitala

21. Wiitala was a commercial diver who, by March 1996, had worked for Dan Gilbert for approximately 13 years; which practically speaking, was his entire commercial diving career. Wiitala began recreational SCUBA diving about 1979. Four years later, he attended a six-month course at a commercial dive school in Houston and was hired by Gilbert (either when Gilbert was with Taylor or as he started G&G) three months after graduating. Wiitala started with Gilbert's company as a dive tender, a job he described as one of setting up dive stations, waking the divers, tending to a diver while he is in the water including holding his hose, and following directions. Additionally, at the end of day, the dive tender broke down the dive station and stowed and refueled equipment as directed. Wiitala went to work with immediate expectations of becoming a diver, but as the newest employee he expected also to do the more menial work. Wiitala described his progression from diver to dive supervisor as accidental.

Q. When did you first act as a dive supervisor for G&G?

A. That, I couldn't tell you. Several years.

---

[55] USCG Investigation, Vol. 4, IO exhibit 40, (Gilbert statement, pg. 70-72)
[56] USCG Investigation, Vol. 4, IO exhibit 40, (Gilbert statement, pg. 70-71)
[57] USCG Investigation, Vol. 4, IO exhibit 40, (Gilbert statement, pg. 16)

16732
2 June 2000

FORMAL INVESTIGATION INTO THE COMMERCIAL DIVING ACCIDENT ABOARD
THE MOBILE OFFSHORE DRILLING UNIT CLIFF'S DRILLING RIG NO. 12 ON
4 MARCH 1996, WITH LOSS OF LIFE

> Q. And what had you done in that process to become qualified to be a dive
> supervisor?
>
> A. I don't know. I wish I knew, or I would have not done it.
>
> Q. When did you know you were ready to be a dive supervisor?
>
> A. I more or less got crowded into it. I never wanted to be.[58]

22. Wiitala later changed his estimate of the time to become a dive supervisor at G&G to five
years. He quit working for G&G approximately 10 months after the death of Brian
Pilkington.[59]

23. Wiitala indicated that compressors failed from time to time while on G&G diving jobs.
When that happened, it was the dive supervisor's responsibility to diagnose the problem. For
Wiitala, the process was simple; it would be obvious if the motor side quit because the
compressor is loud and when it went silent it meant the motor had quit. But, if the
compressor side quit, but not the motor, he would know by checking the air gauges.[60]

Brian Pilkington

24. Pilkington was a 23-year-old commercial diver with two years diving experience at the time
of the diving casualty. Pilkington graduated from University Prep High School in Seattle,
WA and became a certified SCUBA diver at the age of 21. Pilkington attended a commercial
dive school, Divers Institute of Technology, Inc., in Seattle and graduated in February 1994.
When he graduated, Pilkington was certified Level II in Ultrasonic Testing, Liquid Penetrant
and Magnetic Particle by the American Society for Nondestructive Testing. Pilkington also
received a certification deeming him proficient to perform maintenance and repair on the
SuperLite 17 & 27 Helmets and KMB-18 & 28 Band Masks.[61] After graduating, Pilkington
was first employed by Professional Divers of New Orleans and in 1995 he moved to
Houston, TX with his wife, Julia, to work for G&G Marine. There was insufficient evidence
to determine how many dives Pilkington made with G&G before 4 March 1996. The best
evidence would have been G&G's dive logs. However, Gilbert testified that G&G
maintained dive logs only until the end of each pay period and then threw them away.
Gilbert indicated that Pilkington's dive logs for G&G had been destroyed.[62] The testimony
indicates only that Pilkington had dived on several jobs for G&G before 4 March.

---

[58] Wiitala, testimony, Vol. 1, pg. 120, 145-146
[59] Wiitala, testimony, Vol. 1, pg. 146; Wiitala, testimony; Vol. 1, pg. 121
[60] Wiitala, testimony, Vol. 1, pg. 192-193
[61] USCG Investigation, Vol. 5, IO Exhibit 45, (Diving Records of Brian Pilkington)
[62] USCG Investigation, Vol. 4, IO Exhibit 40, (Gilbert Statement, pg. 91 – 94)

- 14 -

16732
2 June 2000

FORMAL INVESTIGATION INTO THE COMMERCIAL DIVING ACCIDENT ABOARD
THE MOBILE OFFSHORE DRILLING UNIT CLIFF'S DRILLING RIG NO. 12 ON
4 MARCH 1996, WITH LOSS OF LIFE

4 March 1996

25. On the evening of 3 March 1996, Gilbert contacted Pilkington and Wiitala to send them to a hull inspection job on Rig 12 out of Sabine Pass, Texas. Wiitala initially refused the job because he believed Pilkington was inexperienced and he did not know Austin. Wiitala reasoned that the team would be too small and Wiitala's responsibilities would be too great.[63] ". . . I figured I was going to be the only one out there doing everything or shouldering everything. And I didn't want any part of it."[64] Wiitala testified that after his initial refusal, Gilbert called back to promise Texas NDE would supply two additional divers. The dive team would total five: Wiitala, Austin, Pilkington and two divers from Texas NDE. Only then did Wiitala accept the job.[65]

26. Gilbert testified that after talking to Wiitala and Pilkington on the evening of 3 March 1996, he went to the G&G facility to prepare a load out list of equipment needed for the Rig 12 job.[66] Among the equipment on the list, two umbilicals were slated by Gilbert to be taken on the job. Gilbert stated that Pilkington arrived at G&G about 30 minutes later and together they gathered the equipment and loaded it into the bed of Pilkington's Nissan pickup truck. Gilbert said that during this process, he went into the office to get timesheets and dive logs to be delivered to Wiitala. Gilbert says that while he was in the office, Pilkington finished loading and checking the equipment to ensure it matched the loadout list. Gilbert instructed Pilkington to meet Wiitala at a roadside stop on Interstate 10 between Houston and Sabine Pass at 0500 hours the next morning.[67]

27. Coast Guard regulations require that a diving supervisor be appointed in writing and the appointment be given to the person-in-charge before diving begins.[68] The diving supervisor is required to provide an operations manual to the vessel's person-in-charge before diving begins; the manual is required to be at the dive location when diving begins.[69] According to Wiitala, Gilbert would customarily designate the dive supervisor for G&G diving jobs by inserting an appointing letter under the plastic cover of the operations manual sent to the dive location. Gilbert did not appoint a dive supervisor or send a company dive operations and safety manual to the Rig 12 dive location.[70] He testified that he expected a Texas NDE employee to be dive supervisor for the job.[71]

[63] Wiitala, testimony, Vol. 1, pg. 265.
[64] Wiitala, testimony, Vol. 1, pg. 172
[65] Wiitala, testimony, Vol. 1, pg. 171-172
[66] USCG Investigation, Vol. 4, IO exhibit 15, (G&G equipment list)
[67] USCG Investigation, Vol. 4, IO exhibit 40, (Gilbert statement, pg. 56-57)
[68] 46 CFR 197.210
[69] 46 CFR 197.420
[70] Wiitala, testimony, Vol. 1, pg. 147-148
[71] USCG Investigation, Vol. 4, IO exhibit 40, (Gilbert statement, pg. 104-105)

- 15 -

16732
2 June 2000

FORMAL INVESTIGATION INTO THE COMMERCIAL DIVING ACCIDENT ABOARD
THE MOBILE OFFSHORE DRILLING UNIT CLIFF'S DRILLING RIG NO. 12 ON
4 MARCH 1996, WITH LOSS OF LIFE

28. Early on the morning of 4 March 1996, Pilkington met Wiitala on Interstate 10 as directed. They drove in Pilkington's truck to Sabine Pass where they were to meet a crew boat to take them to Rig 12.[72] Wiitala testified that he expected a three-person dive team to meet them in Sabine Pass, but instead they met only Austin. Nevertheless, the group did not talk about the problem or make any effort to call for more divers. No one appears to have stopped to examine whether there were enough divers to proceed safely. Wiitala testified that he did ask Austin where the other two divers were, but did not remember Austin's response. Wiitala testified that he was angry about the situation, nevertheless, he did nothing about it.[73] The team made an aborted attempt to reach Rig 12 on a crew boat too small for the sea state, which was described as choppy with two to four foot seas.[74] After returning to the dock and boarding a larger vessel, Austin, Wiitala, and Pilkington arrived at Rig 12 at about 1100 hours.[75] Upon their arrival at Rig 12, the group waited two hours to unload their gear because another dive team was loading its gear to depart the vessel.[76]

29. On 4 March 1996, Coast Guard inspectors arrived on Rig 12 at 1030 hours and worked on the vessel until 1630 hours.[77] During that time, although they knew commercial diving operations were underway, they did not visit the dive operation or inspect the dive station, its manning, or equipment.[78]

30. When the Coast Guard inspectors arrived on Rig 12, they met with the class society surveyor and rig personnel to plan the day's inspections. According to the break-in marine inspector that day "[w]e agreed that ABS would handle the entire inspection with regards to the underwater portion of the exam. *The meeting left me with the impression that ABS would also inspect the topside diving gear as well as the underwater progress of the diving operations.*"[79] At the time of the Rig 12 inspection, the break-in marine inspector had completed the basic marine inspector course at the Coast Guard's Reserve Training Center in Yorktown, VA. Diving operation inspections were not taught in that course. He had not attended the outer continental shelf inspector school taught jointly by the Coast Guard and industry to Coast Guard marine inspectors.

31. Contrary to the break-in inspector's perception, the class surveyor did not believe dive supervision was an area of overlapping responsibility with the Coast Guard. The ABS

---

[72] Wiitala, testimony, Vol. 1, pg. 180
[73] Wiitala, testimony, Vol. 1, pg. 180-181
[74] Champagne, testimony, Vol. 1, pg. 39-40
[75] Wiitala, testimony, Vol. 1, pg. 181-182; Townsend, testimony, Vol. 3, pg. 115
[76] Wiitala, testimony, Vol. 1, pg. 182-183
[77] Townsend, testimony, Vol. 3, pg. 114, 116-117
[78] Wiitala, testimony, Vol. 1, pg. 269; Austin, testimony, Vol. 2, pg. 239
[79] USCG Investigation, Vol. 6, IO Exhibit 66, (Statement of T.L. Thomson dtd 12 May 1999) [emphasis added]; Near the end of the hearing, ABS objected to admission of this exhibit unless Thomson was made available for cross-examination. At the time, neither the IO nor the Parties in Interest were disposed to examine LT (jg) Thomson so late in the process. The IO agreed not to enter the statement. After further consideration, the IO determined that this information is relevant and necessary.

- 16 -

16732
2 June 2000

FORMAL INVESTIGATION INTO THE COMMERCIAL DIVING ACCIDENT ABOARD THE MOBILE OFFSHORE DRILLING UNIT CLIFF'S DRILLING RIG NO. 12 ON 4 MARCH 1996, WITH LOSS OF LIFE

surveyor (who had performed well over 100 SEILODs) had no expectations of supervising the dive because diving operation inspection was not within the mandate of ABS. ABS surveyors do not inspect diving operations as an ordinary part of their work and the ABS Rules have no provisions for inspecting dive procedures or equipment. Furthermore, the ABS surveyor had never inspected a diving station, nor was he familiar with diving operations.[80]

32. At the hearing, the Coast Guard senior marine inspector for Rig 12, LT Julio Martinez, agreed with the ABS surveyor that the Coast Guard, not ABS, was responsible for inspecting dive operations. At the time of the hearing, three years after the inspection, Martinez vaguely remembered being on board Rig 12 on 3 March and believed that no diving operations were underway that day. But, he had no memory of visiting Rig 12 on 4 March.[81] Martinez testified that he would typically inspect a diving operation, if one were underway when he performed a MODU exam. To do this, he would use the Coast Guard's MODU/SEILOD job aid, CG-840H-1 (9-92) and ensure that all the items listed in the job aid were on board and available.[82]

33. When the team dive team reached Rig 12, the vessel was in the bottom-bearing mode in 37 feet of water at West Cameron Block 83.[83] The vessel was approximately eight miles south, south-east of the Sabine Pass East Jetty Light, 9.8 miles from the closest point of land. When the group reported aboard, Austin presented himself to Ronald Townsend and Buddy Horton. Horton coordinated a meeting between the supervisor of the other dive team, American Oilfield Divers, (AOD had cleaned Rig 12's legs and was familiar with the layout of the mat and legs), the ABS surveyor, and Austin to plan the upcoming job. Based on Austin's conduct, Townsend and Horton believed Austin was the dive supervisor even though Austin did not deliver the diving operations and safety manual to Townsend as the dive supervisor is required to do.[84] Townsend did not ask for or examine the diving supervisor's designation, as he is required to do by 46 CFR 197.402 (a) (2) (i). Neither Horton nor Townsend requested the safety and operations manual or diving supervisor written designation from Austin, Wiitala or Pilkington. Horton also assumed Austin was the dive supervisor based on past inspection jobs Austin had performed for Cliffs.[85]

34. Austin, on the other hand, did not consider himself the dive supervisor. He considered himself only a diver and NDT expert. He expected only to dive to do the magnetic particle

---

[80] Everett, testimony, Vol. 2, pg. 327-328, 350
[81] Martinez, testimony, Vol. 2, pg. 130 - 131
[82] Martinez, testimony, Vol. 2, pg. 156-157; See USCG Investigation, Vol. 4, IO Exhibit 31, (MODU Drydock Inspection Book, pg. 20-22, Diving Supervisor appointed in writing, Live Boating variances, Log Books, operating manual, equipment, etc . . .)
[83] N 29-34.7/W 093-41.5; See USCG Investigation, IO Exhibit 69 (Canadian Workers' Comp. Bd. Study) for some discussion of commercial diving dangers in this depth of water.
[84] Townsend, testimony, Vol. 3, pg. 145; See too 46 CFR 197.420
[85] Horton, testimony, Vol. 2, pg. 18, 20, 25, 36

- 17 -

16732
2 June 2000

FORMAL INVESTIGATION INTO THE COMMERCIAL DIVING ACCIDENT ABOARD
THE MOBILE OFFSHORE DRILLING UNIT CLIFF'S DRILLING RIG NO. 12 ON
4 MARCH 1996, WITH LOSS OF LIFE

testing, but expected to have no other control over the diving operations. "I was the -- to look
for terms, I guess, would be the prime contractor; and I subcontracted two divers from
G&G."[86] While Austin talked to Townsend and Horton, Wiitala and Pilkington set up the
dive station on the port side of Rig 12 (See Figure 4 below).

35. The dive station (See Figure 5) consisted of a Quincy 325 air compressor connected by a 30-
foot air hose to a 30-gallon volume tank. The volume tank was connected to an air manifold
(a.k.a. air rack). Two high-pressure air bottles also were connected to the air rack to provide
a secondary air supply if needed. The umbilical leading from the air rack to the diver's
helmet consisted of an air hose, a communications line, a pneumofathometer, a lifeline, and
the line from the NDT probe to the NDT monitor.[87] Next to the air rack was the
communication box with batteries. Located nearby was the NDT scope used to interpret
thickness readings measured by the probe operated by the diver.[88] The team set the
compressor air intake upwind from the exhaust of the compressor's diesel engine.[89]

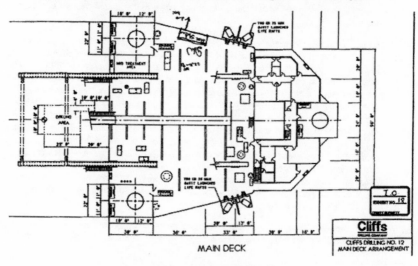

MAIN DECK

Figure 4: Main Deck Rig 12

[86] Austin, testimony, Vol. 2, pg. 225
[87] See USCG Investigation, Vol. 4, IO Exhibit 51, (Photograph of umbilical)
[88] Wiitala, testimony, Vol. 1, pg. 191
[89] Wiitala, testimony, Vol. 1, pg. 253

- 18 -

472

16732
2 June 2000

FORMAL INVESTIGATION INTO THE COMMERCIAL DIVING ACCIDENT ABOARD
THE MOBILE OFFSHORE DRILLING UNIT CLIFF'S DRILLING RIG NO. 12 ON
4 MARCH 1996, WITH LOSS OF LIFE

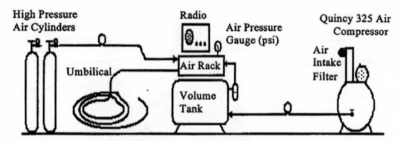

Figure 5: Schematic representation of Dive Station

36. Before the first dive, the dive team discovered their video cable was incompatible with the video equipment on board. They also discovered they had only one dive umbilical on-scene. Wiitala called Gilbert to request a compatible video cable be sent to the site. Wiitala did not raise the issue of the missing second dive umbilical or request another umbilical be sent to the dive site.[90]

37. Wiitala decided the team would begin ultrasonic testing while waiting for the video cable to be delivered.[91] Wiitala decided to send Pilkington down first to conduct the underwater portion of the ultrasonic testing. Ultrasonic testing was the least technical part of the dive and best suited for the less experienced diver. The testing required Pilkington to carry a lightweight probe called a transducer to pre-selected spots on Rig 12's hull. Pilkington was to hold the probe against the hull while an operator on the surface, Austin, interpreted the readings. One of the tools attached to Pilkington's dive belt was a roofing axe secured by a three-foot lanyard.[92] The axe was used to clean barnacles and rust from the hull so that the probe could be placed against clean metal. It could not be secured except at the end of the lanyard. Wiitala explained that when the diver worked underwater, he would hold the axe and transducer in one hand and pull himself along with the other. If the axe dropped, it fell to the diver's feet.[93]

38. While preparing to dive, Pilkington discovered he had forgotten to bring his weight belt. Wiitala testified that he was angry about the lapse and expressed his anger to Pilkington. Nevertheless, Wiitala loaned his weight belt to Pilkington so that the dive could begin. There was little discussion about using a bailout bottle. Wiitala testified that his personal bottle was available, but was set up to connect to his own helmet. Wiitala testified that Pilkington could

---

[90] USCG Investigation, Vol. 4, IO exhibit 40, (Gilbert statement, pg. 60-61)
[91] Wiitala, testimony, Vol. 1, pg. 197-198
[92] Wiitala, testimony, Vol. 1, pg. 239
[93] Wiitala, testimony, Vol. 1, pg. 239, 242-244

- 19 -

16732
2 June 2000

FORMAL INVESTIGATION INTO THE COMMERCIAL DIVING ACCIDENT ABOARD
THE MOBILE OFFSHORE DRILLING UNIT CLIFF'S DRILLING RIG NO. 12 ON
4 MARCH 1996, WITH LOSS OF LIFE

have used Wiitala's bailout bottle, but "Brian chose not to mess with it because the dive was
so shallow and seemed so easy."[94]

39. At about 1330 hours, Pilkington entered the 65 to 70 degree water for the first time.[95]
Pilkington wore a neoprene wet suit and his own Kirby, Morgan SuperLite 27 Dive Hat (See
Figures 6 & 7).[96] He also wore Wiitala's weight belt and a harness with a quick release to
which the umbilical, a knife and axe were attached. A three-foot lanyard attached the roofing
axe to the diver's belt.[97]

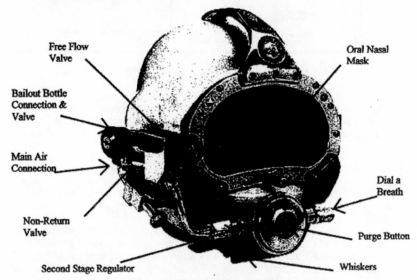

Free Flow
Valve

Oral Nasal
Mask

Bailout Bottle
Connection &
Valve

Main Air
Connection

Dial a
Breath

Non-Return
Valve

Purge Button

Second Stage Regulator

Whiskers

Figure 6: SuperLite 27 Dive Hat

40. Due to the gap between the deck of Rig 12 and the water, Pilkington was lowered to the
surface in a personnel basket (also known as a Billy Pugh basket) attached to a crane
operated by rig personnel. Rig 12 had three legs, two at the stern and one at the bow. An
AOD diver had attached a down line to the mat of the rig and relayed to Wiitala "that the

---

[94] Wiitala, testimony, Vol. 1, pg. 315-317
[95] See USCG Investigation, Vol. 6, IO Exhibit 67, (Second Pilkington Investigation dated 17 August 1998,
MC96003402)
[96] Serial Number 50609
[97] Wiitala, testimony, Vol. 1, pg. 315 – 330; 270 - 300

16732
2 June 2000

FORMAL INVESTIGATION INTO THE COMMERCIAL DIVING ACCIDENT ABOARD
THE MOBILE OFFSHORE DRILLING UNIT CLIFF'S DRILLING RIG NO. 12 ON
4 MARCH 1996, WITH LOSS OF LIFE

down line was tied to the bow leg . . .when in fact it was tied to the stern, or vice versa."[98]
During the investigation, no one was able to explain why AOD had been hired to clean the 40
test spots and Texas NDE -- with its own set of divers -- was hired to do the testing. Since
Pilkington had not dived on a MODU before, he relied on Wiitala to give him directions to
the test sites. Misunderstanding about the orientation of the dive line confused the initial
dive attempt and Wiitala ordered Pilkington to abort the dive so that the team could start
again. When Pilkington reentered the water, he began conducting ultrasonic gauging at
about 1345 hours. The gauging continued for about three hours with Pilkington periodically
moving from one area to another. The work was described as "light," requiring little effort
from the diver other than moving from one spot to another.[99] Wiitala continued to talk to
Pilkington by radio; he testified that Pilkington periodically reported that he felt fine and that
the work was going well.[100] Wiitala described the sounds he heard over the communications
line as the normal sounds connected with a dive. Wiitala heard a background "whoosing"
indicative of air free flowing in the helmet. "Just kind of – he [Pilkington] probably just had
it [the free-flow valve] cracked open a little bit. I mean, you can hear a free flow when it
runs, and he had it running definitely. . . . But obviously not to the extent that I thought he
did."[101] Wiitala did not actively tend the umbilical. "I don't recall if I was standing on it
with one foot or had somebody else holding it for me, . . ." Meanwhile, Austin was
monitoring the NDT instruments and not involved in supervising or tending the diver.[102]

41. Wiitala testified that when Compressor 2 was first put on line, the gauges showed 150 psi.
Three or four times during the dive, however, Wiitala noticed that the pressure dropped to 90
psi.[103] Each time Wiitala saw the pressure drops, he told Pilkington to close his free-flow
valve to allow the compressor to regain pressure (See figure 6).[104] According to Wiitala,
"You open this valve up [free flow valve] and you get quite a bit of air flow [in the helmet]. .
. . It gives you a little extra air if you feel like you need a breather. Some guys need it – I
always leave mine on just a little bit to keep everything defogged, keep everything
circulating. Some guys really hog it on. . . . [meaning] [j]ust leave it too far on. And you're
kind of overflowing the compressor's capability."[105]

[98] Wiitala, testimony, Vol. 1, pg. 204
[99] Wiitala, testimony, Vol. 1, pg. 210
[100] Wiitala, testimony, Vol. 1, pg. 213-214
[101] Wiitala, testimony, Vol. 1, pg. 206 - 209
[102] Wiitala, testimony, Vol. 1, pg. 262-265
[103] Wiitala, testimony, Vol. 1, pg. 194, 215, 219
[104] Wiitala, testimony, Vol. 1, pg. 196
[105] Wiitala, testimony, Vol. 1, pg. 217

16732
2 June 2000

FORMAL INVESTIGATION INTO THE COMMERCIAL DIVING ACCIDENT ABOARD
THE MOBILE OFFSHORE DRILLING UNIT CLIFF'S DRILLING RIG NO. 12 ON
4 MARCH 1996, WITH LOSS OF LIFE

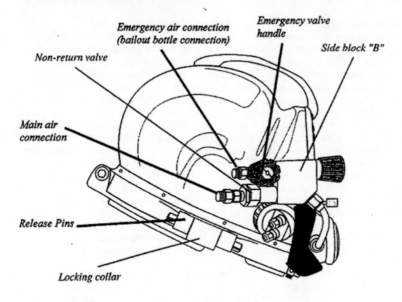

Figure 7: Side view of SuperLite-27 helmet

42. At about 1645 hours, Austin was watching the ultrasonic gauging monitor while Wiitala operated the air rack and directed Pilkington.[106] Wiitala checked the pressure gauge and saw that the pressure had again dropped to 90 psi. Wiitala told Pilkington once again to close his free flow valve, but Pilkington said that the valve was already closed. At this point, Wiitala realize there was a larger problem. Over the next several minutes Wiitala had a garbled conversation with Pilkington, during which Pilkington's manner became increasingly frantic and his breathing rapidly increased to the point it was apparent he was hyperventilating. "He [Pilkington] just kinda went into a whirl. He wouldn't really talk to me on an even keel, and he wouldn't respond to me. I mean, it just got away from him."[107] During the conversation, Pilkington complained of not being able to breathe and said that he heard a hissing noise. Pilkington speculated that he might have forgotten to tighten the airline to his helmet before

---

[106] Wiitala, testimony, Vol. 1, pg. 202
[107] Wiitala, testimony, Vol. 1, pg. 221

16732
2 June 2000

FORMAL INVESTIGATION INTO THE COMMERCIAL DIVING ACCIDENT ABOARD THE MOBILE OFFSHORE DRILLING UNIT CLIFF'S DRILLING RIG NO. 12 ON 4 MARCH 1996, WITH LOSS OF LIFE

his dive and thought the line might have worked free.[108] Wiitala testified that Pilkington had not previously complained about his breathing.[109] As Pilkington continued to hyperventilate, Wiitala pulled on his umbilical to bring him to the surface. Wiitala discovered that the hose was fouled and he couldn't pull Pilkington up. Wiitala instructed Pilkington to unfoul himself so that Wiitala could haul him up, but Pilkington didn't respond.[110]

43. Wiitala then took Compressor 2 offline and changed the valve configuration on the air rack to feed Pilkington's umbilical from one of the standby high-pressure air bottles. According to Wiitala "[he] blew through" the air cylinder in 15 minutes, meaning that the bottle was used up in that amount of time.[111] Wiitala testified two high-pressure air bottles had been brought to Rig 12 but only one was pressurized.[112] The one high-pressure air bottle Wiitala was able to use contained 2250 psig of compressed air.[113] As the high pressure air bottle quickly depressurized, Pilkington continued to hyperventilate, and then his breathing "dropped to calm, controlled breathing, almost like he went to sleep."[114]

44. At 1650 hours, Townsend, the OIM, was told there was a problem at the dive station. Townsend ran to the station and discovered that rig personnel were stringing together 150 feet of oxygen-acetylene cutting torch hose to create a makeshift air line. The intent was to attach the line to Austin's dive helmet to supply Austin with pure oxygen from a welding torch high-pressure oxygen bottle.[115]

45. Wiitala had decided to send Austin down as a rescue diver because Austin was already in his wetsuit and it would have taken Wiitala too long to get dressed out.[116] Wiitala described his decision this way.

> It would have took me forever to get in my rig . . . . To be honest with you, my first reaction was to go in the water. I was going for my hat and realized it was incomplete. Or, to make it complete, it would be like, for lack of a better description, dressing an astronaut. I had to make up the suit and the whole nine yards.[117]

46. Several witnesses indicate that it took 15 to 20 minutes to configure the makeshift airline to Austin's helmet. A safety rope was wrapped around Austin's waist and he was lowered into the water by the same personnel basket used for Pilkington. Elapsed time from when Wiitala

---

[108] Wiitala, testimony, Vol. 1, pg. 220-223, 226
[109] Wiitala, testimony, Vol. 1, pg. 213-215
[110] Wiitala, testimony, Vol. 1, pg. 221 - 226
[111] Wiitala, testimony, Vol. 1, pg. 222-225, 235
[112] Wiitala, testimony, Vol. 1, pg. 235, 322
[113] Wiitala, testimony, Vol. 1, pg. 225
[114] Wiitala, testimony, Vol. 1, pg. 223
[115] Wiitala, testimony, Vol. 1, pg. 235, 237
[116] Wiitala, testimony, Vol. 1, pg. 234
[117] Wiitala, testimony, Vol. 1, pg. 302-303

- 23 -

477

16732
2 June 2000

FORMAL INVESTIGATION INTO THE COMMERCIAL DIVING ACCIDENT ABOARD
THE MOBILE OFFSHORE DRILLING UNIT CLIFF'S DRILLING RIG NO. 12 ON
4 MARCH 1996, WITH LOSS OF LIFE

decided to send a diver down to Pilkington to when Austin went into the water was
approximately 20 minutes.[118] Austin made an initial dive but quickly returned to the surface
complaining that the airline was too short and that he needed additional weight (indicating
that he could not overcome the natural buoyancy of his neoprene wet suit). Rig personnel
found several shackles and configured them so that they could be secured around Austin's
waist. Additional air hose was attached for greater diving range and Austin began his second
dive. After several minutes he returned to the surface and announced that he had found
Pilkington's motionless body below, but could not bring him up because a line restrained him
from floating free. Austin asked for wire cutters to use to free Pilkington and started to make
a third dive. However, just before re-submerging, Austin decided he was not able to continue
and refused to perform the dive.[119] Wiitala immediately put on Austin's helmet and entered
the water. Wiitala reached Pilkington on his first try and grabbed Pilkington's hand to let
him know help had arrived. Wiitala noted a steady stream of bubbles pouring from the
whiskers of Pilkington's helmet (See figure 6).[120] Wiitala found Pilkington floating at a 45-
degree angle to a horizontal plane, with a small amount of water in his helmet. Wiitala saw
that Pilkington's axe had become fouled on a pipe running horizontally along the deck of the
mat. Wiitala cut the lanyard connecting Pilkington's axe to his dive belt and pulled him to
the surface.[121]

47. Townsend testified that he boarded the personnel basket to assist in the rescue effort and that
when Wiitala brought Pilkington to the surface, Townsend grabbed the umbilical to pull
Pilkington toward the personnel basket.[122] Townsend testified that as he pulled the
umbilical, Pilkington's diving harness came free and then the airline came free from
Pilkington's helmet.[123] Wiitala then shoved Pilkington toward the basket and Townsend
hauled Pilkington into the basket.[124] Wiitala testified that he reached up while in the basket
and depressed the locking collar's four release pins so the helmet would come off (See figure
7).[125] Townsend also testifies that the helmet was taken off in the basket as it was hoisted
onto Rig 12's deck.[126] On the other hand, Steve Champagne, an independent contractor
working on Rig 12, testified that when Pilkington was placed on the deck of Rig 12,
Pilkington's helmet was still attached and locked to his diving collar. Champagne noted this
because he had trouble taking Pilkington's helmet off to administer CPR. Champagne said
that, while Pilkington was on the deck of Rig 12, Champagne was not able to release the
helmet, causing Wiitala to have to remove it and allowing about a cup of water to spill from
the mask. While Champagne struggled to release Pilkington's helmet, he noticed that the

[118] Champagne, testimony, Vol. 1, pg. 40
[119] Wiitala, testimony, Vol. 1, pg. 237-238; Townsend, testimony, Vol. 3, pg. 123
[120] Wiitala, testimony, Vol. 1, pg. 246, 317; Whiskers refer to black plastic vents on both sides of the helmet.
[121] Wiitala, testimony, Vol. 1, pg. 238-239, 245-248
[122] Townsend, testimony, Vol. 3, pg. 122-125
[123] Townsend, testimony, Vol. 3, pg. 125-127
[124] Townsend, testimony, Vol. 3, pg. 129, 142
[125] Wiitala, testimony, Vol. 1, pg. 249
[126] Townsend, testimony, Vol. 3, pg. 129-130

- 24 -

16732
2 June 2000

FORMAL INVESTIGATION INTO THE COMMERCIAL DIVING ACCIDENT ABOARD THE MOBILE OFFSHORE DRILLING UNIT CLIFF'S DRILLING RIG NO. 12 ON 4 MARCH 1996, WITH LOSS OF LIFE

airline was still connected to the helmet.[127] Despite the conflicting testimony, all witnesses agreed that when Pilkington's helmet was removed, his face was blue.[128] Champagne and others began to administer CPR immediately.[129] The elapsed time for the rescue was approximately 30-40 minutes.[130]

48. About 8 minutes after CPR began, at around 1800 hours, a helicopter arrived on board Rig 12.[131] Pilkington was quickly hoisted into the helicopter and transported to St. Mary's Hospital in Port Arthur, TX; elapsed time was 13 minutes from the deck of Rig 12 to the hospital.[132] Doctors at the hospital attempted to resuscitate Pilkington for several hours, but he was pronounced dead at 2230 hours.[133] No one at the Coast Guard formal hearing was able to testify whether Pilkington displayed any signs of life when was brought back on board Rig 12. However, Dr. John Clark of the Navy Experimental Diving Unit speculated, based on the hospital reports, that the rescuers found or were able to restore a heartbeat (see Finding of Fact 62 below).

Post Casualty Events

49. An autopsy of Pilkington's body found that his lungs were boggy and congested and his stomach had no residual food fragments. The coroner concluded that Pilkington's cause of death was drowning.[134]

50. Cliffs properly notified the Coast Guard of the casualty and completed all necessary Coast Guard documentation.

51. Coast Guard Investigating Officers did not attend Rig 12 after the accident and did not secure Compressor 2 as part of the original investigation. By the time of this hearing, Compressor 2 had been disassembled and was not available for examination.

52. On 6 March 1996, Gilbert directed Lawdermilk to take Compressor 2 to McKenzie Equipment Co., Inc. (McKenzie) in Houston. Gilbert spoke to McKenzie's service manager. "I told him we had a compressor that we needed checked out, and I wanted him to look at it and give me a letter back saying that it was in good condition; it was running; it was maintaining pressure at 150 psi or it wasn't."[135] McKenzie would not certify the compressor

---

[127] Champagne, testimony, Vol. 1, pg. 28-39; See too Wiitala testimony, Vol. 1, pg. 373
[128] Wiitala, testimony, Vol. 1, pg. 250
[129] Townsend, testimony, Vol. 3, pg. 131
[130] Champagne, testimony, Vol. 1, pg. 42; Linzy, testimony, Vol. 1, pg. 101
[131] Champagne, testimony, Vol. 1, pg. 44; Townsend, testimony, Vol. 3, pg. 133; Linzy, testimony, Vol. 1, pg. 97-98
[132] Linzy, testimony, Vol. 1, pg. 105
[133] USCG Investigation, Vol. 4, IO exhibit 44 (Death Certificate of Brian Pilkington)
[134] USCG Investigation, Vol. 4, IO exhibit 27, (Autopsy report of Brian Pilkington)
[135] USCG Investigation, Vol. 4, IO exhibit 40, (Gilbert statement, pg. 32)

- 25 -

16732
2 June 2000

FORMAL INVESTIGATION INTO THE COMMERCIAL DIVING ACCIDENT ABOARD
THE MOBILE OFFSHORE DRILLING UNIT CLIFF'S DRILLING RIG NO. 12 ON
4 MARCH 1996, WITH LOSS OF LIFE

as being functional and did not produce such a letter. Gilbert testified that someone from
McKenzie called him back to say that the compressor would run and would hold pressure at
150 psi, but if the compressor wasn't repaired, " . . .you could have problems down the
road."[136] The McKenzie employee told Gilbert that the repairs were so extensive it would be
more cost effective to replace the compressor than repair it. Gilbert then directed McKenzie
to replace the compressor. A McKenzie mechanic, Guy Kirby, broke down Compressor 2
and produced a deficiency report:

-Valve seat on head bad

-Unit needs overhaul – oil carryover

-Valves are not holding – needs new rings, bad carbon buildup

-Needs 110823-325 Overhaul Kit

-Rings HP

-Rings LP

-Air Filter

-6609 Head

Kirby concluded his write up by recommending Gilbert replace Compressor 2 rather than
repair it.[137] Lawdermilk testified that when he returned to McKenzie's to pick up
Compressor 2, a mechanic reported that the compressor's main problem was that a rag had
been sucked through the cylinder.[138]

53. About two months after Compressor 2 was examined, a McKenzie employee, Marty
Husband, was asked by the owner, Mary Ann McKenzie, to gather any available paperwork
on the examination.[139] In the course of his investigation, Husband questioned Guy Kirby
about Compressor 2 and gathered the deficiency report described above and contained in IO
Exhibit 19. Husband described the exhibit. "Well, it's a teardown. It's basically a teardown
inspection whereby Guy tore the compressor down, estimated what was wrong with it and
what it would take to repair it as far as cost."[140] Husband described McKenzie's process for
evaluating compressors. "[T]hey put it on a test standard run. They try and pump up
pressure and maintain pressure with the compressor. . . It's done on every unit. And if it
doesn't hold, then they start to disassemble it, which is usually the head section comes off
first. So, that's what I say, basically what he found were the heads – the seats and the heads
were bad. They had a lot of oil carryover and bad rings. So, based on the cost of the parts
versus the cost of a new one, it exceeded 50 percent, which we would normally recommend a

---

[136] USCG Investigation, Vol. 4, IO exhibit 40, (Gilbert statement, pg. 33-34)
[137] USCG Investigation, Vol. 4, IO exhibit 19, (Invoice from McKenzie to G & G Marine)
[138] Lawdermilk, testimony, Vol. 1, pg. 485-486
[139] Husband testimony, Vol. 1, pg. 420
[140] Husband testimony, Vol. 1, pg. 387

- 26 -

16732
2 June 2000

FORMAL INVESTIGATION INTO THE COMMERCIAL DIVING ACCIDENT ABOARD
THE MOBILE OFFSHORE DRILLING UNIT CLIFF'S DRILLING RIG NO. 12 ON
4 MARCH 1996, WITH LOSS OF LIFE

replacement."[141] Husband testified that the oil carryover, bad rings, heads, and seats Guy
Kirby described as bad were compressor parts, not engine parts.[142]

54. Several months after the casualty, as part of civil litigation related to the casualty, a handwritten page of notes was discovered and identified as the dive log of Dan Wiitala for 4
March. Wiitala's notes, made nearly contemporaneously with the casualty, begin by
indicating that "[C]ompresser [sic] was not keeping up to 150 psi but maintained 80 psi."[143]

55. Lawdermilk also was deposed during the civil litigation in August 1997. He described a
conversation he had with Wiitala on the night of 4 March 1996 about the Rig 12 dive. "He
[Wiitala] had said that they had gotten out on the job and the compressor wasn't working
right; so, he worked on it a little bit, got it holding air for a little while. And they initiated the
job and was almost done with the dive that Brian was on when the compressor started losing
air."[144] Lawdermilk went on to testify about the mechanical condition of Compressor 2 prior
to the Rig 12 job.[145]

> Q. Was that [Compressor 2] one of what you considered to be the three working
> compressors?
>
> A. It wasn't working properly, but it was one of the compressors that we used.
>
> Q. Was it normally used as a primary source of air?
>
> A. No.
>
> Q. Had you been having problems with that particular compressor?
>
> A. Yes.
>
> Q. For how long a period of time?
>
> A. I can't say exactly, but probably two to three jobs prior to that.
>
> Q. And what type of problems had you been experiencing with that compressor that was
> ultimately taken out to the Cliffs job?
>
> A. It wouldn't – the pilot valves weren't functioning.
>
> Q. What are pilot valves?

---

[141] Husband testimony, Vol. 1, pg. 387-389
[142] Husband testimony, Vol. 1, pg. 391
[143] See IO Exhibit 70
[144] See IO Exhibit 71
[145] See IO Exhibit 71

- 27 -

16732
2 June 2000

FORMAL INVESTIGATION INTO THE COMMERCIAL DIVING ACCIDENT ABOARD
THE MOBILE OFFSHORE DRILLING UNIT CLIFF'S DRILLING RIG NO. 12 ON
4 MARCH 1996, WITH LOSS OF LIFE

A. They're the air pressure source which controls the air pressure and the air volume.

Q. So, if you've got a pilot valve that's malfunctioning on a compressor, would that affect the ability of the compressor to hold air?

A. Sure.

Q. Would it affect the ability of the compressor to pump the proper volume of air?

A. Sure.

Q. And for at least two or three jobs, this particular compressor that was involved in Brian Pilkington's accident had had problems holding air?

A. Yes.

56. Several days after the casualty, Mr. Peter Pilkington, Brian's father, visited the G&G facility in Houston, Texas. Peter Pilkington found Brian's Kirby, Morgan SuperLite 27 helmet sitting on the floor of the G&G warehouse. Peter Pilkington confiscated the helmet and took it home. Peter Pilkington stated after the hearing that the helmet was not adjusted while in his custody.

57. Slightly more than a year after the accident, Pilkington's helmet was sent for examination to the Navy Experimental Diving Unit (NEDU) in Panama City, Florida. Mr. Peter Pilkington reports that the helmet was not used, repaired or adjusted while it was in his control, before being sent to NEDU. NEDU found that Pilkington's Kirby, Morgan SuperLite 27 diving helmet's demand regulator was not set according to the manufacturer's specifications. NEDU tested the helmet as it was set up when Pilkington used it. In the initial test, NEDU found that, at 80 psig, the helmet would perform "reasonably well to a depth of 33 fsw . . . which would supply gas to a moderately hard working diver, although the respiratory effort would be high, far exceeding the NEDU performance goal."[146] NEDU then tested the helmet at the air pressures recommended for the Kirby, Morgan SuperLite 27. In the words of NEDU, "Interestingly, during the set up, as supply pressure was increased to 165 psig, the helmet experienced free-flow from the second stage regulator at approximately 100 psig. This free-flow condition at 100 psig necessitated making a demand regulator internal adjustment prior to supplying the helmet with an optimum supply pressure of 165 psig. This suggests that either the regulator was adjusted anticipating a supply pressure less than the manufacturer's recommended minimum or that the regulator was improperly adjusted."[147]

---

[146] psig "pounds per square inch gauge"; fsw "feet of salt water"
[147] USCG Investigation, Vol. 4, IO exhibit 26, (SuperLite diving hat report, pg. 2)

- 28 -

16732
2 June 2000

FORMAL INVESTIGATION INTO THE COMMERCIAL DIVING ACCIDENT ABOARD
THE MOBILE OFFSHORE DRILLING UNIT CLIFF'S DRILLING RIG NO. 12 ON
4 MARCH 1996, WITH LOSS OF LIFE

58. At the formal hearing to investigate Pilkington's death, 22-24 June 1999, Master Chief Petty
Officer Brick Bradford, a U.S. Navy master diver, testified about surface supplied air diving
practices. Master Chief Bradford offered his opinion on a number of diving safety issues
related to the casualty. He first discussed Austin's YMCA SCUBA training and whether that
training was enough to allow Austin to work safely as a surface-supplied air commercial
diver.

> Q. Based on [what you've heard about Austin's training], do you think that qualifies a
> person to be a dive supervisor?
>
> A. No, I do not.
>
> Q. Why not?
>
> A. And I would like to expand and say I don't believe that qualifies you to be a
> commercial diver either.
>
> Q. Okay. Why not?
>
> A. The issue of a commercial diver, first: He has no formal training in the rig that he's
> using. He knows nothing of the operational – it's possible that he knows nothing of
> the operational characteristics of the equipment, how to maintain that equipment, how
> to set that equipment up for use, how to properly use that equipment, how to recover
> from a possible emergency relating to that equipment. If he's doing – and it's
> obvious surface-supplied diving is the intended purpose of the SuperLite 27, may not
> be familiar with decompression procedures and those kind of things.[148]

59. In addition to Master Chief Bradford's analysis of Austin's capabilities, he also analyzed
Wiitala's experience and ability to be a dive supervisor. In summary, he said that experience
as a diver alone does not qualify a person to be a dive supervisor. The Master Chief referred
to his own career in the U.S. Navy as an example. Master Chief Bradford said that after
graduating from Navy diving school and working as a Navy diver, if he had been asked
whether he could perform as a dive supervisor, "I would have told them I felt like I could
have done it."[149] But, the Master Chief indicated, after he went to school to be trained as a
dive supervisor, he learned how much more was demanded of a supervisor than he had
known.[150]

60. Master Chief Bradford analyzed the predive procedures exercised by the G&G Marine
employees before Pilkington began his dive.

---

[148] Bradford testimony, Vol. 3, pg. 183-184
[149] Bradford testimony, Vol. 3, pg. 185-186
[150] Bradford testimony, Vol. 3, pg. 185-186

- 29 -

16732
2 June 2000

FORMAL INVESTIGATION INTO THE COMMERCIAL DIVING ACCIDENT ABOARD
THE MOBILE OFFSHORE DRILLING UNIT CLIFF'S DRILLING RIG NO. 12 ON
4 MARCH 1996, WITH LOSS OF LIFE

Q. From everything that you've heard so far . . ., regardless of whether it was done in the
exact same fashion or . . . the same methodology that the Navy would do it, did the
predive preparation occur, in your estimation, in a safe way?

A. No. . . . A diving supervisor was not assigned . . nobody [was] in charge. . . There is
no – there is a lack of verification, if you will, as to whether or not the compressor
has, in fact, been checked for a proper level of oil; that strain relief – if you use strain
relief as your interface hoses between the compressor and the volume tank, are
attached; that these connections are, in fact, secure, wrench tight; that they have been
soap tested; that they're free from kinks, free from being stepped on; that they have
been visually inspected for cuts, nicks, gouges, and other deformities; that the intake
is, in fact, free from obstruction; that the intake is upstream of the exhaust – not only
the prime mover; if it's a diesel or an engine, but also upwind from any other
potential sources of carbon monoxide.

There is also the inspection of the umbilical itself, walking that out; the attachment to
the hat. There is the inspection in the predive procedures for the hat itself. In this
particular case . . . I see a problem in the industry. As a commercial diver, you are
expected to show up on the site with your own hat. As I have heard, the company
will provide you with the umbilical. You make the connection and you go to work.
So, therefore, you have a great amount of variation as to whether or not any
maintenance is done on the hat itself; and at that interface [the helmet/hose
connection] you're setting yourself up for trouble. . . . And I see that as an industry
problem.[151]

61. Master Chief Bradford believed that, because the umbilical was secured to Pilkington's dive
harness, there was little potential that Pilkington's main airline had come loose during his
dive. The Master Chief felt it was possible Pilkington had inadvertently unscrewed his main
airline from his helmet near the end of his dive. The Master Chief characterized that scenario
as "plausible".[152] But, he said "I have heard testimony that suggested, that we're asked if he
went and checked the connection and felt that it was loose and attempted to tighten the
connection and that, perhaps, then he went the wrong way. I believe that that is plausible. . . .
But that would have been – that truly is secondary, in my mind, to – to the first issue, which
is the guy did not have an adequate air supply and that corrective action was not taken in a
timely manner when discovered."[153] Master Chief Bradford concluded that, during his dive,
Pilkington experienced a condition called Hypercapnia.[154]

62. Dr. John Clark, the Scientific Director for the Navy Experimental Diving Unit also testified
at the formal hearing on 22 – 24 June 1999. Dr. Clark adopted the analysis of Dr. David

---

[151] Bradford testimony, Vol. 3, pg. 199-201
[152] Bradford testimony, Vol. 3, pg. 215, 218
[153] Bradford testimony, Vol. 3, pg. 218-219
[154] Bradford testimony, Vol. 3, pg. 215

- 30 -

16732
2 June 2000

FORMAL INVESTIGATION INTO THE COMMERCIAL DIVING ACCIDENT ABOARD THE MOBILE OFFSHORE DRILLING UNIT CLIFF'S DRILLING RIG NO. 12 ON 4 MARCH 1996, WITH LOSS OF LIFE

Youngblood made during the civil litigation.[155] Dr. Clarke added his own observations as follows:

> Most divers, if they're working hard and begin to sense a buildup of CO_2, will ventilate, as this diver did, with a steady flow valve [free flow valve]. Then if this happens more than once or twice, typically the diver would stop work, take more of a breather; and once he's caught his breath again and things are back under control, continue working.

> From what I heard in the testimony yesterday, apparently the diver was operating a steady flow valve repeatedly and only closed the steady flow valve when the – somebody topside explained to him that he was going to lose gas pressure unless he did that. That situation undoubtedly crests to a point of panic. To me, the cause of panic would be the realization that he did not have enough gas perhaps, also if he could not make an escape to the top; but that is purely conjecture.

> *Obviously the diver was not getting the gas he needed*, whether it was from low ops from a compressor or due to the leakage of the gas umbilical. I certainly have no evidence to suggest that it's one or the other. I cannot tell. I don't see any evidence of that.

> Looking at the autopsy results, we have an indication that the diver, while being ventilated on a ventilator – and I'm assuming he did attain signs of rhythm again once he was in the hospital. Otherwise, he probably would not have been on the ventilator. In other words, the C.P.R. was effective in sustaining him to get his heart going. . . .

> [A]lthough some divers can work with a helmet that's putting out a low gas supply, other divers – and not necessarily do I mean inexperienced divers, but just other divers prefer to work with higher flow levels for their gas. Some divers will tolerate a large amount of CO_2 in their bloodstream and get along just fine. I personally have worked with divers who have exercised very vigorously under hyperbaric conditions and claim that they're very happy – they're very comfortable, and then suddenly go unconscious because, in fact, they were comfortable because they weren't breathing hard; but at the same time their arterial CO_2 was steadily climbing, steadily climbing and finally reached a point where unconsciousness snuck up on them and they were totally unaware and boom, they were out like that [indicating the test subject lost consciousness].

> And the other divers, which I basically consider to be safer divers, are those who do not like the feeling of having their gas restricted, who like keeping their arterial CO_2 levels down and want a lot of gas. Eventually they'll reach a point when they feel they're not getting enough gas, and they'll stop. "I'm not doing this anymore" or "I'm going to stop and take a breather, catch my breath, ventilate," whatever.

---

[155] See USCG Investigation, Vol. 4, IO exhibit 28 (Statement of Dr. David Youngblood).

16732
2 June 2000

FORMAL INVESTIGATION INTO THE COMMERCIAL DIVING ACCIDENT ABOARD THE MOBILE OFFSHORE DRILLING UNIT CLIFF'S DRILLING RIG NO. 12 ON 4 MARCH 1996, WITH LOSS OF LIFE

I suspect all these things were going through Brian's mind at the time, and he undoubtedly did stop and ventilate himself. However, in spite of those efforts, if his gas supply was still wanting, his mental confusion would get progressively worse; and at some point he might have started taking actions that were not in his best interest.

It is possible – again, solely conjecture – that in the confusion, he may have reached back and started releasing something he shouldn't have [referring to the possibility that Pilkington disconnected his main airline from his helmet]. I have no idea. But what we do know is that in the course of sustaining a large carbon dioxide insult, you become very anxious. It sounds like Brian was becoming anxious. Of course, if somebody cut off our air supply, anybody would become anxious; but CO_2 alone can do that. And then you begin to be increasingly confused, mentally, and not able to think straight and not able to – at one point eventually, to not even be able to respond to what is being said by topside. You're not aware of anybody else talking to you. You're totally involved in yourself. It's a strange and very dangerous state that you end up in; and if the situation is not remedied immediately, then eventually CO_2 can reach such high levels that you can convulse and become unconscious. Of course, at that point, if you have one in a helmet, then partial drowning is more or less inevitable. It will happen. . . .

One question is how would water get into the helmet? That, to me, makes me believe that, perhaps, the umbilical was connected because in the course of making large respiratory efforts, it's quite possible to create negative pressures inside the helmet, enough negative pressure to balloon the neck dam backward and actually pull water up past the neck dam.

It's also possible to pull water in through the exhaust valves. It's one of the concerns we have about using a helmet like this, as it is, for contaminated water diving. If you're making large respiratory motions, you will get water coming backwards through the exhaust valve.[156]

63. Dr. David Youngblood, a consultant in the civil litigation, offered the following analysis of the casualty:

Based upon my review, I have reached the following opinions: Brian Pilkington commenced his inspection dive from the MODU early in the afternoon of 4 March 1996. There is no record of a pre-dive equipment check or an in-water check for leaks, but there would have been a flurry of bubbles initially since the water was cold and he was wearing only a neoprene wetsuit with no provision for hot water supply. Sudden immersion in cold water causes a marked increase in breathing rate, and, depending upon his position in the water the bubbles from his exhaust could have obscured any leaks.

---

[156] Dr. John Clark, testimony, Vol. 2, pg. 85-91 [emphasis added].

- 32 -

16732
2 June 2000

FORMAL INVESTIGATION INTO THE COMMERCIAL DIVING ACCIDENT ABOARD
THE MOBILE OFFSHORE DRILLING UNIT CLIFF'S DRILLING RIG NO. 12 ON
4 MARCH 1996, WITH LOSS OF LIFE

He began his underwater task of applying the ultrasonic device to sites on the mat
previously cleaned by the AOD crew (in the relative comfort of hot water suits) but soon
began to experience heavy breathing resistance in the demand mode, requiring a switch to
free flow mode. This caused problems: the single compressor (there was no secondary
or standby compressor) was unable to maintain adequate air pressure or flow on open
circuit. Each attempt to "catch his breath" by switching to free flow brought admonition
from topside to cease "free flow" to allow the faulty compressor to attempt to restore the
pressure.

This cycle was repeated over several hours while Brian Pilkington attempted to complete
his task despite the inadequate helmet ventilation. We can only estimate how inadequate
it might have been since the compressor often fell to 80 psi or below – well below the
optimal pressure for proper helmet function – and we can only estimate what the effect of
300 feet of hose and a possible leak at the helmet attachment might have been.[157]
Simulations in a hyperbaric chamber have shown that the ability of the regulator to
deliver adequate air at low pressures is severely compromised, particularly at high flow
demands such as maximum exertion or even panic.

In a situation such as this the diver adapts by altering his breathing pattern. He begins to
take long, slow breaths in order to avoid "bottoming out" the regulator. This alternative
is subtle and almost subconscious in the early stages, but unless the diver is completely at
rest, carbon dioxide begins to accumulate in the body. This "waste gas", the exhaust
from the body's metabolic engine, has very definite and deleterious effects: it begins to
drive the respiratory control center in the brain, which, in turn, drives the respiratory
"pump", the lungs, diaphragm, and chest to increase the air flow.

This drive can be consciously controlled to a degree: that's what happens when you hold
your breath. But conscious control requires an intense concentration and alertness.
These qualities are short-lived as CO_2 accumulates in the body, since CO_2 is a potent
narcotic, dulling the senses while driving the respiratory pump to work ever harder. The
harder the respiratory muscles are forced to work the more CO_2 they produce.

As CO_2 accumulates in the body, it also causes blood vessels in the skin and the brain to
dilate and deliver more blood. Since Brian Pilkington had no hot water suit, only a
wetsuit which flushed cold water over his skin as he moved about, the CO_2 accumulation
caused a rapid heat loss from the skin and the body's core, especially the brain. A cold
brain cannot concentrate. Thinking becomes fuzzy and confused, and simple situations
become complex and dangerous. Brian Pilkington's hatchet slipped through the mat and
the lanyard held him down. At another time it would have been a trivial entanglement, an

---

[157] Youngblood based his analysis on the testimony arising out of the civil litigation. That testimony differs
somewhat from the testimony adduced at the Coast Guard's formal hearing. At the hearing, Wiitala testified that
Compressor 2's gauge only dropped to about 90 psi. However, at the civil litigation and in Wiitala's dive log for the
Rig 12 dive, evidence was developed to show that the pressure went lower. See FOF 42 and 54.

- 33 -

16732
2 June 2000

FORMAL INVESTIGATION INTO THE COMMERCIAL DIVING ACCIDENT ABOARD
THE MOBILE OFFSHORE DRILLING UNIT CLIFF'S DRILLING RIG NO. 12 ON
4 MARCH 1996, WITH LOSS OF LIFE

easy extrication. With his consciousness clouded by CO_2 accumulation and
hypothermia, he panicked.

As panic ensued he struggled violently, producing even more CO_2, until the
concentration was high enough to cause unconsciousness. By this time, the violent,
uncontrollable drive to breathe against a "bottomed out" regulator had created cycles of
negative pressure inside the helmet. The helmet is attached by a thin rubber neck dam or
seal, and when pressure in the helmet becomes negative, water is sucked between the
neck and the seal. This water accumulated in the lower part of the helmet as long as
Brian was upright and struggling, but when he succumbed to the narcotic effects of the
ever-increasing CO_2, he lost consciousness and fell forward. The face plate and mask
filled with water and he inhaled it.[158]

Analysis:

Helmet Flooding

1. As indicated by Dr. Clark, enough water entered Pilkington's helmet to cause him to
   asphyxiate and drown.[159] The amount of water was relatively small, described by Wiitala as
   less than a cup.[160] The NEDU report shows there were no material defects in the helmet or
   helmet's assembly indicating that the flooding was not the result of a helmet malfunction.[161]

2. There are several ways the helmet may have flooded. In every instance though, the
   precipitating event leading to the flooding would be a reduction of air volume and pressure to
   the diver's helmet. One scenario, which would result in helmet flooding, would be if low air
   pressures from Compressor 2 allowed water to enter the helmet under the neck dam.[162] The
   neck dam is designed to be functionally watertight, but if normal operating air pressure is not
   maintained in a helmet, water can seep under the neck dam as it flexes while the diver works.

3. Water also may have entered Pilkington's helmet if he experienced a complete interruption in
   his air supply. In that case, his demand regulator would have stopped working (called
   "bottoming out" the regulator). At that point, every time Pilkington inhaled he would have
   progressively evacuated the air in his helmet creating negative pressure. Pilkington would

---

[158] See USCG Investigation, Vol. 4, IO exhibit 28 (Statement of Dr. David Youngblood).
[159] See FOF 62
[160] See Finding of Fact (FOF) 46, 47, 49
[161] See FOF 54; See too USCG Investigation, Vol. 4, IO Exhibit 26 (SuperLite Diving Hat Report)
[162] See USCG Investigation, Vol. 5, IO Exhibit 50 (picture of neckdam)

- 34 -

16732
2 June 2000

FORMAL INVESTIGATION INTO THE COMMERCIAL DIVING ACCIDENT ABOARD
THE MOBILE OFFSHORE DRILLING UNIT CLIFF'S DRILLING RIG NO. 12 ON
4 MARCH 1996, WITH LOSS OF LIFE

have continued to gasp for air and violent attempts to breathe may have sucked water
between the neck dam and the seal into his helmet.[163]

4. Finally, water may have entered Pilkington's helmet through the emergency air connection.
In a last ditch attempt to trouble-shoot his emergency, Pilkington may have reached for the
emergency valve handle directly adjacent to the main air connection. This connection is
typically used to couple the bailout bottle to the helmet. When not used, the only barrier
preventing water from entering the helmet is the emergency supply valve (See figure 7).
When Pilkington's regulator bottomed out, he may have instinctively opened his emergency
supply valve, the standard procedure taught in commercial dive schools, and allowed water
to enter his helmet. If the emergency valve was opened, water would only have entered the
helmet if the air pressure inside the helmet was extremely low (indicating an almost total
interruption in air supply and pressure). Even the smallest pressure above ambient would
have forced air out of the emergency valve which would have prevented water from
entering.[164]

Hypercapnia

5. Master Chief Bradford, Dr. John Clark, and Dr. David Youngblood all concluded that during
Pilkington's dive, he experienced a condition called Hypercapnia.[165] Inadequate ventilation
of surface supplied helmets can cause Hypercapnia, which is an excess accumulation of
carbon dioxide (CO_2) in the diver's bloodstream and tissues. Carbon dioxide is naturally
created from the body's own metabolic processes. In diving, the buildup of CO_2 in the body
can be exacerbated by a higher than normal concentration of CO_2 in the breathing medium,
poor ventilation, or because something interferes with the natural process of gas exchange in
the lungs. Fresh air contains about 0.033 percent CO_2. Proper carbon dioxide level in the
body is maintained by breathing a sufficient amount of air to dilute the carbon dioxide
generated by the body and delivered to the lungs. If helmet ventilation is inadequate, an
increase in the CO_2 level in the helmet will occur, producing an excess of carbon dioxide
present in the gas breathed.[166]

6. An excess of carbon dioxide affects the brain differently than does a lack of oxygen
(Hypoxia). However, similar symptoms such as confusion, inability to concentrate,
drowsiness, loss of consciousness, and convulsions can result from Hypercapnia. Such
effects become more severe as the level of CO_2 increases. A diver breathing a gas
containing 10 percent CO_2 will generally lose consciousness after a few minutes. Breathing

---

[163] FOF 42, 43, 62
[164] FOF 62
[165] FOF 61
[166] U.S. Coast Guard Investigation, Vol. 4, IO Exhibit 53, (U.S. Navy Dive Manual, Vol. 1, Chpt 3)

16732
2 June 2000

FORMAL INVESTIGATION INTO THE COMMERCIAL DIVING ACCIDENT ABOARD
THE MOBILE OFFSHORE DRILLING UNIT CLIFF'S DRILLING RIG NO. 12 ON
4 MARCH 1996, WITH LOSS OF LIFE

15 percent CO_2 for any length of time will cause muscular spasms and rigidity. [167]
Headache, cyanosis, unusual sweating, fatigue, and a general feeling of discomfort may warn
a diver if they occur and are recognized, but they are not very reliable warnings.
Hypothermia also can mask the buildup of carbon dioxide because the respiration rate
increases initially on exposure to cold water.[168]

7. A diver who loses consciousness because of excess carbon dioxide in his breathing medium,
and does not aspirate water, generally revives rapidly when given fresh air. Increasing the
level of CO_2 in the blood stimulates the respiratory nervous center to increase the breathing
rate and volume, and the heartbeat rate is often increased. Ordinarily, increased breathing is
definite and uncomfortable enough to warn a diver before the level of CO_2 in the air
becomes very dangerous. However, variables such as work rate, depth, and the composition
of the breathing mixture may produce changes in breathing and blood mixture that could
mask any changes caused by excess CO_2. In cases where the partial pressure of CO_2 is
above 0.5 atmospheres absolute, the shortness of breath usually associated with excess
carbon dioxide may not be excessive and may go unnoticed by the diver, especially if he is
breathing hard because of exertion. In these cases the diver may become confused and even
slightly euphoric before losing consciousness. For this reason, a diver must be particularly
alert for any marked change in his breathing comfort or cycle (such as shortness of breath or
hyperventilation) as a warning of Hypercapnia.[169]

Fatigue

8. There is insufficient evidence to track the details of Pilkington's activity before his Rig 12
dive, but it is clear that at the time of the dive, he had had little rest over the previous 24
hours. Pilkington went to the G&G facility on the evening of 3 March to help load the dive
equipment.[170] When the load out was complete, Gilbert told Pilkington to meet Wiitala at
0500 hours the next morning at a roadside stop on Interstate 10. Pilkington met Wiitala as
directed, and then proceeded to Sabine Pass, TX to load the dive gear on a crew boat to
depart for Rig 12 the morning of 4 March.[171] The team made an aborted attempt to reach Rig
12 on a small crew boat in seas so rough the boat had to return to the dock. The team then
transferred the equipment to a second vessel and proceeded to Rig 12 again.[172] When they
arrived on Rig 12, Pilkington helped set up the dive station and prepared to dive.[173] Finally,
Pilkington made a three hours dive in 65 to 70 degree water.[174] "In cold water, [a diver's]
ability to concentrate and work efficiency will decrease rapidly. Even in water of moderate
temperature (60 degree F to 70 degree F), body heat loss can quickly bring on diver

---

[167] NOAA Diving Manual, Section 2.1.3.2
[168] U.S. Coast Guard Investigation, Vol. 4, IO Exhibit 53; (US Navy Dive Manual, Section 3-5.2)
[169] U.S. Coast Guard Investigation, Vol. 4, IO Exhibit 53; (US Navy Dive Manual, Section 3-5.2 [emphasis added])
[170] See FOF 25
[171] See FOF 28
[172] See FOF 28
[173] See FOF 28
[174] See USCG Investigation, Vol. 6, IO Exhibit 67, (Second Pilkington Investigation dated 17 August 1998)

- 36 -

16732
2 June 2000

FORMAL INVESTIGATION INTO THE COMMERCIAL DIVING ACCIDENT ABOARD
THE MOBILE OFFSHORE DRILLING UNIT CLIFF'S DRILLING RIG NO. 12 ON
4 MARCH 1996, WITH LOSS OF LIFE

exhaustion."[175] Finally, after the dive, an autopsy was done on Pilkington's body and the
pathologist reported that Pilkington had no food in his stomach during the dive.[176]

Compressor 2

9. Helmet manufacturers establish a minimum/maximum supply pressure for their equipment.
    On diving jobs, the diving supervisor typically will adjust the airflow to the diver to create a
    pressure inside the diver's helmet above the manufacturer's minimum requirements. In the
    case of the Kirby, Morgan SuperLite 27 the manufacturer recommends a minimum air
    pressure supplied to the helmet of 115 psig with a normal recommended pressure between
    135-165 psig over bottom pressure. Generally, the diving supervisor will increase the over
    bottom air supply to a higher setting if the diver is working hard. The diving supervisor
    determines the correct over bottom pressure for a diver's helmet by calculating the ambient
    pressure at the depth of the dive in feet of salt water (fsw) or feet of fresh water (ffw). The
    diving supervisor multiplies the depth by .445 for salt water or .432 for fresh water. The
    result is the pressure exerted by the water at the depth the diver is working. The supervisor
    then adds that pressure to the recommended manufacturer's minimum recommended helmet
    pressure to determine that job's safe working pressure. On 4 March, working in 28 feet of
    salt water, Pilkington needed 127 psig to meet the manufacturer's minimum safe operating
    requirements for the Kirby, Morgan SuperLite 27 helmet he was wearing.[177] The air pressure
    demand made by Pilkington's helmet on Compressor 2 was well within the normal operating
    tolerances of a Quincy 325 Compressor.

10. The standard output in actual cubic feet per minute (acfm) for a Quincy 325 compressor is
    18.6 acfm at 175 psig at maximum rpm and 8.3 acfm at 175 psig at minimum rpm.[178] The
    demand of a Kirby, Morgan SuperLite 27 helmet at the manufacturer's recommended air
    pressure (115 psig to 165 psig over bottom pressure) is 8.0 acfm when adjusted to free-
    flow.[179] Therefore, a properly functioning Quincy 325 should be able to supply a free-
    flowing Kirby, Morgan SuperLite 27 helmet continuously without "bottoming out", since the
    free flow demand of the helmet is less than the standard output of the compressor.

---

[175] USCG Investigation, Vol. 4, IO Exhibit 53, (U.S. Navy Dive Manual, Vol. 1, pg. 4-15)
[176] See FOF 49
[177] See USCG Investigation, Vol. 4, IO Exhibit 53, (U.S. Navy Dive Manual, Vol. 1, Chapter 6-3.2, Feb. 1993);
    MMP [minimum manifold pressure, psig] = 115 psig + (28 fsw x .445 psig/fsw) = 127 psig.
[178] USCG Investigation, Vol. 6, IO Exhibit 72; (Quincy QR-25 Brochure)
[179] USCG Investigation, Vol. 4, IO exhibit 26, (SuperLite diving hat report); USCG Investigation, Vol. 5, IO exhibit
    53, (U.S. Navy Dive Manual, Vol. 1, Table 6-2, Feb. 1993)

16732
2 June 2000

FORMAL INVESTIGATION INTO THE COMMERCIAL DIVING ACCIDENT ABOARD
THE MOBILE OFFSHORE DRILLING UNIT CLIFF'S DRILLING RIG NO. 12 ON
4 MARCH 1996, WITH LOSS OF LIFE

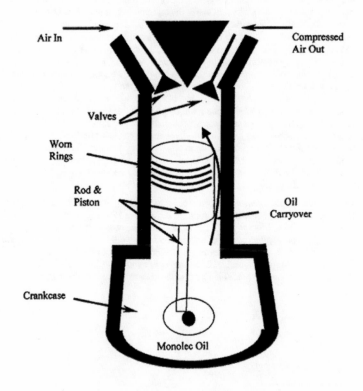

Figure 8: Representation of piston / cylinder assembly

- 38 -

16732
2 June 2000

FORMAL INVESTIGATION INTO THE COMMERCIAL DIVING ACCIDENT ABOARD
THE MOBILE OFFSHORE DRILLING UNIT CLIFF'S DRILLING RIG NO. 12 ON
4 MARCH 1996, WITH LOSS OF LIFE

11. Quincy 325 compressors have a cylinder and piston assembly that compresses air and sends it to a volume tank to be used by the diver. Air enters the cast iron cylinder through the air intake valve on the piston downstroke and is compressed during the piston upstroke. The compressed air is heated and forced out of the cylinder through the outlet valve to be stored in the volume tank. The compressor's piston, crankshaft, and connecting rods are lubricated every rotation of the crankshaft by oil in the crankcase. The piston rings keep the sides of the cylinder clean by scraping the oil from the sides on the downstroke. This keeps oil from entering the cylinder's upper headspace. However, if the rings deteriorate, through wear or lack of maintenance, the oil will blow by the rings and invade the head and valve assembly. The oil then mixes with the compressed air being sent to the volume tank and becomes a component of the diver's breathing air (See Figure 8).

12. When a diver inhales oil-saturated air, he risks developing a malady called Lipid Pneumonia. Lipid Pneumonia was a common affliction of caisson workers and deep-sea divers who, in the early days of diving, experienced excessive oil in their diving medium. Oil would coat the lung alveoli (air sacks), interrupting gas exchange at the interface between the gas in the lungs and the surface of the alveoli (external respiration). This is one reason why the hydrocarbon limit for divers' air is very low, 25-parts per million (PPM) total hydrocarbons and 5 mg/m^3 oil vapor. 5 mg/m^3 is approximately two one thousands of an ounce dispersed in a cubic meter.

13. All oil lubricated low-pressure air compressors used for surface supplied diving are equipped with two types of filters. At the suction side (air inlet) of the compressor an intake air filter prevents the air compressor from ingesting contaminants. Additionally, oil-lubricated compressors used for diving are equipped with a moisture/oil separator and a discharge filter. The moisture separator removes most of the condensation formed during the compression. The moisture/oil separator and filter also remove much of the lubricating oil that mixes with the condensate resulting in an emulsification. The discharge filter serves two functions: it filters particulates that pass through or are generated inside the compressor due to wear or damaged components, and picks up the final traces of oil that get by the moisture/oil separator. Moisture/oil separators require very little maintenance while the discharge filter requires periodic changes in accordance with the manufactures recommended intervals.

14. Evidence that Pilkington's casualty resulted from a poorly performing compressor comes from Pilkington's own helmet.[179] Pilkington's helmet regulator had been adjusted to compensate for low pressures. It is unlikely that Pilkington's regulator adjustments were accidental since, while attending diving school in Washington, Pilkington had been certified proficient to perform maintenance and repair on Kirby, Morgan SuperLite 27 helmets.[180] As

---

[179] USCG Investigation, Vol. 4, IO exhibit 26, (SuperLite diving hat report)
[180] See FOF 24

- 39 -

16732
2 June 2000

FORMAL INVESTIGATION INTO THE COMMERCIAL DIVING ACCIDENT ABOARD
THE MOBILE OFFSHORE DRILLING UNIT CLIFF'S DRILLING RIG NO. 12 ON
4 MARCH 1996, WITH LOSS OF LIFE

was stated in the NEDU report, Pilkington's helmet strongly suggests that the regulator had
been purposely adjusted in the expectation it would be used with under-performing
compressors. NEDU's report also indicates that Pilkington almost certainly never received
air pressures above 100 psi from Compressor 2 during his dive on 4 March, since 100 psi or
more would have free flowed his helmet.[181]

15. Dan Wiitala testified at the hearing that Compressor 2 produced 150 psi of air during most of
Pilkington's dive, but that two or three times Wiitala noticed the air pressure had dropped to
80 – 90 psi. Wiitala testified that when Pilkington closed his free-flow valve, the pressure
returned to 150 psi. Much of the evidence adduced at the hearing and during the civil
litigation, however, contradicts Wiitala. Lawdermilk testified that Compressor 2 had
experienced trouble on two or three diving jobs prior to the Rig 12 job. He testified that the
compressor's pilot valve was not working properly.[182] A pilot valve is a device placed
between the compressor and the volume tank. It ensures the compressor supplies air to the
volume tank. When a pilot valve malfunctions, it can fail to signal the compressor to send
more air to the volume tank. If that occurs, the diver will deplete the volume tank as he
works and the compressor will not replenish the tank. Wiitala's own log made on 4 March
1996 says that Compressor 2 would not "keep up to 150 psi but maintained 80 psi."[183] This
is supported by the fact that when Gilbert sent Compressor 2 to McKenzie's to have it
function tested, it would not hold pressure and was in such disrepair that it was deemed more
cost effective to replace rather than repair it.[184] Finally, the NEDU report indicated that
Pilkington's helmet regulator was set in such a way that it would free-flow if it received
pressure above 100 psi. Wiitala testified at the hearing that he talked to Pilkington during the
dive and heard only noises typical of a free-flowing helmet that was "cracked open a little
bit."[185] The background noise in a helmet with a second stage regulator free flowing at 150
psi would have been much more pronounced than the noise Wiitala said he heard. The
weight of the evidence contradicts much of Wiitala's testimony and strongly suggests that his
testimony about Compressor 2 is not credible.

16. Gilbert's testimony about Compressor 2 is also contradicted by the weight of other evidence.
Gilbert testified that "someone" from McKenzie told him that Compressor 2 would hold
pressure at 150 psi.[186] However, Marty Husband, a McKenzie employee testified that when
his company received a compressor for maintenance, an employee would routinely put it on a
"standard run" to see if it would pump up to and maintain standard pressure. Husband
testified that if the compressor did not maintain pressure, McKenzie's routine practice was to
tear it down to troubleshoot the problem.[187] The fact that McKenzie tore down Compressor 2

---

[181] See FOF 57
[182] See FOF 55
[183] See FOF 54
[184] See FOF 52, 53
[185] See FOF 40
[186] See FOF 52
[187] See FOF 53

- 40 -

16732
2 June 2000

FORMAL INVESTIGATION INTO THE COMMERCIAL DIVING ACCIDENT ABOARD
THE MOBILE OFFSHORE DRILLING UNIT CLIFF'S DRILLING RIG NO. 12 ON
4 MARCH 1996, WITH LOSS OF LIFE

and found numerous problems is persuasive evidence that Compressor 2 would not pump up
to and maintain standard pressure for a properly functioning Quincy 325 air compressor. The
weight of the evidence indicates that Compressor 2 never supplied air pressure above 100
psi. The most likely reason Pilkington's helmet was not adequately ventilated is that
Compressor 2 was not producing adequate air quantity, pressure, or quality.

G&G Maintenance

17. Gilbert claimed G&G had a maintenance program. He described it as a process where
equipment was checked just before it was used, by whichever G&G employee planned to use
it.[188] After Al May, the full-time equipment maintenance person left G&G, the company did
not replace him. G&G stopped performing the Coast Guard required compressor air quality
testing about a year after May left and this was not an isolated maintenance oversight.[189] 46
CFR 197.450 requires dive supervisors to ensure compressor air quality is tested every six
months and after every repair or modification. However, since the testing requires air
samples be sent to a laboratory, the owner is in the best position to ensure that testing is done.
G&G compressors routinely failed on diving jobs; so much so that the employees became
skilled at trouble shooting and repairing them at the job site.[190] Lawdermilk testified that
Compressor 2 had malfunctioned before the Rig 12 job and had not been repaired before
being sent out on 4 March 1996.[191]

18. G&G often would not buy replacement parts to do ordinary equipment upkeep. G&G
employees would use red shop rags as air intake filters for compressors. Lawdermilk
indicated there was a strong likelihood that a shop rag weighted down by marbles had been
used as an air intake filter on Compressor 2. Lawdermilk also testified that when he went to
McKenzie's to pick up Compressor 2 after the accident, the mechanic reported that a rag had
been sucked through the cylinder. If a shop rag was sucked into Compressor 2's air inlet, a
complete interruption of airflow to the diver could have resulted.[192]

Wiitala

19. Wiitala believed he was qualified to be a tender and a diver for G&G as soon as he left
commercial diving school. "I mean, I had gone to school for it. I feel like if you went to
school to learn how to fly a plane, when you get out, you fly a plane."[193] Even though his
progression to dive supervisor was unstructured and accidental, he also believed he was
qualified to be a dive supervisor.[194] Nevertheless, even after having worked for Gilbert and

---

[188] See FOF 15, 16, 17, 18; See too USCG Investigation, Vol. 4, IO exhibit 40, (Gilbert statement, pg. 44-47)
[189] See FOF 15, 16, 17, 18; See 46 CFR 197.450 for air testing regulations.
[190] See FOF 23
[191] See FOF 17
[192] See FOF 17, 52
[193] Wiitala, testimony, Vol. 1, pg. 145
[194] See FOF 21; See too, Wiitala, testimony, Vol. 1, pg. 146

- 41 -

16732
2 June 2000

FORMAL INVESTIGATION INTO THE COMMERCIAL DIVING ACCIDENT ABOARD THE MOBILE OFFSHORE DRILLING UNIT CLIFF'S DRILLING RIG NO. 12 ON 4 MARCH 1996, WITH LOSS OF LIFE

G&G for 13 years and at least eight years as a dive supervisor, Wiitala did not consider himself the dive supervisor on 4 March 1996. He testified that his conversation with Gilbert the night before convinced him that Austin would be the dive supervisor; a conclusion supported by the fact that Gilbert failed to send a designation letter or operations manual to Rig 12.[195]

20. Wiitala went aboard Rig 12 angry that Texas NDE had not supplied the two promised additional divers and was determined to not be saddled with dive supervisor responsibilities. Despite adopting a narrow view of his responsibilities, Wiitala attempted to do some of the work he characterized as dive supervisor-type duties.[196] Wiitala called Gilbert to send out another video cable; he directed Pilkington to make the first dive and while Pilkington was in the water, Wiitala directed Pilkington's movements. Wiitala also worked the dive station, monitoring the gauges, communicating with Pilkington, and managing the air rack.

21. Regardless of his intent, Wiitala was undoubtedly the *de facto* dive supervisor on Rig 12. This was consistent with past practice since, of the three divers on Rig 12, only Wiitala had ever been appointed as dive supervisor by G&G. Before the dive, Wiitala, Austin, and Pilkington overlooked many red flags that should have resulted in suspension of diving operations. But, of the three, Wiitala was unquestionably the best able to identify the problems.

22. Wiitala's initial concerns about the Rig 12 dive were piercingly accurate. When he turned down the job, Wiitala diagnosed the problem as being a lack of personnel to carry out the job. But, when that problem manifested itself on Rig 12, Wiitala failed to request two additional divers be added to the dive team. He also failed to request a second umbilical and, during Pilkington's dive, he failed to recognize the danger signal associated with repeatedly bottoming out Compressor 2 and repeatedly having to tell Pilkington to close his free-flow valve -- an indication that Pilkington was probably laboring for air.[197]

23. A strong indication of the root cause of Pilkington's casualty is reflected in Wiitala's own emergency response. Wiitala came to understand that Pilkington was not receiving enough air only after Pilkington said that he might have forgotten to tighten his airline. Wiitala responded almost instantly by taking Compressor 2 off-line and replacing it with a high-pressure air bottle. Wiitala clearly gave little credence to the possibility that Pilkington had failed to secure his airline. Wiitala's actions were consistent with his analysis, probably accurate, that Compressor 2 was malfunctioning.[198]

24. When Wiitala finally grasped the nature of the problem, he decided to send Austin down to effect a rescue. He made the decision because Austin was already in a neoprene wetsuit with

---

[195] See FOF 21, 25, 27
[196] See FOF 25, 28, 37, 40, 41, 42
[197] See FOF 28, 36; See too Dr. Clarke, testimony, Vol. 2, pg. 109-110
[198] See FOF 42, 43

16732
2 June 2000

FORMAL INVESTIGATION INTO THE COMMERCIAL DIVING ACCIDENT ABOARD
THE MOBILE OFFSHORE DRILLING UNIT CLIFF'S DRILLING RIG NO. 12 ON
4 MARCH 1996, WITH LOSS OF LIFE

a diving collar to which a helmet could be attached; on its face a rational decision. But, Wiitala overlooked several problems. Since there was no umbilical available, 20 minutes were wasted stringing together welding hose to supply oxygen to a helmet. Additionally, when Austin was put in the water he found the neoprene suit made him so buoyant he could not dive to Pilkington and more time was wasted making a weight belt out of shackles. Finally, all of this time was wasted because Austin, the least experienced diver by far, simply did not have the skill to effect a rescue under emergency conditions with improvised equipment. Wiitala indicated at the hearing that he had a Bailout Bottle available and set up for his helmet but he did not attempt to use it during the rescue because he would have had to don his entire wetsuit.[199]

25. In the end, Wiitala was able to don Austin's helmet without a collar, dive to Pilkington, and bring him to the surface – an evolution that took one dive and a matter of minutes. Wiitala's lack of effective control of the situation and obvious poor judgement before and during the rescue attempt indicates that, despite his many years in the diving industry, he had little understanding of the forces at work on 4 March 1996.[200]

Tending

26. There is insufficient evidence to determine whether Pilkington attempted line pull signals during his dive. Wiitala's testimony indicates that at worst he was "tending" Pilkington's umbilical by standing on it and at best, he may have had an untrained rig hand holding the line.[201] Wiitala likely would not have been able to feel line pulls with his foot and a rig hand would likely not have recognized line pull signals if they were made. G&G's safety and operations manual stated that the company complied with the ADC Consensus Standards.[202] The ADC Consensus Standards say that a dive tender "shall not be assigned any other task while the diver is under water."[203]

27. Based on the analysis above, the level of tending done to Pilkington's umbilical was inadequate. Nevertheless, Coast Guard regulations do not describe what is required of a dive tender and Wiitala's efforts, however slight, may have met the letter of the regulations.[204]

Backup Air Supply

28. When Wiitala switched over to the high-pressure air bottle, the bottle drained to ambient pressure in 15 minutes.[205] The second high-pressure air bottle was not pressurized and

---

[199] See FOF 45, 46
[200] See FOF 46
[201] See FOF 40
[202] See FOF 13
[203] See USCG Investigation, Vol. 5, IO Exhibit 57, (ADC Consensus Standards, pg. 3-14)
[204] See 46 CFR 197.432(c)
[205] See FOF 43

16732
2 June 2000

FORMAL INVESTIGATION INTO THE COMMERCIAL DIVING ACCIDENT ABOARD
THE MOBILE OFFSHORE DRILLING UNIT CLIFF'S DRILLING RIG NO. 12 ON
4 MARCH 1996, WITH LOSS OF LIFE

Wiitala was not able to use it as a secondary air supply. Had it been full, another 15 minutes of air would have been available to Pilkington. Under normal circumstances, a high pressure air bottle of that capacity should supply about 75 minutes of air for a properly working Kirby, Morgan SuperLite 27 helmet with the free flow valve open.[206] One likely explanation for the bottle emptying so quickly can be found in the second stage regulator of Pilkington's helmet. The device is a spring biased demand regulator that can be externally adjusted with the helmet's "Dial-a- Breath" knob (See Figure 6) to fine tune the amount of air reaching the diver each time he inhales. The second stage regulator also has an internal adjustment which can be adjusted to set the general air pressure working parameters of the helmet. As the NEDU report indicates, Pilkington's second stage regulator internal adjustment had been set so that it would free flow, literally stay wide open, at any pressure above about 100 psi. The most likely reason the high pressure air bottle emptied in only 15 minutes is that the 150 psi of air the high pressure air bottle sent to the diver forced the second stage regulator to stay open until the bottle emptied. This, indirectly, also is evidence that Compressor 2 never produced or sustained the 150 psi of air as Wiitala claimed. Had Compressor 2 produced that volume and pressure of air, Pilkington would have experienced an almost continuous blast of air far beyond what any diver would feel comfortable; even those who tend to "hog it on." Another indicator that Wiitala's claim of almost continuous pressure at 150 psi is skeptical is that Wiitala stated that when he talked to Pilkington, he heard background noise consistent with the free flow valve being "cracked open a little bit." Had Pilkington's helmet been free flowing at the pressure Wiitala's testimony suggests, the background noise would have been obvious and likely would have impeded communications. Regardless of the above possibilities, the fact remains that there was not enough air to supply Pilkington along with a diving rescue operation. In fact, the dive team relied on a highly dangerous 100% oxygen gas bottle to supply the rescue diver.

Bailout Bottle

29. Pilkington did not dive with a bailout bottle.[207] No Coast Guard regulation required him to use a bailout bottle when diving in less than 130 feet of water.[208] Wiitala claimed that he offered to let Pilkington use his bailout bottle. But, Wiitala also indicated that he had expressed his irritation when Pilkington borrowed his weight belt. It is reasonable to presume that Pilkington was not eager to borrow even more equipment from his boss; especially equipment that would require reconfiguring before Pilkington could use it.[209]

---

[206] USCG Investigation, Vol. 5, IO exhibit 53, (U.S. Navy Dive Manual, Vol. 1, Chapter 6-3.2, Feb. 1993);

T [min] = (33 fsw/ (D [dive depth] + 33 fsw)) x V [volume of air available] / F [helmet free flow rate]; where, V = (Pf [cylinder pressure] – Pmf [minimum cylinder pressure]) / 14.7 psig x C [floodable volume of cylinder], Pf = 2250 psig, Pmf = 220 psig, C = 8 cubic feet (ft^3), F = 8 cubic feet per minute (cfm), D = 28 feet salt water (fsw)

[207] See FOF 38
[208] 46 CFR 197.346(g)
[209] See FOF 38

- 44 -

16732
2 June 2000

FORMAL INVESTIGATION INTO THE COMMERCIAL DIVING ACCIDENT ABOARD THE MOBILE OFFSHORE DRILLING UNIT CLIFF'S DRILLING RIG NO. 12 ON 4 MARCH 1996, WITH LOSS OF LIFE

<u>Second Dive Hose</u>

30. It was argued at the hearing that Pilkington caused his own death when he failed to abort his dive while knowing there was no back-up umbilical. It also was argued that Pilkington should have aborted his dive when he first noticed equipment problems.[210] The same criticism could be applied to Austin and Wiitala; they all had the opportunity to withdraw from the dive operation. Based on the testimony developed at the hearing, we know that Pilkington knew that there was no second dive umbilical available. However, there is insufficient evidence to determine what other unsafe conditions he knew about, either before or during the dive. The reasoning goes that if he knew about unsafe working conditions, Pilkington should have refused to work. Brett Gordon addressed this issue comprehensively in an article. To summarize Gordon's findings, workers have the right to refuse unsafe work under the Occupational Safety and Health Act, but they seldom do. In fairness, the same forces perhaps driving Pilkington to go ahead with the dive in the face of identified problems also may have been driving Austin and Wiitala to complete the dive.

> Employees in the United States have a right to refuse unsafe work in cases where the employee has a reasonable belief that performance of the work constitutes an imminent danger of death or serious physical injury [29 CFR 1977.12(b)(2) (1992)]. This has proven to be a strict standard that is rarely met by the employee. The employee has the burden of showing a reasonable belief under the circumstances and that the action taken was in good faith as 'any employee who acts in reliance on the regulation falls on the employee and he runs the risk of discharge or reprimand in the event a court subsequently finds that he acted unreasonably or in bad faith.' [Whirlpool Corp. v. Marshall, 445 U.S. 1, 21 (1980)]. More importantly, the regulation 'does not require employers to pay workers who refused to perform their assigned tasks in the face of imminent danger,' [Id. At 19]… In practice, the employee is forced to choose to either remain at a task while exposed to a substantial risk of harm, or be without work for a period of time until the dispute is resolved. An employee in these circumstances has little incentive to refuse unsafe work because the slim chance of proving the reasonableness of the belief in court does not outweigh the greater potential for lost pay.

> In addition to the limited scope of an employee's right to refuse dangerous work, an employee in the United States fears employer retaliation by exercising this right, despite an anti-retaliation provision in the OSH Act. [29 U.S.C. 660(c) (1988)]. The anti-retaliation provision of the OSH Act only protects an employee who proves that the refusal to perform a task was both reasonable and in good faith…

---

[210] See USCG Investigation, Vol. 6, IO Exhibit 68, (Parties in Interest Proposed Findings of Fact)

16732
2 June 2000

FORMAL INVESTIGATION INTO THE COMMERCIAL DIVING ACCIDENT ABOARD
THE MOBILE OFFSHORE DRILLING UNIT CLIFF'S DRILLING RIG NO. 12 ON
4 MARCH 1996, WITH LOSS OF LIFE

Few employees are successful in their claims under the anti-retaliation provision
in cases where they refuse unsafe work or file a complaint with OSHA. In 1989,
only 559 of the 3,342 discrimination complaints filed by employees with OSHA
resulted in litigation referrals by the Secretary of OSHA in U.S. district courts,
and even fewer claims were actually successful.[Cite omitted][211]

Main Airline Connection

31. Wiitala's testimony raised the questions of whether Pilkington's main airline was secured to
his helmet when he began his dive and whether Pilkington may have loosened the connection
when he was underwater. Wiitala testified that before Pilkington quit talking, Pilkington said
that he might have forgotten to tighten his airline.[212] The reasoning is that Pilkington may
have reached up to his main air connection (See figure 7) and, while trying to tighten the
fitting, loosened it instead. Master Chief Bradford opined that it was "plausible" that
Pilkington had loosened his main airline connection near the end of his dive.[213] I disagree.
The eyewitness testimony on this issue is contradictory, but some facts are undisputed.
Townsend says that when he tried to pull Pilkington into the personnel basket, Pilkington's
safety harness came free and the umbilical detached from Pilkington's helmet. Champagne,
on the other hand, clearly remembers the hoses being connected to Pilkington's helmet when
Champagne reached to remove the helmet on the deck of Rig 12.[214] Wiitala saw
Pilkington's helmet underwater during the rescue and distinctly remembers seeing the line
attached to the helmet and bubbles coming from the "whiskers" of Pilkington's helmet --
indicating that air was going through the helmet fitting to Pilkington's respirator.[215]

32. The most compelling undisputed fact on this question is that Pilkington was apparently still
alive, although unconscious, when he was brought back to the deck of Rig 12. This shows
that, even at the end of his dive, Pilkington received enough air to sustain life, but not enough
to sustain consciousness.[216] It is possible that Pilkington failed to tighten his air hose to his
helmet causing enough air to leak from the connection to make him blackout. The facts
though, do not support the theory. Pilkington's dive lasted three hours with him doing
relatively light work and moving constantly around the mat of Rig 12. Wiitala testified that
three or four times during the dive, he noticed Compressor 2's pressure gauge slip from about
150 psi down to 90 psi. But when Wiitala told Pilkington to close his free flow valve,
Wiitala testified that the system pressure returned to 150 psi. According to Wiitala, this was
Compressor 2's normal operating pressure, indicating that when Pilkington closed his free-

---

[211] Brett R. Gordon, "COMMENT: EMPLOYEE INVOLVEMENT IN THE ENFORCEMENT OF THE
OCCUPATIONAL SAFETY AND HEALTH LAWS OF CANADA AND THE UNITED STATES", 15 Comp.
Lab. L. 527, 1994
[212] See FOF 42
[213] See FOF 61
[214] See FOF 47
[215] See FOF 46
[216] See FOF 63

- 46 -

16732
2 June 2000

FORMAL INVESTIGATION INTO THE COMMERCIAL DIVING ACCIDENT ABOARD
THE MOBILE OFFSHORE DRILLING UNIT CLIFF'S DRILLING RIG NO. 12 ON
4 MARCH 1996, WITH LOSS OF LIFE

flow valve, the system returned to its maximum pressure and inferentially, proving that the system was practically airtight.[217]

33. Pilkington also did not loosen his main air connection completely at the end of his dive. All the eyewitness agreed that Pilkington's airline was connected to his helmet when he was brought to the surface.[218] There also is no evidence that Pilkington adjusted his hose connection during his dive, prior to raising the question to Wiitala. Therefore, for the loose hose connection theory to be possible, Pilkington would have had to: 1) wrongly suspect his main air connection was loose, and 2) misadjust the connection allowing a fraction, but not all the air in the line to escape, resulting in an almost instantaneous blackout.

Coast Guard Marine Inspectors

34. Had the Coast Guard marine inspectors inspected the dive station on 4 March 1996, they would likely have discovered at least three violations of Coast Guard regulations.

   1) 46 CFR 197.201(a) and (b) [Failure to designate dive supervisor in writing and failure to deliver designation to person-in-charge prior to diving];

   2) 46 CFR 197.420(A)(1) and (2) [Failure to provide operations manual to person-in-charge and have at dive location]; and

   3) 46 CFR 197.482(d)(2) [Failure to log compressor air test results].

The marine inspectors were required by Coast Guard policy to inspect the diving station. The Marine Safety Manual clearly states that "[i]nspection of diving equipment and facilities *shall* be conducted when diving operations occur on . . . vessels inspected for certification..."[219] The marine inspectors were also strongly guided to conduct dive safety inspections by NVIC 1-89. "The underwater survey should not be conducted unless the inspector is satisfied that the equipment and procedures being used by the divers will provide a safe and meaningful examination of the ship. Safety must be foremost on the minds of all those working together on the actual diving operation."[220]

35. If the Coast Guard marine inspectors had inspected the dive station, they could have made some useful judgements about the dive team's qualifications by asking whether a dive plan had been completed and a pre-dive safety checklist and job hazard analysis had been done. However, if the inspectors had looked only at the divers' qualifications, they would have had

---

[217] See FOF 41, 42. Note Analysis para. 19; Wiitala's testimony about Compressor 2's max pressures is extremely suspect. Nevertheless, it can be inferred that the pressure gauge indicated max pressure for Compressor 2, regardless of whether it was 150 psi or something less.

[218] See FOF 46, 47

[219] Marine Safety Manual, Vol. II, Chapter 16.E.1 (emphasis added)

[220] See FOF 2 – 8 and 29, 30, 31, 31; See too USCG Investigation, Vol. 4, IO Exhibit 30 (NVIC 1-89, enclosure 1, para. 5.f.)

- 47 -

16732
2 June 2000

FORMAL INVESTIGATION INTO THE COMMERCIAL DIVING ACCIDENT ABOARD THE MOBILE OFFSHORE DRILLING UNIT CLIFF'S DRILLING RIG NO. 12 ON 4 MARCH 1996, WITH LOSS OF LIFE

trouble deciding whether they were qualified to dive safely. Wiitala was a graduate of a dive school and had been a commercial diver for 12 years.[221] Pilkington was a graduate of a reputable dive school in the State of Washington and had already made several shallow water dives for G&G.[222] Only Austin was not a graduate of a dive school, but he had dived for Cliffs on two previous occasions.[223] Since commercial divers are not required to be licensed, or even to attend diving school, the inspectors would have been hard-pressed to judge whether the Rig 12 diving job could proceed safely based solely on the divers' credentials.

Conclusions:

1. The apparent cause of the death of Brian Pilkington was drowning. Pilkington inhaled water into his lungs, which disrupted gas exchange causing him to asphyxiate.

2. A contributing cause of the death of Brian Pilkington was that water entered Pilkington's helmet. There is insufficient evidence to determine how water entered the helmet. However, the weight of evidence indicates the most likely path of ingress was under the neckdam, drawn in as Pilkington gasped for air when he suffered a loss of air pressure. In the alternative, water may have entered the helmet through the emergency air connection if Pilkington opened the valve and concurrently experienced a complete loss of air pressure.

3. A contributing cause of the death of Brian Pilkington was that he succumbed to Hypercapnia (too much carbon dioxide in the blood), causing him to pass out and his face to fall forward in his helmet allowing him to inhale water.

4. A contributing cause of the casualty was Pilkington's fatigue, lack of nourishment, and hypothermia, which masked the symptoms of Hypercapnia.

5. Pilkington succumbed to Hypercapnia because Compressor 2 produced inadequate air volume or pressure to properly ventilate and remove Carbon Dioxide from his helmet. Compressor 2 probably never produced more than 80-90 psi during the Rig 12 dive.

6. Compressor 2 produced inadequate air volume and pressure to properly ventilate Pilkington's helmet because its valves would not seat and its pilot valve was not working properly, preventing the compressor from pressurizing the volume tank to a pressure above 80-90 psi as air pressure in the tank was depleted by the diver.

7. Since no air quality tests were done for Compressor 2, there is insufficient evidence to prove conclusively that air mixed with oil contributed to this casualty. Nevertheless, the

---

[221] See FOF 21
[222] See FOF 24
[223] See FOF 11

- 48 -

16732
2 June 2000

FORMAL INVESTIGATION INTO THE COMMERCIAL DIVING ACCIDENT ABOARD THE MOBILE OFFSHORE DRILLING UNIT CLIFF'S DRILLING RIG NO. 12 ON 4 MARCH 1996, WITH LOSS OF LIFE

compressor teardown conducted by Guy Kirby and recorded at IO Exhibit 19 indicates that Compressor 2 almost certainly produced oil tainted air as oil blew by the compressor piston rings entering the head assembly to be sent downstream to the diver. A contributing cause of the casualty may have been that Pilkington was debilitated by the early stages of Lipid Pneumonia when he breathed oil saturated air, reducing the partial pressure of air sent to him and impeding gas exchange in his lungs.

8. A contributing cause of the casualty was G&G's failure to do compressor air testing.

9. Compressor 2 produced inadequate air volume and pressure and probably tainted air because G&G had an inadequate maintenance program that did not routinely check and repair Compressor 2, allowing it to fall into disrepair.

10. G&G did not have a good maintenance and repair program because it did not have anyone exclusively responsible for equipment upkeep. Instead, Dan Gilbert claimed to have titular charge of equipment maintenance but expected all employees when they used equipment to detect and repair mechanical problems.

11. G&G did not have a person primarily focused on equipment repair and upkeep because it did not hire anyone to do that job when Mr. Al May, the former shop manager, left G&G in 1990 or 1991.

12. A contributing cause of the casualty was G&G's poor quality control practices. G&G allowed poorly maintained equipment to be sent to jobs and not enough equipment to be sent to jobs. The fact that there is a question about whether Pilkington tightened the airline to his helmet before beginning his dive indicates lax pre-dive preparation by G&G employees.

13. A contributing cause of the casualty was that G&G failed to appoint a diving supervisor in writing, or in the alternative, Texas NDE failed to provide a diving supervisor.

14. A contributing cause of the casualty was that Ronald Townsend, the OIM, failed to require that a diving supervisor, appointed in writing, present to him the written appointment along with an operations and safety manual.

15. There is insufficient evidence to prove definitively that a red shop rag was ingested into the compressor air intake, but a contributing cause of the casualty may have been that a rag was ingested into Compressor 2's air intake reducing the air volume and pressure passing to Brian Pilkington.

16. A contributing cause of the casualty was that Pilkington's axe fouled in the mat piping of Rig 12, restricting Pilkington's ability to be pulled to the surface.

- 49 -

503

16732
2 June 2000

FORMAL INVESTIGATION INTO THE COMMERCIAL DIVING ACCIDENT ABOARD
THE MOBILE OFFSHORE DRILLING UNIT CLIFF'S DRILLING RIG NO. 12 ON
4 MARCH 1996, WITH LOSS OF LIFE

17. A contributing cause of the casualty was the anxiousness and confusion brought on by carbon dioxide poisoning (Hypercapnia) which debilitated Pilkington's ability to think and respond to directions from the dive supervisor.

18. A contributing cause of the casualty was the dive team's inability to quickly muster a coordinated rescue attempt.

19. A contributing cause of the casualty was lack of a standby diver. A ready standby diver likely would have been able to save Pilkington's life. Lack of a ready standby diver with his own gear and air supply created an almost 30 minute delay in the rescue attempt.

20. G&G did not supply an adequate secondary air supply when it sent a high-pressure air bottle to the dive site that was not fully pressurized.

21. There is insufficient evidence to tell whether Pilkington attempted to communicate through line pulls. But, when Wiitala didn't tend the umbilical in his hand, Pilkington was unable to communicate to the surface through line pull signals. A contributing cause of the casualty may have been lack of communication between Pilkington and the surface.

22. Dan Wiitala did not have the training or temperament to be a dive supervisor.

23. Kirk Austin did not have the training or experience to be a standby diver or dive supervisor.

24. G&G was not in compliance with its own manning requirements as set out in its safe practices and operations manual in that a dedicated dive tender was not available.

25. A contributing cause may have been the helmet's internal adjustments made to the regulator affecting how the regulator responded to intermediate pressure. The adjustment was set in an unusual position allowing free-flow at normal operating pressures. This unusual setting indicates that Pilkington had experienced inadequate compressor air volume and pressure from G&G compressors and had adjusted his second stage regulator to compensate for the low air pressures. The setting probably explains why the first high-pressure air bottle drained so quickly.

26. The fact that the Rig 12 Operations Manual that was onboard at the time of the casualty– not the G&G safety and operations manual -- had not been approved by the Coast Guard did not contribute to the casualty or delay the emergency response, including the evacuation of Pilkington to the hospital.

27. A tertiary air supply (bailout bottle) may have saved Brian Pilkington's life.

28. Brian Pilkington's air hose was connected to his helmet. He did not fail to tighten it prior to diving nor did he loosen it during the dive.

- 50 -

504

16732
2 June 2000

FORMAL INVESTIGATION INTO THE COMMERCIAL DIVING ACCIDENT ABOARD THE MOBILE OFFSHORE DRILLING UNIT CLIFF'S DRILLING RIG NO. 12 ON 4 MARCH 1996, WITH LOSS OF LIFE

29. A contributing cause of the casualty was that the Coast Guard marine inspectors failed to inspect the diving station as required by the Marine Safety Manual. Marine Inspectors should have inspected the dive station on Rig 12 in accordance with Marine Safety Manual Vol. II, Chapter 16.E.1. If they had, they likely would have determined that the diving operation lacked a dive supervisor appointed in writing, a dive operations manual, and a log with air test results for Compressor 2. This would likely have resulted in delay of diving operations and another compressor being used, increasing the chance Pilkington would have survived. The marine inspectors failed to meet the expectations of Marine Safety Manual Vol. II, Chapter 16.E.1.

30. Coast Guard marine inspectors likely did not inspect the diving station because at least one of them believed that the ABS surveyor would oversee safe diving operations during the NDT portion of the hull inspection.

31. Coast Guard marine inspectors should not have relied on the ABS surveyor to oversee diving operations to ensure diving safety. That was an inappropriate attempt to delegate Coast Guard authority.

32. The Rig 12 SEILOD was governed by NVIC 12-69. NVIC 12-69 does not impose a requirement for the Coast Guard to do safety-related analysis of the diving operations before approving a SEILOD.

33. NVIC 1-89 is more generally relied on by marine inspectors than is NVIC 12-69. NVIC 1-89, although literally not applicable to the Rig 12 SEILOD, clearly established an expectation for OCMI's to analyze SEILOD proposals to ensure diving operations can be conducted safely. By the standards set in NVIC 1-89, MSO Port Arthur failed to meet Commandant expectations to analyze the ability of the diving contractors to safely carry out a SEILOD on Rig 12.

34. The liveboating diving variance requested by Cliffs for the Rig 12 SEILOD was not necessary since Rig 12 was in a bottom bearing mode and was not self-propelled. The diving variance granted by MSO Port Arthur did not contribute to the casualty.

35. There is no evidence that drugs or alcohol contributed to this casualty.

36. There is evidence that Kirk Austin and Texas NDE, and/or Dan Gilbert and G&G Marine failed to designate a diving supervisor in accordance with 46 CFR 197.210.

37. There is evidence that G&G Marine and/or Dan Gilbert failed to provide an air compressor system with an efficient filtration system as required by 46 CFR 197.310 (c).

- 51 -

505

16732
2 June 2000

FORMAL INVESTIGATION INTO THE COMMERCIAL DIVING ACCIDENT ABOARD
THE MOBILE OFFSHORE DRILLING UNIT CLIFF'S DRILLING RIG NO. 12 ON
4 MARCH 1996, WITH LOSS OF LIFE

38. There is evidence that G&G Marine and/or Dan Gilbert failed to provide a primary breathing gas supply sufficient to support a diver and standby diver for the duration of the planned dive in accordance with 46 CFR 197.340.

39. There is evidence that Ronald Townsend failed to carry out the responsibilities of the Person-in-Charge of Rig 12 as required by 46 CFR 197.402.

40. There is evidence that Dan Wiitala failed to carry out the responsibilities of the diving supervisor as set out in the regulations listed below. Wiitala correctly pointed out that he was never appointed diving supervisor for the Rig 12 dive. However, when he began to act as the diving supervisor, he assumed responsibility for carrying out all of the dive supervisor duties, not just those he could easily accomplish.

    a. 46 CFR 197.404: Responsibilities of the diving supervisor

    b. 46 CFR 197.410: Dive procedures

    c. 46 CFR 197.420: Failure to provide ops manual

    d. 46 CFR 197.432: Failure to continuously tend diver in the water

    e. 46 CFR 197.450: Failure to conduct breathing gas tests

    f. 46 CFR 197.480 & 482: Failure to maintain a logbook

41. There is evidence that the senior marine inspector on board Rig 12, LT Julio MARTINEZ, USCG, failed to follow the requirements of Marine Safety Manual, Vol. II, Chapter 16.E.1 by not ensuring that the dive station was inspected on 4 March 1996 while diving operations were underway on a vessel inspected for certification. This matter has been forwarded to the Commander, Eighth Coast Guard District for further investigation.

42. There is evidence of a violation of 18 USC 1112 (Manslaughter) by G&G Marine and/or Dan Gilbert. This matter has been forwarded to the Commander, Eighth Coast Guard District for further investigation.

43. With the above exceptions, there is no evidence of actionable misconduct, inattention to duty, negligent or willful violation of law or regulations on the part of licensed or certificated personnel; nor evidence of any other failure of inspected equipment or material; nor evidence that any other personnel of the Coast Guard or of any other federal agency, or any other person contributed to this casualty.

- 52 -

16732
2 June 2000

FORMAL INVESTIGATION INTO THE COMMERCIAL DIVING ACCIDENT ABOARD
THE MOBILE OFFSHORE DRILLING UNIT CLIFF'S DRILLING RIG NO. 12 ON
4 MARCH 1996, WITH LOSS OF LIFE

Recommendations:

1. Commandant should require bailout bottles for all commercial diving operations, regardless of depth. The bailout bottles should have sufficient capacity to supply a diver with an appropriate volume of air at the deepest depth being worked. The facts of this case do not strongly support a recommendation for bailout bottles. Nevertheless, all diving experts consulted by the Investigating Officer agreed that bailout bottles come in so many sizes and configurations, and are so inexpensive that every dive should begin with the presumption that a bailout bottle will be used.

2. Commandant should require all unused auxiliary gas ports on diver worn life support equipment to be capped or blanked during all commercial diving operations. This will remove the possibility of water entering a diver's helmet if he inadvertently opens an emergency valve.

3. Commandant should require a standby diver dressed out and with a separate air supply, ready to quickly deploy for all commercial diving operations regardless of depth.

4. Commandant should require diving stages for all commercial diving operations regardless of depth, except where they would be impractical. This will speed entry to the water for divers and rescue divers and remove the need for rescue operations to work from personnel baskets. In this casualty, the rescue operation was itself so slow that using a crane operated Billy Pugh basket as a rescue platform did not significantly add to the delay. Nevertheless, there is no question that a diving stage at water level would have speeded up the rescue.

5. Commandant should require the Diving Supervisor and the Master or Person-in-Charge to develop a site specific rescue plan designating the equipment and personnel that will be used for a rescue or removal of an injured diver from the water for all commercial diving operations.

6. Commandant should require that, prior to any commercial diving operation, the Diving Supervisor describe the rescue plan to all members of the diving team.

7. Commandant should require the Diving Supervisor to complete a Job Hazard Analysis before every commercial diving operation. See IO Exhibit 57, ADC Consensus Standards, pg. 3-9 to 3-10b.

8. Commandant should require Diving Supervisors to complete a pre-dive safety checklist suitable to the type of diving equipment and procedures to be used, prior to all commercial dive operations. See IO Exhibit 53, Navy Dive Manual, pg. 4 –37 to 4-49.

9. Commandant should consider changing Coast Guard regulations to ensure accountability of commercial diving contractors for maintaining records and logs for their diving equipment.

- 53 -

16732
2 June 2000

FORMAL INVESTIGATION INTO THE COMMERCIAL DIVING ACCIDENT ABOARD
THE MOBILE OFFSHORE DRILLING UNIT CLIFF'S DRILLING RIG NO. 12 ON
4 MARCH 1996, WITH LOSS OF LIFE

Commandant should also make minor changes to Coast Guard regulations in addition to
those described above to ensure Offshore Installation Managers play a more active role in
pre-dive safety preparations. Present Coast Guard diving regulations place record keeping
responsibilities on diving supervisors. Diving supervisors are appointed on a job to job basis
and their designation ends when the diving job they supervise ends. Many of the record
keeping responsibilities, however, are continuous and must be completed between diving
jobs, away from the dive site. The following recommended regulation changes illustrate how
the commercial diving contractor and Offshore Installation Manager could be given a more
responsible role in the record keeping and pre-dive safety processes.

a. At 46 CFR 197.204 [Definitions], Commandant should add a definition "Commercial
Diving Contractor" to describe the person or business that provides commercial
diving services.

b. At 46 CFR 197.484 (a) [Notice of casualty], after the words "person-in-charge",
Commandant should include the words "Diving Supervisor or Commercial Diving
Contractor."

c. At 46 CFR 197.486 [Written report of casualty], after the words "person-in-charge of
a vessel or facility", Commandant should include the words "or Diving Supervisor or
Commercial Diving Contractor."

d. Commandant should change 46 CFR 197.210 [Designation of diving supervisor] as
follows:

"The Commercial Diving Contractor shall designate in writing a Diving
Supervisor for each commercial diving operation. The Diving Supervisor shall
present the written designation to the Master or Person-in Charge."

e. Commandant should change 46 CFR 197.402 (2) (i) [Responsibilities of the person-
in-charge] as follows:

"Prior to permitting any commercial diving operation to commence, the Master or
Person-in-Charge shall examine the Diving Supervisor's written designation to
ensure it is complete as required by §197.210."

f. Commandant should cross-reference 46 CFR 109.109 [Responsibilities of master or
person in charge] with 46 CFR 197.402 [Responsibilities of person-in-charge].

g. Commandant should change 46 CFR 197.480 (c) [Logbooks] as follows:

(c) The Diving Contractor and the Diving Supervisor conducting commercial
diving operations from a vessel or facility subject to this subpart shall maintain a
logbook for making the entries required by this subpart.

- 54 -

508

16732
2 June 2000

FORMAL INVESTIGATION INTO THE COMMERCIAL DIVING ACCIDENT ABOARD
THE MOBILE OFFSHORE DRILLING UNIT CLIFF'S DRILLING RIG NO. 12 ON
4 MARCH 1996, WITH LOSS OF LIFE

(d) The logbook required to be maintained by this subpart shall be taken to the jobsite for every commercial diving operation and shall be available for inspection by the Master or Person-in-charge, the United States Coast Guard, or any other cognizant agency.

(e) The Diving Contractor shall retain the logbook required to be maintained by this subpart for a period of not less than three years.

h. Commandant should change 46 CFR 197.482(d) [Logbook entries] as follows:

(d) The Diving Contractor and the Diving Supervisor shall insure that a record of the following is maintained: . . .

(e) The Diving Contractor and the Diving Supervisor shall insure that copies of each of the records required under paragraph (d) are included in the operations manual required by 46 CFR 197.420. The records required under paragraph (d) must be maintained by the Diving Contractor for a period of not less than three years.

i. At 46 CFR 197.420 [Operations manual], Commandant should add the following:

(e) The operations manual must contain copies of the records required to be maintained by 46 CFR 197.482 (d) and (e).

j. At 46 CFR 197.450 [Breathing gas tests], Commandant should change the words "The diving supervisor shall ensure that" – to

The Diving Contractor shall ensure that –

k. At 46 CFR 197.450 [Breathing gas tests], Commandant should add the following:

(d) The Diving Contractor shall maintain the above stated test records for a period of not less than 3 years.

10. Commandant should require the Dive Supervisor and Master or Person-in-Charge to execute a Declaration of Inspection verifying their respective duties have been competed before any commercial dive operation begins. See 46 CFR 35.35-30 for an example of the concept as it is applied to oil transfers.

11. At 46 CFR 197.204 [Definitions], Commandant should include a definition of "Diving Tender". Commandant should consider adopting the description of Diver Tender set out in the Navy Dive Manual. See IO Exhibit 53, Section 4-8.5.3.

- 55 -

509

16732
2 June 2000

FORMAL INVESTIGATION INTO THE COMMERCIAL DIVING ACCIDENT ABOARD
THE MOBILE OFFSHORE DRILLING UNIT CLIFF'S DRILLING RIG NO. 12 ON
4 MARCH 1996, WITH LOSS OF LIFE

12. At 46 CFR 197.204 [Definitions], Commandant should include a definition of "Dive Tending" or "Tending."

13. Commandant should consider limiting the duties of a dive tender to only tending the dive umbilical during a commercial diving operation, as illustrated by the following wording.

At 46 CFR 197.432 (c)[Surface-supplied air diving], Commandant should add the words:

; the person tending the diver shall have no other duties while the diver is under water;

14. At 46 CFR 197.204 [Definitions], Commandant should consider consolidating the definitions "*Commercial diver*" and "*Diver*" into one inclusive definition.

15. Commandant should establish minimum manning standards for all diving operations. Commandant should consider adopting the standards set out in the ADC Consensus Standards. See IO Exhibit 57, pg. 3-24 to 3-29.

16. Commandant should establish commercial diving qualification standards for Commercial Divers, Commercial Diving Tenders, and Commercial Diving Supervisors. Commandant should consider adopting the standards set out in the ADC Consensus Standards. See IO Exhibit 57, pg. 2-3 to 2-8.

17. In the absence of a diver qualification program, Commandant should publish criteria for OCMI's to use when reviewing SEILOD applications to evaluate qualifications of divers to safely conduct diving operations.

18. Commandant should examine NVIC 12-69 and NVIC 1-89 to determine whether the older one should be cancelled and incorporated into the newer.

19. Commandant should require dive operation inspection training for all marine inspectors.

20. Commandant should remove the diving component from the MODU Inspector PQS workbook and establish a separate Performance Qualification Standards workbook for diving operations.

21. Commandant should evaluate the adequacy of the MODU/SEILOD job aid, CG-840H-1 (9-92), to determine whether additional inspection items should be added to the diving checklist (pg. 20 – 22). See IO Exhibit 31.

22. Commandant should publish guidance emphasizing that Coast Guard marine inspectors should not attempt to delegate dive safety enforcement duties to any third party, including classification society surveyors.

16732
2 June 2000

FORMAL INVESTIGATION INTO THE COMMERCIAL DIVING ACCIDENT ABOARD
THE MOBILE OFFSHORE DRILLING UNIT CLIFF'S DRILLING RIG NO. 12 ON
4 MARCH 1996, WITH LOSS OF LIFE

23. Commandant should require dive casualty investigation training for all marine safety casualty investigators.

24. Commandant should consider tasking Coast Guard divers to assist in the investigation of diving casualties. In this case, the IO was assisted by a former Coast Guard diver and a U.S. Navy Master Diver, both with exceptional insight. However, previous investigators to this casualty did not have those valuable resources. The Marine Safety Manual recommends that an IO investigating diving casualties have diving experience, but there are few IO's available with that background.

25. Commandant should consider seeking an agreement with the Navy Experimental Diving Unit and the U.S. Navy Diving School to provide assistance in Coast Guard diving casualty investigations.

26. Commandant should establish a working group of industry experts to examine ways to improve safety practices in the commercial diving industry. The working group should consider whether the Coast Guard should adopt by reference the ADC Consensus Standards for commercial diving operations where they do not conflict with Coast Guard regulations. The group also should consider whether the Coast Guard should require oil-free compressors be used on commercial diving operations. During this investigation, industry experts made many excellent recommendations to improve safety in the industry, many of which could not be included in this report because they were beyond the scope of the investigation. If a group is convened, it should seek input from Marine Safety Office Houston-Galveston, which recently initiated a commercial diving safety awareness and compliance program.

27. Commandant should forward a copy of this investigation to OSHA for consideration.

28. Commandant should forward a copy of this investigation to the Association of Diving Contractors.

29. Commandant should forward copies of this investigation to all Eighth Coast Guard District Coastal OCMI's.

30. This casualty investigation should be closed.

T. D. BEISTLE
Investigating Officer

- 57 -

511

16732
2 June 2000

FORMAL INVESTIGATION INTO THE COMMERCIAL DIVING ACCIDENT ABOARD THE MOBILE OFFSHORE DRILLING UNIT CLIFF'S DRILLING RIG # 12 ON 4 MARCH 1996, WITH LOSS OF LIFE

INVESTIGATING OFFICER'S EXHIBIT LIST

I.O. EXHIBIT NO. 1 – Reporter's Oath

I.O. EXHIBIT NO. 2 – Letter to LCDR Thomas D. Beistle from Commander, Eight Coast Guard District, dated June 3, 1999

I.O. EXHIBIT NO. 3 – Designated Party In Interest letter to Mr. Dan Wiitala from LCDR Thomas D. Beistle dated June 8, 1999

I.O. EXHIBIT NO. 4 – Designated Party In Interest letter to Ms. Martha Adams from LCDR Thomas D. Beistle dated June 8, 1999

I.O. EXHIBIT NO. 5 – Designated Party In Interest letter to Mr. Kirk Austin from LCDR Thomas D. Beistle dated June 8, 1999

I.O. EXHIBIT NO. 6 – Designated Party In Interest letter to Mr. Dan Gilbert, c/o Kenna Seiler, from LCDR Thomas D. Beistle dated June 8, 1999

I.O. EXHIBIT NO. 7 – Designated Party In Interest letter to Mr. Dan Gilbert, G & G Marine, from LCDR Thomas D. Beistle dated June 8, 1999

I.O. EXHIBIT NO. 8 – Designated Party In Interest letter to Mr. Peter J. Pilkington from LCDR Thomas D. Beistle dated June 8, 1999

I.O. EXHIBIT NO. 9 – Designated Party In Interest letter to Cliffs Drilling Company from LCDR Thomas D. Beistle dated June 8, 1999

I.O. EXHIBIT NO. 10 – Designated Party In Interest letter to Mr. Ronald Townsend from LCDR Thomas D. Beistle dated June 8, 1999

I.O. EXHIBIT NO. 11 – Designated Party In Interest letter to Mr. Ronald Townsend, c/o Cliffs Drilling Company, from LCDR Thomas D. Beistle dated June 8, 1999

I.O. EXHIBIT NO. 12 – Letter to parties of interest discussing telephone conference from LCDR Thomas D. Beistle dated June 20, 1999

I.O. EXHIBIT NO. 13 – Affidavit of Donnie Henry

I.O. EXHIBIT NO. 14 – Scheduled time log and job log from Steve Champagne

I.O. ECHIBIT NO. 15 – Materials list dated March 4, 1996

I.O. EXHIBIT NO. 16 – G & G Marine Manual

I.O. EXHIBIT NO. 17 – Hand-drawn diagram from Dan Wiitala

I.O. EXHIBIT NO. 18 – Diagram, Cliffs Drilling No. 12 Main Deck Arrangement Diagram

I.O. EXHIBIT NO. 19 – Invoice from McKenzie to G & G Marine

I.O. EXHIBIT NO. 20 – Direct Interrogatories to the Custodian of Records for McKenzie

I.O. EXHIBIT NO. 21 – Excerpt deposition testimony of Dan Wiitala, p. 39 & 40

I.O. EXHIBIT NO. 22 – Excerpt deposition testimony of Dan Wiitala, p. 237

- 58

16732
2 June 2000

FORMAL INVESTIGATION INTO THE COMMERCIAL DIVING ACCIDENT ABOARD THE MOBILE OFFSHORE DRILLING UNIT CLIFF'S DRILLING RIG # 12 ON 4 MARCH 1996, WITH LOSS OF LIFE

I.O. EXHIBIT NO. 23 – Cliffs personnel count dated March 4, 1996

I.O. EXHIBIT NO. 24 – Coast Guard 2692 Report

I.O. EXHIBIT NO. 25 – Curriculum Vitae of Dr. John Clarke

I.O. EXHIBIT NO. 26 – SuperLite diving hat report

I.O. EXHIBIT NO. 27 – Autopsy report of Brian Pilkington

I.O. EXHIBIT NO. 28 – Dr. David A. Youngblood's analysis dated October 17, 1997

I.O. EXHIBIT NO. 29 – Inspection, Work List 835 dated March 4, 1996

I.O. EXHIBIT NO. 30 – NVIC 1-89 dated March 15, 1989

I.O. EXHIBIT NO. 31 – MODU Drydock Inspection Book

I.O. EXHIBIT NO. 32 – Letter to George "Buddy" Horton from Julio Martinez dated February 26, 1996

I.O. EXHIBIT NO. 33 – Cliffs Drilling Company, Proposal to Conduct Inspection

I.O. EXHIBIT NO. 34 – Excerpt deposition testimony of Kirk Austin, p. 24 & 25

I.O. EXHIBIT NO. 35 – Excerpt deposition testimony of Kirk Austin, p. 27

I.O. EXHIBIT NO. 36 – Excerpt deposition testimony of Kirk Austin, p. 45

I.O. EXHIBIT NO. 37 – Excerpt deposition testimony of Kirk Austin, p. 64

I.O. EXHIBIT NO. 38 – Letter to Texas NDE Technologies from American Bureau of Shipping dated September 25, 1995

I.O. EXHIBIT NO. 39 – Y.M.C.A. card from Kirk Austin

I.O. EXHIBIT NO. 40 – Deposition testimony of Dan Gilbert

I.O. EXHIBIT NO. 41 – McKenzie work order dated September 11, 1998

I.O. EXHIBIT NO. 42 – Transcript of pretrial conference call

I.O. EXHIBIT NO. 43 – Birth certificate of Brian Pilkington

I.O. EXHIBIT NO. 44 – Death certificate of Brian Pilkington

I.O. EXHIBIT NO. 45 – Diving records of Brian Pilkington

I.O. EXHIBIT NO. 46 – Ronald Townsend's Merchant Marine License

I.O. EXHIBIT NO. 47 – Photograph of harness

I.O. EXHIBIT NO. 48 – Photograph of helmet

I.O. EXHIBIT NO. 49 – Photograph of helmet

I.O. EXHIBIT NO. 50 – Photograph of neck dam

- 59

16732
2 June 2000

FORMAL INVESTIGATION INTO THE COMMERCIAL DIVING ACCIDENT ABOARD
THE MOBILE OFFSHORE DRILLING UNIT CLIFF'S DRILLING RIG # 12 ON 4 MARCH
1996, WITH LOSS OF LIFE

I.O. EXHIBIT NO. 51 – Photograph of umbilical

I.O. EXHIBIT NO. 52 – SuperLite Diving Helmet Operations and Maintenance Manual

I.O. EXHIBIT NO. 53 – U.S. Navy Diving Manual

I.O. EXHIBIT NO. 54 – Curriculum Vitae of Dennis Jahde

I.O. EXHIBIT NO. 55 – Advertisements for compressor oils

I.O. EXHIBIT NO. 56 – McKenzie receipts for G & G Marine

I.O. EXHIBIT NO. 57 – Association of Diving Contractors Manual

I.O. EXHIBIT NO. 58 – ACD Memorandum of Understanding for diving certification

I.O. EXHIBIT NO. 59 – Letter to LCDR Thomas Beistle from Steve Duffy, Occupational Safety
    Officer, dated June 21, 1999

I.O. EXHIBIT NO. 60 – Letter to Mr. Steve Duffy, Workers Compensation Board of British
    Columbia, from LCDR Thomas Beistle dated May 10, 1999

I.O. EXHIBIT NO. 61 – Underwater Magazine article

I.O. EXHIBIT NO. 62 – Photograph of orange cylinder

I.O. EXHIBIT NO. 63 – Affidavit of Dan Gilbert

I.O. EXHIBIT NO. 64 – Letter dated June 21, 1999, to LCDR Beistle from Bijan Siahatgar
    discussing parties of interest.
I.O. EXHIBIT NO. 65 – U.S. Coast Guard Inspection Case # MI96008514

I.O. EXHIBIT NO. 66 – Statement of T. L. Thomson dtd 12 May 1999

I.O. EXHIBIT NO. 67 – Second Pilkington Investigation dtd 17 August 1998

I.O. EXHIBIT NO. 68 – Parties in Interest Proposed Findings of Fact

I.O. EXHIBIT NO. 69 – Canadian Workers' Comp. Bd. Study

I.O. EXHIBIT NO. 70 – Diving Log of Dan Wiitala for Cliff's Drilling Rig No. 12 Dive

I.O. EXHIBIT NO. 71 – Deposition testimony of Kevin Todd Lawdermilk

I.O. EXHIBIT NO. 72 – The Quincy QR-25 Brochure

- 60

Some information in this report is being withheld
under 5 U.S.C. Section 552(b)(6).

May 2000 NPRN Linkages

State of the Port Reports

2000 was an active and demanding year for our strategic ports. Beginning with involvement in Y2K activities, through readiness exercises, regional events impacting port security, and outreach efforts, the agencies making up the Port Readiness Committees (PRC) were kept busy. 2001 promises to be even busier, as PRC members continue to exercise outload plans while addressing emerging issues impacting readiness. PRC's have a full schedule of joint exercises, including 13 involving loadouts or mobilization, one involving weapons of mass destruction, and two Sea Emergency Deployment Readiness Exercises (SEDRE). A full listing of exercises can be found at the NPRN website: http://www.marad.dot.gov/nprn/index.html.

Common themes of interest or concern for PRC's were the shortage of resources necessary to ensure readiness; communications between PRC members; and guidance from the national level on the direction of PRC activities.

Port Summaries

New York PRC

A Table Top Exercise (TTX) was conducted in March 2000 in preparation for OPSAIL 2000 and the International Naval Review. The TTX and actual events provided a wealth of lessons learned, especially in the use of security forces to provide protection. Coast Guard Activity New York is currently reorganizing its Port Security program to better address threats to the waterway and its users.

A meeting with the 842nd U.S. Army Transportation Battalion was held in October. The meeting established a baseline for expectations regarding the frequency, scope, and location of expected mobilization efforts. Additionally, risks were identified with respect to security threats, the use of commercial vessels carrying military cargo, and the selection and screening process of commercial vessels. PRC meetings are scheduled for late May and early November 2001.

Hampton Roads PRC

The PRC's semi-annual meetings were used to discuss lessons learned from previous exercises, the FBI's threat assessment process, functions of Military Traffic Management Command (MTMC) and the Deployment Support Command, the Hampton Roads Strategic Port Readiness Reassessment Report, the Incident Command System, and explosive handling issues.

Issues that will be discussed at PRC meetings scheduled for May 2, and November 7, 2001 include the PRC's role in response to terrorist threats and planning for the Port Readiness Exercise (PRX) scheduled in the Fall of 2001

1

May 2000 NPRN Linkages

Wilmington PRC

In 2000, members of the Wilmington PRC developed a web-page; exchanged briefings on agency roles/responsibilities with regard to port security and use of force policies; received a briefing from the North Carolina Army National Guard, 650th Transportation Company on Weapons of Mass Destruction (WMD); and participated in EASTERN READY 00.

Four meetings are scheduled for 2001: 17 February, 19 May, 18 August, and 17 November. Issues that will be addressed this year include updating and utilization of existing contingency plans; increasing focus on domestic terrorism; communications; and maintaining readiness.

Charleston PRC

Agencies from the PRC participated in a PRX (June 2000) and U.S. Coast Guard Group Charleston's small passenger vessel exercise (Spring 2000). The PRX tested member agencies' ability to rapidly deploy combat and support units through the port, respond to a hazardous materials release, respond to and mitigate a WMD incident, and minimize impact to a deployment with the approach of heavy weather.

Port security will be the primary focus of the PRC in 2001. U.S. Coast Guard Marine Safety Office (MSO) Charleston personnel will begin by conducting an assessment of all waterfront facilities. Meetings are scheduled for 18 January and again in the summer.

Savannah PRC

A SEDRE was conducted in March, involving the 3rd Infantry Division. The exercise turned out to be timely, for in August members of the 3rd Infantry deployed to Bosnia in the Italian-flagged vessel GRAN BRETAGNA. Over 540 pieces of DoD equipment were loaded during 24-hour operations, and the ship departed safely and fully loaded 15 hours before the designated time of departure. A Joint Staff Integrated Vulnerability Assessment (JSIVA) was conducted simultaneously with the deployment.

At the November PRC meeting, members discussed results of the JSIVA visit, highlights of the Graham Commission Seaport Security report, and the results of a WMD exercise conducted in June. A PRC meeting is scheduled for April 4, 2001.

Jacksonville PRC

Jacksonville had an extremely active season, capped by the signing of a local Memorandum of Agreement (MOA) between the U.S. Coast Guard MSO, the U.S. Marine Corps Blount Island Command, and Military Sealift Command. The MOA clarifies the roles of the signatory agencies with respect to the Maritime Prepositioning Ship (MPS) Program.

Additionally, the Jacksonville Marine Transportation Exchange (JMTX), formerly the Jacksonville Waterways Management Council, was incorporated in December. The JMTX's mission is to coordinate the safe and environmentally responsible management of the marine transportation system (MTS) in Jacksonville. The JMTX was organized to follow the MTS initiative and is closely modeled after the U.S. Coast Guard's Harbor Safety Committee Guidelines found in the Navigation and Inspection Circular (NVIC) 1-

2

May 2000 NPRN Linkages

00. You can obtain an electronic copy of the NVIC at: http://www.uscg.mil/hq/g-m/nvic/index00.htm. PRC meetings are scheduled for March and July/August.

Corpus Christi PRC

As part of DoD's PHANTOM LIFELINE exercise in October, Ft Hood mobilized several hundred pieces of equipment/cargo via convoy to the Port of Corpus Christi. Overall, the two-week operation showed a high level of efficiency in mobilizing military cargo through Corpus Christi.

In November, MARAD completed the second Port Readiness Assessment for Corpus Christi in 2000. No discrepancies were noted. The PRC will be conducting their first meeting of 2001 in April.

Port Arthur PRC

In addition to participation in a SEDRE and two convoy/fly-aways, the PRC updated the local Port Readiness Memorandum of Understanding (MOU) for the Sabine-Neches waterway, mirroring the national MOU in format and incorporating the newly created Port Readiness Committee Organization chart. The Captain of the Port, on behalf of the members, forwarded a letter to the Army Corps of Engineers expressing their concern over the width of the Sabine-Neches Channel.

Other area activities of note include the formation of a new Port Readiness sub-committee for antiterrorism/force protection, chaired by Military Sealift Command. The purpose of the sub-committee is to better prepare an interagency response before, during and after a military loadout. The PRC will meet quarterly in 2001 to continue their work on readiness issues.

San Diego PRC

The PRC created a security subcommittee to investigate the need for heightened security at local Navy facilities. The subcommittee helped establish a new unit at Naval Station San Diego. The new unit's mission will be to enforce security zones and Restricted Areas protecting Navy assets. The subcommittee also updated the Coast Guard Captain of the Port/Commander, Naval Station San Diego MOU for Security Zones.

The PRC is scheduled to meet in April, July, and October.

Los Angeles-Long Beach PRC

The PRC will meet in March, and again later in the year.

Northern California PRC

The PRC received several presentations during the year. They included a briefing on WMD exercises in the San Francisco Bay area; information about the Bay Area Terrorism Working Group; updates on the Coast Guard's Y2K efforts; an overview of the 834th Transportation Battalion's operations at the Military Ocean Terminal Concord (MOTC), formerly the Naval Weapons Station Concord; and preliminary planning for integrating the 2001 PRX with the annual Harbor Defense Command Unit's BAY WARRIOR exercise.

3

518

May 2000 NPRN Linkages

The Northern California Port Readiness Guide was updated in June. The guide explains the miltary outload organization to PRC members. Quarterly meetings in 2001 will be held March 7, June 6, September 5, and December 5.

Pacific Northwest PRC

PRC members were actively involved in seven deployment briefings conducted by the 833rd Transportation Battalion; seven exercises involving loadout, earthquake, and deployment scenarios; and three mini-SEDREs. Additionally, the 833rd conducted an Integrated Computerized Deployment Systems (ICODES) Battle Drill in January, February, and April.

PRC security workgroup efforts are being incorporated into the Port Readiness Handbook, addressing multi-agency security, communications, command, and control issues. In another effort to improve readiness, the 833rd entered into an Inter-Service Support Agreement with Naval Magazine Indian Island, ensuring continued support of ammunition loadouts. PRC meetings will be held in April and September.

Honolulu PRC

Members of the PRC received briefings regarding the specific equipment/cargo to be moved through the port; loadout transportation requirements; and background information from previous non-military loadouts. The PRC working group focused on revising the local PRC MOA between signatory agencies. The MOA is currently in routing for review and signing.

A PRC meeting is scheduled for the Spring of 2001.

Conclusion

In general, the reports depict local PRC's working to stay abreast of issues that affect readiness and improve communication and coordination between PRC members. The commitment and participation by the full PRC membership is critical to the continued success of our readiness mission

The State of the Port Reports have been submitted to the National Port Readiness Network via the Coast Guard Waterways Security Division. Copies of the annual reports are available upon request.

4

Index

A

ABS (American Bureau of Shipping), 55, 165, 181, 183, 186, 210, 212-13, 230, 300, 311, 348-50, 354, 356, 358, 366-68, 421-25

Abu Musa, 15-17, 19-22, 25, 32, 34, 39, 41, 44-45

ACP (Alternative Compliance Program), 422-23

ADC (Association of Dive Contractors), 52, 108, 164, 205, 207-8, 379-82, 403, 407, 443

Afton (Brian Pilkington's sister), 74, 76, 96, 101, 130, 150-51

Alternative Compliance Program (ACP), 164, 367, 422

American Bureau of Shipping (ABS), 49, 55, 63, 65-68, 78, 119, 121-24, 128-30, 155, 158, 164, 217-18, 270-71, 362, 365, 367-68

AOD, 281-84, 312, 394

Association of Diving Contractors, 52, 107-8, 145-46, 164-65, 169, 203-5, 207, 391, 407, 414

Aunt Beth, 94-95, 97, 101-2, 153, 155

Aunt Cindy, 102

Austin, Kirk, 46-47, 54, 56-57, 61-65, 68-72, 107, 154-55, 179-83, 195, 199, 216-19, 256-58, 270-71, 296-97, 302, 343-65

B

Bauers (compressor), 278

Baumgartner, William, 170

Baynham, Patrick, 442

Beaumont, Texas, 59, 123, 216

Beistle, Thomas, 177-89, 191-98, 200-210, 212-14, 216-22, 224-30, 233, 237-49, 267, 295-303, 307-11, 379-84, 387, 389, 392-402, 438-40

Bell Jet Ranger II, 16

Beth, 153-54. *See also* Aunt Beth

Bob, 102-3. *See also* Uncle Bob

Borne, John, 84, 86, 107, 161, 167, 414

Bradford, Brick, 220, 394-402

Brandom, David, 85-86, 107, 112, 114, 118-24, 126-27, 129, 137, 148, 152-60

Brawand, Walter J., 170

Brian, 15-18, 22-27, 29-33, 35-39, 42-45, 47-50, 52-58, 61-74, 84-87, 91-101, 103-6, 132-36, 147-51, 155-57, 222-24, 226-29

Brooks, Jack, 15

Bush, George Herbert Walker, 11

C

Cal Dive, 441-42

Captain Fels, 109, 161, 164, 166-67, 187-89, 195-96, 320, 343-44

Champaign, Steve, 170, 196, 198, 200-201, 219-22, 224-36

Clapton, Eric, 97-98
  "Tears from Heaven," 98
Clark, John R., 219, 313, 318-20
Cliffs 12, 54-57, 159-60, 169-70, 174-75,
      196-97, 210, 213, 220-21, 236, 271,
      288, 297-99, 301-2, 324-25, 339, 365
Cliffs' Drilling, 53, 57, 107, 119, 122-23,
      125, 129, 154-55, 158, 197-98, 208,
      302, 312, 403, 406, 419
Coast Guard, 66, 106-9, 112-13, 142-47,
      162-64, 167-71, 188-93, 195-97,
      215-17, 342-43, 367-68, 377, 410-11,
      417-24, 437-41, 443-44
Coast Guard Marine Safety Office, 177,
      216, 219
COI (Certificates of Inspection), 209, 301,
      325, 330, 368, 422

D

David. *See* Brandom, David
divers
  commercial, 139, 170, 173, 189, 282,
      332, 347, 363, 399-400
  saturation, 115, 168-69, 175
dive safety manual, 361
Doyle, Howie, 208
Dubai, 18-19, 100, 175

E

Eagle (compressor), 278
Eighth Coast Guard District, 216, 219
Eunice (Brian's mother-in-law), 74, 80-81,
      84, 88, 141
Everett, Ron, 55-57, 68-70, 72, 181, 186,
      296, 306, 343, 365-68, 392
Everett, Ronald, 219, 365

F

Fels, William H., 107. *See also* Captain Fels

G

G&G Marine, 47-49, 61-62, 78-79, 107-8,
      122-24, 141-43, 145-46, 154-55,
      203-7, 237-42, 249-50, 267, 280-81,
      283-88, 380-84, 418-19
Gilbert, Danny, 47, 49, 52, 62, 72-73, 78-
      80, 110-11, 154-55, 157-58, 202-3,
      207, 211-12, 218-19, 243-44, 369-85,
      439-40
Gorton, Slade, 142
Grandpa Fred, 75, 102-4
Guy Kirby, 201, 213-14, 219, 274, 280, 411

H

Henn, Jeremy, 219
Henrie, Donny, 198-201
Hill Rivkins Loesburg O'Brian Mulroy, and
      Hayden, 124
Hofsommer, Eric, 168, 174
Horton, Buddy, 57-58, 61-64, 67-70, 72,
      181-84, 208, 219, 295-312, 343, 360, 377
Humphrey, Jim, 97
Husband, Marty, 201, 213-14, 219, 274-80,
      319, 374

I

IMO (International Maritime Organization),
      171, 422, 424
Inslee, Jay, 170
International Maritime Organization (IMO),
      171, 422, 424
International Oilfield Divers, 385
ISM (International Safety Management), 421

J

Jack. *See* Brook, Jack
Jahde, Dennis, 219, 403-7
Jim, 91-93, 95, 97-98, 163
Julie (Brian's wife), 47-48, 50, 73-75, 77-
      79, 81, 83-85, 91-92, 96, 116-18,
      121-22, 124-25, 127-28, 130, 141,
      152-54, 156-58

K

Karen, 74-76, 79, 81, 84-86, 88, 91-93, 96-
      97, 103, 116-18, 120-22, 124, 137,

141, 151-54, 157-58, 160
King, Fred, 184-85, 200, 219
Kramek, Bob, 424-25
Kranz (captain), 107, 109

L

LaFlamme, John, 219
Lare, Jerry, 184-85
Leonard, Erick, 98

M

Marion, Tom, 177-79, 191, 195, 199
Martin, Dana, 36-39, 43-45, 121, 123-24,
    128-30
Martinez, Julio, 58, 321, 411
Masude (*Umm Khanur*'s captain), 24-32,
    34, 99-100
Miko, John C., 109, 113
Mosele, Franklin, 175
Mosele, Thomas, 174-76, 216, 218, 303-12,
    320, 346, 366-68, 375, 379-84, 392,
    411, 414
Mr. Bill, 22-23, 27-29, 32, 36-37, 40-42, 45

N

NAVIC (Navigation and Vessel Inspection
    Circular), 187-88, 194-97, 208, 210,
    213, 366
Navigation and Vessel Inspection Circular
    (NAVIC), 188, 304
Nebels (Peter Pilkington's clients), 97

P

Patton, Robert, 102
Pilkington, 77-78, 82-83, 113-14, 123-24,
    151-52, 177, 182-84, 187-88, 196-98,
    201-2, 207-10, 325-26, 373-76, 379-
    80, 415-20, 426-39
Pilkington, Brian, 75, 98, 100, 113, 171,
    183-85, 190, 194, 196, 203, 215-16,
    220, 376, 386, 419-20, 437-39
    accident of, 92, 147
    death of, 82, 93, 110, 114, 118, 122, 128,

138, 143, 172
    funeral of, 91, 145
Pilkington, Fred, 166, 184, 426, 436
Pilkington, Jamie, 18, 42, 50, 75-76, 103,
    130, 139, 150-51, 158, 416
Pilkington, Julie, 123, 125
Pilkington, Martine Cote Brian S., 13
Pilkington, Pete, 79, 179, 183-84, 186-90,
    193-95, 197-99, 201-3, 206-13, 303,
    323-43, 346-65, 371-78
Pilkington, Peter, 122-24, 187, 215-16, 415,
    418-19, 437
Pilkington, Peter J., 3-4, 130, 176, 217-18
Plagge (lieutenant), 160, 163-64, 169, 418-
    20
Pluta (admiral), 191
Port Arthur, 47, 53, 56, 58, 68, 71-75, 77,
    80-81, 107, 110, 145, 159-60, 162,
    164-65, 202, 438-39
Portingale, Bill, 22. *See also* Mr. Bill
Provost Umphrey, 86, 106, 112, 153, 158,
    160
Putti, George, 21-22

Q

Quincy 325s, 212, 370, 373

R

Rashid Construction of Dubai, 16
Reverend Willard, 92
Richey, Thomas K., 113

S

Saxon, Ross, 108, 111, 145-46, 203-7, 219,
    242, 381, 407, 443
Seiler, Kena, 128, 142, 177-79, 183-84,
    202, 204, 207, 210-12, 214
Sellas, Kenna, 122-23, 128
Shah, 21, 35, 38
Sharja, 19-20, 31, 34
Siahatgar, Bijan, 121, 123-25, 128-29, 143,
    149, 179, 182, 184-86, 188-90, 198-
    200, 206-8, 270, 308, 310, 390-91,
    403-7
Stepp, Frances, 439, 441-42

Storm, Hanna, 135-37
subca, 15

T

Tatum, Ed, 184-85
"Tears from Heaven" (Clapton), 98
Townsend, Ron, 66, 72, 181-82, 184, 208,
   213, 218-19, 298-300, 310, 343-44,
   390, 392-94

U

Umm Khanur, 19, 22-25, 27-28, 30, 32,
   34-37
Umphrey, Walter, 84, 158, 167
Uncle Bob, 49, 102
Uncle Brian, 98, 103
United Arab Emirates, 15, 17, 19, 103, 131,
   416
United States Coast Guard, 49, 55, 57-58,
   65, 106-8, 145, 147, 153, 161, 163-
   65, 169, 193, 207, 347, 349, 367-68
United States Navy Seal, 115, 175

V

Veentjer, John, 408

W

Walker, Joe, 174-78, 180, 183-84, 186, 188-
   90, 192-93, 196-201, 203-7, 211-13,
   216, 230-36, 249-74, 278-80, 385-90,
   393-94, 406
Walker, Ric, 220, 384-91
Walker, Rod, 170
Wellborn, J. G. Blake, 107, 109, 112, 145,
   160, 188, 192-93, 196
Wiitala, Dan, 46-47, 51-54, 56-58, 60-73,
   78-80, 106-7, 110, 181-83, 202, 237-
   71, 361, 365, 392, 400-401, 410,
   417-18
Wilson, Jim, 170
Wright, Mark, 351-52

Y

Youngblood, David, 115, 313, 318, 386,
   388-90